PHILOSOPHY OF EDUCATION

Essays and Commentaries

Edited by

HOBERT W. BURNS
SYRACUSE UNIVERSITY

CHARLES J. BRAUNER
PURDUE UNIVERSITY

Foreword by
ROBERT H. BECK
UNIVERSITY OF MINNESOTA

THE RONALD PRESS COMPANY · NEW YORK

THIS IS FOR

Carol
Charles
Janifer
Joanne

OUR CHILDREN

—and Blanche

Foreword

There are unmistakable signs that the philosophy of education has entered an era of renewed vigor and excellence. This book—*Philosophy of Education: Essays and Commentaries*—is one of these signs.

I cannot but be impressed with how well students will fare with these essays. Each of the four parts of the book has full, scholarly, but not overwhelming, introductions uniformly written with awareness of the history of the ideas under review. For the student, this means that although he is treated to a first-rate introduction to the most recent development in philosophy—Logical Empiricism—he will not have been led to think of the history of philosophy as a tediously enduring wasteland. In addition, Professors Burns and Brauner frequently provide him with a précis of every important point in an essay.

The craftsmanship is expert; the skill in organization and presentation will appeal to the professional. Equally attractive is the fairness maintained throughout. To sense this fairness, one has only to read through Part II of the book where metaphysics is treated to the lion's share of the section. The editors themselves may feel more at home in Logical Empiricism, but this has not stayed them from honoring, by adequate review, the classic stances of metaphysics.

Craftsmanship is further attested by the design of the book. The section on ethics in Part II is an illustration. In the first place, Burns and Brauner have not represented Idealistic ethics by an essay whose language and examples date is as "old" and, for the young student, therefore, out-of-date. Nor has their sample of Idealistic thought on ethics been written by someone clearly out of touch and out of sympathy with modern social science. J. Donald Butler's "The Role of Value Theory in Education" is selected. Butler has not written simply as an Idealist. Like Burns and Brauner, Butler is aware of the several views an able, contemporary philosopher can hold. His essay is a sample of both an Idealistic approach and a skillful philosophic analysis. So, too, in rounding out the section on ethics with the classic statement of John Dewey in "Theory of Valuation" and of Charles L. Stevenson in "The Nature of Ethical Disagreement," the editors have coupled the presentation of two noted moderns, the one as much as the other manifestly able. In a word, no viewpoint is under-represented or set up as a strawman. The student will be hard pressed to find his prejudices against a position supported by the fact that the disfavored view has been voiced by a weak essay. However firm in a philosophy, the student will find it easy to take seriously each position presented.

In acknowledging impartiality and adequacy in coverage I did not intend to draw attention away from the care Burns and Brauner have given to the design of the book conceived as an instrument for learning and for teaching. Both the extended introductions and the brief but excellent Overviews have been written with a gimlet-like style conserving words and clarity without loss of even subtle meaning. I would offer the introductions to the "categories" of metaphysics, epistemology, and ethics in Part II as paradigms of presentation. No one of these has been written down but neither are the introductions or overviews uninstructive. I learned from each and refer, for an example, only to one, the disarmingly clear treatment of the several forms of Idealism.

The generosity of space alloted Idealism simply signals the intent of Burns and Brauner to permit students a fair opportunity to know the classic tradition. Each of us is indebted for the success of the editors in securing "Idealism as a Philosophy of Education." Louise Antz is one of the most gifted of contemporary students in the philosophy of education, yet has been far too modest in setting out her ideas. In a word, Burns and Brauner have persisted in their search for the best representations of commanding positions in the field. We are the beneficiaries of their determination to mine the best, not simply the best "representatives" of viewpoints, but the most stimulating.

Perhaps the quality of freshness is most evident in the fourth and concluding part of the book. I was struck, and I think others will be also, by the success contributors to Part IV have had in carrying water on both shoulders. It is uncommon to find those who are as at home in the dimension of theory as they are sensitive to the realities of practice. Students will find it difficult not to be informed by these essays.

Unfair as it is to single out one from seven essays of Part IV the student will wish to give special attention to B. Paul Komisar's "Should We Meet the Needs of Students?" It is a first-rate example of the analytical approach, whose theory had been exemplified earlier in the essays "Philosophy and Knowledge" by A. J. Ayer and "The Nature of Ethical Disagreement" by Charles L. Stevenson, both of which appear in Part II.

Komisar's essay must give pause to anyone who would employ the term "needs." It is, then, with special care that I judge *Philosophy of Education: Essays and Commentaries* to be a volume that will meet the needs of students undertaking a first venture in the philosophy of education, and of those others who have progressed to the point where they wish to contrast the several philosophies of education as well as those who teach philosophy of education and have waited a combination of up-to-date readings woven together by scholarly but simple explications of both text and background. Burns and Brauner have not made it easy for those who "would go out and do likewise."

Robert H. Beck
University of Minnesota

Preface

This book of essays has been prepared for beginning students of educational philosophy. The subject matter deals with ends and means, scope and sequence, method and content—in short with philosophy of education as a distinct discipline.

An introduction to the ideas under review precedes each of the four parts of the book, and a précis accompanies many essays. These interstitial commentaries interpret the original ideas of the contributors and draw together and unite the topics. It is hoped that the commentaries in conjunction with the essays will extend, broaden, or act as a catalytic agent upon the understanding of the student of educational philosophy.

The difficult task of identifying titles to be reviewed was greatly facilitated by the many members of the Philosophy of Education Society who gave generously of their time to not only nominate candidates for reproduction, but also help judge them. Space unfortunately prohibits recognition of all these educational philosophers, much less adequate recognition of the importance of their efforts to the construction of the book. Needless to say, despite their friendly advice, guidance, and criticism, the authors alone accept responsibility for the selections and essays included in (or excluded from) the book.

The editors are particularly indebted to Professors Frederick C. Neff of Wayne State University and Van Cleve Morris of Rutgers University who provided us with intellectual guidance and stimulation during the formulation of the book; Professor Robert H. Beck of the University of Minnesota, who generously gave of his time to read the manuscript and provide a Foreword; Professor Gustavo F. J. Cirigliano of the University of La Plata, in Argentina, who also read and criticized the manuscript; and to four graduate assistants whose many efforts combined to smooth the path of publication: Norman Adams, Syracuse University; John Mallan, Syracuse University; Marie Parnell, Rutgers University; and Henry Woessner, Syracuse University.

A debt of gratitude is also owed to the many authors and publishers who so graciously permitted their work to be reproduced in this anthology, and especially to those who prepared essays specifically designed for inclusion in this volume. Individual acknowledgments are found at the beginning of the selection.

Hobert W. Burns
Charles J. Brauner

March, 1962

Contents

Part I

The Nature of Educational Philosophy

Part II

The Divisions of Philosophy

xi

Part III

Philosophies of Education

Part IV

From Theory to Practice

Part I

The Nature of Educational Philosophy

Introduction: Man, Maps, and Philosophy

> Philosophy begins in wonder. And, at the end, when philosophic thought has done its best, the wonder remains. There may have been added, however, some grasp of the immensity of things, some purification of emotion by understanding.
>
> *Alfred North Whitehead*

With what he has inherited and what he has invented, man has cultivated his own wonder. He has wondered about all things— Why is . . . ? What is . . . ? Where is . . . ? How is . . . ? —and he has expressed his wonderment in many ways.

Because he is a wanderer as well as a wonderer, he is a maker of maps; when he wonders he explores, when he explains he maps the regions explored. Some make maps with brush and charcoal, others with nouns and verbs, still others with numbers alone. Drawings etched on the walls of prehistoric caves no less than paintings recently dripped from the brushes of Jackson Pollock offer direct expression and explanation of man's wonder. The geocentric universe of Ptolemy, the heliocentric universe of Galileo, the mechanistic universe of Newton, and the expanding universe of Einstein all testify to yet another dimension of man's wonderment and explanation.

Beyond the direct expression of the arts, yet short of the boundary of scientific explanation, lies a no man's land of wondering. He who works there is the philosopher. His work, often bridging the direct, expressive domain of the arts and the indirect, abstract realm of science, implies not only the creativity of the artist but the discipline of scholarship and logical thought which distinguishes explanation from expression.

This worker ventures out beyond fact in his exploration of the meanings of human experience, but while he may lose touch with fact now and again, he never loses contact with experience. He may be the physicist who speculates about the nature of the cosmos, and he may well expect that astronomers will eventually confirm as fact his speculative conclusions; he may be the metaphysician who speculates about the nature of human nature, dealing with insights into the spiritual qualities of man which he never

3

expects scientists will confirm or deny. Yet both would be philosophers and both would be thinking substantively, thinking about the lay of the land out there in that no man's land of wondering. Both would be drawing a map of that unexplored territory, for the map-making of philosophers takes many forms.

The political philosopher may draw maps of the direction society must follow if it is to stay on the high road of democracy; the social philosopher may chart the overpasses to be constructed and the bypasses to be closed in order to accommodate changes in social terrain caused by the upheavals of automation and nuclear technology; the educational philosopher may be readying not merely a new map with changed place names and detours indicated around construction areas, but a whole new atlas—drawn to a new scale, with a new projection, using new tools and techniques.

Substantive philosophy, the philosophy of science, of history, of politics, of education, of religion, deals with the real and the ideal; it speaks on any subject. But in going beyond the language of science it deliberately loosens its hold on precise meaning and description in order to expand its power to account for things not clearly observed but well imagined; yet it must stop short of the artist's poetic license lest in making a statement it abandon all cognitive meaning, lest the maps it produces become blurred and indistinct, causing later travelers to lose their way in that no man's land because they miss the trees for the forest.

Some of the workers who cultivate this in-between land are better at pruning plants sown and cultivated by earlier philosophers; some attempt to improve the strain by taking a cutting from here and there, grafting them one to the other; others specialize in trying to increase the yield of established fields by applying new techniques to already well-worked land; a few attempt to till new soil, caring but little if the sticks and stones in virgin lands blunt their plows somewhat, for they are interested in pushing back the boundaries of philosophy and opening up new frontiers for exploration; and a very, very few plant germinal seeds in fertile fields, the fruits of which may lead to a new or hardier species of philosophy.

It takes many talents to explore, map, till, plant, and care for the area between what is factually known and what is a direct expression of feeling. Wonder is at once a simple yet complex activity, and the maps men make to express and explain their wonderment are equally simple yet complex.

THE MAP IN THE BACKGROUND

Cultural anthropologists have pointed out that a given way of classifying nature influences what an observer will see and how he will wonder about what he has seen. Linguists demonstrate that a given language influences the ways in which one organizes his experiences, and how one reasons about his experience is conditioned by the grammar he uses. Psychologists indicate that one generally perceives what he expects to perceive, and that these perceptual sets influence behavior, for perception is the prelude to action. Sociologists report that social pressures subtly yet perceptibly dictate the range of human experiences open to men and thus influence the kinds of experiences men seek or avoid.

Such maps in the background cannot be ignored; they guide the human adventure. For instance, the Hopi Indian who believes that the ritual rain dance will influence the coming of the rain relies on a map in the background that is unreadable by most of us. The primitive tribesman, whose map indicates a personalized world in which his subjective wishes actually count for something in the objective run of natural events, can elicit from his map a word picture of this kind:

> The earth is my home,
> It is powerful.
> Water speaks in foam,
> It is powerful.
> There sits a hill,
> It is powerful.
> I go now to kill,
> I am powerful.

But an altogether different map of man's relationship to nature is conveyed by Lewis Mumford, in the following statement about time as one of the key ideas in the modern, scientific map:

> The clock . . . is a piece of power-machinery whose "product" is seconds and minutes: by its essential nature it dissociated time from human events and helped create the belief in an independent world of mathematically measurable sequences: the world of science.

The primitive tribesman and the sophisticated scientist speculate in different ways about the world they share in common, and each draws a map based on his speculations. But no man's map is exclusively one or the other. In some spheres of our lives we may be more primitive than scientific, as when we rely on maps such as those suggested by astrology, mental telepathy, or the power of prayer to guide our human, earthly behavior. Nevertheless, we normally depend upon a map in which a natural order of events is by and large divorced from human events, human aspirations. Few indeed, for example, are those who might commit suicide on the basis of an unfavorable horoscope, who telepathize rather than telephone, or pray for a flat tire to fill with air. Such actions in the face of *ordinary* events would bring one's sanity into question, for our *extraordinary* maps are reserved for extraordinary circumstances. Prayers are clearly more appropriate in a fox-hole than in an auto mechanic's grease pit; the humorous incongruity of the assertion that "There are no atheists in the grease pits!" illustrates that different maps are used on different occasions. Prayer is most appropriate in a foxhole, when there is little else to be done, when an "ordinary map" no longer serves to guide. Given the existence of ordinary and extra-ordinary maps, that very fact indicates that in daily affairs we put more faith in the accuracy of the ordinary map drawn by the scientist, and only when unusual, extraordinary circumstances arise do we seek for the guideposts to be found on other kinds of maps.

Even so, even in providing a map based on factual information and verifiable theory, science itself requires a map of its own to guide the exploration of the unknown; in a certain strange sense a map of the unknown is needed before the unknown can be explored—or, at least, tools appropriate to the exploration are required. These useful tools, the method and language of science, themselves have a map already built into them, and this map in the background influences *how* men will wonder as well as *what* they will wonder about. What men know or believe, or think they know or believe, directs what they look for; and what they look for largely determines what they are likely to find. That which is accepted as making sense sets a precedent for what will be accepted as sensible thereafter, and what is not roughed-in on the map in the background is not likely to be drawn in on the map in the foreground.

The map in the background changes, of course, but gradually and not on all fronts at once. As each human reflects on the surroundings in which he grew, so too does philosophy reflect upon the science and thought which preceded it and from which it grew. Clearly, the more the philosopher knows about the map of the scientist, the more he can wonder about; but even more important, though the maps of science and philosophy are distinct, the less different they will be. Staking out the boundaries of the areas to be mapped by science and philosophy is the required intellectual survey which precedes serious map-making.

SCIENCE AND PHILOSOPHY

It has been said, perhaps in jest but certainly in truth, that philosophy is its own first problem. That is surely the case if the first problem of any discipline is to provide a clear-cut definition of its field of inquiry. Philosophy is as old as, or older than, science; but there is as yet no such definition. It is sad but true that a great deal of philosophic energy, or at least a great deal of the energy of philosophers, is spent trying to define just what philosophy and the philosophy of education is or should be.

Writing in the recent *Encyclopedia of Educational Research,* B. Othanel Smith correctly notes that even though

> The philosophic study of education is an ancient subject, dating in the Western World to Greek thought . . . its domain has never been clearly staked out, especially at points where it touches upon systematic philosophy and more recently on educational science.

The subject-matter pie of the universe can be sliced up as we so please for, as Benjamin Lee Whorf reminds us, "We cut nature up, organize it into concepts, and ascribe significances as we do, largely because we are parties to an agreement to organize it in this way." Most are agreed that the first cut is the deepest and the easiest: divide the pie in half between the physical and the behavioral sciences. The logic of this division is simple enough for obviously there is a difference between physics, astronomy, and biology, on the one hand, and psychology, anthropology, and sociology, on the other hand. But wherein does philosophy fit? Certainly it is not one of the physical sciences—although it does indeed deal with atoms, stars, and life itself. It does not appear to be one of the behavioral sciences—although it does indeed deal with mind, man, and society. It seems not to be a science of any kind, physical or behavioral, even though it cuts across all areas of science.

Unless philosophers are to go without their dessert, without their fair share of the subject-matter pie, they need to define the area of inquiry properly to be called philosophic. Usually this is done, weakly, with a negative definition, by comparing it to science at least to show what philosophy is not.

If we date the beginnings of philosophy with the Milesian school (*ca.* 700 B.C.), and if we date the beginnings of science at about the same time, we note that there was no substantive distinction made between them. Philosophy was the search for wisdom, a search usually starting with assertedly self-evident truths, perhaps incorporating some empirical observations along the way, and always ending with the logically certain and the absolutely true. In this earliest sense philosophy was a *process;* it was often called "moral science." (In the United States we use the title Professor of Philosophy, but universities in many parts of the world still use Professor of Moral Science.) Science, by contrast, was looked upon as any body of conclusions, any organized or systematized body of information, such as geography, ethics, astronomy, or astrology. In this sense science was a *product;* it was often called "natural philosophy." (Again, in some foreign universities the title Professor of Natural Philosophy is used to describe scientists.) The earliest distinctions between science and philosophy were therefore made in terms of means and end, of process and product.

Later, by the time of Aristotle (*ca.* 384–322), a new kind of distinction came to be drawn; it was a distinction of orientation in the process of inquiry. Some thinkers continued to initiate inquiry by relying on principles believed to be self-evident; thus philosophy continued to be rationally oriented. Others, questioning the validity of assuming something to be true in advance of the search for truth, preferred to initiate inquiry on the basis of observation; thus science came to be empirically oriented. Science was then clearly differentiated from philosophy because it no longer followed a theory of inquiry that began with self-evident truths, proceeded to reason logically from these indubitable premises to a conclusion which followed, and then sought empirical data to confirm these a priori principles, reasoning, and conclusions—and so much the worse for the facts if they did not agree with reason. Rather science started with a set of observations or empirical facts, reasoned to probable conclusions or generalizations in a hypothetico-deductive manner, and then returned these conclusions to experience for auditing and testing—and so much the worse for the reasoning if it did not agree with the facts.

Despite this distinction there was no real conflict between science and philosophy, at least in the minds of the Greeks; even though both might be paths to truth, philosophy was the superior path because it relied on man's faculty of reason, not upon the mundane, grubby, narrow, restricted, earthly procedures of empiricism. The empirical method was useful, to be sure, for such tasks as the collection and classification of data; but what was ultimately real, of infinite value, were not the earthly things revealed by science but the heavenly things revealed by philosophy. Since no amount of data collecting, inductive classification, or experimentation could answer questions about the soul of man, the spirit of God (or the gods), or the good life, science became subservient to philosophy.

By the time of Galileo (1564–1642) the distinction between science and philosophy had grown into a separation, for where the prior superiority of philosophy to science precluded conflict between them, the rise of experimental science—greatly aided by Francis Bacon's (1561–1626) "new method" of induction—challenged the centuries-old inordinate-subordinate relationship. The essential characteristic of experimental science, the empirical testing of conclusions with the validity of conclusions utterly dependent upon repeatable and publicly shared experience, posed a threat to all areas and modes of inquiry that could not or would not submit conclusions to the test of experience. Philosophical conclusions, mostly being ethical, metaphysical, or logico-mathematical in nature, simply did not lend themselves to this kind of verification, so the separation of science from philosophy became a divorce.

The Renaissance of the fourteenth century, the Reformation of the sixteenth century, and the Enlightenment of the eighteenth century not only gave rise to the birth of modern science, but also gave rebirth to secular philosophy, with the consequence that the gap between science and philosophy narrowed. In the twentieth century, recent scientific advances have been joined with contemporary philosophic thought to reduce this gap to a minimum; the distinction between them today, as generally accepted by scientists and philosophers, is that "science" and "philosophy" are terms used to describe the division of labor in inquiry. The distinction between science and philosophy is maintained, but the differences are narrowed.

This is best illustrated, perhaps, by the fact that many contemporary scientists are capable and practicing philosophers, and vice versa. While we may think of Bertrand Russell, Hans Reichenbach, or Alfred North White-head as philosophers, how explain the fact that all are well grounded in, and have made important contributions to, science? Albert Einstein, in the public image, was thought of as the prime example of a scientist; yet he never conducted an experiment per se, and his work, as he once declared, was made possible only by a "philosophic breakthrough." And who can draw the line between science and philosophy such that Ernst Mach, F. S. C. Northrup, Percy Bridgman, or Carl Hempel can be classified as one or the other, but not both? These are academic questions, of course, since we know that the subject-matter pie cannot be sliced neatly into discrete pieces without doing some injustice to the pie as a whole and each piece of it—not to mention the cook. Any division is therefore arbitrary, justified only in programmatic terms, and subject to revision whenever required.

Therefore, if philosophy, whatever else it may or may not be, is an attempt at systematic reflection in order to "see things steadily and see them whole," then philosophy needs and must incorporate into its maps scientific facts to assist it in that task; and if science, whatever else it may or may not be, is an attempt at systematic investigation, then science needs and must incorporate into its maps philosophic principles to help in the genesis of hypotheses, the evolution of concepts, the construction of theories, and the guidance of inquiry.

He who inquires is both philosopher and scientist; he has two hats. When he attempts to formulate and ask meaningful questions he is primarily the philosopher; when he attempts to answer those questions he is primarily the scientist. Not all meaningful questions, however, are philosophic; nor do all meaningful questions admit of a scientific answer. For instance, the very question "What is a meaningful question?" is a philosophic question that does not admit of a scientific response—but clearly that question is meaningful for science. Or, the question "Do intelligent beings exist on other planets?" is a scientific question that does not admit of a philosophic answer —but just as clearly that question is meaningful for philosophy.

Perhaps today philosophy is most clearly distinguished from science by virtue of the kinds of questions asked and the methods used to answer them. When Plato asked "What is knowledge?" in his *Theaetetus*, or "What is justice?" in his *Republic*, he was asking questions which outrun the ability of science alone to answer. Facts do not yield answers to such questions, although facts constitute an invaluable element in the answers.

By the same token, when educational philosophers ask "What is education?" or "How do we know?" or "What is of value?" they are not asking scientific questions. That is, they are not asking the sociologist to give them a factual description of our educational system; they are not asking the psychologist to provide an empirical description of learning; nor do they want a cross-cultural analysis from the anthropologist. But when they ask "What is education like in Palo Alto, in Syracuse, in Lafayette?" or "What do tenth graders know about non-Euclidian geometry?" or "What are the objectives of education on Easter Island?" then they *are* asking the sociologist, the psychologist, or the anthropologist for empirical "this-is-the-situation" answers.

If there appears to be a confusion between the first and second set of questions, it lies in their formulation; it is a confusion between *ought* and *is* questions, between *definitional* and *existential* answers, between philosophy and science. When the educational philosopher asks "What is education?" he is actually asking "What *should* education be?" or "What shall we *mean* by 'education'?" When he asks "What is knowledge?" he is not only asking *"What* do we know?" and *"How* do we know?" but also "What do we *mean* when we use the verb *to know?"* When he asks "What is of value?" he is not asking a question about what people do in fact prize so much as he is asking one about what they should prize, why they should prize, and how these prizings can be justified.

These questions are qualitatively different from distinctly scientific questions. When the educator asks "What is the best (i.e., the most effective) way to teach reading to third graders?" or "What is the influence of socio-economic class position upon academic achievement?" or "How can the school plant be earthquake-proofed?" he is not posing questions with a direct ought dimension in them. The ought dimension to these has already been determined and answered; there is no longer any question of oughtness involved, for these questions imply that the pertinent value questions have already been asked and answered. To ask "How should fractions be taught?" may appear to be a philosophic question since it includes the word *should*, but this is deceptive since the mere asking of this question presupposes the prior value judgment that we *want* children to learn fractions. The *should* in that question is *instrumental;* it represents a concern with means to ends. Thus to ask "How should we teach cursive script?" is to ask what educational practices are required if we are to achieve the end of producing pupils who can do something more than print; it is to ask what course of action is needed (i.e., most effective) if our value judgment that we want children to be able to write cursively is going to be translated from a philosophic good to an empirical fact. To ask a "how to" question is to ask an empirical question, and the answer to such an inquiry tells us "this (means) will produce that (end)."

Yet in education, as in all other areas of life, it is not enough to have a technology—to know that X will produce Y. We must also know, that is, make the value decision, that we want Y; we must adjudge Y to be desirable. Since education is manifestly a moral enterprise, at least resting on the root valuation that it is better to know than to be ignorant, all educational questions have an inescapable axiological and epistemological dimension. But obviously education is also an empirical affair, so it has an inescapable scientific dimension as well. To ignore the philosophic dimension is to condemn the educative process to a blind intellectual wandering, devoid of a rudder for guidance, bound by the tradition of tradition, and haltered by habit. To ignore the scientific dimension is to divorce education from reality, to deny it the radar-like guidance of scientific generalizations, base actions on decisions starved for facts, and condemn it forever to rule-of-thumb, by-guess-and-by-golly procedures. Just as philosophy and science cannot be separated (although they can and must be distinguished) neither can the philosophy of education be separated from the science of education.

This is so because facts alone do not determine anything; bare facts are not only nude but mute. They take on a voice only when someone speaks for them, only when their mute presence is interpreted by someone in the light of some set of principles, standards, ends in view—in fine, in the light of philosophy. Facts alone do not dictate any course of action, much less the scope and sequence of an educational program. Programmatic courses of action in education are ascertained not merely by the facts of a given situation, but more importantly by our value preferences with respect to desired and anticipated outcomes.

There are two basic and persisting questions in education: What *should* be done? and how *can* it be done? These are the "ought" and "is" questions, the philosophic and scientific questions. The answers to these questions will of course change and vary from time to time and place to place, but the questions themselves are constants in the educational equation.

Simple logic indicates there are no means without ends (although there might be ends without means for their realization, or means that realize unanticipated ends); consequently an intelligent answer to a scientific question about means awaits the prior answering of a philosophic question about ends. Ends and means in education cannot be organically separated, although they can be logically distinguished for purposes of analysis, or brutally torn asunder through ignorance. They are cut from the whole cloth of education, a cloth that can be tailored into the cloak of learning only when philosophic thought and scientific methodology combine to give pattern and material to education. In this way science provides the necessary factual background for education and the philosophy of education.

Clearly, man wonders least about what he knows best. We seldom wonder, for instance, if the sun will rise tomorrow although we often wonder about what it might shine on. As the scientific method, when applied to education, produces more and more precise information about the process of education, and as increasingly reliable predictions are available for the use of educators, the boundaries of the map of things known are extended. As these frontier areas are opened up, we wonder less and less about them; what was once new and challenging becomes the tame and commonplace. But these hard-won patches of factual data, newly torn from the no man's land, provide the ground for new wonder, for new philosophic exploration. Using the gains made by educational science as background from which to move out into less explored regions, the philosopher of education secures to himself the greatest possible advantage. But unfortunately science has not always provided such a solid background.

Before the sciences of human behavior matured, and before reliable information about schools and education became available, often philosophy alone provided the sole intellectual basis for mapping out a program of instruction. Without sufficient factual information to plot a chart of how people learn, or to help decide what people should learn, educators had to rely on the dead-reckoning of intuition, pure reason, and personal experience. They came to rely heavily on a personalized philosophy of education. In this sense educational philosophy provided some kind of substantive thinking about teaching and learning, and it set a precedent for the type of educational theory used in recent times to undergird practices in such areas as curriculum, administration, supervision, and methodology. Even today, despite the claims of many who decry the "progressivization" of the schools, education remains governed more closely by principles and practices taken from nineteenth century philosophies of education than it is by knowledge drawn from the behavioral sciences and guided by a contemporary philosophy of education.

In this century, and most especially in the recent years, the behavioral sciences began to provide empirical information which took some educational questions out of the no man's land of wondering and put them clearly in the region of the known.

(In point of fact, while the universe may be expanding, the map of philosophy is diminishing. As science has advanced it has laid claim to territory traditionally in the domain of philosophy. Perhaps the first area to be wrested from philosophy was physics; then, in time, such areas as astronomy and physiology. More recently psychology and sociology have declared their independence from philosophy; for example, when "mind" or mental behavior was in the realm of philosophy, and since learning obviously had to do with education, and education with mind, theories of learning were then subject to the jurisdiction of educational philosophy. Today, however, with the independence of psychology from philosophy rather firmly established, the educational philosopher who talks about how children learn either speaks as an educational psychologist, basing his remarks on empirical data provided by psychological theory and investigation, or he talks nonsense. The educational philosopher is therefore restricted in the range of his remarks *qua* philosopher of education; he may talk about what children should learn, why they should learn, or when they should learn—if the "when" question is of subject matter sequence and not a psychological question about readiness. There are some, most notably the analytic philosophers, who claim that the subject matter of philosophy has been reduced to the analysis of language, and educational philosophy thus reduces to the analysis of terms and concepts used in education.)

Intelligence tests, aptitude inventories, attitude surveys, information questionnaires, interest reports, and ability diagnoses developed early in this century led some educators to anticipate a golden age of educational science, an age in which educational maps would be almost completed and the areas left open to wonderment considerably reduced. Developments in educational psychology and sociology, as well as information borrowed from other areas of science, seemed on the verge of disclosing a comprehensive and substantive theory of human nature and learning that would replace the older maps drawn on the basis of philosophic wandering. Science seemed about to provide a background of advanced bases from which educators could finally hit the target and determine just what the aims and means of education should be. Educational thinkers were ready to abandon speculative, rationalistic theories of education in favor of substantive statements based on scientific investigation.

In the first flush of enthusiasm, instead of wondering so much about what should be done, they directed their attention to understanding what had been done, what was being done, and what could be done. They were ready, even eager, to accept as the basis for all educational thinking the same background picture of empirical information that science had supplied as the basis for common sense reasoning about the physical world of objects and events; they were ready to use this purely descriptive and solidly factual background as the basis for educational programs that could and would bear the stamp "inspected, tested, and approved by Educational Science."

This scientizing of education was halted when educational philosophers of all persuasions simply pointed out that the "scientific method of determining the ends of education" through such techniques as job descriptions, activity analyses, and consenses of experts was deceptive and deluding. Valuable as such information may be, it does not and could not, without some kind of guidance, answer questions such as whether or not the schools should continue to reflect a current socioeconomic situation or whether the schools could or dared to build a new social order.

Science and philosophy are inextricably involved in the educative process. When educators base their programs upon philosophy alone it is lop-sided and devoid of content; but more often educators tend to base their programs on science alone and, by implication, deny the need and value of philosophy in the solution of problems. But strangely enough *that* is to assert a philosophic position. Put otherwise, those educators who consider themselves "on the firing line" in education and therefore deny the practicality of theory in favor of the practical and non-theoretical are simply arguing that no theory is the best theory—in the same way that some ultraconservatives argue that no government is the best government. And *that* theory, as Frank Albrecht has noted, has failed every time it has been put seriously to the test. Fact and theory are inescapable in education, but the validity of the facts and the level of the theory are variables in the educational enterprise.

THE PROBLEM OF CATEGORIES: WHAT KIND OF MAPS?

The arbitrariness of the categorization of thought about education into schools of educational philosophy indicates one of the problems in map-making: what should be the tools, or criteria, of categorization? In truth, this is to ask what kind of maps should be drawn, for the maps will reflect not only the cartographer's skill but the tools used to collect and analyze his data.

Should philosophy of education be identified by an a priori definition of the subject matter? By the kinds of questions asked by those who are educational philosophers? By the kinds of answers provided? By the operations performed in formulating, asking, and answering questions? By some, all, or none of these criteria?

The first alternative, in which philosophy of education is defined in terms of its "own" subject matter, is very appealing. The trouble is that there is no great consensus among philosophers or educators as to just what this subject matter does, or should, consist of. Some, perhaps the heirs of the medieval view that philosophy is queen of all the sciences, refuse to be pinned down and insist any subject matter is ultimately philosophical, that any subject matter carries some implications for education. Others, perhaps overly impressed by the sciences' desertion of the queen, have reduced her to an intellectual harlot who serves only a sterile function in the analysis of verbal intercourse; philosophy of education thus becomes one of the hand-maidens of the harlot queen, along with philosophy of science (i.e., linguistic analysis of scientific terms and concepts), philosophy of history (i.e., linguistic analysis of historical terms and concepts), philosophy of religion (i.e., linguistic analysis of religious terms and concepts), etc.

As for the second alternative, if all educational philosophers were agreed on the pertinent questions, then different answers to the same questions would provide a basis for the categorization of philosophies of education. That is, it might be claimed that the subject matter of philosophy of educa-tion is the material (e.g., possible educational relations between man and society, nature and supernature) giving birth to the questions; the different answers given, when lumped into those of a kind, would comprise the different philosophies of education. But this assumes educational philosophers are agreed on the pertinent questions to be asked—which they are not. Some consider the asking of the question "What is the *ultimate* end of education?" pertinent, even vital, to educational philosophizing; others insist this is a meaningless question, incorporating into the very question a philosophic bias (i.e., an example of smuggling conclusions into premises). Thus it is evident that philosophers of education are divided over the *kinds* of questions prop-erly to be asked; there is some general agreement, of course, but there is also violent disagreement—enough so that it would be inaccurate to cate-gorize philosophies of education either, or only, on the basis of different questions asked or different answers given—even if it is assumed these are different answers to the same questions. Perhaps it would be possible to categorize philosophies of education in terms of *bodies* or *sets* of different questions and different answers (each to his own, so to say) so that each philosophy of education would have a unique set of questions and answers. This is possible, naturally, but then it might be concluded that philosophy of education is either the sum of all the questions asked (and the material giving birth to them), the sum of all the answers given (and the methods yielding them), or both. But these definitions of philosophy of education might be so vague as to be meaningless: how would one differentiate philosophy of education from other disciplines, on this view?

Perhaps the *differentia* of philosophy of education lies not so much in questions asked or answers given as in the methods employed to pose questions and secure answers. Insofar as educational philosophy is a process, method is important. Yet, is (any) method exclusive to philosophy? Certainly not the method of science. Nor that of logic. Nor reason, nor intuition, nor revelation—all of which have been used by philosophers of education at one time or another. There *is* method to, and in, philosophy of education; and philosophies of education might be categorized by the (fundamental or primary) method used. It is on this basis, for example, that philosophies are often identified as "rational" or "empirical"; but even so it is a question of emphasis because no rational philosophy denies the uses of experience and no empirical philosophy denies the uses of reason.

There is a middle ground between the royalists who respect no boundaries and who would define their philosophic subject matter as roughly equivalent to the outer limits of the universe, and the linguists who so respect certain kinds of boundaries that they have legislated philosophy of education out of a substantive existence and reconstituted it as a prophylactic method of the whole by which to cleanse education of verbal infection, but this middle ground is no more productive of a satisfactory and acceptable definition than are the extremes.

Apparently it is not possible to define philosophy of education in terms of a unique, distinctive subject matter—or, at least, it has not been done in the last 2000 years to the satisfaction of educational philosophers. Nor can it be defined in terms of a unique, distinctive methodology. Nevertheless, philosophers of education are agreed that they do have both subject matter and methodology; they feel sure the beast exists, and like the seven blind men and the elephant, each has his own idea of it but none can say for sure what the "true" or "whole" nature of the beast is, or should be.

This plurality of definitions is exhibited in the six essays to follow. The first, an official statement of The Philosophy of Education Society, represents as close to a consensus as has been achieved by those who are experts in the field, and by those representing all different points of view in the field. It is not so much a map as an analysis of the tools and techniques of map making.

The second essay, by John Dewey, defines philosophy as the general theory of education; or, put conversely, education is seen to be the practical application of philosophy. In this short essay Dewey does not draw his map (this he does elsewhere) so much as he indicates the relationship between maps and travelers in education.

In the third essay Earl Cunningham sketches in the broad outlines of two different maps of similar territory (as, for example, the difference between a Mercator and polar projection), the Aristotelian and the operational.

Charles Virtue, in the next essay, examines the similarities and differences among four maps: those drawn by Dewey, Alfred North Whitehead, Theodore Brameld, and Harry S. Broudy. George Newsome, in the fifth essay of this section, considers the activities of the map-makers, of educational philosophers, and argues that philosophy of education should produce explorers rather than memorizers of maps already drawn.

Finally, in the sixth and last essay, Kingsley Price attacks the problem somewhat differently. Instead of drawing a new map, reviewing old maps, examining the tools of map-making, or observing the actions of those who draw maps, he asks "What is a map?"—and then by example gives his definition of the field to be explored and mapped by educational philosophers.

∽

OVERVIEW

There is an old saying that if all the philosophers in the world were laid end to end they still wouldn't reach a conclusion. In the following article a majority of the members of The Philosophy of Education Society did reach a conclusion, a conclusion about the nature of their field (and without being laid end to end).

The statement is equally as interesting for its implicit conclusion (i.e., agreement about the field of educational philosophy can be achieved only when generalizations are used) as it is for the explicit conclusion authorized by the Society. This should not be taken as criticism, however, since the Society makes it quite clear that this was an attempt to define only the common, minimal characteristics of philosophy of education.

The article identifies three characteristics common to all "philosophies of" —philosophy of education, philosophy of science, philosophy of history, etc. These are (1) the possession of unique tools of inquiry (e.g., logic, theory of meaning) and categories (e.g., epistemology, metaphysics); (2) the use of these to examine judgments and standards of judgments; and (3) the possession of a unique body of subject matter—the substantive which constitutes the *of* in *philosophy of*.

From this it follows that one philosophizes about education (or, *is* a philosopher of education) when one uses these tools to examine the alternative criteria being suggested as desirable guides for educational behavior. This process of philosophizing about education involves three logically distinguishable, but empirically inseparable, phases.

    1. The *analytic,* or descriptive, phase which involves making clear the nature of the criteria which guide educational choices

2. The *evaluative,* or critical, phase which involves the close inspection of those criteria, the identification and inspection of alternative criteria, and the assessment of each (the latter evidently conducted in terms of an unspecified *metacritical* criterion)

3. The *speculative,* or hypothetical, phase which involves the framing of new alternatives for the conduct of education through this prior examination and synthesis of older standards and practices

The distinctive nature of the discipline of the philosophy of education, then, is characterized by (1) the possession of theoretical tools and techniques which are common to all philosophy, (2) the use of these to make and evaluate decisions particularly pertinent to the field of education, and (3) its unique dependence upon education as the designated subject-matter area for these theoretical operations.

The Distinctive Nature of the Discipline
of the Philosophy of Education

*A Statement by the Philosophy of Education Society**

We make a distinction between disciplines or modes of inquiry such as psychology, sociology, administration, engineering and philosophy, and the persons who utilize these disciplines. Our attention is to the disciplines persons employ rather than to the persons who employ the disciplines.

What philosophy of education ought to be and do is a highly debatable matter insofar as differing answers come from differing philosophical positions. This statement, therefore, attempts only to delineate the basic, common, or minimal characteristics of the discipline within which we find these differing answers and positions.

A. The various philosophies—philosophy of education, art, science, politics, religion and history among them— share three characteristics which help distinguish philosophy from other fields of endeavor:

1. Unique theoretical tools consisting of hypotheses, concepts and categories (such as meaning, truth, value, method).

2. The employment of these tools in the examination of the criteria, assumptions and/or reasons which guide assessments, judgments and choices.

* This statement was prepared by the Committee on the Nature and Function of the Discipline of the Philosophy of Education, of The Philosophy of Education Society, composed of the following members: Nathaniel Champlin, Chairman, Wayne State University; David Adams, Western Michigan University; Otto Krash, Hunter College; Robert Mason, University of Pittsburgh; and Francis Villemain, University of Toledo. The report of the Committee was adopted by the Society at its 1953 annual meeting. Reprinted by permission from *Educational Theory,* IV (January, 1954), 1–3.

3. A scholarly acquaintance with events, practices, circumstances, and/or ideas relevant to that which the philosophy is *of* (that is, education, art, politics, science or religion).

When this critical examination is directed to the criteria and the conceptual tools of the different philosophies we have what some would call "pure" or "general" philosophy, and what others would call the philosophy of philosophy.

The philosophies of education, art, science, religion and history may then be viewed as distinctive philosophic disciplines which achieve their distinctiveness by virtue of that to which they direct their critical and reflective attention. All are philosophies, or philosophy, because of the kinds of conceptual tools and skills employed. Each is a distinctive philosophy because of the domain, subject matter, problem area, or activity about which it theorizes and speculates. Moreover, the theorizing and speculating of one philosophy, say, the philosophy of education or the philosophy of art, may provide conceptions and ideas which act to modify the theorizing of another, say, the philosophy of history or, even possibly, "pure" philosophy. Each philosophy may be considered a resource for others.

We may, through contrast and comparison, locate differences within philosophy. Some have used the terms *realism, idealism* and *experimentalism* to note these differences. Called philosophic positions or "families," they have been differentiated further. Realism, for example, may include such differences as are noted with the terms *sense-realism, materialist realism* and *classical realism. Idealism* and *experimentalism*

also admit of family differences. In the case of the latter we hear of *logical empiricism, bio-social instrumentalism* and *Peircian pragmatism.* This is to say that the philosophy of education, art, science, history, or politics may be qualified by such terms as *realist, idealist,* or *experimentalist* philosophy of education, art, science, history or politics. Such terms (others have been suggested) are used to distinguish the different criteria and grounds used in establishing philosophical concepts, hypotheses and categories.

B. The term *education* may refer to any deliberate effort to nurture, modify, change and/or develop human conduct or behavior; or it may refer to organized schooling. For purposes of consensus we adopt the latter (institutionalized schooling).

Wherever education, thus defined, is taking place we find:

1. Preferences for certain procedures, resources and goals (methods, means and ends) implicit or explicit in the undertaking.
2. The employment of criteria, guides or reasons with which procedures, resources and goals are determined and established.

This is to say that teachers, administrators and others caught up in the educational enterprise, are making choices for desirable procedures, resources and goals in terms of implicit or explicit, critical or uncritical, criteria or reasons. When, prior to choosing, educators delineate and examine alternative criteria and grounds for the selection and rejection of these procedures, resources and goals, they are being critical about the choices they make.

The criteria guiding educational choices and policies may be consistent with the theories and concepts of one philosophical position (e.g., idealism, realism or experimentalism), or with some combination from the alternative positions. Therefore, in order that educational choices and policies be *philosophically* critical they must be made in view of the delineation and examination of alternative philosophical criteria: and anyone, thus oriented, is working within an area that is included in the subject matter of the discipline of the philosophy of education.

Putting it another way: when we (1) single out and examine the criteria and assumptions guiding the choices being made in education, and (2) conduct our examination in terms of the concepts and categories of philosophy, we are working within the discipline of the philosophy of education. This discipline is alternative to other educational disciplines such as administration, psychology, and pedagogy. (This is not to say that competence in one discipline precludes competence in one or more other disciplines.)

C. Three interrelated phases of philosophic thought devoted to education are to be noted. These phases may be viewed as conditions for establishing the "content" of the discipline of the philosophy of education.

1. The *descriptive-analytical* task of the philosopher of education may be in the articulation of (making explicit) the criteria which, in fact, guide the choices made in educational circles. This task may include relating these criteria to philosophic positions, and examining them in terms of consistency, meaning, expectation, and method.

2. The *critical-evaluative* task of the philosopher of education may be in the framing of alternative criteria provided by the philosophy of education. This task may include locating criteria for assessing these alternatives for purposes of determining the more adequate and/or "reasonable" criteria.

3. The *speculative* task of the philosopher of education may be in the forging or framing of new alternatives for use in philosophy, education, and/or the discipline of the philosophy of education.

D. In those institutions having courses in the philosophy of education, we should have provision for the study of, and the gaining of skills in, the conceptual materials (content) peculiar to the discipline. The teaching personnel should be equipped with, and trained in, the conceptual tools and skills peculiar to the discipline.

In those institutions having no place for the philosophy of education, we have, nevertheless, philosophically oriented conceptions and theories "hidden" in, or screened by, policies (administrative-curriculum), and other courses (educational psychology, pedagogy, "methods," and "principles"). Unless these philosophic materials are singled out for special examination they are uncritically assumed and fostered.

〜

OVERVIEW

Although by far the oldest article in the present collection, the following essay by John Dewey can still be classified as one of the most contemporary statements concerning the interaction between philosophy and education. Originally written in 1911 and published for the first time in 1913, the theme of the essay—that philosophy is the general theory of education—was later expanded by Dewey to become one of the central ideas in his famous book, *Democracy and Education.*

In that text Dewey insists that "Philosophy [is] a form of thinking, which, like all thinking, finds its origin in what is uncertain in the subject matter of experience, [and] which aims to locate the nature of the perplexity and to frame hypotheses for its clearing up . . ." Philosophy is not a set of transempirical dicta handed down from some ivory tower; it is a process rooted in the soil of earthly problems—not the shifting skies of metaphysical speculations. The philosophic *act* (or, philosophizing) occurs when habitual behavior no longer serves to guide human conduct adequately and, turning away from habit, one reflects on the status quo in order to plan a new, future course of action. In this sense, philosophy is a process rather than a product; it is a unique form of behavior rather than a unique collection of facts and myths. It is the process of intelligently planning future ends and means.

To grasp the organic relationship that Dewey sees between philosophy and education it is necessary to view education as a much broader phenomenon than mere schooling. Education involves *all* of the institutions and individuals that influence attitudes and dispositions. True enough, the school is such an agency—but so are the home and the church, the sloganeering of Madison Avenue, a Legionnaire parade, and the old swimming hole, not to mention such obvious moulders of human predispositions as television, motion pictures, radio, newspapers, and magazines. Any organization, from the Boy Scouts to the neighborhood gang on the corner, from the local saloon to the international bank, is educative (or miseducative) to the degree it forms or modifies attitudes. In Dewey's words, "Every place in which men habitually meet, shop, club, factory, saloon, church, political caucus, is perforce a school-house."

When the school is set apart from its social context, when schooling is unconcerned with issues in the larger environment, then it ". . . tends to become a routine empirical affair unless its aims and methods are animated by a . . . survey of its place in contemporary life as is the business of philosophy to provide." Philosophy, which is the process of ordering ends and means so as to develop a theory concerning the achievement of a desired future, is thus related to education in a practical sense—for education, consciously geared to this ideal, becomes the vehicle by which to realize this future.

Given this dichotomy, there are two extremes: either education can consist of unguided, habitual behaviors, or it can be an education which is deliberately guided by philosophy. Dewey, of course, elects the latter course of action and the logic of his argument is simple: human dispositions lead to interests; interests lead to the formulation of purposes; purposes lead to efforts; efforts lead to certain socio-individual consequences (the nature of which depend upon the initial dispositions); and education is the process by which these initial dispositions are formed.

Thus Dewey functionally links a broadly conceived education with a philosophy grounded in experience. Since, in his words, ". . . education is the process through which the needed [social] transformation may be accomplished," education becomes the translation of philosophy into a deliberately conducted practice.

Philosophy Is the General Theory of Education

John Dewey*

We have to judge every educational institution and practice from the standpoint of that "whole of experience" which calls it into being and controls its purpose and materials. There exist not merely the principles by which the existing system of education is made effective, but also the principles that animate the entire range of interests of the whole life of the community and that make the existing system what it is. An interpretation and valuation of the educational system in the light of this inclusive social context is the larger and more human view of which we spoke. It utilizes the contributions of science in all its branches to give society an insight into what sort of thing it is

undertaking in the training of its members, and it gives society a clearer consciousness of the meaning of the educational office so largely performed by instinct and custom.

The connection of education and philosophy is, however, even closer and more vital than this [foregoing] sketch of the principles of education, as distinct from the science of education, would indicate. *Philosophy may be defined as the general theory of education; the theory of which education is the corresponding art or practice.* Three interlinked considerations support this statement: (i) Men's interests manifest their dispositions; (ii) these dispositions are formed by education; (iii) there must be a general idea of the value and relations of these interests if there is to be any guidance of the proc-

* *Cyclopedia of Education,* Paul Monroe (ed.), (New York: The Macmillan Co., 1913), Vol. IV, pp. 699–700. Reprinted by permission of Ellis Monroe and Jeanette Monroe Bassett.

ess of forming the dispositions that lie back of the realization of the interests. (i) If at any time the various values of experience are out of harmony with one another, the ultimate cause of the difficulty lies in men's habitual attitudes toward life: the habits of judging and of emotional appreciation that are embodied in their habits of action. Interests, attitudes, dispositions, fundamental habits of mind are mutually convertible terms.

(ii) If we but consent to extend the term education beyond its narrow limitation to schooling, we shall find that we cannot stop short in this extension till we have broadened it to cover all the agencies and influences that shape disposition. Not merely books and pictures, but the machinery of publication and communication by which these are made accessible must be included—and this means the use made of railway and telegraph as well as of the printing press, the library, and the picture gallery. Ordinarily daily intercourse, the exchange of ideas and experiences in conversation, and the contacts of business competition and coöperation are most influential in deciding the objects upon which attention is fixed and the way in which attention is given to them. Every place in which men habitually meet, shop, club, factory, saloon, church, political caucus, is perforce a schoolhouse, even though not so labelled. This intercourse is in turn dependent upon the political organization of society, the relations of classes to one another, the distribution of wealth, the spirit in which family life is conducted, and so on. Public agitations, discussions, propaganda of public meeting and press, political campaigns, legislative

deliberations, are in this regard but so many educational agencies. In brief, every condition, arrangement, and institution that forms the emotional and imaginative bent of mind that gives meaning to overt action is educational in character.

(iii) There are but two alternatives. Either these agencies will perform their educational work as an incidental and unregulated by-product, molding men's mind blindly while conscious attention is given to their other more tangible products; or men will have an idea of the results they wish to have attained, will judge existing agencies according as they achieve or come short of these ends, and will use their idea and their estimate as guides in giving the desired direction to the working of these agencies. This brings us, again, to philosophy, which, as we have seen, is the attempt to develop just such an idea. This is what is meant by saying that philosophy is, in its ultimate extent, a general theory of education; or that it is the idea of which a *consciously guided education* is the practical counterpart.

It is, of course, possible to exaggerate the importance of philosophy even when it is conceived in this vital and human sense. Reflection is only one of the forces that move our action, and in the thick of events it gives place to necessities of more urgency. But on the other hand, reflection is the only thing that takes us out of the immediate pressure and hurly-burly of overt action. It is a temporary turning aside from the immediate scene of action in order to note the course of events, to forecast probable and possible issues, to take stock of difficulties and resources, to bring to explicit consciousness evils that may be remedied, to plan a future course of action. Philosophy cannot create values by thinking about them, by defining and classifying and arranging them. But by thinking about them, it may promote discrimination as to what is genuinely desirable, and thereby contribute to subsequent conduct a clearer and more deliberately settled method of procedure in attaining what is desired.

There is always danger that the student of philosophy will become simply a student of philosophic traditions, of something that is conventionally called philosophy but from which philosophic life has departed because the genuine problem in life which called out the formulation has departed from consciousness. When philosophic distinctions are approached from the standpoint of their bearing upon life through the medium of the educational process in which they take effect, the perplexity, the predicament, of life which generates the issue can never be far from recognition.

∽

OVERVIEW

Lawrence Thomas, building on Charles Peirce's shrewd observation that it is not possible to doubt all things at once, noted that philosophy "clarifies and criticizes the various alternative assumptions about the ultimate nature of the universe and man, some of which [assumptions] men must take as the foundation of any consistent, comprehensive viewpoint on life." Since there is no view without a point of view, there are some things—in each given situation—which must be taken for granted, else all other things lose their perspective for lack of a reference point.

It is in this spirit that Earl Cunningham initiates the following article with the promise that if one will "Outline for [him] the major assumptions in a man's world-view . . . [he] will outline for [us] the patterns which his institutions are most likely to be like."

Implicit in Thomas' definition and Cunningham's promise is the assertion that there are many and conflicting world-views, as indeed there are. Historically speaking, philosophy has been characterized by two major themes, two major points of view, two major ways of "looking at things." For purposes of identification these are often distinguished from each other by the use of such word pairings as rational and empirical, supernatural and natural, absolute and relative, closed and open, or traditional and modern.

It is true that polarized categories in any field ignore finer distinctions; that the setting of black against white ignores the multiple shades of grey. Nevertheless, just as the art critic often stands back to observe the macrocosmic differences between a Renoir and a Degas as they hang side-by-side before he moves in to make his detailed evaluation of each, so too is it useful for the neophyte philosopher of education to begin his observations and evaluations with an elementary, two-valued "this or that" comparison of the large world picture. Cunningham provides the tools necessary for this job by outlining, simply and clearly, the first principles of an Aristotelian and a more contemporary world-view.

Philosophy, he suggests, can be defined as the organization of beliefs about man and his universe, about how and what man knows and values. The basic theme of his essay is that these beliefs are not (or, at least, should not be) held *in vacuuo,* but that they guide man's behavior and shape his institutions—and given different sets of belief, different behaviors and institutions will emerge. Thus, for Cunningham, philosophy makes a difference: if one adheres to a rationalistic set of first principles, drawn for instance from the thought of Plato, Aristotle, St. Thomas Aquinas and Jacques Maritain, he will believe and behave differently from one who adheres to an empirical set of first principles, perhaps drawn from Heraclitus, Francis Bacon, David Hume, and John Dewey.

Put in an educational context, Cunningham implies that differing first principles lead to differing philosophic positions, these different philosophic positions lead to different philosophies of education, from which eventuate different educational policies and practices; thus there is a functional connection between what one actually does in the classroom and what set of first principles one takes to be valid.

The philosophy of education, as process, appears when man applies his first principles to the institution of education; or, put otherwise, the philosophy of education, as product, consists of those implications for educational curriculum, purposes, and methodology which are drawn from first principles.

In his essay Cunningham not only explicates the fundamentals of two generic positions in philosophy, and relates these to education, he re-emphasizes the important fact that somewhere, at some time, at some point, one *must* make assumptions. But he also reminds us that these assumptions, these philosophic acts of faith, need to be made explicit—we should not let them be smuggled into our intellectual baggage. They need to be identified, examined, and perhaps most important, doubted.

The importance of doubt, for those who are fortunate enough to take a newspaper carrying Jack Kent's cartoon strip entitled, "King Aroo," was recently illustrated in a clever manner. They may remember the situation when the Prime Minister came upon King Aroo and the Doubting Tomcat, and a veritable river of tears flowed from the eyes of the cat.

"What's the matter with him?" asked the Prime Minister of King Aroo.
"He's the Doubting Tomcat," replied the King, "and I'm afraid I upset him."
"How?"

"I told him he was such a good doubter," answered King Aroo, "that he could probably doubt anything."

At which point the tearful flow increased as the Doubting Tomcat sobbed, "And try as I may, I can't doubt his words!"

All of which humorously underscores Peirce's dictum that we cannot doubt all things at once, Thomas' assertion that some set of assumptions lie embedded in each *Weltanschauung,* and Cunningham's insistence that each of these world-views be examined to see which is most appropriate in guiding the construction of our educational institutions.

(P.S. Do you think that the Doubting Tomcat can doubt that he doubts?)

First Principles for a Modern Philosophy of Education

Earl C. Cunningham*

"Outline for me the major assumptions in a man's world-view and I will outline for you the patterns which his institutions are most likely to be like," is a rather accurate way to epitomize the role of philosophy in human affairs. Social institutions, unless haphazard, are operational externalizations of assumptions which are thought to be basic and structural to the nature of things.

As used in this study "world-view" means a synoptic summary of beliefs and assumptions which men form around such concepts as the following:

1. The origin, nature, and destiny of the universe;
2. The origin, nature, and purpose of man;
3. The origin, nature, and limits of knowledge; and
4. The origin and nature of value.

* Reprinted by permission from *Educational Theory,* V (January, 1955), 1–12.

Further, and as used in the study, "first principles" means the specific assumptions men project as answers to such general concepts as listed above under "world-view." These first principles, in turn, provide meaning, purpose, and direction for institutional development.

Three things are proposed in this study. *First,* because the presuppositions of this proposed philosophy of education stand in opposition to traditional or Aristotelian presuppositions, and because the current attack on education stems out of an apparent move to re-establish Aristotelian assumptions, Part I is a summary statement of Aristotelian *first principles* as these are related to the above world-view concepts. *Second,* Part II is an attempt to pour meanings into the above world-view concepts in ways which are consonant with modern empiricism. *Third,* Part III is a statement, in synoptic form, of assumptions which serve as first principles for our proposed philosophy of education.

ARISTOTELIAN FIRST PRINCIPLES

Traditional educational philosophy grew out of an amazing complex of ideas—to insist that it is strictly Aristotelian in origin would be inaccurate. Aristotle, Plato, Plotinus, Augustine, Aquinas, are but a few who had a "hand" in our traditional philosophy. However, for reasons of convenience, we are going to speak of this complex as Aristotelian. We turn to a summary of the following Aristotelian first principles:

ON THE ORIGIN, NATURE, AND DESTINY OF THE WORLD. The universe is brought into completed and static existence through motion imparted to primitive matter (potentiality) by Pure Form (God). God surrounds the cosmic spheres and maintains them in motion by his eternal activities.

The universe is a hierarchy of levels. At one end is the passivity of sheer matter. Through an ascending order of form-and-matter one reaches the highest level, which is Pure Form. Form, which is self-energizing, is purposive and teleological. Everything in nature is *directed* toward a *final purpose*. Realization of capacities, which are predetermined by Form, becomes the end of the animate and inanimate world. Nature is under the permanent control and guidance of a transempirical God or Form.

ON THE ORIGIN, NATURE, AND PURPOSE OF MAN. Man is simply an admixture of *form and matter,* with a preponderance of form, the main differentia of which is rationality. Man's origin is bound up, of course, in the initial activity when Pure Form imposed particularized forms on inert matter.

Man has a soul, which is divided into three parts: the vegetative, the will, and reason. Reason is the guiding agency. Since the cosmos is teleological, and since reason is the chief differentia setting man apart from the animal world, and since the *final purpose* of everything in nature is the realization of capacities, then the final purpose of man is realization of his capacity of rationality. . . . The Platonic-Christian variant on this must be noted: Man is a special creation of God; the rational element in man is structurally independent of matter; and the ultimate destiny of the soul of man is restoration to its original home in Plato's perfect world or the Christian heaven.

ON THE ORIGIN, NATURE, AND LIMITS OF KNOWLEDGE. The essence of Form is rationality. By virtue of the preponderance of form over matter, man is at the top of the hierarchy of created things in the natural world. Now since form is characterized by rationality and since man is predominantly form, he is, therefore, predominantly rational. But to be a rational animal is to be a *thinking* animal; and to think one must have a method—thus, Aristotle develops his science of logic. Aristotelian *science* will stand further examination.

1. The inductive process is ancillary to his science. Induction serves only to find particular cases through which the active reason is able to intuit *universal* and *necessary* principles.
2. These universal principles once intuited, are unqualifiedly true. Form, when apprehended through reason, is infallible. *Truth is absolute.*

3. As stated under the nature of the world, the active reason intuits that nature is a hierarchy of forms with Pure Form at the top and approaching sheer matter at the bottom. Now these forms (common nouns) are static *classes of things*. Knowledge of nature becomes an elaborate system of classifying particulars into pre-determined classes. (The principle of classification being purposive, not arbitrary.) *Knowledge thus becomes absolute.*

4. Scientific method presupposes absolute primary truths. The big job of Aristotelian science is *deduction* of specific truths from absolute general truths through the instrument of the syllogism.

5. A later Christian application of these Aristotelian principles again seems apropos: Deriving their *universal* and *necessary* truths from Biblical revelation, the Scholastics also arrived at *absolute* particular truths through an application of the "science" of Aristotle.

On the Origin and Nature of Value. Both traditional philosophers of education and the Scholastics rejected the *golden mean* of the *Nicomachean Ethics* and turned to the absolutistic systems of Plato and Augustine. We must look to these for our guide: Morality is grounded (with Plato) in a perfect, transcendent world. The *real* world is this transcendent world—Justice, Beauty, Truth, Righteousness, the Good, *all* are immutable ideas existing in the perfect world. Through Plato's doctrines of *remembrance* and *participation,* man's reason enables him to know these perfect Ideas. Mundane morality is thus patterned after the perfect Ideas. Thus, through reason *man may know that moral standards are absolute, immutable, eternal.* The

Christian tradition grounds its morality differently but arrives at the same place with Plato: *Values are eternal.*

To summarize Aristotelian first principles:

1. The world came into being through the activity of a *prime mover.*
2. The world is teleological throughout.
3. Everything in nature has a purpose or function. This function is realization of super-imposed capacities.
4. Man is a rational being. His chief function is realization of his capacity of rationality.
5. In the Platonic-Christian pattern, man, standing in unique relation to God through special creation, finds his chief aim in eternal salvation.
6. Truth is an absolute.
7. Moral standards are absolutes.

A CONTEMPORARY WORLD-VIEW

The origin, nature, and destiny of the universe. Our assumptions concerning the origin of the universe are governed by two criteria: (1) the concept of *parsimony,* and (2) knowledge, to be genuine and informative, must be capable of *public* verification.

We are not concerned with origins. We prefer to accept the universe as a *given.* So far as we are concerned, it has always been. Traditional Aristotelians reject this because, as they argue, that which will cease to be, at one time did not exist; if at one time it did not exist, then it could not be the efficient cause of itself. Since everything we know in the world of sense at one time did not exist, then we must posit an unmoved First Cause to get the universe in original motion.

We reject this Aristotelian-Thomistic argument on the grounds of parsimony and reaffirm our assumption that the universe is a given. We reason as follows: Explanations should not be expanded beyond necessity. *Somewhere in the causal series of explanation of origins of the universe we must stop arbitrarily.* Aristotelians insist upon positing an unknown to explain a known. We prefer to stop before we begin—that is, arbitrarily, with what is given in primary experience, which is the known world. . . . Since our data are all of a phenomenal nature, we insist that warrantable inference will not permit us to posit a noumenal or trans-empirical order. Hence, the world of nature is all we can know, and, since it is all that we know, we will keep our generalizations within our data. This yields only a natural order which must be accepted as a given.

We accept Heraclitean change or flux as providing the most reliable picture of the world, with this qualification: Heraclitus posited a *law* of change behind the phenomena of change. We would delete this law of change and describe the universe as one of flux—not through necessity, but from empirical observation. Natural laws are statistical generalizations. There is nothing in the principle of causation which allows us to assume either immutability or inevitability of natural law. It is, as Hume so aptly expressed it, expectancy based on habit. The only necessity is psychological expectancy. This in no sense disturbs the concept of uniformity of nature, nor does it lessen or impair the predictive function of law. It simply recasts both uniformity and predictability in terms of probabilities. This point of view affords us a universe that yields only problematic knowledge; *never certainty.*

The fundamental stuff of the universe is atomic (we prefer to follow Karl Pearson's concept of the atom [as defined in his *Grammar of Science*]: "Atom and molecule are intellectual conceptions by the aid of which physicists classify phenomena and formulate the relationships of their sequences"). All that happens is change within atomic structure and function. Differences in things are purely quantitative and due to chance organization of atomic elements. Existence can be attributed only to that which is quantitatively measurable.

The universe is characterized by novelty. We deny the Aristotelian-Christian concept of a completed, static, closed world, wherein the only change possible is, as Dewey writes [in *Reconstruction in Philosophy*], ". . . the monotonous traversing of a previous plotted cycle. . . ."

We prefer to affirm a world which is open at both ends; where "potentiality" actually means the emergence of the new; where "development" may mean new forms, mutations, novelty; wherein classes are not fixed and wherein variability is limited only by chance arrangements and combinations of elements.

Regarding the destiny of the universe we can only surmise: If the principle of the conservation of energy proves to be correct, then nothing can be destroyed. If the principle of entropy is correct, energy is slowly being dissipated and lost. It may be that in an infinitely variegated universe for every action there is a counter action—if this be true we could well be back into the Heraclitean "strife of opposites" where organization and disorganization oppose each other and thus maintain a relative equilibrium. . . . But of one thing we feel relatively certain, whatever does happen, and anything can, it can be explained in terms of mechanics. Certainly we find no empirical evidence to support the traditional view that the world is moving toward some predetermined ethical end.

ON THE ORIGIN, NATURE, AND PURPOSE OF MAN. Man is a cosmic accident. A fortuitous collocation of atoms combined and organized in a unique way. He is an emergent from and a part of nature in the same sense as are other species in the animal kingdom. He did not have to be, except in retrospect. Somewhere along the vast reaches of evolutionary time, chance, variable mutations favorable to survival occurred, and, through the hereditary transmission of these favorable survival characters, the cosmic stage was set for his eventual emergence. . . . And so man is, as Randall writes [in *The Making of the Modern Mind*], ". . . a tiny speck on a third-rate planet, revolving about a tenth-rate sun, drifting in an endless cosmic ocean."

Man is nature at the level of self-consciousness. There is no reason to attempt to set him apart as non-continuous with evolutionary processes. In a sense, man's rational capacity is no more unique than the wings of a bird or the fins of a fish. Each of these followed particular adaptive, selective routes in the struggle for existence; each developed adequate survival organs.

Again, we reject the teleological explanation that birds have wings so they can fly; man has rational capacities so that he can reason. Rather, birds fly because they have wings; man reasons (if he does) because he has rational capacities. Any qualitative uniqueness man has—such as being created only a little lower than the angels—he can ascribe to his own self-laudatory proclivities (observe his modesty in classifying himself as a *primate!*).

This is no attempt to belittle man's remarkable capacities—his artistic and literary creations, his towering philosophical structures, his inventive genius. It is argued here that perhaps man's greatest capacity is his ability to recognize the limits of his rational competency and to stay strictly within those limits. (Perhaps this is what Korzybski meant by the suggestive title of his book, *Manhood of Humanity*. Certainly this is the meaning of Comte's Positivism.) By nature, man's rational ability is limited. Maturity demands that all we can do when faced with this fact is to acknowledge and to accept it. As Spinoza once argued, either man is rationally competent or he is not: If he is, he needs take no recourse in external forces; if he is not, then he is unable to take recourse in external forces. In either case, recourse to external forces is unwarranted. In our philosophy we choose to affirm man's rational competency while admitting its limitations.

The only purposes man has are those he sets for himself. As we have already said, he is a cosmic accident. Inanimate nature is indifferent to his being or not being. We reject the old biological assumption that nature is concerned with perpetuating the species. We hold nature to be neutral. Man is a purposing animal. He evaluates his existent world and judges conditions as desirable or undesirable. If undesirable, he can project meliorative programs by which to attain desired goals, etc. We must maintain a sharp differentia between cosmic purposes *for* man and man as the *proposer* of purposes. We reject the former; we accept the latter.

ON THE ORIGIN, NATURE, AND LIMITS OF KNOWLEDGE. The organism at birth is a *tabula rasa*. We reject completely the concept of *a priori* knowledge. We will grant a Kantian *a priori* of *capacity,* but must reject his specific faculties and categories—which are patterned after Aristotle.

Knowledge begins with sensory experience and must always be reducible to it. Knowledge is not of objects of the external world but with relations which the observer established with the external world. It is meaningless at the present time to speak about "knowing things as they really are." We know "things" only in relation.

The organism is active and selective in the learning process. In a strict sense the learner becomes a part of the known. In our opening sentence in this section we spoke of the *organism* as a *tabula rasa.* We approach learning here somewhat as a Gestaltist—as interaction between the organism and the environmental complex. When seen in this manner, "mind" loses its substantive character and becomes participial or adverbial.

Assuming the empirical nature of knowledge, several qualifications seem apropos:

1. Non-empirical explanatory concepts (hypotheses) must possess predictive functions which can be verified by observation and experiment.
2. Elaborate controls are necessary for empirical discovery.

3. Empirical discovery is relative to the range of data, to available measuring devices, and to prevailing systems of explanation and interpretation.
4. Empirical discovery must always be subjected to further empirical verification as the ranges of data, etc., are altered.
5. Empirical discovery can yield only problematic solutions.
6. Empirical truth flows out of satisfactory consequences, which are the outgrowth of relations between projected hypotheses and controlled methods of verification.
7. Since man is a *biological* organism concerned with adaptation and adjustment to his environment, and since he is a *rational* organism capable of differentiating between actual existents and desired optimal ideals, knowledge (know-how) becomes an *instrument* through which man seeks to reconstruct his environment in terms of his desired, ideal ends. This is in no sense a limiting concept; the most abstruse subjects can find a niche in this system.
8. Since knowledge is instrumental, we indicate a most vigorous concern with the methodologies and operations by which it is established. For these methods and operations we turn to the canons of scientific research.

ON THE ORIGIN AND NATURE OF VALUE. Our system of ethics is tied in with and flows from certain assumptions found in the above sections. For the sake of clarity we indicate these assumptions:

1. The natural order comprises the totality of things.
2. Man is a chance emergent in the evolutionary process.

3. At birth, the organism is a *tabula rasa,* but with rational and idealizing capacities.
4. Intelligence constitutes man's chief differentia from the rest of the animal kingdom.

Man makes his ideals, his values. A thing is valuable because it is valued. From our point of view these ideals should not be formed in a vacuum, but at the points of tension where men experientially are confronted with the inadequacies of existents, and where they envision what they believe to be the more optimally desirable. An ideal, then, stands for what an individual or a group would like to have in preference to what they actually do have.

This interpretation of the ideal leads, of course, to a plurality of "goods" or ends. It negates any universalized, unitary good such as found in Plato or Christianity. There is not The Good, but a multitude of *goods.* And these *goods* are shifting, moving, changing—coming into and going out of experience as the exigencies of life force or neutralize the individual's attention. . . .

This interpretation of ideals makes moral good atomic—nominalistic—individualistic. Good is not a noun however much philosophical idealists have sought to make it one. "Good" is meaningless unless identified with specifics. . . . As William James once wrote, *to be good a thing or a quality must be so judged for definite,* assignable, reasons.

Further, and flowing from our atomic conception of "good," is the added assumption that since each good is unique, then each good is of equal worth within every other good. Any arbitrary, qualitative hierarchy of goods

breaks down. As Dewey writes [in *Reconstruction in Philosophy*], ". . . every moral situation is a unique situation having its own irreplaceable good. . . ."

A moral situation arises where the individual is confronted with alternative possibilities, and where these alternatives pose issues which involve the welfare of the individual (this may be applied with equal cogency to any self-determined group or community). Decision becomes moral when the question of "oughtness" is asked: which alternant *ought* I choose? We are willing to let this sense of oughtness carry the weight of a Kantian categorical imperative, except that we demand the right to stipulate the "why" of ought. To this we proceed.

We stipulated earlier that man's chief differentia is rationality. There is no better place to begin applying intelligence than in moral situations. "Applying intelligence" means that the individual explores possible or probable consequences of each alternant; that he ponders and deliberates; that he walks clear around the problem so as to face every angle of implication; that he contrives hypotheses; and that he searches for methods for testing these hypotheses. As Dewey writes [in *Reconstruction in Philosophy*],

"Reason, always an honorific term in ethics, becomes actualized in the methods by which the needs and conditions, the obstacles and resources, of situations are scrutinized in detail, and intelligent plans of improvement are worked out."

Intelligence is most productive of desired consequences when it operates under a system of experimental and verifiable controls—controls which arise in experience and are justified through further experience.

The fact is that a moral good is a consequent of a plan of action. One can never know, except *a posteriori,* that a plan of action will result in a moral good. But we are operating on the assumption that an assumed good (that which we project into the future as anticipated good) is much more likely to turn out to be a good (*a posteriori*) if selected and pursued in terms of intelligent method.

Moral action or behavior is thus shifted from non-reflective, habitual conformity to externally imposed "laws," to intelligently thought out methods. This use of the intelligence is best exemplified in the canons of scientific method. . . . This brings us back to our earlier question, "Which way *ought* I to choose?" And our categorical imperative is, "*I ought to choose the way of systematic intelligence.*" If one will do this in morals, he is most likely to find that consequences will take care of themselves. *It may be that attaining the good is more a matter of method than anything else.* . . .

It is at this point of intelligent method that modern religious humanism and liberal protestantism break down. They see with clear insight the hiatus between existent social practices and more optimal possibilities. The liberal Protestant assures us that "if people will just love one another all these problems will be solved," while the humanist seems content to beat the drums for a generalized, utopian "good life." Neither has been able to see, apparently, that the moral situation can be resolved only by specific methods of intelligence. They still try to solve moral problems either by citing clichés or applying generalities. We believe that they can be solved best through controlled intelligence as expressed in scientific method. . . .

∽

OVERVIEW

One of the most interesting sociological phenomena of life in the ivory tower is the split between the "academicians" and the "educationists" (a student, taking courses both in the Teachers College and the Department of Philosophy at Columbia University, once observed that "120th Street"— which separates TC from the main campus—"is the widest street in the whole world").

This gap exists, and historically it has been at its widest between the general philosophers in the liberal arts departments of universities and the educational philosophers in the schools of education in universities. The former have often looked down their noses at the latter, suggesting that educational philosophers are not philosophers at all because they deal with the subject matter of professional education ("if," they sniff, "professional education has any subject matter"), and not philosophy *qua* philosophy. The latter, in their turn, have been prone to write off general philosophers as impractical dabblers in things esoteric, uninterested in and unable to make a significant contribution to the solution of the real problems of a real world—most especially, to the problems of education.

The cold war in *academia* goes on, but as Charles Virtue notes in his conclusion to the following article, there are some signs that the gap is being narrowed. Educational philosophers, he thinks, are coming to realize, more and more, that general philosophy is the matrix of the philosophy of education; and general philosophers are coming to see, more and more, that there is a truly philosophic base to many of the most pressing contemporary problems of education.

But Virtue is not interested in a sociological analysis of human relations with the American university, except as it serves his purpose of demonstrating that the gap is actually incongruous since general philosophy is the mould and the matrix of educational philosophy. The logic of his argument runs like this: (1) general philosophy consists of the subject matter divisions called ontology, epistemology, and axiology; (2) educational philosophy is organically related to general philosophy, if not actually dependent upon it; therefore (3) educational theory is the application of ontological, epistemological, and axiological considerations to educational problems.

For our present purposes the virtue of Virtue's essay is that in illustrating his thesis he utilizes the thought of John Dewey, Alfred North Whitehead, Theodore Brameld, and Harry S. Broudy; in so doing he not only makes his point clear, he serendipitously provides a simplified perspective of the educational/general philosophy of each of these individuals. In this way he builds upon the foregoing essay in which Cunningham identified the two basic sets of first principles by which philosophies can be differentiated. Virtue takes a step beyond the "this or that" rule of division; by reviewing Dewey and Brameld, on the one hand, and Whitehead and Broudy, on the other, he does indeed follow the categorization process suggested by Cunningham. The former pair are generally identified as subscribing to a "modern" set of first principles, while the latter pair are "Aristotelian" to a greater or lesser extent. More important is the fact that Virtue provides clues as to subcategories within each of these major positions. While Dewey and Brameld are both in the Pragmatic tradition, there are important differences in their philosophic thought and their educational recommendations. Similarly, Whitehead and Broudy are in the Realistic tradition, but here too there are important philosophic and educational differences within this tradition.

Virtue begins his analysis by asserting that Dewey's educational philosophy is inseparable from his general philosophy; more, he insists that the validity of Dewey's educational theories is ultimately rooted in his general philosophy—most particularly in Dewey's concept of democracy. From this he concludes that an examination of Deweyan thought confirms the thesis that general philosophy is basic to educational philosophy.

Where Dewey took a sociological premise (i.e., a theory of democracy) as his starting point, Virtue notes that Whitehead starts with a religious premise. Thus where Dewey's thought was axiological in the beginning ("Democracy is good"), Whitehead's was ontological ("God exists"). (It should be pointed out that Whitehead's concept of God and religion involves creative, rather than mystical, experiences.) Since Whitehead's philosophy springs from and returns to the theme of creativity, education for him must be creative—not merely repetitive, not merely traditional.

From this, Virtue again concludes that a man's educational philosophy cannot be fully grasped without a prior comprehension of his general philosophy.

The philosophic Reconstructionism of Theodore Brameld, Virtue indicates, recognizes quite explicitly that the philosophy of education is a "special perspective within" ontology, epistemology, and axiology, thus once again revealing the integral function of philosophy in educational theorizing. Since, in Brameld's view, philosophy is the identification and elaboration of the beliefs widely held in a culture (beliefs about reality, knowledge, and value), philosophic beliefs will not only vary from culture to culture but in any given culture there will be contrasting and competing philosophies. The task of philosophy is not only to act as a mirror reflecting cultural beliefs, however; its larger task is to help a culture solve its problems. Philosophy serves a heuristic purpose with reference to cultural crises. Now a problem arises: of the alternative philosophic systems, which one is best equipped to deal with the contemporary crisis culture? Brameld (in his *Patterns of Educational Philosophy*) makes the case for Reconstructionism; but Virtue, who has led us to the brink of the problem neither saves us nor pushes us off. Rather he leaves us cliff hanging, waiting for the next episode which will never come, for at the moment of decision he reminds us that he is not using his essay to examine competing philosophies in order to determine which is "best," but that he is concerned to show the Reconstructionism of Brameld, like the Experimentalism of Dewey and the Organism of Whitehead, once again demonstrates the fact that educational philosophy draws its sustenance from general philosophy. Here is philosophic brinksmanship at its best.

As his final case in point, Virtue describes the Realistic philosophy of Broudy, noting that from this basic position Broudy develops an educational philosophy. Broudy urges educators to start with what they have at the beginning, namely, an educational problem. Then by persistent analysis of the problem it can be pushed back and back until its philosophic roots are exposed; and Broudy is convinced that the budding and flowering of such problems is clear evidence of philosophic roots somewhere hidden. Once the philosophic aspect of a problem is identified, progress toward a solution may proceed more smoothly and efficiently since the deepest issues at hand are more clearly understood. Broudy describes this method as the ". . . systematic discussion of educational problems on a philosophical level—i.e., the probing into an educational question until it is reduced to an issue in metaphysics, epistemology, ethics, logic, or esthetics, or a combination of these."

Virtue takes this as dramatic evidence that many educational philosophers do in fact (and all should) draw upon general philosophy to help them resolve problems in educational theory and practice.

Running through Virtue's argument, like the chain stitch in a sewn garment, is the implicit belief that given different answers to ontological, epistemological, and axiological questions, we will see not only a difference in general philosophies but a consequent difference in educational philosophies, and therefore, differences in educational policies and practices. But the fabric of his argument is like the fabric of the garment: if the chain stitch is pulled out, if the assumption is invalid, the entire fabric dissolves into a mass of tangled strings.

Virtue concludes by pointing out that as general and educational philosophers come to appreciate the role each might play in the understanding and improvement of the educational enterprise, sociologists will begin to report a thawing out of the cold war between academic and educational philosophers, and an armistice, if not a peace treaty, may be achieved.

General Philosophy and the Philosophy of Education

Charles F. Sawhill Virtue*

The thesis of this paper is that general philosophy is the matrix of educational philosophy, and that responsible evaluation of philosophies of education requires at least a modest exposure to metaphysics, epistemology and axiology. One would not expect to make

* Reprinted by permission from *Educational Theory*, VIII (October, 1958), 203–212.

sense of the educational theories of Plato or of Rousseau, to cite two historical examples, without some acquaintance with Plato's theory of ideas as ontological forms, or of Rousseau's romantic naturalism in ethics; so one can hardly deal intelligently with John Dewey's educational instrumentalism without coming to terms with his larger concept of experience. Why should a widely read Thomistically grounded educational journal some years ago denounce Dewey as "Public Enemy Number One"? Not primarily because of his "progressive" methods, considered as teaching techniques, for there is nothing in Thomism which inhibits psychologically "advanced" techniques of learning as such. What the Thomists object to is Dewey's naturalistic concept of experience, with its ethical correlates and its final indifference to theism.

The major philosophers of education have always known that their educational theories were special applications of their basic ontological, epistemological and axiological theories. Conversely, the great philosophers have always recognized the teaching-learning process as integral in experience and hence a source of basic concepts. When Socrates wanted to illustrate the relation of formal structure to mind he picked an intelligent but untaught slave boy and led him through what was really a classroom exercise in plane geometry. John Locke's theory of mind as a *tabula rasa,* a blank tablet, whereon experience writes, is obviously a figure taken from academic learning situations; Descartes' notion of "innate ideas"—e.g., the ideas of number, of logical truth and falsity—reflects his experience as an exceptionally rational school boy, largely teaching himself and finding these necessary rational forms emerging in his own understanding. . . .

The inseparability of general philosophy and the philosophy of education may be shown directly by a summary exposition of the philosophies of two major philosophers of the Twentieth Century, John Dewey and Alfred North Whitehead, and two contemporary philosophers of education, Theodore Brameld and Harry S. Broudy. Both Dewey and Whitehead wrote on education. Brameld is in the general Dewey instrumentalist tradition, but develops his theory in his own distinctive way; Broudy, while not a Whiteheadian, yet has a feeling for objective value and ontological being, which, like Whitehead's realism, grows out of the realistic metaphysical tradition of Plato and St. Thomas Aquinas.

JOHN DEWEY'S INSTRUMENTALISM

John Dewey is known to educational theorists primarily for his *Democracy and Education* and the never-ending stream of articles and editorials and speeches with which he enriched and remolded American education. He is the fountainhead of Instrumentalist, Experimentalist, Progressive and Reconstructionist educational theory. To Conservatives, Essentialists, Thomists and other Realists, Dewey is the summation and the symbol of all that is wrong with contemporary American education.

Professional philosophers sometimes dispute as to what is most basic (or what actually came first chronologically) in Dewey's thought—his educational ideas or his general instrumentalist principles. The truth seems to be that they were inseparable in his thought. Dewey once commented that the academic philosophers seemed to have largely disregarded his *Democracy and Education,* though he himself thought it the best expression of his basic ideas.

The opening sentences of the Preface of *Democracy and Education* set the tone for the entire book:

The following pages embody an endeavor to detect and state the ideas implied in a democratic society and to apply these ideas to the enterprise of education. The discussion includes an indication of the constructive aims and methods of public education as seen from this point of view, and a critical estimate of the theories of knowing and moral development which were formulated in earlier conditions, but which still operate in societies nominally democratic, to hamper the adequate realization of the democratic ideal. As will appear from the book itself, the philosophy stated in this book connects the growth of democracy with the development of the experimental method in the sciences, evolutionary ideas in the biological sciences, and the industrial reorganization, and is concerned to point out the changes in subject matter and method indicated by these developments.

Dewey thus announces the aim and the method of his educational philosophy; its validity is located in its theory of the nature and origin of democracy; its success is to be measured by the extent to which it contributes to a realization of the democratic ideal.

Academic philosophers have been more concerned with Dewey's derivation of his ideas from the experimental method in the sciences and the concept of evolution in the biological sciences. For this reason they have paid more attention to Dewey's books like *The Quest for Certainty, Experience and Nature* and *Art as Experience* than to his essays on education. In these books Dewey elaborates his basic theories of the nature of experience—that it is primarily practical, the functioning of active organisms interacting with an environment that both makes possible their careers and frustrates the complete fulfillment of their innate potentialities. Only a person who has soaked himself in these critical, epistemological and methodological studies can appreciate the profundity of Dewey's educational theories. With Dewey, general philosophy and the philosophy of education are obverse and reverse of the same coin. In 1897, more than a quarter of a century before Dewey wrote *Experience and Nature,* he asserted in his *Pedagogic Creed:*

I believe that consciousness is essentially motor or impulsive . . . Ideas (intellectual and rational processes) also result from action . . . What we term reason is primarily the law of order or effective action.

The total life work of John Dewey thus illustrates the thesis that general philosophy is basic to the philosophy of education. Concepts originating in analysis of the learning situation are adequately defined, illuminated, and criticized only in the more general disciplines of epistemology, ethics, and metaphysics. The philosophy of education may be the actual starting point for a general philosophy and may contribute distinctive ideas to that general philosophy, but these ideas are validated by their ability to be co-ordinated with more general aesthetic, ethical, epistemological, and metaphysical principles.

ALFRED NORTH WHITEHEAD'S PHILOSOPHY OF ORGANISM

Alfred North Whitehead is better known as a general philosopher than as a philosopher of education, though among college and university teachers Whitehead's essays on education have had a great deal of influence. If Dewey's thought is basically sociological and psychological and centered largely upon the processes of education, Whitehead's is basically mathematical and metaphysical, centering on the problems of rational implication in logic and mathematics and the interrelation of events that constitute actual process. Whitehead's great book, *Process and Reality,* is one of the major works in the history of Western philosophy. It might be described as a twentieth century version of Plato's *Timaeus,* Whitehead having the advantage of modern quantum and relativity physics. Whitehead calls his philosophy "the philosophy of organism," though, curiously enough, he makes scarcely any reference to the biological sciences. One of the central ideas in the philosophy of organism is the idea of sociality, though again, Whitehead is not directly concerned with social and political theory. Whitehead, speaking metaphysically, calls any actuality, such as a rock, a society. This is by no means an affectation, but a serious and profound usage of the term. The primary humanistic source of Whitehead's thought, corresponding to Dewey's reliance on democratic social experience, is religion. Religious experience is for him our deepest sense of the tragically harmonious quality of universal process. It is an experience in which subjectivity and objectivity are merged in contemplation of creative beauty. Here is Whitehead's description of religion, taken from the chapter on Religion and Science in *Science and the Modern World:*

Religion is the vision of something which stands beyond, behind, and within, the passing flux of immediate things; something which is real, and yet waiting to be realized; something which is a remote possibility, and yet the greatest of present facts; something that gives meaning to all that passes, and yet eludes apprehension; something whose possession is the final good, and yet is beyond all reach; something which is the ultimate ideal, and the hopeless quest.

and then he adds:

The fact of religious vision, and its history of persistent expansion, is our one ground for optimism. Apart from it, human life is a flash of occasional enjoyments, lighting up a mass of pain and misery, a bagatelle of transient experience.

Now, what of Whitehead's philosophy of education? Whitehead was not a professional educationist. He wrote no book on the theory and practice of education. He was, however, profoundly concerned with education. First of all, as a mathematician, he wrote on the principles of mathematics in relation to elementary and secondary education. In a more general vein he addressed meetings of school principles and teachers in Great Britain; he considered technical education and the relations of science and literature. His most directly psychological and sociological thought is perhaps an essay on "The Rhythmic Claims of Freedom and Discipline," and a closely related essay on "The Rhythm of Education." Whitehead wrote on education as a mathematician, a teacher, a philosopher concerned with the meaning and value of life. He was profoundly concerned that education be creative; that it enlist the deepest drives of life; that it promote personal growth and social sensitivity; that it enlarge both our sense of order and our feeling for adventure, our loyalty to achieved goods and our creative freedom. These ideas can all be read in the small volume of collected essays, *Aims of Education and Other Essays*. The quality of his thought can be apprehended in the closing words of Chapter 1 of this book, which was Whitehead's Presidential Address to the Mathematical Association of England, forty years ago when Great Britain was engaged in its first desperate struggle of this century, World War I:

When one considers in its length and in its breadth the importance of this question of the education of a nation's young, the broken lives, the defeated hopes, the national failures, which result from the frivolous inertia with which it is treated, it is difficult to restrain within oneself a savage rage. In the conditions of modern life the rule is absolute, the race which does not value trained intelligence is doomed. Not all your heroism, not all your social charm, not all your victories on land or at sea, can move back the finger of fate. Today we maintain ourselves. Tomorrow science will have moved forward yet one more step, and there will be no appeal from the judgment which will then be pronounced on the uneducated.

We can be content with no less than the old summary of educational ideals which has been current at any time from the dawn of our civilization. The essence of education is that it be religious.

Pray, what is religious education?

A religious education is an education which inculcates duty and reverence. Duty arises from our potential control over the course of events.

Where attainable knowledge could have changed the issue, ignorance has the guilt of vice. And the foundation of reverence is this perception, that the present holds within itself the complete sum of existence, backwards and forwards, that whole amplitude of time, which is eternity.

Is not the relation between general philosophy and the philosophy of education beginning to be clear? In Dewey we have a philosopher primarily impressed by the nature of social experience. When Dewey was in China he was hailed by the Chinese, because of the sociological basis of his philosophy, as "the American Confucius." Whitehead, on the other hand, is, in Chinese terms, the Taoist, the philosopher of infinite creativity. The educational philosophy of neither of these major thinkers can be grasped in its wholeness apart from their general philosophic commitments; and neither of them can be adequately evaluated without recourse to that basic analysis and total vision which is the true concern of general philosophy.

THE RECONSTRUCTIONISM OF THEODORE BRAMELD

The two philosophers of education to be presented here enjoy nothing like the prestige and wide influence of Dewey and Whitehead; but in the schools of education their textbooks are widely used and their ideas are typical of kinds of theories future teachers are asked to organize their thinking about. They are thus of great importance to the future of American education. Their impact on elementary and secondary education is immense.

Professor Brameld's admirable textbook *Patterns of Educational Philosophy* first reviews what he terms the major educational philosophies in America today, Progressivism, Essentialism and Perennialism; it then presents his own system, Reconstructionism. Progressivism is sufficiently well known to need no explanation here: It is Dewey's Instrumentalism, the doctrine that all ideas as well as all skills are simply instruments for fuller living. Essentialism is the doctrine that there are certain items of knowledge, certain skills (e.g., spelling), and certain attitudes (e.g., industriousness) that are essential both to the success of the individual and the security of the race. Perennialism is the doctrine that there is a set of beliefs—e.g., belief in God, belief in moral standards, such as the Golden Rule—which is the constantly recurring framework of good living. It is these "perennial" beliefs which should be the main concern of education. [Essentialism and Perennialism are variants of what the layman usually calls "old-line" or conservative theory of education] Brameld, then, really presents the familiar Conservative-Progressive split in educational theory, with two examples of each.

A major excellence of Brameld's educational thinking is that he recognizes educational philosophy as a special perspective within three of the major fields of general philosophy, namely, ontology (theory of the nature of things, e.g., material or spiritual), epistemology (theory of the kinds and the validity of knowledge), and axiology (theory of various sorts of value, e.g., the aesthetic and ethical or moral). Brameld then points out another truism, that philosophy on all its levels is the identification and critical elaboration of the beliefs of a culture. Modern culture, especially American culture, he describes as a "crisis culture," and says that there

are cultural ways of dealing with crises. These ways are sufficiently designated by the terms Conservative, Liberal, Reactionary and Reconstructionist. The crucial cultural problem, and *a fortiori*, the central problem of the philosophy of education, is then the problem of choice among these (and possibly other) ways of dealing with our crisis-culture. How shall these alternatives be appraised? Brameld's answer is that the choice must be made by an appraisal of the assumptions these attitudes toward culture make in their final ontology, epistemology, and axiology.

"Both education and philosophy," he writes, "are themselves intrinsic with culture, primitive or civilized. On the one hand, philosophy can be regarded now as the effort of a culture to become conscious of and articulate to itself. On the other hand, education is the effort of a culture to reinforce and carry out the beliefs expressed through philosophy.

Reconstructionism is identified by Brameld as "a philosophy of vision."

A self-conscious and critical Utopianism, a radical perspective oriented toward the potentialities of an emerging cultural Renaissance, a philosophy of magnetic foresight.

The common denominator of its beliefs is a passionate concern for the *future* of civilization.

As for ontology, Reconstructionism is frankly instrumentalist.

Thus it agrees that experience and nature (recall the title of one of Dewey's greatest books) constitute both the form and content of the entire universe. By *experience* is meant the pulsating, vibrant stuff of life—"things and ideals," feeling and thought, the whole ebb and flow of personality, society, earth, sky. By *nature* is meant the world within reach of scientific experimentation and understanding, a world of disorder and order, of flux and stability, of strife and harmony.

It follows that the reconstructionist, too, is hostile toward other-worldly philosophies, certainly toward any metaphysics that tries to establish the primacy of any supposed realm of *super*-nature over that of nature. Equally he is hostile to objective systems of pre-established order, whether these be of a realist or an idealist variety. From his point of view, "nature," always an elusive term, suggests primarily an evolving reality in which humanity, while the most important manifestation of nature, is but one segment of the dynamic infinitude of soil, water, mountain, plants, animals.

Reconstructionism's area of sharper concentration begins to be delineated when it analyzes and interprets *social* reality—particularly group experience.

The reconstructionist accepts the naturalistic, this-worldly ontology of progressivism but stresses more heavily that aspect he regards as most important to reconstructing our culture. . . . Two mutual features peculiarly relevant to his concern are, first, the cultural determinants of human experience, and second, history. The former is considered in terms of group conflicts, group allegiances, and group conditioners; the latter in terms of a philosophy of history as social struggle, as expansion and contraction of freedom, as organisms, and as future.

If the purpose of this essay were to recommend a philosophy of education, this would be the place to analyze and evaluate Brameld's Reconstructionist theory—its naturalistic ontological assumptions, its culture-determined values, its theory of history as social struggle, its special emphasis upon the emerging future. Brameld's revision of

Instrumentalism makes Reconstructionism the cutting-edge of left-wing educational theory in the United States. Our purpose, however, is not to choose among competing theories, but to see their relation to general philosophy.

The dilemma of philosophy is this: Thought must always begin *somewhere;* but any one *where* must be defined in terms of other *where:* as the mathematicians and logicians say, any term must be integral to a set of terms. Brameld makes his ontological terms relative to his cultural—i.e., his socio-historical terms. There is no reason why he should not do this. A philosopher may select whatever sort of data seem to him most important for his base line, measuring the relative importance of other data relative to them. Any academic philosopher would say that it is the consideration of which data to begin with that is the crucial problem of philosophy. Brameld's own reiterated pleas for objectivity in teacher-training, his warnings against indoctrination and smug narrowness, demonstrate that he wants critical, not acquiescent, thought by the students who are to be the future teachers. Assuming this critical awareness, he makes a plea for "defensible partiality." But can anyone expect competent critical judgment from students who have not had training in basic general philosophy?

HARRY S. BROUDY'S REALISTIC PHILOSOPHY OF EDUCATION

Harry S. Broudy's Realistic philosophy of education, elaborated in his useful, recent book *Building a Philosophy of Education*, illustrates the interconnectedness of general and specialized philosophy by its very antithesis to Brameld's Reconstructionism. Through Broudy's whole book there runs a sort of wonder at the marvelous experience of being a self-conscious creative personality in this extraordinary universe. To use a phrase of one of the major American axiologists, Broudy's world is "a value-charged universe." The great business of life, says Broudy, is to become creatively aware of the potentialities of life and to realize these potentialities in creative act. Broudy's realism is thus in the Platonic-Aristotelian-Thomistic-Leibnitzian-Whiteheadian tradition of ontological Realism as contrasted with the Protagorean-Cartesian-Humeian-Jamesian-Deweyan empirical tradition of Brameld's Reconstructionism.

Seeing the human situation in this light, Broudy views education as the rational guidance of the learning of the nature of the real to the end that the individual may share in the real values of being. And his theory of the philosophy of education is that it is the clarification and deepening of the way the guided learning process takes account of these values. Broudy's Realism is thus an axiologically oriented variant of the general position of Essentialism. He is careful to explain that this general position does not inhibit him from profiting from the psychological, sociological, and methodological insights of the Instrumentalists.

Broudy begins by distinguishing two general methods in the philosophy of education: (1) the adoption of a general philosophical point of view and an exploration of the ways in which this point of view can be made effective in education—which is Brameld's method; and (2) the use of the methods of philosophy itself in the discussion of educational problems. This second approach entails the analysis of educational problems into their final presuppositions and implications. Broudy chooses the second method, with judicious recourse to the first for his practical conclusions. He describes his type of procedure as

the systematic discussion of educational problems on a philosophical level—i.e., the probing into an educational question until it is reduced to an issue in metaphysics, epistemology, ethics, logic, or esthetics, or to a combination of these.

When these issues are reached, then rational men must do the best they can to recognize

those structures in the universe, man and society that are normative for man's striving toward the good life.

Broudy's approach is thus not only ontologically, but methodologically, diametrically opposed to Brameld's. Whereas Brameld not only begins with, but moves constantly toward, an anthropological-sociological view of education, Broudy begins with a classical rationalistic-realistic interest in the structure of being, and moves toward an analysis of educational situations in terms of their ultimate place in a rational world-view.

Broudy's concern with education is with its role in promoting human good. In the beginning of his chapter "Education and Values," he points out that establishing the aim of education entails judgment as to the features of the good life. The form of the good life, he describes as entailing self-determination, self-realization, and self-integration. The cultural theory of value proposed by naturalistic anthropologists, Broudy observes, leads to the familiar dilemma of the relativity of all values. The school, he says, must face the problem of the divergence of moral (and other) standards in the community. Deep lying differences, he says, are not negotiable by appeal to fact or to scientific theory; for facts mean nothing until they are interpreted, and interpretation is the business of philosophy.

When disagreements and controversy reach this level . . . it is a matter of metaphysics, epistemology, and ethics to find a common evaluation that is more significant than a cultural accident.

The school has only a limited number of alternatives about value standards:

(1) It can follow the elections and promote the norms of the group that wins;
(2) It can try to represent in its teachings the norms of all important segments of the community, at one time or at different times;
(3) It can try to avoid those materials and studies on which there are any serious disagreements in the community; or
(4) It can try to set up and adhere to a standpoint that cuts across group preferences by taking its norms from some conception of the nature and destiny of man himself.

Broudy implicitly endorses the fourth alternative when he says:

If all we have said about knowledge has any truth at all, and if what we have said about the school as an agency devoted to the transformation of life through knowledge is not complete nonsense, then it follows that the norms and standards of the school should be as universal as knowledge can help to make them.

Broudy then examines theories of value and proposes a realistic theory of value as "the relation between structures of things and the structure of human nature."

This concept of value locates the objectivity of value in the real structure of being, and its subjectivity in consciousness.

Having established his theory of value, Broudy turns to a specific list of values—bodily, economic, recreational, associational, character, intellectual, aesthetic, and religious—and discusses the role of the school in relation to each of these.

Broudy's conservative Realistic philosophy of education shares with Brameld's progressive Reconstructionist philosophy the philosophic virtue of beginning with a general attitude toward life and then analyzing educational concerns in the light of this basic worldview. Since Broudy attempts to see life as a whole, and since he sees the educational process as the guidance of life toward all its potentialities, he avoids over-emphasis on the purely intellectual aspects of education, keeping in mind, for example, character and aesthetic qualities in all phases of school work. On the other hand, he does stress the unique intellectual function of the school in contrast to the home, the church, and other institutions of society.

Broudy's educational Realism depends, he says, upon a realistic epistemology—namely, that there is truth to be discovered and that learning consists in discovering truth. Hence,

The discovery of the nature of the world, the social order and of ourselves is the material upon which the pupil is to perfect the habits or tendencies of acquiring, using, and enjoying truth. . . . All learning (is) a means for purifying the aesthetic, ethical, political, and social experience of the pupil by subjecting it to intellectual discipline.

Broudy's Realistic philosophy of education runs directly counter to Brameld's Reconstructionism in its ontology and its theory of knowledge, and therefore in many of its pedagogical applications.

GENERAL PHILOSOPHY AND THE PHILOSOPHY OF EDUCATION

The split between general philosophy and the philosophy of education, amounting to a practical divorce in most colleges and universities, has not been planned by anyone. It has occurred largely because of the haphazard growth of higher education in America and the more theoretical concerns of academic philosophers as compared with the immediately practical demands made upon the philosophers of education. There are now signs that mutual concern for the well-being of American education is prompting a lessening of the gap between them. . . .

Perhaps the long war is ending and academic philosophers will recognize the perspicuity with which the philosophers of education have applied their general principles to the baffling problems of educational content and method. Philosophers of education may find it obvious that the basic issues of education are simply the basic issues of life in an educational context, and agree with the academic philosophers that if these issues are not treated with deep seriousness, then

"all the voyage of their life
is bound in shallows and in miseries."

∿

OVERVIEW

In a frontal assault on a, if not the, major problem in philosophy of education, George Newsome opens the following essay by raising questions about the meaning of the term "philosophy of education." As the editors have indicated in their remarks introducing Part I of this volume, this is no small problem and its solution will be no small task.

Perhaps smarting from the superior attitude of general philosophers toward philosophy of education, an attitude which Charles Virtue considered in the previous essay, Newsome chides those general philosophers who do not hesitate to define philosophy of education even though they have yet to define philosophy, their own field (e.g., see the *Harvard Educational Review*, Spring, 1956). Newsome readily admits that philosophy of education is in some way related to general philosophy, but he stoutly maintains that the former cannot be defined in terms of the latter until academic philosophers determine just what philosophy is. The logic of this is impeccable, though perhaps it is gratuitous to assert that philosophy of education is obviously related to general philosophy and, in the same breath, deny that there is any acceptable (or, at least, accepted) definition of philosophy.

Newsome also refutes those who would define philosophy, and hence philosophy of education, in terms of its (unique) subject matter. It is not so much that philosophy lacks a substantive content, he reasons, as it is that philosophers are notorious for picking and choosing their own subject matter and treating it as they please. With such eclectic subject-matter practices it is not impossible to define philosophy in terms of subject matter; but it would be highly impractical, since such a broad definition would not serve to differentiate philosophy from other areas of inquiry.

Some suggest that philosophy deals with the problems of men, and its definition must flow from this fact. That philosophy does or should deal with human problems is agreeable to Newsome, and he suspects that all philosophers would assent to this. But he implies that while to say philosophy deals with such problems is a true statement, it is a meaningless one for definitional purposes; since psychology, sociology, medicine, etc., *ad inf.,* *ad naus.,* all deal with the problems of men.

Then, having demonstrated that there is no general agreement concerning the meaning of philosophy, he goes on to show that neither is there such an agreement concerning the meaning of education. Even if "philosophy" and "education" could be adequately defined, there is another problem: can philosophy *of* education be defined by using these two definitions and linking them with a sentential connective such as "of" or "and"? He thinks not. To do this is to suggest that philosophy of/and education would then imply *two* subject matters, *two* areas of inquiry, *two* sets of problems of men. Such a bifurcation he rejects out of hand.

With this initial analysis out of the way, Newsome proceeds to identify three basic approaches to the problem of definition. The first holds that educational philosophy is nothing but a special point of view toward education; the second, that it is the application of philosophy to education; the third, that philosophy is to be defined as the general theory of education.

After examining these alternatives in some detail he reaches the following conclusions: First, if philosophy of education involves nothing more than a unique viewpoint toward education, then the educational philosopher can only operate on a common-sense level; he is little more than a cracker-barrel philosopher with somewhat more than a passing interest in the schools, and philosophy of education as subject matter is non-existent, hence indefinable. Second, if educational philosophy involves the application of general philosophy to educational problems, then the philosopher of education is literally all mixed up; he is half philosopher and half educator, and educational philosophy is merely the hand servant of general philosophy. Third, if philosophy is the general theory of education then the educational philosopher is a philosopher in his own right (as are philosophers of science, philosophers of art, philosophers of history); but this does not mean the educational philosopher should teach the same subjects general philosophers teach, nor does it mean he should take leave of schools of education and join departments of philosophy. Rather he should, and now Newsome reaches his conclusion, ". . . engage in philosophic activity, exercise the function of a philosopher, and think and act philosophically." Only in this way can philosophers do their job, an important phase of which is to explain *how* philosophers philosophize and *how* theorists theorize, and on the basis of this the philosopher of education might help in the construction of some useful theories to guide education.

Newsome's approach to the problem of defining philosophy of education is at once encouraging and discouraging. In asking that the definition be couched in somewhat operational terms; that is, in terms of what philosophers do, he avoids the temptation to make the definition depend upon a social consensus. But if the definition is to be based on an analysis of what philosophers actually do, then, as Newsome pointed out earlier, the definition will be so broad as to be ineffective, since philosophers shy away from any limitations on their professional activities.

When he exhorts philosophers to exercise the function of a philosopher, to think and act philosophically, to engage in philosophic activity, it is an exhortation bound to cause frustration; for it begs the real question: lacking a definition of philosophy, how is it possible to know the functions of philosophers or the kind of activities in which they should engage, to know what philosophic thought and action are? The philosopher is indeed one who does these things, and one who does these things is indeed a philosopher. But that is a tautology and leads no closer to a clear definition.

However, even if Newsome has failed to solve the problem—and he has not claimed that he has done so—he is keeping company with some of the ablest minds of the century. Further, by focusing attention on the problems involved, his essay has served the philosophy of education clearly and well.

Educational Philosophy and the Educational Philosopher

*George L. Newsome, Jr.**

Considerable attention has been given by educators, educational philosophers, and philosophers to a definition of the term "philosophy of education." Writers of texts on the subject, teachers of educational philosophy and related studies, and philosophers have all sought to define philosophy of education, state its peculiar aims, subject matter, scope, and the like, or to advocate in its place some autonomous discipline of education. . . .

Needless to say, various conceptions of educational philosophy which can be found in these many sources show that philosophy and educational philosophy can be, and in fact have been, defined in different ways. Philosophers, who have not yet defined their own discipline except to their own personal satisfaction, nevertheless, do not hesitate to try to define educational philosophy. This situation, however, is probably to be expected and, on the whole, might prove valuable in that it might highlight areas of agreement and disagreement and bring forth new and valuable ideas.

Philosophy of education, no doubt, has something to do with philosophy, since the term "philosophy" is used. Philosophers, as we know, have not yet reached agreement upon a definition of philosophy. Such statements as "philosophy is an attempt to comprehend

reality," "philosophy is an attempt to rationalize experience," or "philosophy is an attempt to see reality steadily and see it whole" all depend upon what one means by "reality," "experience," or "wholeness." Similarly, attempts to define philosophy in terms of its subject matter have failed. Philosophers select their own subject matter and treat it as they see fit. Philosophers, it seems, hold different opinions regarding the particular characteristics of philosophy as a branch of knowledge, although they seem generally to agree that it is not a special form of activity apart from human problems. In short, about all that philosophers can agree upon concerning philosophy as a discipline is that it has something to do with the problems of men. Educational philosophers might possibly reach a similar agreement concerning educational philosophy.

Educational philosophy, no doubt, pertains to education. Education, like philosophy, is a term that is difficult to define. It can be defined in many ways, from the narrowness of formal schooling to the generality of life. The indications are that philosophers and educators have not yet come to any very general agreement upon a definition of education.

If definitions of philosophy and of education cannot generally be arrived at, then any attempt to define philosophy of education in terms of them is

* Reprinted by permission from *Educational Theory*, IX (April, 1959), 97–104.

hopeless. Even if definitions of philosophy and of education were established it seems doubtful that philosophy of education could be defined by mechanical linking of the two definitions with an "and" or "of." Such a mechanical linkage would presuppose two separate subject matters, two fields of endeavor, two sets of problems, and the like. Secondly, it is presupposed that two such fields linked together would give the field of educational philosophy in which the educational philosopher finds the problems of his concern. It is highly doubtful that this is actually the case. The idea of defining educational philosophy in terms of a definition of philosophy, on one hand, and a definition of education, on the other, is a gross oversimplification of the problem.

COMMON APPROACHES TO DEFINING EDUCATIONAL PHILOSOPHY

How can the problem be effectively approached? First, let us look at several alternative approaches. Some of the more common approaches may be classified as follows:

1. Regard educational philosophy as a point of view toward education.
2. Regard educational philosophy as the application of philosophy to education.
3. Regard philosophy as the generalized theory of education.

Under each of these generalized classifications there are various differences that should be noted, especially in the case of the second classification.

The first approach to educational philosophy seems to range from the common sense notions of "practical" schoolmen to systematic philosophies. Sometimes one hears or reads statements about educational philosophy that suggest that it is more or less one's own personal outlook and uncritical beliefs about education. For example, an elementary school principal expressed her philosophy of education by singing a little song called "Let's all Get Together." One often hears such expressions as "my philosophy of audiovisual aids is . . . ," or "my philosophy of lunchroom management . . . ," and the like, which also suggest common sense notions.

In a similar manner, one frequently encounters ideas concerning educational philosophy which suggest that people are by nature idealistic, realistic, and the like. These natural inclinations, however, need to be developed by formal study of "rival and conflicting" systems of philosophy. Such formal study will enable one, it is implied, to find his "philosophical home" and enable him better to formulate a "philosophy of life." Educational philosophy, then, becomes a study of philosophical systems in connection with education. Most of those texts in educational philosophy which set forth, system by system, such classical positions as idealism, realism, and the like seem to make these assumptions and imply this view of educational philosophy.

The second approach to educational philosophy is probably the most common approach of all. The idea of applying philosophy to education does not mean that there is agreement as to how philosophy is to be applied, nor what is to be applied. Philosophy might be applied by applying the answers philosophers have given to various questions that might be of concern to education. Philosophy might also be applied to education by utilizing the methods, tools, techniques, and such, of philosophy in investigating problems of formal schooling. Philosophy can be applied to education in yet another way. One might utilize "world frames," systems of philosophy, and the like, to explain or interpret education. Finally, one can apply philosophy to education by deducing educational implications from systematic philosophies.

The view that educational philosophy is an applied discipline in the sense that it is the application of "unique theoretical tools" to problems of formal schooling warrants further consideration. This view was apparently one that emerged from efforts of educational philosophers to make their field of study academically respectable. They, no doubt, wished to show that it possessed a "distinctive nature," and this distinctiveness was found in the "unique theoretical tools" employed and in what the philosophy was *of*. The theoretical tools named in the report of the committee could hardly be called unique to philosophy of education, nor for that matter even to philosophy. Sciences both natural and social utilize hypotheses, concepts, and categories, and ideas of meaning, truth, value, and method which were termed "unique theoretical tools." They also employ these tools in much the same manner as the report suggested. The idea of defining a field of study or work in terms of "unique tools" falls short of expectations. Carpentry, plumbing, auto mechanics, or any other ac-

tivity can not be defined in terms of its tools alone. The artisan must also be considered. The committee, however, refused to consider the person using the tools. If they employed a person alleged to be a carpenter on this basis, they might be most disappointed in the results of his work, even though it is often recognized that a workman can be judged by the *condition* of his tools. Finally, in limiting educational philosophy to problems of formal schooling, the committee seems to have sawed off the limb that they were sitting on. How can one effectively deal with problems of education in isolation from the other activities of life?

The third approach to educational philosophy is probably one that has not received much attention. As Professor Axtelle has said, ". . . Dewey's conception of philosophy as the general theory of education is not only one of his most profound insights, but one of the most profound insights in the history of thought." The insight, however, does not seem to have occurred to very many educators and educational philosophers. Indeed, it might well have never been evident to any except Dewey himself. Just what does this insight mean? What is implied in the idea that philosophy is the generalized theory of education?

Dewey thought that philosophy might be described in terms of the problems of social life; that it *could not* be defined in terms of subject matter; that it was reflective thinking which had generalized its place, value, and function in experience; and that it was the general theory of education. Such reflective thinking, however, required freedom to think and to inquire, with no prior guarantee of the outcomes. He said [in *Experience and Nature*]:

Freedom of thought denotes freedom of thinking; specific doubting, inquiring, suspense, creating, and cultivating of tentative hypotheses, trials, or experimentatings that are unguaranteed and that involve risks of waste, loss, and error. Let us admit the case of the conservative; if we once start thinking, no one can guarantee where we shall come out, except that many objects, ends, and institutions are surely doomed. Every thinker puts some portion of an apparently stable world in peril and no one can wholly predict what will emerge in its place.

Dewey also thought that philosophy was not concerned with furnishing solutions to so-called practical and immediate problems, but rather in locating significant problems and devising methods for dealing with them, or as he stated it [in *Democracy and Education*]:

Philosophy is thinking what the known demands of us—what responsive attitude it exacts. It is an idea of what is possible, not a record of accomplished fact. Hence it is hypothetical, like all thinking. It presents an assignment of something to be done—something to be tried. Its value lies not in furnishing solutions (which can be achieved only in action) but in defining difficulties and suggesting methods for dealing with them.

The fact that philosophy was hypothetical in character did not lead Dewey, however, to think that it was in any way a special discipline, or that it was in any way unrelated to the world of men and things. In fact, he urged [in *Democracy and Education*] that:

Unless philosophy is to remain symbolic—or verbal—or a sentimental indul-

gence for a few, or else mere arbitrary dogma, its auditing of past experience and its program of values must take effect in conduct.

All of these conceptions of educational philosophy suggest a role for the educational philosopher. That is, the way in which one conceives of educational philosophy indicates the functions of the educational philosopher. If educational philosophy be thought of as a common sense view of education, then the educational philosopher functions at the common sense level. If educational philosophy is the study of "conflicting philosophies" or systems with a view of helping students find a comfortable philosophical home, then the educational philosopher is concerned with demonstrating conflicting systems and guiding students into consoling and personally satisfying positions. Where educational philosophy is conceived as an applied discipline, the educational philosopher is half philosopher and half educator whose chief function is to take what philosophy may give him and apply it as he can to education. The chances are that he is not a philosopher in his own right, but rather one who borrows from philosophy. As a borrower he borrows ideas, conceptual tools, methods, and the like, from philosophy, or he borrows systems which might be milked for educational implications. When the educational philosopher becomes a borrower, he is expected to return what he borrows, and, in some cases, pay interest on the loan as well. In any case, the borrower is servant to the lender. On the other hand, if philosophy is viewed as the general theory of education, the educational philosopher must be a philosopher in his own right.

THE EDUCATIONAL PHILOSOPHER AS A PHILOSOPHER

What does it mean to say that the educational philosopher should be a philosopher in his own right? First of all, it does not mean that he has to be a teacher of those studies usually found in philosophy departments, nor that he has to be a member of group, faculty, or department labelled "philosophy." It does mean, however, that he must engage in philosophical activity, exercise the functions of a philosopher, and think and act philosophically. To do these things, he must think reflectively, think freely, doubt, inquire, cultivate hypotheses, infer consequences, think what the known demands, analyze, synthesize, and project ideas. Secondly, to be a philosopher does not mean that such thinking need be done apart from education, nor that it be restricted to education. The philosopher does not just think, he must think about something. What he thinks about are problems of men, what the known objects and events of life demand, what seems possible; in short, human experience and nature. Education, then, if it be life, or related to life, must be a concern of the philosopher. The philosopher can not effectively deal with education alone, however, for he cannot treat education separately from the rest of experience. In short, he cannot explain education merely in terms of education.

Were educational philosophers more concerned with defining philosophy in terms of philosophizing instead of in terms of distinctiveness of knowledge, their efforts might be more fruitful. The first two views of philosophy of education have notable shortcomings. They either fall into the trap of common sense or lead to what Sidney Hook called the "garrulous absurdities" of supposing that an educational philosophy might be deduced from some systematic cosmology. Let it be admitted that such educational philosophies can, and have, been deduced; but to suppose that they are more than symbolic and verbal is yet to be seen. It might be well to ask such philosophers how they know what they are doing. (For example, see Otto Krash, "How Do Philosophers Know What They Are Doing?" *Educational Theory,* V [July, 1955], 167–171. Krash suggests that failure to accept the principles of change and continuity leads to dogmatism and *a priori* reasoning. Are philosophers doing this when they seek to deduce educational theories from fixed systems?) Both of the first two views of educational philosophy seem to tend toward the formation of what has been termed useless theories of education. Foster McMurray has said:

While educational philosophers engage at second-hand controversies of systematic philosophy and in finding implications for education, practical educators with no training in theory proceed with their own task of constructing and changing school programs.

Unfortunately for educational philosophers who hold the first two positions concerning educational philosophy, McMurray's statement cannot be easily dismissed nor well refuted in the light of factual evidence.

The alternative to the present dilemma is to stop thinking of educational philosophy as a self-contained discipline and begin to show concern for the functions of educational philosophers as philosophers. Disciplines suggest disciples, not philosophers. What can educational philosophy offer in this age of anxiety, conservatism, and transition? Could the answer be philosophical thinking, rather than stories about philosophies and ghosts from the philosophical cemetery? The challenge of philosophy seems to be to press forward, not regress; to philosophize, not merely talk about philosophy; and to seek to make students philosophers, not merely disciples. It is not the mission of philosophy to console the timid and fainthearted, nor to defend vested interests, nor to publicize current practice. The aim of philosophy is criticism and vision, not complacency and hindsight. The means are critical and reflective thinking. The instrument is the educational philosopher upon whom so much depends.

If this conception of educational philosophy were accepted, the educational philosopher might come to feel less like a second-hand dealer in philosophy operating a shabby establishment on the lower end of academic avenue. Instead, he might come to think of himself as a philosopher and educator, a critic of the total culture, and as a thinker capable of developing new alternatives to present problems. He would not need to limit his activities to problems of institutions labelled schools. The school and its problems would be viewed in the total life situation of our times. The educational philosopher would not allow any subject matter boundary lines to prevent him from examining issues that were of living significance, for such issues could not be foreign to education formal or informal.

Although educational philosophers do not seem to have taken so radical and comprehensive a view of their field of scholarship, there now seem to be indications that a growing number of them are working in this direction. For example, Myron Leiberman (*Education As a Profession*) and Lawrence G. Thomas (*The Occupational Structure and Education*) indicate that educational philosophers are bringing philosophy to bear upon real problems that heretofore have been outside the customary domain of educational philosophy. Theodore Brameld, in seeking to develop a reconstructed philosophy of education, has drawn upon many fields of scholarship and dealt with a number of pressing problems. Recent periodical literature also seems to reveal that there are a growing number of philosophers in education who are philosophizing about real and pressing social and educational problems. Finally, the quality of recent philosophizing in education seems to be of a high order. These trends point to the maturing of educational philosophy as a significant field of scholarship.

With the maturing of educational philosophy it might be expected that philosophers will give more attention to their own activity. They are likely to become more critical of what they do when they philosophize, and also more concerned about their role as philosophers. In so doing, they might become more concerned with the *how* of philosophizing and theory building. Just how do philosophers philosophize and build theories? Educational philosophers seek also to explain education. Explaining is one of the chief tasks of the philosopher; it is the foundation of his theories, or probably what his theories are designed to do. Questions of how philosophers explain and theorize raise questions concerning the use of categories and classification, language form, definition, models, logic of inquiry and explanation, and ideas of systematic methods of explaining, such as concepts of description and causation. More careful inquiry into questions of this sort might well help educational philosophers explain education in a more effective manner, and help them to build theories that cannot be labelled "useless." Such inquiry might also help overcome a situation which has been described as follows [by Frederick E. Ellis]:

The need for perspective and direction in such a critical area as education is plainly evident and to this end the discipline of history and philosophy of education can make increasingly significant contributions. One must add, however, that rigorous and scholarly research of high excellence in the discipline is conspicuously lacking. . . . There is great assiduity in accumulating knowledge about things educational, but disconcerting lack of systematic, integrating theory which would give meaning and significance to our efforts. . . . The fragmentary and ragbag character of a great deal of current educational research indicates slight evidence of the construction of such a theoretical framework.

∽

OVERVIEW

Of the many attempts to answer the question "What is the philosophy of education?" the following essay by Kingsley Price is among the most direct, the most clear, and the most sophisticated. Many who have posed the question have approached it as if in search of the philosophic Holy Grail; that is, they have been searching for *the* answer, an answer which would identify once and for all the essence or the substance, or both, of philosophy of education. Price is asking a different question, however. He asks, "What is *a* philosophy of education?" and since the questions we ask determine the answers we get, Price's answer is somewhat unique. While his answer may be unique, his procedures are not radically different; yet it is worth noting that he is among the first, with Israel Scheffler, of the contemporary "analytic philosophers" to tackle the problem. For this and other reasons, the following article is as interesting for its methodology as it is for its conclusion.

As George Newsome commented in the preceding essay, there is as yet no clarity or precision of meaning in the words "philosophy" and "education," and Price is in accord with this view. But where Newsome did not stop to provide such a definition, simply because his business lay elsewhere, Price does.

The word "philosophy," he begins, refers to two kinds of processes and their products. The first process is that of analysis; the activity of trying to understand a word, clarify an idea, or grasp a concept. The product of this process, at least when it is successful, consists in the achievement of meaning; the clear understanding of a word, idea, or concept. The second process peculiar to philosophy is the persistent activity of trying to answer *specific kinds* of questions. These specific kinds of questions, of course, are those posed by metaphysics, epistemology, axiology, ethics, esthetics, and logic—the "traditional" subject content of general philosophy. The particular processes used in answering these questions are legion; but varied as they may be they are all attempts to answer ontological questions (e.g., What exists?), epistemological questions (e.g., What does it mean to say "I know"?), etc. The product of this answering service is Philosophy with a capital P. That is, the product is a body of propositions centered about each of the specific question areas, the sum of which represents "a" Philosophy. Philosophy, then, has both method and content. Methodologically it is the process of analysis and questioning. Contextually it consists of a body of propositions, whose meaning is clearly understood, purporting to answer certain kinds of questions.

Given this definition of philosophy, Price then defines "education" as ". . . the academic discipline which endeavors to understand [the] deliberate process" of transmitting the arts and sciences. Education thus conceived has two parts, the factual part and the recommending part. The first consists of *all* the information gathered or gatherable ". . . which bears upon the life of children and of adults." In this broad sense there is virtually no information which does not become a part of the factual aspect of education. But, as Price indicates, were education nothing more than this first part, it would be equivalent to human ecology. However, there is another side of education, the recommending part, and it is here that the mass of information is put to use. It is the raw material from which recommendations for the conduct of education are constructed. These are recommendations concerning the aims and methods of instruction, curriculum, guidance, supervision, administration, etc. This aspect of education consists of a body of procedural and contextual recommendations about the transmission of the arts and sciences; and education is the academic discipline which attempts to understand and explain this.

Only after offering these definitions of "philosophy" and "education" does Price come to grips with the prime question. But given these definitions, that question is seen to be considerably less perplexing; for, as he observes, to ask " 'What is a philosophy of education' is to ask what a philosophy of such a discipline is." To ask that general question is to ask three specific questions, all three of which stem from the earlier definition of philosophy. The first of these is "What is an analysis of education?"; the second, "What is a metaphysics of education?"; and the third, "What is an ethics of education?".

After an examination of these questions, Price reaches the following answers. First, the analysis of education consists in the process of clarifying the elements (terms or activities) of the educative process which are confused or confusing. Second, there is no such thing as the metaphysics of education (a conclusion which will disappoint many). Third, there is no such thing as *the* ethic(s) of education; rather there are many ethics *for* (the guidance of) education. That is, with reference to the third conclusion, the recommending part of education involves valuations and judgments about what the goal recommendations of the educative process should be. These recommendations constitute the ethics of education.

In sum, the philosophy of education consists of the linguistic and logical analysis of the terms used in education, and the examination and justification of the recommendations proposed for the over-all direction of education.

Here, agree or disagree, is a clear and firm definition of philosophy of education. It is not a definition of *the* philosophy of education, nor is it a definition of *a* philosophy of education—it is rather a definition of "philosophy of education" without an article. It is a definition that does not make educational philosophy the camp follower of general philosophy, although they would both travel together; it does not make educational philosophy an autonomous discipline, although it is seen as a distinct discipline; and it is precise enough to give meaning and content to the philosophy of education.

What Is a Philosophy of Education?

*Kingsley Price**

In this essay, I shall ask and try to answer the question, "What is a philosophy of education?" and I shall do this for two reasons. The first is that it is a question which is interesting in itself; the second is that although few possess a clear notion as to what kind of thing a philosophy of education is, many are required, upon occasion, to produce, or to profess allegiance to one. Decisions of the greatest practical importance are often made to depend upon our success or willingness in this particular; so that it is not only entertaining, but useful as well, to elicit a clear idea of the philosophy of education. Before attempting an answer to the question, it will be well to remove some of the obscurity which it harbors.

* Reprinted by permission from *Educational Theory*, VI (April, 1956), 86–94.

MEANING OF "PHILOSOPHY" AND "EDUCATION"

The obscurity from which the question suffers springs largely from unclarity as to the words "philosophy" and "education." Let us consider the first one first.

PHILOSOPHY. The word "philosophy" has frequently been used to refer to activities of two different sorts as well as to their results. The first activity is analysis; and while there is much dispute among philosophers as to the nature of analysis, there is little difficulty in recognizing it when it occurs. It is a certain way of trying to understand a word, to clarify an idea, or to comprehend a concept. It is well exemplified in the early parts of Plato's *Republic* and in *Moby Dick* where Melville is concerned to understand the concept "whale." ". . . How shall we define the whale . . . ," he writes, "so as conspicuously to label him for all time to come. To be short . . . a whale is *a spouting fish with a horizontal tail.* There you have him. However contracted, that definition is the result of expanded meditation."

When analytical activity succeeds, it affords an understanding of words, of ideas, or of concepts, and its results are expressed in the statements of the philosophers who perform the analysis. But it is impossible to lay down any bounds to such statements, for it is impossible to decide, *a priori,* what words, ideas, or concepts we shall find unclear. Plato wished to understand the term "justice" more thoroughly, and Melville, the concept "whale." But in advance of the fact, no one could have known that analyses of these terms would be needed. We may, nonetheless, quite properly hold that analytical philosophy is constituted not only by the activity of analysis, but also by all those doctrines which human beings reach by way of that activity.

The second kind of activity often described as philosophical is that of trying to answer questions of certain sorts. These are the questions of metaphysics, ethics, epistemology, aesthetics, and logic. They are questions such as these: "Is there any characteristic or group of characteristics which every existing thing must possess and which nothing else may possess," the metaphysical question; "What is the nature of moral goodness and moral rightness, and what things are properly judged in these terms," the ethical question; etc.

The activities by which people have sought to answer these questions are extraordinarily diverse. Usually, they have relied in some measure on analysis. Some have borrowed knowledge from the empirical sciences. Many have found help in theology and religion. Others have sought to answer them by appeal to what they regarded as a peculiarly philosophical insight or peculiarly philosophical method. And still others have supposed that an intuition, in one way or other mystical, lay at the bottom of their answers. But however diverse, all these activities have in common the purpose of providing answers to the traditional questions of philosophy; and it is for this reason that I mention it as a second kind of activity referred to by that word.

This second kind of activity results in philosophical theories—in metaphysics; ethics, epistemology, etc. Metaphysics comprises all those theories which purport to set down the nature of existing things; ethics, all those theories which concern themselves with the nature of the morally right and good as well as with the place of their habitation. And about metaphysics and ethics, there are two things particularly to be noticed. The first is that all metaphysical theories agree with each other in one way, and disagree in another; the second, that all ethical theories exhibit, with respect to each other, a corresponding conformity and difference. The agreement in which metaphysical theories participate is suggested by the question which each attempts to answer. This is the question whether there are any properties which must be possessed by all the things that exist and by nothing else; and the agreement between metaphysical theories consists in their recognition of a single world of existing things. It is the same world which is the subject of metaphysical discourse, whether that discourse be idealist, materialist, or even mystical; for it is the same world which the first declares to be throughout mental, the second thoroughly material, and the third a troublesome illusion.

The disagreement between metaphysical theories results from divergent applications of the distinction between appearance and reality. Idealism holds that all things which exist are really mental, however much some may appear to be corporeal. Materialism asserts that all things are really material however much some may appear to be mental. And mysticism contends that nothing really is what is seems (it is not in point here to catalogue the various metaphysical theories, but it seems to me that all involve the dis-

tinction between appearance and reality).

We should note here what this agreement and disagreement between metaphysical theories amount to. The agreement amounts to this: that there is a body of non-metaphysical truths about the world which no metaphysical theory alters; the disagreement to this: that each metaphysical theory supplements these truths with its peculiar insight. If idealism is true, mountains are mental; if materialism is true, they are material; and if mysticism is true, they are illusions of troubled souls. But no matter which is right, and even if none should be, the character of the mountains, although it should consist of appearances only, remains unchanged. Their constitution, their past, and their future—all this is logically independent of any and all metaphysical theories. What they really are can at most supplement what they appear to be; it cannot modify it. And all non-metaphysical truths, like those which comprise that chapter of geology devoted to mountains, owe no allegiance to any metaphysical theory.

The second point particularly to be noticed is that ethical theories exhibit, with respect to each other, a corresponding conformity and difference. All these theories are answers to two questions; first, "What things are good, right, etc.?"; and secondly, "What is the nature of goodness, rightness, and like concepts?" The agreement consists in the common recognition of a single body of moral precepts; no ethical theory can create a new moral obligation. An ethical writer who claimed to have discovered, by philosophical reflection alone, hitherto unknown moral truths would be thought a charlatan or a fool. And ethical theories agree as to what particular actions are morally right, and what particular states of affairs morally good. That is, they agree in their answers to the first question.

There is disagreement between ethical theories as to the nature of rightness, goodness, and the like. Some hold that moral goodness is a trait accessible only to reason; others, that it is some quality like pleasantness, the possession of which is open to empirical verification; and others still, that it properly characterizes nothing, being, like love or rage, a human response to things, although subtly different from these. But the single body of moral precepts, agreed upon by all ethical theories, is logically independent of the doctrines peculiar to each, in a way analogous to the way in which the body of non-metaphysical truths, agreed to by all metaphysical theories, is logically independent of the doctrine in which the peculiar contribution of each consists. Whatever is right, is right, no matter what one's theory may be as to the nature of rightness; just as whatever exists, exists, no matter what one's theory may be as to the characteristics which every existing thing must exhibit. And the statements that are true about what exists and what is right do not vary with the theories which we hold on peculiarly metaphysical and ethical topics.

EDUCATION. The word "philosophy" is properly used to refer to analysis as well as to its results, and to the traditional questions of metaphysics, ethics, etc., as well as to their answers. We have noticed that in this second part of philosophy there are theories which, though divergent in content, also betray a certain kind of agreement. But this elucidation of the word "philosophy" does not take us all the way in the elucidation of our question; and in order to complete that elucidation, we must establish a meaning for the word "education."

Concerning this word, we should notice that writers have used it in a good many divergent ways. Space does not permit a consideration of most of them here. It is necessary, however, to mention two. According to the first use, "education" refers to the process of deliberately transmitting the arts and sciences (the word "arts" is used here in its broader and older sense), and of fostering contributions to them. According to the second, "education" refers to the academic discipline which endeavors to understand that deliberate process. I shall employ the word in this second way.

Education thus understood contains two parts. These are the factual and the recommending parts. The first consists of information of greatly varied sorts gleaned from other academic disciplines and from common sense. History, psychology, sociology, anthropology, many other fields of knowledge and native wit, yield information which bears upon the life of children and of adults. And all this information constitutes the factual part of the academic discipline of education.

But were this all of the subject, education would be indistinguishable from human ecology. The information assembled would simply describe in a general way the career of the human being from infancy onward, together with his relations to nature and society. It is the purpose to which this information is put which distinguishes education as a discipline. This purpose is the development of objectives for, and methods of, instruction, guidance, administration, and the like. And the second part of education consists in a set of recommendations as to the manner of conducting the process of transmitting and fostering the arts and sciences based upon the facts assembled in the first part.

"Education" means the academic discipline which attempts to understand the deliberate process of bequeathing and of improving the arts and sciences. And this discipline consists of a certain set of facts drawn from many sources as well as a set of recommendations based upon them as to the way in which this process may be most usefully dispatched.

To ask, then, "What is a philosophy of education?" is to ask what a philosophy of such a discipline is. And now we have gone a little way toward understanding, if not toward answering, our question.

ANALYSIS, METAPHYSICS, AND EDUCATION

When we ask the question "What is a philosophy of education?" we are asking either one or all of three different questions; and these different questions flow from the complex meaning of the term "philosophy." The first of these questions is "What is an analysis of education?"; the second, "What is a metaphysics of education?"; the third, "What is an ethics of education?" It might be supposed that our question should be resolved not only into these,

but into three other questions as well. It might be supposed, that is to say, that our question asks, "What is an aesthetics, an epistemology, and a logic of education?" For these disciplines, we saw, were included among those referred to by "philosophy" in its second sense. But no one, to my knowledge, ever thought to phrase such questions, and I cannot well imagine, in the absence of concrete contexts, what such questions would come to. For these reasons, the last three questions are not regarded as parts of the topic of our primary interest.

Let us consider the first question "What is an analysis of education?", and let us remember that "education" refers to the academic discipline. The first question, then, asks something about a body of statements, i.e., the statements in which the academic discipline is couched; and what it asks concerns the manner in which certain words, ideas, or concepts function in that body. The answer to the question is that an analysis of education is the activity of clarifying whatever elements in that discipline may prove to be obscure, as well as the doctrines which embody the results of that activity.

Let us consider, next, the question "What is a metaphysics of education?" —the second part of the complex question into which our original one was resolved. Many have felt a certain lack with regard to the factual part of education, and the deficiency they have had in mind springs from the belief that every statement of fact is in need of explanation. A statement of fact is one, belief in whose truth or probability relies heavily upon observation of the fact referred to, or of some other fact connected with it; and it is this reliance upon observation which has been thought to give rise to the difficulty. Although we should observe all the facts and exhaustively describe them, many have believed, we should not thereby have explained any one of them. For the question "Why is this description of the world true or probable and not some other conceivable description?" always remains intelligible. And since this is so, there is need for some statement or body of them, belief in whose truth or probability does not rely upon observation, which precludes the truth or probability of other conceivable descriptions of the facts, and which guarantees the description which observation supports. An explanatory statement is one which does not suffer from the deficiency of statements of fact, but does show in the way indicated why certain statements of fact are correct.

A metaphysical theory has been thought to explain statements of fact in the sense just made out. Thus, for example, those who have espoused idealism seem, often, to have believed that the truth or probability of certain scientific doctrines was explained by it, and explained in the sense that their truth or probability was required by idealism, while the falsity of rival doctrines was also required by it. Similar claims have been made for metaphysical theories of other sorts.

We may now set down a fuller understanding of the second part of our question. To ask "What is a metaphysics of education?" is to inquire as to the nature of an explanation of its factual part, and to inquire, moreover, as to the explanation of that part in terms

of a theory of existence. It is to indicate a need for a theory of existence which will explain the truth or probability of its factual part. And a philosophy of education is not only an analysis of its obscure constituents, but a metaphysical explanation of the facts upon which its recommendations rest as well.

A consideration of the third part of our question, "What is an ethics of education?" is reserved for a later part of this essay. Here I wish to consider the importance and validity of the two parts thus far discussed.

It is quite clear that the first of these questions, the question concerning the analysis of education, is of much importance; for understanding what an analysis of education is, enables us to see that there is great need for it. There are many words, ideas, or concepts in the discipline of education, both in its factual and recommending parts, which are obscure beyond all management. Consider, for example, such terms as "integrated," "child-centered," "the whole person," "core curriculum," "on-going process," "experience," "shared experience," "citizenship," "loyalty," "disloyalty," "enrichment," "growth," "need," "meaningful," "value." It is doubtful that many have a very clear notion as to the use of these terms, and certain that some employ them rather to signal an attack or justify a defense than to make clear statements of fact or intelligible recommendations. Yet it is in such terms that entire programs are praised or condemned, and personnel evaluated. Such jargon serves well to rally the faithful and to disperse the enemy, but because of its obscurity it serves but ill in the statement of educational facts and educational recommendations. Part of a philosophy of education would be an analysis of this jargon. An understanding, let alone an agreement, among professional educators can be accomplished only when such an analysis is provided.

While understanding what an analysis of education is enables us to see the need for analytical work, the situation is different with respect to a metaphysics of education. Our discussion of theories of this sort led to the view that a metaphysics of education is a theory which explains the truth or probability of the factual part of education; and employing the phrase in this way, a good many philosophers have thought that such theories did really exist.

[Rupert C. Lodge], for example, describes the realistic or materialistic metaphysics of education as follows: "The realist would educate the individual to become an unresisting bit of matter, permeable to physical law and opening himself entirely to its almighty influence." In this brief description of realism or materialism, the following points seem to be involved: (1) that every existing thing is material—the metaphysical theory, and (2) that empirical facts about the individual can be put correctly only in statements which exemplify physical or material laws. [J. Donald Butler] exemplifies our point even more clearly when, in expounding idealism in education, he writes: ". . . we will try to deal with the salient characteristics of a typically idealist education. First, we will describe the pupil as seen through idealist eyes. Then we will state the objectives of education as idealists conceive them. And finally, we will discuss somewhat specifically a half dozen factors among those comprising the educational process under idealist direction." 'Describing the pupil as seen through idealist eyes' seems pretty clearly to be 'giving an idealist explanation of statements of fact concerning him.'

It is the view of these writers that a metaphysical theory explains the factual part of education, but they seem to believe that it does a good deal more as well. Our first author, for example, suggests that if materialism is true, then the recommendations of education are all instances of the injunction to obey the laws of nature whose influence is, in any case, "almighty." Our second author holds clearly that "objectives of education as idealists conceive them," together with 'factors of the educational process under idealist direction,' are recommendations founded upon a factual description of the pupil explained in idealist fashion. Both authors seem to hold that the facts about human life require certain recommendations—that in the light of these facts, some recommendations are wrong, others futile, and still others right or correct. They seem to say, further, that because of this connection between right recommendations and statements of fact in education, a metaphysical theory which would assure the latter also would guarantee the former. So many have thought that a metaphysical grounding of the facts of education served as well to validate its recommendations.

That the recommendations of education in some way depend upon its facts, no one can deny; but that these facts are not susceptible of metaphysical guarantee, everyone ought to agree. For statements of educational facts profess, in metaphysical language, to record appearances, and if correct, they are non-metaphysical truths. But as we saw earlier, all non-metaphysical truths are logically independent of metaphysical theories, and the statements of fact with which education is concerned are therefore also logically independent of any metaphysics. They are so because the sciences of psychology, history, sociology, anthropology, etc., from which education draws its statements of fact are not required by any particular metaphysical theory. Whether idealism, materialism, or any other alternative metaphysical theory is the true one is not a question which makes any difference to the sciences. And the belief of some metaphysicians that their theories serve to explain scientific knowledge is vain. Consequently, though some metaphysical theory may be the true one, there is no need to know it in order to secure the factual part of education, or to ground the recommendations derived therefrom. The second part of our question, "What is a metaphysics of education?" is idle; there can be no such thing.

ETHICS AND EDUCATION

What may we say concerning the third part of our question, namely, the nature of an ethics of education? Concerning this question, we should notice that ethical theories endeavor to answer at least two questions: first, "What is the nature of 'goodness' and 'rightness'?" and second, "What things are good and right?" And it might be supposed, first, that an ethics of education is simply a part of a very large collection of statements as to all the things

that are good and right. It might be supposed, that is to say, that an ethics of education is simply that part of the answer to the second question of ethics which pertains to educational practices. But if this were the case, it is clear that an ethics of education would be nothing different from the recommending part of that discipline, itself. It would say over again the things which are said in the second part of education. But it is clear that educational recommendations and an ethics of education are different things, for there is more to ethics than the simple fact of issuing injunctions and making recommendations.

Secondly, it is often supposed that an ethics of education is a statement of the objectives educators entertain for the programs in which they participate. But this, too, is a mistake; for to state one's intentions is not to produce an ethical theory of any sort, but only to inform others as to what one is about. The stating of intentions, while often described as a philosophical activity, is a very different thing from an ethical theory; for such a theory is motivated by an effort not simply to produce injunctions or reveal intentions, but to justify some statement as to the nature of goodness and rightness, or some judgment in which these ideas are involved.

We should emphasize, thirdly, that constructing a theory of this kind is distinct both from making recommendations and from stating intentions. To recommend and to express oneself require little more than the desire to do so. To justify a statement or a judgment of the kind mentioned above, on the other hand, requires the giving of reasons for it. The giving of reasons consists in the endeavor to show that the recommendations we have made or the intentions we have entertained are valid. Suppose, for example, that we were to find in the second part of education the recommendation that children should be allowed to develop their own interests without let or hindrance from the instructor. The repetition of this injunction clearly would not constitute a philosophical or ethical treatment of it, nor would the mere statement that so to proceed is the intention of some educator. But the question whether this is a valid recommendation is one which we think of as a peculiarly ethical question. For what it asks is whether the proposed action actually is a good or right one. An ethics of education involves a certain way of dealing with the recommendations which educators make in their attempts to distinguish valid from invalid proposals, the genuinely good or right from the genuinely wrong or bad, as well as the statements which embody the results of those attempts.

It should be noted that this question cannot be answered fully without some consideration of the first of the questions in terms of which ethics is understood. We cannot know that some proposed action is genuinely right, or some state of things genuinely good, without having some notion as to the nature of "rightness" or "goodness." For if we were ignorant as to the nature of either, our judgment might assign a moral character to some action or state of things which was undeserving of it; confusion might secretly take the place of understanding. And in this way the entirety of ethics is involved in the ethics of education.

In the second part of education, there are two distinct kinds of recommendation; and we may now observe that in the ethics of education, there is a corresponding division of topics. In education, we discover, first, a great many statements to the effect that something should exist. Some of these statements pertain to societies of various sorts; and others, to persons of various sorts. Thus, Plato recommends the existence of an aristocratic state and an aristocratic man; Dewey, the democratic state and the democratic man; and Rousseau, the less corrupted state and the innocent man. These we may call "goal recommendations." Statements of the second sort recommend particular procedures in the daily business of education. Thus, Plato recommends that the young guardians should be made to view battles; Dewey, that school activities should be predominantly cooperative; and Rousseau, that the young gentleman should be long isolated from his fellows. Statements of this sort we may call "subordinate recommendations." Subordinate recommendations, it is clear, secure their force from goal recommendations; for it is because certain social and personal states of affairs are entertained as the objectives of education that the particular methods of educating, embodied in subordinate recommendations, are urged upon us.

The ethics of education must consider the recommendations of both these kinds; and with respect to each kind, it must consider at least two questions. With respect to goal recommendations, it must ask whether the objectives are genuinely good, and are not mistakenly thought to be so; and what the reasons are which justify its answer to that question. And with respect to subordinate recommendations, it must ask similar questions: whether the methods recommended are genuinely valid, and what the reasons are for or against their validity.

The ethics of education may be construed either as the activity of considering the nature of goodness and rightness, the validity of the goal recommendations of education as well as of its subordinate recommendations, and the giving of reasons for or against such recommendations; or as a body of statements which incorporate such considerations.

Two morals are to be drawn from this understanding of the phrase "ethics of education." The first is that ethical writers on education must be quite clear as to the kind of reasons which tell for or against the recommendations of that discipline. It is easily supposed by many that ethical recommendations receive their support in the same way as do other kinds of statement, that reasons for them are premises from which they can be deduced, or inductive evidence which renders them probable. There is not space, here, to show why this view is dubious. We can only note its dubious character, and observe that clarity in ethics of education demands a clear understanding of the relation which makes one thing an ethical reason for another.

The second moral is that, in the beginning at least, there is no such thing as *the* ethics of education. We have seen that there are several different kinds of ethical theory; and we may now add that within each, there is much variation from one particular theory to another. Each particular ethical theory provides us with its own unique ethics of education; for although there should be one single coherent body of valid educational recommendations—a view which seems inevitable to the writer [but a view which] does not preclude the variation of goal recommendations in time and place, nor a variation of subordinate recommendations—each ethical theory would supplement the statement of those precepts by its unique understanding of the nature of goodness and rightness. In the beginning, at least, the pragmatic ethics of education, for example, is only one among many other such theories. In the end, after careful consideration of the claims of the various theories, one might well offer his allegiance to one as opposed to the rest. To accept one from the outset, however, as many have done, is a dogmatism against which our second moral warns; while to accept one upon reflection, where cognitive superiority manifests itself, is an obligation which philosophy imposes.

CONCLUSION

When we ask, "What is a philosophy of education?" we are asking, "What is an analysis of education, a metaphysics of education, and an ethics of education?" And this complex question is answered by saying that an analysis of education is a clarification of whatever terms are obscure in it, that a metaphysics of education is a theory of existence intended to explain its factual part, and in that way to ground its recommendations; and that an ethics of education is a justification of the two kinds of recommendation it contains, including a consideration of the question as to the nature of goodness and rightness, and presupposing an understanding of the nature of ethical reasons.

We have seen that there is great need for analytical work, and that metaphysical theories cannot explain the facts of education. We may now add that this failure on the part of the metaphysics of education need not be much lamented. Those who desire a justification of the recommendations of education, and who would have thought this to be found in its metaphysics may still find it in their philosophy. For it is this function which is the peculiar contribution of ethics to the philosophy of education.

∽

Part II

The Divisions of Philosophy

Introduction: Charts, Categories, and Philosophy

> "When *I* use a word," Humpty Dumpty said in rather a scornful tone, "it means just what I choose it to mean—neither more nor less."
>
> "The question is," said Alice, "whether you *can* make words mean so many different things."
>
> "The question is," said Humpty Dumpty, "which is to be master— that's all."
>
> *Lewis Carroll*

Humpty might well be speaking for the philosopher who wishes to use his words precisely and clearly in order to preserve the integrity of his meaning. Alice might be speaking for the puzzled student, wondering if the philosopher can indeed invest common language with uncommon meaning. Like the beginning student in philosophy, Alice is not a little shocked and surprised to discover that a given word can have many meanings; that the other side of the word-coin does not have one and only one true meaning, but that different philosophers often put different meanings to a word—"reality," for instance.

Words are verbal labels that are pasted onto ideas, the better to identify and classify their content or meaning, in much the same way a housewife puts labels on her preserves to classify jams and jellies.

Language, the way we arrange and order words to preserve the meaning of experience, is very probably the most important tool invented by man. Some languages are flexible, some are fairly rigid; some yield pastel-like shades of meaning, while others let us describe our experiences only in black-and-white terms. For instance, Eskimos are said to have seventeen different words to describe the phenomenon we simply call "snow."

Culture conditions language, and whether we express the subtleties of experience with finely shaded meanings or linguistically trample roughshod over them greatly depends on the language culture places at our command. To illustrate this, consider again the case of the housewife labeling her preserves. If she has just canned some berries she might describe what she has been doing by saying, "I put some ——— in this jar" (using "strawberries,"

"berries," "fruit," or even "food" to complete the sentence). Any of those alternatives would be meaningful to us because we share a common culture and language—and we understand, implicitly at least, the system of categories in the language. That is, if she had said "strawberries," we could infer "berries," "fruit," and "food." But now suppose that this housewife can speak Chinese and wanted to make the same report to a Chinese who had never experienced the joys (and woes) of the canning season. She might fill in the blank with *yangmei, tsaumei, shewigwo,* or *gwo,* and communication would take place, even though there would have been no meaning-for-meaning exchange here. That a one-to-one translation is not possible is seen in the following comparison:

strawberries	yangmei, tsaumei
berries	—
fruit	shewigwo
—	gwo

Thus "berries" is more inclusive than either *yangmei* or *tsaumei,* but not as inclusive as *shewigwo.* The housewife, being fluent in Chinese, might be able to coin a term which describes the English meaning of "berry," but it would be quite lengthy. On the other hand, *gwo* can mean "fruit" or "nuts," or both.[1]

As a final example of the importance of language and culture to philosophy, consider that much of our prized Western philosophy (e.g., Plato or Aristotle) simply does not make sense in Arabic! What to us may seem sensible and logical is, to the Arab, senseless, illogical and, perhaps worse yet, bad grammar.

In the attempt to cope with our environment, to explain and understand our lives and our universe, to find or put meaning into experience, we must rely on language; and insofar as philosophy represents one important phase of this attempt it cannot escape language or culture. Alice's problem is perennial. Indeed, if this is one of the first books about philosophy you have read, and if you happen to be a student in a philosophy class for the very first time, pause now to reflect on one of your present philosophical problems: Is it not that the vocabulary, the nomenclature, of philosophy is puzzling and frustrating to you? Are you not trying, like Alice, to discover the meanings of words used by philosophers, words which you have used in other context and with other meanings, but which are now labels pasted onto different ideas? If this *is* your present problem, you are not alone; philosophic novices spend most of their time putting labels on intellectual

1 This illustration was drawn from Charles F. Hockett, "Chinese v. English: An Exploration of the Whorfian Theses," in *Language in Culture,* ed. Harry Hoijer (Chicago: The University of Chicago Press, 1954), pp. 106–123.

containers, stacking the containers on a conceptual shelf, and trying to arrange the labels, containers, and shelves (just as the housewife does with her jams and jellies) in a neat, logical, orderly way.

The problem is one of organization, classification, categorization. Which labels go on what containers, and what containers go on which shelves? Just as the housewife has to decide to use the word "berries" rather than "strawberries," "blackberries," or "blueberries," whether the blueberries should be to the right of the blackberries, and those to the left of the strawberries, and whether berries or whole fruits should be on the upper, middle, or lower shelves, so too do students of philosophy have a similar task. Where the housewife labels food the student labels ideas; and each necessarily relies on words to express their systems of classification. The word, the label used, to a very great extent, will determine where the container goes. Professional philosophers, just like beginners, have category problems.

Philosophic concepts are slippery things; no sooner is one labeled epistemological than an ontological dimension becomes apparent; no sooner is an idea put into the cubbyhole marked Aristotelian than some Pragmatic part of it protrudes; no sooner is Plato labeled an Idealist than it is noted the label Realist may also be applied to his thought with equal justification. The problem of categorization is a persistent one in philosophy; it is equally persistent as a pedagogical problem. For purposes of instruction (a purpose hopefully to be served by this book), how *should* philosophic ideas, concepts, positions, or points of view be organized and classified?

They might be categorized in terms of schools, but no philosophic system is built of patented components that are exclusively members of that system. Worse, when philosophers are categorized as members of this school or that, but not more than one, some violence is done to their thought. Still, there is great merit in using such labels as Idealism, Realism, Thomism, Pragmatism, or Logical Empiricism to encapsulate general modes of thought. The categories of supernaturalism and naturalism to classify philosophic thought also are useful, for these labels give the reader some indication as to the contents of the container so labeled. Of course, there is the question whether or not two labels are sufficient for many different containers. Again, the labels rational and empirical can be used to identify philosophic containers, and there is some justification for this kind of categorization even though no philosopher or philosophic system is purely and exclusively rational or empirical. One final alternative might be to classify containers as to their substance rather than their content; that is, as the housewife might speak of glass jars, tin cans, paper cups, or plastic holders, philosophers might use the categories of monism, dualism, and pluralism to distinguish one kind of container from another.

The choice of labels and categories in philosophy is crucial and painful. It is crucial because distinctions do exist and need to be identified and preserved; it is painful because philosophic categories almost invariably serve as a Procrustean bed for philosophers and their concepts. Consider, for example, St. Thomas Aquinas. If his philosophy is categorized by school he is (obviously!) a Thomist—but, perhaps, in the same way Karl Marx was categorized when he protested, "Je ne suis pas Marxiste!" Aquinas is a Thomist, but he is just as obviously some kind of Realist. He is clearly a supernaturalist, but he claims his philosophizing begins with human perception of natural events. He epitomizes reliance on reason, yet his subject matter for reflection is drawn from empirical experience. As for "quantity," he is clearly and only a dualist—but, unfortunately, not all Realists are dualists, not all supernaturalists are rationalists, etc., so there is no generalization to guide the business of categorization.

How then, for pedagogical if not philosophical purposes, shall philosophies be categorized? Whatever the answer, it is arbitrary; some will use this system of charts and categories, others that system. This confusion is perpetuated by lack of agreement among authors of textbooks. In three of the most popular texts in philosophy of education the classification systems vary. One author speaks of Pragmatism, Romantic Naturalism, Idealism, Naturalistic Realism, Rational Humanism, and Catholic Supernaturalism; the second refers to Naturalism, Idealism, Realism, and Pragmatism; and the third writes about Progressivism, Essentialism, Perennialism, and Reconstructionism, yet all are covering the same basic material. This is the problem of "isms" in philosophy. Lacking a criterion to distinguish one philosophy from any other or each from all others, different authors use different schemata. There are no completely satisfactory niches in which to pigeonhole philosophic thought, thus categories are superimposed on philosophies, since philosophies are not built to fit preestablished categories.

While the problem of classifying philosophies is not satisfactorily solved, there has been more success in the classification of the subject matter of philosophy. That is, there is general agreement that philosophic subject matter can be divided into three main categories: metaphysics, the theory of reality; epistemology, the theory of knowledge; and ethics, the theory of value.

PEDAGOGICAL PLAN OF THIS ESSAY

Part II of this book is designed to provide essays in the three major areas of philosophy; the editors' chapters in Part II are designed to provide an introduction to those essays, in the hope that their value may be enhanced..

The very best introduction would be to read a book or take a course in the history of philosophy; but if you have not had that course perhaps the pages to follow will substitute temporarily. Simple sense, however, indicates that the editors' chapters are not a book, nor is one book a course. So in these chapters the editors have decided *not* to divide the available space equally between metaphysics, epistemology, and ethics, but to emphasize the former at the expense of the latter two. The reason for this (and we trust it is pedagogically sound) is that our experience indicates your instructor in the philosophy of education, given the limited course time of only one semester, will wisely choose to emphasize in his class discussions the epistemological and ethical aspects of philosophy since these are most directly pertinent to education.

Consequently, this chapter will be devoted to a review of the major theories of reality. Even so, we have tried to touch upon epistemology and ethics, as well as to offer a sense of the historical continuity in philosophy, and we are hopeful that the emphases of this chapter will join with those of your instructor to give you a rounded grasp of what philosophy is all about.

The Category of Metaphysics

Metaphysics deals with the ultimate or essential nature of this and all possible universes in a synoptic, comprehensive way. The metaphysician tries to give a description of reality not by identifying and enumerating every single thing that exists but by finding some common denominator of reality, by speculating on the ultimate material of reality, and using that to create an all-encompassing *Weltanschauung* (world-view).

One purpose of this essay, to be accomplished in the pages to follow, is to provide some introductory comments about theories of reality. Of course, such discussion requires some system of classification—thus once again raising the old problem of putting labels on containers. Perplexing as this task is, it is necessary for pedagogical purposes if no other. The task is somewhat eased because answers to the questions "What is the *ultimate* nature of reality?" or "What is the *ultimate* constitution of world-stuff?" ask not only about the quality of reality, but also about quantity. That is, such questions ask not only *what* kind but *how many* kinds. Taking the quantitative question first, answers take one of three forms. Some philosophers claim there is ultimately only *one* kind of world-stuff, and all things that exist—from fireplugs to unicorns, from Marilyn Monroe to ideas of justice—can be reduced to and expressed in terms of some single, unitary world-stuff. This position is called *monism*. Some monists say reality is eventually seen to be nothing but spiritual (e.g., Idealism), while others argue for nothing but the physical (e.g., Materialism).

Some philosophers deny reality is "nothing but" one quality or substance, insisting that reality ultimately reduces to *two* kinds—usually the spiritual and the physical—and, therefore, this metaphysical position is called *dualism*.

A third general position is to deny the either-or alternatives of monism and dualism by arguing that reality simply cannot be reduced to one or two kinds, and affirming that many, many different kinds exist. This position is *pluralism*.

Given these three basic alternatives it is possible to categorize metaphysical positions on that basis. Combining these metaphysical categories with generalized schools of philosophy (and bearing in mind the interests of students, who are anxious to put labels on containers), the classification system illustrated can be used for the pedagogical purposes of this essay. Remember, however, that philosophy does not have a neat, logical system of categorization automatically built into it, so some injustices and inaccuracies are made through the necessary arbitrariness of any such outline. See pp. 76–77 for the classification outline.

IDEALISTIC MONISM: OVERVIEW

There are many answers to the basic ontological question (which, by definition, asks about the meaning of existence per se), and as we have seen, one answer is that the constitution of all that which exists is, in the final analysis, of one kind. This belief that reality consists in one kind of world stuff is a monistic approach to that part of metaphysics called ontology. There are different kinds of monisms, but when a philosopher makes an argument that reality ultimately reduces to Mind or Spirit, he is making an Idealistic argument. That is, his monism is Idealistic (remember that philosophers mean idea-istic) because he puts an emphasis on *mind* as the key to reality, because in his view reality is indeed mental or spiritual in the final analysis. Matter, physical things like the stars in the firmament or the stars in Hollywood, may have existence (depending on the variety of Idealism at hand; see below) but matter is not ultimately real.

Idealists from Plato to Butler are agreed that reality is quantitatively one and qualitatively mental. Yet by no means is there a party line, for Idealistic philosophers differ in their interpretation of reality. For purposes of this essay these differences can be given the following labels: Formal Idealism, which we will associate with Plato; Subjective Idealism, of which George Berkeley is the best example; Spiritual Idealism, sometimes more accurately identified as Kantian Realism; and the Absolute Idealism of Georg Hegel.

Formal Idealism: Plato. Almost any school child can identify Plato as a philosopher, and almost any college student can identify him as an Idealist. A few graduate students, perhaps testing their powers of interpretation, might dare to use the phrase Platonic Realism in expectation of confounding those undergraduates who have been taught to equate philosophic Idealism with the great Plato. It may be that these graduates can make a defensible case (by arguing that Plato's analysis can be seen to be dualistic rather than exclusively monistic). Even so, the undergraduates have not been miseducated: Plato's thought is indeed most often taken as the prototype for Idealism.

Plato is celebrated for this theory of ideas; hence he is generally said to be the first Idealist. Platonic Idealism rests on the distinction between *appearance* and *reality,* and out of his analysis of this distinction grows his theory of ideas.

According to Plato, the world we experience through our senses—the moon we see, the tree we touch, the okra we taste, the perfume we smell,

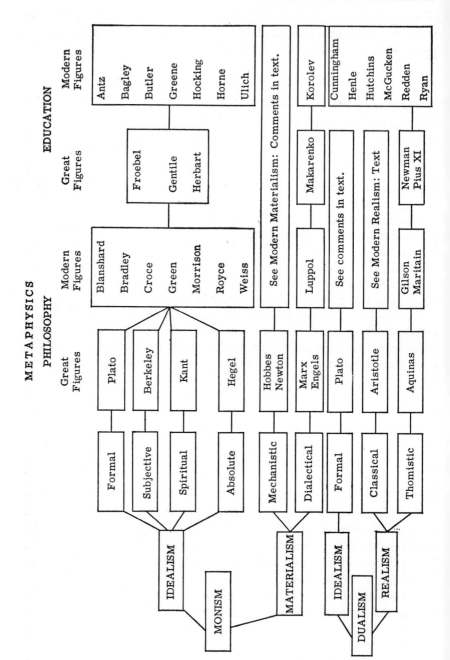

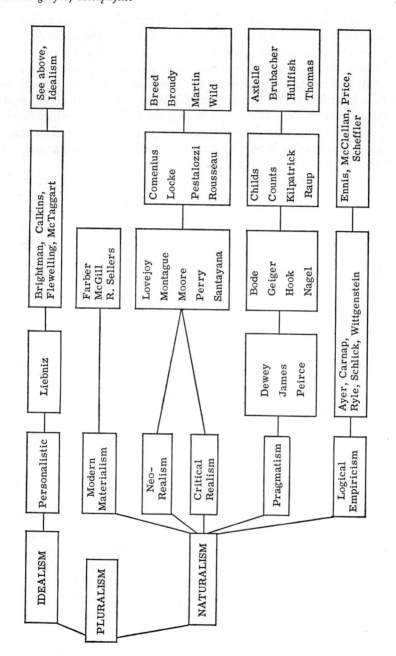

the poem we hear—does not constitute the real world. It is but a carbon copy of the real world, and a smudged carbon at that. It is the world of appearance, and while it apparently exists (or exists apparently) it is not real, not ultimately real. It could not be, reasoned Plato, for the ultimately real is constant and unchanging, whereas the world we experience through perception is an inconstant, changing world. What is real is stable; change is the opposite of stability, so it cannot be real; the world of experience changes, and even as we perceive these changes, our perceptions themselves change. So, clearly, perception is unreliable and the sensible world we experience is not the real world, not true reality.

How do we know this? In his famous analogy of the cave (see Book VII of *Republic*) Plato compares us to prisoners in cave, bound in such a way that we must look at the wall in front of us. Behind us is a fire, and all we can perceive, given this situation, are the dancing, changing shadows on the wall—the shadows of objects behind us and our own shadows. Naturally, never having been out of the cave, or even able to turn around and look at the objects or fire behind us, we consider these shadows as real, having no idea that they are reflections of the real things beyond our senses (and not very good reflections, at that). Only when we escape from the cave do we realize how horribly mistaken we were about the true nature of reality. Only then do we come to know how our perceptions deceived us into believing the apparent was the real.

The world of appearance is thus but a copy of the real world, which is the world of ideas. (Plato uses "idea" and "form" interchangeably, and it is from this that his philosophy can be labeled Formal Idealism.) In the realm of ideas is to be found the ideal bed, of which all sensible beds are copies; the ideal, or the idea of, circle, of which all sensible circles are copies; and the ideals of justice, truth, and beauty which serve as the forms or molds of particular things or practices which we label good, true, and beautiful. Thus the universe *is* and *appears;* matter exists, true, but its shape, its form, its very existence, depends on the corresponding idea.

Consider, for example, a painting by DaVinci or a statue by Rodin. Clearly both picture and figure have material existence—they are ontological facts. But just as clearly they existed as an idea in the minds of their creators *before* they existed in the world of appearance. DaVinci's "Mona Lisa" and Rodin's "The Thinker" existed in the mind before they existed in paint and metal. "Mona Lisa's" haunting smile was an idea, existing in mind, before it existed in paint; so, too, the contemplative attitude of "The Thinker." Thus matter is the raw material upon which mental forms, or ideas, are impressed. The idea is prior to, it is independent of, the material. *It* is ultimately real, not its manifestations. So goes Plato's theory of ideas, by which reality is seen to be idea-(1)-istic or form-alistic.

As a theory of reality, Platonic, or Formal, Idealism has both logical and ontological aspects. Logically it offers an explanation of generalizations (i.e., general terms or universals). For example, there are many kinds of dogs—Golden Retrievers, Dachshunds, Collies, Beagles, and Heinz 57's—all of which we identify with the general term "dog." Yet, what is meant by the term "dog" in general? Goldens are similar to Beagles and Beagles to Wolfhounds, but by "dog" we seem to mean something that is different from any particular dog, yet similar to all dogs. Thus a Golden is a dog because its nature is common to any or all other dogs—but just how? The answer to *that* question is still up for grabs, according to some philosophers (others say it's a pseudoproblem), but even so it is clear that, in order to communicate, we need words like "dog," and so they are in some way pertinent and meaningful. The general meaning put to them by Plato would have them refer not to particular dogs but to the idea of dog—in rough, to the "dogginess" which has real and eternal existence in the world of ideas, and which is manifested in the world of appearances through particulars. Fido—that smelly old creature you love—exists; but when he dies, he is gone forever. Not so for the ideal dog, or "dogginess," which is eternal and unchanging, hence ultimately real. Thus the logical aspect of the theory of ideas explains the meaning of general terms.

The ontological aspect has been suggested in the previous paragraph: The meaning of the word "dog" is dependent on dogginess, thus particular dogs depend on the ideal dog—which exists only in the realm of ideas. So it is, once again, that ideas are the ontologically real.

In sum, while the graduate student might argue that Plato is a Realist, he is generally identified as an Idealist because he believed the real world was not the world of things we see, hear, feel, taste, or smell, but the world of ideas—the things we know by reason rather than by experience. And, since his ideas were creative forms, we have given his philosophy the generic label Formal Idealism.

Subjective Idealism: Berkeley. The famous Irish bishop, George Berkeley (1685–1753), gave a renewed emphasis to Idealism after it had suffered severe blows at the hands of John Locke (1632–1704).

Locke's philosophizing had reached a skeptical conclusion with regard to reality: The world we experience really doesn't exist, but the world that really does exist is not knowable. As a man of God, Anglican Berkeley was upset with the popularity of Locke, because from such a philosophy the existence of God could not be conclusively demonstrated; thus he set out to destroy Locke's Realism. To do this he took as true the bulk of Locke's epistemology, and agreed with Locke that there is nothing in the mind (i.e., ideas) that is not first in the senses (i.e., experienced), and that which we know is ideas. However, he discarded Locke's ontology which, combined with his epistemology, led to skepticism (perhaps even solipsism) and reconstituted the whole thing into a Subjective Idealism.

In his analysis Berkeley concludes that there are no objects independent of the mind—hence his idea-ism. Yet, he does maintain the existence of physical objects (contrary to some of his interpreters who claim he denies physical existence), so he has the task of explaining and justifying the existence of material objects.

As an empiricist he admits that the only evidence for the existence of material objects is our experience with them. From this he reasons that, all things considered, not only is it true that our perception provides us with evidence of the existence of a material object, it is the *only* evidence we have. But more, since this is the case, the very existence of the object is dependent upon our experience with it—it is, so to speak, as if it were created in experience. (Some misinformed Pragmatists make the same argument in behalf of Dewey, but Dewey never maintained this point of view.)

From this conclusion, from the belief that an object exists only as it is given in experience, came the Berkeleyan dictum: *esse est percipi* (to be is to be perceived). Thus the existence of a thing depends on its being perceived. Taken at face value, Berkeley's conclusion appears absurd, for simple logic indicates that if the dictum "to be is to be perceived" is true, then "to be perceived is to be" is equally true—and no intelligent individual would hold, for example, that the furniture we perceive in illusions, dreams, and hallucinations is real (i.e., has physical existence). Similarly, the same simple logic indicates that if "to be is to be perceived" is true, then "not to be perceived is not to be" (i.e., things not seen don't exist) is also true. Thus when you fall asleep reading this book it disappears (you like that?); or when you say goodnight to your steady, he or she ceases to exist the moment you turn your back! This comes close to the intellectual isolation of solipsism, and such would be the consequence of Berkeley's dictum if taken at face value.

Berkeley does *not* want it taken at face value, however, as these famous limericks suggest:

> There once was a man who said, "God
> Must think it exceedingly odd
> If he finds that this tree
> Continues to be
> When there's no one about in the Quad."

> "Dear Sir: Your astonishment's odd,
> *I* am always about in the Quad
> And that's why the tree
> Will continue to be,
> Since observed by Yours faithfully, God."

What Berkeley has in mind, then, does not have reference to human perception but to God's perception—and thus he builds God into the system. *To be,* therefore, involves the existence of an idea in the mind of God; and that is the *ultimate* reality.

In sum, Berkeley's philosophy rests on the belief that ideas are the product of mind, and mind is the product of Mind. We know, for instance, that our minds produce some ideas, but we also know we have some ideas that were not created by us; yet we do have these "foreign" ideas which are similar in kind to those we create, so it must be that these ideas are the product of another mind. That other and superior Mind we call God, and He is the author of all ideas—and therefore of reality.

In essence, Berkeley avers that matter cannot exist except as ideas, thus nature exists, but only subjectively in the mind and is dependent upon the most perfect Subject or Mind—God—for existence. In this manner it is labeled as Subjective Idealism.

Spiritual Idealism: Kant. The great Immanuel Kant (1724–1804) undertook—most notably in his *Critique of Pure Reason* and *Critique of Practical Reason*—to retrieve Idealism from the pit of subjectivity into which Berkeley had cast it. He attacked Berkeley's Idealism, perhaps mistakenly, on the ground that it falsely asserted material objects are actually nothing but fictitious entities in a subjective mind. To Kant this was an untenable position, for he was convinced that material objects do exist (and not merely in a mind), and that we can know them.

His interest was primarily epistemological. That is, he was concerned to answer, in a way more satisfactory than Idealists had, the traditional questions of epistemology: What can we know? What do we know? How do we know? and How can we be sure? In fine, what is knowledge? He concluded that we can only know our experiences. For instance, we have a sensation of, say, perceiving the fiery tail of a comet or the wagging tail of a dog, and because our minds function in a certain way, this sensation is received by them—but according to Kant, as with Locke, it is impossible for us ever to know the cause of the sensations we receive. From this analysis it follows that a natural world does exist although, unfortunately, we can never know this world of things in themselves; without our minds we could not know about this external world of things, and even with our minds we cannot know what that physical world would be, or is, like in and of itself.

To distinguish between the world in itself and the world as it appears to us through sensations, Kant used the terms "noumenal" and "phenomenal." The former, consisting of things in themselves (*ding-an-sich*), is as such unknowable; the latter, the world of appearance, is indeed knowable—but what we know, then, are our own sensations, experience, ideas. In a clear sense this is subjectivism, albeit not extreme subjectivism or solipsism since, for Kant, these experiences and ideas are not exclusively private or personal. That is, when Kant makes a proposition about a material object, when he says "Trees exist," he is reporting a certain experience, he is affirming the receipt of certain sense data. This is subjective, yet he fully expects that you and I would offer the same report concerning our sense data if we were in his situation. Kant thus uses the safety value of sharability to move from subjective (private) to intersubjective (public) confirmation of phenomenal events.

Here Kant faces a problem. If, as Berkeley said, material objects exist only in our minds, then science—that is, physical science—is impossible. Kant avoids that by affirming the existence of objects which do exist independently of mind, yet all we know are our perceptions—the phenomenal world of appearance. How then build a science? How then distinguish between true and false perceptions, between authentic sense data and the sense data of hallucinations, in order to distinguish between Aesop and Einstein? To satisfy this requirement, Kant built into his Idealism the concept of causality in nature; in this way we are able to differentiate between strictly private experience, which yields no science, and public experience, which is basic to science.

Kant related causality to his concept of universal laws, some of which deal with objective relations (i.e., physical laws governing the behavior of objects) and some of which deal with subjective relations (i.e., moral laws governing the behavior of men). As we reflect on our experience we can conceive of a universe in which *all* events occur strictly according to the physical laws of nature; thus the idea of a God who causes all this is not strictly necessary since such an idea is not necessarily entailed by our experience. On the other hand, Kant continued, as we reflect on our experience we can equally well conceive of a universe in which a God is indeed the cause of everything, and although we cannot directly experience this, we can behave as if this were indeed the real, or true, universe.

Given these logical alternatives, the purely mechanistic universe governed by strictly physical laws and devoid of a God, or a universe in which all is governed by God, Kant chooses the latter even though it is only the former we sense directly. He chooses as he does because, he argues, it is only in this kind of universe that man can be assured of his essential integrity—and in which morality and immortality, freedom and freedom of will, could exist. This choice, this idea of the universe, is moral and regulative; it provides moral direction for human guidance and makes possible the good life.

In sum, Kant postulates two worlds: the noumenal, unknowable world of things in themselves, and the phenomenal, knowable world of experience. Which is the real world? The former, because man is moral, morality presupposes a God, so we must therefore conclude that a God exists and the real world is essentially spiritual. On the basis of this explanation of ultimate reality we can label Kant's philosophy Spiritual Idealism.

Absolute Idealism: Hegel. Just as Kant found Berkeley's Idealism too subjective, so in his turn did Georg Hegel (1770–1831) find Kant's Idealism too subjective. Kant's metaphysical and unknowable thing in itself, seemed to Hegel to corrupt the unity of reality and he set about establishing Idealistic monism on a firm basis. Still, he found value in Berkeley's epistemology, as taken from Locke and passed through Kant so, while he did try to overcome the problem of a thing in itself, he was even more concerned with unifying, expanding, and perfecting Idealism as a philosophic system.

Pursuing the end in view of correcting Kant's conclusions about the noumenal and phenomenal worlds, Hegel argued that this two-worldism was actually a dualism repugnant to Idealistic monism. He undertook to retrieve Kant from this dualism by pointing out that an entity, such as a thing in itself, which is said to possess no sensible or knowable attributes, is at one with an entity which has no real existence; further, to speak of an entity or object which does not exist is to speak of nothing real, and therefore to speak of nothing. In fine, Hegel strips Kant's noumenal world of any kind of existence other than nominal; that is, he argues that Kant's thing in itself is an abstraction.

Richard Hoenigswald, writing on the "Philosophy of Hegelianism" in *Twentieth Century Philosophy,* not only points out Hegel's antipathy to the tortured metaphysics of Kant but gives an insight into Hegel's concept of unity and absoluteness:

> . . . metaphysics never means for Hegel the deviously and surreptitiously arrived-at knowledge of things outside of knowledge, but rather the unity toward which every thinkable claim to definiteness with reference to every other claim is oriented. This unity depends upon nothing outside itself. . . . For this reason it may be called "absolute." For it *is* absolutely everything; and everything that exists in a manner free from all limitations of mere individual viewpoints, and so, from all "abstractions" of reflection, is just that unity alone.

The bone of contention between Absolute and other Idealists is found when the body of experience is examined. Berkeley, for example, took sense experience as the ground and warrant for epistemology and ontology; in so doing he tended to downgrade consciousness or pure reason. Hegel, on the other hand, refuses to restrict experience to sense experience, and broadens the term to include consciousness, imagination, reason, perception, moral interests—in fact, everything. He thus uses "experience" as an all-inclusive term (as Dewey was to do after him). This bone of contention is further splintered by the Hegelian approach to mind. Other Idealists had maintained that since ideas are the product of mind, the existence of an idea therefore implies the prior existence of a mind, although mind does not necessarily imply ideas, because mind need not produce ideas. (As many school teachers affirm!) For Hegel, however, the relationship between mind and idea is reciprocal; each implies the other in a biconditional logic. This "utilization" of mind and idea helped eliminate the dualism Hegel saw in Kant's metaphysics.

Hegel is really driving toward a simple ontological point: reality is not something outside of experience, to be known by experience; it is not "in our heads" to be known through introspection of ideas or the working of our mind; reality *is* experience. It is experience broadly conceived; it is the comprehensive systematization of experience into a unified, synoptic, Gestalt-like whole. When other Idealists protest this Hegelian formulation, the Absolute Idealist freely admits we can, do, and should distinguish between "things as they really are" and "things as I see them in my mind," but he insists this is a *logical differentiation* done within the context of experience and does not in any way imply or require an ontological division between (my) (our) experience and reality. It is in this sense that reality is unitary and absolute.

Yet clearly, ideas vary, experiences vary, and while reality may be absolute and whole, it is surely not homogeneous. There are, for Kant, levels of reality—a hierarchy of "real," "realer," "realest." Hegel argues that as we examine our individual and social experience, we conclude that all the subject matters of experience—things or objects, ideas or subjects—are in some way related. That is, while each datum of reality is in some way connected to all other real data, some enter into close and stable relationships (e.g., the conjugal family) while others partake only of a distant, unstable relationship (e.g., third cousins, thrice removed); some are broad in that the relationship is quite pervasive (e.g., the generality of $E = mc^2$), others are narrow in that the relationship is restricted (e.g., the particularity of Cadillac usage). Accordingly, there are levels of reality.

How determine the more from the less real? Why, by an analysis of "being and becoming." That is, a thing (or event, person, relationship) is real to the degree it moves toward and fulfills its true nature or realizes its full potential. Thus, oak and acorn are real, but the tree enjoys a higher level of existence than the seed because it has fulfilled its potential. Thus the real is judged in terms of the ideal, and that which is ultimately real is the ideal; those things which have moved through "becoming" to "being" *are.*

That is, they have their complete existence; they are real because they *are*.

Things are what they are, and become what they will be, according to Hegel, due to the dialectic method or nature of reality; this dialectic is the dynamic in Hegel's Absolute Idealism for it is the catalytic agent in reality. Less poetically, it is a method, a logic, by which we can know reality. This dialectic method has three stages: the thesis (an Idea), the antithesis (Nature), and the synthesis (Spirit); or to fill the logical form with another triadic content, the thesis (a thing), the antithesis (a different thing), and the synthesis (a new thing based on the old).

Change and progress—all becoming—result from the dialectic process of reality, and they can be understood and explained when thought (mind and ideas) is based on a dialectical logic. Put most simply, the dialectic is a forward-moving process involving some present, on-going situation which represents the thesis. Out of this current state of affairs some difficulty or contradiction arises, and this represents the antithesis. Between these two a struggle or conflict ensues, and the resolution of this is the synthesis. It should be noted, however that neither the thesis nor the antithesis "wins" the struggle and emerges victorious and intact, while the other goes down to total defeat and destruction. Rather, the synthesis represents elements of both the original thesis and the consequent antithesis; and even though it is based on both, contains elements of both, and grew out of the struggle between both, it is genuinely new, unique, and different. It is, in short, a *new* situation, a *new* thesis—and so the dialectic process begins anew, ever anew, yet new forever.

Reality, for Hegel, is thus explained; levels of reality are thus explained. But what is Absolute Reality, The One, The Absolute? It is a single (monistic), all-inclusive whole universe as a unified and coherent system, culminating in Pure Spirit or Absolute Mind. J. Donald Butler puts it well in his *Four Philosophies:*

> Then phenomenal world with all of its manifold interrelationships is throughout a manifestation of Infinite Mind realizing itself in finite and temporal processes. At bottom the so-called physical world is Idea; this is the foundation it rests upon. At top, the far-off end toward which it moves is Mind, Spirit, the Infinite Idea, fully realized for itself.

In sum, Hegel believed that reality is a dialectic evolution from mind to nature to God—a philosophic Tinkers-to-Evers-to-Chance, with the completion of the play representing All. The universe is an organic whole, but a developing whole in terms of the dialectic process. Reality, in this meaning, *is* (or alternately, is *in*) a process of evolution, a process of becoming. It moves toward the ultimate Idea; it evolves into Being (God); it becomes Spiritual and Absolute. Because Hegel believed that ultimate reality is an absolute, total, unified Spirit, we have labeled his philosophy Absolute Idealism.

Idealistic Monism: A Final Word. As we have seen, there is no party line which all who would be called Idealists must follow. Indeed, although we have been considering the metaphysical aspects of Idealism under the ontological rubric of "monism," there is a brand of Idealism known as Personalism (*infra,* pp. 98–101) which is not even monistic.

There is a central theme, however, running through all Idealistic approaches to the question of reality, and that is the emphasis on mind, ideas, and consciousness. Reality *is* mind to the modern Idealist; but this was not always so.

Plato, whom we label the father of Idealism, believed that ultimate reality consisted of forms, and material was "compressed to fit" these forms which were perfect, therefore ideal. In that sense Formal (form-al) Idealism took non-material ideal forms as the ultimately real.

Later Idealists tended to substitute ideas for these Platonic ideals as the building blocks of the universe, hence an emphasis on idea-ism rather than ideal-ism. In that sense Idealism posited An Idea, an Ultimate Idea, as real.

More recently, Idealists have begun to push ideal-ism and idea-ism to the side, in favor of mind as the ultimately real, on the thesis that ideals and ideas are not primary but secondary, since they are products of mind. Both Absolute Idealism and Personalistic Idealism approach reality from this point of view (although they disagree on the oneness or manyness of mind). Other modern Idealists, admitting the importance of ideals, ideas, and mind, prefer to focus their attention on the concept of consciousness as the key to reality. Withal, modern Idealists see mind and mental processes as basic, so modern Idealism is sometimes labeled Mentalism.

What is common to Idealistic monism, then, is the root metaphor that reality is, and can be understood only in terms of, mind.

MATERIALISTIC MONISM: OVERVIEW

The historic argument among monists is whether the ultimate oneness of reality is mental or material. As we have seen, monistic Idealists make an argument that material objects are, if not illusory, secondary to and derived from mind. Monistic Materialists, to the contrary, argue that matter is prior to mind, that mind grew out of matter. Hence matter is the ultimately real.

While there is much intraparty strife among Materialists, they agree that matter is prior to mind, that in the course of natural evolution inanimate matter became animate, and that in the case of humans at least, matter became thinking. Thus mind is reduced to matter; or more accurately, the mental activities generally associated with the mind are actually the functioning of a completely material brain—and "mind" becomes an adverb (a description of a process) rather than a noun (an existent). On this point Materialists from Democritus to Sellars, including such as Hobbes and Marx are agreed. For purposes of this essay only two kinds of Materialism, Mechanistic and Dialectical, will be discussed; since the other major branch, Modern Materialism, will be considered as a pluralistic rather than monistic approach to reality.

Mechanistic Materialism. Briefly put, the metaphysics of Mechanistic Materialism holds that reality is matter in motion. By "matter" is meant those physical entities which are "hard," which are active, and which exist externally to us and independently of us. In this context "hard" means that matter is persistent, it does not go away even though we may so will it, thus it resists or persists; "active" means that matter is constantly in motion, and consequently "this" bit of matter affects all other matter; "external" means that matter is not a manifestation of an idea, be it yours, mine, or God's; and "independent" means its existence in no way depends on us, our will, or our perceptions.

This kind of Materialism began with the very earliest of Western philosophers—the pre-Socratics such as Democritus (*ca.* 460–380) and Leucippus (*ca.* 480–440)—when the thesis of atomism was first laid down. These philosophers held that everything in the universe, from sand to air, from man to the gods, were ultimately composed of hard, solid, homogeneous, indivisible, and invisible particles. Since the thesis held all reality consisted of these, and since they were all made of the same stuff, reality was One. Yet, in One (i.e., matter) there were many (i.e., particles of matter), but no one of the many could be further reduced. That is, no one of them could be separated from any of the others, thus the pre-Socratics called them atoms (*atoma; a,* not, and *tome,* divisible).

Since atoms exhausted the content of reality, and since they were constantly in motion, it followed that all attempts at explanation had to be in terms of physical laws which described how atoms moved. That is, the only subject matter of inquiry had to do with the kinds of relationships between atoms, and the different kinds of atoms. As B. A. G. Fuller summarizes this early atomism, ". . . all qualitative difference was reduced to and explained in terms of quantitative difference, and all qualitative change was reduced to and explained in terms of movement in space."

In fine, Materialism had its beginning with atomism, which held there is but one world-stuff matter—that is, atoms in motion. Notice, however, that these atoms are *in motion*—hence "nothing" as well as "something" must exist. If atoms are moving, matter could not be solid since they require room to move around in; hence these early Greeks utilized the concept of *space,* which they referred to as a void or as nothingness. In this way they provided all the intellectual tools necessary for the later construction of Mechanistic, Dialectical, and Modern Materialism; atoms (matter), motion (energy), and "the void" (space).

The materialistic foundation laid by the pre-Socratics was undermined by the Idealism of Plato, the supernaturalism of Christianity, and the (unfortunate!) loss of Democritus' writings.* Only an undercurrent of Materialism flowed through philosophy, in the thought of such as Francis Bacon (1561–1626) and Thomas Hobbes (1588–1697) until its revival in the eighteenth century and its flowering after Isaac Newton (1642–1727).

We are all well aware of the historical struggle between science and theology (e.g., Copernicus, Galileo, the heliocentric theory, and the Church), and even though Martin Luther was no staunch advocate of physical science, his Protestant Reformation helped open the door for the return of Materialism since physical science had not thrived well on a philosophic diet of Christian supernaturalism. But with the Reformation of the sixteenth century, the Renaissance of the seventeenth century, and the Enlightenment of the eighteenth century, Materialism flourished as never before.

Though the Mechanistic Materialism of the eighteenth and nineteenth centuries differed in many respects from that of the Greeks, it built on and refined the earlier principles of reductionism and atomism.

Although it was Plato who capitalized on the problem of appearance *vs.* reality, pre-Socratic Materialists were aware that the true nature of reality might not be as it appeared (i.e., physical in nature), and that their perception might be in error. Plato, as we have seen, did argue that perception is an unreliable guide to reality; he insisted that the world is not as it appears, and when reduced to its ultimate form, reality is ideal. But before that the Materialists had noted that there are many, many kinds of things in the world, and it did not seem reasonable to them that all of these could be equally real, all without some common denominator. In the search to reduce the many to a few, and the few to One—in the search for the common denominator of reality—they struck upon the principle of reductionism. This principle holds, simply, that complex things and events can be reduced to their constituent or elementary parts, that the whole is the sum of the parts, and that the complex whole is to be understood by reducing it to

* It is said that his works were as proliferate, literate, and entertaining as Plato's, and since much of Plato's work is an attempt to refute the empiricism, materialism, and relativism of such as Democritus and Protagoras, it is interesting to speculate about the course of philosophy —indeed, of Western civilization—had these works not perished and been available in their entirety for continuous examination.

the simple, to the elementary, to the basic. Mechanistic Materialism, no less than Greek Materialism, took as valid the principle of reduction.

The second principle inherited from these Greeks was that of atomism. We have seen how, on application of the principle of reductionism, the Greeks concluded that the building blocks of reality were atoms of matter; that is, these atoms were said to be hard particles, infinitesimally small, and different from each other in size, shape, weight, and speed. Later Materialists kept the atomic principle, although (thanks to the rise of science) they were considerably more sophisticated about the nature of atoms—for instance, the "ultimate unit" of matter was not seen to be an atom in the gross, but something even more basic such as a proton or neutron. (Modern Materialists still accept this principle, although they speak of such things as electrons and neutrinos as the basic units of matter.)

The Mechanistic Materialists added something to Greek Materialism: the principle of mechanism. It is true that the atomists spoke of determinism, and it is true that mechanism is a form of determinism (or alternately, that determinism is a function of mechanism), but the mechanism of the recent centuries is considerably different from the determinism of the early centuries. Mechanistic Materialism holds that events occur (i.e., matter moves in a certain way) due to some *antecedent* set of physical conditions; further, all events are "determined" in this sense where there is no determiner (God). They happen. But they don't just happen; they happen *because*—because they *had* to happen due to some combination of physical conditions. Chance, as a principle of science or philosophy, was ruled out; the universe was not open (i.e., not open to new, basic creation and not open to sheer chance) but closed, fixed, final. The world machine was complete, it was "wound-up" and all that remained was to watch it run on and on forever, hoping to catch a clue as to the perpetual motion of the mainspring.

Pedagogues usually draw on David Hume's metaphor of the pool table to explain the universe as seen by Mechanistic Materialists: Consider that the universe is a pool table (better yet, a billiard table since no pockets are required), consider that the billiard balls are atoms, and consider that the balls are always moving (recall the basic thesis of Materialism is matter in motion). Given those considerations, it follows that the balls in motion will hit each other, will recoil from the cushions, etc., but they will never come to rest. They might slow down, but they'll speed up again when another ball hits them. Now, if we only knew the position of each ball at a given moment, and if we knew how fast they move, then we could calculate the position of any ball at any time in the past, present, *or future*. That is, we could predict with 100 per cent certainty. (In a certain sense that is what astronomers do when they "turn back the sky," in celestial exhibitions, to the day when Christ was born, Caesar murdered, or when they move ahead to show the sky in the year 1984.)

In sum, mechanistic philosophers view reality as material, an all events, be they physical or psychical, are either forms or functions of matter in motion. In this sense metaphysics is reduced to physics, and physics becomes the method of discovering and understanding antecedent reality by means of uncovering the mechanical nature of the universe. For its emphasis on matter as real, it is Materialism; for its emphasis on the kind of movement, it is mechanistic—hence, for matter in motion we have the label Mechanistic Materialism.

Dialectical Materialism. In the formulation of his Absolute Idealism, Hegel introduced a new logic—the dialectic process—consisting of a thesis, antithesis, and synthesis. Out of any given situation (thesis) grows a contradictory situation (antithesis), and the resolution on the struggle between these opposites evolves into a new situation (synthesis) containing elements of its antecedents but yet is new and unique. This synthesis becomes the new thesis, and the dialectic process thus continues unabated.

In the formulation of Materialism, reality was reduced to particles with material qualities, and Mechanistic Materialism, under the stimulus of Newtonian physics, came to view the universe as a complicated machine which was operating in accord with some set of fixed, immutable, eternal physical laws.

Karl Marx (1818–1883) and Friedrich Engels (1820–1895), the cofounders of Dialectical Materialism, rejected both Idealism and Mechanism, but from the former they took the Dialectic and from the latter they took Materialism. If we could write philosophic equations, it might be said that Democritus divided by Hegel yields Marx (another such fanciful equation reports that Parmenides divided by Heraclitus yields Plato). In any case, as the saying goes, Marx stood Hegel's dialectic on its head (i.e., made matter rather than mind the subject matter of dialectic process) and emerged with one of the most well-known philosophies of recent times.

Marx criticized Hegelianism for its misinterpretation of the dialectic and Mechanistic Materialism for its static ontology. To elaborate on the latter point first, Marx saw that mechanism made allowance for change as alteration but not as innovation. This accounted for the slow change of evolution but not the abrupt change of revolution. Since he took constant innovation as one of the characteristics of reality, he had to separate Materialism from mechanism; he had to "open" the closed universe. Convinced that innovation was a "constant property" of reality, Marx undertook to explain its nature—for clearly no system emphasizing revolution could be said to be satisfactory if it did not incorporate within it a theory of innovation.

Accordingly, and now we come to the second point, Marx radically modified the Hegelian dialectic so as to become his theory of innovation. That is, it is matter that is changing or undergoing a dialectical and evolutionary development, not Mind. The divorce of the dialectic from Idealism and the separation of mechanism from Materialism gave Marx the means to marry the dialectic to matter, the issue of which is Dialectical Materialism.

There are three principles to the dialectic process as seen by Marx: the transformation of quantity into quality (and vice versa), the unity of opposites, and the negation of the negation. The first of these explains the emergence of new qualities or innovation through transformation; the second explains how actively opposite elements unite temporarily to promote change, to cause the transformation; and the third explains evolutionary development, or progress. Let us illustrate these separately.

First, the principle of quantitative transformation is based on the ontological assumption of Materialism: things exist, therefore they can be counted (i.e., matter is quantitative); qualities exist, too, but they are simply representative of quantitatively different arrangements of matter. Thus, at a certain crucial point in material quantification (Hegel calls it the *nodal line*), a thing becomes a different thing—it is *transformed* from this into that by reason of a quantitative change. Simply put, a change in quantity causes a change in quality. The most obvious example of this principle is illustrated by the three states of H_2O: liquid, solid, gas. Thus a qualitative change of state occurs when water becomes ice through freezing or vapor through boiling. Yet the change from water to ice, while evolutionary in the sense that it takes time, is revolutionary at the nodal point where water *becomes* ice. At this crucial point water ceases to exist and ice comes into existence, both at once, and thus the transformation is effected. The following conversation, taken from Jules Vern's *From the Earth to the Moon*, illustrates the principle of transformation:

"It is known now [said Barbicane] that heat is only a modification of motion. When water is warmed—that is to say, when heat is added to it—its particles are set in motion."

"Well," said Michel, "that is an ingenious theory!"

"And a true one, my worthy friend; for it explains every phenomenon of caloric. Heat is but the motion of atoms, a simple oscillation of the particles of a body. When they apply the brake to a train, the train comes to a stop; but what becomes of the motion which it previously possessed? It is transformed into heat, and the brake becomes hot. . . ."

Second, the principle of the unity of opposites is also based on an ontological assumption of Materialism: reality is essentially contradictory, but these "opposites in reality" are not irreconcilable. This principle is traceable to pre-Socratics, such as Heraclitus who maintained that reality is a process of becoming and, for this to be so, a thing must be the same as itself yet different from itself—that is, a changing thing is a unity of opposites.

(In passing, it is interesting to note that dialectical logic, like Heraclitian logic before it, was based on the assumption that the Aristotelian rule of logic called the Law of Identity is invalid. This rule holds that a thing cannot both be itself and something else—thus either A is A or it is not A, it cannot be both. Dialectical logic holds that A can indeed be A and non-A at the same time. It is even more interesting to note that in both instances the logical system is geared to the ontological system; but the question of which came first is a "chicken and egg" problem—although it is evident that man sees before he thinks, and thus his experience shapes his logic.)

By way of illustrating the identity of opposites, consider Marx's example of a debt: he says that debts and assets are not two different kinds of things, but essentially the same thing—for what is negative to the debtor is positive to the creditor. Thus, in his own words, "Positive and negative are supposed to express an absolute difference. The two however are at bottom the same; the name of either might be transformed to the other." As another example, consider the identity of opposites involved when Columbus sailed west to reach the East.

Third, the principle of the negation of the negation contains both a physical and a metaphysical basis. The physical basis is the scientific fact of evolution; the metaphysical basis is the belief in "built-in" progress—that evolution, while unending, nevertheless moves in a certain direction. Thus natural development is like a spiral, always moving upward toward higher levels and newer syntheses. The phrase "negation of the negation," of course, refers to the continually on-going dialectical process in which each developmental stage (the thesis) is the negation of a prior stage (the "old" synthesis), and in which each new stage always contains the seeds of its own destruction so that it too will eventually be negated. One meaning of this is that, if the series of quantitative-qualitative change is an infinite series, then nothing in the universe is fixed, final or immune to change.

To illustrate Dialectical Materialism at work, think (as Marx would have us do) in economic terms: take as the thesis the feudal manor as an economic system, and as the antithesis the rise of towns and cities. History records this struggle, the collapse of feudalism, and the emergence of capitalism as the synthesis. The new thesis, then, is capitalism; and out of this grows the antithesis of socialism—and, according to Marxists the coming synthesis is obvious to all who read the handwriting on the wall of history. The point of the illustration just made is of thought and reflection; it is a tool to be used. Where Mechanistic Materialism was passive toward the material universe, Marxian Materialism is active; it is concerned not with contemplation, but with action. The Marxist wants to change the world, and his philosophy (so he believes) tells him how to do so.

This underscores an important point: for each economic system or each method of production, there is an appropriate and corresponding social system, and a change in the former requires a change in society. What this boils down to, of course, is the Marxian dictum that in order to change society one must change the economic system, or, more specifically, if we want to change human nature we must first change the way people make a living. At this stage it takes no great logician—Aristotelian, dialectical, or otherwise—to see the role of class struggle in Dialectical Materialism. The opening words of the Communist Manifesto, after the Preface, call attention to this: "The history of all hitherto existing society is the history of class struggles. . . ."

In sum, Marx revised both Materialism and the dialectic to form the philosophy which asserts that matter is the basic reality, that matter evolved according to the dialectic, and that this is most obviously manifested in the economic determination of socio-political change. For reasons now obvious this form of monism is labeled Dialectical Materialism.

IDEALISTIC DUALISM: A NOTE

In the introductory paragraphs of this essay, under the topic of Formal Idealism, it was pointed out that Platonic thought had set the stage for monistic types of Idealism. Yet, at the same time, it would be equally defensible to speak of Plato as a dualist because he argued that the two ontological reals are form and matter.

On the basis of this argument he opposed the World of Ideas to the World of Sense, made the first prior and primary, but still joined these two worlds into the universe of reality. On that view Plato can be labeled a dualist. The essentials of Platonic metaphysics have been noted already, and a re-reading of that section bearing in mind the concept of dualism will indicate the legitimacy of labeling the form-matter dualism of Plato as an Idealistic Dualism.

REALISTIC DUALISM: OVERVIEW

Dualism obviously refers to "twoness"; by definition, any theory which reduces reality to two kinds is dualistic. In metaphysics, for instance, there is the Platonic dualism of form and matter, the Thomistic dualism of God and nature, or the Cartesian dualism of mind and matter. In most metaphysical dualisms the pairs are "opposites," and one member is said to be of more importance than the other—although both are equally real and irre-ducible—and is thus "first among equals."

It is much more difficult to define Realism—perhaps because those philosophers who call themselves Realists (e.g., Classical Realists, Neo-Realists, Critical Realists) do not agree upon a common set of principles; or perhaps it is because of the very way in which the word "real" is used. Yet, despite this catch-as-catch-can nomenclature, there are four meanings generally put to Realism:

1. Realism is the belief that matter (i.e., the physical world) is independent of cognition; consequently human experience and knowledge are of an independent, external world and this world is not in any way affected by our awareness of it.
2. Realism is the belief that the universe cannot be reduced to forms, ideas, or minds; consequently something (i.e., matter) would continue to exist even if all men, minds, ideas, or consciousness did not exist. On this view, the tides would rise and fall so long as the moon orbits, even if every single human was destroyed in an atomic war.
3. Realism is the belief that ideas (i.e., the Ideal world) are independent of material objects; consequently while experience may be with sensible ob-jects, knowledge is of the ideas giving form to these objects. On this view, circles and justice, triangles and beauty, would exist even if there were no mathematics, social organization, or art.
4. Realism is the belief that universals exist, and that they exist independently of the particulars which manifest the existence of these universals. On this view, "red" or "redness" has an existence separate and independent from red flags, red sweaters, red lipstick, red blood, etc., and thus if no particular with the property we call "red" existed, "redness" would nevertheless exist. (The theories contrary to this kind of Realism are called nominalism, where universals are said to be names, and conceptualism, where they are said to be ideas.)

Given these definitions of Realism the problems inherent in talking about it are obvious. For instance, definitions two and three are clearly contra-dictory, for two is Materialistic in nature while three is Idealistic; yet both are Realisms. Definition one is an epistemo-ontological relation of two, thus one and two taken together constitute what has been called Modern Real-ism. Definitions one and four, however, when taken jointly, can be said to constitute Classical Realism. What then of definition three, which is rejected by both Classical and Modern Realists? It is, as we have seen, a Platonic conception (although it is somewhat similar to definition four), and for that reason we have treated it above as an aspect of Idealistic dualism. The elimination of Platonic Realism leaves Classical and Modern Realism to be considered; yet, since this section deals with dualism, and since most (but not all) Modern Realists are pluralists, we will consider here only Aristotle and Thomas Aquinas.

Classical Realism: Aristotle. Plato's most famous student, Aristotle (384–322), did not agree with Platonic metaphysics, nor did he agree with Democritus and other atomists; consequently, in developing his own meta-physic he followed the rule of the golden mean by mediating the Material-ism of the pre-Socratics and the Idealism of the Socratics.

Beginning with the assertion that "first philosophy" (i.e., metaphysics) is the analysis of *being,* and aware that language and metaphysics are in-separable, Aristotle undertook to identify the ways in which the verb *to be* can be used; that is, he sought to identify the predicates appropriate to existence. He found ten of these, which he labeled "categories." The Aristotelian categories, and illustrations of each, are as follows:

1. *Substance:* "John is a *man.*"
2. *Quality:* "John is a *rational* man."
3. *Quantity:* "*All* men are mortal."
4. *Relation:* "Syracuse, N.Y., is (*east, west*) of Syracuse, Sicily."
5. *Place:* "Syracuse is *in* (New York, Sicily)."
6. *Time:* "It is *later* than you think."
7. *Condition:* "John is a *slave.*"
8. *State:* "John is *tired.*"
9. *Action:* "John is *walking.*"
10. *Passivity:* "John is *listening.*"

It should be noted that some of these categories are not clearly differentiated one from the other; even so, Aristotle maintained that these exhaust the possibilities of thought and action (i.e., everything can be classified under one of these). Thus when he reflected upon these ten predicates he con-cluded that they must be predicated of something—of some *thing*—so he concluded that the first of them, substance, is the prime category and there-fore the prime nature of reality. Without it—without *substance*—to possess quality or number, etc., all the other nine categories are disembodied. Only if the first exists can the others exist, for it is only in terms of substance that the others *are.* Here, then, is the basic building block in Aristotelian meta-physics: substance is the basic reality; reality is substantial.

This did not complete his analysis of *being,* for he had to consider form. He rejected the Platonic theory of form, and denied Plato's assertion that form has an independent existence or an existence separate from substance. He merged form and matter into a substantial union, for (he argued) matter never exists but that it has some kind of form, and every form that exists is the form attached to some object. If, therefore, both matter and form have existence, and if one never exists without the other, then it can only follow that substance (the ultimately real) is manifested through the combination of form and matter in particular objects.

(At this point it should be made clear that Aristotle by "matter" did not mean only the physical; he also meant the intellectual—ideas—for he believed that some matter is sensible [e.g., a tree] and some is intelligible [e.g., the idea of cause and effect]. *Being,* then, is the marriage of ideas as form and the physical as material into a substantial union.)

This leaves the problem of *becoming:* how does an object come to be? He identifies four causes, all of which combined explain *becoming:* the formal cause, the material cause, the efficient cause, and the final cause. Let us consider these, using art as an example.

The artist, before he begins to paint, has an idea of what he is about to create; this idea corresponds to what the finished picture will be like, it is the idea that guides the artist before and during his work. This represents the formal cause, since the form in the mind of the artist will cause the finished product. Still, an idea is not a painting. That is, he needs the materials of work and to some extent these materials influence the finished product (e.g., one cannot paint without colors or sculpt without marble, ice, wood, etc.); this represents the material cause. Too, he needs the implements of art: brushes, paint, canvases, and so on. Insofar as these tools of the trade affect (and effect) the final product, they are the efficient cause. Finally, there is the reason underlying the whole project, the purpose of the painting—and this is the final cause.

All of these causes taken together explain the creation of something, they explain *becoming.* Yet it is the fourth of these causes, the final cause or the purposive cause, that gives us the true clue to *becoming,* because matter does not seek any kind of form but a certain kind of form. The boy seeks to become a man, the acorn an oak; so we see clear evidence of purpose in all matter. The boy cannot truly become a woman, nor the acorn a birch; that is not their ultimate purpose. For Aristotle, then, the sum of all this added up to a purposive universe, devoid of sheer chance (but possessed of error and evil). It was for him a teleological universe, in which purpose dictated events.

In sum, Aristotle held that both ideas and matter had existence, that form and matter were inseparable and eternal. Thus, since both are real and neither is reducible to the other, we label Aristotle a dualist and a Realist.

Scholastic Realism: St. Thomas Aquinas. As shown in the preceding section, Aristotle was not "a member" of a philosophic school called Realism; if anything he provided the bricks and mortar with which the school could be built by later philosophers—and it was built, and his name was engraved on the founder's plate. Aristotle was a Realist in *attitude* more than anything else.

By the same token, St. Thomas Aquinas, who was greatly impressed with Aristotelian thought (he called Aristotle "The Philosopher," as if there were none other), was a Realist, if for no other reason than his belief in the existence of matter, in the reality of matter.

He also believed in the reality of God, and this conjoined with his belief in the reality of matter to form his dualism which was composed of the natural and supernatural. Nature and supernature, God and matter, both exist—although Aquinas believed God created matter out of a void, and therefore the supernatural is primary since it is prior to the natural. By Aquinas' definition, primary matter is being-in-potential, and concrete or "hard" matter comes into existence whenever God so wills it. Potential matter becomes real matter, then, in the supernatural creative act—and all that was thus caused to exist owes its existence to Him who exists without cause or is His own cause: God. Even so, God (supernature) and matter (nature) co-exist in an ontological reality; this is the essential point of Thomistic dualism.

In a certain sense, then, Thomistic dualism is a blend of early Greek Materialism and later Greek Idealism; it is a blend of the Idealistic Plato and the Realistic Aristotle, with the heavier dosage being Aristotelian; it is a blend of two monisms into a dualism, yet it is not the simple addition of the two, because Christianity had entered the philosophic scene.

Thomism, *qua* philosophy, cannot be well understood without Thomism *qua* theology; the variable of Christ and His Church was added to the ontological equation. Historically, Thomism grew out of Scholasticism (i.e., Aquinas emerged as the most influential of the Schoolmen), and often today the terms "Thomistic philosophy," "Scholastic philosophy," and "Catholic philosophy" are used interchangeably. The Scholastics were a group of middle-centuries Catholic philosophers who were interested in reconciling the philosophic beliefs of the ancient Greeks with the theological beliefs of the medieval Church. For many centuries such a reconciliation, accomplished by St. Augustine (354–430), was between Platonic Idealism and early Christianity. But with the passage of time changes occurred in Christianity both as practiced and intellectualized (i.e., in theology), and the Augustinian formulation came under attack from those who would divorce Church dogma from Platonic Idealism and remarry it to Aristotelian Realism. This was most notably accomplished by Aquinas, whose works were taken as orthodox after his canonization in 1323.

As a realist in the Aristotelian sense, Aquinas argued that universals were real and manifested their existence in particular objects; in this way he explained the relationship of similar things by attributing an essential nature to existential objects. For example, consider a tree: it does have leaves and limbs, height and weight, and shape or size, but these are not the properties which make a tree a tree. These are merely external manifestations—"accidents," he called them—of the tree. It is true that these accidents *differentiate* one kind of tree from another, but that which indicates the similarity of birch to maple to oak to redwood is the universal of "treeness," and this universal (i.e., the essence) exists in every single tree (i.e., a particular). But while each universal exists, and manifests its existence, in a correlative particular—so that treeness makes trees; doginess, dogs, etc.,— all universals exist in God. Thus it is God who made matter and gives it its form, for nature is the substantial union of universal and material so as to produce the furniture of the universe.

Being, therefore, is crucial to Aquinas' metaphysics, for things are real in the degree that they *are*. That is, *being* involves both being and becoming, actuality and potentiality. In this hierarchy God *is;* He is complete; He is the perfect being; hence He is the Ultimately Real. Below Him are those nearest to Him in being—the angels, the saints, humans, animals, and, at the bottom, inanimate matter.

In sum, Thomism represents the twin realities of God and nature, with the former transcending the latter; for this is labeled dualistic. And because it asserts the objective existence of matter, an existence not dependent on knowers or experiencers, it is labeled Realistic.

METAPHYSICAL PLURALISM

By way of review, we have seen that monism is a term used to describe an ontology that reduces the universe and everything in it to one kind of stuff, such as ideas in mind or matter in motion.

Dualism, on the other hand, reduces the universe to two kinds of stuff, such as mind and matter or God and nature.

Pluralism, however, represents the thesis that such monistic or dualistic reductions are in error because reality is composed of many (i.e., at least three and more like innumerable) kinds, none of which are reducible.

For purposes of this essay Idealism will be represented by Personalism, while Naturalism will be broken down into Modern Materialism, Neo- and Critical Realism, and Pragmatism.

Personalistic Idealism. When tracing their family tree Personalists are prone to go back as far as Heraclitus (*ca.* 562–470) or Anaxagoras (*ca.* 500–430), and trace it through to Rene Descartes (1596–1650) and Gottfried Liebniz (1646–1716), yet it is still fair to say this kind of Idealism is a rather modern development.

It is true that some Heraclitian fragments may support Personalistic Idealism, but other fragments equally well support Materialism. It is true that Anaxagoras affirmed that mind is the basis of existence, but this does not draw a clear line of demarcation between Personalism and other varieties of Idealism. It is true that Descartes, using the method of systematic doubt in order to find the indubitable, came up with the "personalistic" maxim *cogito ergo sum* ("I think, therefore I am"); yet Descartes is not generally considered to be a Personalist or even an Idealist. And, finally, it is true that Liebniz, in constructing his monadic world-view, might well be called the founder of modern Personalism (if a seventeenth-century philosopher can be said to be modern). Now, all this is true, and he who wants a full understanding of Personalism would do well to start with the pre-Socratics and work forward through the history of philosophy, paying especial attention to such as Liebniz.

Nevertheless, for those who want to get to the matter at hand (without, so to speak, going to the historical root of the matter), it is possible and justifiable to look upon Personalism as a rather modern variant of Idealism and turn to modern thinkers such as Edgar Brightman (1884–1953), Mary Calkins (1863–1930), and Ralph Flewelling (1871–1960) for an interpretation of Personalistic Idealism.

The *differentia* of Personalism, as contrasted with other Idealisms, is that the former is pluralistic while the latter (as noted earlier) are monistic. There are other differences, of course, some subtle and some gross, but the traditional Idealistic insistence on monism strikes the Personalist as a case of throwing out the baby with the bath. That is, Personalists feel that monistic Idealists, in building a block uinverse composed of mind, stratified into levels of reality, and culminating in One Mind, manage to lose personal identity in the process. Perhaps the forest is seen whole and steadily, but the individual trees are ignored—and, after all, were it not for the trees there'd be no forest.

With other Idealists, the Personalist agrees ultimate reality is Mind, but unlike them he does not believe it is One Mind. Rather, reality is mind in the plural—minds—and ultimate reality is not One Mind but many individual minds. Further, these minds are not unattached non-material entities which are part of, but randomly wandering in, the universe; they have a home, each has a home, in some individual, in some person. Mind is thus personal, since it cannot exist without individual persons. It is plural, not only because there are many persons, but because the separate and personal existence of each individual is a harsh fact of reality.

What of material objects in this Personalistic, pluralistic, Idealistic frame of reference? Because he *is* an Idealist he is going to reduce matter to mind, so that material objects are (ultimately seen to be) either ideas or minds. If they are minds, they enjoy a personal identity; if ideas they cannot be detached from mind, so they are ideas in mind, partaking of the individuality of a mind. Reality in this sense is seen to be a kind of Group mind or Group think—a community of minds, or persons with minds—which is in the last analysis mental in nature.

But, is that not to make a monistic argument? That is, when the Personalist insists ultimate reality is completely and only mental, is he not returning to the old familiar monism of traditional Idealism? The Personalist thinks not. He thinks not because he, unlike other Idealists, does not reduce and distill reality into One Mind, but into many minds. His pluralism is not a pluralism of kind (i.e., qualities of reality), for there is only one kind: mind. His is a pluralism of that one kind (i.e., quantity of reality) because there are many minds, not One Alone which is Absolute, Eternal, All-Embracing, and Final.

Personalism is pluralistic for these reasons and more. Brightman, for instance, does not agree with Hegel that experience is coterminous with that which persons experience, for if this were the case then persons would be absorbed into experience and would lose their individual reality. This he does not want to happen (an emotional argument), and this he does not see happen (an empirical argument). Thus, for the Personalist, experience is not reality; certainly not so in a cosmic or macrocosmic sense, only when it is personal—not when it is depersonalized and viewed as an abstraction independent of persons or individual minds. And that is irrefutable, Brightman and Calkins argue, because the only kind of experience we can talk about in any meaningful way is personal experience. Hence, there can be no impersonal, absolute reality since there is no impersonal, absolute experience.

Even further, the Personalist joins with other Idealists in admitting (even demanding) that the existence of mind is the necessary prerequisite of experience; and since this is so he wonders how some Idealists then conclude mind *is* experience or reality. He prefers to conclude that the only experience we ever have is personal and subjective, the only mind of which we are constantly aware is our own, so if we are to make any statements about reality in terms of mind and experience we must not only separate mind from experience but preface both of those terms with the word "personal," for all, ultimately, is personal. To do otherwise, he feels, is to build a logic which cannot help but depersonalize reality, destroy individualism, and force us to the weird and dangerous conclusion that ultimate reality resides in an Absolute Mind which is unexperiencable and unknowable—and therefore opens the gates of the city of philosophy to a supernatural mysticism which, in the name of reason, destroys reason; and, worse, rather than encourage the exercise and development of individual, personal minds, some Personalists believe Absolute Idealism demands conformity and unity to the One Absolute Mind—a consequence to be devoutly avoided for its social as well as philosophical implications.

In sum, Brightman, Calkins, Flewelling, et al., are generally agreed that reality consists of individual minds and the ideas which are products of this pluralism of minds. As one manifesto states, "The universe is completely mental in nature . . . [and] the total universe is a system of selves or persons. . . ." It is due to this emphasis on individuals and individuality, on persons and personalities, that we label this philosophy Personalistic Idealism.

Naturalistic Pluralism. Simply defined, naturalism takes nature as the ultimate ontological category. To go beyond this definition, however, is not so simple for it entails a definition of nature. Perhaps at this point it would be useful to go about defining "nature" backwards by indicating what naturalists do not mean by it.

First and obviously they do not divide it into the supernatural and the "merely" natural; thus transcendental notions do not transcend all of nature but, contrariwise, are within nature. Second, and equally obvious, they do not equal nature or reality with the mentalism of Idealism or the narrow atomism of Materialists; both mind and matter are within nature and thus natural. In fine, still going about it negatively, there is nothing that is not natural.

Positively, then, nature is all inclusive. It incorporates man and his experience, his works and his ideas, his knowledge and his values. Nature is coterminous with reality in its broadest sense; nature is all there is, and all there is is natural.

Modern Materialism. The ontological lines separating Modern Materialism from other pluralistic naturalisms are hard to draw; it is similar to, yet different from, Realism and Pragmatism. Because that is so perhaps the best way to illustrate it is to contrast it with the monistic materialisms, indicating how contemporary materialism has outgrown "push-pull, click-click" mechanism and the "hup, two, three; hup, two, three" of the Marxian dialectic.

These earlier materialisms, as was noted, benefited greatly from the scientific revolution starting with Francis Bacon's *Novum Organum* and propulsed by Isaac Newton's welding together of the previously unrelated fields of astronomy and mechanics into a mechanistic physics. These materialisms got their support from physical science and pledged their philosophic fealty to that same science, come what may. What came, of course, was the Einsteinian philosophico-scientific revolution; but by this time the philosophic categories of mechanism and the dialectic had hardened and these materialisms grew into a scientistic dogma by breaking the vow to experimental science. Thus, while claiming to be scientific and seeking to bask in the light of physics, they have not actually kept pace or faith with modern science.

Dialectical Materialism, as interpreted by Vladimir Lenin (1870–1924) and Josef Stalin (1879–1953), broke philosophic faith with Marx and Engels by dogmatizing their philosophy into an eternal verity—something undesired by Marx and Engels, since they believed Dialectical Materialism should and would change as physical science changed. In this sense, materialism based on Newtonian mechanics or Marxian dialectics is no longer entitled to be called scientific materialism, and that title has been assumed by the rightful heir: Modern Materialism.

As would be expected, Modern Materialism draws upon the formulation of ancestral materialisms when it repeats that inanimate matter is (was) prior to animate matter, and as a result of physio-biological evolution rational, purposeful organisms (that's us) developed. It adds to this classical formulation two new aspects: first, it is pluralistic; second, it introduces the concept of "integrative levels."

The atomistic monism of earlier days is discarded in favor of a pluralism of materials, where not atoms but electrons are basic; even more, these Modern Materialists may not even be materialists since they conceive energy, not hard matter to be the nature of reality (note, too, they do not speak of "ultimate" reality). They still cling to the principle of reductionism, however, as their reduction of matter to energy (e.g., $E = mc^2$, thermonuclear explosions) indicates. In short, the contemporary materialistic philosopher does not originate a description of matter; he asks the physical scientists, and their answer is his definition.

As for its concept of integrative levels, this is now fundamental to Modern Materialism. This concept emerged when the explanations of Mechanistic Materialism, based on strictly chemico-physical principles, and the explanations of Dialectical Materialism, based on those principles plus the dialectical metaphysic, proved inadequate to keep in step with recent scientific developments. This concept does not deny the heurism of physical or chemical explanation, but it also insists on biological and psychological explanations of reality. It thus introduces psycho-biological considerations which are supplementary to, and contemporary with, chemico-physical considerations. The "new" biology is based on a theory of levels; that is, animate and organic matter is organized differently on the different levels of material animation (see example below) and each level is integrated within itself, and within the next higher and next lower level.

For example, consider the case of John Jones, *homo sapien*. John is alive, hence he is organic (when, unfortunately, John dies he will become inorganic). John is a system in himself, that is, he is (so to speak) the sum of his respiratory system, digestive system, nervous system (including his brain), his skeletal system, etc. Each one of John's component systems is composed of sub-systems, and so on, until we get down to his cells or further (e.g., the work now being done on the DNA concept, etc.). With the exception of the first level, every other level contains all lower levels in it, and the "highest level" is, of course, John himself in all his human splendor.

Obviously this theory of integrative levels (and the theory applies to all kinds of organic matter, from an amoeba to the Pope) automatically rejects both the mechanism of some materialisms and the vitalism of all Idealisms. The rejection of mechanics as an explanation of material man is welcome, for who wants to be a mechanical man, merely working as an infinitesimal part of a huge cosmic machine? But the rejection of vitalism, of mind, *that* seems to be another matter (if you will excuse the pun)! Yet, Modern Materialism, along with its naturalistic cousins, Realism and Pragmatism, does just that: mind is *another level of matter* in the system of integrative levels. Put generally, mind is defined from a psycho-physical viewpoint; put specifically, mental behavior is a psycho-biological phenomenon; put clearly, no mental activity takes place except as a corresponding neuro-physiological activity takes place; and put bluntly, mind as such does not exist, since "mind" is a term used to describe the functioning of the brain. (Thus "mind" has no more mystery about it than "lightning," even though both phenomena may lack adequate explanation at this time.) That, of course, is taken by all naturalists, as putting the *coup de gras* to any philosophy which depends upon a non-material metaphysics (e.g., Idealism and Thomism).

In sum, contemporary materialism claims to be in harmony with, and dependent on, contemporary science and the scientific method. That affinity gives it the label Modern, and its basic theme gives it the label Materialism.

MODERN REALISM: OVERVIEW

The spirit of Realism can be traced, as shown above, to Aristotle, but the ontological manifestations of this spirit are not easily catalogued and labeled for the reason that the glue which binds Realists together is more epistemological than metaphysical.

Generally speaking, however, Realists agree that the physical universe exists, that it is an orderly universe, and that it can be known. Beyond this most general kind of agreement it is dangerous to speak of Realism without using a qualifying term such as "Aristotelian," "Thomistic," "Neo-" or "Critical." In this section on Modern Realism, Neo-Realism and Critical Realism will be considered.

As a background, it should be noted that these contemporary Realisms are not only reactions against Idealisms and narrow Materialisms but an attempt to move beyond the Representative Realism of John Locke which, as noted earlier, led to problems of skepticism if not solipsism. Locke's Realism was called representative because he believed that real objects or substances do have ontological existence and these real objects force or cause us to have ideas about them, so reality is represented by ideas it produces. For Locke, then, we do not know reality directly but only indirectly; what we know directly are our experiences or ideas which resemble the external reality and thus reality is represented in our minds by the ideas it somehow causes us to have.

This onto-epistemological account does not satisfy contemporary Realists, and the rejection of Representative Realism created a vacuum filled by the Modern Realists.

Neo-Realism. Historically speaking, some authorities have dated Neo-Realism from Alexius Meinong (1853–1920), Edmund Husserl (1859–1938), Alfred Whitehead (1861–1947), Bertrand Russell, and G. E. Moore (1873–1958), and while Realistic strains are found in all of these great figures we are arbitrarily going to date Neo-Realism as of 1910. The authority for this date is William P. Montague (1873–1953), who relates that a group of American philosophers joined together in that year to found what they called The New Realism.

Although these Neo-Realists were not harmonious in their metaphysical convictions (e.g., some were monists, some dualists, and some pluralists; some transcendental, some naturalists), they did share in common some epistemological beliefs which had certain ontological dimensions. These common commitments seemed to be as follows:

1. Knowledge of an object in no way influences the ontological status of that object; to say "it is known" does not modify the "it *is*." This can be labeled the ontological principle.
2. Particular objects of knowledge (e.g., a chair) do not depend on awareness or consciousness for their existence; if they are real they exist independently of subjective consciousness. This can be labeled the existential principle.
3. Universals (e.g., redness) of which we may be aware continue to subsist even when we are not consciously aware of them; thus universals such as numbers or colors subsist because our awareness of the existence of a particular number or color does not injure the independent subsistence of those universals. This can be labeled the subsistential principle.

4. Particulars and universals are directly known, and knowledge of these existents and subsistents is not dependent upon intermediate, Lockian mental images; thus objects of knowledge are presented, not represented, to us. This can be labeled the presentative principle.

In sum, as Montague notes, the intention of the Neo-Realists was to reconstitute Realism as a viable philosophy by adding the concept of abiding universals and subtracting from it the concept of epistemological dualism. While these were primarily epistemological considerations, they have clear ontological presuppositions, to wit: Ultimate reality consists of a world of being in which particulars exist, and a world of essences in which universals subsist.

Critical Realism. Critical Realism can be dated from 1920, in the same way Neo-Realism was, for in that year another group of Realists—disagreeing with the Neo-Realists—met to modernize Realistic philosophy.

As before, the Critical Realists represented no central agreements as to metaphysics since they were—like all modern philosophers—basically interested in epistemological questions. Consequently some of them were dualists, though most were pluralists; some were spiritualistic, though most were naturalistic; but all were Realists in some sense of the definitions earlier identified.

Critical Realism holds, with all other Realisms, that objects do have an existence independent of knowledge of them, and knowledge does not affect this existence. In this they agree with what we have labeled the Neo-Realists' ontological principle. But Critical Realists offer an amendment to that principle: an externally existing object is what it is only by virtue of its relationship with other objects. We might label this the principle of relativism.

The result of this ontological amendment does not injure the external or objective existence of objects, but it modifies their independence since it affirms that objects cannot be completely independent of other objects—all are part of what we might call an ontological environment or an objective network. On this view we cannot know any object in isolation but only and always in terms of its relations; e.g., iron is heavier than horsehair only in terms of some relational field and it is what it is only in terms of that field. If, for example, the "normal" field in which objective relationships lead us to conclude a bar of gold is heavier than an equal volume of steel is changed by an electro-magnet, then the objective relations—and therefore the objects themselves—are changed with regard to some "objective properties." Imagine that the bar of gold and this book are placed in a vacuum; in that environmental field both objects fall equally, and this change in the "normal" nature of the objects is due to a change in the "normal" nature of their relational field.

Now consider that people are objects as well as bars, books, and stars. Thus a human factor enters the onto-epistemological calculations of the Critical Realists, for people stand in (some kind of) relation to objects. Thus if an object is what it is in terms of its relationship to other objects, and if humans can be said to be objects, then what non-living objects are is in some way related to us as knowers. For instance, the redness of the pencil is not only dependent on the pencil, but also on the light that illuminates it—and perhaps even on the eye that sees it.

But this is going too far for the Critical Realists; as good Realists they are insistent on demanding that material objects are independent of cognition, and that cognition in no way alters their ontological status. Thus their relativity is restricted to objects alone, and humans are ruled out of that part of the ontological environment.

In sum, Critical Realism postulates that the universe is composed of two kinds of relational events; material things, in which objects are relational, and mental "things," or ideas, which are internally related among themselves and somehow externally related to the objective world. This is apparently a rejection of Neo-Realism's principles of presentation and subsistence. That is, it is an epistemological dualism even though it may be an ontological pluralism. It is a Realism for reasons abundantly clear, but because it rejects the simple, direct, "naive" epistemology of the Neo-Realists for a more complicated position it has been labeled Critical.

Realism: A Final Word. As indicated earlier, and as illustrated in the text, the ontology of Realists is a many-splendored thing. It is a metaphysical mosaic containing monism, dualism, and pluralism, things and ideas, naturalism and supernaturalism. Yet in this diversity there is unity, for Realism is Realism at least because it firmly and faithfully holds that there *is* a physical world existing independently of the men and minds that exist in it. That conviction is the *sine qua non* of all Realists, and the word "Realism" is most accurately used when it refers to just that metaphysical belief.

PRAGMATISM

Pragmatism is usually said to be America's unique contribution to philosophy, in spite of the fact that Kant coined the term (*pragmatisch*) and in spite of the fact that its roots can be traced back to such ancient Greeks as Anaximander (*ca.* 611–547) and Protagoras (*ca.* 481–411). Even though Pragmatism is not divorced from the mainstream of Western philosophy, it is peculiarly American; and its founders—Chauncey Wright (1830–1875),

Charles Peirce (1839–1914), William James (1842–1910), and John Dewey—have given its metaphysics a uniquely American twist.

Some philosophers (Pragmatists among them) claim Pragmatism lacks a metaphysic, that it is really little more than a theory of meaning grown into an epistemology, with a naturalistic ethic added for good measure (if you will again excuse the pun), and that it is not therefore a philosophy. The accuracy of this judgment hinges on one's definition of philosophy, of course, and while Pragmatists believe theirs is a complete philosophy they readily (and happily) admit it is not an all-inclusive philosophic system in the grand European tradition; indeed, they generally believe that such soup-to-nuts systems are intellectual relics of the horse and buggy days of philosophy. And, admitted or not, Pragmatism does have a metaphysic if we define that category as containing a description of the universe as a whole (no pun intended).

James indicated the heart of a Pragmatic theory of reality when he said that the word "universe" was a misnomer and suggested we speak of a "pluraverse." Pragmatists, then, are pluralists. Peirce gave another clue when he coined the word "tychism," by which he meant that absolute (i.e., sheer) chance exists and is evident in the nature of the pluraverse. Wright contributed to the naturalistic metaphysic of Pragmatism not only by denying that the universe is harmonious or intentional in itself, but by calling the physical order of nature mere "weather," doing and undoing without end. And Dewey, for his part, took these clues, added others, and solved the metaphysical problem for Pragmatism.

Reality is experience in the Pragmatic metaphysic; perhaps that should be spelled with a capital letter—Experience—in keeping with Idealism, Materialism, etc. To say experience is real—as almost any philosophy will admit—is not the same thing as saying experience is reality. And to say that reality is experience is not to deny reality (i.e., existence) to things or ideas, for Pragmatists are not subjectivists claiming objects reduce to ideas or experience, nor are they materialists claiming ideas reduce to matter; rather they claim that experience is primary and both subjects and objects emerge from and are known in experience. This conception of experience is strange to philosophers, and puzzling to students. It is drawn directly from Wright's assertion that natural events are in the way of being ontological weather; Dewey, seizing upon this, once said that since experience is the name given to natural affairs, he suggested we say "it experiences" in the same way we say "it snows" or "it rains." In a very certain sense, then, the root theme of Pragmatism—experience—is metaphysical.

We have noted that Pragmatists are pluralists, for nature is not merely material or physical, but includes all that exists; and further, as naturalists, all that exists is natural and experiential. Nor is nature predetermined, determined, or orderly in any final metaphysical sense. It is not predetermined because the only purposes in nature are human purposes; it is not deterministic because it is an open universe, a universe "with a hole in the top," a universe in which chance and change play important roles; it is not an orderly universe in and of itself but, by use of the scientific method, it can be ordered.

In sum, Pragmatism holds that reality includes everything—ideas and Idealists, matter and Materialists, values and fears—and that these cannot be reduced to monisms or dualisms. Further, it sees creation and the emergence of the novel as a constant process in an evolving pluraverse, and argues that all of these things take place in, or are a result of experience. For that reason Pragmatism is often labeled (as Dewey himself once suggested) Experimentalism.

LOGICAL EMPIRICISM

In the same way that Idealism has been characterized as "tender-minded" and Pragmatism "tough-minded," we might characterize Logical Empiricism (nee Logical Positivism) "hard-nosed." It is hard-nosed because its founders and followers wanted to build a no-nonsense-allowed kind of philosophy in which vagueness, mysticism, and downright follishness would not be tolerated. To rule out such philosophic evils and errors they built their philosophy on a rock of meaning: the verifiability criterion of meaning.

This rule is specifically designed to admit as meaningful only those assertions which are, or are capable of being, logically or empirically demonstrated to be true. In this "logically" refers only to analytic systems (e.g., mathematics) which are devoid of empirical content and are therefore true or false by rules of usage, a special kind of social convention; "empirically" refers to observable conditions in the experiencable world. There have been several attempts to formulate successfully such a criterion of meaning, and the spirit which Logical Empiricists hope to encapsulate in their rule runs something like this: a proposition is meaningful if and only if it is capable of being scientifically or empirically tested—at least in principle.

On this view, of course, most of what has historically passed as metaphysics is automatically ruled out of philosophy as meaningless—and this is precisely one of the ends in view of Logical Empiricists. Gone is the Platonic world of forms, the Berkeleyan all-seeing God—and, in fact, *all* Idealism. Gone too is much, but not all, of Materialism; most of Classical Realism, considerable areas of Modern Realism; and some of Pragmatism.

What is left? Certainly not metaphysics as conventionally known. That is,

Logical Empiricists talk about several kinds of metaphysics—inductive, deductive, intuitive, and transcendental—and all but the first are judged to be meaningless (albeit entertaining poetry). And the first, on inspection, turns out to be a metaphysics that is tautologically equivalent to the descriptions of reality supplied by science. Reality, then, is whatever scientific evidence shows it to be.

Logical Empiricists are really not interested in building a new kind of metaphysics, because they are simply not interested in building a philosophic system. Rather, they would prefer to alter radically philosophic methods—and the result of that would be a radical alteration in philosophy. They are methodists, interested in supplying philosophy with a new tool: linguistic analysis. While it is not our purpose here to expound on linguistics or logic, it should be said that on this view philosophy *qua* philosophy becomes the analysis of language.

Thus, when the language of traditional metaphysics is put under this logico-linguistic microscope and examined for content it is found to suffer from gluttony of words and malnutrition of meaning: deductive metaphysics is guilty of using fables to produce ontological facts, intuitive metaphysics inexcusably confuses beliefs with knowledge (and worse), and transcendental metaphysics is populated with all sorts of intellectual idiocies, beginning with its attempt to explain the unexperienced and unexperiencable through experience (e.g., using experience to deny the validity of experience).

In sum, this point of view denies the validity of traditional metaphysics. Its "metaphysic," the verifiability theory of meaning, is deliberately antimetaphysical. It is not, as Herbert Feigl reminds us, a metaphysic which describes reality as "nothing but" (i.e., monists and dualists) or as "something more" (i.e., pluralists), but goes about trying to discover "what is what," and what is scientifically meaningful. For these reasons we can label Logical Empiricism tough-minded and hard-nosed.

THE ESSAYS TO COME

The following two essays, by Curt J. Ducasse and Lawrence G. Thomas, build on the foregoing comments and complete the section on metaphysics.

Ducasse's essay has pedagogical value because it examines the question of metaphysical reality from several points of view, the better to help us understand what is involved when we "take a position" about reality. Thomas' essay, on the other hand, has pedagogical value because it is written from a metaphysical position that, for philosophical neophytes, is often very difficult to understand or appreciate.

Ducasse, then, stands outside and helps us look into metaphysical positions; Thomas stands inside and helps us look at one such position.

~

OVERVIEW

Perhaps the most persistent problem in philosophy deals with the nature of reality. Thales, an ancient Greek thinker, postulated that the world-stuff of reality was water, for which conclusion he has since earned the title "water metaphysician." Anaximander believed in an "Indefinite Something" from which opposites (hot and cold, right and wrong, up and down) come and to which they return. Ananimenes claimed air was the ultimately real; Xenophanes held out for earth; Pythagoras for numbers; Heraclitus for fire; Parmenides for the changeless; and Zeno for the changing.

In the attempt to solve this problem the question of quantity arose: Is reality one or many? Monistic? Dualistic? Pluralistic? Until recently monism received the vote of most philosophers, and the issue came to be whether ultimate reality is mental or material. For many years it was generally considered that either the Idealists or Materialists represented the only tenable alternative answers to the problem, or perhaps those who (like the Scholastics) took a dualistic position.

Idealism has generally held that mind (Mind, God, Spirit) existed before matter and brought matter into existence; mind and its products (ideas) are prior and therefore initially and ultimately real; the material is subsequent to, and dependent upon, mind and therefore less real.

Materialism, to the contrary, has generally held that matter existed before mind; that in the natural course of evolution matter became living and eventually, in the brains of certain animals, thinking.

In recent years philosophers, somewhat unhappy with the limited range of choice posed by the definition of the problem, and drawing upon newer developments in philosophy and science, began to reconsider the fundamental assumptions underlying the formulation of the problem of reality. Many of these philosophers, after such an examination, have held that the problem is actually a pseudo-problem; and, in consequence, recent philosophic work has tended to be more analytic.

This analytic movement has marked an important difference in the approach to the problem of reality. Traditionally the philosophic question has been "What is the ultimate nature of reality?" or "What is real?" The contemporary approach has been to ask, "How do we use the word 'real,' how can we use the concept 'real,' and what are the justifications for these usages?" This approach represents, in part, a shift in attitude toward the whole of philosophy and not toward the one problem of reality. The following essay is an excellent example of this shift in general philosophy and it doubly serves our present purposes since it also presents a critical scrutiny of established ontological problems.

Curt J. Ducasse uses his essay to identify five general ways in which the word "real," and its cognates "really" and "reality," can be used. These might be called professional, descriptive, existential, relevant, and ontological.

Professional usage is technical usage; that is, lawyers talk about *real* property, mathematicians talk about *real* numbers, and building contractors talk about *real* estate. In professional usage the word "real" has a given, accepted meaning; its meaning is legislated by members of the profession involved and is accepted by the practitioners of the profession as valid. It has meaning only within those confines, for, by way of example, no mathematician would maintain that there are unreal numbers as well as real numbers, nor would any lawyer talk about unreal property (although he might well talk about intangibles). These professional usages are not directly pertinent to the solution of the philosophic problem, yet they do indeed show one way in which the concept of "real" has meaning.

Descriptive usage is very common, in normal and philosophic discourse, for quite often the word "really" is used to differentiate between appearance and existence—between what seems to be the case and what actually is the case. For example, one might say of a dog that "Fido appears to be vicious but he really isn't"; or one might say of a stick placed in a water tumbler that "It appears to be bent but it really isn't"; or one might say of railroad tracks extending toward the horizon that "They appear to merge into a monorail but they really don't." Descriptive usages of this type are actually predictions, and therein lies the clue to their analysis.

To say that Fido is really ferocious is to say (if we take words seriously) that he views the postman as a food-substitute, that he has about as much use for children as he has for cats, that he clearly prefers the company of your mother-in-law to yours. Those (so we say) are the manifestations of *real* ferocity, and if Fido is ferocious then he must possess each and every one of those qualities that constitute the true signification of fierceness. If he lacks some or all he may still *appear* ferocious (let us imagine that Fido is an English bulldog) but he is not *really* so. It is true that every description contains the seeds of a prediction; thus to describe something as real is to make predictions about the behavior or qualities of that thing, and if these behaviors or qualities are not borne out in experience then the description is in error.

On analysis it is therefore seen that the statement "This is really a vicious dog" is merely to assert that the sentence "This is a vicious dog" is a true sentence; the word "really" qualifies the statement, not the dog. When the concept of reality is used in this way it is used only to emphasize something, to reassure someone that the sentence or assertion is indeed true despite apparent evidence to the contrary. It is, partially at least, an emotive usage designed to emphasize something (as when, for example, a young lady, kissed on the first date, exclaims "Really!" to emphasize something or other).

Existential usage of the concept of reality is exemplified by propositions such as "Unicorns don't *really* exist," or "Popeye isn't a *real* sailor," or " 'Mauritius' is a *real* nation." One meaning of this usage is the same as the truth-claim meaning of descriptive usage. To say that Unicorns don't really exist is the same as saying the assertion "Unicorns exist" is not a true assertion. But another meaning is different: to say that something is real is to say that something exists and, as Ducasse points out, this calls for an analysis of the infinitive "to exist."

Ducasse makes this analysis and concludes that if something exists it must exist somewhere and at sometime. That is, existence is dependent upon a spatio-temporal matrix; time and place are necessary predicates of reality, and if something is said to be real but cannot be located in time or place then the "reality" involved is, at best, non-cognitive. To say that "Lucifer's desk is real" is to say that "Lucifer's desk exists" (and, of course, it would be redundant to say "Lucifer's desk really exists"); but the truth or falsity of this existential assertion is ultimately dependent upon the specification of the spatio-temporal conditions of the desk's existence. Lacking these specifications the concept of reality involved is not cognitive and, therefore, no valid ontological statement is being put forth.

What has been identified as "relevant usage" of the concept of reality involves usages where the reality of something is dependent upon particular frames of reference. Put otherwise, the answer given to the question "What is real, or really so," depends upon a frame of reference which is relevant to the purposes and interests of the moment. It might be said, for example, with equal justification, that H_2O is really a liquid (or a gas, or a solid); the reality herein strictly depends upon the context at hand. It would be irrelevant to tell the iceman that he should not consider the weight of his load since ice is *really* a gas, and everyone knows gas is not heavy. In this type of relevant usage the opposite case (for instance, "H_2O is not really a gas") means only that H_2O may on occasion be liquid or gaseous. But for present purposes those possibilities are simply irrelevant, not of interest, or inappropriate to a specific frame of reference. Here, then, reality is dependent upon interest and purpose, and a claim that reality is independent of these is an irrelevant claim.

A final usage is ontological. Here the word "real" is used to describe a *Weltanschauung*—an over-all, synoptic frame of reference. The tests of truth and falsity, proof and disproof, probability and possibility, simply are not pertinent since the assertion of what is real is an assumption rather than a conclusion. To assume an ontological position, Ducasse asserts, means that one *has taken and is occupying some position* with respect to what one says or believes or assumes the characteristics of reality to be. It is to take a stand which might hold, for instance, that anything which is real must have the characteristics of C_1, C_2, C_3 . . . C_n—and without these characteristics that something is simply not real.

Here we have come full circle, for this is the usage intended by those who claim that ultimate reality has the characteristic of (water, air, fire, earth, number, mind, or material). That is, the Idealist insists that reality is mental and to be real is to be mental; the Materialists insist that reality is material and to be real is to be material . . . or that reality is dualistic, pluralistic, and so on.

It is important to note that these are positions, points of view, assumptions, or presuppositions; they are not statements of fact or hypotheses to be submitted to test since they are by their nature untestable. They serve to indicate a position taken from among all the positions that might have been taken; and he who takes one such position and claims this is the "true" position has deceived himself, for such positions are neither true nor false, but are simply "positions taken" and no more (that is, truth and falsity are not proper predicates of reality in this sense). To claim that reality is mental or material, air or fire, is not to solve an ontological problem or make a justifiable claim about reality; it is, in Ducasse's words, "either stating the ontological position (one) chooses to take, or else dealing with only a pseudo-problem. . . ."

The Method of Knowledge in Philosophy

C. J. Ducasse*

Even among philosophers, the part of philosophy called metaphysics enjoys today no great popularity, but rather is the subject of many strictures. Some of its critics allege that its prob-

* Reprinted by permission from *University of California Publications in Philosophy,* Vol. 16, No. 7 (1945). The Howison Lecture for 1944.

lems are too remote from those of plain men to have any practical importance. Hence they urge philosophers to forget them and to occupy themselves instead with the problems of social and political philosophy. Others claim that the age long failure of metaphysicians to settle their differences is enough to show that any answers proposed to the questions they discuss cannot represent knowledge, but only personal opinions or temperamental preferences. And others yet contend that the problems of metaphysicians are not genuine problems at all and hence cannot be solved, but that they can be eliminated by bringing to light the false assumptions on which they rest. . . .

I believe, then, that although some of the problems metaphysicians have discussed are indeed pseudo problems, and that some others, although genuine, do not belong to philosophy at all, nevertheless certain others of them are, or contain, genuine problems, which are philosophical and are perfectly capable of solution. . . .

I believe, thus, that metaphysics, or, more generally, theoretical inquiry in philosophy, can reach results having title to the name of knowledge. But I also believe that, for this, the modes of investigation used must be purged of the defects which have too often made philosophical inquiry heuristically barren and thus tended to bring it into disrepute. These defects have been such as looseness of inference, ambiguity of terms, confusion of issues, inadequate testing of hypotheses; and they seem to me traceable in the main to two sources.

One of these sources is the assumption, widespread even among philosophers, that in philosophy it is possible to reach knowledge through reasonings carried on in the vague terms of ordinary language without bothering to use a technical apparatus of thought. But the truth is that as soon as inquiry, whether in philosophy or elsewhere, comes to questions more difficult than those which everyday experience or casual reflection is able to answer, a technical terminology becomes a *sine qua non* of fruitful thinking. For a technical term is simply a term whose meaning is known exactly; and hence, not to bother to use technical terms is not to bother to think with precision. One can easily imagine how far chemistry or geometry, for instance, would have progressed if chemists had not bothered to use more exact conceptions of alcohol, of acid, or of ether; or mathematicians, of points, planes, or circles; than the vague conceptions those words stand for in ordinary language. The situation of philosophy is no different. Unpopular as a plea for technical language in philosophy is sure to be today, the fact must be faced that at the point where one ceases to be superficial, there, technical language, far from making for unintelligibility, is on the contrary the only means of being intelligible and of making dependable inferences. This is true in the sciences and equally so in philosophy.

Technical terms, however, must not be confused with jargon terms. A jargon term is not necessarily precise. It is merely one which is not understood by most persons because it designates things with which only a comparatively few persons occupy themselves. Thus, every trade, art, and craft, as well as every science, has its own jargon. But the jargon terms of the sciences—unlike most of those of the trades or the crafts—get defined exactly; and therefore, in addition to being esoteric like the latter, they become technical.

On the other hand, even terms in common use—such as alcohol, acid, and circle; or, in philosophy, property, truth, substance, proposition, and so on—become technical terms as soon as their meaning is stated exactly.

Philosophers, it is true, have sometimes defined their terms, and sometimes, although more rarely, defined them with some precision. This brings me to the second of the two sources of defective method in philosophy to which I alluded a moment ago. It is that to specify exactly the meaning of a term is not enough to insure that it will be an effective implement for the winning of knowledge. For this, what is needed besides is that its meaning shall not be assigned to it arbitrarily, but shall represent characters which there is reason to believe are possessed by the things the term is used to think about.

Unfortunately, the definitions offered by philosophers have often failed to satisfy this capital requirement, and have then represented mere speculations. Of course, speculation, which is but the making of hypotheses, is just as legitimate and indeed necessary in philosophy as in the natural sciences; but before any conclusions can be based on a speculation, adequate testing of it is as indispensable in philosophy as elsewhere.

Why then have philosophers so often failed to test adequately, or at all, the hypotheses that constituted the definitions they gave of their terms? The chief reason, I believe, has been that they have not realized clearly enough the nature of the facts by which these hypotheses could be tested empirically. Because of this, the testing has too much been limited to a checking of the mutual consistency of the various hypotheses entering into a system—the system as a whole, however, being then left more or less hanging in the air for lack of empirical verification of its hypotheses.

But every genuine problem has data; that is, facts not themselves questioned, about which the problem is and by reference to which any proposed solution of it can be empirically tested. And since in philosophy what these facts are is often not very obvious, one of the basic maxims of knowledge-yielding method in philosophy should be that, when a question is to be investigated, one should not only ask oneself just which facts it is about, but also state them explicitly. Actually, however, they are too often merely alluded to, as if oneself and everybody else already understood quite well what they are.

The procedure I suggest will not only make clear the way to test empirically any hypothesis made about those facts, but will also greatly facilitate compliance with a second, equally important methodological maxim. It is that one should again not be content merely to name or allude to the question which is to be answered about the facts one has listed, but that the question too should be stated as explicitly and unambiguously as possible. Observance of these two maxims will automatically lead one to distinguish, and to treat separately, each of the several questions one's initial vague statement of a problem may unawares have been propounding all at once. This will not only clear away such difficulties as confusions breed, but will also be of positive help in solving the questions one isolates, for a sharply formulated question is one of the most fertile sources of ideas.

These two maxims, however, are not so easy to comply with in philosophy that they need for this only to be accepted. The concrete nature of the method they define, as well as the power this method may possess to solve the problems to which it is applied, can be made fully clear only by an example. In the remainder of my remarks I shall therefore illustrate its use by applying it to the central and most ancient of the problems of metaphysics.

This problem is commonly referred to merely as that of the nature of reality, but it is sometimes formulated more explicitly. A. E. Taylor, for instance, describes metaphysics as "a systematic and impartial inquiry as to what we really mean by the familiar distinction between 'seems' and 'is,' that is to say, a scientific inquiry into the general characteristic by which reality or real being is distinguished from mere appearance, not in one special sphere of study, but universally."

But even this formulation fails to specify the data of the problem. Moreover, it tends to suggest that the data of the problem as to the nature of reality are of the same logical type as would be, for instance, those of a problem as to the nature of chalk, or of rubber; and therefore that to solve it we must compare concrete samples of real being with concrete samples of merely apparent or unreal being, and observe what characteristics differentiate the former from the latter. But that the problem is not of this logical type is perhaps sufficiently shown by the fact that since some philosophers are idealists, some materialists, and others adherents of still other doctrines, samples of real be-

ing could not be picked without begging in the very act what the contending philosophers would regard as the question at issue.

To avoid this, the data to which we look as starting point must be of quite a different kind. I submit that they can consist only of concrete examples of the manner or manners in which the word "real" or its cognates, "really" and "reality," are used predicatively. That is, our data will have to consist of statements such as that a certain substance, which seems to be paper, is really asbestos; or that mermaids do not really exist; or that trees far away appear blue but in reality are green; and so on. Such concrete instances of the predicative use of the word "real" or its cognates constitute the factual data which a hypothesis as to the meaning of those words must fit and by reference to which its tenability can be empirically tested; for the problem then is as to what those words mean as applied in the given examples.

Of course, I take it that what we are interested to analyze is examples which, like those given, illustrate commonly accepted usage; but it is worth noting that if examples of some freak usage of those same words were given instead, then, if it interested us to do so, we could analyze equally well the meaning those words had there. The essential point is that either no applications of those words are given us, and then we can make them mean anything we please; or else concrete examples of some applicative usage of them are furnished, and then we have data by which to test empirically the soundness of any proposed definition of what they mean in that particular sort of context. A definition of them so reached will be a so-called real or objective definition, as distinguished from an arbitrary, merely verbal definition.

Our second maxim of method, it will be recalled, enjoins us to state explicitly what we are seeking to discover about the data the first maxim requires us to list. In the present case, then, what we wish to discover is the meaning the word "real" or its cognates have in the sample statements we take as data. Any hypothesis as to this will therefore have the form of a definition of the word concerned; and since a definition is good if and only if it is exactly equivalent to the term defined, the test of the adequacy of any definition that occurs to us will consist in the possibility of replacing the term defined by the definition proposed, in any of the sample statements taken as data.

But what will be the test of that possibility itself? It will be, I submit, that this replacement shall not result in making false any of the statements that were true, nor in making true any that were false, nor in altering the truth or the falsity of any other statement implying or implied by the given ones. For this test will be met automatically if a definition expresses a genuine equivalence, and will not be met unless it does.

The nature of the method I propose having now been described in general, let us next apply it in particular to the problem of the nature of reality, and see what it will do for us.

As soon as, in compliance with it, we begin listing statements in which the word "real" or one of its cognates

is used predicatively, the suspicion forces itself upon us that the word may mean one thing in some of them, and something else in certain others. We are therefore led to divide our sample statements into several groups and to scrutinize each group separately.

The first may well consist of examples in which the adjective "real" is evidently used in some special, purely technical sense. In law, for instance, real property is contrasted with personal or portable property, and "real" therefore means nonpersonal or immovable. In mathematics, certain numbers are called real numbers and contrasted with imaginary numbers, although both kinds are real enough, in an ordinary sense of the term, to be accurately described and fruitfully employed by mathematicians. Again, in logic real definitions are contrasted with verbal or nominal definitions, although words are just as real, in an ordinary sense, as are things other than words. It is clear that no problem involving the distinction between reality and appearance arises in connection with these or possible other equally technical uses of the word "real." We may therefore dismiss them from consideration.

The group we come to next is much more significant. It consists of statements such as that a certain dog looks or seems or appears ferocious, but is not so really or in reality; or that a certain seemingly valid argument is really fallacious; or that the stone in a certain ring, although it appears to be glass, is a real diamond; or that a certain substance seems to be paper but is in reality asbestos; and so on. All these, let it be noted, are descriptive statements. That is, in each some entity, for example a substance, is given, and the hypothesis is offered that it is of a certain kind, for example, of the kind called paper. For the sake of generality, let us call E the entity given in any of them, and call K the kind to which it is claimed to belong; and let us note that, whatever the kind K may be, there is always some set of characters, a, b, c, d, such that, if and only if a given entity possesses all of them, it is of kind K. This simple analysis puts us in position to describe exactly the occasions which give rise to the question as to whether a given entity E really is, or only appears to be, of a kind K.

They are occasions on which only some of the characters of E are manifest to observation, and on which these manifest characters—which constitute the appearance of E at the time—happen to be the same characters as would be manifest in the existing circumstances if E should happen to be of kind K.

For example, under present circumstances, the color, shape, texture, and flexibility of the sheet I hold are manifest to observation; they are its present appearance; whereas the combustibility of it, if it be combustible, is not now manifest. But further, the color, flexibility, and other now manifest characters of the sheet, are the same characters as would be manifest under present circumstances if the sheet were of the kind called paper.

Now, if the things which in our past experience manifested this same color, flexibility, and so on, did later turn out in most cases to possess also combustibility and the remaining char-

acters of paper, then what we naturally say in the present case is that this sheet seems or appears to be paper; that is, its present appearance is the same as that of paper.

Furthermore, if, on applying the proper tests, we find that this sheet does have also those remaining characters of paper, then we express this by saying that it not only appears to be paper, but really is paper; whereas, if it turns out to lack some of them, what what we say is that, although it appears to be paper, it is not really so, or is not real paper.

Thus, in terms of an entity E, and of a set of characters a, b, c, d, all of which must be possessed by it if it is to be of kind K, but only some of which are at the time manifest in it, we have defined exactly the types of situations which govern the use of the notions of appearance and reality in cases where the nature of the thing a descriptive statement describes consists of a complex of characters. When on the contrary a single character is concerned, as when we say that the trees on a distant hillside appear blue but really are green, the analysis of "really" is very different. We shall consider it farther on at the appropriate place.

What now can we conclude is the qualification introduced by the words "real" or "really" in statements of the kind we have been examining? A moment's reflection makes evident that in our example what is qualified as "real" is not in fact the paper itself at all, for paper does not have two species—one called real paper and the other unreal or seeming paper. What is not really paper is not paper at all. Rather, what is qualified is the descriptive proposition,

"This is paper," and the effect of inserting the word "really" into it is simply to assert that that proposition is true: to say "This is really paper," is exactly the same as to say, "Truly, this is paper," or "That this is paper, is true."

Accordingly, the occasions on which we say "This is really paper," instead of simply "This is paper," are occasions on which we wish to assert that, notwithstanding some item of evidence to the contrary, it is true that this is paper. On the other hand, the occasions on which we say simply "This is paper," are those on which we are answering the question "What is this?" without anything having suggested that it is not paper.

These remarks complete the analysis of the notion of reality as it enters in statements of the type we have been examining. I turn now to examples of a different kind. They consist of existential assertions; that is, of assertions which, instead of answering as before the question "What is this?" answer the question "Are there any so and so's?"

Instances of existential assertions in which the notion of reality enters would be that, in reality, no mermaids exist; that the man called Hamlet by Shakespeare did not really exist; that Utopia is an imaginary country but that Spain is real; that there is really such a psychological state as hypnosis; or that black swans really exist but green swans do not.

In some of these statements, it looks as if "is real" means simply "exists," but in others the notion of reality clearly is additional to that of existence. The examples which are of the latter

sort may be dealt with first and briefly, since in them the import of the word "really" or of either of its cognates is essentially the same as in the descriptive statements we have considered. That is, in existential statements too, its import is to assert that the statement in which the word enters is true notwithstanding some doubt or item of evidence to the contrary.

For example, the sort of occasion on which one would naturally say "mermaids do not really exist," or "mermaids are not real," instead of simply "no mermaids exist," would be one on which, perhaps, a child had been reading a story about mermaids or had seen a moving picture representing some. For the simplest explanation of such a story or picture would naturally be that there are mermaids, and the story or picture therefore constitutes an item of circumstantial evidence that mermaids exist. The import of the statement that mermaids do not really exist would thus be that that evidence is misleading—that, in spite of it, the truth is that mermaids do not exist.

In such examples, realness is thus not a character differentiating one species of existence from another and inferior species called unreal or seeming existence; any more than, in our earlier example, realness differentiated one species of paper from an inferior one called seeming or unreal paper. In both groups of examples alike, what the word "really" or either of its cognates qualifies is the statement itself in which it occurs, and its force is the same as that of the adverbs "truly" or "certainly."

Let us now return to the sort of assertions in which "is real" is used simply as synonymous with "exist." Our task here is then to analyze the meaning of "to exist." This will not only make explicit the meaning of these assertions, but also clarify by contrast that of assertions—such as those just discussed and certain others yet to be considered—in which the notion of reality is added to that of existence.

The question as to what exactly it means, to say that something of a given kind K exists, is best approached by limiting attention at first to cases where what is in view is specifically physical existence, as distinguished from, for example, mathematical or psychological existence.

In all such cases, the assertion that there exists something of a kind K is, I submit, exactly synonymous with the assertion that something of that kind is somewhere; that is, occupies some place in space at some time. It is important to notice, however, that an assertion of existence may be more or less determinate.

For example, least determinately, one might assert that there are black swans, or, which is the same thing, that black swans exist; that is, are at some place, not specified.

But, somewhat more determinately, the assertion made might be instead that there are black swans somewhere within a specified region—for instance, in Australia.

Or thirdly and now quite determinately, the assertion made might be that there is a black swan here now; that is, at the specific place to which one is pointing at the time.

These examples make evident that, in the phrases "there is" or "there are," one is using the word "there" not in some idiomatic sense but literally, that is, as indicative of spatial location whether completely indeterminate or partially or wholly determinate. In these phrases, moreover, temporal location also is indicated, likewise more or less determinately, at least by the past, present, or future tense of the verb, and often through specification by date of some period or particular moment also.

Physical existence, thus, is essentially spatiotemporal ubiety; and that which has or lacks ubiety, that is, is or is not present at some place at some time, is always some what or kind—which may be a kind of substance, or of property, or of relation, or of activity, or of change, or of state, and so on.

When existence other than physical is in view—for instance, mathematical existence—the meaning of existence is closely analogous. The difference is only that the place concerned is a place in some order other than the space-time order.

Thus, for example, the assertion that a square root of 9 exists, but no square root of 3, means that the character "being square root of 9" characterizes a certain place in the order of the whole numbers, namely, the determinate place called 3; whereas the character "being square root of 3" characterizes none of the places in the series of whole numbers.

In any assertion of existence, thus, no matter whether it be more particularly one of physical existence, or of mathematical, or psychological, or mythological, or other existence, two components always are essentially involved, namely, a what and a where. And generically a where or place is the sort of thing specifiable in terms of ordinal relations; that is, of relations such as between, next to, beyond, among, outside of, and so on.

This analysis, it should be noted, incidentally results in making explicit also the meaning possessed by the word "reality" when it is used not as an abstract term synonymous with "realness," but as a concrete, denotative term; as, for example, in such statements as that reality is exclusively material, or exclusively mental, or of both these kinds, or of the nature of will, and so on. When the word "reality" is so used, it means "everything that exists." It is obvious that reality in this sense is not the opposite of appearance, but of non-existence, or nothing.

At this point, it may be remarked in passing that when the word "reality" is used thus denotatively, then that, if anything, which it denotes, is known to us, that is, known to us to exist, only if our existential judgments or other existential apprehensions are true. Hence, if their truth (or erroneousness) is to be something ascertainable at all, it cannot possibly be defined as correspondence (or noncorrespondence) to reality, that is to something known at all to exist only if those very apprehensions or judgments of existence happen to be true.

We shall now examine next a use of the word "really" or its cognates radically different from any we have so far considered. An example of it would be the statement that the wood of the table is really a cloud of minute particles at relatively vast distances from one another; and another example, that water is really a compound of oxygen and hydrogen.

When this is asserted about water, the word "really" cannot have the same meaning as when we say that the liquid in a given glass is really water. For the statement that water is really H_2O evidently does not mean that water only seems to be water but in truth is something else; nor does it mean that it only seems to have the familiar properties of liquidity, tastelessness, capacity to quench thirst and fire, and so on, but has instead of these the property of being analyzable into oxygen and hydrogen; nor does it mean simply that it is true that the composition of water is H_2O.

What it means, I submit, is that, for certain purposes, such as some of those of chemists, the property of being analyzable into and synthesizable out of hydrogen and oxygen is the important or relevant property; whereas for such purposes the other, more familiar properties of water are irrelevant.

In statements of this type, then, the definition of realness which, at the time they are made, tacitly governs the use in them of the word "really" is that to be real is to be relevant to the purposes or interests which rule at the time. In such cases, the opposite of "to be real" is thus not, as before, to be a deceptive appearance, nor to be nonexistent, but to be irrelevant, unimportant, insignificant, negligible, of no interest or value for the purposes ruling at the time.

Additional examples belonging to this group would be such statements as that the real way to talk to a mob is such and such; that you really must do this or that; that such and such a proposal is not realistic; that nothing is more real than an idea; that such and such a consideration is very real; and so on. The example mentioned earlier, in which we say that the trees on the distant hillside seem blue but really are green, analyzes in a manner slightly different from that in which we say that water is really H_2O; but in it, too, realness consists in relevance to interests or purposes postulated as for the time ruling. For, evidently, that the trees display the color blue when they are observed from far away is exactly as true as that they display the color green when they are observed from a distance of a few feet. The two properties are perfectly compatible; and the trees truly possess both. Which color we say the trees "really" have is therefore a matter only of whether only the near point of observation is relevant to the purposes which rule us at the time (as when they are the ordinary practical or scientific purposes), or of whether on the contrary any point of observation we have chosen is relevant to our then ruling purposes (as when we are landscape painters).

We have studied so far four main types of statements in which the word "really" or one of its cognates figure. The four types differed markedly in certain respects, but they were nevertheless alike in a respect to which attention must now be called, namely, all of them were statements of something or other that had the status of hypothesis. That is, what they formulated was in each case something that was either true or false, and was therefore susceptible of being more or less fully verified or confuted.

But now we must notice yet another group of statements in which the notion of reality enters, but which express not hypotheses at all, but something else altogether, to which the categories of truth, falsity, probability, confirmation, proof, or disproof do not apply at all. What they express I shall call ontological positions.

Just what an ontological position is, as distinguished from a hypothesis in which the notion of reality figures, will become clear if we return to the tacit major premise which, as we saw, was assumed by the assertion that water really is H_2O. That tacit premise, it will be recalled, was that to be real is to be relevant to certain of the purposes of chemists. Now, to adopt this or any similar major premise for one's activities through a given time is to take a position as to what, for the time, one will mean by "being real." And to be governed, even if unawares, by such a major premise at a given time is to be then occupying a position as to what it is to be real. That is, the statement of such a major premise is the statement of an ontological position. It is always of the form "to be real is to have such and such a character."

An ontological position, thus, is essentially of the nature of an exclusive or basic interest in the things which have a certain character; it is a rule one adopts as to what things one will regard as alone of interest, or will rank as basic or primary. For example, the ontological position that to be real is to have a certain character C would consist in interest exclusively or basically in things having this character; it would be the rule of admitting to consideration only the things having character C, or at least of positing them as fundamental and absolutely prior in interest or importance.

Now, an ontological position may be consciously embraced, or it may be occupied unawares. It may be occupied by many persons, or by few. It may be congenial to one person, and repugnant to another. It may be occupied at a certain moment, and relinquished the next in favor of a different one. But just because an ontological position is not a contention at all but essentially an interest at the time ruling, an ontological position cannot be true or be false; nor therefore can it be shown more or less probably true than another, or be refuted, or be proved. These possibilities exist only in the case of hypotheses.

The ontological position, for example, which natural scientists, while functioning as such, occupy, is that to be real is to be perceptually public or implicit in what is so. But it is evident that these words do not formulate a hypothesis as to properties empirically discoverable in some concretely given entity called reality; for no empirical facts one might adduce could prove or disprove what those words expressed, or render it probable, doubtful, or improbable. Plainly, they describe no hypothesis at all, but simply the criterion by which the things in which the natural sciences interest themselves are distinguished from the things these sciences ignore.

Truth, falsity, and probability are thus categories logically incongruous to ontological positions—as inapplicable to them as would be the predicates thirsty or bitter to logarithms or to algebraic equations. Ontological positions may only be occupied or not occupied, be embraced or abandoned. This analysis of their nature and logical status, I may say, seems to me in essential agreement with conclusions reached by Professor J. Loewenberg in a penetrating article entitled "The Question of Priority" which he published some years ago; and I therefore look to him hopefully for moral support in a conception of the nature of ontological positions which, I realize, is likely to shock many philosophers.

Additional instances of ontological positions that have been held or might be held would be that to be real is to be introspectively observable or implicit in what is so; that to be real is to be individual; that to be real is to be unique and changeless; that to be real is to be free from contradictions; that to be real is to be a coherent whole; and so on.

There is one ontological position, however, worth special mention here. It is the one occupied by any ontologist —and therefore by ourselves here now —at the time he is engaged in an inquiry as to the nature of reality. This position is that to be real is to be relevant to the problem of the nature of reality, appearance, and unreality. Evidently, it is a position different from the idealistic, or materialistic, or other conclusion as to the nature of reality, which an ontologist may believe his reflections on the subject eventually dictate.

But this very remark now leads us to ask whether our inventory of the variety of statements in which the notion of reality figures has been complete. Is there any problem as to the nature of reality which is a genuine, not a pseudo problem, but which we have not yet considered? It might be contended that such metaphysical doctrines as idealism, materialism, voluntarism, and so on, purport to be answers to a question about reality distinct from all those we have examined. An adequate scrutiny of this contention would require more time than I can now dispose of, but I can indicate briefly why I believe it to be mistaken.

The statement, for example, that reality is exclusively mental may be construed in either one of two ways. First, it may be taken as but another way of saying that to be real is to be either a mind or a mind's idea. If so, it is evidently the statement of what we have called an ontological position, not of a hypothesis; and, as pointed out, it is then not the sort of thing which either is true or is false. It only declares the primacy, for the idealist, of minds and their ideas, and his intent to construe everything in terms of them.

But the statement that reality is exclusively mental may be interpreted otherwise. In it, the word "reality" may be taken denotatively, that is, taken to mean "everything that exists." The statement that reality is mental then means that only minds and their ideas exist.

In ordinary usage, however, the words "mental things" denote only such things as feelings, thoughts, volitions, hopes, memory images, and so on, or the minds comprising them; whereas such things as the wood of the table, which, beyond question, also exists, are normally denoted by the words "material things." I submit, therefore, that the statement that reality is exclusively mental, as meaning that everything which exists is minds and ideas—or similarly, that reality is exclusively material—cannot possibly be true unless some meaning at variance

with the customary is forced, *ad hoc,* by means of the qualification "really," either on the verb "to exist," or else on the adjective "mental," or "material."

A materialist, for example, might say that what he contends is that nothing which is not material has real existence. But then this would be but saying that the realm of material existence is the only one he chooses to acknowledge—the only one of interest to him. Thus, because he would be restricting his assertion to a particular realm of existence, which he elects to rank as alone or supremely interesting to him, he would in fact again not be stating a hypothesis as to the nature of everything that exists, but again only declaring the ontological position he chooses to take.

But instead of using the word "really" to limit arbitrarily the scope of "to exist," one might use it instead to stretch, equally arbitrarily, the denotation of the terms "mental" or material."

An idealist, for example, might say that what he maintains is that everything which exists is really mental, that it really consists of minds and their ideas. But then, since, beyond question, the wood of this table can be sawed, scraped, sandpapered, soaked in oil, and so on, it would automatically follow that minds, or their ideas, can in some cases be sandpapered, soaked in oil, used as a table, and so on. But these are the very kinds of operations we mean when we speak of material operations.

I submit, therefore, that to assert that the wood on which such operations can be performed is mental would not be to reveal a hitherto unsuspected but verifiable property of the wood. It would only be to reveal that one has arbitrarily elected to employ the word "mental" to denote not only the things it is customarily used to denote, but also those customarily denoted by the word "material." To do this, however, would be exactly the same logically, and just as futile, as proposing to say henceforth that white men are really Negroes, or that Negroes are really white men. This would not be revealing any hitherto hidden fact as to the color of their skins, but only tampering wantonly with language.

But the idealist who asserts that reality is mental, or the materialist who asserts it to be material, usually believes himself to be revealing some generally unrecognized fact about such things as wood, or about such things as thoughts, and thus to be solving a genuine problem. Yet, as I have briefly tried to show, he is in truth doing no such thing, but either stating the ontological position he chooses to take, or else dealing with only a pseudo-problem, which evaporates when one distinguishes and analyzes as we have done the different meanings the word "reality" or its cognates have in the several sorts of contexts in which they function in the language.

There is, however, a genuine problem as to mind and matter. But it is not as to whether everything is mental or nothing material, or everything material and nothing mental. For there is no doubt at all that some existing things have and others do not have the properties, such as those I have mentioned, which we mean when we speak

of material properties; nor that some existing things have and others do not have the properties we mean to refer to when we speak of mental properties. The datum of the genuine problem as to mind and matter is that certain things, such as wood, in fact are called material and not mental, and others, such as thoughts, in fact are called mental and not material. And the problem itself is as to what exactly the words "material" and "mental" mean as so applied and so denied.

Then, when this has been discovered, the further problem arises as to what, in the light of the discovery, may be the relation between mind and matter. But the remarks which have preceded show that the relation cannot possibly be that of identity.

In concluding, let me say that the analyses I have offered of the several meanings of the word "reality" or its cognates may well have contained mistakes. But the method of inquiry we have used, which has required that the several kinds of contexts in which these words occur be not just alluded to but be unambiguously specified by concrete examples, has thereby furnished the very facts by reference to which the correctness of those analyses can be empirically tested, and the analyses rectified if need be.

I hope, however, that the results we have obtained by that method in our discussion of the ancient problem as to the nature of reality may be judged sufficiently sound and substantial to recommend the use of the same method in dealing with other philosophical problems.

OVERVIEW

As Ducasse has shown in the preceding essay, philosophers often use the concept of reality to identify an ontological position, a position which undergirds their epistemologies and axiologies. The taking of an ontological first principle gives meaning and coherence to an entire philosophic system; it is the ontological glue which binds all the pieces of a system together in harmony and unity, and often the extended and fully developed position cannot be understood unless this first ontological assumption is grasped.

Historically speaking, there were but two major variables in all ontological formulations: subject and object (mind and matter). Those in the Idealist tradition hold that subjects (cosmic mind, ideas, universal spirit, or God) are prior to objects (cosmic furniture such as stars, chairs, planets, animals, or trees), and ontological reality is therefore ultimately mental. Those in the materialist tradition hold the reverse and, in consequence, ontological chicken-and-egg arguments dot the pages of the history of philosophy.

Recently, with the development of Experimentalism,[1] a third force in the ontological war has emerged; a third force holding that *experience* is prior while both subjects and objects are secondary and derived phenomena. This position is so radically different from traditional philosophic formulations about reality that non-Experimentalists have had some trouble grasping its meaning and import. This is understandable since, so to speak, Experimentalists not only want to play in the ontological game but they want to change the rules of the game.

As is logical, philosophers holding to a more traditional ontology have attempted to understand Experimentalism within their traditional frame of reference. This attempt, sincere as it is, has been foredoomed to failure—one cannot truly comprehend Einstein from a Newtonian point of view, bull fighting from an S.P.C.A. point of view, or California weather from a Floridian point of view. To understand Experimentalism, Einstein, the *corrida,* and California weather, one must change his point of view—at least temporarily. It is tautological that there is no view without a point of view and, given different points of view, different views are had. It is just as obvious that long-held viewpoints are not easily or lightly surrendered, even momentarily for purposes that are temporary. Thus the ontology of Experimentalism has remained somewhat mysterious and difficult to comprehend for those bound by their own ontological perspectives.

---

[1] A term used, for present purposes, interchangeably with Pragmatism and Instrumentalism.

In an attempt to overcome these psychological as well as expository difficulties, Lawrence G. Thomas, in the following essay, undertakes to explain the ontology of Experimentalism from a non-Experimentalist point of view. This is a dangerous but challenging undertaking; dangerous because the chances of misunderstanding are multiplied by the mixing of radically different philosophic positions (can one obscurity be explained in terms of another?), and challenging because literary as well as philosophic skills must be fused to preserve meaning in such alien surroundings.

Thomas carries it off, however, thanks largely to the masterful "analogy of the ocean" in which he depicts individual subjects and objects as waves on the great ocean of experience—an ocean that is in continual movement, and from which waves emerge and take on individual identities and are differentiated as subjects and objects before they sink back into the restless, ever-creative ocean of experience.

The Ontology of Experimentalism

*Lawrence G. Thomas**

One of the major problems in achieving an understanding of philosophies different from one's own is the difficulty of shifting from one frame of reference to another. Hard as this is, it is a crucially needed skill in a democracy. In a country committed to a pluralism of religions, politics, and educational policies, an understanding of the opposition's viewpoint is essential to peaceable negotiation, compromise, and co-existence. On the one hand, there is a strategic advantage in understanding the views one is opposing as well as the view one is advocating. To misunderstand an opponent is one form of under-estimating him. It is more important to know his philosophy than to know his numbers. On the other hand, mutual understanding often allays fears, widens the area of acknowl-

edged common ground, and opens the road to cooperation. When the understanding is widespread, former enemies in the opposition are often transformed into needed critics and stimulating challengers. As much as I am committed to experimentalism as a philosophy of life, I would dread the day, were it likely to come, when no other philosophy was actively held.

Sometimes a person professes to seek understanding of an opposing philosophy by examining its logical structure from the premises of his own position, usually concluding, of course, that the opposing view is inconsistent and irrational. To look at a differing philosophy solely from the postulates and premises of one's own viewpoint is to invite a caricature of the other philosophy. Disciples of the other viewpoint are then likely to appear, at the best, dull-witted and, at the worst, viciously anti-intellectual.

* Reprinted by permission from *Educational Theory*, VI (July, 1956), 177–183.

A more scholarly and objective way to seek understanding is to examine the philosophy in terms of its own assumptions and presuppositions. This method, however, while providing knowledge of differences between philosophies, often leaves these differences incomparable and unnegotiable because there is no common frame of reference. The experimentalists, at this point, usually appeal to the consequences of these differences in educational policy and practice as the test of significance, while the classical philosophies usually appeal to the consistency and comprehensiveness with which each philosophy answers the speculative questions of men. These, obviously, are not common frames of reference.

This paper is an attempt to promote understanding between two opposing viewpoints through a third approach, so seldom tried that little information exists on its possible success. It consists of reversing the customary approach mentioned first above. Instead of inviting a disciple of a classical philosophy to examine the logic of experimentalism from his own premises, I propose to explain a basic aspect of experimentalism in terms of the kind of questions a classical bias would raise. This means raising questions about experimentalism which are really foreign to this philosophy, but these questions will be raised by me, a sympathetic disciple of experimentalism, in an effort to get wider understanding of this philosophy, instead of by an opponent who would have to resist constantly the temptation to caricature this philosophy. To become specific, this paper will discuss the implications of experimentalism for an ontology from the viewpoint of the kind of questions that various types of realists, including the scholastics, would be likely to raise.

THE NATURE OF EXPERIENCE IN EXPERIMENTALISM

A familiar as well as useful starting point is the nature of experience. The realist holds that experience is a secondary notion, that a subject and an object must exist in reality before an experience can take place between them. Experiencing, in the realist's view, is the process of bringing together these two independent, antecedent entities into a knowing relationship. From the viewpoint of the subject, experiencing is any conscious awareness. Experience, if it is accurate, discloses to the subject the objects which actually exist independently of his experience. The purpose of experiencing is to gain knowledge of what is.

In contrast, the experimentalist regards experience as much broader than conscious awareness. Upon inspection, it exhibits a cyclical character, usually expressed in the phrase "doing and undergoing." Conscious awareness is only one quality or aspect of experiencing. Unconscious doing and undergoing also takes place and is the source of many of our problems. Subconscious doing and undergoing is probably the source of our insights and hunches.

The phrase "doing and undergoing" direct attention to the subjective features of experience. It is the subject who is doing and undergoing. The objects in his experience are the products of his doing and undergoing. His experience does not discover or disclose objects antecedently given. Rather his experience *achieves* objects, by differentiation and abstraction, through the cycle of doing and undergoing. The quality of his perception, influenced as it is by his past experiences and his present purposes and values, makes an ineradicable contribution to the nature of the objects perceived. The meaning of objectivity thus shifts from a revelation of what is actually "out there" to agreement among various observers on the content of their shared experiences—i.e., objectivity means intersubjective corroboration.

While this description of experience indicates a great deal about the nature and status of external objects in experience, it does not tell us enough about the nature and status of the subject. It suggests that the subject may be a "given," the agent which *has* experiences, while the world of objects is constructed out of the subject's perceptions. The usual answer to this suggestion is to affirm that the subject, too, is modified and changed by what he undergoes in the interaction process. This answer, however, is seldom persuasive to realists. They also acknowledge that the subject is modified by his experiences but insist that there must be a subject given before there can be any modification of it. They feel justified, therefore, in accusing experimentalists of postulating a "given" subject who then constructs the character of the external world solely out of his perceptions. This interpretation places the experimentalist position perilously close to the solipsism of subjective idealism, a conclusion which realists frequently and happily draw, thinking they have experimentalism tagged for sure.

Although the conception of experience as doing and undergoing is an important aspect of the experimentalist position, it is obviously misleading if not analyzed further. The essence of the experimentalist view is that experience or experiencing is a basic, primary condition, logically prior to either objects or subjects. Experience, in Dewey's words, "recognizes in its primary integrity no division between act and material, subject and object, but contains them both in an unanalyzed totality." Instead of starting with a subject who *has* experiences, experimentalism starts with an experiencing process which can, upon analysis, be differentiated into subjects and objects. In a remarkably clear but seldom quoted passage, Dewey says (in *Experience and Nature*):

> In the first instance and intent, it is not exact nor relevant to say 'I experience' or 'I think.' 'It' experiences or is experienced, 'it' thinks or is thought, is a juster phrase. Experience, a serial course of affairs with their own characteristic properties and relationships, occurs, happens, and is what it is. Among and within these occurrences, not outside of them nor underlying them, are those events which are denominated selves.

Such a view of experience leads inevitably to relativity. The "given" is experience; the derived are the subjects and objects. Only experience is just what it is, the flowing totality of all events and reference points. The nature of subjects as well as of objects is relative, contextual, depending on the experiential situation. The relativity of objects to frames of reference has become popularized in the work of physical scientists—e.g., the position of stars, the relation of weight to rate of movement, the Doppler effect in hearing sound waves. The relativity of subjects or selves to situations is perhaps less widely acknowledged, although the recent rise of phenomenological psychology may popularize this idea too. Everyday experience, of course, provides many examples. Perhaps in most situations we identify our selves with the boundaries of our skin, but on occasion our selves become identified with our families, our home towns, our profession, our nation, and sometimes even humanity. In the other direction, our essential selves are occasionally much smaller than the limits of our bodies. Wartime experience showed that a soldier who regarded his gangrenous leg as not-self, as a threat to the continuing life of his "real" self, had much better prospects of recovery from an amputation than one who continued to regard his diseased leg as part of his essential self.

THE NATURE OF ONTOLOGY IN EXPERIMENTALISM

Having made the point that pragmatism takes the undifferentiated flow of experience as the starting point for philosophic thought, Dewey then gives all his attention to its functional significance when analyzed into familiar subjects and objects. The problem to be attacked by empirical method, he says, "is to note how and why the whole is distinguished into subject and object, nature and mental operations. Having done this, it is in a position to see *to what effect* the distinction is made; how the distinguished factors function in the further control and enrichment of the subject matters of crude but total experience." This endeavor, of course, is valuable, sound, and characteristically pragmatic.

But instead of going on into these practical tests of an adequate and significant analysis of experience, this is the point where I should like to turn attention in the other direction, toward ontological questions. Some of my experimentalist colleagues have expressed some doubt that an ontology can be reliably inferred from the experimentalist conception of experience, and considerable conviction that it would not be useful even if it were possible. I share their doubts about the possibility but not about the usefulness. The attempt will be worthwhile if it affords other philosophers, especially realists, a new insight into the logical structure of experimentalism and a further clarification of its differences from their views.

Something of the ultimate nature of subjects and objects has already been indicated. They are twin-born in the differentiating transactions of on-going experience. The nature of the subject at any given time is dependent on the objective circumstances, just as the nature of the object is dependent on the differentiating perceptions of the subject. Of course, the subject and object are not created *de novo* in each situation. There is continuity and endurance as well as novelty from situation to situation. But any inquiry into the nature of an object requires explicit reference to surrounding conditions, including the perceiving observer. The nature of the object consists of the relationships which both connect it to, and distinguish it from, the perceiving subject and other perceived objects in the environment. Similarly, any inquiry into the nature of the subject's self requires explicitly reference to surrounding conditions. His selfhood consists of relationships with environments of the past, present, and anticipated future. In short, when the ultimate nature of one's self and one's environment is sought, the experimentalist finds that they dissolve into relationships within the flow of experience.

This conclusion is not unique to experimentalism. Hegel held that objects, rather than existing in themselves and taking on relationships to other things, really existed *in* their relationships. The modern realist, James Feibleman, has said the same thing in these words:

In place of the old relations of a primary substance, we now have the substance itself consisting of primary relations. Or in other words, there is no longer any final substance as such: an object having incidental relations with other objects. The object itself consists in its relations with the rest of existence. This leads away from the notion of stubborn things having incidental use, to the notion of stubborn use constituting, incidentally, things.

The distinctive feature of the experimentalist conclusion is that the source or home of these relationships is experience. Reality is experience, and experience is reality; the two concepts are co-terminous. When Dewey uses the phrase "it experiences" to indicate what is logically prior to the expression "I experience," the "it" is an expletive, having the same meaning as it does in the phrase, "it is raining." By the phrase "it experiences," Dewey means simply that experiencing is going on, so far at this initial level without distinguishable subject or object. This is as far as I have found Dewey going into the realm of ontology.

THE ULTIMATE NATURE OF EXPERIENCE

But for those interested in a systematic ontology, the next question is what is the ultimate nature of this subject-less and object-less experience which is held to be synonymous with reality. This is the kind of problem which Dewey once recommended solving by turning one's back on it. It is not the kind of question that can be answered by the empirical method in philosophy. Empirical method can deal with perceived reality, for it consists of all the objects, connections, and generalizations which have some direct reference to empirical events from the viewpoint of some self. This, to the experimentalist, is the realm of truths and verifiable meanings. But speculations about the nature of a projected reality beyond empirically explorable events are only logical in their actual or human meaning. Hence, since they are only logically implied, they can be tested as consistent or inconsistent with certain axioms or postulates, but they cannot be asserted as either true or false empirically.

However, there is still another reason why this ontological question is considered unanswerable and even meaningless by most experimentalists. One can seek answers about the nature of something only when an observer in a frame of reference is specified. Therefore, how can one inquire into the nature of experience when it is initially assigned the status of an unanalyzed totality prior to the emergence of perceiving subjects and perceived objects? Even realists should be able to see the logical nature of this difficulty. If they do, they would be quite right in blaming the difficulty on the basic premises of the experimentalist's position.

Most realists avoid this difficulty by starting from different premises. They assume that reality is much wider than experience and that reality consists ultimately of essences or primary substances which secondarily take on relations with each other. Experience is then only one kind of relationship which brings a subject-essence into contact with an object-essence. Experience performs no creative function in evolving subjects and objects, as it does for the experimentalist, but merely performs the function of disclosing the characteristics of the objective world through the senses. Experience is important, but the human mind is not limited to this access to the objective world. Reason can and should transcend this kind of experience. The job for reason is to occupy the role of the cosmic observer in seeking the ultimate nature of reality. If reason, starting from sense experience but unconfined by it, can assume the role of the cosmic observer, a systematic description of the ultimate nature of reality then becomes logically possible.

This contrast of basic premises may help realists to see the logic of the experimentalist position. It may also help them to see why the experimentalist is logically cut off from any cogent means of answering questions about the ultimate nature of experience when it is conceived initially in its primary integrity, undivided into subjects and objects. Without a subject occupying a specified viewpoint, the experimentalist cannot legitimately attempt the task of converting the events and affairs of experience into cognitive objects for communication to others. This comes about because the experimentalist postulates the continuum of experience as logically prior to self-conscious subjects and objects of knowledge. Most realists, on the other hand, postulate the existence of subjects and objects as logically prior to experience. Usually these subjects and objects are conceived to exist as essences, taking on relations with each other as they become known in the ordinary world of experience.

How does one make a choice between these two starting points? Both are conceivable. Either one can underpin philosophical systems which are internally consistent. Philosophers in the classical tradition sometimes make their choice on the grounds that one choice is more plausible than the other, that one choice is congenial to reason while the other is repugnant to reason. But such grounds amount to a confession of a personal or temperamental bias. There is good evidence for believing that, after a period of conditioning and adjustment, most persons would find that the opposing starting point had acquired an acceptable "feel." For instance, we initially feel that the sun rises in the east and sets in the west, but we easily and readily assert that the sun really remains comparatively fixed while the earth revolves.

I'm still having trouble getting the "feel" of the Einstein conception of space as boundless, limited, and curved, but I no longer consider it repugnant to reason. Experimentalists recommend that the choice between the two starting points be decided on the basis of their respective logical consequences in the economical interpretation and effective guidance of ordinary human experience. This, too, is an expression of bias, even though it is one I happen to like. In short, temperament is likely to have more influence than philosophic analysis in determining one's choice of starting points. Recognition of this probability could do much to promote mutual respect and cooperative endeavors among professional philosophers.

THE VIEWPOINT OF AN "INDEPENDENT COSMIC OBSERVER"

As evidence of my confidence and faith in this point, I should like to propose that we deliberately violate frames of reference for a moment and look at the experimentalist's picture of experience from the viewpoint of a cosmic observer. This cosmic observer, let us imagine, is apart from the engulfing sweep of experience as conceived by the experimentalist. His capacity to observe is not evolved out of the continum of experience nor bound by it. He is an independent entity, equipped solely with passive, camera-lens senses to observe things as they really are. In effect, this cosmic observer is having a realist-type experience of the experimentalist conception of experience. If you can go along with this generous spirit of make-believe, how would the experimentalist view of reality appear to him?

The closest physical analogy I can imagine is a great ocean of experience in continual movement. Individual subjects and objects emerge as waves, follow a course for awhile, and eventually sink back into the sea, but there are always more waves, going on forever. If our cosmic observer wonders how he distinguishes the waves from the ocean, he will probably decide it is a matter of degree. When the crests are high enough and the troughs deep enough, waves are clearly distinguishable. It is easier to distinguish waves from each other (i.e., objects from each other) than it is to distinguish waves from the sea (i.e., objects from experience). In fact, our cosmic observer cannot be quite sure that he is really observing the sea. All he really sees is waves and the differences (troughs) between them, but the whole thing needs some sort of integrating setting, which can be called the sea. The sea of experience is sensed intuitively rather than directly observed.

If he were to concentrate on individual waves (objects) in this ocean, he would see each wave developing a unique character as it interacted with its immediate environment. In the course of each wave, he would see novelty yet similarity, change yet continuity. As each wave moves forward, it varies in shape and is constituted of different molecules of water at any given time, and yet there is enough continuity to preserve its identity in the eyes of the cosmic observer. The place and power and effect of a wave at any given moment gives it an undeniable individual reality, and yet, if he watches long enough, he notes that each wave is ultimately insubstantial, dissolving back into the ocean of experience. Ultimately, he concludes, there is only the ebb and flow of relationships in experience, in spite of the immediate appearance of individual objects as waves. This conclusion means that reality consists ultimately, not of terms or essences as self-contained existents, but of relationships or processes, which constitute and exhaust the meanings of things or essences. Hence, in answer to the ontological question raised by the realists, experiencing in its most primitive form is a restless, differentiating continuum of relationships, quite similar to Northrup's conception of ultimate reality as an undifferentiated but differentiatable aesthetic continuum.

This excursion into the imaginary world of a passive, contemplative cosmic observer may have value for both the realists and the experimentalists. If it has provided answers to questions which realists believe should be raised about any philosophical system and which they believe the experimentalists fail to answer, it may give them the

"feel" of the experimentalist position. And if it has also shown why experimentalists cannot logically undertake this kind of analysis of their postulate regarding the primary character of experience, except in a spirit of make-believe, it may give the realists increased understanding of the experimentalist position. For the experimentalists, this excursion into an imaginary perspective on their basic postulate may be of value in two respects. First, although it has no veridical meaning for their position, it may afford them some aesthetic enjoyment in a realm of speculative thought toward which they have traditionally been merely hostile and contemptuous. Second, it may give them, in turn, greater insight into the bias of the realist position so that their subsequent relations with realists need not be devoted exclusively to polemics and proselytizing. In short, both groups may profit as much from seeking to understand each other as from seeking to understand the truth, even as a relative truth. And they could make no greater contribution to the survival of a democratic culture of plural perspectives.

〜

The Category of Epistemology

A theory of knowledge is an explanation of what is to be meant by "knowledge" and "truth"; out of this emerges another evidence of the inseparability of philosophy and language, for a theory of knowledge is based upon a linguistic analysis of the verb *to know*.

The functions to be served by a theory of knowledge are multiple, but most importantly it should explain how we move from appearance to reality; it should explain the relation between mental content and the object of knowledge. An adequate theory of knowledge should provide answers to such questions as these:

1. What are the conditions, both necessary and sufficient, of knowledge?
2. What is the external nature of the object before the mind when we internally cognize it?
3. How can we be justified in asserting the existence of a material object?
4. What are the relations between premises and conclusions that permit us to assert the truth of the latter?
5. What does it mean to make a universal statement, and under what conditions are we justified in asserting such generalizations?
6. What kind of mental activities are involved in the knowing process, especially with regard to perception and reason?

From this analysis it can be seen that there are three aspects to the problem of knowledge: the ontological, the psychological, and the logical. The ontological aspect suggests the question, *"What* do we know?"; thus it deals with the metaphysical status of objects of knowledge, and a satisfactory answer to this question requires a theory of reality. The psychological aspect suggests the question, *"How* do we know?"; thus it deals with the human processes (perception, reason) of coming to know, and a satisfactory answer to this question requires theories of perception and mind. The logical aspect combines questions about the *what* and *how* of knowing because it deals with propositions about the process and product of knowledge; that is, what is claimed to be known can only be expressed in a proposition, so the object of knowledge is a partial function of the language which expresses the knowledge claim. Likewise, the proposition which expresses a knowledge claim is a partial function both of the object of knowledge and the method of knowing. Thus a satisfactory answer to this aspect requires a theory of meaning.

When writing his story the good epistemologist, like the good journalist, will answer the questions Who?, What?, When?, Where?, Why?, and How? *Who* knows or can know? *What* is known or can be known? *When* does knowledge occur and *how long* does it last? *Where* is knowledge, or the world-stuff that gives rise to knowledge? *Why* do we know, or want to know? *How* do we know, and how can we be certain of our knowledge? A set of answers to these questions would constitute a fairly complete philosophy, not merely epistemology, because adequate answers require certain metaphysical and ethical considerations as well.

THREE EPISTEMOLOGICAL CATEGORIES

All of these questions presuppose a first question: Is knowledge possible; can we know? Historically speaking there have been three answers to this question: "Yes," "No," and "Yes, but." Let the labels *dogmatist, skeptic,* and *fallibilist* identify these three answers. The dogmatist believes that in order to have knowledge we must first have some self-evident propositions which are certain (i.e., not open to any doubt) and which have not been deduced from any other propositions. Further, the dogmatist asserts that we do have such propositions, and therefore he says, "Yes, we can and do know— certainly." The skeptic agrees with the dogmatist that in order to know anything we must first have some certain and uninferred propositions, but he denies that any exist; we do not have them, he says, and we cannot ever have them. Therefore he concludes, "No, we cannot know." The fallibilist, however, does not agree that we must have a set of certain and uninferred propositions if we are to know. With the dogmatist he agrees that certain (i.e., absolute) knowledge is dependent upon self-evident truths, but with the skeptic he denies that such truths or propositions exist—hence he denies the possibility of absolute knowledge. But he does not deny the possibility of knowledge, so his answer is, "Yes, but . . ." The "but" means that he believes we can have knowledge, but it will never be 100 per cent certain; consequently, all the knowledge we can ever have will be probable, dependent, contingent, and relative.

In fine, the dogmatist thinks it is a waste of time to talk about whether or not knowledge is possible because he believes it is a fact that we do have certain, self-evident, synthetic *a priori* truths. The skeptic agrees that an epistemological dialogue is somewhat fruitless, because he is convinced that, since there are no self-evident propositions to start with, every single proposition must rest on another by inference, and so on into an infinite regression; thus he believes that, since there is no proper foundation for epistemology, any house of intellect must be built of cards. The fallibilist agrees with the skeptic that there is no perfect foundation on which to build knowledge, so he suggests that instead of trying to build it on the base of certain and uninferred propositions we must build it on something else that is certain: immediate experience. Thus, to the major question in epistemology—"Are there any judgments which require no prior judgment?"—three answers are offered. "Yes," says the dogmatist, "self-evident truths." "No," says the skeptic, "there are none." Says the fallibilist, "Yes, there is something that is certain and infallible—but it is immediate experience, not propositions or truths."

Clearly the major differences here are between the dogmatist and the fallibilist; that is, they are at least willing to argue about the *what* and *how* of knowledge—the skeptic simply sits and laughs at what he believes to be a *pons asinorum* in epistemology. We will want to explore these two positions, but first let us put the skeptic out of his misery so the discussion can go on without any loose ends. The skeptic is very simply extinguished: when he is asked "Can we have any knowledge at all?" his answer is "No!" But on analysis, we see that by saying "No" he is saying "Yes," and thus defeating his whole position. That is, if we do not and cannot know, then it is impossible to know that we cannot know. Thus the skeptic who denies the possibility of knowledge cannot—by the terms of his own premise— make such an assertion. This dismissal of skepticism is no mere sophistry, for if one is absolutely to deny the possibility of knowledge he must admit that he knows something; to wit: he *knows* that there is no possibility of knowledge. And this, as we have seen, is logically untenable. Consequently it must be concluded that some kind of knowledge is possible. We are left, then, with the dogmatist and the fallibilist; with they who claim knowledge is absolute and certain, and assert we have such; and with they who claim the only knowledge we have or can have is relative and probable. The first, since they base their theory of knowledge on reason, can be labeled *rationalists;* the second, since theirs is based on experience, can be labeled *empiricists;* and the history of philosophy is marked by epistemological battles between rationalism and empiricism.

Bearing in mind the pedagogical objective of developing the theses of rationalism and empiricism, but being aware of the limitation of space, the objective can perhaps best be achieved by a brief review and analysis of one of the Platonic dialogues, *Theaetetus.* The instructional value in this approach is that the *Theaetetus,* being the first critical attempt to solve the problem of knowledge, established the theme of the epistemological debate that has gone on for more than two thousand years. Further, it is a direct confrontation of rationalism with empiricism (although Plato naturally loads the dice in favor of the former), and thus is an ideal springboard for pedagogical purposes.

RATIONALISM VS. EMPIRICISM

The *Theaetetus* represents the first step in the development of a Platonic (Idealist) theory of knowledge, but an appreciation of this is dependent upon an awareness of his objectives in writing the *Theaetetus*. Plato was vitally interested in the promotion of the good life; that is, he wanted to discover if virtue could be taught, for if it could be then education would become the means to the end of the good life. In an earlier dialogue, *Protagorus,* Plato equated virtue with knowledge and concluded that the knowledgeable man would be a good man and, conversely, that the good man is a knowledgeable man; thus, for Plato, morality rests on true knowledge of the good—not on mere opinion or social consensus of the good. The key to understanding Platonic Idealism is to remember that epistemology and ethics are joined in an inseparable union.

Equally important to remember is the fact that Plato was concerned to justify his other-worldly metaphysic—that ontological realm of ideas which he believed was Reality. To do this he had an epistemological task; he had to demonstrate that empiricism implied a skepticism. That is, he had to prove that empiricism implied the impossibility of having any knowledge at all. If he could do this, if he could destroy the empiricist thesis that experience yields knowledge, then he could reassert the obvious fact that we *do* have knowledge and conclude that whatever knowledge we have could not possibly be a result of experience. Consequently, if that be true, and if we do know, then there must be another source of knowledge that is not empirical. And indeed there is, Plato finds (but not in the *Theaetetus*) that other source is reason.

The *Theaetetus* thus poses the question, Does knowledge depend on experience?, and answers it in the negative. In arriving at this answer Plato attempts to wound fatally empiricism through the Socratic technique of concept examination. Nominally, the dialogue subjects the empiricism of Heraclitus ("all is flux and change") and Protagorus ("man is the measure of all things") to a rational examination which is designed to demonstrate their impossibility.

Briefly put, the Protagorean thesis is that man is the measure of all things—knowledge and good—and that man is an inconsistent measure, therefore nothing is certain and absolute. Thus all is changing, with the exception of the Law of Change (although the rate and direction of change changes), so knowledge, which depends upon human experience, is relative rather than absolute. Plato violently objects to this empiricism, and attempts to refute it by adopting an argument of this sort: if what appears to us is true, and if our knowledge is dependent upon our senses, then truth is relative upon our senses; yet, on this view, it follows that there is no way by which mistaken opinion (i.e., false claims to knowledge) can be shown to be erroneous.

The dialogue opens with Socrates asking Theaetetus, What is knowledge? Theaetetus, who represents a form of naive empiricism, scratches his head and responds that knowledge is perception; or, tautologically, perception is knowledge. Given this answer, Socrates indicates that on this view knowledge is impossible because if we accept experience or perception as valid then no established and repeatable body of knowledge could exist. That is, Socrates notes that the Protagorean doctrine of "everything changes," if taken literally, refutes the possibility of evidence being repeatable. To hold to that theme would be self-defeating since it would preclude common, sharable knowledge. Further, Socrates makes a pragmatic argument: nobody acts on the basis of constant change, nobody acts as if there is no common pool of knowledge; and, even more, people do not depend only upon their perceptions and experiences, they also rely on experts—hence we implicitly and pragmatically assume that knowledge is not strictly dependent upon individual perception or experience.

In fine, Plato makes the following criticisms of Theaetetus' theory of knowledge and perception: if man and nature constantly change, then the object of knowledge and the means of knowing (perception) must change —thus we could never have the same perception twice, so it would be impossible to repeat evidence, and consequently it would be impossible to have reliable knowledge.

Plato is willing to accept Theaetetus' theory of perception as central to the empiricist thesis because he believes it demonstrably precludes experience as a source of knowledge. Yet, as we have seen, we do have knowledge, so there must be another source of knowledge besides experience—and there is: the mind. Plato, with impeccable logic, points out that if one instance can be cited in which we know something without reference to experience, then empiricism is discredited and rationalism is made viable. And, argues Plato, there are many things we know that are not dependent upon perception—for instance, we know that every event has a cause, and this truth is discovered by reason alone, for no quantity or quality of sense experience will let us perceive this truth.

Once again Socrates asks Theaetetus, What is knowledge?, and this time he replies, Knowledge is true opinion. But this is shown to be unsatisfactory, and when Theaetetus tries to amend that answer by saying knowledge is true opinion rationally analyzed, Socrates also scoffs at this. The dialogue comes to an end not by developing and defending an Idealistic theory of knowledge but simply by knocking down an empiricist theory of knowledge. In this sense the basic question of the dialogue, What is knowledge?, is left unanswered.

In subsequent dialogues, however, Plato does develop a theory of knowledge and, strangely enough, after discrediting Protagoras' assertion that man is the measure Plato turns right around and endorses it. That is, Plato said that man is truly the measure because there lie in him certain innate, universal concepts or ideas which are basic to knowledge. Now we see that Plato's disagreement with Protagoras was not so much on man as the measure but upon *how* man measured; Protagoras argued that experience was the yardstick, but Plato insisted man measures through reason. This disagreement, as noted earlier, still characterizes epistemological debate—it is the controversy between rationalism and empiricism.

In building his rationalistic theory of knowledge Plato argued that the soul comes into the world carrying with it, as part of its "factory equipment," true ideas. These ideas came to be known in a pre-earthly existence, a sort of immortality-in-reverse theory, in which the soul resided in the world of reality (and not in the world of appearance, which is the human world). This kind of knowledge is conceptual knowledge, not sense knowledge; more harshly, it is the only knowledge, the senses yielding mere opinion. Conceptual knowledge, being perfect and being dependent upon reason, reveals the true nature of things, their essences; but sense experience reveals only the manifestations of things.

Today we might argue that such a theory of knowledge is unacceptable; who, for instance, will maintain that we know what we know because we remember it from a prior existence? Very few; but many will still support the core of the rationalistic argument: the human knower has the power or the potential or the ability to know because this facility is built right into him. That is, rationalists argue that man can know because he is a rational animal, and his ability to reason is an inherent and integral part of his human nature—indeed, it is what makes him human. Plato believed that man comes equipped with a complete stock of ideas, and knowledge emerges when he remembers; Aristotle believed that man comes equipped with an intellect, and knowledge comes when it is exercised; Aquinas believed that man comes equipped with the seeds of knowledge implicit in his mind, and knowledge comes when experience and reason combine to fertilize these seeds; and so on for all rationalists.

But rationalism has not won the day in epistemology. Later empiricists faulted Plato for playing an intellectual shell game: they insist that he used perception to disqualify perception. That is, they admit Plato clearly showed that some perceptions are erroneous and that no perception is absolutely perfect—but to do this he used even other perceptions. For example, the antiempirical argument that the perception of a stick in a glass of water leads us to conclude wrongly the stick is bent, and offers this as evidence that perception is unreliable, is itself an unreliable argument because the assertion that the stick is really straight, not bent, itself depends upon even other perceptions. Thus the argument is not whether perception is unreliable, but which (kinds of) perceptions are most reliable. And this takes us straight into fallibilism and theories of knowledge based on experience and probabilities.

Empiricism holds that all knowledge is derived from experience; there is no other source. We may reason, true, but we do not reason in a vacuum—we reason (reflect) upon experience; we may admit authoritative (but not authoritarian) claims as knowledgeable, true; but such an appeal to authority must be based on experience if it is to be valid. For the empiricist knowledge is not of another world, known by reason alone; it is knowledge of this world, known by shared and tested experiences. The purpose of knowledge is not to "know Ultimate Reality," but to enable man to predict the future, to live a better life. In fine, epistemology is a method of verifying or justifying beliefs or ideas that are expressed in propositions (i.e., knowledge claims).

Propositions that are claims to know have their source in experience and are tested in further experience; although there are several ways of verifying (veri-fy; to *make* true, not to discover the true) knowledge claims, the ultimate test is observation—and thus empiricism reaffirms with modifications the initial position taken by Theaetetus. The knowledge claim that "It is snowing today in Syracuse" is to be verified by direct observation; if my senses, or yours, or all who are in Syracuse and take the trouble to look out the window, confirm that statement then we say the knowledge claim is verified, it is true, we *know* it is snowing today in Syracuse. In the same way we come to know, for instance, that dogs bark, leaves fall from trees, unmarried men follow pretty women (married or not), and that there is but one fire-house in Lafayette.

But experience does not directly yield all we know; more often than not we must wind through a labyrinth of experiences and reasons, in a hypothetico-deductive manner, before we can identify the direct experience required that will let us assert a knowledge claim is true. For instance, consider the propositions "The sun moves" (or even "The earth moves"), "This is a brass key," "Caesar crossed the Rubicon," "There were no humans on the earth in the year one million B.C.," or "Matter consists of electrical charges." None of these knowledge claims can be known directly through perception or immediate experience—but, insists the empiricist, if we are to credit them we must find a method of figuring out the kind of present ex-perience we will take as sufficient warrant for the truth of such knowledge claims. All of our knowledge, therefore, is experiential, and most of it, in one way or another, is indirect (who needs to be run over by a train, for instance, to know that trains can reduce animate matter to inanimate?).

That last example of the train gives the clue to the method of an empirical epistemology: many knowledge claims can be verified only by the use of inductive inferences based on direct observation, and the knowledge so provided is probable. The import of this is methodo-logical: empiricism relies upon an inductive logic to mediate experience, to predict future experiences, and thus a theory of probability is necessarily built into empiricism. That is not the case with rationalism, not only because rationalists generally put their emphasis on a deductive logic, but because rationalists simply are not willing to call probable knowledge "knowledge"—you will remember that by knowledge they mean a proposition which is certain and uninferred or, if inferred, is inferred from self-evidently true premises. No empiricist can offer that kind of knowledge and, indeed, he denies that kind of knowledge exists.

How does the empiricist view the problem of knowledge? What does he mean by the use of the verb *to know?* Generally speaking, he means three things. When someone says, "I know x," he means the proposition express-ing the knowledge-claim is true, he believes in the truth of the proposition, and he has some kind of empirical evidence to support the knowledge claim. If I say, "I know it takes two days for a letter to get from Syracuse to Lafayette," then (a) I am offering that as a true proposition, (b) I believe it, and (c) I have some kind of evidence to back up my belief.

The question of what will be admitted as evidence to verify the claim is crucial, and unless the claim itself can indicate the pertinent evidence re-quired it is a spurious claim, it is meaningless. Further, the evidence must be public and repeatable. In the case of the postal service between New York and Indiana, the knowledge claim is based on past experience, but the claim is valid only to the degree that future experience confirms it. When I say, "I know it takes two days for a letter to reach Lafayette from Syracuse," I am implying that anyone who drops a letter in a Syracuse mailbox on Monday will, if he jets to Lafayette, see his letter received on Wednesday. But note now that it's possible the letter will arrive Tuesday or Thursday (or not at all; that's happened too)—thus we see that the knowledge involved is not certain, not absolute, but relative and probabilistic. The knowledge claim boils down to the proposition that "If one mails a letter to Lafayette from Syracuse on Monday, the probabilities are _____ that it will arrive on Wednesday." The blank, the probability statement, is filled in on the basis of past experience and future expectations (and can be estimated by the low cost of insuring a letter); therefore, the knowledge claim is justified only in terms of its *predictive content.*

If knowledge is probable it is not certain. Can we live with probable knowledge? The empiricist argues not only that we can but that we must—since there is no other kind. But he takes away whatever sting there may be to this by noting that some events are so stable, so constant, that we can know them with nigh-absolute probability. For instance, we know the probabilities that the sun will rise tomorrow are fantastically high in our favor (even if we also know, i.e., predict, that the day will come when it won't rise); we know the probabilities that the federal government will tax our income for the next twenty years are against us, but we don't know it for sure; we know that a college education will probably yield a higher lifetime earning power, and we know that the Yankees will probably win the pennant next year. But in all cases our knowledge is contingent and probable, based on past experience which produces our future expectations —and the validity of every knowledge claim is tested in the crucible of continuing experience.

THE CATEGORY OF TRUTH

Before closing the section epistemology some mention of the concept of truth is required. Approaches to truth are dependent upon a theory of knowledge, and a theory of truth might be labeled rational or empirical depending upon the method of admitting candidates for truth to the corpus of reliability.

Generally speaking, there are four approaches to truth; the coherence theory, which is most closely identified with Idealism; the correspondence theory, which is identified with Realism; the instrumental theory, which is identified with Pragmatism; and the verifiability theory which is identified with Logical Empiricism.

According to the coherence theory, truth is represented by the systematic coherence of judgments and ideas, and an idea is tested for its truth content by comparing it with ideas already known to be true. Thus a candidate for truth can be tested by determining if it "fits," if it coheres. An idea might be said to be true if it is implied by other ideas known to be true, or if in conjunction with some ideas, it helps to imply other known true ideas. Thus the constellation of existing ideas sets the precedent by which new ideas—especially maverick information—will be judged.

According to the correspondence theory, truth is represented by the degree of correspondence between an idea or a statement and the objective state of affairs the idea purports to describe. The test for truth is whether or not the candidate does indeed describe objective reality, when the idea or statement is compared with the fact. For example, the idea or statement that "Saturn has nine rings" is true or false in terms of the actual objective fact—it depends upon whether or not Saturn actually does have nine rings, thus positing an external reality against which internal perceptions are to be judged.

According to the instrumental theory, truth is represented by the practical consequences or effectiveness of an idea, and the test for truth is whether or not the idea works for a specifically postulated end—whether it successfully guides and predicts behavior. It should be noted that the Jamesian theory of truth, that an idea is true if it is successful in satisfying human desires, is at odds with the Peirce-Dewey theory of truth, in which the truth of an idea or statement is measured by its success in facilitating inquiry and increasing the predictive ability of humans.

Finally, according to the verifiability theory, an idea or statement is true when it is empirically verified, when its predictive content has been tested and found accurate. Logical Empiricists also talk quite a bit about logical truth or truth by convention; what is meant here is that some ideas or propositions are found to be true by an inspection of meaning alone. Logico-mathematical systems are analytic, for instance, and any component of such a system (e.g., $2 + 2 = 4$; P and Q implies P) is valid or invalid by reference to the parent system.

These theories of truth are not mutually exclusive. Pragmatism and Logical Empiricism, to take an example, are so spiritually close as philosophies that either system could and does incorporate the "other's" theory of truth. By the same token, rationalists usually rely on a coherence or correspondence theory of truth, although some Empiricists (e.g., Modern Realists) do so as well.

THE ESSAYS TO COME

The following three essays, by Alfred J. Ayer, Rachel Goodrich and John Dewey, exemplify three quite different approaches to the problem of knowledge.

Ayer, writing from the standpoint of Logical Empiricism uses his essay to examine the questions "What *do* we mean, what *can* we mean, when we use the verb *to know?*" Goodrich, writing from a Neo-Thomist position, makes an argument that will admit as valid extra-sensory or supernatural claims to know. Dewey, writing in the Pragmatic tradition, lays the foundation for a theory of knowledge that is based on human disposition rather than definition, and action rather than reflection.

∽

OVERVIEW

Much contemporary philosophy involves the search for meaning because it is clearly evident that our claims to know are dependent, in large degree, upon the language in which the claim is couched. This search, often entitled *philosophic analysis,* frequently begins with concept examination. That is, in this philosophic strategy the opening tactic in the campaign for clear speech often involves posing the question "What (do) (can) we mean by ———?," with the concept under analysis filling in the blank.

In the following essay that blank is completed by the insertion of the verb *to know,* and Alfred J. Ayer, a noted philosophic analyst, initiates his solution to the problem of knowledge with an analysis of the uses and abuses of that verb. His approach to the problem is not indirectly guided by an earlier positivistic theory of meaning which held that, in Ludwig Wittgenstein's terms, the meaning is the use.

One very common use of "know" involves being familiar with some object of knowledge, as when one claims to be acquainted with some person, place, thing, or event. For example, this usage is indicated when one asserts "Oh, yes, I know John Jones well!" or "How well I know San Francisco!" This is a common usage, one that is especially employed by name droppers (e.g., substitute "President Kennedy" or "Mickey Mantle" for "John Jones") when they wish to appear knowledgeable.

Another usage indicates that the knower has undergone some kind of experience or participated in some kind of event; as, for instance, when one says "I know what it is to be (afraid) (happy) (fearful) (sick)." Knowledge in this sense is experiential.

A third common use means that one is able to categorize. That is, when one is possessed of the ability to distinguish or separate one thing or event from another. In this use most people have knowledge in that they can distinguish gin from vodka, but "true" knowledge is represented by those who can distinguish, identify, and categorize more subtle differences. For instance, the wine taster who can distinguish micro-differences in taste, body, and bouquet is more knowledgeable than he who finds little difference between Gallo, Mogen David, and Harvey's Bristol Cream.

From this kind of elementary analysis Ayer goes on to examine other possibilities—for instance, Does knowing consist of being in a special state of mind?—and concludes that knowing involves "having the right to be sure." That is, the necessary and sufficient conditions of knowing or having knowledge are that (1) what is known must be true, (2) the knower must be sure of what he knows, and (3) the knower must have adequate evidence to demonstrate that what he surely knows is true.

With such a conclusion as this Ayer subtly but clearly reformulates the definition of the problem of knowledge; the question "can we know" is now seen not to be dependent upon the discovery of what knowledge "is," but dependent upon the kind(s) of justification adduced in support of surety—on the evidence. Put otherwise, the problem of knowledge is not "What is Knowledge?" but "How can we use the verb *to know* with assurance?" Thus the question of evidence is central to the satisfactory formulation of a theory of knowledge yet, even so, the criteria of satisfactory evidence must not be built into the theory. In Ayer's terms,

> This right [to be sure] may be earned in various ways; but even if one could give a complete description of them it would be a mistake to try to build it into the definition of knowledge, just as it would be a mistake to try to incorporate our actual standards of goodness into a definition of good.

The answer to the "meta-epistemological" question, "how do you know you know?," is thus left open—in this essay at least. An approach to the entire problem is found in the book from which this essay is taken, as well as Ayer's earlier work, *Language, Truth, and Logic.*

Philosophy and Knowledge

A. J. Ayer*

THE METHOD OF PHILOSOPHY

It is by its methods rather than its subject-matter that philosophy is to be

* Reprinted by permission from *The Problem of Knowledge* (New York: St. Martin's Press, Inc., 1956), pp. 1–34.

distinguished from other arts or sciences. Philosophers make statements which are intended to be true, and they commonly rely on argument both to support their own theories and to refute the theories of others; but the arguments which they use are of a peculiar character. The proof of a philosophical statement is not, or only very seldom, like the proof of a mathematical statement, it does not normally consist in formal demonstration. Neither is it like the proof of a statement in any of the descriptive sciences. Philosophical theories are not tested by observation. They are neutral with respect to particular matters of fact.

This is not to say that philosophers are not concerned with facts, but they are in the strange position that all the evidence which bears upon their problems is already available to them. It is not further scientific information that is needed to decide such philosophical questions as whether the material world is real, whether objects continue to exist at times when they are not perceived, whether other human beings are conscious in the same sense as one is oneself. These are not questions that can be settled by experiment, since the way in which they are answered itself determines how the result of any experiment is to be interpreted. What is in dispute in such cases is not whether, in a given set of circumstances, this or that event will happen, but rather how anything at all that happens is to be described.

This preoccupation with the way things are, or are to be, described is often represented as an enquiry into their essential nature. Thus philosophers are given to asking such questions as: What is mind? What sort of a relation is causality? What is the nature of belief? What is truth? The difficulty is then to see how such questions are to be taken. It must not be supposed, for instance, that a philosopher who asks What is mind? is looking for the kind of information that a psychologist might give him. His problem is not that he is ignorant of the ways in which people think and feel, or even that he is unable to explain them. Neither should it be assumed that he is simply looking for a definition. It is not as if philosophers do not understand how words like 'mind' or 'causality' or 'truth' are actually used. But why, then, do they ask such questions? What is it that they are trying to find out?

The answer to this, though not indeed the whole answer, is that, already knowing the use of certain expressions, they are seeking to give an analysis of their meaning. This distinction between the use of an expression and the analysis of its meaning is not easy to grasp. Let us try to make it clear by taking an example. Consider the case of knowledge. A glance at the dictionary will show that the verb 'to know' is used in a variety of ways. We can speak of knowing, in the sense of being familiar with, a person or a place, of knowing something in the sense of having had experience of it, as when someone says that he has known hunger or fear, of knowing in the sense of being able to recognize or distinguish, as when we claim to know an honest man when we see one or to know butter from margarine. I may be said to know my Dickens, if I have read, remember, and can perhaps also quote his writings; to know a subject such as trigonometry, if I have mastered it; to know how to swim or drive a car; to know how to behave myself. Most important of all, perhaps, are the uses for which the dictionary gives the definition of 'to be aware or apprized of,' 'to apprehend or comprehend as fact or truth,' the sense, or senses, in which to have knowledge is to know that something or other is the case.

All this is a matter of lexicography. The facts are known, in a sense, to anyone who understands the English language, though not everyone who understands the English language would be competent to set them out. The lexicographer, *pace* Dr. Johnson, is required to be something more than a harmless drudge. What he is not required to be is a philosopher. To possess the information which the dictionary provides about the accredited uses of the English word 'to know,' or the corresponding words in other languages, is no doubt a necessary qualification for giving an analysis of knowledge; but it is not sufficient. The philosopher who has this information may still ask What is Knowledge? and hesitate for an answer.

We may discover the sense of the philosopher's question by seeing what further questions it incorporates, and what sorts of statement the attempt to answer it leads him to make. Thus, he may enquire whether the different cases in which we speak of knowing have any one thing in common; whether, for example, they are alike in implying the presence of some special state of mind. He may maintain that there is, on the subjective side, no difference in kind between knowing and believing, or alternatively, that knowing is a special sort of mental act. If he thinks it correct to speak of acts of knowing, he may go on to enquire into the nature of their objects. Is any limitation to be set upon them? Or, putting it another way, is there anything thinkable that is beyond the reach

of human knowledge? Does knowing make a difference to what is known? Is it necessary to distinguish between the sorts of things that can be known directly and those that can be known only indirectly? And, if so, what are the relationships between them? Perhaps it is philosophically misleading to talk of knowing objects at all. It may be possible to show that what appears to be an instance of knowing some object always comes down to knowing that something is the case. What is known, in this sense, must be true, whereas what is believed may very well be false. But it is also possible to believe what is in fact true without knowing it. Is knowledge then to be distinguished by the fact that if one knows that something is so, one cannot be mistaken? And in that case does it follow that what is known is necessarily true, or in some other way indubitable? But, if this does follow, it will lead in its turn to the conclusion that we commonly claim to know much more than we really do; perhaps even to the paradox that we do not know anything at all: for it may be contended that there is no statement whatsoever that is not in itself susceptible to doubt. Yet surely there must be something wrong with an argument that would make knowledge unattainable. Surely some of our claims to knowledge must be capable of being justified. But in what ways can we justify them? In what would the processes of justifying them consist?

I do not say that all these questions are clear, or even that they are all coherent. But they are instances of the sort of question that philosophers ask. The next step is to see how one would try to answer them. Once again, it will be best to take particular examples. Let us begin with the question whether the various sorts of knowing have any one thing in common, and the suggestion that this common feature is a mental state or act.

COMMON FEATURES OF KNOWLEDGE

Except where a word is patently ambiguous, it is natural for us to assume that the different situations, or types of situation, to which it applies have a distinctive common feature. For otherwise why should we use the same word to refer to them? Sometimes we have another way of describing such a common feature; we can say, for example, that what irascible people have in common is that they are all prone to anger. But very often we have no way of saying what is common to the things to which the same word applies except by using the word itself. How else would we describe the distinctively common feature of red things except by saying that they are all red? In the same way, it might be said that what the things that we call 'games' have in common is just that they are games; but there there seems to be a difference. Whereas there is a simple and straightforward resemblance between the things whose colour we call 'red,' the sort of resemblance that leads us naturally to talk of their having an identical quality, there is no such simple resemblance between the things that we call 'games.' The *Oxford English Dictionary* defines a game as 'a diversion of the nature of a contest, played according to rules, and de-

cided by superior skill, strength, or good fortune.' But not all games are diversions, in the sense of being played for fun; games of patience are hardly contests, though they are decided by skill and luck; children's games are not always played according to rules; acting games need not be decided. Wittgenstein,[1] from whom I have taken this example, concludes that we cannot find anything common to all games, but only "a complicated network of similarities" which "overlap and crisscross" in the same way as the resemblances between people who belong to the same family. "Games," he says, "form a family."

This is a good analogy, but I think that Wittgenstein is wrong to infer from it that games do not have any one thing in common. His doing so suggests that he takes the question whether things have something in common to be different from the question whether there are resemblances between them. But surely the difference is only one of formulation. If things resemble one another sufficiently for us to find it useful to apply the same word to them, we are entitled to say, if it pleases us, that they have something in common. Neither is it necessary that what they have in common should be describable in different words, as we saw in the case of 'red.' It is correct, though not at all enlightening, to say that what games have in common is their being games. The point which Wittgenstein's argument brings out is that the resemblance between the things to which the same word applies may be

[1] Ludwig Wittgenstein, *Philosophical Investigations,* Part I, paragraphs 66, 67, pp. 31–32.

of different degrees. It is looser and less straightforward in some cases than in others.

Our question then becomes whether the different sorts of cases in which we speak of something's being known resemble one another in some straightforward fashion like the different instances of the colour red, or whether they merely have what Wittgenstein would call a family resemblance. Another possibility is that they share a common factor the possession of which is necessary to their being instances of knowledge, even though it is not sufficient. If knowledge were always knowledge that something is the case, then such a common factor might be found in the existence of a common relation to truth. For while what is true can be believed, or disbelieved, or doubted, or imagined, or much else besides being known, it is, as we have already noted, a fact or ordinary usage that what is known, in this sense, cannot but be true.

But can it reasonably be held that knowledge is always knowledge that something is the case? If knowing that something is the case is taken to involve the making of a conscious judgment, then plainly it cannot. A dog knows its master, a baby knows its mother, but they do not know any statements to be true. Or if we insist on saying that there is a sense in which they do know statements to be true, that the dog which knows its master knows the fact that this is his master, we must allow that what we call knowing facts may sometimes just be a matter of being disposed to behave in certain appropriate ways; it need not involve any conscious process of judging,

or stating, that such and such is so. Indeed, we constantly recognize objects without troubling to describe them, even to ourselves. No doubt, once we have acquired the use of language, we can always describe them if we choose, although the descriptions that we have at our command may not always be the descriptions that we want. "I know that tune," I say, though its name escapes me and I cannot remember where I heard it before; "I know that man," though I have forgotten who he is. But at least I identify him as a man, and as a man that I have met somewhere or other. There is a sense in which knowing something, in this usage of the term, is always a matter of knowing what it is; and in this sense it can perhaps be represented as knowing a fact, as knowing that something is so. Much the same applies to the cases where knowing is a matter of knowing how. Certainly, when people possess skills, even intellectual skills, like the ability to act or teach, they are not always consciously aware of the procedures which they follow. They use the appropriate means to attain their ends, but the fact that these means are appropriate may never be made explicit by them even to themselves. There are a great many things that people habitually do well, without remarking how they do them. In many cases they could not say how they did them if they tried. Nor does this mean that their performances are unintelligent. As Professor Ryle has pointed out,[2] the display of intelligence lies in the manner of the performance, rather than in its being accompanied or preceded by any con-

[2] Gilbert Ryle, *The Concept of Mind*, Chap. 2.

scious recognition of the relevant facts. The performer does not need to tell himself that if such and such things are done, then such and such will follow. He may, indeed, do so, but equally he may not: and even when he does it is not because of this that his performance is judged to be intelligent. This point is convincingly established by Professor Ryle. But once again, if we are prepared to say that knowing facts need not consist in anything more than a disposition to behave in certain ways, we can construe knowing how to do things as being, in its fashion, a matter of knowing facts. Only by this time we shall have so extended our use of the expression "knowing facts" or "knowing that something is the case" that it may well become misleading. It may be taken to imply that the resemblances between the different ways of having, or manifesting, knowledge are closer and neater than they really are.

DOES KNOWING CONSIST IN BEING A SPECIAL STATE OF MIND?

It should by now be obvious that if "knowing a fact" is understood in this extended sense, it need not be even partially a description of any special state of mind. But suppose that we confine our attention to the cases in which knowing something is straightforwardly a matter of knowing something to be true, the cases where it is natural in English to use the expression "knowing that," or one of its grammatical variants. Is it a necessary condition for having this sort of knowledge, not only that what one is said to know should in fact be true, but also

that one should be in some special state of mind, or that one should be performing some special mental act? Is it perhaps a sufficient condition, or even both necessary and sufficient? Some philosophers have maintained not only that there are such cognitive states, or acts, but that they are infallible. According to them, it is impossible for anyone to be in such a state of mind, unless what it purports to reveal to him is really so. For someone to think that he knows something when he really does not know it, it is not enough, in their view, that he should be mistaken about the fact which he claims to know, that what he thinks true should actually be false; he must also be mistaken about the character of his mental state: for if his mental state were what he took it to be, that is a state of knowledge, he could not be mistaken about the fact which it revealed to him. If this view were correct, then being in a mental state of this kind would be a sufficient condition for having knowledge. And if, in addition, one could not know anything to be true without being in this state, it would be both necessary and sufficient.

An obvious objection to this thesis is that to credit someone with the possession of knowledge is not to say that he is actually displaying it, even to himself. I know some facts of ancient history and I do not know them only on the rare occasions when I call them to mind. I know them at this moment even though I am not thinking of them. What is necessary is that if I were to think of them I should get them right, that if the subject comes up I am in a position to make statements which are authoritative and true. It is not necessary that I should continually be making these statements, or even that I should ever make them, provided that I could make them if the occasion arose. This point is sometimes made by saying that the verb "to know" is used to signify a disposition or, as Ryle puts it, that it is a "capacity" verb.[3] To have knowledge is to have the power to give a successful performance, not actually to be giving one.

But still, it may be said, however intermittent these performances may be, it is surely necessary that they be given at least once. They need not be public, but even if they are only private they must in fact occur. It would be absurd to say that someone knew a truth, which he had never even thought of, or one that he had thought of but not acknowledged to be true. Let it be granted that the most common use of the English verb "to know" is dispositional. It is not even the only correct use—we do sometimes speak of knowing in the sense of coming to realize—but let that pass. The important point is that the dispositions which are taken to constitute knowing must sometimes be actualized. And the way in which they are actualized, so this argument continues, is through the existence of a special mental state.

But what is this state of mind supposed to be? The reply to this may be that it is unique in character, so that it cannot be analysed in terms of anything else. But what then is the evidence for its existence? It is indeed true that one is not reasonably said to know a fact unless one is completely sure of it. This is one of the distinctions between

knowledge and belief. One may also be completely sure of what one believes, in cases where the belief is refused the title of knowledge on other grounds; such as that it is false, or that, although it is true, the reasons for which it is held do not come up to the standard which knowledge requires. But whereas it is possible to believe what one is not completely sure of, so that one can consistently admit that what one believes to be true may nevertheless be false, this does not apply to knowledge. It can indeed, be said to someone who hesitates, or makes a mistake, that he really knows what he is showing himself to be unsure of, the implication being that he ought, or is in a position, to be sure. But to say of oneself that one knew that such and such a statement was true but that one was not altogether sure of it would be self-contradictory. On the other hand, while the respective states of mind of one who knows some statement to be true and another who only believes it may in this way be different, it does not seem that there need be any difference between them when the belief is held with full conviction, and is distinguished from knowledge on other grounds. As Professor Austin puts it, 'Saying "I know" is *not* saying "I have performed a specially striking feat of cognition, superior, in the same scale as believing and being sure, even to being merely quite sure": for there *is* nothing in that scale superior to being quite sure.'[4] And it may very well happen that even when people's beliefs are false they are as fully convinced of

---

[3] *Ibid.*, pp. 133–134.

[4] J. L. Austin, "Other Minds," *Supplementary Proceedings of the Aristotelian Society,* XX, 171.

their truth as they are of the truth of what they know.

Moreover, though to be convinced of something is, in a sense, to be in a particular state of mind, it does not seem to consist in any special mental occurrence. It is rather a matter of accepting the fact in question and of not being at all disposed to doubt it than of contemplating it with a conscious feeling of conviction. Such feelings of conviction do indeed exist. There is the experience of suddenly coming to realize the truth of something that one had not known before: and may it be that similar experiences occur when one is engaged in defending a belief that has been put in question, or when one finally succeeds in resolving a doubt. But for the most part, the things that we claim to know are not presented to us in an aura of revelation. We learn that they are so, and from then on we unquestioningly accept them. But this is not a matter of having any special feelings. It is not certain that to have a feeling of conviction is even a sufficient condition for being sure; for it would seem that a conscious feeling of complete conviction may co-exist with an unconscious feeling of doubt. But whether or not it ever is sufficient, it clearly is not necessary. One can be sure without it. And equally its presence is not necessary for the possession, or even for the display, of knowledge.

The fact is, as Professor Austin has pointed out,[5] that the expression "I know" commonly has what he calls a "performative" rather than a descriptive use. To say that I know that something is the case, though it does imply

[5] *Ibid.*

that I am sure of it, is not so much to report my state of mind as to vouch for the truth of whatever it may be. In saying that I know it I engage myself to answer for its truth: and I let it be understood that I am in a position to give this undertaking. If my credentials do not meet the usual standards, you have the right to reproach me. You have no right to reproach me if I merely say that I believe, though you may think the less of me if my belief appears to you irrational. If I tell you that I believe something which I do not, I am misinforming you only about my mental attitude; but if I tell you that I know something which I do not, the chances are that I am misinforming you about the truth of the statement which I claim to know, or if not about its truth, then about my authority for making it. In the same way, to say of some other person that he knows that such and such is so is not primarily, if at all, to describe his state of mind; it is first of all to grant that what he is said to know is true; and, secondly, it is to admit his credentials. If we consider that his credentials are insufficient, whether on the ground that he is not, as we say, in a position to know, though others might be, or, possibly, because we hold that what he claims to know is something for which neither he nor anyone could have the requisite authority, then we will not allow that he really does know what he says he knows, even though he is quite sure of it and even though it is actually true.

But here it may be objected that this excursus into philology is beside the point. Let it be granted that the expression "I know" is not always used in English to signify a cognitive mental state. Let it be granted even, what is very much more doubtful, that it is never so used. The fact remains, it may be argued, that these cognitive states, or acts, exist. When they do occur, they are sufficient for knowledge. Furthermore, their existence is the only authority worth having, so that if our ordinary use of words were strictly philosophical, which it obviously is not, they would be not only sufficient for knowledge, but necessary as well.

Now I do not deny that ordinary usage is capable of improvement, or even that some improvement might be made in it on philosophical grounds. Philosophers, like scientists, are at liberty to introduce technical terms, or to use ordinary words in a technical sense. But this proposal to restrict the application of the verb "to know" to cases where the knowledge consisted in someone's being in a cognitive mental state would not be fortunate. For the consequence of accepting it would be that no one could ever properly be said to know anything at all.

The reason for this is that there cannot be a mental state which, being as it were directed towards a fact, is such that it guarantees that the fact is so. And here I am not saying merely that such states never do occur, or even that it is causally impossible that they ever should occur, but rather that it is logically impossible. My point is that from the fact that someone is convinced that something is true, however firm his conviction may be, it never follows logically that it is true.[6]

[6] Except in the rare cases when the truth of the statement in question is a logical condition of its being believed, as in the assertion of one's own existence.

If he is a reliable witness and if he is in a good position to assess the truth of whatever statement is in question, then his being convinced of its truth may provide us with a strong reason for accepting it; but it cannot be a conclusive reason. There will not be a formal contradiction in saying both that the man's state of mind is such that he is absolutely sure that a given statement is true, and that the statement is false. There would indeed be a contradiction in saying both that he knew the statement to be true, and that it was false; but this, as has already been explained, is because it enters into the meaning of the word "know" that one cannot know what is not true. It cannot validly be inferred from this linguistic fact that when someone is considering a statement which he knows to be true, it is his state of mind that guarantees its truth. The statement is true if, and only if, what it states is so, or, in other words, if the situation which it describes is as it describes it. And whether the situation really is as it is described is not to be decided merely by examining the attitude which anyone who considers the statement has towards it, not even if the person who considers it knows it to be true. If philosophers have denied, or overlooked, this point, the fault may lie in their use of such expressions as "state of knowledge." For if to say of someone that he is in a state of knowledge is merely to describe his condition of mind, it does not entail that there is anything which he knows; and if it does entail that there is something which he knows, then, as we have seen, it does not merely describe his condition of mind. Since the expression is in any case artificial, it may be understood in either of these ways, though I suppose it would be more natural to take it in the second sense, as signifying the opposite of being in a state of ignorance. What we may not do is use it in both senses at once, for they are incompatible; an expression cannot refer only to a condition of mind, and to something else besides. The mistake should be obvious when it is pointed out, but it has not always been avoided. And the result is that a condition of mind, ambiguously referred to as a state of knowledge, is wrongly thought to be sufficient to guarantee the truth of the statements upon which it is supposed to be directed.

But unless some states of mind are cognitive, it may be said, how can we come to know anything? We may make the truth of some statements depend upon the truth of others, but this process cannot go on forever. There must be some statements of empirical fact which are directly verified. And in what can this verification consist except in our having the appropriate experiences? But when these experiences will be cognitive: to have whatever experience it may be will itself be a way of knowing something to be true. And a similar argument applies to a priori statements, like those of logic or pure mathematics. We may prove one mathematical statement by deducing it from others, but the proof must start somewhere. There must be at least one statement which is accepted without such proof, an axiom of some sort which is known intuitively. Even if we are able to explain away our knowledge of such axioms,

by showing that they are true by definition, we still have to see that a set of definitions is consistent. To conduct any formal proof, we have to be able to see that one statement follows logically from another. But what is this seeing that one statement follows from another except the performance of a cognitive act?

The bases of this argument are sound. We do just have to see that certain proofs are valid, and it is through having some experience that we discover the truth or falsehood of any statement of empirical fact. In the case of some such statements, it may even be that our having certain experiences verifies them conclusively. This is a point which will have to be considered later on. But in any such case what verifies the statement, whether conclusively or not, is the existence of the experience, not the confidence that we may have in some description of it. To take a simple example, what verifies the statement that I have a headache is my feeling a headache, not my having a feeling of confidence that the statement that I have a headache is true. Of course if I do have a headache and also understand the statement, I shall undoubtedly accept it as being true. This is the ground for saying that if I have such an experience, I know that I am having it. But, in this sense, my knowing that I am having the experience is just my having it and being able to identify it. I know that I am having it inasmuch as I correctly take it as verifying the statement which describes it. But my justification for accepting the statement is not that I have a cognitive, or any other attitude towards it: It is simply that I am having the experience. To say that the experience itself is cognitive is correct, though perhaps misleading, if it is merely a way of saying that it is a conscious experience. It may still be correct if it is a way of saying that the experience is recognized for what it is by the person who is having it, though, as we shall see later on, such recognition can be mistaken. It is not correct if it is taken as implying that the experience either consists in or includes a process of infallibly apprehending some statement to be true.

Similarly, what makes it true, for example, that the conclusion of a syllogism follows from the premises is that the inference exemplifies a law of logic. And if we are asked what makes the law of logic true, we can in this and in many other cases provide a proof. But this proof in its turn relies upon some law of logic. There will come a point, therefore, when we are reduced to saying of some logical statement simply that it is valid. Now to be in a position to say that such a statement is valid we must be able to see that it is so, but it is not made valid by our seeing that it is. It is valid in its own right. Of course if "seeing" here has the force of "knowing," then the fact that the statement is valid will indeed follow from the fact that it is seen to be so. But once again this makes only the verbal point, that we are not, in this usage, entitled to talk of "seeing" something to be true unless it really is true. It does not prove that there are, or can be, any mental states of intuition which are such that their existence affords an absolute guarantee that one really is, in this sense, seeing what one thinks one sees. It

must always remain possible that one is mistaken. Admittedly, if someone thinks that he may have been mistaken in accepting some logical statement which had seemed to him evidently true, there may be nothing for him to do but just look at it again. And if this second look confirms the first, his doubts may reasonably be put to rest. But the truth of the statement in question still does not logically follow from the fact that it continues to strike him as self-evident. Truths of logic make no reference to persons: consequently, they cannot be established by any mere description of some person's mental state. And this holds good whatever the mental state may be.

This is not to say that we do not know the truth of any *a priori* statements, or even that we do not know some of them intuitively, if to know them intuitively is to know them without proof. Our argument no more implies this than it implies that we cannot know any empirical statements to be true. It is designed to show, not that we do not have the knowledge which we think we have, but only that knowing should not be represented as a matter of being in some infallible state of consciousness: for there cannot be such states.

This point is important, if only because their neglect of it has led philosophers into difficulties which might have been avoided. In Berkeley's well-known phrase they "have first raised a dust, and then complain, we cannot see."[7] Starting from the premise that consciousness, in the sense of cognitive awareness, must always be conscious-

[7] George Berkeley, *The Principles of Human Knowledge,* Introduction, section iii.

ness *of* something, they have perplexed themselves with such questions as what consciousness is in itself and how it is related to the things, or facts, which are its objects. It does not seem to be identical with its objects, yet neither does it seem to be anything apart from them. They are separate, yet nothing separates them. When there is added the further premise that consciousness is also self-conscious, the problem becomes more complicated still. In attempting to solve it existentialist philosophers have gone so far as to deny the law of identity and even to speak of "the nothing" as if it were a special sort of agent, one of whose functions was to divide consciousness from itself. But apart from their own obvious demerits, these are reactions to a problem which should not arise. It depends upon the initial mistake of assuming that a naive analysis in terms of act and objects yields an adequate account of knowledge.

Other philosophers, besides the existentialists, have make the mistake of treating knowledge as though it consisted in the possession of an inner searchlight. How far, they then ask, can the searchlight reach? Is it confined to the present or can its rays illuminate the past? Is not remembering a way of knowing? But does it then follow that the past is still real? Perhaps the light can even play upon the future. But how can it be possible to inspect what does not yet exist? It is commonly assumed that we can train the searchlight upon our own conscious states. But can it ever go beyond them? Do physical objects come within its scope? Do the thoughts and feelings of others? Some philosophers have held

that moral and aesthetic values can be objects of knowledge. Numbers and abstract entities have also been included. Indeed Plato seems to have thought that these were the only things that could be really known. Religious persons have claimed to be acquainted with a deity. And does not the experience of mystics suggest that the rays can penetrate beyond the actual world? But must there then not be a suprasensible reality? For it is taken for granted that whatever the searchlight can illuminate must in some manner exist.

Not all these questions are fictitious. There are genuine problems about the character and extent of what can be known. But this fashion of presenting them is a great impediment to their solution. It suggests that all that need be done to discover what it is possible to know, and consequently what is real, is to examine the states of mind of those who lay claim to knowledge. But, setting aside the question how such an examination could be made, it would be little to the purpose. The most that it could reveal would be that the subjects were having certain experiences and that they were convinced of the truth of whatever it was that these experiences led them to assert. But this would not prove that they knew anything at all, except, possibly, that they were having the experiences in question. It would still have to be established by an independent argument that the experiences disclosed the existence of anything beyond themselves. And there is another way in which this talk of knowing objects is misleading. It fosters mistaken views of the dependence of questions about the criteria of knowledge upon questions about reality. Thus followers of Plato are apt to make such pronouncements as that "the perfectly real can alone be perfectly known":[8] but it is not clear even what this means unless it is merely a portentous way of saying that one cannot know what is not the case. We shall see, for example, that the fact that historical statements can be known does not oblige us to conclude that the past is real, unless to say that the past is real is just a way of saying that there are historical statements which are true. In this, as in other cases, it will be found that questions about the possibility of knowledge are to be construed as questions about the analysis of different types of statement and about the grounds that there may be for accepting them.

The mistaken doctrine that knowing is an infallible state of mind may have contributed to the view, which is sometimes held, that the only statements that it is possible to know are those that are themselves in some way infallible. The ground for this opinion is that if one knows something to be true one cannot be mistaken. As we remarked when contrasting knowledge with belief, it is inconsistent to say "I know but I may be wrong." But the reason why this is inconsistent is that saying "I know" offers a guarantee which saying "I may be wrong" withdraws. It does not follow that for a fact to be known it must be such that no one could be mistaken about it or such that it could not have been otherwise. It is doubtful if there are any

facts about which no one could be mistaken, and while there are facts which could not be otherwise, they are not the only ones that can be known. But how can this second point be reconciled with the fact that what is known must be true? The answer is that the statement that what is known must be true is ambiguous. It may mean that it is necessary that if something is known it is true; or it may mean that if something is known, then it is a necessary truth. The first of these propositions is correct; it restates the linguistic fact that what is not true cannot properly be said to be known. But the second is in general false. It would follow from the first only if all truths were necessary, which is not the case. To put it another way, there is a necessary transition from being known to being true; but that is not to say that what is true, and known to be true, is necessary or certain in itself.

If we are not to be bound by ordinary usage, it is still open to us to make it a rule that only what is certain can be known. That is, we could decide, at least for the purposes of philosophical discourse, not to use the word "know" except with the implication that what was known was necessarily true, or, perhaps, certain in some other sense. The consequence would be that we could still speak of knowing the truth of *a priori* statements, such as those of logic and pure mathematics; and if there were any empirical statements, such as those describing the content of one's present experience, that were certain in themselves, they too might be included: but most of what we now correctly claim to know would not be knowable, in this al-

[8] Dean Inge, "Philosophy and Religion," *Contemporary British Philosophy* (First Series), p. 191.

legedly strict sense. This proposal is feasible, but it does not appear to have anything much to recommend it. It is not as if a statement by being necessary became incapable of being doubted. Every schoolboy knows that it is possible to be unsure about a mathematical truth. Whether there are any empirical statements which are in any important sense indubitable is, as we shall see, a matter of dispute: if there are any they belong to a very narrow class. It is, indeed, important philosophically to distinguish between necessary and empirical statements, and in dealing with empirical statements to distinguish between different types and degrees of evidence. But there are better ways of bringing out these distinctions than by tampering with the meaning, or the application, of the verb "to know."

DISCUSSION OF METHOD: PHILOSOPHY AND LANGUAGE

We have now answered some of the questions which are raised by a philosophical enquiry into the nature of knowledge. It has been found that there is no very close resemblance between the different instances which are correctly described as instances of knowing, and in particular that to know something does not consist in being in some special state of mind. Here are facts which we can be said to know intuitively, but these intuitions cannot be infallible. It has further been shown that the conception of objects of knowledge can be philosophically misleading, and that while there is a sense in which one cannot be mistaken if one knows

that something is so, this does not imply that what one knows is itself necessary or indubitable. The whole discussion was introduced as an example of philosophic method. Let us therefore consider, for a moment, how these conclusions have in fact been reached.

An important part of our procedure has been to put these general questions about knowledge to the test of particular instances. Thus the proof that one can know an object, in the sense of being able to recognize it, without making any conscious judgment about it, is that it is possible to find examples of such recognition where there is no evidence that any judgment is made. The proof that knowing how to do something need not include the ability to give an account of the way in which it is done is just that there are many things which people know how to do without there being able to give any such accounts. To discover that there need be no difference, in respect of being sure, between knowing and believing, we need only look at cases in which it turns out that someone does not know what he thought he knew. Very often the reason for this is that what he thought he knew was false. Consequently, he could not have known it, he only believed it. But there is no suggestion that his mental state was different from what it was supposed to be. Had what he claimed to know been true he would, in these circumstances, have known it. In such cases we show that what might be thought to be a necessary factor in a given type of situation is really not necessary, by finding examples in which it does not occur. This is essentially a method of disproof: we cannot so decisively show that a certain factor is necessary, merely by finding examples in which it does occur; we have to be able to see that its presence is logically required by the fact that the situation is of the given type. At the same time we may test the view that it is so required by searching for counter-examples. That none are forthcoming is at least an indication that it is correct. There is a certain analogy here with scientific reasoning, except that it is not so much a matter, as in the scientific case, of discovering whether there are any counter-examples as of deciding whether there could be. The question if whether there is anything that we should be prepared to count as an exception to the suggested rule. Thus the proof that knowing, in the sense of "knowing that," is always knowledge of some truth is that it would not otherwise be reckoned as knowledge. But it is not always so clear whether or not we should be prepared to admit exceptions. And one way of finding out is to examine carefully whatever might appear to be a doubtful case.

It does not matter whether the examples taken are actual or imaginary. In either case we describe a situation in order to see how it should be classified. Or if there be no doubt as to its classification, we may redescribe it in such a way as to bring to light certain features of it which might otherwise be overlooked. The argument therefore depends upon considerations of language; in the present instance upon the ways in which we use, or propose to use, the verb "to know." But this does not mean that it is an argument about words, in any trivial sense, or that is especially tied to the English language.

We are concerned with the work that the word "know" does, not with the fact that it is this particular word that does it. It is for this reason that we can spare ourselves a sociological investigation into the ways in which people actually do use words. For it would not matter if the popular practice were different from what we took it to be, so long as we were clear about the uses that we ourselves were ascribing to the word in question. And in talking about these uses we are talking about the uses of any words in any language that are, or may be, used in the same way. It is therefore indifferent whether, in this manner of philosophizing, we represent ourselves as dealing with words or as dealing with facts. For our enquiry into the use of words can equally be regarded as an enquiry into the nature of the facts which they describe.

Although we have not been in any way concerned with setting up a formal system, the argument has also been developed by means of deductive logic. Thus the proof that no cognitive state of mind could be infallible depends upon the logical truism that if two states of affairs are distinct a statement which refers to only one of them does not entail anything about the other. If the statement that someone is apprehending, or intuiting, something is to be regarded purely as a description of his state of mind it cannot follow from it that what he apprehends is true. A similar argument was used by Hume to prove that knowledge of causal relations "is not, in any instance, attained by reasonings *a priori*."[9] "The effect,"

[9] David Hume, *An Enquiry Concerning Human Understanding,* Part I, section iv, paragraph 23.

he says, "is totally different from the cause, and consequently can never be discovered in it."[10] Or again, "there is no object, which implies the existence of any other if we consider these objects in themselves, and never look beyond the idea which we form of them."[11] As Hume puts them, these statements are not obviously tautological; but they become so when it is seen that what he is saying is that when two objects are distinct, they are distinct; and consequently that to assert the existence of either one of them is not necessarily to assert the existence of the other.

When they are formulated in this way such statements may seem too trivial to be worth making. But their consequences are important and easily overlooked. The proof of this is that many philosophers have in fact maintained that causality is a logical relation and that there can be infallible acts of knowing. To refute them satisfactorily, we may need to do more than merely point out the logical mistake. We may have to consider how they could have come to be misled, what are the arguments which seem to support their view, how these arguments are to be met. In general, it will be found that the points of logic on which philosophical theories turn are simple. How much of moral theory, for example, is centered upon the truism, again remarked by Hume, that "ought" is not implied by "is," that there can be no deductive step from saying how things are to saying how they ought to be. What is difficult is to make the consequences of such truisms palatable, to

discover and neutralize the motives which lead to their being denied. It is the fact that much philosophizing consists in persuasive work of this sort, the fact also that in all philosophy so much depends upon the way in which things are put, that gives point to the saying that philosophy is an exercise in rhetoric. But if this is to be said, it must be understood that the word "rhetoric" is not to be taken, as it now very often is, in a pejorative sense.

It is not my purpose to give an exhaustive list of philosophical procedures. Those that I have described are typical and important, but they are not the only ones that will come within our notice. In particular, it will be seen that philosophers do not limit themselves to uncovering the criteria which we actually use in assessing different types of statement. They also question these criteria; they may even go so far as to deny their validity. In this way they come to put forward paradoxes such as that matter is unreal or that no one can ever really know what goes on in the mind of another. In themselves such statements may seem merely perverse: their philosophical importance comes out in the discussion of what lies behind them.

KNOWING AS HAVING THE RIGHT TO BE SURE

The answers which we have found for the questions we have so far been discussing have not yet put us in a position to give a complete account of what it is to know that something is the case. The first requirement is that what is known should be true, but this is not

---

10 *Ibid.*, paragraph 25.
11 David Hume, *A Treatise of Human Nature*, Book I, Part III, section vi.

sufficient; not even if we add to it the further condition that one must be completely sure of what one knows. For it is possible to be completely sure of something which is in fact true, but yet not to know it. The circumstances may be such that one is not entitled to be sure. For instance, a superstitious person who had inadvertently walked under a ladder might be convinced as a result that he was about to suffer some misfortune; and he might in fact be right. But it would not be correct to say that he knew that this was going to be so. He arrived at his belief by a process of reasoning which would not be generally reliable; so, although his prediction came true, it was not a case of knowledge. Again, if someone were fully persuaded of a mathematical proposition by a proof which could be shown to be invalid, he would not, without further evidence, be said to know the proposition, even though it was true. But while it is not hard to find examples of true and fully confident beliefs which in some ways fail to meet the standards required for knowledge, it is not at all easy to determine exactly what these standards are.

One way of trying to discover them would be to consider what would count as satisfactory answers to the question, How do you know? Thus people may be credited with knowing truths of mathematics or logic if they are able to give a valid proof of them, or even if, without themselves being able to set out such a proof, they have obtained this information from someone who can. Claims to know empirical statements may be upheld by a reference to perception, or to memory, or to testimony, or to historical records, or to scientific laws. But such backing is not always strong enough for knowledge. Whether it is so or not depends upon the circumstances of the particular case. If I were asked how I knew that a physical object of a certain sort was in such and such a place, it would, in general, be a sufficient answer for me to say that I could see it; but if my eyesight were bad and the light were dim, this answer might not be sufficient. Even though I was right, it might still be said that I did not really know that the object was there. If I have a poor memory and the event which I claim to remember is remote, my memory of it may still not amount to knowledge, even though in this instance it does not fail me. If a witness is unreliable, his unsupported evidence may not enable us to know that what he says is true, even in a case where we completely trust him and he is not in fact deceiving us. In a given instance it is possible to decide whether the backing is strong enough to justify a claim to knowledge. But to say in general how strong it has to be would require our drawing up a list of the conditions under which perception, or memory, or testimony, or other forms of evidence are reliable. And this would be a very complicated matter, if indeed it could be done at all.

Moreover, we cannot assume that, even in particular instances, an answer to the question How do you know? will always be forthcoming. There may very well be cases in which one knows that something is so without its being possible to say how one knows it. I am not so much thinking now of claims to know facts of immediate experience, statements like "I know that I feel pain," which raise problems of their own into which we shall enter later on. In cases of this sort it may be argued that the question how one knows does not arise. But even when it clearly does arise, it may not find an answer. Suppose that someone were consistently successful in predicting events of a certain kind, events, let us say, which are not ordinarily thought to be predictable, like the results of a lottery. If his run of successes were sufficiently impressive, we might very well come to say that he knew which number would win, even though he did not reach this conclusion by any rational method, or indeed by any method at all. We might say that he knew it by intuition, but this would be to assert no more than that he did know it but that we could not say how. In the same way, if someone were consistently successful in reading the minds of others without having any of the usual sort of evidence, we might say that he knew these things telepathically. But in default of any further explanation this would come down to saying merely that he did know them, but not by any ordinary means. Words like "intuition" and "telepathy" are brought in just to disguise the fact that no explanation has been found.

But if we allow this sort of knowledge to be even theoretically possible, what becomes of the distinction between knowledge and true belief? How does our man who knows what the results of the lottery will be differ from one who only makes a series of lucky guesses? The answer is that, so far as the man himself is concerned, there need not be any difference. His procedure and his state of mind, when he is said to know what will happen, may be exactly the same as when it is said that he is only guessing. The difference is that to say that he knows is to concede to him the right to be sure, while to say that he is only guessing is to withhold it. Whether we make this concession will depend upon the view which we take of his performance. Normally we do not say that people know things unless they have followed one of the accredited routes to knowledge. If someone reaches a true conclusion without appearing to have adequate basis for it, we are likely to say that he does not really know it. But if he were repeatedly successful in a given domain, we might very well come to say that he knew the facts in question, even though we could not explain how he knew them. We should grant him the right to be sure, simply on the basis of his success. This is, indeed, a point on which people's views might be expected to differ. Not everyone would regard a successful run of predictions, however long sustained, as being by itself a sufficient backing for a claim to knowledge. And here there can be no question of proving that this attitude is mistaken. Where there are recognized criteria for deciding when one has the right to be sure, anyone who insists that their being satisfied is still not enough for knowledge may be accused, for what the charge is worth, of misusing the verb "to know." But it is possible to find, or at any rate to devise, examples which are not covered in this respect by any established rule of usage. Whether they are to count as instances of knowledge is then a question which we are left free to decide.

It does not, however, matter very greatly which decision we take. The main problem is to state and assess the grounds on which these claims to knowledge are made, to settle, as it were, the candidate's marks. It is a relatively unimportant question what titles we then bestow upon them. So long as we agree about the marking, it is of no great consequence where we draw the line between the different levels of distinction. If we choose to set a very high standard, we may find ourselves committed to saying that some of what ordinarily passes for knowledge ought rather to be described as probable opinion. And some critics will then take us to task for flouting ordinary usage. But the question is purely one of terminology. It is decided, if at all, on grounds of practical convenience.

One must not confuse this case, where the markings are agreed upon, and what is in dispute is only the bestowal of honours, with the case where it is the markings themselves that are put in question. For this second case is philosophically important, in a way in which the other is not. The sceptic who asserts that we do not know all that we think we know or even perhaps that we do not strictly know anything at all, is not suggesting that we are mistaken when we conclude that the recognized criteria for knowing have been satisfied. Nor is he primarily concerned with getting us to revise our usage of the verb "to know," any more than one who challenges our standards of value is trying to make us revise our usage of the word "good." The disagreement is about the application of the word, rather than its meaning. What the sceptic contends is that our markings are too high; that the grounds on which we are normally ready to concede the right to be sure are worth less than we think; he may even go so far as to say that they are not worth anything at all. The attack is directed, not against the way in which we apply our standards of proof, but against these standards themselves. It has, as we shall see, to be taken seriously because of the arguments by which it is supported.

I conclude then that the necessary and sufficient conditions for knowing that something is the case are first that what one is said to know be true, secondly that one be sure of it, and thirdly that one should have the right to be sure. This right may be earned in various ways; but even if one could give a complete description of them it would be a mistake to try to incorporate our actual standards of goodness into a definition of good. And this being so, it turns out that the questions which philosophers raise about the possibility of knowledge are not all to be settled by discovering what knowledge is. For many of them reappear as questions about the legitimacy of the title to be sure. They need to be severally examined; and this is the main concern of what is called the theory of knowledge.

∽

OVERVIEW

It is an axiom that the questions we ask determine, to great extent, what we know; by the same reasoning the way in which the problem of knowledge is formulated determines what a satisfactory solution to the problem will be.

Ayer's rules for the solution of the problem, as outlined in the previous essay, were such that all scientific statements or statements based on sense experience can be candidates for admission to the body of knowledge, but metaphysical statements can never move beyond mere candidacy.

These rules strike some philosophers as unnecessarily harsh for, as Rachel Goodrich argues in the following article, to restrict knowledge to sense experience is to prohibit the epistemological justification of spiritual, religious, and moral knowledge.

Writing from the standpoint of Neo-Thomism she outlines a Thomistic theory of knowledge—a proposed solution to the problem of knowledge—which would be unacceptable if Ayer's rules (and those of others who speak as strict empiricists) were adopted.

According to St. Thomas, knowledge does indeed start with the senses; but, contrary to some views, knowledge is not a mere inference from the senses. Rather our human senses stand as middleman in the knowing transaction; they are the catalytic agent between the objects of knowledge that exist in the external, objective world and our human knowledge of those objects. A crucial difference between empiricists and Thomists occurs at this point. The empiricist looks on initial sense experience itself as the clearest and most certain element in the knowing process—raw data uncontaminated. By contrast, the Thomist sees initial sense experience as unrefined knowledge most contaminated; confusion enters with sense experience the way static enters with a radio signal—only successive stages of intellectual filtering can isolate the pure signal. The empiricist views sense experience as a pure element found in nature, the Thomist sees it as a natural deposit in which the ore must be melted from the rock. For the Thomist, the senses serve the purpose of experiencing particular objects of knowledge (e.g., Bulldogs, Fido, Golden Retrievers, Spot, Pekes, or Heinz 57) while the intellect abstracts from these sense reports the universals involved (e.g., dogs or dogginess). Put otherwise, every existent object has both its essence and its accidents; in Thomistic nomenclature these accidents are those properties of the object that are variable,[1] while the essential property is fixed and stable—and true knowledge is knowledge of essentials, not of particulars or accidents.

The mind is able to grasp these intelligibles, these essentials, because the distinctive feature of the rational human mind is that it contains within it the seeds of knowledge (but not in a Platonic sense of innate ideas or concepts stored in the mind from a pre-earthly existence and remembered when

---

[1] For example, the curly hair of a Labrador Retriever as opposed to the straight hair of a Dachshund, short tails as opposed to long tails, thick foot pads as opposed to sensitive pads, and so on.

stimulated by the senses or jogged by reasoning). In colloquial terms it might be said these seeds of knowledge, or the potential to know, are part of the built-in equipment of the human knower, f.o.b. at birth.

Knowing, or knowledge, comes about when the mind adequately and accurately conceives an object; or, to put in the context of truth, since truth and knowledge are related in the knowing process, truth is discovered by the mind when our idea of a thing accurately corresponds with the thing itself. Truth is the correspondence of an idea, thought, or statement with an objective fact or condition; and we are said to know when our ideas do indeed correspond to objective reality. This correspondence theory of truth is generally held by all Realist philosophers, not by Thomists alone, although there are sophisticated differences among "Representative Realists," "Presentative Realists," and other forms of philosophic Realism.

Thus the senses do lead to knowledge for the Neo-Thomist; but, as Goodrich indicates, there is other knowledge than sense knowledge. We do have earthly knowledge of such things as trees, fireplugs, Boyle's Law, dogs, statistical correlations, or the structure of the nervous system; but we also have knowledge of such things as God, angels, absolute moral principles, the idea that the whole is greater than the part, and other eternal verities—and *that* knowledge did not come to us through our senses.

If we do have that sort of knowledge, and the Thomist argues that we obviously do, then there must be another source of knowledge; and to restrict knowledge to sense experience is to foreshorten our intellectual horizons and needlessly cast many of our knowledge–hopes (things we would like to know about, and can know about) into the discard pile.

Goodrich not only provides an outline of a Neo-Thomistic theory of knowledge, but she shows how this borrows from and lends to—in a unitarian consistency—concepts about the nature of man and the nature of the universe.

Neo-Thomism and Education

Rachel M. Goodrich*

During the year 1957 the London University Institute of Education published, under the title *Education and the Philosophic Mind*, a series of lectures concerned with "anything in the

* Reprinted by permission from the British *Journal of Educational Studies*, VII (November, 1958).

philosophic thought current in our universities that was capable of fertilizing the work of teachers," and one of the lectures, delivered by Father Lawson, discussed Neo-Thomist ideas. In the United States these ideas have long been familiar in the sphere of education through the writings of Jacques Maritain and others, and since I believe that British educational thinking cannot afford to ignore them, this paper is an attempt to follow up Father Lawson's lead in exploring the educational significance of Neo-Thomism. I shall not here concern myself with St. Thomas' direct educational teachings, which are admirably set forth by Maritain in his book *Education at the Crossroads,* and elsewhere. I want rather to discuss two or three more general Thomist doctrines which have important implications for education.

First, however, I must face the charge frequently made that Neo-Thomism is merely reviving an outmoded synthesis of Aristotelianism with Christian Orthodoxy, and thus is irrelevant for education, as for all departments of modern living. This surely is to misunderstand doubly. For in the first place, Neo-Thomism is no mere revival. "Neo-Thomism," writes Copleston, "is not merely a museum piece; it is a living and developing movement of thought, deriving its inspiration from Aquinas, but conducting its meditation on his writings, in the light of subsequent philosophy, and of subsequent cultural developments in general."[1] And in the second place St. Thomas himself was far more than a mere synthesiser. He was certainly concerned to relate the findings of the human reason with the truths of the Christian Revelation, and also the Greek tradition of thinking with the Hebrew, but he radically transformed Aristotle in the process and the result was a profoundly original philosophy proper to St. Thomas. The originality,

according to his great modern interpreter, Etienne Gilson, consists partly in the fact that as a metaphysician he adopts an "existentialist" as distinct from an "essentialist" approach. For Plato, and even for Aristotle, the core of reality was to be found in the notion of "essence." Beings, or substances, consisted of form and matter—(form being the intelligible element which enables things to be classified and known in terms of concepts, and matter that which distinguishes individuals within the class or species) and it was through concepts that men came to understand the "essential" nature of substances. We move here, it is plain, amid abstractions and in a world of thought rather than of actuality. It was St. Thomas' great achievement that while accepting these categories of substance and essence, and of form and matter, he passes beyond them to a deeper level of reality by affirming an "act-of-being" which is prior to essence and constitutes the living actuality of each existent thing. Because of this preference for the dynamic principle of "existence" over the static concept of "essence" Thomism may claim to be an existential philosophy with a fascinating kinship to, but also a radical dissimilarity from, the modern form of existentialism. Now just how far this existential emphasis is explicit in St. Thomas' own writings, and how far it is a modern development of his ideas is perhaps debatable, but it is after all with the writings of the Neo-Thomists that we are concerned, and such development only serves to establish Thomism as a living and flexible system of thought; and as we discuss one or two Thomist doctrines in greater detail, it will become apparent how

[1] F. C. Copleston, *Aquinas* (London: Pelican), p. 250.

illuminating the existential interpretation can be.

It is clearly impossible in a short paper to cover the vast canvas of the *Summa,* which ranges over the cosmos in its treatment of God, the Angels, and the whole visible creation including man; nor does our earth-bound vision easily follow the order appropriate to St. Thomas. I propose, therefore, to start at the human end, though not as Father Lawson, in the lecture I referred to, with the Thomist doctrine of the human person, but rather with the Thomist theory of knowledge. For it is here, I believe, that Thomism makes its most characteristic contribution to education, and here is the congenial starting point for the modern thinker who is above all preoccupied with epistemology.

The empiricist position of the dominant contemporary British school is an exceedingly narrow one—for the critique of reason from Descartes to Kant, followed by the modern linguistic critique, has landed us with the restriction of knowledge to the sphere of sense experience, not only in its original, but also in its final term since only that is knowledge which can, in principle, be empirically verified. Scientific knowledge then alone is valid. Now the dazzling achievements and promises of the scientific movement perhaps account for the strange fact that many modern philosophers accept with equanimity this radical restriction, which reduces their own function to that of mere logicians; but it is not inconceivable that, as the glamour of science wears off a little, men will not insist on returning to ask the fundamental metaphysical questions, concerning

man's nature and destiny, freedom, immortality and the existence of God. Indeed some men still persist in continuing to ask them even now, and it is surely worth considering an alternative theory of knowledge which permits of the possibility of our attaining some true, even if limited, understanding of the nature of things, and which thus liberates our thinking into wider horizons. Such a theory of knowledge can be drawn from the writings of St. Thomas, though he does not formulate an explicit epistemology; and an admirably lucid explanation of it is to be found in summary in Dr. E. L. Mascall's *Word and Images,* and in more detail in his *Existence and Analogy.*

Its basic tenet is that the human mind is not (as Kant believed) confined only to discursive reasoning but that it has also an intuitive power of apprehending the intelligible and grasping truth. The mind, in medieval terms, consists both of "ratio" and "intellectus." St. Thomas fully agrees with the moderns that sense experience is the starting point, but would reject the view that knowledge consists in an inference from sensation. He would say rather that in perception man uses sense experience as the medium of intellection and through it is able to grasp the intelligible nature of its object.

And just what does the intellect apprehend? Here St. Thomas follows Aristotle in saying that sense experiences the material particulars, and intellect abstracts the intelligible forms as concepts. But this leads to a very unsatisfactory and artificial conclusion that —as Mascall puts it, "The sense can receive particulars but cannot know them; while the intellect can know but can only know universals." He shows, however, that the existential interpretation can solve the difficulty. For the intellect does not stop short at the concept, but in a second movement of "judgment" affirms the universal and affirms its actual existence in the particular, and in both these operations it is intimately connected with the senses in the unity of the perceptual act.[2]

If we would go beyond this description of the mechanism of knowing to ask how it is that the mind is able to grasp the intelligible, the answer is to be found, says Gilson, in the fact that man's mind contains within it the principle or germ of knowledge—not in the form of innate ideas which St. Thomas denies—but in power, at the very first contact with experience, to conceive certain self-evident principles (either simple ones such as the notion of being or unity, or complex ones such as that the whole is greater than the part, or that every event is caused), and these first principles become constitutive of our future thinking.

Man's mind then we may say is apt for the apprehension of the intelligible, but there is also that in things which renders them apt to be apprehended—and here Josef Pieper brings out an interesting connection with the Christian doctrine of creation. "It is the creative fashioning of things by God which makes it possible for them to be known by men."[3] Their intelligibility resides in the fact that they have been creatively thought by God—and truth for

St. Thomas thus has a double reference. Truth consists first in the things themselves as creatures corresponding with the archetypal thoughts of God; and only secondarily applies to true judgments of the human intellect, which, as itself God's creation, is able to conform itself adequately to its object. In this second sense, truth is to be defined as the adequation of the intellect with the thing, an adequation never fully achieved however, since the very creatureliness which makes thing intelligible to us also prevents our ever reaching full comprehension of even the humblest creation, since to do so would be to think as God.

Here then is what has come to be known as the correspondence theory of truth, which, as it stands, needs some development if it is to face up to modern critical theory—and some such developments have already been indicated. For instance, the power of intellectual apprehension cannot now be assumed but must be justified, and this may perhaps be attempted from the empirical standpoint if we accept the contention of D. J. B. Hawkins that basic experience itself is too narrowly conceived and must be widened to permit at least of the distinction between "having a sensation and being aware of a sensation," which "primitive awareness of fact is also the beginning of thought";[4] and this if I understand the argument rightly, might be regarded as equivalent to the basic apprehension of the "intellectus." Secondly, the Realist theory of knowledge is challenged by the modern insistence on the subjectivity

[2] E. L. Mascall, *Existence and Analogy* (London: Longmans), pp. 54–57.

[3] Josef Pieper, *The Silence of St. Thomas* (London: Faber & Faber), p. 61.

[4] D. J. B. Hawkins, *Crucial Problems of Modern Philosophy* (Sheed & Ward), pp. 126, 133.

of perception; but here Dr. Mascall makes an important suggestion that Thomist epistemology should not be interpreted as naive Realism if we remember that the intelligible world we apprehend need not be structurally isomorphic with the world of sensible experience. So that we can grant in the sensible sphere the subjectivity demanded by modern relativity theories, without surrendering the essential objectivity of our understanding of the intelligible structure of reality. And thirdly, as regards the linguistic attack on the feasibility of discourse about metaphysical realities, we must note that the difficulty was keenly appreciated by St. Thomas himself, and that one possible solution lies in the development and refinement of the Thomist doctrine of analogy.

And what then, if we can accept it, is the significance of the Thomist theory of knowledge? To adopt it would, as I implied at the outset, be to reinstate a second kind of thinking alongside that of the scientist—a thinking which, says Mascall, "requires not detachment from the object but involvement with it, not the restriction of attention to the sensible surface but penetration beneath it to the intelligible metaphysical being, not ratiocination but contemplation,"[5] though the word contemplation must not mislead, since it here denotes an intellectual insight derived through sense experience, and is distinct from the directly given spiritual vision of the mystic.

And this re-instatement of the contemplative element in human thinking would have a direct and profound edu-

[5] E. L. Mascall, *Words and Images* (London: Longmans), p. 65.

cational implication. For while freely acknowledging the importance of scientific method, and remaining fully alive to the contemporary need for increased scientific education, we should have to resist, both in the matter and method of education, any exclusive emphasis on scientific thinking. It is, of course, generally agreed that humane subject matter must be retained in the curriculum of every child. But from the Thomist standpoint more is involved. Whatever the subject of study, pupils must be not only taught to think discursively, critically and analytically with a problem-solving purpose in mind, but must also be encouraged and inspired to think disinterestedly and "contemplatively," and to acquire what is sometimes described as a capacity for intellectual wonder. Now it is not easy to see what this means in practical terms of the classroom. But may it not be said that, in some small degree, contemplative thinking is fostered whenever a pupil is led to grasp and appreciate the real significance of a logical or mathematical argument; or helped to gain genuine insight into some human character of literature or history; or prompted and encouraged to ponder those speculative questions which arise so naturally in the minds of adolescents, and to which no precise and clear-cut scientific answers can be given? And if, as Mascall suggests, intellectual wonder is effectively evoked by the "stupendously surprising character" of the natural world, may it not be the occasional duty of our schools to lure children away from their urban environment of human artifacts into country surroundings, and there to confront them with some thought-provoking natural mysteries? And finally, is there not a strong case, with our more intelligent pupils for introducing them, during their last school years, to some actual philosophical study, as a systematic training in contemplative thinking? Though here let it be said that it is not only Philosophy and the Humanities which can inculcate the beginnings of wisdom, but that as Maritain argues, the natural sciences, if they are taught not only for the sake of practical application but essentially for the sake of knowledge, provide man with a vision of the universe, and a sense of the sacred, exacting, unbending objectivity of the humblest truth, which play an essential part in the liberation of the mind, and here perhaps is an important key to the problem of educating the specialist liberally, not only by nourishing his mind with humane subject matter, but by training him to think in the most fully human way.

So much for direct educational implications: there are equally important indirect consequences of holding the Thomist theory of knowledge. For this permits us to ask, and to give reasoned answers, to two questions vital for the defining of educational aims—"What is the nature of man?" and "What is the nature of the Universe?"

The answer to the first comprises the Thomist doctrine of the human person. St. Thomas here strikes an admirable balance between Idealism of all types which stresses spirituality at the expense of the body, and on the other hand of all types of Materialism for which mind is a mere by-product of physical processes. Man is to be conceived neither as an incarnate angel nor as a mere biological organism, but rather, in the words of Maritain, as "a horizon in which two worlds meet."[6] For the human person is a close-knit unity of body and soul, together forming one substance. The soul for St. Thomas, as for Aristotle, is widely conceived as the organizing principle of life in all animate beings, and the rational powers. Its relation to the body is that of form to matter: it constitutes the body as a human body, and conversely if separated from the body cannot be spoken of at all as a human person. However, St. Thomas as a Christian and existentialist thinker transforms Aristotle's doctrine radically. Matter cannot, as with Aristotle, be the sole principle of individuation, nor soul the impersonal form common to the species, for to the Christian the human soul is both unique and immortal. Aquinas does not, says Mascall, "accept a pre-determined scheme of universals and particulars, applying in exactly the same mode to all types of being from the electron to the angel."[7] He starts with the living world of diversified creatures in which individual and specific characteristics are variously combined, and where man, deriving his natural individual characteristics through his human body, possesses also incommunicable spiritual individuality can survive death; for, though the body depends for its very existence upon the soul, the converse is not true, and the soul transcends the physical by exercising what Father Lawson describes as "activities in its own right of thinking, under-

[6] Jacques Maritain, "Thomist Views on Education," *Modern Philosophies and Education* (Chicago: University of Chicago Press), p. 78.

[7] E. L. Mascall, *Words and Images*, p. 62.

standing and willing": but nevertheless the insufficient doctrine of the soul's immortality is completed by the Christian doctrine of bodily resurrection which shall reconstitute the essential unity of the human person.

It is, however, not only balance but a right perspective which is found in this Thomist picture of human nature, for the two elements of body and soul are not to be regarded as indistinguishable or of equal significance. "We cannot insist too much on this," writes Gilson, "that the constitutive functions of the body and soul in the human composite are very unequal. If we consider the problem for the basic point of view of the act of being that of the soul in no way depends upon the body's. The reverse is true."[8] St. Thomas affirms the unity of soul with body, which is the medium for securing the soul's good, and never to be regarded as an evil or illusory thing, yet at the same time he insists on the primacy of the spiritual within the human person.

And all this has clear educational implications vital in an age of technology and automation in which personal values are in peril. Thomism rightly asserts the fundamental educational aim in terms of shaping the human person, subordinating to this all social and vocational claims whatsoever. And again it rightly asserts the freedom and responsibility of each individual in face of the deterministic trend in much educational psychology. Granting this right perspective, however, the insistence of Thomism on psychosomatic unity affords as Maritain says "a philosophic key for the sound interpretation of

great modern discoveries in neurology and psychiatry"; and it results, incidentally, in a proper appreciation of physical education interpreted not only as Gymnastics and Athletics, but also as the training of physical and aesthetic skills, and the perfecting of sense experience as the gateway to knowledge.

And now for our second question—and obviously the most significant of all —What is the nature of the universe? Here the Thomistic doctrine of knowledge makes its most important contribution, not only to education but to our modern life in general. For it offers us the possibility of a reasonable basis for the Christian revelation, in that it shows how natural reason may establish the two truths of God's existence and His creation of the Universe. This is clearly not the time and place to discuss in detail St. Thomas' five proofs for the existence of God (the arguments based on motion, efficient causality, necessary being, degrees of perfection, and design); and indeed modern commentators stress that these are to be interpreted as variations on a single theme. "The Thomistic proofs," says Gilson, "for the existence of God amount, in the last analysis, to a search beyond existences which are not self-sufficient, for an existence which is self-sufficient, and which, because it is so, can be the first cause of all others."[9] This is a thoroughly existential position in which God is conceived as "He Who Is"—in terms of self-subsistent being—whose existence can be apprehended through His effects on His creatures. The argument rests on the claim that the human mind is capable of apprehending the

[8] Etienne Gilson, *The Christian Philosophy of St. Thomas Aquinas* (Gollancz), p. 196.

[9] *Ibid.*, p. 81.

contingency of finite beings, and also of grasping the relation of dependency. Today, it is these apprehensions which are stressed rather than the elements of syllogistic demonstration in St. Thomas' writing. "The argument," writes Mascall, "that if beings exist that are not self-sufficient they derive their being from a being that is self-sufficient is not merely the deduction of one proposition from another by the rules of logic; it results from an understanding of the very nature of non-self-sufficient being . . . What is necessary, in short, if we are to pass from a belief in the existence of finite beings to a belief in the existence of God is not so much that we should thoroughly instruct ourselves in the laws and procedures of formal logic, as that we should thoroughly acquaint ourselves with finite beings and learn to know them as they really are,"[10] a task incidentally which involves all the discipline of contemplative thinking. And he concludes: "The Five Ways are not really five different methods of proving the existence of God, but five different aids to the apprehension of God and the creature in the cosmological relation." We have here, then, not proof in the sense of impregnable logical demonstration, but if we can accept, as I believe we can, the basic assertion, of the Realist theory of knowledge, we have a valid apprehension of God in His creatures based on a natural understanding of finite beings and thus firmly rooted in the empirical world.

There are of course other religious approaches, with their own logic, some relying wholly on the authority of divine revelation, others on the experiences of personal encounter. But, it would seem to me, Thomism is uniquely important in that it provides, as it were, a publicly valid natural theology, which is a necessary basis for the acceptance of the far richer and more significant truths of revelation at a time when God's very existence is widely questioned; and which can moreover serve to objectify the findings of personal religious experience which can never be self-authenticating.

The Thomist position results then in the re-instatement of certain basic religious truths as knowledge in their own right, and this surely is of the greatest educational importance as justifying the giving of religious instruction. Of course, a problem remains as to the precise form of this instruction since the religious truths accessible to human reason are by no means coterminous with the whole body of revealed truth which is diversely interpreted; but at least we are delivered from the dilemma as to whether or not it is a legitimate educational purpose to indoctrinate religiously at all. Acknowledgment of the validity of religious and metaphysical knowledge, moreover, restores to the curriculum a rightful element of hierarchy, and renders possible, in place of our discrete and warring specialisms, a unified "view" of knowledge in Newman's sense, in which all the sciences, natural, human, and divine, have their appointed place as reflections of a unified reality creatively though in the mind of God.

And now for some final estimate of the educational significance of the Thomist revival. In an interesting paper on the Christian idea of education re-

[10] E. L. Mascall, *He Who Is* (London: Longmans), pp. 61, 73.

cently delivered at the Kent School, Connecticut, Dr. Pollard spoke thus: "My thesis is that the most fruitful and significant category within which to consider this subject of the Christian idea of education is that of Renaissance,"[11] and he argued that the classical tradition was rediscovered in the fifteenth century, but that we today need a recovery of our Hebraic heritage. With this I heartily agree and I believe that Neo-Thomism has an important part to play in such a renaissance. Doubtless the Biblical Tradition is of primary import, but the scriptures are essentially non-philosophical, and a theological revival alone might be insufficient to combat the metaphysical deficiencies of our day, and to reinstate natural theology, which, in a critical age, is the indispensable ally of revealed religion. There is, moreover, a peculiar virtue in the Thomist synthesis of natural and divine knowledge in an age which cries aloud for a new synthesis to assimilate the scientific revolution. Nor does the category of renaissance

[11] E. Fuller (ed.), *The Christian Idea of Education* (New Haven, Conn.: Yale University Press), p. 2.

imply stale repetition—indeed it was the classical Renaissance which gave birth to the whole body of modern thought. A Hebrew renaissance would no doubt have similarly creative results. As for the Thomist tradition, it has already, as I have tried to show, revealed itself capable of development (and no doubt far more development is indicated), while at the same time recovering an urgently needed truth— that is, a trust in the intuitive power of the human intellect. It has, of course, its limitations. It has for example been accused of over-intellectualism, though let us never forget that the arguments of St. Thomas in the end gave place to his silence—and that he left the *Summa* incompleted because, as he said, "All that I have written seems to me nothing but straw . . . compared to what I have seen and what has been revealed to me." Of all philosophic systems his is surely the most comprehensive and spacious, and I am certain that modern educational thinkers cannot afford to neglect all the hard thinking, fruitful wisdom and wide charity that are to be found with him whose appropriate title is the Angelic Doctor.

OVERVIEW

Just as the urban planner involved in slum clearance projects often tends to tear down old institutions and familiar landmarks, to bulldoze the ground clean and clear before he constructs his new edifices, so too did John Dewey often introduce his new philosophical ideas by first attacking and attempting to clear away the old, traditional points of view. To ease the curiosity of the sidewalk superintendents architects often put up signs or slogans to describe, in a glittering generality or a flashy phrase, how the new low-cost public housing unit would be superior to the old, run-down tenements; and by the same token the followers of Dewey often use cliches as verbal shortcuts to describe the edifice Dewey was abuilding on epistemological grounds.

Such educational slogans are not adequate substitutes for intellectual discourse about theory; but they can serve the practical purpose of polarizing and encapsulating substantively different points of view. In this case a quick peek into Dewey's epistemological edifice can be gained by glancing at the following slogan-like definitions (and their denied alternatives): For Dewey,

Knowledge is relative	(not absolute)
Knowledge is contextual	(not independent)
Knowledge is hypothetical	(not categorical)
Knowledge is hypothetical	(not intrinsic)
Knowledge is active	(not passive)
Knowledge is created	(not discovered)

Perhaps all of these thumb-nail (or, thumb-nose) descriptions are included in the assertion that knowledge grows out of the problem solving process, that it is the intellectual crown which caps an active attempt to resolve a doubt, ease an irritation, smooth a path, or restore habitual behavior.

The seeds of knowledge lie dormant in experience (recall Thomas' analogy of experience as a great ocean), and grow within yet out of experience. More specifically, knowledge is the outgrowth of inquiry, where (according to Dewey's *Logic*),

Inquiry is the controlled or directed transformation of an indeterminate situation into one that is so determinate in its constituent distinctions and relations as to convert the elements of the original situation into a unified whole.

The main principles of Dewey's problem solving method—imbalance, problem formulation, data gathering, hypothesis, experimentation, verification—are, as a result of constant reformulation, reinterpretation, and discussion, so well known and so readily available elsewhere that they do not require extensive restatement or treatment here. In point of fact, so much attention has been paid to the process of inquiry (i.e., to the method of coming to know) that the *antecedent* conditions of inquiry have often been neglected, overlooked, or misinterpreted even by such philosophers as Bertrand Russell, A. J. Ayer, and Hans Reichenbach. Dewey, however, pays especial attention to the antecedent conditions of inquiry for he is aware that what we know grows out of the questions we ask. F. S. C. Northrup, for instance, applauds Dewey's logic by declaring (in *The Logic of the Sciences and Humanities*) that

Dewey has the correct answer to our question concerning the positive method to be used in initiating inquiry. His prescription is correct because it affirms a tautology, the tautology, namely, that one must begin inquiry with what one has at the beginning, namely, the problem.

But Northrup, too, misinterprets Dewey's theory of knowledge for Dewey does not mean to say (nor does he say) that inquiry starts with a problem. Rather, he insists that it must begin with what there is at the beginning: *an indeterminate situation.* When this indeterminate situation is subjected to inquiry then it is transformed, psychologically as well as logically, into a problematic situation; and it is out of this problematic situation that a specific problem is defined and only then are the more formalized steps in the problem solving process undertaken.

The components of the antecedents to inquiry are the indeterminate situation, the problematic situation, and the definition of the problem. Because these antecedent conditions have often been neglected and because the logical distinction between them is so easily blurred (which in turn may result in a blurred or unsatisfactory solution), a brief analysis of the terms and concepts involved in Dewey's epistemology will be helpful.

By *situation* is meant a total experiential matrix, for all situations are pluralistic, not monistic. Dewey offers this definition:

> What is designated by the word "situation" is *not* a single object or event or set of objects and events. For we never experience nor form judgments about objects and events in isolation, but only in connection with a contextual whole. This latter is what is called a "situation."

If a situation is a contextual whole, then the indeterminate situation is that kind of situation in which the components—subjects, objects, events, and relationships—are, as Dewey describes them, "disturbed, troubled, ambiguous, confused, full of conflicting tendencies, obscure . . ." It is the indeterminate situation that, by its very nature, provokes inquiry. It is important to note that it is *the situation* that possesses the traits of disturbance, ambiguity, confusion, and obscurity; these are the qualities of the situation itself, not merely of the inquirer.[1] This distinction plays such a key role in Dewey's pragmatic epistemology that he was very careful to identify the difference between the doubtful situation and the doubtful inquirer:

> *We* are doubtful because the situation is inherently doubtful. Personal states of doubt that are not evoked by and are not relative to some existential situation are pathological. . . . It is, accordingly, a mistake to suppose that a situation is doubtful only in a "subjective" sense.

It is out of this indeterminate situation that the problematic situation evolves; the indeterminacy which is inherent in such a situation is logically

---

[1] It should be noted that attributing such properties to the situation itself is an ontological statement; it is to say something about the nature of experience as such.

antecedent to the problematic situation. When attention is turned toward an indeterminate situation, when an inquirer initially cognizes the indeterminate situation as presenting difficulties to be identified, then—and by that token—it is transformed into a problematic situation. The catalyst in this transformation is intellectual; it involves a human judgment about the situation. That is, no situation is problematic until it is so judged by a knower who is in that situation; it is this value judgment that qualifies the situation, that changes it from an indeterminate to a problematic situation—and insofar as the person making this judgment is himself a part of the situation his very action in adjudging it problematic entails a qualitative change in the situation: it is no longer merely indeterminate, it is now problematic.

This distinction between an indeterminate and problematic situation may seem of verbal importance only, but it is considerably more than that since it is at this stage of inquiry that human values shape the balance of the process of coming to know. Dewey says that the

indeterminate situation might have been called a *problematic* situation [but] this name would have been, however, proleptic and anticipatory. The indeterminate situation becomes problematic in the very process of being subjected to inquiry.

The indeterminate situation is precognitive; because the doubtfulness that characterizes it is *in* the situation itself there can be nothing intellectual or cognitive in it at that stage of inquiry. But what logically follows is that this non-cognitive, indeterminate situation is the necessary precondition of cognitive inquiry. When, therefore, cognition or reflection is directed toward it the problematic situation emerges:

The first result of evocation of inquiry is that the situation is taken, adjudged, to be problematic. To see that a situation requires inquiry is the initial step in inquiry.

Here Dewey has made the distinction, often overlooked by other logicians, between the "given" and the "taken." What is given to an inquirer is an indeterminate situation and this, being given, is the logical starting place of inquiry; what is taken by the inquirer is the problematic situation.

The definition of a specific problem, or of specific problem areas, is the next step in this theory of knowledge. The distinction just made between the indeterminate and problematic situation is logically fine and empirically accurate, but in itself does not carry the process of inquiry very far. It is the first necessary step in the definition of a specific problem, for it is out of the problematic situation that specific problems to be solved are evolved. In Dewey's words,

A problem represents the partial transformation by inquiry of a problematic situation into a determinate situation. It is a familiar and significant saying that a problem well put is half-solved.

The definition of a problem, therefore, clearly suggests that the inquirer is well along into the process of coming to know. Thus, when Northrup and others (*supra*) assert that inquiry begins with the definition of the problem they are glossing over some subtle empirical features preceding formal inquiry, features which require logical distinction. But even with this extended attention to the antecedents of inquiry many philosophers (most publically "A," to whom a letter from Dewey was appended in *Knowing and the Known*) have not fully grasped the meaning and importance of these antecedent conditions, especially of the problematic situation. Attempting to explain the meaning of the word "problematic" to "A," Dewey said:

> That word stands for the existence of something questionable, and hence provocative of investigation, examination, discussion—in short, inquiry. However, the word "problematic" covers such a great variety of occasions for inquiry that it may be helpful to specify a number of them. It covers the features that are designated by such adjectives as confusing, perplexing, disturbed, unsettled, indecisive; and by such nouns as jars, hitches, breaks, blocks—in short, all incidents occasioning an interruption of the smooth, straightforward course of behavior and that deflect it into the kind of behavior constituting inquiry.

The problematic situation which constitutes an antecedent condition of inquiry thus assumes an importance prior, but not superior, to the method of inquiry: the technique of solution emerges from the problem as defined by the inquirer, and because the resolution of the problem is dependent upon the technique of the solution it follows that the solution is, in turn, dependent upon the definition of the problematic situation and the analysis of the specific problem.

Since the indeterminate situation is given, and the problematic situation is taken, error cannot be a logical property of the antecedent conditions of inquiry; yet, if the constituents of the problematic situation are misunderstood or misanalyzed in the formulation of a specific problem, then the error which occurs there must necessarily be reflected in the solution of the problem. Dewey says:

> From the standpoint of the conduct of inquiry it directly follows that the nature of the problem as well as the solution to be reached is *under* inquiry; failure in solution is sure to result if the problem has not been properly located and described.

Just as inquiry initiates with an indeterminate situation, so too does it terminate with the transformation, or reconstruction, of that into a determinate situation. Put otherwise, the solution of the inquirer, to be judged successful, must make determinate an originally indeterminate situation. To do this it is not only necessary to transform an indeterminate situation into a problematic situation, but to define accurately the problem. The problem is solved, accordingly, when a once indeterminate situation becomes determinate; in the ultimate meaning of the word that is the pragmatic test for Dewey. He summarizes this method of inquiry, or theory of coming to know, thus:

> Inquiry is the directed or controlled transformation of an indeterminate situation into a determinately unified one. The transition is achieved by means of operations of two kinds which are in functional correspondence with each other. One kind of operation deals with ideational or conceptual subject-matter. This subject-matter stands for possible ways and ends of resolution. . . . The other kind of operation is made up of activities involving the techniques and organs of observation. Since these operations are existential they modify the prior existential situation, bring into high relief conditions previously obscure. . . . The ground and criterion of the execution of this work of emphasis, selection and arrangement, is to delimit the problem in such a way that existential material may be provided with which to test the ideas that represent possible modes of solution. Symbols, defining terms and propositions, carry forward both ideational and existential subject-matters in order that [the problem may be solved].

What is crucial in Dewey's epistemology, therefore, is the ideational identification and formulation of the problem by the inquirer. The indeterminate and problematic situations provide the existential matrix from which the problem is given and taken; once the familiar elements in the problematic situation have been recognized it is possible to define what remains—the unfamiliar, doubtful elements—in terms of an end in view. These processes, while an empirical part of the method of inquiry, are primarily philosophic in nature for it is the problem situation and its characteristics as revealed by philosophic analysis that must guide inquirers to those facts which are relevant to defined problems and, once those facts are identified, to the relevant hypotheses and eventually to the relevant methods of testing and verifying.

The establishment of this end in view (i.e., the desired solution to a problem) is reflective in nature. It is part of what has been called "trial by imagination" because the end in view, in this ideational trial, is seen to resolve an indeterminate situation; this intellectual rehearsal becomes the basis for a trial in experience. In this sense philosophy provides guidance to the experimental conditions of inquiry and influences, if it does not direct, the solution of problems.

From a pragmatic point of view, then, the method of coming to know is dependent upon value judgments in the beginning and the end. In the beginning because inquiry starts with the transformation of an indeterminate situation into a problematic situation, and this transformation—being judgmental—is valuational in nature. In the end because the solution chosen or found, of all possible solutions that might have been chosen or found, is judged strictly in terms of the problematic situation as evaluated earlier. Put simply, the solution satisfies or it does not satisfy; if it is satisfactory it is so only in terms of the original situation which is now, by virtue of some achieved end-in-view, determinate in all its aspects.

This method of inquiry, this epistemology, is appropriate to any area of human activity; it is not restricted, and should not be, Dewey argued, to physical science. Thomas, for instance, argues that the Deweyan formulation "is not restricted to science. It is logically appropriate to any area of human inquiry . . ." Victor Lenzen, describing Einstein's theory of knowledge, said that "he [Einstein] initiates his critical reflections concerning theoretical physics with an analysis of concepts which serve to interpret common experience."

The point being made, of course, is that from the pragmatic viewpoint the fundamental (indeed, the only) subject matter of inquiry is human experience. It is for this reason, among others, that Dewey often referred to his philosophy as "experimentalism" rather than "pragmatism."

In the following essay Dewey discusses the three central themes in his epistemology: a theory of meaning, a theory of knowledge, and a theory of truth.

The Instrumental Theory of Knowledge

John Dewey*

I. MEANINGS, VALID AND INVALID

Ghosts, centaurs, tribal gods, Helen of Troy and Ophelia of Denmark are as much the meanings of events as are flesh and blood, horses, Florence Nightingale and Madame Curie. This statement does not mark a discovery; it enunciates a tautology. It seems questionable only when its significance is altered; when it is taken to denote that, because they are all meanings of events, they all are the same kind of meaning with respect to validity of reference.

* Reprinted by permission from *Intelligence in the Modern World*, ed. Joseph Ratner (New York: The Modern Library, 1939), pp. 925–945.

Because perception of a ghost does not signify a subtle, intangilble form, filling space as it moves about, it does not follow that it may not signify some other existential happening like disordered nerves, a religious animistic tradition; or, as in the play of Hamlet, that it may not signify an enhancement of the meaning of a moving state of affairs. The existential events that form a drama have their own characteristic meanings, which are not the less meanings of those events because their import is dramatic, not authentically cognitive. So when men gather in secret to plot a conspiracy, their plans are not the less meanings of certain events because they have not been already carried out; and they remain meanings of events even if the conspiracy comes to naught.

The proposition that the perception of a horse is objectively valid and that of a centaur fanciful and mythical does not denote that one is a meaning of natural events and the other is not. It denotes that they are meanings referable to different natural events, and that confused and harmful consequences result from attributing them to the same events. The idea that the consciousness of a horse as now present and of a centaur differ as perceptions, or states of awareness, is an illustration of the harm wrought by introspective psychology, which, here as elsewhere, treats relationships of objects as if they were inherent qualities of an immediate subject-matter, ignoring the fact that causal relationships to unperceived things are involved. The matter of the cognitive validity of the horse-perception and the cognitive invalidity of the centaur-perception is not an affair of intrinsic difference in the two perceptions, which inspection of the two states of awareness as such can ever bring to light; it is a causal matter, brought to light as we investigate the causal antecedents and consequents of the events having the meanings.

In other words, the difference between assertion of a perception, belief in it, and merely having it is an extrinsic difference; the belief, assertion, cognitive reference is something additive, never merely immediate. Genuinely to believe the centaur-meaning is to assert that events characterized by it interact in certain ways with other now unperceived events. Since belief that centaur has the same kind of objective meaning as has horse denotes expectation of like

efficacies and consequences, the difference of validity between them is extrinsic. It is capable of being revealed only by the results of acting upon them. The awareness of centaur meaning is fanciful not simply because part of its conditions lie within the organism; part of the conditions of any perception, valid as well as invalid, scientific as well as esthetic, lie within the organism. Nor is it fanciful, simply because it is supposed not to have adequate existential antecedents. Natural conditions, physiological, physical and social, may be specified in one case as in the other. But since the conditions in the two cases are different, consequences are bound to be different. Knowing, believing, involves something additive and extrinsic to having a meaning.

No knowledge is ever merely immediate. The proposition that the perception of a horse is valid and that a centaur is fanciful or hallucinatory, does not denote that there are two modes of awareness, differing intrinsically from each other. It denotes something with respect to causation, namely, that while both have their adequate antecedent conditions, the specific causal conditions are ascertained to be different in the two cases. Hence it denotes something with respect to consequences, namely, that action upon the respective meanings will bring to light (to apparency or awareness) such different kinds of consequences that we should use the two meanings in very different ways. Both acts and consequences lie outside the primary perceptions; both have to be diligently sought for and tested. Since conditions in the two cases are different, they operate differently. That is, they belong to different histories, and the matter of the history to which a given thing belongs is just the matter with which knowledge is concerned.

The conscious or perceived affair is itself a consequence of antecedent conditions. But were this conscious or apparent (evident, focal) consequence the only consequence of the conditions, if there were not other as yet unapparent consequences, we should have absolutely no way to tell in what sequence of events a perception belongs, and hence absolutely no way of determining its validity or cognitive standing. It is because conditions which generate the perception of a horse have other and different consequences that the perception (and similarly of those which generate the idea of the centaur), that it is possible to make a distinction between the value in knowledge of the two ideas. By discovering the different sequential affairs to which they respectively belong we can differentiate their import for knowledge. Failure to recognize this fact is the ultimate condemnation, it may be remarked in passing, of idealistic theories of knowledge, which identify knowledge with immediate consciousness. If an all-inclusive consciousness were to exist, it would be a piece of esthetic scenery, interesting or tedious as the case might be, but having no conceivable cognitive standing.

That a perception is cognitive means, accordingly, that it is used; it is treated as a sign of conditions that implicate other as yet unperceived consequences in addition to the perception itself. That a perception is truly cognitive means that its active use or treatment is followed by consequences which fit

appropriately into the other consequences which follow independently of its being perceived. To discover that a perception or an idea is cognitively invalid is to find that the consequences which follow form acting upon it entangle and confuse the other consequences which follow from the causes of the perception, instead of integrating or coordinating harmoniously with them. The special technique of scientific inquiry may be defined as consisting of procedures which make it possible to perceive the eventual agreement or disagreement of the two sets of consequences. For experience proves that it is possible for great disparity between them to exist, and yet the conflict not be perceived or else be explained away as of no importance.

II. KNOWLEDGE AS INSTRUMENTAL AND HYPOTHETICAL

There is no miracle in the fact that tool and material are adapted to each other in the process of reaching a valid conclusion. Were they external in origin to each other and to the result, the whole affair would, indeed, present an insoluble problem—so insoluble that, if this were the true condition of affairs, we never should even know that there was a problem. But, in truth, both material and tool have been secured and determined with reference to economy and efficiency in effecting the end desired—the maintenance of a harmonious experience. The builder has discovered that his building means building tools, and also building material. Each has been slowly evolved with reference to its fit employ in the entire function; and this evolution has been checked at every point by reference to its own correspondent. The carpenter has not thought at large on his building and then constructed tools at large, but has thought of his building in terms of the material which enters into it, and through that medium has come to the consideration of the tools which are helpful.

Thinking is adaptation to an end through the adjustment of particular objective contents. The thinker, like the carpenter, is at once stimulated and checked in every stage of his procedure by the particular situation which confronts him. A person is at the stage of wanting a new house: well, then, his materials are available resources, the price of labor, the cost of building, the state and needs of his family, profession, etc.; his tools are paper and pencil and compass, or possibly the bank as a credit instrumentality, etc. Again, the work is beginning. The foundations are laid. This in turn determines its own specific materials and tools. Again, the building is almost ready for occupancy. The concrete process is that of taking away the scaffolding, clearing up the grounds, furnishing and decorating rooms, etc. This specific operation again determines its own fit or relevant materials and tools. It defines the time and mode and manner of beginning and ceasing to use them. Logical theory will get along as well as does the practice of knowing when it sticks close by and observes the directions and checks inherent in each successive phase of the evolution of the cycle of experience. The problem in general of validity of the thinking process as distinct from the validity of this or that process arises

only when thinking is isolated from its historic position and its material context.

In the course of changing experience we keep our balance in moving from situations of an affectional quality to those which are practical or appreciative or reflective, because we bear constantly in mind the context in which any particular distinction presents itself. As we submit each characteristic function and situation of experience to our gaze, we find it has a dual aspect. Wherever there is striving there are obstacles; wherever there is affection there are persons who are attached; wherever there is doing there is accomplishment; wherever there is appreciation there is value; wherever there is thinking there is material-in-question. We keep our footing as we move from one attitude to another, from one characteristic quality to another, because of the position occupied in the whole movement by the particular function in which we are engaged.

The distinction between each attitude and function and its predecessor and successor is serial, synamic, operative. The distinctions within any given operation or function are structural, contemporaneous, and distributive. Thinking follows striving, and doing follows thinking. Each in the fulfilment of its own function inevitably calls out its successor. But coincident, simultaneous, and correspondent within doing is the distinction of doer and of deed; within the functions of thought, of thinking and material thought upon; within the function of striving, of obstacle and aim, of means and end. We keep our paths straight because we do not confuse the sequential and functional relationship of types of experience with the contemporaneous and structural distinctions of elements within a given function. In the seeming maze of endless confusion and unlimited shiftings, we find our way by the means of the stimulations and checks occurring within the process in which we are actually engaged. Operating within empirical situations we do not contrast or confuse a condition which is an element in the formation of one operation with the status which is one of the distributive terms of another function. When we ignore these specific empirical clews and limitations, we have at once an insoluble, because meaningless, problem upon our hands.

All knowledge, as issuing from reflection, is experimental in the literal physical sense of experimental. Thinking, or knowledge—getting, is far from being the armchair thing it is often supposed to be. The reason it is not an armchair thing is that it is not an event going on exclusively within the cortex or the cortex and vocal organs. It involves the explorations by which relevant data are procured and the physical analyses by which they are refined and made precise; it comprises the readings by which information is got hold of, the words which are experimented with, and the calculations by which the significance of entertained conceptions or hypotheses is elaborated. Hands and feet, apparatus and appliances of all kinds are as much a part of it as changes in the brain. Since these physical operations (including the cerebral events) and equipments are a part of thinking, thinking is mental, not because of a peculiar stuff which enters into it or of peculiar non-natural activ-

ities which constitute it, but because of what physical acts and appliances do: the distinctive purpose for which they are employed and the distinctive results which they accomplish.

That reflection terminates, through a definitive overt act,[1] in another non-reflectional situation, within which incompatible responses may again in time be aroused, and so another problem in reflection be set, goes without saying. Certain things about this situation, however, do not at the present time speak for themselves and need to be set forth. Let me in the first place call attention to an ambiguity in the term "knowledge." The statement that all knowledge involves reflection—or, more concretely, that it denotes an inference from evidence—gives offense to many; it seems a departure from fact as well as a wilful limitation of the word "knowledge."

(1) It may well be admitted that there is a real sense in which knowledge (as distinct from thinking or inquiring with a guess attached) does not come into existence till thinking has terminated in the experimental act which fulfils the specifications set forth in thinking. But what is also true is that the object thus determined is an object of knowledge only because of the thinking which has preceded it and to which it sets a happy term. To run against a hard and painful stone is not of itself, I should say, an act of knowing; but if running into a hard and painful thing is an outcome predicted after inspection of data and elaboration of a hypothesis, then the hardness and

---

[1] For emphasis I am here exaggerating by condensing into a single decisive act an operation which is continuously going on.

the painful bruise which define the thing as a stone also constitute it emphatically an object of knowledge. In short the object of knowledge in the strict sense is its objective; and this objective is not constituted till it is reached. Now this conclusion—as the word denotes—is thinking brought to a close, done with.

If the reader does not find this statement satisfactory, he may at least recognize that the doctrine set forth has no difficulty in connecting knowledge with inference, and at the same time admitting that knowledge in the emphatic sense does not exist till inference has ceased. Seen from this point of view, so-called immediate knowledge or simple apprehension or acquaintance knowledge represents a critical skill, a certainty of response which has accrued in consequence of reflection. A like sureness of footing apart from prior investigations and testings is found in instinct and habit. I do not deny that these may be better than knowing, but I see no reason for complicating an already too confused situation by giving them the name "knowledge" with its usual intellectual implications. From this point of view, the subject-matter of knowledge is precisely that which we do not think of, or mentally refer to in any way, being that which is taken as matter of course, but it is nevertheless knowledge in virtue of the inquiry which has led up to it.

(2) Definiteness, depth, and variety of meaning attach to the objects of an experience just in the degree in which they have been previously thought about, even when present in an experience in which they do not evoke infer-

ential procedures at all. Such terms as "meaning," "significance," "value," have a double sense. Sometimes they mean a function: the office of one thing representing another, or pointing to it as implied; the operation, in short, of serving as sign. In the word "symbol" this meaning is practically exhaustive. But the terms also sometimes mean an inherent quality, a quality intrinsically characterizing the thing experienced and making it worthwhile. The word "sense," as in the phrase "sense of a thing" (and non-sense) is devoted to this use as definitely as are the words "sign" and "symbol" to the other. In such a pair as "import" and "importance," the first tends to select the reference to another thing while the second names an intrinsic content.

In reflection, the extrinsic reference is always primary. The height of the mercury means rain; the color of the flame means sodium; the form of the curve means factors distributed accidentally. In the situation which follows upon reflection, meanings are intrinsic; they have no instrumental or subservient office, because they have no office at all. They are as much qualities of the objects in the situation as are red and black, hard and soft, square and round. And every reflective experience adds new shades of such intrinsic qualifications. In other words, while reflective knowing is instrumental to gaining control in a troubled situation (and thus has a practical or utilitarian force), it is also instrumental to the enrichment of the immediate significance of subsequent experiences. And it may well be that this by-product, this gift of the gods, is incomparably more valuable for living a life than is the primary and intended result of control, essential as is that control to having a life to live.

Words are treacherous in this field; there are no accepted criteria for assigning or measuring their meanings; but if one use the term "consciousness" to denote immediate values of objects, then it is certainly true that "consciousness is a lyric cry even in the midst of business." But it is equally true that if someone else understands by consciousness the function of effective reflection, then consciousness is a business —even in the midst of writing or singing lyrics. But the statement remains inadequate until we add that knowing as a business, inquiry and invention as enterprises, as practical acts, become themselves charged with the meaning of what they accomplish as their own immediate quality. There exists no disjunction between esthetic qualities which are final yet idle, and acts which are practical or instrumental. The latter have their own delights and sorrows.

The intellectual definition or delimitation assigned to the "given" is as tentative and experimental as that ascribed to the idea. In form both are categorical, and in content both are hypothetical. Facts really exist just as facts, and meanings exist as meanings. One is no more superfluous, more subjective, or less necessitated than the other. In and of themselves as existences both are equally realistic and compulsive. But on the basis of existence, there is no element in either which may be strictly described as intellectual or cognitional. There is only a practical situation in its brute and unrationalized form.

What is uncertain about the facts as given at any moment is whether the right exclusions and selections have been made. Since that is a question which can be decided finally only by the experimental issue, this ascription of character is itself tentative and experimental. If it works, the characterization and delineation are found to be proper ones; but every admission prior to inquiry, of unquestioned, categorical, rigid objectivity, compromises the probability that it will work. The character assigned to the datum must be taken as hypothetically as possible in order to preserve the elasticity needed for easy and prompt consideration. Any other procedure virtually insists that all facts and details anywhere happening to exist and happening to present themselves (all being equally real) must all be given equal status and equal weight, and that their outer ramifications and internal complexities must be indefinitely followed up. The worthlessness of this sheer accumulation of realities, its total irrelevancy, the lack of any way of judging the significance of the accumulations are good proofs of the fallacy of any theory which ascribes objective logical content to facts wholly apart from the needs and possibilities of a situation.

The more stubbornly one maintains the full reality of either his facts or his ideas, just as they stand, the more accidental is the discovery of relevantly significant facts and of valid ideas—the more accidental, the less rational, is the issue of the knowledge situation. Due progress is reasonably probable in just the degree in which the meaning, categorical in its existing imperativeness, and the fact, equally categorical in its brute coerciveness, are assigned only a provisional and tentative nature with reference to control of the situation. That this surrender of a rigid and final character for the content of knowledge on the sides both of fact and of meaning, in favor of experimental and functioning estimations, is precisely the change which has marked the development of modern from medieval and Greek science, seems undoubted.

To learn the lesson one has only to contrast the rigidity of phenomena and conceptions in Greek thought (Platonic ideas, Aristotelian forms) with the modern experimental selection and determining of facts and experimental employment of hypotheses. The former have ceased to be ultimate realities of a nondescript sort and have become provisional data; the latter have ceased to be eternal meanings and have become working theories. The fruitful application of mathematics and the evolution of a technique of experimental inquiry have coincided with this change. That realities exist independently of their use as intellectual data, and that meanings exist apart from their utilization as hypotheses, are the permanent truths of Greek realism as against the exaggerated subjectivism of modern philosophy; but the conception that this existence is to be defined in the same way as are contents of knowledge, so that perfect being is object of perfect knowledge and imperfect being object of imperfect knowledge, is the fallacy which Greek thought projected into modern. Science has advanced in its methods in just the degree in which it has ceased to assume that prior realities and prior meanings retain fixedly and finally, when entering into reflective situations, the characters they had prior to this entrance; and in which it has realized that their very presence within the knowledge situation signifies that they have to be redefined and revalued from the standpoint of the new situation.

III. EXPERIMENTAL VERIFICATION AND TRUTH

That fruitful thinking—thought that terminates in valid knowledge—goes on in terms of the distinction of facts and judgment, and that valid knowledge is precisely genuine correspondence or agreement, of some sort, of fact and judgment, is the common and undeniable assumption. But the discussions are largely carried on in terms of an epistemological dualism, rendering the solution of the problem impossible in virtue of the very terms in which it is stated. The distinction is at once identified with that between mind and matter, consciousness and objects, the psychical and the physical, where each of these terms is supposed to refer to some fixed order of existence, a world in itself. Then, of course, there comes up the question of the nature of the agreement, and of the recognition of it. What is the experience in which the survey of both idea and existence is made and their agreement recognized? Is it an idea? Is the agreement ultimately a matter of self-consistency of ideas? Then what has become of the postulate that truth is agreement of idea with existence beyond idea? Is it an absolute which transcends and absorbs the difference? Then, once more, what is the test of any specific judgment? What has become of the correspondence of fact and thought? Or, more urgently, since the pressing problem of life, of practice and of science, is the discrimi-

nation of the relative, or superior, validity of this or that theory, plan, or interpretation, what is the criterion of truth
within present non-absolutistic experience, where the distinction between
factual conditions and thoughts and the
necessity of some working adjustment
persists?

Putting the problem in yet another
way, either both fact and idea are present all the time or else only one of them
is present. But if the former, why
should there be an idea at all, and why
should it have to be tested by the fact?
When we already have what we want,
namely, existence, reality, why should
we take up the wholly supernumerary
task of forming more or less imperfect
ideas of those facts, and then engage in
the idle performance of testing them by
what we already know to be? But if
only ideas are present, it is idle to speak
of comparing an idea with facts and
testing its validity by its agreement.
The elaboration and refinement of ideas
to the uttermost still leaves us with an
idea, and while a self-consistent idea
stands a show of being true in a way in
which an incoherent one does not, a
self-consistent idea is still but a hypothesis, a candidate for truth. Ideas are
not made true by getting bigger. But
if only "facts" are present, the whole
conception of agreement is once more
given up—not to mention that such a
situation is one in which there is by
definition no thinking or reflective factor at all.

This suggests that a strictly monistic epistemology, whether idealistic
or realistic, does not get rid of the problem. Suppose for example we take a
sensationalistic idealism. It does away
with the ontological gulf between ideas

and facts, and by reducing both terms
to a common denominator seems to facilitate fruitful discussion of the problem. But the problem of the distinction
and reference (agreement, correspondence) of two types or sorts of sensations
still persists. If I say the box there is
square, and call "box" one of a group
of ideas or sensations and "square" another sensation or "idea," the old question comes up: Is "square" already a
part of the "facts" of the box, or is it
not? If it is, it is a supernumerary, an
idle thing, both as an idea and as an
assertion of fact; if it is not, how can we
compare the two ideas, and what on
earth or in heaven does their agreement
or correspondence mean? If it means
simply that we experience the two "sensations" in juxtaposition, then the same
is true, of course, of any casual association or hallucination. On the sensa-
tional basis, accordingly, there is still
a distinction of something "given"
"there," brutally factual, the box, and
something else which stands on a different level, ideal, absent, intended, demanded, the "square" which is asserted
to hold good or be true of the thing
"box." The fact that both are sensations
throws no light on the logical validity
of any proposition or belief, because by
theory a like statement holds of every
possible proposition.

The same problem recurs on a realistic basis. For example, there has recently been propounded the doctrine of
the distinction between relations of
space and time and relations of meaning or significance, as a key to the
problem of knowledge. Things exist in
their own characters, in their temporal
and spatial relations. When knowledge
intervenes, there is nothing new of a

subjective or psychical sort, but simply a new relation of the things—the suggesting or signifying of one thing by another. Now this seems to be an excellent way of stating the logical problem, but, I take it, it states and does not solve. For the characteristic of such situations, claiming to terminate in knowledge, is precisely that the meaning—relation is predicated of the other relations; it is referred to them; it is not simply a supervention existing side by side with them, like casual suggestions or the play of fantasy. It is something which the facts, the qualitative space and time things, must bear the burden of, must accept and take unto themselves as part of themselves. Until this happens, we have only "thinking," not accomplished knowledge. Hence, logically, the existential relations play the role of fact, and the relation of signification that of idea, distinguished from fact and yet, if valid, to hold of fact. In other words, "ideas" is a term capable of assuming any definition which is logically appropriate—say, meaning. It need not have anything to do with the conception of little subjective entities or psychical stuffs.

This appears quite clearly in the following quotation: "It is the ice which means that it will cool the water, just as much as it is the ice which does cool the water when put into it." There is, however, a possible ambiguity in the statement. That the "ice" (the thing regarded as ice) suggests cooling is as real as is a case of actual cooling. But, of course, not every suggestion is valid. The "ice" may be a crystal, and it will not cool water at all. So far as it is already certain that this is ice, and also certain that ice, under all circum-stances, cools water, the meaning-relation stands on the same level as the physical, being not merely suggested, but part of the facts ascertained. It is not a meaning-relation as such at all. We already have truth; the entire work of knowing as logical is done; we have no longer the relation characteristic of reflective situations. Here again the implication of the thinking situation is of some "correspondence" or "agreement" between two sets of distinguished relations; the problem of valid determination remains the central question of any theory of knowing in its relation to facts and truth.

I hope the above statement of the difficulty, however inadequate, will serve at least to indicate that a functional logic inherits the problem in question and does not create it; that it has never for a moment denied the prima facie working distinction between "ideas," "thoughts," and "facts," "existences," "the environment," or the necessity of a control of meaning by facts. It is concerned not with denying, but with understanding. What is denied is not the genuineness of the problem of the terms in which it is stated, but the reality and value of the orthodox interpretation. What is insisted upon is the relative, instrumental, or working character of the distinction—that it is a logical distinction, instituted and maintained in the interests of intelligence, with all that intelligence imports in the exercise of the life functions.

It may prove convenient to take an illustration of a man lost in the woods, taking this case as typical of any reflective situation insofar as it involves perplexity—a problem to be solved. The problem is to find a correct idea of the way home—a practical idea or plan of action which will lead to success, or the realization of the purpose to get home. Now the critics of the experimental theory of logic make the point that this practical idea, the truth of which is evidenced in the successful meeting of a need, is dependent for its success upon a purely presentative idea, that of the existent environment, whose validity has nothing to do with success but depends on agreement with the given state of affairs. It is said that what makes a man's idea of his environment true is its agreement with the actual environment, and "generally a true idea in any situation consists in its agreement with reality." I have already indicated my acceptance of this formula. But it was long my misfortune not to be possessed off hand of those perfectly clear notions of just what is meant in this formula by the terms "idea," "existence," and "agreement" which are possessed by other writers on epistemology; and when I analyzed these notions I found the distinction between the practical idea and the theoretical not fixed nor final, and I found a somewhat startling similarity between the notions of "success" and "agreement."

Just what is the environment of which an idea is to be formed: i.e., what is the intellectual content or objective detail to be assigned to the term "environment?" It can hardly mean the actual visible environment—the trees, rocks, etc., which a man is actually looking at. These things are there and it seems superfluous to form an idea of them; moreover, the wayfaring man, though lost, would have to be an unusually perverse fool if under such circumstances he were unable to form an idea (supposing he chose to engage in this luxury) in agreement with these facts. The environment must be a larger environment than the visible facts; it must include things not within the direct ken of the lost man; it must, for instance, extend from where he is now to his home, or to the point from which he started. It must include unperceived elements in their contrast with the perceived. Otherwise the man would not be lost. Now we are at once struck with the facts that the lost man has no alternative except either to wander aimlessly or else to conceive this inclusive environment; and that this conception is just what is meant by idea. It is not some little psychical entity or piece of consciousness-stuff, but is the interpretation of the locally present environment in reference to its absent portion, that part to which it is referred as another part so as to give a view of a whole. Just how such an idea would differ from one's plan of action in finding one's way, I do not know. For one's plan (if it be really a plan, a method) is a conception of what is given in its hypothetical relations to what is not given, employed as a guide to that act which results in the absent being also given. It is a map constructed with one's self lost and one's self found, whether at starting or at home again, as its two limits. If this map in its specific character is not also the only guide to the way home, one's only plan of action, then I hope I may never be lost. It is the practical facts of being lost and desiring to be found which constitute the limits and the content of the "environment."

Then comes the test of agreement of the idea and the environment. Supposing the individual stands still and attempts to compare his idea with the reality, with what reality is he to compare it? Not with the presented reality, for that reality is the reality of himself lost; not with the complete reality, for at this stage of proceedings he has only the idea to stand for the complete theory. What kind of comparison is possible or desirable then, save to treat the mental layout of the whole situation as a working hypothesis, as a plan of action, and proceed to act upon it, to use it as a director and controller of one's divagations instead of stumbling blindly around until one is either exhausted or accidentally gets out? Now suppose one uses the idea—that is to say, the present facts projected into a whole in the light of absent facts—as a guide of action. Suppose, by means of its specifications, one works one's way along until one comes upon familiar ground—finds one's self. Now, one may say, my idea was right, it was in accord with facts; it agrees with reality. That is, acted upon sincerely, it has led to the desired conclusion; it has, through action, worked out the state of things which it contemplated or intended. The agreement, correspondence, is between purpose, plan, and its own execution, fulfillment; between a map of a course constructed for the sake of guiding behavior and the result attained in acting upon the indications of the map. Just how does such agreement differ from success?

If we exclude acting upon the idea, no conceivable amount or kind of intellectualistic procedure can confirm or refute an idea, or throw any light upon its validity. How does the non-pragmatic view consider that verification takes place? Does it suppose that we first look a long while at the facts and then a long time at the idea, until by some magical process the degree and kind of their agreement become visible? Unless there is some such conception as this, what conception of agreement is possible except the experimental or practical one? And if it be admitted that verification involves action, how can that action be relevant to the truth of an idea, unless the idea is itself already relevant to action? If by acting in accordance with the experimental definition of facts (viz., as obstacles and conditions), and the experimental definition of the end or intent (viz., as plan and method of action) a harmonized situation effectually presents itself, we have the adequate and the only conceivable verification of the intellectual factors. If the action indicated be carried out and the disordered or disturbed situation persists, then we have not merely confuted the tentative positions of intelligence, but we have in the very process of acting introduced new data and eliminated some of the old ones, and thus afforded an opportunity for the resurvey of the facts and the revision of the plan of action. By acting faithfully upon an inadequate reflective presentation, we have at least secured the elements for its improvement. This, of course, gives no absolute guaranty that the reflection will at any time be so performed as to prove its validity in fact. But the self-rectification of intellectual content through acting upon it in good faith is the "absolute" of knowledge, loyalty to which is the religion of intellect.

The Category of Ethics

Ethics, the study of good and bad, right and wrong, constitutes the third major category in philosophy. The first, metaphysics, was an attempt to answer the question "What is?"; the second, epistemology, was an attempt to answer the question "What, and how, do we know?"; the third, ethics, is an attempt to answer the question "What is good?" Ethics involves an analysis of moral concepts and judgments in the construction of a theory of value.

Answers to questions of ethics can be categorized into three major ethical theories: the intuitive theory of ethics, the naturalistic theory of ethics, and the emotive theory of ethics. The intuitive theory holds that while it is impossible to define ethical concepts (and for that reason this theory is often labeled the indefinability theory of ethics), such concepts do in fact exist; further, ethical values have an objective existence as properties or relationships that can only be known intuitively. The naturalistic theory holds that ethical concepts are definable, that they do not have a purely objective (or purely subjective) existence, but they are social creations with a bio-social base in nature; further, they are not to be known through intuition, revelation, or discovery but created by individuals and societies to serve certain purposes. The emotive theory holds that ethical concepts are not factual judgments and therefore they cannot be spoken of as true or false—hence they are cognitively meaningless; the emotivist does not deny the existence of such judgments, he simply insists that they express nothing more than individual and social emotions or attitudes and thus any force they might carry is emotive rather than cognitive.

To use other labels to identify these positions, the intuitive position might be referred to as an objective theory of values because it is held that values reside in objects as properties, or in relationships as properties, but that the goodness or the rightness of these values is in no way dependent upon subjects (people). The emotive position might be referred to as a subjective theory of values because it is held that value expressions are strictly dependent upon people (subjects), and that such expressions can only be grounded in subjective feelings, commitments, and persuasions but never in objective fact. The naturalistic position might be referred to as an instrumental theory of values because, while denying that values are rooted exclusively in either objects or subjects, it holds that valuations are instruments for solving human problems which inescapably involves both an objective and subjective basis.

ETHICAL INTUITIONISM

The basic thesis of this position is that we intuit good and bad, right and wrong, and this is possible because an objective moral order exists in the universe—a moral order that is independent of human hopes and fears, beliefs and wants. Ethical intuitionism can be illustrated by this kind of assertion: "Don't you really know that it is wrong to lie?" or "Really, don't you know that you should be honest?" The argument here, of course, is that *indeed you do know* that it is wrong to lie, cheat, steal, and chase (female) redheads, and conversely, that you do indeed know you ought to be kind to children, dogs, and your wife (especially if she is a redhead). Implicit in such ethical propositions is the concept of obligation: one *ought* to do so and so, one *should* not do so and so. The "should" is not based on social obligation or immediate personal well-being, but on the intuitive realization that that's "just the way things are meant to be." (It was this kind of obligation that led men to conclude they ought not to have slaves.)

Ethical intuitionists admit that moral concepts and relations of this kind cannot be empirically grounded, even though they do carry prescriptions for behavior; the source of moral prescriptions is non-empirical although their manifestation is (or should be) behavioral. When it is admitted that ethics cannot be empirically grounded it is at the same time admitted that rightness and wrongness cannot be empirically analyzed; even so it is claimed that we *do know* that some behaviors are right and some are wrong, and since we so know this we are therefore obligated to act in a way which will conform with these objective ethical concepts. Again, for example, we do know —by intuition—that it is wrong to take food from a starving child or that it is right to help those unfortunates in the "underdeveloped" nations of the world.

The intuitive theory does not divorce itself from fact or reason, however, because the ethical norms we intuit are both rational and factual. For example, the intuitionist would ask, rhetorically, if anyone believes the actions taken at Buchenwald or Maidenek were right—and he would be very greatly surprised if anyone justified such actions in terms of morality (he would not be surprised if they were justified in political terms, but he would hold such a politic was wrong because it was separated from an objectively valid, intuited morality). More simply, he would argue that any action which caused needless suffering is wrong, and that the wrongness automatically follows from such an action in the very same way that the action of drawing an equilateral triangle means that the angles formed by the three sides are equal: the one necessarily entails the other, and just as "we know" a triangle must have three sides, so too do "we know" that certain actions are good or bad.

In sum, this position holds that ethical concepts do exist, that they exist in objects and objective relations, that they manifest their existence in empirical behavior, that such judgments are objectively true or false and thus they obligate us to behave in certain ways. We know all this because we intuit it, and for that reason this position can be labeled ethical intuitionism.

ETHICAL NATURALISM

Ethical naturalism, like intuitionism, gives values cognitive status; unlike intuitionism it insists that values are definable and can be rooted empirically; some naturalists are therefore prone to suggest that value judgments are capable of confirmation or verification, even though they would deny they are objectively true or false; other naturalists are inclined to dismiss the concept of truth as integral to a naturalistic ethics, on the ground that ethics are meaningful but not veridical.

That which binds all ethical naturalists together is their belief that ethical judgments are natural (not supernatural) in the same way that factual judgments are natural; but they disagree upon the natural grounds of definability.

Some naturalists would base ethics on individual interest or approval, thus on the individual level an action is good or right if an individual approves of, or takes interest in, such an action. The higher good, in such a case, involves those actions which promote the general welfare by building upon a multiplicity of individual interests and approvals. On inspection this can be seen to be a socio-individual theory of value because the warrant for ethical judgments rests with society and the individuals in it, and the moral obligation to conform to ethical judgments is strictly social (e.g., customs, mores) and individual (e.g., conscience).

Other naturalists find little fault with such a theory, but argue that there are psychological factors other than merely subjective interests at work. This kind of socio-psychological theory would hold that ethical judgments issue from the psychological nature of the human animal; thus, for instance, we must consider psychological questions dealing with human interests, drives, needs, wants, and satisfactions in the construction of a theory of value.

Another group of naturalists agrees that ethical judgments may be based on such things as interest, needs, and wants, but that the utility of such judgments is tested when they are used as instruments to achieve some end, to resolve some human problem. In this formulation it is possible to cognize values, to know right and wrong, good and bad, but since they serve as guides to action and since the status of value judgments depends upon their success in guiding action, we cannot know *in advance with certainty* whether or not a given action is right or wrong, good or bad. In this sense, values are relative and contingent, not absolute.

In sum, this position holds that ethical concepts do exist, that they do manifest themselves in human behavior (i.e., they reside in an experiential matrix composed of subjects and objects), that while such judgments are not *a priori* true or false they are capable of empirical confirmation, and that they are instruments of action, not dicta of action. The sense of obligation in this formulation is that one should do *this,* if he wants to achieve *that* end; and *that* end is defined to be good or bad in terms of its natural relations with a matrix of subjects and objects. For this reason it can be labeled ethical naturalism.

ETHICAL EMOTIVISM

Emotivism denies the cognitive status of values or value judgments, although it admits that individuals do value and do make value judgments.

On this view value judgments merely express individual and social emotions, not some reflections of a cosmic moral order. The emotivist agrees with the intuitionist that ethical concepts are indefinable or unanalyzable because there is no standard or criterion by which they can be validated; the emotivist then goes on to insist that moral judgments are indefinable simply because they are not cognitive concepts. They are pseudo-propositions, apparently containing some empirical meaning but inspection shows them to be void of content. Thus when I say, "Professor Smith was wrong to flunk Jones because his term paper was submitted late," the emotivist argues that I am saying nothing more than "Smith flunked Jones because his paper was overdue." The "wrongness" merely indicated my disapproval of Smith's action; "wrongness" is not a function of the action, but of my attitude toward it.

On that account the emotivist description is sometimes referred to as the "ugh!, oh!, and ah!" theory since ethical propositions serve to indicate emotive reactions to states of affairs; they also serve to foster attitudes and actions because they take the appearance of imperatives. The sentence "You ought to shut the door!," when said to an errant child, is easily seen to be the command, "Shut the door!" Or, "One ought not to lie" is equivalent to a moral injunction to tell the truth. In all of these examples, the emotivist points out, it is impossible to speak of ethical concepts as veridical.

In sum, the emotivist suggests that when the intuitionist or absolutist calls an action right or wrong, good or bad, the criterion is whether or not that action conforms to the transempirical belief of some higher (usually religious) authority, a belief which is itself not subject to confirmation; "good" means approval by that authority. The emotivist suggests that when the naturalist calls an action moral or immoral, the standard is whether or not that action conforms to social beliefs about the promotion of the general welfare; "good" here means approval by society. But, he concludes, on close analysis it is easily seen that ethical propositions are not cognitive but hortatory, since the expression of a value judgment does not permit its empirical verification but only calls for conformity through emotional persuasion. For this reason we use the label ethical emotivism to describe this approach to ethics.

THE ESSAYS TO COME

The following essays by J. Donald Butler, John Dewey, and Charles L. Stevenson, conclude this section on ethics as well as that part of this book dealing with philosophy *qua* philosophy.

Butler, writing as an Idealist, outlines a theory of value that can ultimately be rooted in the God concept—hence a transempirical ethic. Dewey, writing as a pragmatic empirist, outlines a theory of valuation that is firmly rooted in the concept of human experience—hence a pragmatic ethic. Stevenson, writing as a logical empiricist, analyzes ethical disagreements—such as these that obtain between naturalists and supernaturalists—in terms of attitudinal differences and so provides some basis for examining ethical propositions.

◦

OVERVIEW

The following essay, written by the noted contemporary Idealist, J. Donald Butler, argues that an adequate value theory should take into account two generic kinds of value: the ultimate and the social.

Ultimate values are God-like or rooted in God, Who alone has absolute and ultimate existence; consequently these values partake of this absolute, ultimate status. Social values, on the other hand, are rooted in man—in his societies—and are therefore relative to and dependent upon man and his works. Where absolute values share in God's perfect tenure, social values share in the transciency of human experience, and the latter are thus inferior to the former.

The realization or achievement of values, transcendental or empirical, requires effort. Values exist but they are not *freely* given; rather one must put forth effort to possess them. Some effort is mandatory, or put otherwise, we "owe" interest to them and this debt demands that this obligatory interest be translated into effort. It is in this that Butler asserts that while values do in fact exist one must participate in them to know or realize them; absolute values are the given, social values the taken, but to accept the given or utilize the taken it is necessary to integrate them actively into one's experience.

The criterion of value realization involves the relating of parts to wholes. By way of illustrating this axiological part-whole relationship, it can be seen that the value inherent in a great work of art (say, a Beethoven symphony) is understood and appreciated as a differentiated whole (say, when one unites all the parts of the score into *a* symphony and views it and values it not as a series of related parts but as an integrated whole). This part-whole relationship permeates all values, and the relating of parts to the whole is the *sine qua non* of value realization.

The root value in such a structure lies in being related to God; it is the root since God is the source from which all values flow and to Whom they return. One cannot, therefore, participate in the ultimate, absolute, and most meaningful values unless one first sees and believes that he *is* a part of God's whole. From this it can be seen that the ends of life are divine ends, purposed by God; and since this is so it can only follow that values cannot be separated from God and religion, else one turns one's back on all chance of realizing the ultimately valuable.

This point argues, in fine, that without a God no true value could exist; not because man does not create some of his own socio-individual values, but because without God man wouldn't even exist to do so.

From his preliminary considerations of value, Butler goes on to examine some relations of axiology to education:

First, the process of value realization is clearly an educative process; for this reason education is inescapably value laden.

Second, with the sole exception of churches and clergymen, the schools and teachers constitute the social institution best designed and equipped to assist in the educative process of value realization.

Third, it is patently obvious (although schoolmen often seem not to see the obvious) that all educational objectives stem from a value theory *of some sort*. Objectives or aims of any kind are an expression of value judgments, of the desired or desirable, the valued or valuable.

Fourth, some of the most valuable learning takes place when choices have to be made between competing alternatives, when one's value system is put to the test and one is forced to reach decisions on the basis of reflective, criterial thinking.

Butler concludes by admitting that there is indeed room for axiological disagreement and, in consequence of this he advocates that the schools should be permissive regarding children's value decisions. He summarizes the broad areas of disagreement succinctly and accurately when he states that "Values either are or are not rooted ultimately in God," and because neither the God-centered nor the society-centered belief has been shown satisfactory to all concerned he believes each pupil deserves a free and fair opportunity to build his own value beliefs.

For Butler, and most Idealists, however, values are indeed rooted in God.

The Role of Value Theory in Education

J. Donald Butler*

While my predominant feeling in presenting this paper is a sense of honor that The Philosophy of Education Society invited me to prepare it, another secondary frame of mind has accompanied my efforts such as they are. This is a feeling of indebtedness to the Society for commissioning me to do a job which I very much needed to do for my own good. The assignment first came to me in a context, which was somewhat ironical. A few days before the request came to me in a letter from Professor Broudy, I had just remarked to one of my classes that I had never yet received a good paper in value theory. Since the request came I have been embarrassed by an assignment which called upon me to produce something on the subject which at least would not be less than I had expected from my students.

In preparing this paper, I have assumed, I hope not mistakenly, that I

* Reprinted by permission from *Educational Theory*, IV (January, 1954), 69–77, 86.

could say something about general value theory. Noting that [the previous speaker's subject matter was] not focused solely on general value theory, I assumed that I could say something about general value considerations without transgressing. Consequently, the first part of my paper attempts to state some of my basic beliefs concerning value which are necessarily involved in the value aspect of education.

Looking at education within the general framework of my value theory, I have also dealt, in part two of this paper, with certain close relationships between axiology and the educative process. The final and third part of my paper attempts to depict the educational institution of society as an institution which ideally, at least, should be largely permissive with respect to value experience and value judgments.

A. PRESUPPOSITIONS

There are certain presuppositions concerning value which help to define the general frame of reference within which I necessarily work as I try to deal specifically with the role of value theory in education. While I recognize that it is quite beyond the reasonable scope of this paper to discuss axiology in general; yet I think it necessary to make at least four of my presuppositions explicit.

1. The first of these has to do with the ontology of values. It is that some values have the status of ultimate existence. Such values have this status not because they are independent realities, but because they are in and of the nature of God, who alone has ultimate and absolute existence. Of course, there is almost an infinite number and variety of values which do not have this status but are relative to the human scene alone and have the same kind of transiency that human experience has. Some of these values are instrumental; eventually they are means to other ends or to ultimate values. Some of them are terminal values, being enjoyed for what they are at the time without ever becoming means to other ends, or only indirectly being means to ultimate ends. Others are positive contraditions of ultimate values, perversions of value, negating and undermining the affirmative and abiding in value experience.

Value, very broadly defined it seems to me, refers to any particular quality as distinguished from a quantitative element; in a sense the whole essence side of reality is value. A color quality, for instance, although an elemental value, is a value. I wouldn't compare it in importance at all with an ultimate value, but nevertheless it is a value and may serve an ultimate purpose, at least indirectly. There is a vast range of value experience in which there are many different kinds of value and much room for variety. Many values are only temporal and temporary in their significance. This does not mean that they are wrong values or that they are right values; it does mean that they are more relative to the temporary existence of our human orbit than they are to God. But they are still values. However, they do not have the abidingness of ultimate values, which are in and of God. While I do not wish to draw a sharp line of separation, I do wish to distinguish between things which are temporary, temporal, transient, and relative to our individuality and to our humanness, as over against the ultimate values which are implicit and inherent in God in what He is bringing into being in the coming Divine Society. As I think of values, I use categories referring to the ultimate and the temporary, but I also use categories referring to the instrumental and the intrinsic. There may be something intrinsic about certain very elementary values which forbid our regarding them as instrumental except in a sense which is clearly indirect. While such elementary values may be indirectly instrumental to ultimate values, they are themselves temporal and not ultimate. They are at the same time indirectly instrumental values because they are a part of the value experience men need to have in order to enter into ultimate values. Ultimate values are real basic existences which have an ontology; their ontology is that they are rooted in God. They have just as much reality as so-called laws of nature. For me the so-called objective laws of nature have been overly objectified. It seems to me that these are little more than manifestations of the orderly way in which God works. They are not rigid structures as it were, as in positivism for instance. The qualities of person which are implicit in the nature of God are just as real as this orderly way of working. Values do not have a separate impersonal objective existence comparable to the ideas of Plato. Ultimate values are real and objective because they are in and of God and not because they stand "out there," as it were, somewhere between God and man as so-called objective realities. I am unable to define ultimate values apart from the person in whom they are resident. If you ask me if love is an ultimate value, I must say "Yes"; but I must also say, "the love which we know because of what God is." And with any other value I would have to do the same. All values have to be related to persons. All essence in the last analysis is either that which is in and of person or that which is the relation of persons.

The negations or perversions of value remain to be discussed, for however we define value we are confronted by the actuality that value can be contradicted or subverted and commonly is, rather than being realized or achieved. It is at this point that I find that I have a measure of agreement with pragmatism. Pragmatism roots all value, as I understand it, in the human social process. I agree that this is the orbit of a vast range of values, some of which are instrumental, some terminal, and most of them temporal as compared to ultimately abiding values which are rooted in God or sustained by Him. While ultimate values have their foundation in God, and by virtue

of this have a constancy which none of the values have whose basis of existence is the human social process, evil which is the negation of or perversion of value, whether temporal or ultimate, has its orbit also in the human individual-social process.

2. The second presupposition has to do with the need for effort in the possession of value. It is that all values, whether ultimate or temporal, are enjoyed and possessed only as the human subject, individual or collective, participates or becomes engaged in active efforts or relations by which he (or it) moves from present actual fact to a new situation in which the old fact is replaced by newly realized value. Values are what they are in essence largely because there are individual persons to possess and enjoy them. This is the subjective side of value. The presupposition that ultimate values have their existence in and of God does not imply that our possession of them is automatic and without effort. There is a subjective element in value experience which is comparable to the subjective element in Berkeley's treatment of knowledge. There is effort and activity in which we as individuals have to engage in order to enter into values. Now this does not at all mean salvation by merit or salvation by works. It does mean, however, that we have to reach out and embrace, we have to enter in and participate; there must be some kind of refraction through our experience in order for us to enter into values. This does not mean that values are dependent upon individuals; ultimate values are extant. The individual only realizes values as he enters into them. I am attempting in this presupposition to

parallel Berkeley's knowledge treatment with a value treatment which has the same pattern. Values are existent but we have to participate in them in order to enter into them; they do not just automatically transpose into our experience from the order objective to us.

3. The third presupposition supplies a criterion as a guide in the realization of value. It is that values are realized in the great majority of value situations by relating parts and wholes, if not exclusively in this manner. Logical values result from correctly recognizing whole-part relations. Aesthetic values are possessed when a work of art is understood and appreciated as a differentiated whole. Social values are realized when an individual recognizes his place as no more than a part in the total society and is willing to grant to all other individuals their due privileges. Religious values arise as the individual practices his relation to God, the total Person, in worship, fellowship, and service. This part-whole value principle commends itself to me as a very inclusive principle and one which is futuristic, or in theological terms, eschatalogical, in its prospect. For if and when parts are in their places fulfilling their normal ends as parts, and are evaluated in this context, and if and when wholes are known as wholes and not conglomerations of parts, then all will be harmonized in a living whole, established in God who alone is, constituting that eventual divine order in which the many are in and of the One.

This strongly implies that the root value for me is in being effectively related to God—a root value because it is the value from which all other values stem. This can be compared to what I understand as the root value of pragmatism, namely, relatedness to the social process, because it is the soil out of which all value grows. Now the principle that I have stated here is comparable to this but quite entirely different; it is that the root value is in being related not to society but to God. The intention, however, is not to set up an antithesis between God and society, except as sources of value.

But such a fundamental relation as this is not established by the part assuming to be related to the whole; it must rather be initiated by the One reaching out to relate the many to Himself. This I believe is what Christ is to man looked at from the value side. He is the one God entering into the life process of the many, even in the face of hostility, and giving himself to each and all, that His existence might be theirs and they might thereby partake of the One. Not only does our knowledge situation require that there be Incarnation if God is to be revealed; but our value situation calls for atonement if we are to be related to God and partake of the values which are resident in Him. But although this relation is made possible by Christ, it nevertheless does not thereby become a value of human experience automatically. And this is to refer our attention again to the educational problem. Even though Christ may reach out to us, we need to respond, embrace, and participate in order to enter into ultimate value.

While what I am attempting to say does presume upon the epistemology of our relation to God, the singular task at hand is to deal with the value side of this relation. I have contended so far that men can only partake of ultimate value by being related to God and being in and of Him. I would like to contend further that the only way in which we can be in and of God is for Him to be broken. How can those who are created, as it were, outside of God, who are creatures and not God, and who have in a measure their own autonomy, their own privacy, and their own individuality—how can they partake of that which God is unless God chooses to share that which He is, in and of Himself? In the nature of the case, given these conditions, an opening must be made by God and man must be invited in. And that means not only overture to us from God, which is Incarnation, but it also means atonement in which the one who is Incarnate is also broken.

My phrasing may suggest that this conception is built by means of individualistic categories alone. But individualism is not intended. This conception is intended to be just as organic as individual. I do not regard society, human or divine, as a collection of individuals, but rather as a living organic whole. Enlightened Protestant Christians are at some pains to correct the individualism of fundamentalist Christianity. And they should be, for this individualism and the mechanistic view of society which is its companion are corruptions which have more affinity for naive naturalism than for the Christian Faith.

4. The fourth and last presupposition has to do with the nature of man, more specifically, his moral condition. We cannot view value theory, it seems to me, as though we ourselves are ob-

jective spectators who can think with complete and full impartiality about our value problems. As problems they involve us, and because the problems have to do with values, we are predisposed toward the solution. One way in which we are predisposed is to desire a solution which is advantageous to ourselves or to our group. Another more basic way in which we are predisposed is that not only are we concerned about the means by which a good life is lived, but we are concerned about the ends which constitute a good life. Because of this, our situation as men is a radical situation. If it were true that the true ends of our lives were so implicit in our beings, that our conscious decisions scarcely bring into question the chief ends of life, our situation would not be so radical; but actually our value concerns and judgments focus more upon the goals of a good life than upon the things instrumental to it. Consequently, when we rebel against a destiny which is not what we desire that it should be, our revolt is a radical one pointed at the level of ends and not just at the level of means. We choose the destiny which we desire in preference to any other alternative.

Now, if it is true that the true ends of human life are divine ends, integral to a divine society whose existence is rooted in God, then when we reject these ends for those of our own desiring, there is a finality about our choice which brings down the curtain not only upon an orbit of value experience, but of existence as well. Achieving values which are ultimately good is a big enough problem at the level of means; we need the fellowship of the Divine Spirit and the Divine Community in order to be sustained in such good means unto such good ends. But when we reject this fellowship we turn our backs both upon the ends and the means of realizing them. It is impossible to separate ultimate value from the ultimate Community.

B. EDUCATION AND AXIOLOGY

Now, to turn directly to educational concerns which involve value theory. I would like to observe that there is an essential and very close relation between education and axiology. There are four aspects of this close connection which I now see very clearly.

1. The first of these refers back to my second presupposition: the necessity for human subjects to participate in the realization of values in order for them to achieve them and enjoy them. If it is true, as I maintain, that whatever the ontology of a value is, persons or societies must be actively engaged in its actualization or they cannot possess it and enjoy it for themselves; then value realization is an educative process and necessarily involves people in a growth and development which is educational at its heart. It might be said that this is an educational dimension which is indigenous to axiology as such.

2. The second aspect of the close relation between education and axiology I should like to mention involves a characterization of the school as a unique institution in society. The uniqueness of the educational institution of society looked at in the light of value theory is that it is more especially a value-realizing institution than is any other institution with the exception of religion.

I have not been able to explore this adequately, as of course its validation involves a whole philosophy of social institutions. Whatever else the institutions of society do, they do seek to realize value. Business seeks economic value for its investors and aims, with varying degrees of honesty, to offer its patrons some other value the return from which is this same economic value. Government at its best seeks to maintain and further achieve values of social order, general welfare, and the common good, although this is always corrupted by the intention to gain other values which are not so generally enjoyed.

But my impression is that there is in almost all other institutions a kind of factualism in addition to value-seeking, which is foreign to education. With reference to the individual pupil, education begins with him as he is at any given stage in his growth and nurture and seeks to convey him into a stage of development and value achievement which is not now actual. Socially, education begins with its society or culture as it is at a given point in history. It may make itself a completely subservient tool of that society or culture and thereby conceive its intention as conforming the new generation and so conserving the values, good or bad, which are actual in that culture. It may, however, and we hope it more commonly will, conceive of its function as reconstructive as well as conservative. In this event there enters a strong futuristic and axiological element into the educational task. The school not only conserves, it certainly does not destroy, what is good in the culture, but its vision reaches quite beyond this objective to conveying the society into a new orbit of value possession, in which that which is desired but is not now actual fact becomes more than an ideal or an objective, namely a present realized possession of the culture.

3. A third aspect of the connection between axiology and education is the necessary relationship between educational objectives and value theory. Any objectives which can be conceived for any phase of life are an expression, consciously or unconsciously, of value judgments. And when objectives are proposed for education, whether general or specific, whether by teachers or administrators for individual classes or schools, or by national bodies such as the Educational Policies Commission, some answers to value problems are implicit in these objectives.

The significant imperative which this relation forces upon us is that if our aims and objectives are to be adequate, they require that we be thoroughgoing in our value thinking. This is one of the strategic points at which more adequate attention should be drawn to the role of value theory in education. Except for educational philosophers, it seems to me that virtually no one connected with education is aware of the connection between value theory and the formulation of objectives. Furthermore, there is not the needed comprehension of value problems necessary to the formulation of a value theory. Needless to say, none possesses a value theory unless the most popular superficial talk about values can be called such. And because of this vacuum in value thinking, there is not an adequate context for the formulation of educational objectives. Regardless of the value judgments which may be made of the essence of given educational objectives, those objectives can not be adequately conceived unless they are formulated in the light of a value theory which is embraced with full cognizance of the problems involved, and which the theory is designed to answer. This, in turn, will involve equally responsible thinking in metaphysics and epistemology.

This underscores, as can be done at several comparable points, the importance of adequate background in philosophy of education as an essential requirement for all who become connected with the schools in any professional way. It also suggests the wisdom of encouraging lay discussions of the purposes and functions of our schools with the help of as expert guidance as can be secured. Such discussions should relate specifically educational concerns to as broad generalities as possible, in the hope that at the grass roots people may come to wise and discerning value judgments within the context of which to carry forward the educational functions of the community.

4. A fourth consideration concerning the relation of axiology and education is the significance for children and youth of their value problems and decisions.

The point at which the really vital learnings can take place is the point at which decisions have to be made between alternatives. While it is granted that there is a maturation dimension according to which the psychological appropriateness of decisions must be determined (younger children having more decisions made for them and being shielded from strenuous decisions where great hazard is a possibility, with an increasing reluctance on the part of adults to intervene as a child progresses from preadolescence through early and middle adolescence to adulthood), yet it must be recognized that the making of value judgments and decisions is central to education. Parents and teachers ought to be cautious in making decisions for their children or shielding them from difficult decisions; they should turn the occasions for such judgments and decisions to educational ends.

Value problems are the first reflective steps of maturing youth. They provide the first occasion for reflective decisions; therefore, value concerns in education are of unique importance, with all children, but especially with adolescents because in their struggles and tensions are the early occasions for genuinely reflective decision.

Of course it may be unlikely that every child can become a philosopher who builds for himself a theory of value, relates this value theory to a metaphysics, and validates both by a theory of knowledge. But every child must come eventually to live his own life with some measure of responsibility. The closer he can approach a theory of value within which his value judgments can make some real sense, the more adequate and responsible he can be in facing the demands of life. It is for this purpose that his value experiences can be made educational. A given value problem and the decisions which resolve it do not comprise the whole story of value experience. Value problems constitute, it seems to me, the first significant reflective steps of maturation. No doubt they are preceded in childhood and somewhat in pre-adolescence by problems of causality, the kind of inquisitive concern which is expressed in questions regarding how the world came to be and where babies come from. But real responsible reflection begins with value problems.

C. SCHOOLS SHOULD BE PERMISSIVE REGARDING VALUE DECISIONS

All of these considerations regarding the relation of axiology and education seem to me to point in the direction of an educational institution which is predominantly permissive in relation to the value decisions of growing children and youth. The schools should freely provide opportunity for value consideration, decision and realization; they should not withhold consideration, predetermine or force value decisions, and then expect value realization to go on within this predisposed framework.

Of course, actually there are many vested interests pressing in upon the schools which are uneasy about open discussion and objective analysis of the particular province which they are concerned to have protected from such consideration. The present witch-hunt phenomenon is an instance of political and economic vested interests seeking to prevent freedom of discussion which might encourage or give birth to opposing loyalties. Another area in which free discussion is commonly prevented by such pressures is in the area of religious or antireligious loyalties. On the one hand some religious interests prefer schools in which there is a kind of rationalistic control of the doctrine which is taught. Though diametrically opposed, a secular way of life, virtually equivalent to a religion in order of devotion, is nevertheless very similar to religious thought control in the desire to see that a scientific world-view is taught. By way of carrying the example further it seems to me that the solution is in neither of these alternatives and that neither alternative gives discerning attention to the value issues involved.

While of course there are many decisions about the education of their children which must be made by parents, by elected authorities, by administrators, and by teachers, there are also many decisions which must be made by pupils which are an essential part of education and apart from which genuinely educative activity cannot go on. I am often surprised at the number and extent of decisions it is commonly assumed that parents, teachers, administrators, and school officials must make. Many of these decisions, it seems to me, are going to be remade by the pupils in spite of the decisions that have already been made for them. And, I believe that most decisions which call for review by the pupils are rightly pupil decisions in the first instance anyway. The value concerns of growing children and youth call for such indigenous decisions by them, and with respect for these our schools should be more permissive than dominant.

1. There are certain very general values which the adult community, as expressed in the direction of school life, must prize. The first of these is that it will prize itself. It will prize its own community life as a vital matrix into which new generations are born and in which they grow and are nurtured. It will prize its heritage not so much as a fixed fund which is transmitted from generation to generation, but as a living stream of which the present generation is a living cross-section and the present living expression. The adult community as expressed in its direction of school life will prize and respect the child. It will respect the child by not thinking of him as one who is to be conformed only to what is the present adult culture. It will rather respect the child as a measured, but distinct object of hope for the future. It will also respect the child as a person, as a soul with a destiny, a destiny which may reach beyond the human culture and the human orbit. And it will be concerned not to place any ceiling over this destiny restricting it to temporal boundaries. The adult community will also value its subgroupings. While it should move by majority decisions, majorities should not be so dominant and so devoid of understanding as not to leave place for the healthy dissent and nonconformity of minorities.

2. While one could get lost completely among the trees if he were to attempt to consider the specific value areas in which pupil decisions are made, yet some endeavor should be made to indicate what some of these are, at least by representation. One of the most common areas of value experience where youth finds it necessary to make decisions is the realm of ethics. As children become pre-adolescents and especially as they grow into adolescence and adulthood, they are confronted with many problems of right and wrong. This is one important area in which maturation and certainly education calls for thoughtful judgment. Social questions concerning war and peace, race, and class distinction also press in upon youth, especially in this time of tension and quiet revolution. With boys, the certainty of early military service increases the urgency by

making it very personal and immediate. Varying somewhat with individual presuppositions, home and community backgrounds, religious, political, and economic problems evoke some serious thinking and call for some measure of judgment. Such problems are important in themselves, but they are also important because they can open out into even more fundamental metaphysical and epistemological concerns. However, they are not likely to serve such a worthy end if they are intercepted prematurely by a dominating or over-solicitous sponsorship. The truly educative concern will meet such occasions for serious thought with an attitude which permits genuine deciding by children and youth; it will not offer the shortcut of ready-made answers, nor will it shield efficiently from the real hazards of genuine decision-making.

3. In addition to decisions which have just been described respecting the evaluation of specific values, there are other decisions having to do with the whole of value experience which should be regarded as areas in which decisions have to be made in the process of maturing. These are judgments concerning the foundations of and nature of value. It seems to me that any education would be superficial which did not make some provision for judgment concerning such fundamental considerations, however fully it makes provision for specific value judgments. These general value concerns mentioned now in the light of the pupil's learning experience relate to the basic presupposition with which this paper began, and also constitute a final conclusion. My argument regarding the place of these presuppositions in education is that instead of education being authoritarian with these or other presuppositions made explicit as the rational basis of the education provided, or instead of the schools being authoritarian by opposing such principles or precluding study of them and judgment concerning them, education should rather be an open-ended process providing occasion for decision about such basic loyalties as these.

a. Values either are or are not rooted ultimately in God. Now, what I am saying is that instead of our teaching that they are or instead of our teaching the antithesis of this presupposition, our education should be so constructed that every pupil is at least given an opportunity to make a decision about this very belief.

b. Similarly being related to God is either the foundation of all value realization by an individual or a society, or else it is irrelevant. My argument is that instead of begging the question on this presupposition, education should be so constructed that there is no occasion for decision concerning this important concern.

c. And finally, either man is able of himself to relate himself to God, or such other matrix out of which it is believed that values arise, or else he needs to be related by a power or a Person beyond himself. Again my contention is that education should not answer this question for the pupil but instead provide the occasions in which the learner will come to make his own decision, a decision which he will necessarily make for himself eventually when and if it is really made.

OVERVIEW

It is very fashionable in philosophic circles today to insist that factual and normative propositions are of clearly different kinds, that normative propositions cannot be grounded in fact, and consequently that an "empirical theory of value" is at best a contradiction in terms or at worst an impossibility.

Dewey, however, considers this dualism just one more manifestation of the philosophic dragon that requires slaying. In his attempt to demonstrate that values can be, or are, grounded in experience he makes a very simple argument:

1. People do *in fact* prize, desire, or value certain existential situations; these can be said to constitute (under certain conditions) ends in view.
2. Ends in view serve as plans or guides to behavior so that prized existential situations (ends) can be realized; ends in view are thus means to ends.
3. Propositions about values are thus propositions about existential means and ends; they are "if–then" in nature and, being hypothetical in nature, are no less susceptible to the empirical test than any scientific "if–then" generalization.

It may be objected that, given this formulation of a theory of value, value propositions can never be completely or finally verified—thus we are cast adrift in a sea of moral relativity with no firm, immovable star to guide us. Quite so, Dewey would have to say. But be not dismayed; rather he would point out that *all* empirical science (and for Dewey there is no other kind) is relative and contingent, that no scientific proposition can ever be completely or finally verified. In values as in science, he would insist, there is no final word—there is only the latest word.

Theory of Valuation

*John Dewey**

. . . Because valuations in the sense of prizing and caring for occur only when it is necessary to bring something into existence which is lacking, or to conserve in existence something which is menaced by outside condi-

tions, valuation *involves* desiring. The latter is to be distinguished from mere wishing in the sense in which wishes occur in the absence of effort. . . .

If 'valuation' is defined in terms of desire as something initial and complete in itself, there is nothing by which to discriminate one desire from another and hence no way in which to measure

* Reprinted by permission from *Theory of Valuation* (Chicago: The University of Chicago Press, 1939).

the worth of different valuations in comparison with one another. Desires are desires, and that is all that can be said. Furthermore, desire is then conceived of as *merely* personal and hence as not capable of being stated in terms of other objects or events.

When, however, desires are seen to arise only within certain existential contexts (namely, those in which some lack prevents the immediate execution of an active tendency) and when they are seen to function in reference to these contexts in such a way as to make good the existing want, the relation between desire and *valuation* is found to be such as both to make possible, and to require, statement in verifiable propositions. (i) The content and object of desires are seen to depend upon the particular context in which they arise, a matter that in turn depends upon the antecedent state of both personal activity and of surrounding conditions. Desires for food, for example, will hardly be the same if one has eaten five hours or five days previously, nor will they be of the same content in a hovel and a palace or in a nomadic or agricultural group. (ii) Effort, instead of being something that comes after desire, is seen to be of the very essence of the tension involved in desire. For the latter, instead of being merely personal, is an active relation of the organism to the environment (as is obvious in the case of hunger), a factor that makes the difference between genuine desire and mere wish and fantasy. It follows that valuation in its connection with desire is linked to existential situations and that it differs with differences in its existential context. Since its existence depends upon the situation, its ade-

quacy depends upon its adaptation to the needs and demands imposed by the situation. Since the situation is open to observation, and since the consequences of effort-behavior as observed determine the adaptation, the adequacy of a given desire can be stated in propositions. The propositions are capable of empirical test because the connection that exists between a given desire and the conditions with reference to which it functions are ascertained by means of these observations. . . .

Appraisals of courses of action as better and worse, more and less serviceable, are as experimentally justified as are nonvaluative propositions about impersonal subject matter. In advanced engineering technologies propositions that state the *proper* courses of action to be adopted are evidently grounded in generalizations of physical and chemical science; they are often referred to as *applied* science. Nevertheless, propositions which lay down rules for procedures as being fit and good, as distinct from those that are inept and bad, are different in form from the scientific propositions upon which they rest. For they are rules for the use, in and by human activity, of scientific generalizations as means for accomplishing certain desired and intended ends.

Examination of these appraisals discloses that they have to do with things as they sustain to each other the relation of *means to ends or consequences.* Wherever there is an appraisal involving a rule as to better or as to needed action, there is an end to be reached: the appraisal is a valuation of things with respect to their serviceability or needfulness. If we take the examples given earlier, it is evident that real estate is appraised for the purpose of levying taxes or fixing a selling price; that medicinal treatments are appraised with reference to the end of effecting recovery of health; that materials and techniques are valued with respect to the building of bridges, radios, motor-cars, etc. . . .

There is always some observation of the *outcome attained* in comparison and contrast with that intended, such that the comparison throws light upon the actual fitness of the things employed as means. It thus makes possible a better judgment in the future as to their fitness and usefulness. On the basis of such observations certain modes of conduct are adjudged silly, impru-dent, or unwise, and other modes of conduct sensible, prudent, or wise, the discrimination being made upon the basis of the validity of the estimates reached about the relation of things as means to the end or consequence actu-ally reached. . . .

The conclusions reached may be summarized as follows: (1) There are propositions which are not merely about valuations that have actually oc-curred (about, i.e., prizings, desires, and interests that have taken place in the past) but which describe and de-fine certain things as good, fit, or proper in a definite existential relation: these propositions, moreover, are *gen-eralizations,* since they form rules for the proper use of materials. (2) The existential relation in question is that of means-ends or means-consequences. (3) These propositions in their general-ized form may rest upon scientifically warranted empirical propositions and are themselves capable of being tested by observation of results actually at-tained as compared with those in-tended. . . .

Let the connection between prizing and valuation be admitted and also the connection between desire (and inter-est) and prizing. The problem as to the relation between appraisal of things as means and prizing of things as ends then takes the following form: Are desires and interests ('likings,' if one prefers that word), which directly ef-fect an institution of end-values, inde-pendent of the appraisal of things as means or are they intimately influenced by this appraisal? If a person, for ex-ample, finds after due investigation that an immense amount of effort is required to procure the conditions that are the means required for realization of a desire (including perhaps sacrifice of other end-values that might be ob-tained by the same expenditure of ef-fort), does that fact react to modify his original desire and hence, by definition, his valuation? A survey of what takes place in any deliberate activity provides an affirmative answer to this question. For what is deliberation except weigh-ing of various alternative desires (and hence end-values) in terms of the con-ditions that are the means of their exe-cution, and which, as means, determine the consequences actually arrived at? There can be no control of the opera-tion of foreseeing consequences (and hence of forming ends-in-view) save in terms of conditions that operate as the causal conditions of their attainment. The proposition in which any object adopted as an end-in-view is statable (or explicitly stated) is *warranted* in just the degree to which existing con-ditions have been surveyed and appraised in their capacity as means. The sole alternative to this statement is that no deliberation whatsoever occurs, no ends-in-view are formed, but a person acts directly upon whatever impulse happens to present itself.

Any survey of the experiences in which ends-in-view are formed, and in which earlier impulsive tendencies are shaped through deliberation into a *chosen* desire, reveals that the object finally valued as an end to be reached is determined in its concrete makeup by appraisal of existing conditions as means. However, the habit of completely separating the conceptions of ends from that of means is so ingrained because of a long philosophical tradition that further discussion is required.

1. The common assumption that there is a sharp separation between things, on the one hand, as useful or helpful, and, on the other hand, as *intrinsically* good, and hence that there exists a separation between propositions as to what is expedient, prudent, or advisable and what is inherently desirable, does not, in any case, state a *self-evident* truth. The fact that such words as 'prudent,' 'sensible,' and 'expedient,' in the long run, or after survey of all conditions, merge so readily into the word 'wise' suggests (though, of course, it does not prove) that ends framed in separation from consideration of things as means are foolish to the point of irrationality.

2. Common sense regards some desires and interests as shortsighted, "blind," and others, in contrast, as enlightened, farsighted. It does not for a moment lump all desires and interests together as having the same status with respect to end-values. Discrimination

between their respective shortsightedness and farsightedness is made precisely on the ground of whether the object of a given desire is viewed as, in turn, itself a conditioning means of further consequences. Instead of taking a laudatory view of "immediate" desires and valuations, common sense treats refusal to mediate as the very essence of short-view judgment. For treating the end as *merely* immediate and exclusively final is equivalent to refusal to consider what will happen after and because a particular end is reached.

3. The words 'inherent,' 'intrinsic,' and 'immediate' are used ambiguously, so that a fallacious conclusion is reached. Any quality or property that actually belongs to any object or event is properly said to be immediate, inherent, or intrinsic. The fallacy consists in interpreting what is designated by these terms as out of relation to anything else and hence as absolute. For example, *means* are by definition relational, mediated, and mediating, since they are intermediate between an existing situation and a situation that is to be brought into existence by their use. But the relational character of the *things* that are employed as means does not prevent the things from having their own immediate qualities. In case the things in question are prized and cared for, then, according to the theory that connects the property of value with prizing, they necessarily have an immediate quality of value. The notion that, when means and instruments are valued, the value-qualities which result are only instrumental is hardly more than a bad pun. There is nothing in the nature of prizing or desiring to

prevent their being directed to things which are means, and there is nothing in the nature of means to militate against their being desired and prized. In empirical fact, the measure of the value a person attaches to a given end is not what he *says* about its preciousness but the care he devotes to obtaining and using the *means* without which it cannot be attained. No case of notable achievement can be cited in any field (save as a matter of sheer accident) in which the persons who brought about the end did not give loving care to the instruments and agencies of its production. The dependence of ends attained upon means employed is such that the statement just made reduces in fact to a tautology. Lack of desire and interest are proved by neglect of, and indifference to, required means. As soon as an attitude of desire and interest has been developed, then, because without full-hearted attention an end which is professedly prized will not be attained, the desire and interest in question automatically attach themselves to whatever other things are seen to be required means of attaining the end.

The considerations that apply to 'immediate' apply also to 'intrinsic' and 'inherent.' A quality, including that of value, is inherent if it actually belongs to something, and the question of whether or not it belongs is one of *fact* and not a question that can be decided by dialectical manipulation of the concept of inherency. If one has an ardent desire to obtain certain things as means, then the quality of value belongs to, or inheres in, those things. For the time being, producing or obtaining those means *is* the end-in-view. The notion

that only that which is out of relation to everything else can justly be called *inherent* is not only itself absurd but is contradicted by the very theory that connects the value of objects as ends with desire and interest, for this view expressly makes the value of the end-object relational, so that, if the inherent is identified with the nonrelational, there are, according to this view, no inherent values at all. On the other hand, if it is the fact that the quality exists in this case, because that to which it belongs is conditioned by a relation, then the relational character of means cannot be brought forward as evidence that their value is not inherent. The same considerations apply to the terms 'intrinsic' and 'extrinsic' as applied to value-qualities. Strictly speaking, the phrase 'extrinsic value' involves a contradiction in terms. Relational properties do not lose their intrinsic quality of being just what they are because their coming into being is *caused* by something 'extrinsic.' The theory that such is the case would terminate logically in the view that there are no intrinsic qualities whatever, since it can be shown that such intrinsic qualities as *red, sweet, hard,* etc., are causally conditioned as to their occurrence. The trouble, once more, is that a dialectic of concepts has taken the place of examination of actual empirical facts. The extreme instance of the view that to be intrinsic is to be out of any relation is found in those writers who hold that, since values *are* intrinsic, they cannot depend upon *any* relation whatever, and certainly not upon a relation to human beings. Hence this school attacks those who connect value-properties with desire and interest on exactly the same ground that the latter equate the distinction between the values of means and ends with the distinction between instrumental and intrinsic values. The views of this extreme non-naturalistic school may, accordingly, be regarded as a definite exposure of what happens when an analysis of the abstract concept of 'intrinsicalness' is substituted for analysis of empirical occurrences.

The more overtly and emphatically the valuation of objects as ends is connected with desire and interest, the more evident it should be that, since desire and interest are ineffectual save as they co-operatively interact with environing conditions, valuation of desire and interest, as means correlated with other means, is the sole condition for valid appraisal of objects as ends. If the lesson were learned that the object of scientific knowledge is *in any case* an ascertained correlation of changes, it would be seen, beyond the possibility of denial, that anything taken *as end* is in its own content or constituents a correlation of the energies, personal and extra-personal, which operate as means. An end as an *actual* consequence, as an existing outcome, is, like any other occurrence which is scientifically analyzed, nothing but the interaction of the conditions that bring it to pass. Hence it follows necessarily that the *idea* of the object of desire and interest, the *end-in-view* as distinct from the end or outcome actually effected, is warranted in the precise degree in which it is formed in terms of these operative conditions.

4. The chief weakness of current theories of valuation which relate the latter to desire and interest is due to failure to make an empirical analysis of concrete desires and interests as they actually exist. When such an analysis is made, certain relevant considerations at once present themselves. . . .

(i) . . . That desires as they first present themselves are the product of a mechanism consisting of native organic tendencies and acquired habits is an undeniable fact. All growth in maturity consists in *not* immediately giving way to such tendencies but in remaking them in their first manifestation through consideration of the consequences they will occasion *if* they are acted upon—an operation which is equivalent to judging or evaluating them as means operating in connection with extra-personal conditions as also means. Theories of valuation which relate it to desire and interest cannot both eat their cake and have it. They cannot continually oscillate between a view of desire and interest that identifies the latter with impulses just as they happen to occur (as products of organic mechanisms) and a view of desire as a modification of a raw impulse through foresight of its outcome; the latter alone being desire, the whole difference between impulse and desire is made by the presence in desire of an end-in-view, of objects *as* foreseen consequences. The foresight will be dependable in the degree in which it is constituted by examination of the conditions that will in fact decide the outcome. If it seems that this point is being hammered in too insistently, it is because the issue at stake is nothing other and nothing less than the possibility of distinctive valuation-propositions. For it cannot be denied that propositions having evidential warrant and experimental test are possible in the case of evaluation of things as means. Hence it follows that, if these propositions enter into the formation of the interests and desires which are valuations of ends, the latter are thereby constituted the subject matter of authentic empirical affirmations and denials.

(ii) We commonly speak of "learning from experience" and the "maturity" of an individual or a group. What do we mean by such expressions? At the very least, we mean that in the history of individual persons and of the human race there takes place a change from original, comparatively unreflective, impulses and hard-and-fast habits to desires and interests that incorporate the results of critical inquiry. When this process is examined, it is seen to take place chiefly on the basis of careful observation of differences found between desired and proposed ends (ends-*in-view*) and attained ends or actual consequences. Agreement between what is wanted and anticipated and what is actually obtained confirms the selection of conditions which operate as means to the desired end; discrepancies, which are experienced as frustrations and defeats, lead to an inquiry to discover the causes of failure. This inquiry consists of more and more thorough examination of the conditions under which impulses and habits are formed and in which they operate. The result is formation of desires and interests which are what they are through the union of the affective-motor conditions of action with the intellectual or ideational. The latter is there in any case if there is an end-in-view of any sort, no matter how casually formed,

while it is adequate in just the degree in which the end is constituted in terms of the conditions of its actualization. For, wherever there is an *end-in-view* of any sort whatever, there is affective-*ideational*-motor activity; or, in terms of the dual meaning of valuation, there is union of prizing and appraising. Observation of results obtained, of *actual* consequences in their agreement with and difference from ends anticipated or held in view, thus provides the conditions by which desires and interests (and hence valuations) are matured and tested. Nothing more contrary to common sense can be imagined than the notion that we are incapable of changing our desires and interests by means of learning what the consequences of acting upon them are, or, as it is sometimes put, of *indulging* them. It should not be necessary to point in evidence to the spoiled child and the adult who cannot "face reality." Yet, as far as valuation and the theory of values are concerned, any theory which isolates valuation of ends from appraisal of means equates the spoiled child and the irresponsible adult to the mature and sane person. . . .

The sole alternative to the view that *the* end is an arbitrarily selected part of actual consequences which *as* "the end" then justifies the use of means irrespective of the other consequences they produce, is that desires, ends-in-view, and consequences achieved be valued in turn as means of further consequences. The maxim referred to, under the guise of saying that ends, in the sense of actual consequences, provide the warrant for means employed— a correct position—actually says that some fragment of these actual consequences—a fragment arbitrarily selected because the heart has been set upon it—authorizes the use of means to obtain *it,* without the need of foreseeing and weighing other ends as consequences of the means used. It thus discloses in a striking manner the fallacy involved in the position that ends have value independent of appraisal of means involved and independent of their own further causal efficacy.

We are thus brought back to a point already set forth. In all the physical sciences (using 'physical' here as a synonym for *nonhuman*) it is now taken for granted that all "effects" are also "causes," or, stated more accurately, that nothing happens which is *final* in the sense that it is not part of an ongoing stream of events. If this principle, with the accompanying discrediting of belief in objects that are ends but not means, is employed in dealing with distinctive human phenomena, it necessarily follows that the distinction between ends and means is temporal and relational. Every condition that has to be brought into existence in order to serve as means is, *in that connection,* an object of desire and an end-in-view, while the end actually reached is a means to future ends as well as a test of valuations previously made. Since the end attained is a condition of further existential occurrences, it must be appraised as a potential obstacle and potential resource. If the notion of some objects as ends-in-themselves were abandoned, not merely in words but in all practical implications, human beings would for the first time in history be in a position to frame ends-in-view and form desires on the basis of empirically grounded propositions of the temporal relations of events to one another. . . .

[It] is at least a sign of immaturity when an individual fails to view his end as also a moving condition of further consequences, thereby treating it as *final* in the sense in which 'final' signifies that the course of events has come to a complete stop. Human beings do indulge in such arrests. But to treat them as models for forming a theory of ends is to substitute a manipulation of ideas, abstracted from the contexts in which they arise and function, for the conclusions of observation of concrete facts. It is a sign either of insanity, immaturity, indurated routine, or of a fanaticism that is a mixture of all three.

Generalized ideas of ends and values undoubtedly exist. They exist not only as expressions of habit and as uncritical and probably invalid ideas but also in the same way as valid general ideas arise in any subject. Similar situations recur; desires and interests are carried over from one situation to another and progressively consolidated. A schedule of general ends results, the involved values being "abstract" in the sense of not being directly connected with any particular existing case but not in the sense of independence of all empirically existent cases. As with general ideas in the conduct of any natural science, these general ideas are used as intellectual instrumentalities in judgment of particular cases as the latter arise; they are, in effect, tools that direct and facilitate examination of things in the concrete while they are also developed and tested by the results of their application in these cases. . . .

There is no need to deny that a general and abstract conception of health finally develops. But it is the outcome of a great number of definite, empirical inquiries, not an *a priori* preconditioning "standard" for carrying on inquiries. . . .

Experience has shown that problems for the most part fall into certain recurrent kinds so that there are general principles which, it is believed, proposed solutions must satisfy in a particular case. There thus develops a sort of framework of conditions to be satisfied—a framework of reference which operates in an *empirically* regulative way in given cases. We may even say that it operates as an "a priori" principle, but in exactly the same sense in which rules for the conduct of a technological art are both empirically antecedent and controlling in a given case of the art. While there is no a priori standard of health with which the actual state of human beings can be compared so as to determine whether they are well or ill, or in what respect they are ill, there have developed, out of past experience, certain criteria which are operatively applicable in new cases as they arise. Ends-in-view are appraised or valued as *good* or *bad* on the ground of their serviceability in the direction of behavior dealing with states of affairs found to be objectionable because of some lack or conflict in them. They are appraised as fit or unfit, proper or improper, *right* or *wrong,* on the ground of their *requiredness* in accomplishing this end.

Considering the all but omnipresence of troubles and "evils" in human experience (evils in the sense of deficiencies, failures, and frustrations), and considering the amount of time that has been spent explaining them away, theories of human activity have been strangely oblivious of the concrete function troubles are capable of exercising when they are taken as *problems* whose conditions and consequences are explored with a view to finding methods of solution. The two instances just cited, the progress of medical art and of scientific inquiry, are most instructive on this point. As long as actual events were supposed to be judged by comparison with some absolute end-value as a standard and norm, no sure progress was made. When standards of health and of satisfaction of conditions of knowledge were conceived in terms of analytic observation of existing conditions, disclosing a trouble statable in a problem, criteria of judging were progressively self-corrective through the very process of use in observation to locate the source of the trouble and to indicate the effective means of dealing with it. These means form the content of the specific end-in-view, not some abstract standard or ideal. . . .

The net outcome is (i) that the problem of valuation in general as well as in particular cases concerns things that sustain to one another the relation of means-ends; that (ii) ends are determinable only on the ground of the means that are involved in bringing them about; and that (iii) desires and interest must themselves be evaluated as means in their interaction with external or environing conditions. Ends-in-view, as distinct from ends as accomplished results, themselves function as directive means; or, in ordinary language, as *plans*. Desires, interests, and environing conditions as means are modes of action, and hence are to be conceived in terms of energies which are capable of reduction to homogeneous and comparable terms. Co-ordination or organizations of energies, proceeding from the two sources of the organism and the environment, are thus both means and attained result or "end" in all cases of valuation, the two kinds of energy being theoretically (if not as yet completely so in practice) capable of statement in terms of physical units.

The conclusions stated do not constitute a complete theory of valuation. They do, however, state the conditions which such a theory must satisfy. An actual theory can be completed only when inquiries into things sustaining the relation of ends-means have been systematically conducted and their results brought to bear upon the formation of desires and ends. For the theory of valuation is itself an intellectual or methodological means and as such can be developed and perfected only in and by use. Since that use does not now exist in any adequate way, the theoretical consideration advanced and conclusions reached outline a program to be undertaken, rather than a complete theory. The undertaking can be carried out only by regulated guidance of the formation of interests and purposes in the concrete. The prime condition of this undertaking (in contrast with the current theory of the relation of valuation to desire and interest) is recognition that desire and interest are not given ready-made at the outset, and *a fortiori* are not, as they may at first appear, starting-points, original data, or premises of any theory of valuation, for desire always emerges within a prior system of activities or interrelated energies. It arises within a *field* when the field is disrupted or is menaced with disruption, when conflict introduces the tension of need or threatens to introduce it. An interest represents not just a desire but a set of interrelated desires which have been found in experience to produce, because of their connection with one another, a definite order in the processes of continuing behavior.

The test of the existence of a valuation and the nature of the latter is actual behavior as that is subject to observation. Is the existing field of activities (including environing conditions) *accepted,* where "acceptance" consists in effort to maintain it against adverse conditions? Or is it *rejected,* where "rejection" consists of effort to get rid of it and to produce another behavioral field? And in the latter case, what is the actual field to which, as an end, desire-efforts (or the organization of desire-efforts constituting an interest) are directed? Determination of this field as an objective of behavior determines *what* is valued. Until there is actual or threatened shock and disturbance of a situation, there is a green light to go ahead in immediate act— overt action. There is no need, no desire, and no valuation, just as where there is no doubt, there is no cause of inquiry. Just as the problem which evokes inquiry is related to an empirical situation in which the problem presents itself, so desire and the projection of ends as consequences to be reached are relative to a concrete situation and to its need for transformation. The burden of proof lies, so to speak, on occurrence of conditions that are impeding, obstructive, and that introduce conflict and need. Examination of the situation in respect to the conditions that constitute lack and need and thus serve as positive means for formation of an attainable end or outcome, is the method by which warranted (required and effective) desires and ends-in-view are formed: by which, in short, valuation takes place.

∽

OVERVIEW

In the following essay Charles L. Stevenson provides a brief but excellent example of philosophic analysis when he examines the nature of ethical disagreement.

He points out that disagreement may be of two kinds: disagreement in belief and disagreement in attitude. The former is that kind of disagreement where proponent and opponent cannot both be right; that is, both beliefs cannot at the same time be true. The latter is that kind of disagreement where both cannot be satisfied; that it, "truth" is not pertinent to the resolution of the disagreement.

On this view he notes that ethical disagreements are disagreements in both belief and attitude, and insofar as science is accepted as a criterion for fixing belief, disagreements in belief are clearly and properly subject to an appeal to science. One would be foolish, in this account, to believe that Kilimanjaro is higher than Everest or that Negroes are inherently inferior to whites since science has shown these to be untrue.

Yet science is not directly pertinent to the resolution of disagreements in attitude—for how is science alone able to show the white Southerner that his attitude toward segregation is "wrong," or to convince Sir Edmund Hillary that it is "more fun" to climb Kilimanjaro than Everest? For that matter, how is one to be convinced that the scientific method is the "best" method even to solve disagreements in belief if one does not have a favorable attitude toward science?

In any case, it is clear that some ethical disagreements involve attitudinal differences—"agreements to disagree"—which, Stevenson maintains, are emotive rather than cognitive. Thus ethics is not a science, nor completely susceptible to the scientific method.

The Nature of Ethical Disagreement

*Charles L. Stevenson**

When people disagree about the value of something—one saying that it is good or right, and another that it is bad or wrong—by what methods of argument or inquiry can their disagreement be resolved? Can it be resolved by the methods of science, or does it require methods of some other kind, or is it open to no rational solution at all?

The question must be clarified before it can be answered. And the word that is particularly in need of clarification, as we shall see, is the word "disagreement."

Let us begin by noting that "disagreement" has two broad senses: In the first sense it refers to what I shall call "disagreement in belief." This occurs when Mr. A believes *p*, when Mr. B believes not-*p*, or something incompatible with *p*, and when neither is content to let the belief of the other remain unchallenged. Thus doctors may disagree in belief about the causes of an illness; and friends may disagree in belief about the exact date on which they last met.

In the second sense, the word refers to what I shall call "disagreement in attitude." This occurs when Mr. A has a favorable attitude to something, when Mr. B has an unfavorable or less favorable attitude to it, and when neither is content to let the other's attitude remain unchanged. The term "attitude"

is here used in much the same sense that R. B. Perry uses "interest"; it designates any psychological disposition of being for or against something. Hence love and hate are relatively specific kinds of attitudes, as are approval and disapproval, and so on.

This second sense can be illustrated in this way: Two men are planning to have dinner together. One is particularly anxious to eat at a certain restaurant, but the other doesn't like it. Temporarily, then, the men cannot "agree" on where to dine. Their argument may be trivial, and perhaps only half serious; but in any case it represents a disagreement in attitude. The men have divergent preferences, and each is trying to redirect the preference of the other.

Further examples are readily found. Mrs. Smith wishes to cultivate only the four hundred; Mr. Smith is loyal to his old poker-playing friends. They accordingly disagree, in attitude, about whom to invite to their party. The progressive mayor wants modern school-buildings and large parks; the older citizens are against these "new-fangled" ways; so they disagree on civic policy. These cases differ from the one about the restaurant only in that the clash of attitudes is more serious, and may lead to more vigorous argument.

The difference between the two senses of "disagreement" is essentially this: the first involves an opposition of beliefs, both of which cannot be true,

* Reprinted by permission from *Readings in Philosophical Analysis,* ed. Herbert Feigl and Wilfrid Sellars (New York: Appleton-Century-Crofts, Inc., 1949), pp. 587–593.

and the second involves an opposition of attitudes, both of which cannot be satisfied.

Let us apply this distinction to a case that will sharpen it. Mr. A believes that most voters will favor a proposed tax, and Mr. B disagrees with him. The disagreement concerns attitudes—those of the votors—but note that A and B are not disagreeing in attitude. Their disagreement is in belief about attitudes. It is simply a special kind of disagreement in belief, differing from disagreement in belief about head colds only with regard to subject matter. It implies not an opposition of the actual attitudes of the speakers, but only of their beliefs about certain attitudes. Disagreement in attitude, on the other hand, implies that the very attitudes of the speakers are opposed. A and B may have opposed beliefs about attitudes without having opposed attitudes, just as they may have opposed beliefs about head colds without having opposed head colds. Hence we must not, from the fact that an argument is concerned with attitudes, infer that it necessarily involves disagreement in attitude.

We may now turn more directly to disagreement about values, with particular reference to normative ethics. When people argue about what is good, do they disagree in belief, or do they disagree in attitude? A long tradition of ethical theorists strongly suggest, whether they always intend to or not, that the disagreement is one in belief. Naturalistic theorists, for instance, identify an ethical judgment with some sort of scientific statement, and so make normative ethics a branch of science. Now a scientific argument typically ex-

emplifies disagreement in belief, and if an ethical argument is simply a scientific one, then it too exemplifies disagreement in belief. The usual naturalistic theories of ethics that stress attitudes —such as those of Hume, Westermarck, Perry, Richards, and so many others—stress disagreement in belief no less than the rest. They imply, of course, that disagreement about what is good is disagreement in belief about attitudes; but we have seen that that is simply one sort of disagreement in belief, and by no means the same as disagreement in attitude. Analyses that stress disagreement in attitude are extremely rare.

If ethical arguments, as we encounter them in everyday life, involved disagreement in belief exclusively— whether the beliefs were about attitudes or about something else—then I should have no quarrel with the ordinary sort of naturalistic analysis. Normative judgments could be taken as scientific statements, and amenable to the usual scientific proof. But a moment's attention will readily show that disagreement in belief has not the exclusive role that theory has so repeatedly ascribed to it. It must be readily granted that ethical arguments usually involve disagreement in belief; but they also involve disagreement in attitude. And the conspicuous role of disagreement in attitude is what we usually take, whether we realize it or not, as the distinguishing feature of ethical arguments. For example:

Suppose that the representative of a union urges that the wage level in a given company ought to be higher— that it is only right that the workers receive more pay. The company representative urges in reply that the workers ought to receive no more than they get. Such an argument clearly represents a disagreement in attitude. The union is for higher wages; the company is against them, and neither is content to let the other's attitude remain unchanged. In addition to this disagreement in attitude, of course, the argument may represent no little disagreement in belief. Perhaps the parties disagree about how much the cost of living has risen, and how much the workers are suffering under the present wage scale. Or perhaps they disagree about the company's earnings, and the extent to which the company could raise wages and still operate at a profit. Like any typical ethical argument, then, this argument involves both disagreement in attitude and disagreement in belief.

It is easy to see, however, that the disagreement in attitude plays a unifying and predominating role in the argument. This is so in two ways:

In the first place, disagreement in attitude determines what beliefs are relevant to the argument. Suppose that the company affirms that the wage scale of fifty years ago was far lower than it is now. The union will immediately urge that this contention, even though true, is irrelevant. And it is irrelevant simply because information about the wage level of fifty years ago, maintained under totally different circumstances, is not likely to affect the present attitudes of either party. To be relevant, any belief that is introduced into the argument must be one that is likely to lead one side or the other to have a different attitude, and so reconcile disagreement in attitude. Attitudes

are often functions of beliefs. We often change our attitudes to something when we change our beliefs about it; just as a child ceases to want to touch a live coal when he comes to believe that it will burn him. Thus in the present argument, any beliefs that are at all likely to alter attitudes, such as those about the increasing cost of living or the financial state of the company, will be considered by both sides to be relevant to the argument. Agreement in belief on these matters may lead to agreement in attitude toward the wage scale. But beliefs that are likely to alter the attitudes of neither side will be declared irrelevant. They will have no bearing on the disagreement in attitude, with which both parties are primarily concerned.

In the second place, ethical argument usually terminates when disagreement in attitude terminates, even though a certain amount of disagreement in belief remains. Suppose, for instance, that the company and the union continue to disagree in belief about the increasing cost of living, but that the company, even so, ends by favoring the higher wage scale. The union will then be content to end the argument, and will cease to press its point about living costs. It may bring up that point again, in some future argument of the same sort, or in urging the righteousness of its victory to the newspaper columnists; but for the moment the fact that the company has agreed in attitude is sufficient to terminate the argument. On the other hand: suppose that both parties agreed on all beliefs that were introduced into the argument, but even so continued to disagree in attitude. In that case neither party would feel that their dispute had been successfully terminated. They might look for other beliefs that could be introduced into the argument. They might use words to play on each other's emotions. They might agree (in attitude) to submit the case to arbitration, both feeling that a decision, even if strongly adverse to one party or the other, would be preferable to a continued impasse. Or, perhaps, they might abandon hope of settling their dispute by any peaceable means.

In many other cases, of course, men discuss ethical topics without having the strong, uncompromising attitudes that the present example has illustrated. They are often as much concerned with redirecting their own attitudes, in the light of greater knowledge, as with redirecting the attitudes of others. And the attitudes involved are often altruistic, rather than selfish. Yet the above example will serve, so long as that is understood, to suggest the nature of ethical disagreement. Both disagreement in attitude and disagreement in belief are involved, but the former predominates in that (1) it determines what sort of disagreement in belief is relevantly disputed in a given ethical argument, and (2) it determines, by its continued presence or its resolution, whether or not the argument has been settled. We may see further how intimately the two sorts of disagreement are related: since attitudes are often functions of beliefs, an agreement in belief may lead people, as a matter of psychological fact, to agree in attitude.

Having discussed disagreement, we may turn to the broad question that was first mentioned, namely: By what

methods or argument or inquiry may disagreement about matters of value be resolved?

It will be obvious that to whatever extent an argument involves disagreement in belief, it is open to the usual methods of the sciences. If these methods are the only rational methods for supporting beliefs—as I believe to be so, but cannot now take time to discuss—then scientific methods are the only rational methods for resolving the disagreement in belief that arguments about values may include.

But if science is granted an undisputed sway in reconciling beliefs, it does not thereby acquire, without qualification, an undisputed sway in reconciling attitudes. We have seen that arguments about values include disagreement in attitude, no less than disagreement in belief, and that in certain ways the disagreement in attitude predominates. By what methods shall the latter sort of disagreement be resolved?

The methods of science are still available for that purpose, but only in an indirect way. Initially, these methods have only to do with establishing agreement in belief. If they serve further to establish agreement in attitude, that will be due simply to the psychological fact that altered beliefs may cause altered attitudes. Hence scientific methods are conclusive in ending arguments about values only to the extent that their success in obtaining agreement in belief will in turn lead to agreement in attitude.

In other words: the extent to which scientific methods can bring about agreement on values depends on the extent to which a commonly accepted body of scientific beliefs would cause us to have a commonly accepted set of attitudes.

How much is the development of science likely to achieve, then, with regard to values? To what extent would common beliefs lead to common attitudes? It is, perhaps, a pardonable enthusiasm to hope that science will do everything—to hope that in some rosy future, when all men know the consequences of their acts, they will all have common aspirations, and live peaceably in complete moral accord. But if we speak not from our enthusiastic hopes, but from our present knowledge, the answer must be far less exciting. We usually do not know, at the beginning of any argument about values, whether an agreement in belief, scientifically established, will lead to an agreement in attitude or not. It is logically possible, at least, that two men should continue to disagree in attitude even though they had all their beliefs in common, and even though neither had made any logical or inductive error, or omitted any relevant evidence. Differences in temperament, or in early training, or in social status, might make the men retain different attitudes even though both were possessed of the complete scientific truth. Whether this logical possibility is an empirical likelihood I shall not presume to say; but it is unquestionably a possibility that must not be left out of account.

To say that science can always settle arguments about value, we have seen, is to make this assumption: Agreement in attitude will always be consequent upon complete agreement in belief, and science can always bring about the latter. Taken as purely heuristic, this assumption has its usefulness. It leads people to discover the discrepancies in their beliefs, and to prolong enlightening argument that may lead, as a matter of fact, from commonly accepted beliefs to commonly accepted attitudes. It leads people to reconcile their attitudes in a rational permanent way, rather than by rhapsody or exhortation. But the assumption is nothing more, for present knowledge, than a heuristic maxim. It is wholly without any proper foundation of probability. I conclude, therefore, that scientific methods cannot be guaranteed the definite role in the so-called "normative sciences" that they may have in the natural sciences. Apart from a heuristic assumption to the contrary, it is possible that the growth of scientific knowledge may leave many disputes about values permanently unsolved. Should these disputes persist, there are non-rational methods for dealing with them, of course, such as impassioned, moving oratory. But the purely intellectual methods of science, and, indeed, all methods of reasoning, may be insufficient to settle disputes about values, even though they may greatly help to do so.

For the same reasons, I conclude that normative ethics is not a branch of any science. It deliberately deals with a type of disagreement that science deliberately avoids. Ethics is not psychology, for instance; for although psychologists may, of course, agree or disagree in belief about attitudes, they need not, as psychologists, be concerned with whether they agree or disagree with one another in attitude. Insofar as normative ethics draws from the sciences, in order to change attitudes via changing people's beliefs, it draws from all the sciences; but a moralist's peculiar aim—that of redirecting attitudes—is a type of activity, rather than knowledge, and falls within no science. Science may study that activity, and may help indirectly to forward it; but it is not identical with that activity.

I have only a moment to explain why the ethical terms, such as "good," "wrong," "ought," and so on, are so habitually used to deal with disagreement in attitude. On account of their repeated occurrence in emotional situations they have acquired a strong emotive meaning. This emotive meaning makes them serviceable in initiating changes in a hearer's attitudes. Sheer emotive impact is not likely, under many circumstances, to change attitudes in any permanent way; but it begins a process that can then be supported by other means.

There is no occasion for saying that the meaning of ethical terms is purely emotive, like that of "alas" or "hurrah." We have seen that ethical arguments include many expressions of belief; and the rough rules of ordinary language permit us to say that some of these beliefs are expressed by an ethical judgment itself. But the beliefs so expressed are by no means always the same. Ethical terms are notable for their ambiguity, and opponents in an argument may use them in different senses. Sometimes this leads to artificial issues; but it usually does not. So long as one person says "This is good" with emotive praise, and another says "No, it is bad,"

with emotive condemnation, a disagreement in attitude is manifest. Whether or not the beliefs that these statements express are logically incompatible may not be discovered until later in the argument; but even if they are actually compatible, disagreement in attitude will be preserved by emotive meaning; and this disagreement, so central to ethics, may lead to an argument that is certainly not artificial in its issues, so long as it is taken for what it is.

The many theorists who have refused to identify ethical statements with scientific ones have much to be said in their favor. They have seen that ethical judgments mold or alter attitudes, rather than describe them, and they have seen that ethical judgments can be guaranteed no definitive scientific support. But one need not, on that account, provide ethics with any extramundane, *sui generis* subject matter. The distinguishing features of an ethical judgment can be preserved by a recognition of emotive meaning and disagreement in attitude, rather than by some non-natural quality—and with far greater intelligibility. If any unique subject matter is postulated, as it usually is, to preserve the important distinction between normative ethics and science, it serves no purpose that is not served by the very simple analysis I have here suggested. Unless non-natural qualities can be defended by positive arguments, rather than as an "only resort" from the acknowledged weakness of ordinary forms of naturalism, they would seem nothing more than the invisible shadows cast by emotive meaning.

Part III
Philosophies of Education

Levels of Educational Theory

The maps used by educators to guide them have varied not only as to content and detail but as to basic orientation. There have been as many guiding North stars as explorers.

Some maps were but rough outlines of the terrain to be crossed, indicating only peaks and valleys. Others were more complete, but their completeness was often a result not only of past explorations but of imaginative projections. Some maps were complete in detail, with all the known and suspected features of the educational landscape entered and labeled. These more complete maps identified all the detours, by-roads, dead ends, and unimproved roads, as well as the thoroughfares, the better to guide the educational traveler on his trip. They indicated the broad highways which had to be followed if education was to get "there" from "here." No matter that some of the charted mountains did not exist, that some of the avoided valleys contained resources to sustain the trip, that some unexplored passes might have been short-cuts; what was important was that the maps existed and educators followed them.

PRACTICAL PRINCIPLES TO GUIDE EDUCATION

The most elementary maps provided practical principles for the conduct of education. Rules of thumb, gleaned from years of trial and error experience, constituted the first and most direct level of educational theory.

For example, Marcus Fabius Quintilian (*ca.* 35–95), decrying the Romanization of the educational theories of Plato and Aristotle, and rebelling against the impracticality of Roman philosophy when applied to education, set down some practical principles to guide education. Examples of this level of educational theory can be found in his *Institutes of Oratory* where, among other rules of thumb, is the assertion that "Some boys are indolent, unless you stimulate them; some are indignant at being commanded; fear restrains some; with other, hasty efforts succeed better."

Reliance upon practical principles was not by any means restricted to the ancients, however. Andrew Bell (1753–1832) and Joseph Lancaster (1778–1838) simultaneously invented the "monitorial method" and argued that it was at once the most practical, efficient, and economic theory of education. This method, wherein the abler or older pupils memorized their lessons and then helped the slower or younger to memorize theirs, employed a military-like discipline within a rigid chain of command to insure classroom control, all the while operating on the implicit rule of thumb principle that "he who has just learned, or learned best, is fit to teach."

With certain noteworthy exceptions it is probably fair to say that the actual conduct of education was guided by such practical, rule of thumb procedures until fairly recent times.

PSYCHO-PHILOSOPHIC PRINCIPLES TO GUIDE EDUCATION

Such simple rule of thumb maps were not restricted to trial and error explorations, however. They were related to more sophisticated pictures when such educational theorists as Comenius and Pestalozzi worked practical principles of education into a broader pattern.

Johann Heinrich Pestalozzi (1746–1827) is often celebrated as the intellectual father of modern education because his methodology, based on the concept of the Object Lesson, has permeated educational thought ever since. In his view the child is created by God and comes into the world possessing in germ all those moral, intellectual, and physical powers which, if developed by natural means offered to him by the very nature of the universe, will enable the child to realize in full all his potentials. The precise educational method required to develop the child, most particularly his intellectual potential, was a procedure which sought out the simplest elements of knowledge so the attention of the learner might be secured, and then, by direct and personal experience, the child would move from this simple object to increasingly abstract concepts. Since this method would normally start with the teacher handling, exhibiting, and presenting an object to the child it became known as the Object Lesson.

A perfect vacuum is as rare in the world of ideas as it is in the world of physics, and Pestalozzi certainly did not develop his theories out of thin air; rather they were considerably influenced by Jean Jacques Rousseau (1712–1778) and Johann Amos Comenius (1592–1670).

More than a century before Pestalozzi was born, Comenius anticipated Pestalozzi's "germ possession" theory. Building on Plato's (*ca.* 427–347) theory of implicit ideas and St. Thomas Aquinas' (*ca.* 1225–1274) theory of man's inherent potential to know, Comenius held that the seeds of erudition, virtue, and piety (i.e., knowledge, morality, and religion) lie dormant within each of us, implanted by God as part of our human nature, and waiting to be brought to flower by our senses and reason. He wrote, in *The Great Didactic,* "To the rational soul, that dwells within us, organs of sense have been supplied . . . and by the aid of these . . . it follows that there is nothing in the universe which cannot be compassed by man endowed with sense and reason."

From such a psycho-philosophic theory of man Comenius developed a set of postulates for the education of man, postulates which he asserted to be in harmony with the nature of the universe itself and, therefore, admirably suited to the natural inclinations of the learner. Education should, he averred, begin early in life; learning should move from the general to the particular, from the easier to the more difficult. Progress must not be rushed, that is, children should not be forced to do that which they do not wish to do, according to their age and motivation. All learning must initially come through sense impressions and, if teaching is to be successful, whatever is to be learned must be applied promptly. Finally, Comenius held that all subject matter must be taught consistently according to one and the same educational method.

Given this brief review, it is easy to see that the fruit of Pestalozzi came from the tree of Comenius'—a tree that, in turn, grew from seeds planted and nourished by such as Plato, Aristotle, Aquinas, and Rousseau. In the same way that rules of thumb led to psycho-philosophic principles, these in turn led to the next level of educational theory.

"LAWS" OF HUMAN NATURE TO GUIDE EDUCATION

Psycho-philosophic principles, such as "all learning begins with the senses" or "what will be learned depends upon the learner's inclinations," soon led to the development of even broader generalizations about education. Newer and bigger maps were being drawn.

Johann Friedrich Herbart (1776–1841), one of the first trained philosophers since the time of Plato to give serious attention to education, rebelled at the attempts of Comenius and Pestalozzi to "practicalize" education. Spurred by this motivation, Herbart attempted to raise the level of educational theory to a scholarly discipline. To achieve this end he took as his first premise the belief that mind is the material of education, and concluded that a theory of education is little more than a theory of mental processes. Once given an understanding of mental processes, Herbart felt, educational programs and practices designed to develop the mind would follow as night follows day.

Still, the mind is not a muscle that can be developed by itself; it must exercise on the sense impressions it receives from the immediate environment. Thus, Herbart reasoned, since learning is a function of experience then the environment in which the child learns assumes a crucial role in educational theory. It is the teacher, therefore, who is of most importance in the Hebartian formulation, for the teacher establishes the learning environment which influences the sense impressions to be received by the child's mind. Consequently the development of the child's mind and character are causally related to the skill and wisdom of the teacher in fostering the learning process.

A philosophic Idealist (i.e., idea-ist; the letter "l" is added for reasons of euphony alone), and successor to the great Immanual Kant (1724–1804) in the chair of philosophy at Koenigsburg, Herbart based his laws of human nature on a theory of ideas. He argued that we learn when we acquire a new idea, but that a new idea can be acquired only when it is compared with other ideas already in the mind. Just as we come to learn the meaning of a new word or a unique experience by looking at it in its context and associating it with similar words and experiences, so too do we learn the meaning of a new idea by associating it with our other ideas. Herbart called this process of learning the new by means of association with the old "apperception." The sum total of our ideas is an apperceptive mass, and it is this mass of associated ideas which permits the learner to acquire new ideas; thus, for Herbart, knowledge is acquired by the mind in a series of associative steps. Such was his theory of mental processes.

His theorizing was a cut above rules of thumb, if only because it indicates how practical principles (e.g., his Five Formal Steps) can be derived from "laws" of human nature. But his "laws," of course, were not the only ones from which dicta for the direction of education could be drawn.

Friedrich Froebel (1782–1852) was a contemporary of Herbart's who had worked briefly with Pestalozzi and had been influenced by Pestalozzi's philosophic Realism. In addition, he was impressed by the romantic naturalism of Rousseau, from which he eventually drew his three point theory of natural development, play activity, and social cooperation.

Even so, the dominant philosophic Idealism of the age infected him and he turned to an absolute Idealism for his root metaphor of life and, therefore, the basis of his educational theories. His Idealism is evident in the postulates upon which he based his educational proposals: that God's universe is an organic whole, of which all lesser organisms (e.g., individual and society) are members; that individuals are organic parts of society, which is itself a natural organism; that the child, in turn, is an organic unity which achieves fullness of being through creative self-activity; and this self-activity, or education, is a completely natural process and follows certain natural laws as legislated by God.

These postulates led him to the principles of natural development, play activity, and social cooperation; these principles pointed up Froebel's belief that the learner is not only an individual but a member of society, and education, if it is to be called successful, must help the child adjust to society. (On this view many claim that Froebel is the father of "life adjustment" theories of education, removing the onus from John Dewey. Even a casual inspection of the family tree of educational philosophy, however, reveals that the great Plato himself might well be charged with that particular paternity suit.)

Education thus conceived involved a natural unfolding of the child's interests and abilities, over a period of time, just as flowers unfold and reveal their charms over a period of time. Obviously there is some kind of similarity between the growing child and the growing flower, between the child's teacher and the flower's gardener, between the kinds of fertilizer required to help each grow and develop its potentials. Too, child and flower both pass through recognizable developmental phases, phases which may be helped or hindered by teacher or gardener and, consequently, it seems perfectly obvious that teacher and gardener can do better if they understand the natural laws of organic development pertinent to growth. Further, either child or flower will grow without teacher or gardener, as the child does if he leaves school and as the flower does when it grows in the wilderness; even so, either organism flourishes best when it has the help of a caretaker. Just as the gardener helps the flower unfold in a realization of all its potential splendor, so too does the teacher help the child realize all his God-given capacities.

This analogy so struck Froebel that he called his school "the children's garden" (*Kindergarten*), and he cast the child in the role of the growing seed and the teacher in the role of the careful, informed gardener. (For a recent philosophic analysis of the flower metaphor see Israel Scheffler's book, *The Language of Education.*)

By stressing the interactive roles of individual and society in the educative process Froebel avoided the overemphasis on sheer intellectualism that characterized Herbartian theory as well as the extreme emphasis on adjustment to social conditions that is to be found in Thomas Hobbes' (1588–1697) educational theories.

A final example of educational theories based upon "laws" of human nature is suggested by John Dewey's (1859–1952) theories. With Froebel, Dewey agreed that education had two faces, the individual or psychological and the social or sociological. Education must then be concerned with the development of the individual *in* society, not the training of a mind or the development of an intellect isolated from society and social considerations.

Clearly the psychological nature of a given child provides one ground for educational procedure and, just as clearly, the nature of a given society provides the other ground; given this dynamic, education occurs as individuals participate in society. But for Dewey this base for education, although accurate, was inadequate; the dynamic was established, but it lacked direction. Whatever else he may or may not have been, Dewey was first and foremost a moral philosopher; his basic commitment was to the social principle of democracy—and it was this kind of social organization that he had in mind when he set forth his educational theories.

Given this dynamic—the child as a problem solving animal and the society as a problem presenting environment—education became a matter of problem solving, with knowledge the inevitable by-product. A more complete presentation of Dewey's theories follows, but for now it should be noted that his "laws" of human nature, when related to learning, contained three essential ingredients: interest, purpose, and effort. Once interest is aroused (and a passing fancy or a whim does not represent interest) the learner will formulate a purpose and, if the interest is persistent and the purpose is internalized (e.g., not imposed by a teacher), then the child will put forth effort to realize his end in view, to solve his problem; and the end result involves learning. It is this effort, or activity, that leads directly to knowledge; learning is coexistent with intelligent activity.

USING THE MAPS TO GUIDE EDUCATION

Educational maps based on rules of thumb were crude and, although educators followed them, they lacked vector. Educational maps based on psycho-philosophic principles were more sophisticated, but the educational traveler had no assurance that the philosopher's sextant was firmly pointed toward the "right" star. Educational maps based on the "laws" of human nature were easily superior to rule of thumb sketches or psycho-philosophic drawings, but, like the former which lacked direction and like the latter which had too many directions, they fell short. Nevertheless, educators still use all three kinds of maps to guide their educational practices.

For instance, the influence of Monitorial rules of thumb is hard to overestimate. Originating in Great Britain, where Bell's and Lancaster's systems initially took root, the Monitorial method rapidly spread to Scandinavia, France, and Germany, where educators followed the Monitorial map for a good many years; even recent studies in comparative education indicate that Monitorial methods, albeit modified, are still used in certain European schools. In 1806 the Free School Society of New York brought the system to the United States and, within a few years, many areas in the East were following the Bell-Lancastrian rules of thumb to guide their educational programs. Adolphe E. Meyer, in his *An Educational History of the American People,* reports that:

> In 1818 Lancaster, then near the height of his pontifical authority, visited America. Received in the grand manner, like a bemedaled warrior, he devoted himself, amid the huzzahs of his marveling fellows, to the promotion of his system, helping to install it in various places, writing and lecturing in its favor, and even, upon invitation, addressing the people's agents and lawmakers in Congress . . .

Eventually its popularity died out, partially due to the introduction of other, "more practical," rules of thumb, as well as to the growing influence of more comprehensive theories of education.

(It is extremely interesting to note that the Monitorial system got off to such a good start in the United States because nineteenth century philanthropic institutions, such as the Free School Society, saw in it the method by which their philanthropic dollars could buy the widest educational influence. More recently contemporary philanthropic institutions, perhaps like the fabled Ford Foundation, in an attempt to find a solution to such problems as the teacher shortage, have sponsored experimental programs involving the use of "assistant teachers" in the classroom and "lay readers" in the home. Whatever the merits or faults of such programs, and whatever may be the implicit definition of "education" that lies buried within such programs, they are without doubt the methodological grandchildren of the Monitorial system. Many philanthropic and educational systems are evidently entranced by the military charm of Monitorial programs.)

Moving from the practical application of rules of thumb to the application of psycho-philosophic principles, consider the Object Lesson stemming from Pestalozzi's theories. The direct empiricism of the methodology, coupled with the rationalization which justified it, had an immense appeal to educators in Europe and the United States. The most famous application of Pestalozzi's theories is represented by the Oswego and Utica experiments of the 1860's, under the direction of Edward A. Sheldon. (The campus of Oswego State College today has a statue of Pestalozzi, a child on the knee and an apple in the hand, in symbolic memoriam of the Object Lesson.)

Following such psycho-philosophic principles as "proceed from the concrete to the abstract, the simple to the complex, and the particular to the general," elaborate maps for the guidance of education were drawn. The principles underlying the Oswego-Utica experiments, and the experiments themselves, were considered so successful that the National Teachers Association (forerunner of the National Education Association) adopted Object Teaching as the official and approved educational methodology. Teacher training institutions, impressed not only with the apparent wisdom of Pestalozzi's educational theories and the methodology which followed these, but also with the recommendation of the National Teachers Association, proceeded to train a generation or more of school teachers who were imbued with conviction as to the validity of the method and the psycho-philosophic principles underlying it.

The more comprehensive the map, the greater its potential application to education. Given the Herbartian "laws" of human nature, for instance, it seemed but a simple task to identify an educational methodology and program based on these "laws." While Herbart provided the outlines of such a methodology in his theory of apperception, it was his followers who formalized and rigidified his ideas into fixed dogma (as all disciples tend to do; the thinker's burden is the true believer). Called the Five Formal Steps, and designed to guide the teacher, Herbartian methodology can be summarized as follows:

1. *Preparation*, in which the teacher explains the purpose of the lesson at hand
2. *Presentation*, in which the new subject matter is analyzed and clarified
3. *Association*, in which the new ideas (i.e., subject matter) are compared and contrasted with the old
4. *Generalization*, in which the new is combined with the old to provide for the construction of a general principle
5. *Application*, in which the learner uses the newly acquired ideas; almost any public school teacher, especially those who have attended a normal school, has been exposed to some variant of this Hebartian methodology

Without doubt the educational maps drawn by Herbart and Pestalozzi have left an indelible imprint on American educational methodology.

Other comprehensive maps, such as those drawn by Froebel and Dewey, have also guided education. The educational principles of Froebel, for instance, had a great influence upon the schools through the work of Horace Mann (1796–1859) and Henry Barnard (1811–1900). These great educators based many of their reform programs on Froebel's theories; the kindergarten, for instance, is now firmly established as an integral part of the public school in most states. The influence of Dewey has also been great, especially upon elementary school education, even though many of the contemporary practices generally labeled "progressive" (i.e., stemming from Dewey's educational thought) would be more properly attributed to Rousseau, Pestalozzi, and Herbart.

The crucial point is, of course, that education is guided by some kind of map, be it the simple map of practical principles, the more complex map based on psycho-philosophic principles, or the rather extensive map drawn from the "laws" of human nature. When all of these maps are joined, in some way, so as to form a grand map of the educational universe, a comprehensive *system* is established.

COMPREHENSIVE SYSTEMS: "THE BIG MAP"

The accolade "philosophy of education" has often been given to these comprehensive systems. A philosophy of education, in this sense, is comprehensive because it incorporates propositions about man and society, knowledge and truth, right, wrong, good and bad, and the nature of reality. It is systematic because such propositions are woven into an intellectual tapestry with each thread dependent upon the others and each contributing to the others, so as to present a network of facts, values, and hypotheses about education.

Perhaps the first such map was drawn by Plato, who set the precedent for all comprehensive systems that have been labeled, generically, "Idealism." Plato's student, Aristotle (*ca.* 384–322), did not himself draw a map that we might specifically label "philosophy of education," but he did leave extensive charts, based on rational surveys of man, nature, and society so as to establish a framework for comprehensive systems generally called "Aristotelian."

St. Thomas Aquinas, for example, drew heavily upon Aristotle's thought when he drew a map to guide Catholic education (a philosophy usually identified as "Thomism" or "Scholasticism"). Another such map, often called "Classical Realism," leans heavily on Aristotelian sketches.

A different type of map, largely dismissing the cartography of both Idealists and Thomists, was drawn by such figures as Charles Peirce (1839–1914), William James (1842–1910), and John Dewey. Alternately identified as "Pragmatism," "Instrumentalism," or "Experimentalism," this map differs uniquely from Idealism, Thomism, or Realism because it was drawn, so to speak, using different rules of map making.

Even more recently a group of philosophers of education, largely in the tradition of Bertrand Russell (1872–   ) and Ludwig Wittgenstein (1889–1951), and using both different rules and different tools, have attempted to demonstrate that map making itself (i.e., the creation of comprehensive systems) is passe. Properly speaking, of course, this point of view—often known as "Logical Positivism," "Logical Empiricism," or simply "analytic philosophy"—should not be classified under the heading "Comprehensive Systems: 'The Big Map'" since it is neither comprehensive nor systematic in the way those terms were earlier defined in this section. Still in all, it *is* comprehensive in that analytic philosophers include almost any subject matter in the scope of their logical operations, and it is systematic because it does represent an orderly, consistent way of attacking problems in education.

Generally speaking, therefore, philosophies of education often represent comprehensive systems which, for purposes of classification, comparison, and pedagogy, have been labeled Idealism, Realism (including Thomism), and Pragmatism. This division of philosophic thought about education into "schools" is of course arbitrary—but there is both logical and pedagogical justification for it.

THE ESSAYS TO COME

The first three of the following eight essays represent what might be called the rational position in philosophy and education. Louise Antz, a contemporary Idealist, offers an application of philosophy to education that has Plato for its intellectual progenitor. Harry S. Broudy, a contemporary Realist who prefers to identify his essay as an exposition of Classical Realism, uses Aristotle as a main intellectual resource. Pius XI, writing ex cathedra, puts forth a theory of education drawn from many Church sources but primarily based on the rationalism of St. Thomas Aquinas.

The next essay, by George Kneller, has been identified as representing what might be called the "non-rational" (*not* irrational) position because it relates modern Existential philosophy to education and, as with Existentialism, is based on an Existentialist rejection of rationalism and empiricism in philosophy.

The succeeding two essays exemplify the Experimentalist-Pragmatic position in educational philosophy. Frederick C. Neff sets forth the philosophic principles of Peirce, James, and Dewey—principles we now categorize as "Pragmatism"—and look upon as the philosophic underpinnings of a great deal of modern education. Theodore Brameld, writing as a Reconstructionist founds his philosophy of education upon the grounds illustrated by Neff but moves beyond the normal conception of Pragmatism to offer a new vision of education.

The two concluding essays do not represent comprehensive philosophic systems so much as they represent "programmatic" approaches to educational problems. Israel Scheffler, drawing upon the work done in recent analytic philosophy has written one of the early essays applying the tools and techniques of philosophic analysis to the problems of education—an essay that has since been followed by a rush of analyses of the language and concepts used in education. Richard W. Dettering, basing his essay on the work of such semanticists as Korzybski and Hayakawa as well as that of philosophic analysts, points out another ramification of the meaning of recent philosophic and linguistic developments for education.

∽

Idealism as a Philosophy of Education

*Louise Antz**

INTRODUCTION

Every philosophy seeks to be universal, that is, to be true of its object wherever that object is found. A philosophy "of," like philosophy of art, of politics, of religion, or of education, combines two universes of discourse, that of general philosophy and that of the principles of the given field of advanced human activity and thought. This field is one common to mankind, but it is one which cannot fruitfully be theorized about philosophically without considerable reference to particular cultures. In application, it must always draw from and be adapted to concrete realities as these are understood in given communities, whether local or international.

America has had very few schools actually founded and maintained on philosophical principles. We are an eclectic people, and our educational thought reflects ideas from all the philosophies, without much effort to understand them theoretically. In the meantime, each philosophy tries to draw people out of the cave into the light of its own sun and to send them

back as better teachers, perhaps not only of the neighbors but of mankind. Idealism owes much to the suns of other philosophies, but believes it has some ultimately fundamental light of its own.

I. THE TERMINOLOGY OF IDEALISM

Idealism is the name which has come to be used for all philosophic theories which give priority to *mind*. Since very few philosophies are materialistic in a radical sense, there are idealistic elements in nearly all philosophies. There is no single meaning for *Idealism,* but a family of meanings; and therefore, no single inclusive definition but a family of definitions. The same is true for the word *mind,* which has a number of synonyms and near synonyms, each with its own history of usage. Further, the word *mind* may stand either for the subject of an experience, that is, for the person thinking; or it may stand for the realm of intelligible, orderly meanings—for the knowable rather than for the knower. Still further, the *subject* of the experience may be either human or divine,

* An original essay written expressly for this volume.

and the objects of thought may be on a human or a divine scale.

Words denoting the experiencing human subject may be *mind, soul, spirit, life,* person, or the Greek terms *psyche, nous, pneuma.* The same words, capitalized, may stand for the Divine Subject, and so may *Logos, Absolute,* and *God.* For mind as objective,[1] as the realm of intelligible meanings, the terms are mind, thought, essences, the intelligible, the true, ideas, the ideal, the realm of mind, the realm of form, the meaningful, reason; and the Absolute, the World Mind, Reason, Nature, the Logos, the Divine Cosmos, the Mind of God, God.

"The Greeks had a word for it." All the meanings denoted and connoted by these terms (and their opposite terms, standing for the inert, the radically passive, the purposeless, the lifeless, the chaotic) were discovered by the Greeks, and they had words for each meaning. I say *words* because each thinker, like a creative artist, saw the nature of things in a partly individual way, and invented or reassigned terms to suit his insight and judgment. This same process went on among Hindu thinkers before the Greeks, and it goes on today. This means that philosophic terms must be understood in their own context.

The word *idea*[2] is Greek, and means

that which is by nature clear and intelligible. It means that which has form, the opposite of the chaotic. But the Greeks derived *idea* from *idein, to see;* and *to see* is a mental activity, rather than the object of the activity. Plato's expression, "To see with the eye of the mind" is a way of saying, "To know through one's power of reason." *Reason* for classical philosophy is the power or structure of mind which enables it to grasp and work with its objects, whether in a cognitive, emotional, aesthetic, practical, or technical way. Today, we almost always use *reason* in a technical way, to mean *reasoning about* something, and so we deprive *reason* of the full meaning it had till modern times. We need a word, since *reason* has been so narrowed, to mean "think-feel" or "understand-appreciate," to denote this unity of mental response.

Primarily, an *idea* is an object of knowledge—something knowable or known. Taken as a guide for action, an *idea* becomes an *ideal.* The perfect or ideal squares and circles of geometry are psychologically suggested by the imperfectly square or circular objects of the sense world, but they themselves are of a very different order of being. They are intelligible objects, visible only to the eye of the mind. They can never, being immaterial, be exactly copied in the material world, but they are the patterns which we follow—roughly or carefully according to the needs of the situation—whenever we make a square or a circular object. The same condition holds for man in relation to the most fundamental of Platonic Ideas, the *Good,* with its special forms, the *True* and the *Beautiful,* and their species, temperance, harmony,

---

[1] "Belief in objective mind is natural. Men naturally believe that there is reason in the sense of discursive thought . . . but a reason that somehow accounts for things and renders their operations intelligible." F. J. E. Woodbridge, *The Realm of Mind* (New York: Columbia University Press, 1926), p. 50.

[2] Greek synonyms for form are *idea, eidos, paradeigma, morphe.* Compare our *idea, idol, paradigm, morphology.*

spiritedness, wisdom, justice, and the like. Through a good education, and through the long effort of reason and wise living, man can come to comprehend them; but again, since they are immaterial, he can embody them only to a degree in his natural life and institutions. But, knowing and loving them, he can through his aspiration toward them avoid the life of mental sloth, of bestial and unreasoning pleasure, and of soul-destroying false ambitions; and Plato felt man can bring harmony and proportion into his soul, making it musical and healthful, fit for this life and for immortality.

FOUR MAIN TRADITIONS IN IDEALISM. Idealisms differ in many respects, including their theories about mind. The oldest tradition is the Greco-Christian *philosophia perennis,* with three fundamental propositions. The first states the assumption of antecedent being; that is, of the indestructibleness of basic reality. The second states the assumption of the competence of human reason; that is, the relation between mind and being is such that being can be known. This principle belongs to both Realism and Idealism and was never seriously challenged before modern naturalism and Pragmatism. The third proposition is that being and value are primal in the universe and are inseparable. Urban[3] calls this "the axiom of intelligibility" and rightly judges it to be the driving force of the entire Greco-Christian philosophical tradition.

The second Idealistic tradition is the distinctly epistemological one, often called *mentalism, spiritualism,* or *sub-*

[3] Wilbur Urban, *Beyond Realism and Idealism* (London: George Allen and Unwin, 1949).

jectivism, since an active mind is a spirit, or the subject that has experiences. *Mentalism* began with Descartes and Berkeley, and many structures have been built on its basic proposition, which states the recognition that human knowledge is always had by a subject; that is, it is always in or for a mind. The name *Idealism* was born with this subjectivist movement. The Greek idealists were usually known as Platonists. *Idea-ism* might have been a better name, since Descartes and Berkeley called perceptions *ideas,* using the old Greek word for things clearly seen. Since Descartes, there has been an uninterrupted epistemological argument among Idealists and Realists over the nature of percepts and their relation to the rest of what we know. No new correctional or synthesizing effort has satisfied all thinkers, and so each has been met by a counterargument. But most philosophers came to agree that a theory transcending both simple epistemological Idealism and simple epistemological Realism is necessary, and many interesting ones have been devised.

The third kind of Idealism, the *organic,* grew out of the effort to solve the problem of uniting subjectivity and objectivity in a satisfactory theory that would account for both the universe and the individual, and for both the objective and the subjective factor in knowing. Kant's work is a major link but full-blown organicism appears in Hegel, with the thesis that not only must mind be organic to being, but being must be organic to mind. Organic philosophies, as the name suggests, think of reality as a complex structure comparable to living things.

Some organic philosophies see mind as wholly impersonal and immanent within the whole. These are, roughly, pantheistic and are found in both the East and the West. Others see mind as both immanent and transcendent, that is, mind pervades all things, making them what they are, but the whole has a transcendent dimension; that is, there is an eternal, purposeful, self-knowing power at the heart of reality which is more than any possible sum of the parts and gives the whole its final character. This concept has sometimes been called *panentheism,* that is, God is transcendent to everything but Himself, but He is in and through all. But however the organic whole is understood, it always is conceived as having a nature of its own. It is absolute, that is, independent: nothing that is or ever will be is beyond it, and its laws are interior to itself; it has a life of its own, it is harmonius within, it is intelligible. The harmony is strikingly a harmony of opposites, but basically of "contraries," not "contradictories."

Some of the opposites which have essentially bipolar relations are: the whole and the part, the subjective and the objective, the personal and the impersonal, the eternal and the temporal, the universal and the particular, the abstract and the concrete, the steady and the fluid, conjunctiveness and disjunctiveness, unity and diversity, being and becoming, the inactive and the creative, the permanent and the novel. Professor Frank C. Wegener's *Organic Philosophy of Education* is a contemporary study of what a philosophy of organism can mean for education.

Personalism, the fourth development, finds its key ideas in the phenomenon of personhood. Much influenced by Hebrew and Christian religious experience, it objects to pantheistic philosophic theories, such as those of Spinoza and Hegel, which see universal reality as divine but impersonal, as objective mind but not subjective self. Personalists also object to theories which care only for the intellectual nature of the human mind, as against the full self, for whom feeling, willing, creating, and decision-making are as integral as is logical thinking. There are large experimentalist and existentialist elements in this type of Idealism, as indeed there are also in the organic type.

AMERICAN IDEALIST PHILOSOPHERS OF EDUCATION. Idealism as a philosophy of education has been represented in America by Emerson, the Alcotts, Harris, Horne, Hocking, Demiashkevich, Thompson, Butler, Wegener, Ulich, and the present writer. Probably the greatest difference among them is in the degree to which theism and personalism do or do not influence their thought. They largely accept the identification of being and value in the perennial philosophy; the theory of Berkeley that *to be* is to be for a mind; the theory of Hegel that there is a unity throughout the universe; the theory that God both transcends the universe and is immanent in it; and they largely accept the Personalist conclusion that the human self is the best key we have to the nature of that of which we are a part.

I have called my own general philosophy *Theistic Idealism,* or *Panentheism,* to convey the conviction that reality is made up of minds, or spirits, and their products. God, the primal spirit, the ground of all being, is both transcendent and immanent. Nature is one of his manifestations, the medium through which human persons are developed, and for which they have, in their own local part of it, some responsibility. Whitehead's conception of reality as an organic universe, shot through and through with dimensions of a bipolar nature, with God the one eternal actual entity, can be interpreted to meet the Idealist's theory that everything is either subjective or objective mind: either mind creating or mind responding to the products of other minds. It is harder to show the eternal actual entity as "personal" or a "self." But theistic Idealists do think that to the *spiritual being* and the *natural being* which are aspects of the whole for so many organicists there must be added the attribute of *personal being*.

No one has expressed better than Martin Buber the ancient Hebrew and Christian intuition that "I-It" and "I-Thou" are the two primary meanings that man knows. "I-It" expresses man's attitude to things, and to man when he is regarded as a thing. "I-Thou" expresses the relation of *meeting,* when face to face each discovers the other as "Thou" and knows himself as an "I." This is what *person* means, this is the ontological reality that justifies Kant's "Treat each person, including thine own self, as an end withal." There comes a time when one finds himself meeting—in his heart, in his mind—an invisible Thou who is recognized as ultimate.

The "I-Thou" relation between a child and an adult, or another child, can be peculiarly real. It is a quintessence of faith, hope, and love. It is the stuff of Paradise; and like every other Paradise known in human life, it is doomed to be broken through the knowledge of good and evil. Broken, but as a value not destroyed. It reappears and is mended in new personal relations. It takes the form of the intellectual understanding that each man is an end in himself and therefore never to be treated as a means only. It is put to work in faithful service, in the private realm and in the public. It is held to with the saving good humor of faith when the spectacle of cruel, power-driven, irrational humanity is enough to make every man doubt all men, and God.

This phrase, the saving good humor of faith, perhaps needs a word of explanation. The true teacher understands it; the one who, through whatever means experience may offer, strives toward the salvation of every child, no matter how dreadful a specimen of delinquent humanity this one or that one may be. The faith that can continue to serve the good in the very pit of evil has an element of gaiety about it, a lightness of heart possible only if one believes this evil is not the last word. The life of Anne Frank illustrates the point perfectly.

II. IDEALISM AND SOME CONTEMPORARY EDUCATIONAL PROBLEMS

MIND AND METHOD. Modern Idealism has no single method, comparable to experiment in Pragmatism or to the systematic structuring of facts in Scientific Realism, as the key to all its work. It doubts there is any such thing as *the* scientific method or *the* philosophic method. Idealists do, of course, make much use of dialectic, and they use various methods, logical, aesthetic, metaphorical, experimental, and others, to develop the meaning of important intuitions. On the whole, methods, including educational methods, develop to fit needs and conditions, and in the last analysis, mind as mind judges its own work. "The truth is, the mind is not subject to 'law' in the same rigid sense that matter is . . . There always remains a certain amount of arbitrary spontaneity in its action, without which it would be dead."[4] This is the wisdom of Peirce. Bosanquet, in a little gem which has unfortunately been allowed to go out of print, writes:

> I confess that all this talk about method in philosophy seems to me rather foolish and wearisome. I only know in philosophy one method; and that is to expand *all* the relevant facts, taken together, into ideas which approve themselves to thought as exhaustive and self-consistent.[5]

Lamprecht writes: "Dialectic was Plato's word for the most determined intellectual effort to bring together systematically every consideration that is relevant to the understanding of any subject or problem. 'According as a man understands or does not understand a subject as a whole,' wrote Plato, 'he is or is not a dialectician.'"[6]

Rouse translates Plato a little differently:

Those who are judged best of the twenty-year-olds (Socrates said) will receive greater honors than the rest; and these must gather together into one connected view all the studies which they followed without order in their education in childhood, to disclose the relationship of the studies to one another and to the nature of real being.[7]

Tillich, whose analysis and use of dialectic is worth anybody's study, says:

> . . . many processes of observation and thought are necessary in order to reach true judgments. The reason is that things hide their true being . . . This discovery is made through a process of preliminary affirmations, consequent negations, and final affirmations. It is made through "yes and no," or dialectically.[8]

A major method is a flexible pattern for ordering things to some purpose. Other methods and techniques are always necessary in a subsidiary fashion. Thus Dewey, in analyzing the components of "an" experience of the sort that ends with the testing of an hypothesis, describes the whole as "a complete act of reflective thinking" and permits within the act itself any methods, including dialectic, which will lead the mind to the needed materials and their interpretation. The case is similar with his analysis of "an" aesthetic experience, where the purpose is different, more contemplative, but the quality of wholeness and mental satisfaction the same. In a parallel fashion, a dialectical experience may include within it hy-

[4] Justus Buchler (ed.), *The Philosophy of Peirce* (New York: Harcourt Brace & World, Inc., 1940), p. 348.

[5] Bernard Bosanquet, *Three Lectures on Aesthetic* (London: Macmillan & Co., Ltd., 1915), p. 3.

[6] Sterling P. Lamprecht, *Our Philosophical Traditions* (New York: Appleton-Century-Crofts, Inc., 1955), p. 48.

[7] W. H. D. Rouse (trans.), *Great Dialogues of Plato* (New York: New American Library, 1956), p. 337 (*Republic,* Bk. VII, 537).

[8] Paul Tillich, *Systematic Theology* (Chicago: The University of Chicago Press, 1951), Vol. I, p. 101.

pothesis making, problem solving, and other means of search and clarification, but close—for the time being—with a luminous sense of insight, of finding oneself on a new mountain top with a new perspective. It may be one that can be elaborated into a hypothesis; it may be one that can only be expressed in a metaphor, because fact-language is too weak for it; it may be so much more mystical than discursive that no expression at all is adequate to it, except a qualitative change in the very feel of life, and therefore in one's living.

Idealists do not believe that scientific methods have a justifiable monopoly on truth, and they regret the use of the term "pseudo-statement" by most Logical Positivists to describe human thought and insight expressed in literature and the other arts. They do not believe that poetry, morality, and religion have only emotive value. There is important knowledge about man and his world which is not accessible to scientific method in the official sense. John Middleton Murry, writing against the idea of literature as pseudo-statement, illustrates with the problem of the accurate description of single objects and the accurate statement of experiences. "When John Clare speaks of the primrose

> With its crimp and crudled leaf
> And its little brimming eye

his is surely an accurate description: but accurate with an accuracy unknown to and unachievable by science."[9] The point is that every object and every experience has both a com-mon and a unique aspect, and the unique aspect, and the unique, or the concrete singular, is communicated not through scientific generalizations but through art. *The fundamental tool of art is metaphor.*

But in fact there is a metaphorical element in all language, including the languages of science; and there are assertorial elements in all art and in religion. Philip Wheelwright[10] argues cogently that all statements are expressive and that scientific propositions are not pure assertions, but rather are limiting cases containing the minimum of meaning beyond the assertorial. Poetic and religious statements, on the other hand, have assertorial meanings to the extent that they contain ideas to which the speaker gives *assent*. The kind of assent here is very frequently intuitional. Whether the criterion of truth be correspondence, pragmatic effect, coherence, or intuition, we discover through a dialectical analysis that each tacitly assumes truth to be that which *ought to be assented to*. Each has an appropriate declaration about assenting. What the intuitionist declares, when his position is pushed to the extreme through dialectic, is this: "We *ought to assent* only, or primarily, to those statements toward which, with our whole mind awake, we respond with an illumined conviction of their rightness."[11]

For personal life, and the life of shared experience, such intuitions are fully as important as are the findings

---

[9] J. Middleton Murry, "Beauty is Truth," *The Symposium—A Critical Review* (October, 1930), p. 498.

[10] Philip Wheelwright, *The Burning Fountain, A Study in the Language of Symbolism* (Bloomington, Ind.: Indiana University Press, 1954), p. 289.

[11] *Ibid.*

of science. Much experience with the arts and with religion helps the learner to evaluate them as they are there expressed. For a creative intuitional life, one must be encouraged in experiences of his own, and in their expression through whatever means he can master. Idealistic educators provide the young, from babyhood on, with richly intuitional literature and art, and help them to recognize and use their own intuitional assents. But here, as elsewhere, dialectic and experiment have roles to play as checks and questioners.

For Idealists, the great mental activities are always methodological; that is, there is always a productive working with whatever aspects of "objective mind" may be at hand. A fair summary of what Idealists see mind doing would be something like this: *First,* mind's chief activity is unifying, with analysis and synthesis the typical subordinate activities. Kant's insistence that mind never perceives things as isolated bits but always in forms, or *Gestalts,* against a background, is relevant here. Analysis means breaking the *Gestalts* down for study; synthesis means reordering the materials. This is always into a new *Gestalt,* for once anything is analyzed it is seen as something other than it was before.

Second, mind's activity is marked by the selection of material. Every teacher knows that whatever may be presented to them, children's minds simply will not all take it in the same way. *Third,* mind discovers and creates values—practical and artistic, for instance, or scientific, moral, social, religious, philosophical. One can't be sure which act comes first, discovery or creation. Many people have to do something creative themselves before their eyes are opened to what has all the time been waiting around them. *Fourth,* the active subjective mind creates itself. It enriches itself, it endangers and rescues itself; it learns its dependencies as well as its independencies, and where it can look for salvation in dire need. It learns that it is not omnipotent and that it is responsible. It identifies itself as *self.*

If these are the typical things that minds naturally do, then the business of schools is to see that they get a chance to do them. All minds are alike in having these basic gifts, but different in degree, and in their taste for the elements in the environment. It is easy to starve a mind by giving it too little to work with, or the wrong things. This fact implies *a foundational principle for educators:* As far as you possibly can, expose each child to the best things of the culture, in all their variety, so that he is not deprived of the opportunity to find his "own," and to decide eventually what to do with it.

A second foundational principle is: Help the student gain the special techniques which will enable him to unify, to select, etc., his chosen undertakings beyond the mere beginner's level. This means great knowledge of subject matter on the part of teachers; much greater than the average teacher is expected to have today. Of course, knowing subject matter means knowing the "doing" of any field, whether language, science, painting, or morality; and pedagogy means knowing how to connect the material and the learner.

The inclusion of morality raises a special point here. There are some things, like living up to the basic norms of the community, which can be expected of everyone. But this is a problem which, more than any other, cannot be handled by the school without the cooperation of the community. It raises the question of discipline as a community-wide responsibility, and the problem of going beyond the community's standards to better ones when those of the community are particularly weak or evil.

A third foundational principle is: Learn to judge the needs and abilities of the learner. Scientific measuring techniques help a great deal, of course, but sheer human insight and understanding are still very necessary. Knowledge of the basic ways in which children *can* be different is of fundamental importance, and here again a judicious mixture of the personal knowledge of the teacher and the findings of science is called for. Anyone who has followed the history of educational psychology knows how slow and difficult, and how often erroneous, has been the process of discovering what sort of a thing native intelligence is. The most recent studies tell us it is not one thing, measurable by one IQ test, but a combination of several different abilities tied-up, as it were, in a bundle. Idealists, of course, will stand by their hunch that the abilities belong to a permanent unifying self, a genuine "I" or "You," but will readily grant the variety of native equipment.

Researchers are now quite sure that the following, among a good many others, some of them not yet discovered, are primal mental abilities: *The space factor,* the ability to visualize objects in space, and to sense how much room there is between them. *The number factor,* which means ability to manipu-

late numbers, but is not the same as the ability to do mathematical reasoning. *Verbal comprehension,* which means the ability to comprehend the meaning of words, and thus to interpret literature. *Word fluency,* the ability to call up words and use them in speech or writing. *The ability to memorize,* which is of several distinct kinds, not all present in the same person: for instance, the ability to memorize intentionally and to recall casual past experience are not the same. *Induction,* the ability to discover the underlying principle in the material one is working with. Thurstone says we do not know whether this ability is associated with creativeness.[12] All normal children have some amount of each ability, but the various abilities in their several degrees come in different "packages" in different children. Child George may be high in abilities T,V,X,Z, but low in S,W,Y. Child Ruth may be high in S,V,X,Y, but low in T,U,W,Z. Experimental studies are being made to learn the effect of different combinations of talents on ease of reading, creative work, total personality configurations, and the like.

SUBJECT MATTER. Idealistic philosophers of education generally agree that the school curriculum should have regard for the abilities and needs of learners, the legitimate demands of society, and the kind of universe we live in. They would urge keeping subject matter liberal, rather than specialized, for as long a time as the student's abilities, financial resources, and interests allow. Subject matter which liber-

[12] Thelma Gwinn Thurstone *et al., What is Intelligence?* (Washington, D.C.: National Education Association).

ates takes the student out of the cave of localism and mere vocationalism. Subjects which widen the student's understanding of humankind are particularly valuable for this, and so are those which open up the world of nature to him. How the subjects are taught is as important as what is taught. The liberal arts are not liberal when taught as mere technical facts for passing examinations, or when not adapted to the student's capacities. The sciences, for instance, should be taught as conceptual orders having unity and fascinating applications; as open on their frontiers and always in need of new thinkers; as human ideas, partly reflecting nature and partly instrumental in dealing with her; as closely related, in a two-way process, to other elements in the culture, especially to social life, the arts, morals, politics, religion, and philosophy. *Thinking like a scientist* is something any student can do on some level, and it is far more important than learning masses of facts and carrying out endless laboratory directives. Dewey urged this truth upon us half a century ago, and many recent studies have shown that education has persistently resisted his plea. Science teachers do not seem to be sufficiently educated themselves to appreciate scientific thinking. (Lest anyone misunderstand, a student majoring in a science needs to learn its facts thoroughly!)

History, the fine arts, and religion make plain man's failures as well as his successes, and thus raise the question of his whole nature, and of the nature of the universe. Teachers in the public schools still tend to avoid teaching these subjects in depth, partly because they have not been educated for it,

and partly in self-protection, since these questions can be controversial. They thus delay, or permanently stunt, intellectual and emotional growth in the learners. Teen-agers and even younger children very much desire the substance and meaning found in the questions which, on an advanced level, make up the branches of philosophy. A better educational world than our own will be able to provide them with this food.

TEACHERS AND THE NEW MACHINES. Idealists believe the most important factor in a child's environment is the quality of the adults who influence him. This judgment in no way denies the influence of the young upon the young. It simply maintains that all the young reflect adult habits, thoughts, qualities, and norms. Wise, firm, loving parents can make up for any number of handicaps, from poverty to the evils in social custom and propaganda, provided their battle with the rest of the environment is not altogether too uneven. Excellent teachers are more important than expensive buildings, though buildings and equipment really suited to teaching and learning aid all teachers. Likewise, in the end any conditions serve children well which prevent the teacher from being regarded by the community as "just a little school-teacher" of not much consequence in the adult world.

The good teacher is a person who opens up new worlds to learners and helps them with the skills and attitudes necessary for understanding, growth, and mastery. He must be a magician here, for the modes of influence, direct and indirect, are many. Every teacher will not reach every pupil; and pupils, because of their own natures and personal histories, need a variety of influential adults. These are reasons for a school's having able teachers who are not too much alike, even though they may well have a basic professional philosophy in common. It is usually desirable, for instance, to have both men and women on the staff; and it is well to include the "parental" and the "tough and businesslike" types, the exuberantly physical and the delicately spiritual, the fact-minded and the theory-minded on a faculty. The more generous and appreciative these teachers are toward each other's idiosyncracies and special gifts, the more chance for everyone's good mental health and growth.

The new devices for teaching, especially television and the "learning machines," are often welcomed as a substitute for live teachers by mechanistic, impersonal people; and they are often rejected by people who fear any change at all from face-to-face teaching. Neither of these attitudes is intelligent. The Idealist, of course, rejects the notion that efficient factual learning is the one great thing in education. But on both philosophic and practical grounds, he can welcome the machines, provided certain conditions are met.

The Idealist who finds in the organic nature of a person the most satisfactory analogy for reality as a whole recognizes that there are mechanical structures and dimensions within the organic. They serve as one of the means of regularity, and they are usually objects of very great beauty, as in the sheer perfection of a deductive system, the delicate balance of a bird's body, or the rhythmic interlocking of gears and pistons in an engine.

The structure and functioning of both the objective world, the realm of "objective mind" as the Idealist would say, and of the self, or the realm of "subjective mind," range from a kind that can be called mechanical to a kind that is sheer flow, uniqueness, or creativity. And any aspect of the life of mind has a place in school. An Idealist would particularly not want to banish the mechanical, because there is nothing so true as that free, creative experience can be impeded, if not made possible, by the lack of basic mechanical skills, whether in the use of a language, the playing of an instrument, the managing of a home, or the mastery of a science. A great many of the methods courses in teachers colleges have been meant to enable teachers to teach the "mechanics" so that all children have good control of them: There has been enormous failure to reach this result for reasons that should be obvious. This writer used to dream of teaching logic so well that everyone would pass the course, and with skill and understanding. But too much variety in student ability, too much absence just on the wrong days, too little chance to find out *just what* was confusing a student, frustrated this aim. Good machines, that provide for individual learning and drill in a thoroughly ordered way, can change all that. The teacher's energy then can go into channeling the child's skills and knowledges into imaginative and creative application of every variety.

The conditions without which we might as well junk the machines include (1) having the machines designed by experts, such as B. F. Skinner, and (2) having administrators and teachers fully prepared to use the machines properly. A real danger is that teachers will be made miserable by principals whose training is not in the wealth of the culture but in public relations, building management, and statistics. New gadgets hastily adopted are commonly a bane, whereas they might actually have the potentiality for being a blessing, if properly employed.

PHILOSOPHY AND PROBLEMS OF DISCIPLINE. There is nothing that frightens the young teacher or wears down the older one so much as difficulties in classroom management, especially when there is little help from the total community and when there is uncertainty as to what the practically and ethically right thing is. The aim of discipline, of course, is to maintain the community, to develop the behavior most fruitful in social growth and in learning, and to strengthen the individual's direction of his own acts according to norms. Idealists are on principle against both authoritarianism and permissivism, but they are for both authority and freedom. The actual conditions and the particular methods that cause trouble or make for success must be learned in part from one's own life, in part from sociology and psychology, and in part from the "know-how" of the profession.

But while sociology and psychology are major sources for reliable data on how to handle typical problems under typical conditions, there remain two facts to consider. One is that the findings of these still young sciences show considerable contradiction and change, within periods as short as five years. The other is that the answers of science do not translate themselves directly into rules for action but must be interpreted within a context of individual facts, of preferred values and of other truths and principles. Philosophy can play a help-ful role here. There is something fairly steady in the principles of a mature philosophy of education. They can help a teacher form his own judgments about new claims, avoid accepting the latest ideas about human behavior as always right and avoid falling into a chilly scepticism. From an Idealistic point of view, there are valuable insights and methods in each of the three major philosophical positions of Realism, Idealism, and Pragmatism, and in those of the newcomers, Existentialism and philosophical analysis. There is also a great deal to be learned from religious thought.

There are different philosophies partly because their creators are each specially interested in certain dimensions of reality. An organic Idealistic philosophy recognizes a number of dimensions each of which has its rights. The late Rupert C. Lodge was wise when he argued that in the practice of business as well as of teaching, use of the differing main principles and methods of Realism, Idealism, and Pragmatism can be valid in differing types of problem situation.[13] Wayne Leys, using a number of historical ethical principles, builds his book *Ethics for Policy Decisions*[14] on a similar concept. The important thing, he believes, is to be able to ask deliberative questions skillfully in order to find out what sort of guide or guides is relevant to the ethical situation facing one. There are times, for instance, when the utilitarian principle of considering the greatest

13 Rupert C. Lodge, *Philosophy of Education,* 2d ed. (New York: Harper & Brothers, 1947).

14 Wayne A. R. Leys, *Ethics for Policy Decisions* (Englewood Cliffs, N.J.: Prentice-Hall, Inc., 1952).

good of the greatest number should be invoked, as by a legislature deciding where to build a new road, or a faculty deciding on a curriculum within given financial limits. But for a teacher personally upset by the behavior of a neurotic student, the question might well be, "What is your scale of values? Are you putting first things first?" Questions of psychology and the Stoic question, "What is within my power?" are also relevant. The main question for a teacher in one situation might well be, "Is my proposed action consistent with my accepted ideals?", while in another situation this question could be quite irrelevant. "What is the actual problem to which I need an answer?" might be the proper question.

This is not an eclectic procedure but rather a discriminating and dialectical one. It could not be used by a person who did not already have a profound conviction that "the good" is something to be striven for. Not all general philosophies but, so far as I know them, all philosophies of education are developed on the assumption that "the good" *means something*. They differ in their understanding of it, but they have a good deal in common, too. Teachers familiar with stable philosophic and religious conceptions of human nature will find it easier to interpret the usefulness and relevance, for discipline and other problems, of the new "facts" and theories poured out by scientific research, and by knights-errant who may or may not be qualified to guide education. They will, also, be more ready to "be all things to all men" when they deal with parents, colleagues, and children representing different faiths and traditions.

EDUCATION FOR THE COMMON-WEALTH. There is a central tradition in Idealistic thought which unites interest in the human being as self, interest in the commonwealth, and interesting education, particularly education for leadership and for judgment of leadership. The tradition today joins with these an urgent desire "to speak for man," "to save the earth." This union of concerns has not been historically true of all Idealists, for they have differed greatly on the relation of the individual to social institutions. On the one extreme is the anti-social interiorized life of the cynics, the ultra-solipsistic egoism of Max Stirner, and the anti-governmental individualism of Walt Whitman. On the other hand is the excessive esteem for social institutions of the later Hegel and the cooperation of the philosopher-educator Giovanni Gentile with Italian fascism. More in the center, with more signs of having learned from the dialectic of experience,[15] are Socrates, Plato, [16] Kant, the earlier Hegel, and Royce; and also recent philosophers of education like Hocking, Horne, Demiashkevich, Butler, and Wegener. In them we find the genuine Idealistic principle which says that the very essence of mind is to be free, and that institutions are needed to encourage and guide the growth of mind; and that the meaning of freedom is to be sought in the whole nature of mind—in its relation to the structure

[15] For an analysis of the power of the "dialectic of experience," see W. E. Hocking, *Human Nature and its Remaking* (New Haven, Conn.: Yale University Press, 1929).

[16] Both the *Republic* and the *Laws* are excessively paternalistic, but to identify their spirit with either communistic or fascistic totalitarianism seems to me a misreading.

of experience and of the objective world, as well as in its subjectivity.

The *Republic* and the *Laws*, each with a great deal to say about education, are essentially in the domain which Walter Lippmann calls the public philosophy; yet the myth of Er, like the dialectical path in the Symposium and the myth of the soul in the Phaedrus, offer reasons for living the good life which are quite other than the demands of citizenship. It is the adventure of the soul in the universe, rather than in the town, which clinches Socrates' claim that the just life is the only humanly acceptable life. Nevertheless, it is in the town, in the give and take between man and man, that the soul discovers its nature and learns to look for its ideals.

One of the most valuable things in Plato is his recognition that a commonwealth fit for civilized man to live in must have excellent men to govern it; men highly trained and widely experienced; wise in the ways of humanity, knowing how to be practical, yet firmly guided by well understood ideals; and ready to spend their lives in the public service. The greatest flaw in Plato's political theory, as Aristotle clearly saw, is the failure to provide for a check on the governors, and for advice to them, through the citizens; also, he fails to see that quite ordinary people are capable of judging the general worth of proposals put clearly before them. The feeling of the citizens that they have a vested interest in the workings of the commonwealth is as important as having the right men in office.

Walter Lippmann, in *The Public Philosophy,* reminds us of the well established fact that "the relation is very close between our capacity to act at all and our conviction that the action we are taking is right."[17] The basic law of the land must reflect something that is higher than the arbitrary will of any individual or nation; something that is binding on "both the Greeks and the Persians"; something that the reason of any human being can accept. This is the basic meaning of natural law. Whether we think its source is God, or Nature, or the accumulated, interpreted experience of the human race, it is there for man to appeal to, beyond Caesar and beyond arbitrary decrees. It is "the right." It makes civility among nations possible.

Our own country was founded on such ideas. They are the very essence of the public philosophy, the framework within which justice and public service can function. Idealists do not think that any verbal formulation of basic ethical and political principles is final, nor that application can be made directly without interpretation. They do think there is plenty of evidence that, unless principles long acceptable to reason and still being refined in such documents as the Declaration of Human Rights of the United Nations are taught and held to within the several commonwealths, education will be poorly supported both financially and spiritually, and in turn will be weak in its own effort to increase personal and social well-being. Our schools, after all, are supported by a society essentially industrial and commercial. Educators are not in control of the dynamics of power. They influence its operations in

17 Walter Lippmann, *The Public Philosophy* (New York: New American Library, 1955), p. 83, 137–138.

the long run through the habits and ideas they develop in the young, and perhaps especially the young who go to college.

The colleges unfortunately do relatively little to see that all graduates are acquainted with the principles of the public philosophy, and with the problems of their use. The present stampede to teach science is mainly for job-getting, and scientists, perhaps more than anybody else, need to be saved from the provincialism of specialization. We can be grateful that leading scientists and technologists are pleading for much more attention to the reading and writing of English, for skill here makes wider self-education in adulthood likely. But the great majority of all students go into business and industry, or into homemaking. There is every temptation in a profit-making society to put the selfish will of the individual first. Our educational services, for both youth and adults, need to make a powerful effort to develop ideas and attitudes of loyalty toward the public good—local and worldwide—for this good is the only thing which can protect the individual in his personal life, giving him the chance to be human.

In the 1930's Michael Demiashkevich, a refugee from Russia, begged America to give a thorough, serious education in the sciences and the humanities to all youths in the upper quarter of the student body, for the sake of an informed public leadership. He argued that this need not take money and time from the teaching of the other students, who should have an equal share of education, according to their needs. It means essentially academic seriousness, more disciplined

thinking, and richer, tougher subject matter for those able to take it. Demiashkevich was a strong critic of the extremist tendencies in "progressive" education, with which, incidentally, he refused to identify John Dewey. Demiashkevich unfortunately used the word "elite" to denote the group of able youth. His book[18] was thoroughly trounced and rejected by almost the whole educational press. I believe his ideas would be much better received today. But we are still not educating people to know what they need in order to live thoughtfully and vote thoughtfully in One World. Operation "The Public Philosophy" is a major one for education.

FOR THE EARTH. Theistic Idealists are often asked, "If you believe in immortality, why do you care about the earth?" All Idealists do not believe in immortality, but for those who do, life eternal is here now, as well as in the future. There is no escape anywhere from the nature of personhood, from the responsibilities, the joys, and the sufferings of being a living human self. Moreover, the theist who loves God loves his universe, especially this part of it which is now home, in all its inexhaustible beauty and wonder. He loves his fellowman, even his enemy. Man, limited natural creature, as well as limited child of God, is the chief source of his own fear, trouble, and despair. Hell is other persons, says Sartre in *No Exit*. But man also learns through man what love is, in all its forms—*philia, eros, agape*. And so, though an Idealist can say with Socra-

18 Michael Demiashkevich, *An Introduction to the Philosophy of Education* (New York: American Book Co., 1935).

tes and Boethius that all of life is a dying to things temporary, and can look at his own death, or the death of the earth, with acceptance and the certainty that God is not dead, this is an attitude radically opposite to indiffer-ence toward this life, toward himself, his fellow man, or the earth. He thinks the necessary moral-political changes that may save us and the earth from Armageddon can come only if men care.

〜

Implications of Classical Realism
for Philosophy of Education

Harry S. Broudy*

Does classical Realistic philosophy have anything to contribute to the solution of current educational problems? Or is such a philosophy of historical interest only in a culture so different from that which sustained Plato and Aristotle?

Educational problems exemplify the problems of an age, because education is the process by which one generation tries to embody its own value pattern in the lives of a younger one. In our own time, we have yet to adjust our ideal of universal education to the fact of individual differences in ability to profit from formal schooling. We still do not know the relation that ought to obtain between financial supporters of education and those who decide what is to be taught. Is there a body of knowledge and techniques essential for every pupil, and if so, who shall determine what is essential?

Such specific questions of educational policy have their roots in more general cultural conflicts; these, in turn, ultimately stir up the philosophical issue of whether or not there is a value pattern that has universal validity. In other words, is there such a thing as truth or are there only ideologies that are relative to historical situations and only as valid as the political power of their adherents?

At the levels of educational policy and practice, ideology is the decisive concept, because the value scheme that controls the aims and procedures of the school is rarely grounded explicitly in an abstract metaphysical or epistemological system. Thus it is belief in the inherent value of free enterprise in our economic affairs, in the inherent rightness of the secret ballot when making political decisions, that shapes policy rather than formal theory about the nature of reality or man. As Reisner has pointed out, the "world-frames" of Plato, Aristotle, and Aquinas are not only much more concrete than their metaphysical systems, which is inevitable, but they also reflect social condi-

* Reprinted by permission from *Proceedings of The Association for Realistic Philosophy*, ed. H. M. Austin (Norton, Mass.: Wheaton College, 1949), pp. 1–15. This view is treated more fully in the author's *Building a Philosophy of Education*, 2d ed. (Englewood Cliffs, N.J.: Prentice-Hall, Inc., 1961).

tions and evaluations of human conduct and life peculiar to such conditions. Hence from a given metaphysical position, diverse educational views have historically been developed.[1]

And yet despite their diversity, all educational systems which claim Classical Realism as a respectable ancestor presuppose a theory of existence and of knowledge that is sharply at odds with philosophical positions that assert relativity of knowledge in general or of moral knowledge in particular as the only universally valid proposition.

It would be unfair to say that only Classical Realism believes in objective standards or that it alone tries to establish their theoretical possibility. But as matters stand the dominant modes of current educational thought either do not operate on this belief or have difficulty in justifying it.

1. Scientism has succeeded in establishing its method in its own areas. But this very success has doomed all experience not in these areas to irrationality or to the status of unarguable culture patterns.

2. Dewey's instrumentalism has valiantly tried to overcome these limitations by urging the validity of scientific thinking in all areas of life; by making thought an instrument of adjustment. But an objective or, at least, a clear-cut standard for "adjustment" it cannot seem to establish. As a criterion, adjustment is no more helpful than the "will of God," because the problem is to adjudicate among diverse modes of adjustment and among diverse interpretations of the "will of God."

3. Idealism does justice to the religious and ethical predilections of modern men, but to many it seems to have elevated the molehill of the "egocentric predicament" into a mountain of the Absolute.

4. Dialectical Materialism reduces our problem to a conflict among ideologies economically determined. But is its hope of reaching an objective truth about ideology anything more than just another ideology?[2]

5. Thomism, even in its modern form, casts its objective standard of truth and value into religious categories which themselves are seen as historically determined and which require faith rather than reason, or in addition to reason, for their acceptance.

In this situation it is not surprising that educators prefer to stick to science and scientific method as long as they can and to label everything else as controversial and dangerous. But education is a practical enterprise. Value judgments cannot be avoided for long. There has to be a standard—and in practice there always is one, viz., the wishes of politically powerful groups, or custom, or expediency. In a democracy, it is inevitable that such demands will be as diverse as they are insistent.

In such a situation our original question gets point. Does Classical Realistic philosophy present and justify a scale of value that can command the rational assent of a modern world? If so, can this be translated into suggestions for the solution of educational problems? While indicating an answer to the first question I will concern myself mainly with the second.

[1] Edward H. Reisner, in *Philosophies of Education* (Chicago: The University of Chicago Press, 1942), pp. 33 ff.

[2] Otis Lee, *Existence and Inquiry* (Chicago: The University of Chicago Press, 1949), p. 175.

I. IMPLICATIONS FOR AIMS IN EDUCATION

It is often charged that American education is confused. In any sense that the accusation is important, it means that educators cannot envision and formulate a unified pattern of values wherewith to regulate the educative enterprise. If professional educators cannot do so, it is because in America today, the "good" life denotes a wide variety of value patterns. If these views agree on anything, it is probably on the principle that there is no valid method for insisting that one is "better" than another.

To rise above this diversity, educators tend to formulate general aims by listing the functions individuals perform in adult life and then converting these into aims of education by prefixing the words "good," "adequate," "worthwhile" to the statement of the function. For example, membership in a family group is a function, worthy home membership is the educational aim; citizenship is a function, good citizenship is the educational aim. We thus get lists of educational aims for health, leisure time, vocations, aesthetic enjoyment. This device, unfortunately, does not remove confusion, because first, it is precisely the *kind* of home, *kind* of leisure activity, *kind* of civic role that people disagree about, and in the second place, these functions remain coordinate in value.

The only remedy for the confusion is a view of human nature and of human society that enables us rationally to assert the relative priority of human functions and to assess the claims of various human groupings. Here we can only state (without attempting to defend) some of the principles of realistic philosophy essential to such a view.

1. There is a "natural" structure or order in the universe independent of our wishing, feeling or desiring.[3]
2. There is a "natural" structure or way of living characteristic of "human being."
3. These structures can be apprehended by human knowing as they are in themselves.
4. The results of such knowledge disclose the norms for individual life and social organization.

In sum, the Realist holds: A "natural order" of human life obtains when all human activities are guided by an end rationally apprehended and rationally willed. When reason discloses that man has the potentiality to live such a life it thereby certifies that actualization of this capacity is the only valid end for genuinely *human* living.

To this end all collective and individual effort in the healthy state strives, and by this end all effort is evaluated. *Man as rational master of himself and of his environment so far as this is possible is therefore the goal of the good life, the good society and of the good school.*

THE NECESSITY OF EDUCATION. Education if it has any distinctive meaning has a special role to play in this perfecting of man. Clearly if man were perfected automatically no education would be needed. The necessity for education is to be found (1) in the fact

[3] For more precise statement and explanation of these principles, cf. John Wild, *Introduction to Realistic Philosophy* (New York: Harper & Brothers, Inc., 1948).

that man's action can be determined by many forces of which reason is only one and rarely the strongest, and (2) in the fact that perfection is not biologically transmitted. We can rely on heredity only for various grades of capacity for perfection.

As to the first fact: the physiological demands of nutrition, safety and reproduction hold the first lien on human activity. They can in a hostile situation become the sole determinants of action with reason subordinated to a mere instrument of their fulfillment. The need for emotional security in the form of social approval is another powerful determinant of human action. It holds the second lien and likewise, when starved or denied, makes reason a slave to its craving.

To arrive at a life where self-mastery and rational direction shall govern requires first that the lower needs be satisfied but not dominant. They must be satisfied, because they are the necessary conditions for higher modes of living, but since their satisfaction does not guarantee a passage to a higher level, another directive factor has to be invoked. This factor is education—the deliberate attempt to help the individual to self-mastery, to provide some of the means for seeing his essential goal, and some of the means for achieving it. The second fact merely points to education as a process that must be applied to each generation as a prerequisite to the cultural continuity of the group.

THE POSSIBILITY OF EDUCATION. This deliberate attempt to produce one mode of life rather than another is possible only because the human infant is so largely undetermined. These potentialities can be actualized in diverse patterns.

THE AIM OF EDUCATION. The aim of education as a distinctive enterprise has to be stated in more specific terms than the good life, because all human enterprises in the natural order have this as their aim. Education has a distinctive aim, however, only if it has a distinctive function. What this function is may be indicated by the following observations:

1. It deals with human beings only, and only insofar as they are in one respect or another immature, unskilled, unperfected, i.e., insofar as they are still potentialities.
2. Education is concerned with the initial phases of actualization. Teaching is the patterning in the individual of modes of actualization that will continue to function after teaching has ceased.
3. Such modes of self-sustaining actualization are habits of doing, habits of choosing, habits of preferring, habits of thinking, and habits of knowing. The word "habit" as a tendency of the organism to respond in terms of previous experience expresses the auto-dynamism of behavior at which education aims.

We can further delimit the function of education:

1. It is an art and not itself a science.
2. It is not a material art, for it does not transform material objects.
3. It is not a political art, for it does not plan or execute social action.
4. It is not coextensive with life, but only one of the means for determining its direction and quality.
5. It is not merely growth, but rather the directing of growth.

These distinctions are of more than academic import. While education is a prerequisite for all the arts, sciences, and the successful functioning of all social institutions, it is not to be identified with any of these unless we are willing to admit that education has no distinct function of its own. What human nature is, education does not determine; that is the business of philosophy and to some extent of science. Nor does it determine the rational form of society or its institutions. Nor does it *qua* education plan for social control and action or carry out such plans.

Education's own unique aim and function is to transform the inherent capacities of the individual for rational self-determination into habits of action, feeling, taste, and thought.

II. IMPLICATIONS FOR CURRICULUM

Inasmuch as the function of education is to actualize human capacity for rationally willed behavior, its successful outcome will be reliable tendencies in the individual to apprehend, use, and enjoy truth in all the situations and tasks of life. Appropriate habits draw their content from the specific tasks a culture imposes. The problem of the curriculum is the selection of means and materials which will develop general capacities into suitable, effective tendencies. There arise in consequence three curricular questions: 1. In the active grasp of what knowledge shall all men be schooled? 2. What skills are needed if one is to apprehend, use, and enjoy truth? 3. What desires and preferences will strengthen and maintain reason-guided habits?

A. GENERAL EDUCATION

1. KNOWLEDGE. The first question can be answered by making a distinction between the functions an individual performs by virtue of his membership in the human race and those he performs by virtue of his specialized place in the social structure or by virtue of special endowments, talents or disabilities. (1) Every man has to function as a member of the natural *sustaining* groups of family, community, state, and world.[4] (2) He lives in a material world that needs to be transformed to maintain human activities. His own body is both an instrument in that world and a part of it. (3) Every individual lives with himself as a particularized route to or away from perfection. As such he needs to apprehend his own nature and potentiality for the life of reason.

Function (1) calls for knowledge of the whole range of social science and philosophy, the minimum essentials of which include:

a. The group structure that the attainment of a Common Good presupposes, its hierarchical order of ends and means, and the essential function of each group distinguished from the accidental ones.
b. The principles of justice governing the apportionment of rights and duties within and among the groups.
c. The history of their development.
d. Discrepancies between actual orders and the natural order.

From function (2) follows the need of knowing the physical sciences, mathematics, and the biological sciences.

4 Wild, *op. cit.,* Chap. 10.

From function (3) follows the study of psychology, literature, philosophy, the arts, and religion.[5]

This listing, of course, covers the totality of human knowledge and I hasten to forewarn against the absurd conclusion that to master this is the principle of the curriculum. Let us remember that education is not science as such and its goal is not mastery of knowledge as such. Rather the mastery at which education aims is of that order required for the establishment of *tendencies* to apprehend, use and enjoy such truth. Education does not end with any level of schooling but schooling is responsible for the dynamic tendencies that are to go on after schooling has ceased. Hence, in *general* education only the most basic principles and the most commonly needed information are essential as the materials for instruction while the process of establishing habits goes on. Of course, no important area of human experience is to be left totally unexplored as teachers pursue the central aim of founding in their pupils abiding dispositions to seek and profit from truth in every area of life.

How much and how well the ingredients of this general education are learned depends upon individual capacity, but human beings vary essentially not in the *kind* of truths they can ap-

prehend but in the levels of generality, or abstractness, or comprehensiveness of knowledge at which they can learn efficiently. The adjustments for such individual differences will be discussed in the section on organization.

2. SKILLS. Since the aim of the educator is not the mastery of subject as such, but rather the development of self-sustaining tendencies (habits) and since skill is an ingredient of habit, it follows that general education will include skills prerequisite for the acquisition, use, and enjoyment of truth.[6]

It is not the purpose of this paper to catalogue the skills. Nevertheless, history has allied Classical Realism with traditional educational procedures so closely that it is necessary to make the following comments:

a. A cultivation of language and number as ends in themselves which leads to verbalism, is not a necessary corollary to Classical Realism. Symbolic skills are to be taught as *instruments* of knowledge, but indispensable instruments, i.e., not replaceable by the moving pictures, radio, or television.

b. Classical Realism needs to divorce itself from that doctrine of 'mental discipline' which holds that the skills of imagining, inferring, comparing, etc., are generic powers that are developed by Latin grammar or mathematics, and thereafter operate automatically in any situation requiring their use. This divorce does not entail the repudiation of the notion of capacities, because the actualization of a general capacity such as imagining consists of particular imaginings in specific situa-

[5] The skills and habits pertaining to the realization of religious values should be included in general education, if there is a universally accepted religious cult. Even a public school system in the United States could incorporate religious instruction into its curriculum if religious values could be stripped of the varied creedal and ritualistic characteristics. So long as this cannot be done—and there is a marked reluctance to do so—religion has to be part of special rather than general education.

[6] Cp. John Dewey, *Democracy and Education* (New York: The Macmillan Co., 1916), pp. 54–55.

tions. To make such skills "general" requires that the learner use them in a wide variety of situations; there is no reliable short-cut through the teaching of any one subject.

c. Classical Realism is also allied historically, but not logically, to a separation between knowledge and the use of it in life situations. Certainly the Aristotelian doctrine of practical wisdom implies no such radical division. The tendency to use knowledge is itself a habit that requires skill and practice. Of all habits, this is probably the most crucial in general education, and the motor skills are no less important in this connection than the noetic ones.

d. If the skills of apprehension and of use are developed to a fairly high degree of competence, the skills of enjoyment are largely taken care of. If the pupil can read so that meanings arise easily and insights into symbolic relationships are not laborious, he can not only apprehend Shakespeare but also enjoy the apprehension. Some mastery of the symbolism and even of the techniques of the fine arts are probably essential to the full enjoyment of art products. There are both skills of impression and expression in the esthetic field, and tendencies to use these in esthetic situations are among the objectives of general education.[7]

This analysis of the curriculum does not imply that each element must be

developed separately or in any particular time sequence. The analysis is necessary, however, if the educator is to understand the content and structure of the habits he hopes to develop. The only valid criterion of education is whether or not the individual manifests those tendencies developed under instruction after the instruction ceases. It may even be the case that in a given social environment these habits will suffer disintegration by powerful pressures, but for this no educational process can take the whole responsibility.

3. PATTERNS OF PREFERENCE. If the pupil deliberates about choices, uses reliable information, and uses it skilfully but does all this merely because the approval of teachers, parents, etc., can thereby be obtained, the habit is still in an unreliable state, and education is not yet completed.[8] Only when the pupil freely chooses to practice his knowledge and skill and derives genuine satisfaction from doing so can we be sure that a reliable habit has been formed. Every well developed habit contains an emotional bias favoring its own exercise.

How to bring about this emotional attachment is probably education's most difficult problem. It is especially difficult whenever there is a discrepancy between the values of the school and those of the community. And in an imperfect state this is always the case. The system of punishments and rewards actually used by a given community attaches pleasure and pain to objects and activities in a way that is not always the way of the school. If a community values material success above moral integrity or acts as if it does; if the com-

[7] Certain tendencies in modern art education would lead to the suspicion that the skill element in enjoyment is subordinated to creativity and spontaneity of expression. But it is unfortunately true that after the period of uncritical childhood is over, we abandon those media where our skill is inadequate to our needs for expression.

[8] Wild, op. cit., Chap. 3.

munity lavishly rewards the titillators of animal pleasures and starves the purveyors of rational pleasures, the school is hard put to it to form predilections in the pupil for moral integrity and rational pleasures.

This fact led Plato in *The Republic* to insist on the isolation of children from their natural parents, and on the careful cleansing of all poetry, drama, and legends. Unless informal education can be controlled, formal education can do relatively little about the love of the good or the attitude of the pupil toward any given value. It is true that formal educational systems in Russia, Japan, and Germany did seem to produce an emotional uniformity as astounding as it was dismaying, but before all the credit is given to the school, it might be well to point out that the forces controlling the schools controlled *all* other educative agencies including the radio and the press. Had not the bulk of the population adopted attitudes that were aggressive, anti-this or pro-that, the schools could not have given them to the children. That is why schools, no matter how well-intentioned, cannot eliminate delinquency from children whose environment puts a premium upon it.

Indeed even on the higher levels of education, where ideas seem most effective in altering attitudes, it is to be noted that the members of the *avant garde* sophomore year are the solid conservatives of the 15-year class. If they persist in their non-conformism, they become isolated into small intellectual cells with little effect on the group as a whole. Unless, therefore, we are prepared to suggest measures as drastic as those adopted in totalitarian countries, the school cannot guarantee a permanent love of the good.

This is not to say that the school can do nothing about value preferences, for if this were the case, it could not help in the formation of habits. That it cannot vouch for the permanence of these preferences is simply due to the fact that the social milieu in which an individual's adult life is lived can reinforce or powerfully modify such preferences. A boy may leave high school with a very respectable mastery of English usage and a strong desire to use English correctly. But let him be thrown in with a group to whom correct English usage is an affectation, and within five years he will either have left the group or have adopted its mode of speaking. The same may be said with respect to tastes in literature and the other fine arts. That the college has more success in establishing fairly permanent tastes is due only in part to the college instruction. More important is the fact that college graduates are more likely to find employment and live their social lives with groups that reinforce such tastes.

Deplorable as this situation is, it does not alter the responsibility of the school for trying to form preferences essential to the habits it is trying to perfect. It may be true, as Mortimer J. Adler points out, that the moral virtues are only secondarily the concern of institutional education,[9] but in every habit whether moral or noetic there is an ingredient of volitional disposition that is the proper concern of formal education.

[9] *Philosophies of Education*, p. 220.

B. SPECIAL EDUCATION

In the subsequent section (III) the question as to how much general education should be given to the individual will be considered. Here let us turn to the kind of education the individual needs to perform his function as a member of the instrumental groups which supply the means for realizing the common good.

It is a commonplace to point out that science and technology based thereon have made it possible for *all* men to have sufficient leisure to perfect their rational natures. What an army of slaves made possible for a few men in the time of Plato and Aristotle, technology, at least theoretically, now makes possible for all mankind. The advent of technology, however, has transformed the quality of work itself. The worker groups include greater and greater numbers of men who need intellectual training of one kind or another to perform their work. Even if we grant that a great deal of this knowledge is "know how" and does not presuppose the scientific knowledge upon which it is based, there is still a wide difference between what goes on in the head of a radio technician, a navigator, a traffic engineer, and what goes on in the head of a ditch digger or a movie ticket-taker. It is to the credit of Dewey that he explicated the intellectual possibilities of gainful occupations—possibilities pretty completely overlooked by Plato and Aristotle.

The noetic habits needed for modern work cannot in a highly complex industrialized society be picked up informally, i.e., by imitation or by simple participation. Some of them have to be given formally. Consequently there arises a conflict between general and specific education in their claims upon the curriculum. In this connection, the following observations are in order:

1. The vocationalists usually overestimate the amount of specialized training needed for the majority of jobs and tend to underestimate the training needed for membership in the sustaining groups of family, community, and state.

2. The vocationalist usually does not realize how much general education (as above outlined) does contribute to employability. On the higher vocational levels this is being understood, witness the recent emphasis on general education in technical and professional schools.

3. The controversy would become less academic if the amount of specific education for given types of work were rationally determined. It would also help if both parties to the debate realized that the capacity of the individual very often sets the limit for the level of both general and special education that he can reach.

On the question of curriculum then, it follows that general education is basic; vocational education supplementary, but necessary.

At a time when vocational ambition threatens to become (if indeed the threat has not been already carried out) the dominant motive in American education, it is understandable that the adherents of Classical philosophy should be somewhat bitter about vocational education and somewhat heroic about the irrelevance of economic value in the justification of the liberal arts curriculum. Three points, however, might be kept in mind. First, for a subject to have economic value does not necessarily disqualify it educationally; in the second place, man in our society is a working animal. Finally, the liberal arts curriculum became firmly entrenched in our culture partly because it did have a vocational value. Latin, for example, was a vocational prerequisite for the statesman, the clergyman, and indeed, for all the learned professions in the Middle Ages. Because the lesser vocations did not at that time require formal preparation, we are too prone to argue that the training they now do require is "merely" vocational.

In spite of all this, the relative position and importance of general and special education is clear, and whenever vocational training becomes dominant in an educational system, it should be regarded as a danger signal, for it means that the education of man as man is being neglected and that the sustaining groups to which man belongs *essentially* are being subordinated to those in which membership does not constitute his essential being.

III. IMPLICATIONS FOR ORGANIZATION

Formal education in any group raises such questions as: Who shall be educated? For how long? By whom? Under what control? These are questions of organization.

It would seem to follow from the principle that all men are rational, that all have a natural right to the education that will allow them to perfect themselves as human beings. It is unfortunately true that the chief propounders of Classical Realism (Plato and Aristotle) proposed and sanctioned social practices that contradict this principle. The principle does, nevertheless, follow from the premises of Classical Realism, and it does not logically entail the three grades of intellect assumed by Plato nor any finite number of such grades. It, therefore, does not commit us to a caste system of education on the one hand, nor to quantitative or qualitative equality of education on the other. Who shall be educated and at what level is a question that can better be answered on empirical grounds than on speculative ones. The individual's right to education is limited only by his capacity to learn and the group's ability to provide opportunity to learn.

Pupils vary with respect to the level of abstraction at which they can learn efficiently. Some can understand calculus; others must stop at applied geometry, and still others cannot go beyond rote arithmetic. In history, some cannot apprehend more than the isolated historical event simply or dramatically described; others can understand sequences of cause and effect; still others can comprehend theories of causation; and a few (mostly candidates for the doctorate) like to discuss the theories about theories of causation.

This abstraction differential, or differences in power to deal with abstractions, is evident on every level of instruction where symbols and ideas, i.e., the noetic skills, are involved. It means that even in general education this differential will determine just what will be taught and on what level. It is also the rational determinant of who should go to high school, college, or university. It is an important factor in the choice of an occupation.

Now since the abstraction differential can be determined empirically, albeit not with perfect precision by intelligence tests, a philosophy of education need not commit itself to either a caste system of education or to a mechanical equalitarianism. The ideal educational system recognizes the individual as a *unique* pattern of value potentials and tries to exploit these to their *maxima*. This uniqueness does not mean that individuals determine the truth nor that there is no truth that everybody ought to apprehend. Rather it is all one truth, but we do vary in the level at which we can assimilate it. By adhering to capacity for learning as a criterion, we can avoid the demand that everyone learn exactly the same thing in the same way, and likewise the notion that the whims of children are true guides for curriculum and organization.

Who shall control education? The agency that has the greatest responsibility for the Common Good.

In the perfect state there would be no discrepancy between the good citizen and the good man, and there would be no question of educational control, because the educator and the statesman would be one in their thinking. But in imperfect states, control must be split into two phases. On the one hand, the construction and maintenance of a school system is a function of the state. On the other hand, questions of curriculum and method cannot safely be left to politicians whose motives may be other than the love of truth and the desire to make men good.

The wise alternative is to give the educators, philosophers, and scientists authority in these matters on the ground that these groups are primarily interested in the discovery and the teaching of truth. Their authority would, therefore, be the authority of truth itself.

In natural science it can be said that scientific method and its results do exert a very powerful compulsion upon the public. Even the most corrupt politician does not try to bribe a chemical reaction. In other areas, unfortunately, there is no body of truth so compelling as to obviate wars of interpretation. Because philosophers cannot agree, and because religious leaders seem a little afraid of agreement, it is the state or the dominant group within a culture that determines what the "truth" in the debatable realm shall be.

It is an old dilemma. Either we commit ourselves to relativity in the field of value and surrender final authority to a power group, or we assert the objectivity of truth in these areas and immediately have twenty candidates for The Truth. For the Absolute and God never speak in public. The hope of reviving Classical Realism rests on the ability of its proponents to shake themselves loose from the countless dogmatists who feel themselves justified by it. Realists must make their claim to truth on philosophical grounds that all men as men can examine rationally. Otherwise intelligent and well-intentioned men will remain what they now regretfully are—the bedfellows of skepticism and relativism. If philosophers can rise above the particularity of race, creed, color, political habits, and cultural peculiarities, there is hope for an objective truth about man as man. Such a truth might well become authoritative for education and even for statesmanship. Once we discern the nature of the universal and essential and make provisions for that, we can allow full play to the peculiarities of the accidental, so that there will be room for a rich and stimulating cultural pluralism.

IV. IMPLICATIONS FOR METHOD

The relevant question to ask about method is: Does it achieve efficiently the results desired? Given the objective to achieve a certain level of mastery in reading, there is *a priori* no *one* method that must be judged best. Insofar as results can be tested and measured, the judgment must wait upon empirical evidence. Although the quotation marks cannot be dispensed with when education is spoken of as a "science," there is hope that questions of method will in time be questions of fact.

Unfortunately, the distinctions between aim, curriculum, and method in education are not always observed in controversy. For example, the doctrine of the child-centered school is at least partially false as a guide for curriculum construction, but as a technique of instruction, it is highly efficient and especially so for the lower levels of abstractive capacity. Dewey's belief in the efficacy of informal education is warranted, but the inference that all education shall be experimental and informal is highly debatable. Method is, in brief, a relatively independent variable, and it is difficult to discern any necessary relationship between any given method

and any specific philosophic position.[10]

The key to general method is the same as the key to organization, viz., the recognition of abstraction differentials in pupils and abstraction levels in subject matter. The fact that formal education becomes necessary when the culture of a group is encased in arbitrary symbols whose meaning can not be picked up informally has given formal education a bias favoring abstractions and unduly favoring minds that deal with them easily. With universal education as a desideratum, this bias will have to be corrected.

CONCLUSION. It would seem then that the question raised at the outset can for the most part be answered in the affirmative. Classical Realism in its basic metaphysical, epistemological, and ethical doctrines can help in the solution of our educational problems. It can contribute most in the clarification of the aim and function of education. It can help us to arrive at policy with respect to curriculum and organization. In the field of method, where education is a practicing art, the science of education and the lessons of experience are definitive; the question of technical means is not in the main a philosophical question, unless the nature of the means becomes inconsistent with the nature of the end.

[10] The relation of the activity method to the epistemological instrumentalism of Dewey offers the least difficulty in this respect, because here thinking, purposive activity, and learning become almost indistinguishable.

Christian Education of Youth

Pope Pius XI*

NATURE AND IMPORTANCE OF EDUCATION

Indeed never has there been so much discussion about education as nowadays; never have exponents of new pedagogical theories been so numerous, or so many methods and means devised, proposed and debated, not merely to facilitate education, but to create a new system infallibly efficacious, and capable of preparing the present generation for that earthly happiness which they so ardently desire.

The reason is that men, created by God to His image and likeness and destined for Him who is infinite perfection, realize today more than ever, amid the most exuberant material progress, the insufficiency of earthly goods to produce true happiness either for the individual or for the nations. And hence they feel more keenly in themselves the impulse toward a perfection that is higher, which impulse is implanted in their rational nature by the Creator Himself. This perfection they seek to acquire by means of education. But many of them, with, it would seem, too great insistence on the etymological meaning of the word, pretend to draw education out of human nature itself and evolve it by its own unaided powers. Such easily fall into error, be-

cause, instead of fixing their gaze on God, first principle and last end of the whole universe, they fall back upon themselves, becoming attached exclusively to passing things of earth; and thus their restlessness will never cease till they direct their attention and their efforts to God, the goal of all perfection, according to the profound saying of St. Augustine: "Thou didst create us, O Lord, for Thyself, and our heart is restless till it rest in Thee."[3]

It is therefore as important to make no mistake in education as it is to make no mistake in the pursuit of our last end, with which the whole work of education is intimately and necessarily connected. In fact, since education consists essentially in preparing man for what he must be and for what he must do here below, in order to attain the sublime end for which he was created, it is clear that there can be no true education which is not wholly directed to man's last end, and that in the present order of providence, since God has revealed Himself to us in the person of His only-begotten Son, who alone is "the way, the truth and the life," there can be no ideally perfect education which is not Christian education.

From this we see the supreme importance of Christian education, not merely for each individual, but for families and for the whole of human society, whose perfection comes from the

* Encyclical Letter *Divini Illius Magistri* of His Holiness Pope Pius XI (New York: The America Press, 1936, pp. 2–36). Reprinted by permission.

[3] *Confess,* I, 1.

perfection of the elements that compose it. From these same principles, the excellence, we may well call it the unsurpassed excellence, of the work of Christian education becomes manifest and clear; for after all it aims at securing the supreme Good, that is, God, for the souls of those who are being educated, and the maximum of well-being possible here below for human society. And this it does as efficaciously as man is capable of doing it, namely, by co-operating with God in the perfecting of individuals and of society, inasmuch as the education of youth makes on the soul the first, most powerful and lasting impression for life, according to the well-known saying of the Wise Man, "A young man according to his way, even when he is old, he will not depart from it."[4] With good reason, therefore, did St. John Chrysostom say, "What greater work is there than training the mind and forming the habits of the young?"[5]

But nothing discloses to us the supernatural beauty and excellence of the work of Christian education better than the sublime expression of love of our Blessed Lord, identifying Himself with children, "Whosoever shall receive one such child as this in my name, receiveth me."[6]

Now in order that no mistake be made in this work of utmost importance, and in order to conduct it in the best manner possible with the help of God's grace, it is necessary to have a clear and definite idea of Christian education in its essential aspects, viz., who

[4] Prov. xxii, 6.
[5] *Hom. 60 in c. xviii Matt.*
[6] Mark ix, 36.

has the mission to educate, who are the subjects to be educated, what are the necessary accompanying circumstances, what is the end and object proper to Christian education according to God's established order in the economy of His divine providence?

I. TO WHOM DOES EDUCATION BELONG?

Education is essentially a social and not a merely individual activity. Now there are three necessary societies, distinct from one another and yet harmoniously combined by God, into which man is born: two, namely the family and civil society, belong to the natural order; the third, the Church, to the supernatural order.

In the first place comes the family, instituted directly by God for its peculiar purpose, the generation and formation of offspring; for this reason it has priority of nature and therefore of rights over civil society. Nevertheless, the family is an imperfect society, since it has not in itself all the means for its own complete development; whereas civil society is a perfect society, having in itself all the means for its peculiar end, which is the temporal well-being of the community; and so, in this respect, that is, in view of the common good, it has pre-eminence over the family, which finds its own suitable temporal perfection precisely in civil society.

The third society, into which man is born when through baptism he receives the divine life of grace, is the Church; a society of the supernatural order and of universal extent; a perfect society, because it has in itself all the means required for its own end, which is the eternal salvation of mankind; hence it is supreme in its own domain.

Consequently, education, which is concerned with the whole man, individually and socially, in the order of nature and in the order of grace, necessarily belongs to all these three societies, in accordance with the end assigned to each in the present order of divine providence.

A. EDUCATION BELONGS TO THE CHURCH

And first of all, education belongs pre-eminently to the Church, by reason of a double title in the supernatural order, conferred exclusively upon her by God Himself; absolutely superior, therefore, to any other title in the natural order.

1. BECAUSE OF HER MISSION. The first title is founded upon the express mission and supreme authority to teach given her by her divine Founder: "All power is given to me in heaven and in earth. Going therefore teach ye all nations, baptizing them in the name of the Father, and of the Son, and of the Holy Ghost, teaching them to observe all things whatsoever I have commanded you, and behold I am with you all days, even to the consummation of the world."[7] Upon this magisterial office Christ conferred infallibility, together with the command to teach His doctrine. Hence the Church "was set by her divine Author as the pillar and ground of truth, in order to teach the divine faith to men, and keep whole and inviolate the deposit confided to

[7] Matt. xxviii, 18–20.

her; to direct and fashion men, in all their actions, to purity of morals and integrity of life, in accordance with revealed doctrine."[8]

2. BECAUSE OF HER SUPERNATURAL MOTHERHOOD. The second title is the supernatural motherhood, in virtue of which the Church, spotless spouse of Christ, generates, nurtures and educates souls in the divine life of grace, with her sacraments and her doctrine. With good reason then does St. Augustine maintain: "He has not God for father who refuses to have the Church as mother."[9]

Hence it is that in this proper object of her mission, that is, "in faith and morals, God Himself has made the Church sharer in the divine teaching office and, by a special privilege, granted her immunity from error; hence she is the mistress of men, supreme and absolutely sure, and she has inherent in herself an inviolable right to freedom in teaching."[10] By necessary consequence the Church is independent of any sort of earthly power as well in the origin as in the exercise of her mission as educator, not merely in regard to her proper end and object, but in regard to the means necessary and suitable to attain that end. Hence with regard to every other kind of human learning and instruction, which is the common patrimony of individuals and society, the Church has an independent right to make use of it, and above all to decide what may help or harm Christian education. And this must be so, because the Church as a perfect society has an in-

[8] Pius IX, *Ep. "Quum non sine,"* July 14, 1864.

[9] *De Symbolo ad Catech.,* XIII.

[10] *Ep. Ency. "Libertas,"* June 20, 1888.

dependent right to the means conducive to its end, and because every form of instruction, no less than every human action, has a necessary connection with man's last end, and therefore cannot be withdrawn from the dictates of the divine law, of which the Church is infallible guardian, interpreter and teacher.

This truth is clearly set forth by Pius X of saintly memory.[11]

Whatever a Christian does even in the order of things of earth, he may not overlook the supernatural; indeed he must, according to the teaching of Christian wisdom, direct all things toward the supreme good as to his last end; all his actions, besides, insofar as good or evil in the order of morality, that is, in keeping or not with natural and divine law, fall under the judgment and jurisdiction of the Church.

It is worthy of note how a layman, an excellent writer and at the same time a profound and conscientious thinker, has been able to understand well and express exactly this fundamental Catholic doctrine:[12]

The Church does not say that morality belongs purely, in the sense of exclusively, to her; but that it belongs wholly to her. She has never maintained that outside her fold and apart from her teaching, man cannot arrive at any moral truth; she has on the contrary more than once condemned this opinion, because it has appeared under more forms than one. She does however say, has said, and will ever say, that because of her institution by Jesus Christ, because of the Holy Ghost sent to her in His name by the Father she alone possesses what she has had immediately

from God and can never lose, the whole of moral truth, *omnem veritatem,* in which all individual moral truths are included, as well those which man may learn by the help of reason as those which form part of revelation or which may be deduced from it.

3. Extent of the Rights of the Church. Therefore with full right the Church promotes letters, science, art, insofar as necessary or helpful to Christian education, in addition to her work for the salvation of souls; founding and maintaining schools and institutions adapted to every branch of learning and degree of culture.[13] Nor may even physical culture, as it is called, be considered outside the range of her maternal supervision, for the reason that it also is a means which may help or harm Christian education.

And this work of the Church in every branch of culture is of immense benefit to families and nations, which without Christ are lost, as St. Hilary points out correctly: "What can be more fraught with danger for the world than the rejection of Christ?"[14]

Nor does it interfere in the least with the regulations of the state, because the Church in her motherly prudence is not unwilling that her schools and institutions for the education of the laity be in keeping with the legitimate dispositions of civil authority; she is in every way ready to cooperate with this authority and to make provision for a mutual understanding, should difficulties arise.

Again it is the inalienable right, as well as the indispensable duty of the Church, to watch over the entire edu-

[11] *Ep. Ency. "Singulari quadam,"* Sept. 24, 1912.

[12] A. Manzoni, *Osservazioni sulla Morale Cattolica,* c. III.

[13] *Cod. Jur. Can.,* c. 1375.

[14] *Commentar. in Matt.* c. xviii.

cation of her children, in all institutions, public or private, not merely in regard to the religious instruction there given, but in regard to every other branch of learning and every regulation insofar as religion and morality are concerned.[15]

Nor should the exercise of this right be considered undue interference, but rather maternal care on the part of the Church in protecting her children from the grave danger of all kinds of doctrinal and moral evil. Moreover this watchfulness of the Church not merely can create no real inconvenience, but must on the contrary be of the greatest value for the right ordering and well-being of families and civil society; since it keeps far away from youth the moral poison which at that inexperienced and changeable age more easily penetrates the mind and more rapidly spreads its baneful effects. For it is true, as Leo XIII has wisely pointed out, that without proper religious and moral instruction "every form of intellectual culture will be injurious; our young people, not accustomed to respect God, will be unable to bear the restraint of a virtuous life, and never having learned to deny themselves anything, they will easily be incited to disturb the public order."[16]

The extent of the Church's mission in the field of education is such as to embrace every nation, without exception, according to the command of Christ: "Teach ye all nations";[17] and there is no power on earth that may lawfully oppose her or stand in her way. In the first place, it extends over all the faithful, of whom she has anxious care as a tender mother. For these she has throughout the centuries created and conducted an immense number of schools and institutions in every branch of learning. As we said on a recent occasion:[18]

Right back in the far-off Middle Ages, when there were so many (some have even said too many) monasteries, convents, churches, collegiate churches, cathedral chapters, etc., there was attached to each a home of study, of teaching, of Christian education. To these we must add all the universities, spread over every country and always by the initiative and under the protection of the Holy See and the Church. That grand spectacle, which today we see better, as it is nearer to us and more imposing because of the conditions of the age, was the spectacle of all times; and they who study and compare historical events remain astounded at what the Church has been able to do in this matter, and marvel at the manner in which she has succeeded in fulfilling her God-given mission to educate generations of men to a Christian life, producing everywhere a magnificent harvest of fruitful results. But if we wonder that the Church in all times has been able to gather about her and educate hundreds, thousands, millions of students, no less wonderful is it to bear in mind what she has done not only in the field of education, but in that also of true and genuine erudition. For, if so many treasures of culture, civilization and literature have escaped destruction, this is due to the action by which the Church, even in times long past and uncivilized, has shed so bright a light in the domain of letters, of philosophy, of art and, in a special manner, of architecture.

All this the Church has been able to do because her mission to educate ex-

15 *Cod. Jur. Can.,* cc. 1381, 1382.

16 *Ep. Ency. "Nobilissima Gallorum Gens,"* February 8, 1884.

17 Matt. xxviii, 19.

18 Discourse to the Students of Mondragone College, May 14, 1929.

tends equally to those outside the fold, seeing that all men are called to enter the kingdom of God and reach eternal salvation. Just as today when her missions scatter schools by the thousands in districts and countries not yet Christian, from the banks of the Ganges to the Yellow River and the great islands and archipelagoes of the Pacific Ocean, from the Dark Continent to the Land of Fire and to frozen Alaska, so in every age the Church by her missionaries has educated to Christian life and to civilization the various peoples which now constitute the Christian nations of the civilized world.

4. HER RIGHTS HARMONIZE WITH OTHERS'. Hence it is evident that both by right and in fact the mission to educate belongs pre-eminently to the Church, and that no one free from prejudice can have a reasonable motive for opposing or impeding the Church in this her work, of which the world today enjoys the precious advantages.

This is the more true because the rights of the family and of the state, even the rights of individuals regarding a just liberty in the pursuit of science, in methods of science and all sorts of profane culture, not only are not opposed to this pre-eminence of the Church, but are in complete harmony with it. The fundamental reason for this harmony is that the supernatural order, to which the Church owes her rights, not only does not in the least destroy the natural order, to which pertain the other rights mentioned, but elevates the natural and perfects it, each affording mutual aid to the other, and completing it in a manner proportioned to its respective nature and dignity. The reason is that both come from God, who cannot contradict Himself: "The

works of God are perfect and all His ways are judgments."[19]

B. THE RIGHTS OF PARENTS

This becomes clearer when we consider more closely and in detail the mission of education proper to the family and to the state.

In the first place, the Church's mission of education is in wonderful agreement with that of the family, for both proceed from God and in a remarkably similar manner. God communicates directly to the family, in the natural order, fecundity, which is the principle of life, and hence also the principle of education to life, together with authority, the principle of order.

The Angelic Doctor, with his wonted clearness of thought and precision of style, says: "The father according to the flesh has in a particular way a share in that principle which in a manner universal is found in God . . . The father is the principle of generation, of education and discipline and of everything that bears upon the perfecting of human life."[20]

1. IT IS ANTERIOR TO THE STATE. The family therefore holds directly from the Creator the mission and hence the right to educate the offspring, a right inalienable because inseparably joined to the strict obligation, a right anterior to any right whatever of civil society and of the state, and therefore inviolable on the part of any power on earth.

2. IT IS INVIOLABLE. That this right is inviolable St. Thomas proves as follows.[21]

[19] Deut. xxxii, 4.
[20] *S. Th.*, 2–2, Q. CII, a. 1.
[21] *S. Th.*, 2–2, Q. X, a. 12.

The child is naturally something of the father . . . so by natural right the child, before reaching the use of reason, is under the father's care. Hence it would be contrary to natural justice if the child, before the use of reason, were removed from the care of its parents, or if any disposition were made concerning him against the will of the parents.

And as this duty on the part of the parents continues up to the time when the child is in a position to provide for itself, this same inviolable parental right of education also endures. "Nature intends not merely the generation of the offspring, but also its development and advance to the perfection of man considered as man, that is, to the state of virtue,"[22] says the same St. Thomas.

The wisdom of the Church in this matter is expressed with precision and clearness in the Codex of Canon Law, Can. 1113: "Parents are under a grave obligation to see to the religious and moral education of their children, as well as to their physical and civic training, as far as they can, and moreover to provide for their temporal well-being."[23]

On this point the common sense of mankind is in such complete accord, that they would be in open contradiction with it who dared maintain that the children belong to the state before they belong to the family, and that the state has an absolute right over their children. Untenable is the reason they adduce, namely, that man is born a citizen and hence belongs primarily to the state, not bearing in mind that before being a citizen man must exist; and existence does not come from the state, but from the parents, as Leo XIII wisely declared: "The children are something of the father and, as it were, an extension of the person of the father; and, to be perfectly accurate, they enter into and become part of civil society, not directly by themselves, but through the family in which they were born."[24] "And therefore," says the same Leo XIII, "the father's power is of such a nature that it cannot be destroyed or absorbed by the state; for it has the same origin as human life itself."[25] It does not however follow from this that the parents' right to educate their children is absolute and despotic; for it is necessarily subordinated to the last end and to natural and divine law, as Leo XIII declares in another memorable encyclical, where he thus sums up the rights and duties of parents: "By nature parents have a right to the training of their children, but with this added duty that the education and instruction of the child be in accord with the end for which by God's blessing it was begotten. Therefore it is the duty of parents to make every effort to prevent any invasion of their rights in this matter, and to make absolutely sure that the education of their children remain under their own control, in keeping with their Christian duty, and above all to refuse to send them to those schools in which there is danger of imbibing the deadly poison of impiety."[26]

It must be borne in mind also that the obligation of the family to bring up

[22] *Supp. S. Th.,* 3 p., Q. 41, a. 1.
[23] *Cod. Jur. Can.,* c. 1113.

[24] *Ep. Ency. "Rerum Novarum,"* May 15, 1891.
[25] *Ibid.*
[26] *Ep. Ency. "Sapientiae Christianae,"* January 10, 1890.

children includes not only religious and moral education, but physical and civic education as well,[27] principally insofar as it touches upon religion and morality.

3. IT IS RECOGNIZED BY CIVIL LAW. This incontestable right of the family has at various times been recognized by nations anxious to respect the natural law in their civil enactments. Thus, to give one recent example, the Supreme Court of the United States of North America, in a decision on an important controversy, declared that it is not in the competence of the state to fix any uniform standard of education by forcing children to receive instruction exclusively in public schools, and it bases its decision on the natural law: the child is not the mere creature of the state; those who nurture him and direct his destiny have the right coupled with the high duty, to educate him and prepare him for the fulfilment of his obligations.[28]

4. IT IS PROTECTED BY THE CHURCH. History bears witness how, particularly in modern times, the state has violated and does violate rights conferred by God on the family. At the same time it shows magnificently how the Church has ever protected and defended these rights, a fact proved by the special confidence which parents have in Catholic schools. As We pointed out recently in

Our letter to the Cardinal Secretary of State:[29]

The family has instinctively understood this to be so, and from the earliest days of Christianity down to our own times, fathers and mothers, even those of little or no faith, have been sending or bringing their children to places of education under the direction of the Church.

It is paternal instinct, given by God, that thus turns with confidence to the Church, certain of finding in her the protection of family rights, thereby illustrating that harmony with which God has ordered things. The Church is indeed conscious of her divine mission to all mankind, and of the obligation which all men have to practice the one true religion; and therefore she never tires of defending her right, and of reminding parents of their duty, to have all Catholic-born children baptized and brought up as Christians. On the other hand so jealous is she of the family's inviolable natural right to educate the children, that she never consents, save under peculiar circumstances and with special cautions, to baptize the children of infidels, or provide for their education against the will of the parents, till such time as the children can choose for themselves and freely embrace the faith.[30]

We have therefore two facts of supreme importance, as We said in Our discourse cited above: the Church placing at the disposal of families her office of teacher and educator, and the families eager to profit by the offer, and entrusting their children to the Church

---

[27] *Cod. Jur. Can.,* c. 1113.

[28] "The fundamental theory of liberty upon which all governments in this Union repose excludes any general power of the State to standardize its children by forcing them to accept instruction from public teachers only. The child is not the mere creature of the state; those who nurture him and direct his destiny have the right coupled with the high duty, to recognize and prepare him for additional duties." U.S. Supreme Court Decision in the Oregon School Case, June 1, 1925.

[29] Letter to the Cardinal Secretary of State, May 30, 1929.

[30] *Cod. Jur. Can., c.* 750, 2; *S. Th.* 2–2, Q. X, a. 12.

in hundreds and thousands. These two facts recall and proclaim a striking truth of the greatest significance in the moral and social order. They declare that the mission of education regards before all, above all, primarily the Church and the family, and this by natural and divine law, and that therefore it cannot be slighted, cannot be evaded, cannot be supplanted.[31]

C. THE RIGHT OF THE STATE

From such priority of rights on the part of the Church and of the family in the field of education, most important advantages, as we have seen, accrue to the whole of society. Moreover, in accordance with the divinely established order of things, no damage can follow from it to the true and just rights of the state in regard to the education of its citizens.

These rights have been conferred upon civil society by the Author of nature Himself, not by title of fatherhood, as in the case of the Church and of the family, but in virtue of the authority which it possesses to promote the common temporal welfare, which is precisely the purpose of its existence. Consequently education cannot pertain to civil society in the same way in which it pertains to the Church and to the family, but in a different way corresponding to its own particular end and object.

1. MEASURED BY THE COMMON GOOD. Now this end and object, the common welfare in the temporal order, consists in that peace and security in which families and individual citizens have the free exercise of their rights, and at

the same time enjoy the greatest spiritual and temporal prosperity possible in this life, by the mutual union and coordination of the work of all. The function therefore of the civil authority residing in the state is twofold, to protect and to foster, but by no means to absorb the family and the individual, or to substitute itself for them.

2. HAS DUTY TO PROTECT. Accordingly, in the matter of education it is the right, or to speak more correctly, it is the duty of the state to protect in its legislation the prior rights, already described, of the family as regards the Christian education of its offspring, and consequently also to respect the supernatural rights of the Church in this same realm of Christian education.

It also belongs to the state to protect the rights of the child itself when the parents are found wanting either physically or morally in this respect, whether by default, incapacity or misconduct, since, as has been shown, their right to educate is not an absolute and despotic one, but dependent on the natural and divine law, and therefore subject alike to the authority and jurisdiction of the Church, and to the vigilance and administrative care of the state in view of the common good. Besides, the family is not a perfect society, that is, it has not in itself all the means necessary for its full development. In such cases, exceptional no doubt, the state does not put itself in the place of the family, but merely supplies deficiencies and provides suitable means, always in conformity with the natural rights of the child and the supernatural rights of the Church.

In general then it is the right and duty of the state to protect, according to the rules of right reason and faith, the

[31] Discourse to the Students of Mondragone College, May 14, 1929.

moral and religious education of youth, by removing public impediments that stand in the way.

3. HAS DUTY TO FOSTER. In the first place it pertains to the state, in view of the common good, to promote in various ways the education and instruction of youth. It should begin by encouraging and assisting, of its own accord, the initiative and activity of the Church and the family, whose successes in this field have been clearly demonstrated by history and experience. It should moreover supplement their work whenever this falls short of what is necessary, even by means of its own schools and institutions. For the state more than any other society is provided with the means put at its disposal for the needs of all, and it is only right that it use these means to the advantage of those who have contributed them.[32]

Over and above this, the state can exact, and take measures to secure, that all its citizens have the necessary knowledge of their civic and political duties, and a certain degree of physical, intellectual and moral culture, which, considering the conditions of our times, is really necessary for the common good.

However it is clear that in all these ways of promoting education and instruction, both public and private, the state should respect the inherent rights of the Church and of the family concerning Christian education and, moreover, have regard for distributive justice. Accordingly, unjust and unlawful is any monopoly, educational or scholastic, which, physically or morally, forces families to make use of government schools, contrary to the dictates of their Christian conscience, or contrary even to their legitimate preferences.

[32] *Ibid.*

4. CAN RESERVE CERTAIN FORMS TO ITSELF. This does not prevent the state from making due provision for the right administration of public affairs and for the protection of its peace, within or without the realm. These are things which directly concern the public good and call for special aptitudes and special preparation. The state may therefore reserve to itself the establishment and direction of schools intended to prepare for certain civic duties and especially for military service, provided it be careful not to injure the rights of the Church or of the family in what pertains to them. It is well to repeat this warning here; for in these days there is spreading a spirit of nationalism which is false and exaggerated, as well as dangerous to true peace and prosperity. Under its influence various excesses are committed in giving a military turn to the so-called physical training of boys (sometimes even of girls, contrary to the very instincts of human nature); or again in usurping unreasonably, on Sunday, the time which should be devoted to religious duties and to family life at home. It is not Our intention, however, to condemn what is good in the spirit of discipline and legitimate bravery promoted by these methods. We condemn only what is excessive, as for example violence, which must not be confounded with courage nor with the noble sentiment of military valor in defense of country and public order; or again exaltation of athleticism, which even in classic pagan times marked the decline and downfall of genuine physical training.

In general also it belongs to civil society and the state to provide what may be called civic education, not only for its youth, but for all ages and classes.

This consists in the practice of presenting publicly to groups of individuals information having an intellectual, imaginative and emotional appeal, calculated to draw their wills to what is upright and honest, and to urge its practice by a sort of moral compulsion, positively by disseminating such knowledge, and negatively by suppressing what is opposed to it.[33] This civic education, so wide and varied in itself as to include almost every activity of the state intended for the public good, ought also to be regulated by the norms of rectitude, and therefore cannot conflict with the doctrines of the Church, which is the divinely appointed teacher of these norms.

5. RELATION BETWEEN CHURCH AND STATE. All that we have said so far regarding the activity of the state in educational matters rests on the solid and immovable foundation of the Catholic doctrine of the Christian constitution of states set forth in such masterly fashion by Our predecessor Leo XIII, notably in the encyclicals *Immortale Dei* and *Sapientiae Christianae*. He writes as follows:[34]

God has divided the government of the human race between two authorities, ecclesiastical and civil, establishing one over things divine, the other over things human. Both are supreme, each in its own domain; each has its own fixed boundaries, which limit its activities. These boundaries are determined by the peculiar nature and the proximate end of each, and

describe as it were a sphere within which, with exclusive right, each may develop its influence. As, however, the same subjects are under two authorities, it may happen that the same matter, though from a different point of view, may come under the competence and jurisdiction of each of them. It follows that Divine Providence, whence both authorities have their origin, must have traced with due order the proper line of action for each. The powers that are, are ordained of God.

Now the education of youth is precisely one of those matters that belong both to the Church and to the state, "though in different ways," as explained above:[35]

Therefore [continues Leo XIII] between the two powers there must reign a well-ordained harmony. Not without reason may this mutual agreement be compared to the union of body and soul in man. Its nature and extent can be determined only by considering, as we have said, the nature of each of the two powers, and in particular the excellence and nobility of the respective ends. To one is committed directly and specifically the charge of what is helpful in worldly matters; while the other is to concern itself with the things that pertain to heaven and eternity. Everything, therefore, in human affairs that is in any way sacred, or has reference to the salvation of souls and the worship of God, whether by its nature or by its end, is subject to the jurisdiction and discipline of the Church. Whatever else is comprised in the civil and political order rightly comes under the authority of the state; for Christ commanded us to give to Caesar the things that are Caesar's, and to God the things that are God's.

Whoever refuses to admit these principles, and hence to apply them to education, must necessarily deny that

---

[33] P. L. Taparelli, *Saggio teor. di Diritto Naturale*, n. 922; a work never sufficiently praised and recommended to university students (cf. Our Discourse of December 18, 1927).

[34] *Ep. Ency. "Immortale Dei,"* November 1, 1885.

[35] *Ibid.*

Christ has founded His Church for the eternal salvation of mankind, and maintain instead that civil society and the state are not subject to God and to His law, natural and divine. Such a doctrine is manifestly impious, contrary to right reason and, especially in this matter of education, extremely harmful to the proper training of youth, and disastrous as well for civil society as for the well-being of all mankind. On the other hand, from the application of these principles there inevitably result immense advantages for the right formation of citizens. This is abundantly proved by the history of every age. Tertullian in his *Apologeticus* could throw down a challenge to the enemies of the Church in the early days of Christianity, just as St. Augustine did in his; and we today can repeat with him:[36]

Let those who declare the teaching of Christ to be opposed to the welfare of the state, furnish us with an army of soldiers such as Christ says soldiers ought to be; let them give us subjects, husbands, wives, parents, children, masters, servants, kings, judges, taxpayers and taxgatherers who live up to the teachings of Christ; and then let them dare assert that Christian doctrine is harmful to the state. Rather let them not hesitate one moment to acclaim that doctrine, rightly observed, the greatest safeguard of the state.

While treating of education, it is not out of place to show here how an ecclesiastical writer who flourished in more recent times, during the Renaissance, the holy and learned Cardinal Silvio Antoniano, to whom the cause of Christian education is greatly indebted, has set forth most clearly this well-established point of Catholic doc-

trine. He had been a disciple of that wonderful educator of youth, St. Philip Neri; he was teacher and Latin secretary to St. Charles Borromeo, and it was at the latter's suggestion and under his inspiration that he wrote his splendid treatise on *The Christian Education of Youth*. In it he argues as follows:[37]

The more closely the temporal power of a nation aligns itself with the spiritual, and the more it fosters and promotes the latter, by so much the more it contributes to the conservation of the commonwealth. For it is the aim of the ecclesiastical authority to form by the use of spiritual means good Christians, in accordance with its own particular end and object; and in doing this it helps at the same time to form good citizens, and prepares them to meet their obligations as members of a civil society. This follows of necessity because in the City of God, the Holy Roman Catholic Church, a good citizen and an upright man are absolutely one and the same thing. How grave, therefore, is the error of those who separate things so closely united, and who think that they can produce good citizens by ways and methods other than those which make for the formation of good Christians. For, let human prudence say what it likes and reason as it pleases, it is impossible to produce true temporal peace and tranquillity by things repugnant or opposed to the peace and happiness of eternity.

6. RELATION OF CHURCH AND SCIENCE. What is true of the state is true also of science, scientific methods and scientific research; they have nothing to fear from the full and perfect mandate which the Church holds in the field of education. Our Catholic institutions, whatever their grade in the educational and scientific world, have

no need of apology. The esteem they enjoy, the praise they receive, the learned works which they promote and produce in such abundance and, above all, the men, fully and splendidly equipped, whom they provide for the magistracy, for the professions, for the teaching career, in fact for every walk of life, more than sufficiently testify in their favor.[38]

These facts moreover present a most striking confirmation of Catholic doctrine defined by the Vatican Council:[39]

Not only is it impossible for faith and reason to be at variance with each other, they are on the contrary of mutual help. For while right reason establishes the foundations of faith and, by the help of its light, develops a knowledge of the things of God, faith on the other hand frees and preserves reason from error and enriches it with varied knowledge. The Church, therefore, far from hindering the pursuit of the arts and sciences, fosters and promotes them in many ways. For she is neither ignorant nor unappreciative of the many advantages which flow from them to mankind. On the contrary, she admits that just as they come from God, Lord of all knowledge, so, too, if rightly used, with the help of His grace they lead to God. Nor does she prevent the sciences, each in its own sphere, from making use of principles and methods of their own. Only, while acknowledging the freedom due to them, she takes every precaution to prevent them from falling into error by opposition to divine doctrine, or from overstepping their proper limits and thus invading and disturbing the domain of faith.

This norm of a just freedom in things scientific serves also as an in-

violable norm of a just freedom in things didactic, or for rightly understood liberty in teaching; it should be observed, therefore, in whatever instruction is imparted to others. Its obligation is all the more binding in justice when there is question of instructing youth. For in this work the teacher, whether public or private, has no absolute right of his own, but only such as has been communicated to him by others. Besides, every Christian child or youth has a strict right to instruction in harmony with the teaching of the Church, the pillar and ground of truth. And whoever disturbs the pupil's faith in any way, does him grave wrong, inasmuch as he abuses the trust which children place in their teachers, and takes unfair advantage of their inexperience and of their natural craving for unrestrained liberty, at once illusory and false.

II. SUBJECT OF EDUCATION

A. THE WHOLE MAN

In fact it must never be forgotten that the subject of Christian education is man whole and entire, soul united to body in unity of nature, with all his faculties natural and supernatural, such as right reason and revelation show him to be; man, therefore, fallen from his original estate, but redeemed by Christ and restored to the supernatural condition of adopted son of God, though without the preternatural privileges of bodily immortality or perfect control of appetite. There remain, therefore, in human nature the effects of original sin, the chief of which are weakness of will and disorderly inclinations.

---

[38] Letter to the Cardinal Secretary of State, May 30, 1929.

[39] *Conc. Vat., Sess.* 3, cap. 4.

"Folly is bound up in the heart of a child and the rod of correction shall drive it away."[40] Disorderly inclinations, then, must be corrected, good tendencies encouraged and regulated from tender childhood and, above all, the mind must be enlightened and the will strengthened by supernatural truth and with the assistance of grace, without which it is impossible to control evil impulses, impossible to attain to the full and complete perfection of education intended by the Church, which Christ has endowed so richly with divine doctrine and with the sacraments, efficacious means of grace.

B. NATURALISM

Hence every form of pedagogic naturalism, which in any way excludes or overlooks supernatural Christian formation in the teaching of youth, is false. Every method of education founded, wholly or in part, on the denial or forgetfulness of original sin and of grace, and relying on the sole powers of human nature, is unsound. Such, generally speaking, are those modern systems bearing various names, which appeal to a pretended self-government and unrestrained freedom on the part of the child, and which diminish or even suppress the teacher's authority and action, attributing to the child an exclusive primacy of initiative and an activity independent of any higher law, natural or divine, in the work of his education.

1. FALSE AND DAMAGING. If any of these terms are used, less properly, to denote the necessity of a gradually more active cooperation on the part of the

pupil in his own education; if the intention is to banish from education despotism and violence, which, by the way, just punishment is not, this would be correct, but in no way new. It would mean only what has been taught and reduced to practice by the Church in traditional Christian education, in imitation of the method employed by God Himself towards His creatures, of whom He demands active cooperation according to the nature of each; for His Wisdom "reacheth from end to end mightily and ordereth all things sweetly."[41]

But alas! it is clear from the obvious meaning of the words and from experience, that what is intended by not a few is the withdrawal of education from every sort of dependence on the divine law. So today we see, strange sight indeed, educators and philosophers who spend their lives in searching for a universal moral code of education, as if there existed no Decalogue, no gospel law, no law even of nature, stamped by God on the heart of man, promulgated by right reason and codified in positive revelation by God Himself in the Ten Commandments. These innovators are wont to refer contemptuously to Christian education as "heteronomous," "passive," "obsolete," because founded upon the authority of God and His holy law.

Such men are miserably deluded in their claim to emancipate, as they say, the child, while in reality they are making him the slave of his own blind pride and of his disorderly affections, which, as a logical consequence of this false system, come to be justified as

---

[40] Prov., xxii, 15.

[41] Wisdom, viii, 1.

legitimate demands of a so-called autonomous nature.

But what is worse is the claim, not only vain but false, irreverent and dangerous, to submit to research, experiment and conclusions of purely natural and profane order those matters of education which belong to the supernatural order; as for example questions of priestly or religious vocation, and in general the secret workings of grace, which indeed elevate the natural powers but are infinitely superior to them, and may nowise be subjected to physical laws, for "the Spirit breatheth where He will."[42]

2. SEX EDUCATION. Another very grave danger is that naturalism which nowadays invades the field of education in that most delicate matter of purity of morals. Far too common is the error of those who with dangerous assurance and under an ugly term propagate a so-called sex education, falsely imagining they can forearm youths against the dangers of sensuality by means purely natural, such as a foolhardy initiation and precautionary instruction for all indiscriminately, even in public; and, worse still, by exposing them at an early age to the occasions, in order to accustom them, so it is argued, and as it were to harden them against such dangers.

Such persons grievously err in refusing to recognize the inborn weakness of human nature, and the law of which the Apostle speaks, fighting against the law of the mind;[43] and also in ignoring the experience of facts, from which it is clear that, particularly

in young people, evil practices are the effect not so much of ignorance of intellect as of weakness of a will exposed to dangerous occasions and unsupported by the means of grace.

In this extremely delicate matter, if, all things considered, some private instruction is found necessary and opportune, from those who hold from God the commission to teach and who have the grace of state, every precaution must be taken. Such precautions are well known in traditional Christian education and are adequately described by Antoniano cited above, when he says:[44]

Such is our frailty and inclination to sin, that often in the very things considered to be remedies against sin we find occasions for and inducements to sin itself. Hence it is of the highest importance that a good father, while discussing with his son a matter so delicate, should be well on his guard and not descend to details, nor refer to the various ways in which this infernal hydra destroys with its poison so large a portion of the world; otherwise it may happen that, instead of extinguishing this fire, he unwittingly stirs or kindles it in the simple and tender heart of the child. Speaking generally, during the period of childhood it suffices to employ those remedies which produce the double effect of opening the door to the virtue of purity and closing the door upon vice.

3. COEDUCATION. False also and harmful to Christian education is the so-called method of "coeducation." This too, by many of its supporters, is founded upon naturalism and the denial of original sin; but by all, upon a

---

[42] John iii, 8.
[43] Rom. vii, 23.

[44] *Dell 'educazione cristiana dei figliuoli,* lib. II, c. 88.

deplorable confusion of ideas that mistakes a leveling promiscuity and equality for the legitimate association of the sexes. The Creator has ordained and disposed perfect union of the sexes only in matrimony and, with varying degrees of contact, in the family and in society. Besides, there is not in nature itself, which fashions the two quite different in organism, in temperament and in abilities, anything to suggest that there can be or ought to be promiscuity, and much less equality, in the training of the two sexes. These, in keeping with the wonderful designs of the Creator, are destined to complement each other in the family and in society, precisely because of their differences, which therefore ought to be maintained and encouraged during their years of formation, with the necessary distinction and corresponding separation, according to age and circumstances. These principles, with due regard to time and place, must, in accordance with Christian prudence, be applied to all schools, particularly in the most delicate and decisive period of formation, that, namely, of adolescence; and in gymnastic exercises and deportment, special care must be had of Christian modesty in young women and girls, which is so gravely impaired by any kind of exhibition in public.

Recalling the terrible words of the divine Master: "Woe to the world because of scandals!"[45] We most earnestly appeal to your solicitude and your watchfulness, Venerable Brethren, against these pernicious errors, which, to the immense harm of youth, are spreading far and wide among Christian peoples.

[45] Matt. xviii, 7.

III. ENVIRONMENT OF EDUCATION

In order to obtain perfect education, it is of the utmost importance to see that all those conditions which surround the child during the period of his formation—in other words, the combination of circumstances which we call environment—correspond exactly to the end proposed.

A. THE CHRISTIAN FAMILY

The first natural and necessary element in this environment, as regards education, is the family, and this precisely because so ordained by the Creator Himself. Accordingly that education, as a rule, will be more effective and lasting which is received in a well-ordered and well-disciplined Christian family; and more efficacious in proportion to the clear and constant good example set, first by the parents, and then by the other members of the household.

It is not our intention to treat formally the question of domestic education, nor even to touch upon its principal points. The subject is too vast. Besides there are not lacking special treatises on this topic by authors, both ancient and modern, well known for their solid Catholic doctrine. One which seems deserving of special mention is the golden treatise already referred to, of Antoniano, on *The Christian Education of Youth,* which St. Charles Borromeo ordered to be read in public to parents assembled in their churches.

Nevertheless, Venerable Brethren and beloved children, We wish to call your attention in a special manner to the present-day lamentable decline in family education. The offices and professions of a transitory and earthly life, which are certainly of far less importance, are prepared for by long and careful study; whereas for the fundamental duty and obligation of educating their children many parents have little or no preparation, immersed as they are in temporal cares. The declining influence of domestic environment is further weakened by another tendency, prevalent almost everywhere today, which, under one pretext or another, for economic reasons or for reasons of industry, trade or politics, causes children to be more and more frequently sent away from home even in their tenderest years. And there is a country where the children are actually being torn from the bosom of the family, to be formed (or, to speak more accurately, to be deformed and depraved) in godless schools and associations, to irreligion and hatred, according to the theories of those who teach common ownership of all things; and thus is renewed in a real and more terrible manner the Slaughter of the Innocents.

For the love of our Saviour Jesus Christ, therefore, we implore pastors of souls, by every means in their power, by instructions and catechizing, by word of mouth and written articles widely distributed, to warn Christian parents of their grave obligations. And this should be done not in a merely theoretical and general way, but with practical and specific application to the various responsibilities of parents touching the religious, moral and civil training of their children, and with indication of the methods best adapted to make their training effective, supposing

always the influence of their own exemplary lives. The Apostle of the Gentiles did not hesitate to descend to such details of practical instruction in his epistles, especially in the Epistle to the Ephesians, where among other things he gives this advice: "And you, fathers, provoke not your children to anger."[46] This fault is the result not so much of excessive severity, as of impatience and of ignorance of means best calculated to effect a desired correction; it is also due to the all too common relaxation of parental discipline which fails to check the growth of evil passions in the hearts of the younger generation. Parents, therefore, and all who take their place in the work of education should be careful to make right use of the authority given them by God, whose vicars in a true sense they are. This authority is not given for their own advantage but for the proper upbringing of their children in a holy and filial "fear of God, the beginning of wisdom," on which foundation alone all respect for authority can rest securely; and without which, order, tranquillity and prosperity, whether in the family or in society, will be impossible.

B. THE CHURCH'S EDUCATIONAL WORKS

To meet the weakness of man's fallen nature, God in His goodness has provided the abundant helps of His grace and the countless means with which He has endowed the great family of Christ, the Church. The Church, therefore, is the educational environment most intimately and harmoni-

[46] Ephes. vi, 4.

ously associated with the Christian family.

This educational environment of the Church embraces the sacraments, divinely efficacious means of grace, the sacred ritual, so wonderfully instructive, and the material fabric of her churches, whose liturgy and art have an immense educational value; but it also includes the great number and variety of schools, associations and institutions of all kinds, established for the training of youth in Christian piety, together with literature and the sciences, not omitting recreation and physical culture. And in this inexhaustible fecundity of educational works, how marvelous, how incomparable is the Church's maternal providence! So admirable too is the harmony which she maintains with the Christian family, that the Church and the family may be said to constitute together one and the same refuge and temple of Christian education.

C. THE SCHOOL

Since, however, the younger generation must be trained in the arts and sciences for the advantage and prosperity of civil society, and since the family of itself is unequal to this task, it was necessary to create that social institution, the school. But let it be borne in mind that this institution owes its existence to the initiative of the family and of the Church, long before it was undertaken by the state. Hence, considered in its historical origin, the school is by its very nature an institution subsidiary and complementary to the family and to the Church. It follows logically and necessarily that pub-

lic schools must not be opposed to but in accord with those other two elements, and form with them a perfect moral union, constituting one sanctuary of education, as it were, with the family and the Church. Otherwise the school is doomed to fail of its purpose and to become instead an agent of destruction.

This principle we find recognized by a layman famous for his pedagogical writings, though these because of their false liberalism cannot be unreservedly praised. "The school," he writes, "if not a temple, is a den." And again: "When literary, social, domestic and religious education do not go hand in hand, man is unhappy and helpless."[47]

1. "Neutral" School. From this it follows that the so-called "neutral" or "lay" school, from which religion is excluded, is contrary to the fundamental principles of education. Such a school, moreover, cannot exist in practice; it is bound to become irreligious. There is no need to repeat what Our predecessors have declared on this point, especially Pius IX and Leo XIII, at times when laicism was beginning in a special manner to infest the public school. We renew and confirm their declarations,[48] as well as the Sacred Canons in which the frequenting of non-Catholic schools, whether neutral or mixed, those namely which are open

[47] Nic. Tommaseo, *Pensieri sull'educazione,* Parte I, 3.6.

[48] Pius IX, Ep. *"Quum non sine,"* July 14, 1864; *Syllabus,* Prop. 48; Leo XIII, *Alloc.* *"Summi Pontificatus,* August 20, 1880; *Ep. Ency. "Nobilissima,"* February 8, 1884; *Ep. Ency. "Quod Multum,"* August 22, 1886; *Ep. Officio "Sanctissimo,"* December 22, 1887; *Ep. Ency. "Caritatis,"* March 19, 1894; etc. (Cf. *Cod. Jur. Can. cum Fontium Annot.,* c. 1374.)

to Catholics and non-Catholics alike, is forbidden for Catholic children and can be at most tolerated, on the approval of the Ordinary alone, under determined circumstances of place and time and with special precautions.[49]

2. "MIXED" SCHOOL. Neither can Catholics admit that other type of mixed school (least of all the so-called *école unique,* obligatory on all), in which the students are provided with separate religious instruction, but receive other lessons in common with non-Catholic pupils from non-Catholic teachers.

The mere fact that a school gives some religious instruction (often extremely stinted) does not bring it into accord with the rights of the Church and of the Christian family, or make it a fit place for Catholic students. To be this, it is necessary that all the teaching and the whole organization of the school, and its teachers, syllabus and textbooks in every branch, be regulated by the Christian spirit, under the direction and maternal supervision of the Church; so that religion may be in very truth the foundation and crown of the youth's entire training; and this in every grade of school, not only the elementary, but the intermediate and the higher institutions of learning as well. To use the words of Leo XIII:[50]

It is necessary not only that religious instruction be given to the young at certain fixed times, but also that every other subject taught be permeated with Christian piety. If this is wanting, if this sacred atmosphere does not pervade and warm the hearts of masters and scholars alike,

[49] *Cod. Jur. Can.,* c. 1374.
[50] *Ep. Ency. "Militantis Ecclesiae,"* August 1, 1897.

little good can be expected from any kind of learning, and considerable harm will often be the consequence.

3. CATHOLIC SCHOOL. And let no one say that in a nation where there are different religious beliefs, it is impossible to provide for public instruction otherwise than by neutral or mixed schools. In such a case it becomes the duty of the state, indeed it is the easier and more reasonable method of procedure, to leave free scope to the initiative of the Church and the family, while giving them such assistance as justice demands. That this can be done to the full satisfaction of families, and to the advantage of education and of public peace and tranquillity, is clear from the actual experience of some countries comprising different religious denominations. There the school legislation respects the rights of the family and Catholics are free to follow their own system of teaching in schools that are entirely Catholic. Nor is distributive justice lost sight of, as is evidenced by the financial aid granted by the state to the several schools demanded by the families.

In other countries of mixed creeds, things are otherwise, and a heavy burden weighs upon Catholics, who under the guidance of their bishops and with the indefatigable cooperation of the clergy, secular and regular, support Catholic schools for their children entirely at their own expense; to this they feel obliged in conscience and, with a generosity and constancy worthy of all praise, they are firmly determined to make adequate provision for what they openly profess as their motto: "Catholic education in Catholic schools for all the Catholic youth." If such education is not aided from public funds, as distributive justice requires, certainly it may not be opposed by any civil authority that does not wish to spurn the rights of the family and the claims of legitimate liberty.

Where this fundamental liberty is thwarted or interfered with, Catholics will never feel, whatever may have been the sacrifices already made, that they have done enough, for the support and defense of their schools and for the securing of laws that will do them justice.

a. CATHOLIC ACTION THROUGH THE SCHOOL. For whatever Catholics do in promoting and defending the Catholic school for their children is a genuinely religious work and therefore an important task of "Catholic Action." For this reason the associations which in various countries are so zealously engaged in this work of prime necessity are especially dear to Our paternal heart and are deserving of every commendation.

Let it be loudly proclaimed and well understood and recognized by all, that Catholics, no matter what their nationality, in agitating for Catholic schools for their children, are not mixing in party politics, but are engaged in a religious enterprise demanded by conscience. They do not intend to separate their children either from the body of the nation or its spirit, but to educate them in a perfect manner, most conducive to the prosperity of the nation. Indeed a good Catholic, precisely because of his Catholic principles, makes the better citizen, attached to his country and loyally submissive to constituted civil authority in every legitimate form of government.

In such a school, in harmony with the Church and the Christian family,

the various branches of secular learning will not enter into conflict with religious instruction to the manifest detriment of education. And if, when occasion arises, it be deemed necessary to have the students read authors propounding false doctrine, for the purpose of refuting it, this will be done after due preparation and with such an antidote of sound doctrine, that it will not only do no harm, but will be an aid to the Christian formation of youth.

In such a school, moreover, the study of the vernacular and of classical literature will do no damage to moral virtue. There the Christian teacher will imitate the bee, which takes the choicest part of the flower and leaves the rest, as St. Basil teaches in his discourse to youths on the study of the classics.[51] Nor will this necessary caution, suggested also by the pagan Quintilian,[52] in any way hinder the Christian teacher from gathering and turning to profit whatever there is of real worth in the systems and methods of our modern times, mindful of the Apostle's advice: "Prove all things: hold fast that which is good."[53] Hence in accepting the new, he will not hastily abandon the old, which the experience of centuries has found expedient and profitable. This is particularly true in the teaching of Latin, which in our days is falling more and more into disuse because of the unreasonable rejection of methods so successfully used by that sane humanism whose highest development was reached in the schools of the Church. These noble traditions of the past require that the youth committed to

[51] *P. G.,* t. 31, 570.
[52] *Inst. Or.,* I, 8.
[53] I. Thess. v, 21.

Catholic schools be fully instructed in the letters and sciences in accordance with the exigencies of the times. They also demand that the doctrine imparted be deep and solid, especially in sound philosophy, avoiding the muddled superficiality of those "who perhaps would have found the necessary, had they not gone in search of the superfluous."[54] In this connection Christian teachers should keep in mind what Leo XIII says in a pithy sentence:[55]

> Greater stress must be laid on the employment of apt and solid methods of teaching and, what is still more important, on bringing into full conformity with the Catholic faith what is taught in literature, in the sciences and, above all, in philosophy, on which depends in great part the right orientation of the other branches of knowledge.

b. GOOD TEACHERS. Perfect schools are the result not so much of good methods as of good teachers, teachers who are thoroughly prepared and well grounded in the matter they have to teach; who possess the intellectual and moral qualifications required by their important office; who cherish a pure and holy love for the youths confided to them, because they love Jesus Christ and His Church, of which these are the children of predilection; and who have therefore sincerely at heart the true good of family and country. Indeed it fills Our soul with consolation and gratitude toward the divine Goodness to see, side by side with religious men and women engaged in teaching, such a large number of excellent lay teachers, who, for their greater spiritual advance-

ment, are often grouped in special sodalities and associations, which are worthy of praise and encouragement as most excellent and powerful auxiliaries of "Catholic Action." All these labor unselfishly with zeal and perseverance in what St. Gregory Nazianzen calls "the art of arts and the science of sciences,"[56] the direction and formation of youth. Of them also it may be said in the words of the divine Master: "The harvest indeed is great, but the laborers few."[57] Let us then pray the Lord of the harvest to send more such workers into the field of Christian education; and let their formation be one of the principal concerns of the pastors of souls and of the superiors of religious orders.

D. THE WORLD AND ITS DANGERS

It is no less necessary to direct and watch the education of the adolescent, "soft as wax to be molded into vice,"[58] in whatever environment he may happen to be, removing occasions of evil and providing occasions for good in his recreations and social intercourse; for "evil communications corrupt good manners."[59]

More than ever nowadays an extended and careful vigilance is necessary, inasmuch as the dangers of moral and religious shipwreck are greater for inexperienced youth. Especially is this true of impious and immoral books, often diabolically circulated at low prices; of the cinema, which multiplies

---

[54] Seneca, *Ep.* 45.
[55] Leo XIII, *Ep. Ency. "Inscrutabili,"* April 21, 1878.

[56] Oratio II, *P.G.,* t. 35, 426.
[57] Matt. ix, 37.
[58] Horace, *Art. Poet.,* v. 163.
[59] I Cor. xv, 33.

every kind of exhibition; and now also of the radio, which facilitates every kind of teaching. These most powerful means of publicity, which can be of great utility for instruction and education when directed by sound principles, are only too often used as an incentive to evil passions and greed for gain. St. Augustine deplored the passion for the shows of the circus which possessed even some Christians of his time, and he dramatically narrates the infatuation for them, fortunately only temporary, of his disciple and friend Alipius.[60] How often today must parents and educators bewail the corruption of youth brought about by the modern theatre and the vile book!

Worthy of all praise and encouragement, therefore, are those educational associations which have for their object to point out to parents and educators, by means of suitable books and periodicals, the dangers to morals and religion that are often cunningly disguised in books and theatrical representations. In their spirit of zeal for the souls of the young, they endeavor at the same time to circulate good literature and to promote plays that are really instructive, going so far as to put up, at the cost of great sacrifices, theatres and cinemas, in which virtue will have nothing to suffer and much to gain.

This necessary vigilance does not demand that young people be removed from the society in which they must live and save their souls; but that today more than ever they should be forewarned and forearmed as Christians against the seductions and the errors of the world, which, as Holy Writ admonishes us, are all "concupiscence of

the flesh, concupiscence of the eyes and pride of life."[61] Let them be what Tertullian wrote of the first Christians, and what Christians of all times ought to be, "sharers in the possession of the world, not of its error."[62]

This saying of Tertullian brings us to the topic which we propose to treat in the last place and which is of the greatest importance, that is, the true nature of Christian education, as deduced from its proper end. Its consideration reveals with noonday clearness the pre-eminent educational mission of the Church.

IV. END AND OBJECT OF CHRISTIAN EDUCATION

A. TO FORM THE TRUE CHRISTIAN

The proper and immediate end of Christian education is to cooperate with divine grace in forming the true and perfect Christian, that is, to form Christ Himself in those regenerated by baptism, according to the emphatic expression of the Apostle: "My little children, of whom I am in labor again, until Christ be formed in you."[63] For the true Christian must live a supernatural life in Christ: "Christ, who is your life,"[64] and display it in all his actions: "That the life also of Jesus may be made manifest in our mortal flesh."[65]

For precisely this reason, Christian education takes in the whole aggregate

---

60 *Confess.*, VI. 8.

61 I John, ii, 16.
62 *De Idoldatria,* 14.
63 Galat. iv, 19.
64 Coloss. iii, 4.
65 II. Cor. iv, 11.

of human life, physical and spiritual, intellectual and moral, individual, domestic and social, not with a view of reducing it in any way, but in order to elevate, regulate and perfect it, in accordance with the example and teaching of Christ.

Hence the true Christian, product of Christian education, is the supernatural man who thinks, judges and acts constantly and consistently in accordance with right reason illumined by the supernatural light of the example and teaching of Christ; in other words—to use the current term—the true and finished man of character. For it is not every kind of consistency and firmness of conduct based on subjective principles that makes true character, but only constancy in following the eternal principles of justice, as is admitted even by the pagan poet when he praises for his two qualities "the man who is just and firm of purpose."[66] And on the other hand, there cannot be full justice except in giving to God what is due to God, as the true Christian does.

The scope and aim of Christian education as here described appears to the worldly as an abstraction, or rather as something that cannot be attained without suppression or dwarfing of the natural faculties, and renunciation of the activities of the present life. Hence it seems to be inimical to social life and temporal prosperity, and contrary to all progress in letters, arts and sciences, and all the other elements of civilization. To a like objection raised by the ignorance and prejudice of even cultured pagans of a former day, and repeated with greater frequency and insistence in modern times, Tertullian has replied as follows:[67]

We are not strangers to life. We are fully aware of the gratitude we owe to God, our Lord and Creator. We reject none of the fruits of His handiwork; we only abstain from their immoderate or unlawful use. We are living in the world with you; we do not shun your forum, your markets, your baths, your shops, your factories, your stables, your places of business and traffic. We take ship with you and we serve in your armies; we are farmers and merchants with you; we interchange skilled labor and display our works in public for your service. How we can seem unprofitable to you with whom we live and of whom we are, I know not.

The true Christian does not renounce the activities of this life, he does not stunt his natural faculties; but he develops and perfects them, by coordinating them with the supernatural. He thus ennobles what is merely natural in life and secures for it new strength in the material and temporal order, no less than in the spiritual and eternal.

B. TO FORM USEFUL CITIZENS

This fact is proved by the whole history of Christianity and its institutions, which is nothing else but the history of true civilization and progress up to the present day. It stands out conspicuously in the lives of the numerous saints, whom the Church—and she alone—produces, in whom is perfectly realized the purpose of Christian education, and who have in every way ennobled and benefited human society. Indeed, the saints have ever been, are

[66] Horace, Odes, III, 3, v. 1.

[67] Apol., 42.

and ever will be the greatest benefactors of society, and perfect models for every class and profession, for every state and condition of life, from the simple and uncultured peasant to the master of sciences and letters, from the humble artisan to the commander of armies, from the father of a family to the ruler of peoples and nations, from simple maidens and matrons of the domestic hearth to queens and empresses. What shall we say of the immense work which has been accomplished even for the temporal well-being of men by missionaries of the gospel, who have brought and still bring to barbarous tribes the benefits of civilization together with the light of the faith? What of the founders of so many social and charitable institutions, of the vast numbers of saintly educators, men and women, who have perpetuated and multiplied their lifework, by leaving after them prolific institutions of Christian education, to the great profit of families and for the inestimable advantage of nations?

C. CHRIST THE MASTER AND MODEL

Such are the fruits of Christian education. Their price and value is derived from the supernatural virtue and life in Christ which Christian education forms and develops in man. Of this life and virtue Christ our Lord and Master is the source and dispenser. By His example He is at the same time the universal model accessible to all, especially to the young in the period of His hidden life, a life of labor and obedience, adorned with all virtues, personal, domestic and social, before God and men.

Now all this array of priceless educational treasures, which We have barely touched upon, is so truly a property of the Church as to form her very substance, since she is the Mystical Body of Christ, the immaculate spouse of Christ and consequently a most admirable mother and an incomparable and perfect teacher. This thought inspired St. Augustine, the great genius of whose blessed death we are about to celebrate the fifteenth centenary, with accents of tenderest love for so glorious a mother:[68]

O Catholic Church, true Mother of Christians! Not only dost thou preach to us, as is meet, how purely and chastely we are to worship God Himself, to possess whom is life most blessed; thou dost moreover so cherish neighborly love and charity that all the infirmities to which sinful souls are subject find their most potent remedy in thee. Childlike thou art in molding the child, strong with the young man, gentle with the aged, dealing with each according to his needs of mind and of body. Thou dost subject child to parent in a sort of free servitude, and settest parent over child in a jurisdiction of love. Thou bindest brethren to brethren by the bond of religion, stronger and closer than the bond of blood . . . Thou unitest citizen to citizen, nation to nation, yea, all men, in a union not of companionship only, but of brotherhood, reminding them of their common origin. Thou teachest kings to care for their people, and biddest people to be subject to their kings. Thou teachest assiduously to whom honor is due, to whom love, to whom reverence, to whom fear, to whom comfort, to whom rebuke, to whom punishment; showing us that whilst not all things nor the same things are due to all, charity is due to all and offense to none.

[68] *De Moribus Ecclesiae catholicae,* lib. I, c. 30.

Let us then, Venerable Brethren, raise our hands and our hearts in supplication to heaven, "to the Shepherd and Guardian of [our] Souls,"[69] to the divine King "who gives laws to rulers," that in His almighty power He may cause these splendid fruits of Christian education to be gathered in ever greater abundance "in the whole world," for

[69] Cf. I Peter ii, 25.

the lasting benefit of individuals and of nations.

As a pledge of these heavenly favors, with paternal affection We impart to you, Venerable Brethren, to your clergy and your people, the Apostolic Benediction.

Given at Rome, at St. Peter's, the thirty-first day of December, in the year 1929, the eighth of Our pontificate.

PIUS PP. XI.

Existentialism and Education

George F. Kneller*

I do not intend this essay to serve as an overall critique of existentialism but as a brief survey of some aspects of it which are relevant to education. Since its emergence as a *cause celebre* at the end of World War II existentialism has attracted a good deal of critical attention, although unfortunately in the English-speaking world it tends to be regarded still as not really a philosophy. On the other hand, it has received only sporadic analysis from an educator's point of view, and then as a rule in articles that do not appear outside educational journals. Although no existentialist has yet attempted a systematic application of his philosophy to the problems of education, I write in the belief that nevertheless existentialism contains within itself an approach to education which is refreshingly different from those of the established philosophic schools and which represents a

* An original essay written expressly for this volume.

powerful counter-attack against the most insidious enemies currently facing our educational system, and indeed our whole society, namely, social conformity and the mechanization of man.

I

It is often objected that we should abandon the term "existentialism" altogether except to refer to the doctrines of Jean-Paul Sartre. Many prominent thinkers labeled "existentialists" have since disowned the title, and with good cause, since here is no philosophy or "ism" in the traditional sense. Attitudes expressed in the writings of Soren Kierkegaard, Friedrich Nietzsche, Martin Heidegger, Karl Jaspers, Jean-Paul Sartre and Gabriel Marcel clearly set them beyond the domains of academic philosophy. To the names I have mentioned may be added those of Blaise Pascal, the novelists Fyodor Dostoevski, Franz Kafka and Albert Camus, the

Russian philosopher Nikolai Berdyaev, and such contemporary theologians as Karl Barth, Martin Buber, Paul Tillich and Reinhold Niebuhr.

These, then, are some common elements in the existentialist outlook:

(1) Philosophy should not consist in the "objective" contemplation of traditional philosophic questions, but should become a *passionate encounter* with the perennial problems of life, and in particular with the inevitability of death, the agony and joy of love, the reality of choice, the experience of freedom, and the futility or fruitfulness of personal relationships. Existentialism is an attempt at philosophizing from the standpoint of the actor rather than the spectator. Philosophy that issues from the intellect alone, that is the product of evenings spent in the book-lined study rather than in the turmoil of life itself, lays claim to a spurious detachment which men in any case cannot truly attain. Rather philosophizing must begin in the individual's passionate awareness of the human predicament, *his own predicament,* which is the finitude and contingency of man's existence. As soon as philosophy loses sight of individual man's condition, it abandons its only moorings and becomes sheer speculation—speculation, moreover, that is no mere harmless juggling with irrelevant abstractions but dangerous, too, for when converted into ideologies, these abstractions exercise a hypnotic effect on the minds of millions.

(2) In Sartre's celebrated aphorism, "Existence precedes essence." That is to say, the sheer brute fact that things exist is logically prior to any essence or definition we may read into them. Ob-

jects exist, and man interprets them; but before he ever regards them as the embodiments of certain characteristics, they simply *are.* The world is *there:* it is concrete and particular, and any essence we abstract out of it is less real than the data from which it is abstracted.

(3) By itself the universe is without meaning or purpose. Contrary to the teachings of theology and the great metaphysical systems, man does not form part of a single cosmic design, because "design" is no more than a concept of mind, and the universe is indifferent to mind. The purposes we think we detect in the universe are nothing but a projection of our own desire for order. But in reality we are simply "cast" into an alien world, for which we were not especially created but within which we must sooner or later die. Our *Angst* or "dread" arises from our awareness of the "absurdity" of this condition, that we are free and yet finite, *in* the world and yet *apart from* it, and withal condemned to death. Man, who knows meaning, must live and die in a world without meaning. In his freedom he transcends the world and through his death he submits to it.

(4) Precisely because man does not form part of any universal system he possesses absolute freedom. In fact his existence may potentially be synonymous with freedom. In striking contrast to the many forms of scientific and philosophic determinism prevalent today, existentialism affirms man's total freedom and consequent responsibility for all his actions. We shall see later how the existentialist analyzes men's attempts to evade the terrible burden

of their freedom, as terrible as the "otherness" of the world in which they live.

(5) Since man is free, he "makes himself." Freedom being pure potentiality until it actualizes itself in deeds, man himself is "nothing" until he acts. He is the sum of his own actions, for each of which he is fully responsible, since he could always have chosen otherwise. In Sartre's words:

What is meant here by saying that existence precedes essence? It means that, first of all, man exists, turns up, appears on the scene, and, only afterwards defines himself. If man, as the existentialist sees him, is indefinable, it is because at first he is nothing. Only afterwards will he be something and he himself will have made what he will be. . . . Not only is man what he conceives himself to be, but he is also what he wills himself to be after this thrust toward existence. Man is nothing other than what he makes himself.[1]

(6) Since man is free, the philosopher must expose, not as an observer only but as one passionately committed to his own point of view, those tendencies in the twentieth century which act to dehumanize man by undermining this freedom, such as the exploitation of human units by the mass media, the subordination of individuals to machines or to an economic system, the tyranny of the majority in the democratic process and of the group in social affairs. Hear what Nikolai Berdyaev says:

Social training and the civilizing of barbarous man may be a beneficial process; but it does not mean the formation of personality. The completely socialized

and civilized man may be entirely impersonal; he may be a slave and not notice that he is. . . . The problem of man is more primary than the problem of society. All the sociological doctrines of man are erroneous; they know only the superficial, objectified stratum in man. . . . The source of slavery is objectivization, exteriorization, alienation. It is slavery in everything; in the acquisition of knowledge, in morals, in religion, in art, in political and social life. . . . Man seeks freedom. . . . There is within him an immense drive towards freedom, and yet not only does he easily fall into slavery, but he even loves slavery.[2]

II

No matter how much existentialists may have in common, they are sharply divided by deep and fundamental differences. Thus Nietzsche, Heidegger, Sartre and Camus are atheists, while Kierkegaard, Jaspers and Marcel are theists. Marcel is a Catholic, Buber a Jew, and Neibuhr, Barth and Tillich are Protestants, while Berdyaev belonged to the Russian Orthodox Church. Again, while Marcel and Jaspers come to moderately optimistic conclusions, Heidegger and Sartre remain profoundly pessimistic. These differences constitute the first major obstacle in any attempt to comprehend the general nature of the doctrine.

A second obstacle in the way of understanding arises from the fact that existentialism, so its adherents maintain, cannot be studied objectively from without, but requires the student to identify himself with its doctrines from

[1] Jean-Paul Sartre, *Existentialism* (New York: Philosophical Library, Inc., 1947), p. 18.

[2] Nikolai Berdyaev, *Slavery and Freedom* (New York: Charles Scribner's Sons, 1944), Chap. 1.

within. The existentialist philosopher does not analyze issues from a safe distance but rather immerses himself in them both intellectually and emotionally. "The dynamic element in my philosophy, taken as a whole," writes Gabriel Marcel,

can be seen as an obstinate and untiring battle against the spirit of abstraction . . . I have played the part of a prosecuting attorney against every philosophy that seemed to me to remain the prisoner of abstractions.[3]

Philosophy must begin in dread, in genuine awareness of the human condition. Unless the student himself adopts the existentialist method of philosophizing, he necessarily misses the message of the movement and hence judges it unfairly.

The very writings of existentialists bristle with stylistic difficulties. And here lies a third obstruction to understanding, that writers employ terms which cannot adequately be translated into English. While Nietzsche's brilliant, aphoristic prose makes him one of the most readable of all philosophers, Kierkegaard's subtle, ironic style and use of the dialectic bewilders any but the most attentive reader. It is Heidegger, however, who has become the existentialist *bete noire* of the Anglo-Saxon world. I quote at random from his magnum opus, *Sein und Zeit* ("Existence and Being"):

'Nothing' is revealed in dread, but not as something that 'is.' Neither can it be taken as an object. Dread is not an apprehension of Nothing. All the same, Nothing is revealed in and through dread,

yet not, again, in the sense that Nothing appears as if detached and apart from what-is-in-totality when we have that 'uncanny' feeling. We would say rather: in dread Nothing functions as if *at one with* what-is-in-totality.[4]

Such a style proves hard going for those brought up on the more mellifluous expressions of Locke, Berkeley and John Stuart Mill. Existentialists also make frequent use of such terms as *angoisse* and *Sorge,* which are translated conventionally into English as "anguish" and "care," but which in the original cast a penumbra of meaning and overtone which no English rendering can convey. Indeed, existentialists sometimes confuse one another. Marcel, for instance, writes of Heidegger's concept, *Sein zum Tode:*

'*Zum Tode sein*' cannot be translated into French. . . . '*Etre vers la mort*' ('to be towards death')—but what does that mean? 'To be destined for death?' Or perhaps 'to be delivered up to death?' Therein lies a far-reaching equivocation . . . There is nothing in all this, to my mind, that is self-evident.[5]

The fact that existentialism lends itself better to literary than to philosophic treatment poses another dilemma. The French existentialists have used the novel and play extensively in order to propagate their views—more successfully, perhaps, than they have used philosophy. Here they can embody the dialectic of ideas in the meeting and conflict of real characters, in whose predicament the reader's mind

[3] Gabriel Marcel, *Man Against Mass Society* (Chicago: Henry Regnery Co., 1952), p. 1.

[4] Martin Heidegger, *Existence and Being* (London: Vision Press, 1949), p. 368.

[5] Gabriel Marcel, as quoted in Jean Wahl, *A Short History of Existentialism* (New York: The Philosophical Library), 1949.

and feelings are simultaneously involved. Sartre and Camus are two of France's leading writers, however much Sartre's *Les Chemins de la Liberte* may differ from *L'Etranger* or *La Peste*. In Germany Heidegger has turned his attention to a philosophic analysis of the poems of *Holderlin*. This peculiar behavior of existentialists means that any adequate comprehension of the doctrine demands literary as well as philosophic accomplishment.

Finally, existentialism has flourished best in conditions of social and economic collapse (in Germany after the First World War and in France after the Second), which seem more conducive than prosperity to the anguished introspection, resonant despair and defiant affirmation which characterize the movement. But for many Americans, who have not had to suffer the real tragedy and devastation of war, the doctrine seems to be just a bit ridiculous; it is "off-beat"—almost unhealthy. The American temperament (if one may use such an abstraction) still remains essentially optimistic, confident that, given the "know how," there is nothing that men cannot achieve once they have set their minds to it. On the other hand, however buoyant this temperament, there is an increasing concern over the growth of conformism, a concern which echoes, though superficially, the existentialist concern for the individual in his struggle against the pressure of the anonymous crowd (*das Man*).

III

Before going further, however, we shall have to wrestle a bit with the formidable components of existentialist ontology, which is essentially phenomenological. Let us look first of all at the contrasting views of four leading existentialists, Heidegger, Sartre, Jaspers and Marcel. Heidegger distinguished Being, here understood as the ultimate reality in which all things share, from existence, which is the sum total of all particular existents. *Dasein,* or human being, differs from all other forms of existence, since it alone is able to relate itself consciously to Being. On the other hand, as the prefix, *Da,* indicates, it is also *there* in the world, bound inescapably to it, and hence limited and finite. An important characteristic of Dasein is *Sorge,* or concern for its own existence. When this concern is directed towards Being itself, it is then authentic, since Being is the true source of Dasein. But when it fractures itself into the myriad humdrum concerns of the day-to-day world, it becomes inauthentic and man evades his true destiny, which is to respond to the call of Being. Man, then, can either live authentically, by deliberately relating himself to Being, or else he can flee from authenticity by immersing himself in the realm of public existence, in the petty cares and pleasures of *das Man*.

Sartre describes two forms of being, *etre en-soi* ("being in-itself") and *etre pour-soi* ("being for-itself"). The former is the being of things and the latter, the being of men. Things are in-themselves because they are not free to be otherwise. Stones, animals, airplanes have no power to choose: they simply exist. Man, on the other hand, is wholly free and hence wholly responsible for what he does. He exists for himself and can choose whatever he wishes. On the other hand, he can seek to escape this freedom by living *in* rather than *for* himself, by attempt-to attain a fixed and permanent character—as a "prohibitionist," for example, or an "anti-semite." When a man says, "I am a prohibitionist," he seeks to characterize himself as something and thus to avoid the responsibility of being continually free. His error lies, not in his love of temperance, which in itself is no bar to authenticity, but in the attempt to abdicate his freedom by becoming the kind of person that can be placed in the usual categories. Men, therefore, can live authentically as free individuals, or inauthentically by attempting to assume fixed characteristics. They can live either in or for themselves, and if they choose the former, all human relationships are doomed to ultimate futility.

According to Jaspers, *Dasein* (or human being) is conscious of transcendent Being, which like a horizon encompasses all forms of finite being. Man realizes that he is related to Being when he becomes aware of certain "ultimate situations" which he cannot avoid, such as death, conflict, suffering, chance and guilt. In the encounter with these situations and through reflection on them he perceives that he can live authentically only to the extent that he consciously relates himself to that Being of which all other beings partake. Philosophy and the authentic life begin in despair, as the individual faces the "ultimate situations," but it ends in affirmation, whereby man sees himself in his true dimension as an aspect of Being itself.

For Marcel, the concept of being is an ontological mystery. It is not a problem which can be discussed and objecti-

fied apart from myself. The question of being does not simply involve but actually implicates my own existence: I am myself in question with the question raised, for indirectly I am affirming my own reality. When I ask What is Being? I also ask the question Who or What am I, that I can indeed ask this question?

Marcel's ontological inquiry starts with a theory of intersubjectivity; it is a theory of *we are* as opposed to *I think*. Here Marcel stresses the element of relation. My existence to be meaningful invokes the presence of a reality other than myself. "We can understand ourselves by starting from the other, or from others, and only by starting from them . . ." Thus ontological inquiry is not solopsistic: "I concern myself with being only insofar as I have a more or less distinct consciousness of the underlying unity which ties me to other of beings whose reality I already have a preliminary notion."[6]

Can being then be equated with existence? The ideal of existence itself is "ambiguous," says Marcel, because it refers to both human beings and things. But a thing, or an object, can hardly partake of being. Things and objects pass away; they can be there and then be there no longer. Hence their existence "is scarcely being at all." *My* existence, on the other hand, does involve being. My existence transcends the there-elsewhere contradiction:

I exist; or again: 'such and such a being whom I love, exists,' the perspective changes; to exist no longer means 'to be there or to be elsewhere;' in other words it

[6] Gabriel Marcel, *The Mystery of Being* (London: Havrill, 1951), Vol. II, pp. 7–8.

means that essentially we transcend the opposition between *here and elsewhere*.[7]

It is true, says Marcel, that I can in a certain sense take hold of my own existence, but on the other hand, my own being cannot be an object of my affirmation. We might be tempted to say that there is always a gap between me and my being. I can narrow the gap, it is true, but "at least in this life I cannot hope to bridge it." In short, being cannot be treated as a datum: "The exigency of being is not a simple desire or a vague aspiration. It is, rather, a deeprooted interior urge, and it might equally well be interpreted as an appeal (for fulfilment)."[8]

IV

The uncompromising affirmation of authentic freedom and individual uniqueness is the stirring message of existentialism for the philosophy of education today. The impact of an educational theory based on existentialism might conceivably turn the tide in the determined struggle that many educators are waging against the notorious tendency to conformity in schools today. Unfortunately the emphasis laid by experimental philosophies on the essentially social nature of human experience has led to the growth of an educational system which encourages the pupil to adapt himself to the ways of his fellows rather than to go off on his own. Such a system admires the achievments of the group over those that are won in isolation, and tends to extol group learning over individual effort. The "well-adjusted" pupil has his

counterpart outside the school in the "organization man" of our big corporations, the executive whose prime virtue is his ability to "get along" well with his business associates; and in politics in the "image-politician," the one who is popular and well-liked by the man in the street, because he can present himself as the latter writ large.

The existentialist asserts that the individual does not necessarily "realize" himself in the group at all, but only exchanges his true self for the anonymous mask of the group. Instead of finding self-fulfilment he actually loses himself. The slick attitudes and gestures of the group and the easily assimilated mannerisms of the class present the merest façade of success, barely concealing the emptiness of the failed human being. How many of our neuroses spring from the stifling of originality within the folds of convention? And "casualness" and "patio living" are no less stifling then the formalism they are supposed to have replaced! The school must encourage the growth of free, creative individuality, not "adjustment" or the insidious pressure to conform that lurks beneath the bland exterior of that overly venerated concept, "team spirit." The individual, declares existentialism, may join the group if he wishes, but under no pressure and of his own free will.

The usual themes of education, one may readily understand, differ widely from the usual themes of existentialism. It is not possible, therefore, to talk about the connection between the two in the same way that one would in the case of a traditional philosophy and education. I shall try, nevertheless, to establish points of contact by using

[7] *Ibid.*, p. 27.
[8] *Ibid.*, p. 37.

such mutually pertinent themes as (1) anguish and death; (2) the individual and the others (*das Man*); (3) knowledge and the knower; (4) values and the individual; (5) the teacher and the student; and (6) the educational process.

(1) Finitude is the most significant feature of the human condition and death the most important event in a man's life. Death should not be regarded simply as the untimely closure of our days or as a longed-for release from age or pain; it is not a merely negative event, the point at which we simply stop living, but rather a positive entity, the goal towards which each one of us is moving every moment of our lives. Man, as I have said, is "cast" into the world, knowing not *why* but simply *that* he exists. And yet, of all the innumerable objects and creatures which share the universe, only man knows that he must die. Aware of his finitude and of the inevitability of death, he is filled with *Angst* or dread.

It is here that philosophy should begin, "on the other side of despair," by attempting to see in the facts of the human condition and man's relation to Being itself. To do so, it must abandon the everyday concept of death as an impersonal event—the inevitable lot of the human race. To be told that a thousand people die every day or even to read in the newspaper of a fatal accident does not move us personally, as it should, but simply provokes the useless reflection that *all people* die. We stifle the thought on which we should reflect which is that *I* must die. Hence we should not dismiss the idea of death as of no importance to us personally, but should keep it continually before us, in the knowledge that our deaths will totally expunge all that we have ever been or thought or done. To live authentically is to live in the ever-present awareness of death. Every choice we make should be made as though it were our last.

There might seem at first to be no place in education for so direct and "melodramatic" a confronting of death. To the young death is either too remote in time, something that happens when one is seventy (which is as distant as eternity itself), or else simply a morose idea to be entertained in fits of depression. Death has no reality in young lives, and counts for nothing compared with getting a car or a girl or a tan. But, surely, if this is the case, the conclusion to be drawn is, not that our schools should dismiss death as irrelevant to the young, but that they must give it the attention it justly deserves. Let our schools take the attitude that it is only the thought of death which makes us truly aware of the values of life. To be conscious of death—our own death—is not to deliver oneself to morbid fantasy but to make possible the enhancement of living. The student should be shown that existence for its own sake does not override all other values, and that it is actually possible to pay too high a price for the privilege of remaining alive. Often it may be finer to die for an ideal than, by preserving one's life, to betray one. History shines with examples of those who willingly made the supreme sacrifice, of mothers who died for their children, soldiers for their country, martyrs for their faith. "Greater love than this hath no man shown, that he laid down his life for a friend." Indeed, the student has before him two magnificent examples that eclipse all others—of Christ in His agony dying for the redemption of mankind, and of Socrates taking the hemlock, that the freedom of the Athenian might be upheld.

Although the teacher should inspire his pupils by describing such examples, his task does not end there. By making them aware of the inevitability and perhaps even desirability of death, he should lead them to examine the quality of their own lives, for the imminence of death is the most potent spur to self-examination. On the other hand, the teacher would be ill-advised to persuade the student that he lives under perpetual sentence of death, although in the existentialist sense this may be true. Rather the student must learn to live his life in the knowledge that some day, a day like this one, life is going to end. Then let him ask himself what he is living for. Is he living to the full as a free man, or is he content simply to exist? When he dies, will it have mattered whether he lived at all? The student is used to having slogans fired at him—from television screens, billboards, politicians, classroom walls and so on. Let him recall, instead, the words of Blaise Pascal, "Live today as if you were to die tomorrow."

(2) Existentialists differ in their views on the relation of the individual to others. For Sartre any man is potentially always in conflict with his neighbor, and all social relationships—whether with one's family, one's friends, one's lover or the state itself—are doomed to frustration. Why is this? According to Sartre man is completely free either to exercise his freedom or to resemble an object. Whenever he comes into contact with another person—even by merely looking at him—he must either dominate the other or be dominated by him. In the first case he denies the other's freedom by treating him as an object. In the second, he denies his own freedom by "objectifying" himself. This conflict reaches its greatest intensity in love, which becomes either sadism, whereby one denies the freedom on one's lover, or masochism, wherein one denies one's own freedom. The only authentic commitment a free man may undertake without sacrificing his own freedom or that of others is one which expands the total area of human liberty. To the extent that a social system restricts freedom, we may cooperate with others to reform or abolish it. We may, for example, take the side of the working class against the bourgeoisie, not on the Marxist principle that the triumph of the proletariat is inevitable, but according to the existentialist view that the working class has not yet attained the freedom to which it has a right.

Less radical in this respect than Sartre, Heidegger argues, not that any social order must inevitably conflict with man's fundamental egoism, but that society in its present form is inimical to that free comradeship of autonomous individuals which characterizes true *Dasein*. Men should be able to choose their own associates and communicate with them as they will. As things are, society (*das Man*) forces the individual to conform outwardly to its own norms in return for taking certain risks in his behalf. It demands no *genuine* self-discipline, but imposes its norms from without. The reaction of the authentic individual is to withdraw from the petty jockeying and noisy garrulity of *das Man,* and keep to the company of a few well chosen comrades.

Marcel and Jaspers disagree with both Sartre and Heidegger, and insist that true freedom or authentic existence leads to a warm participation in the activities of others. As free men we are bound to recognize the freedom of others, and this recognition leads in turn to love and mutual sharing. Nevertheless, participation must remain the authentic interplay of free personalities, not the spurious "togetherness" of the group, which succeeds through whittling down rather than building up the selves of its members. Hence they deplore the depersonalization of man in an industrial society and the influence of the behavioral sciences, which study him, not as a free agent, but as the object of complexes, stimulus-response mechanisms and social interaction.

With their scorn for the inauthentic existence of *das Man,* existentialists condemn the lowering of standards brought about by universal education. If the primary concern of an educational system is with the average rather than the exceptional student, it will substitute the certainty of mediocrity for the possibility of brilliance, and compel the individual to conform to the law of the average. Nietzsche has written:

It might seem to these masses that education for the greatest number of men was only a means to the earthly bliss of the few; (but) the 'greatest possible expansion of education' so enfeebles education that it

can on longer confer privileges or inspire respect. The most general form of culture is simply barbarism.[9]

The contemporary existentialist would not, of course, advocate the Nietzschean view of an education for an elite of potential Supermen. Nevertheless, he insists that equality of educational opportunity shall not be made an excuse for educating all children at the same rate in the same way. Our educational system must permit much greater variety in its methods and organization in order to accommodate itself to the infinitely greater variety of human nature. If schools cannot do this, they should be abolished.

The existentialist is sharply critical of the prevailing tendency to educate children in groups rather than as individuals. He points out that the group will either obstruct the development of its slower members by going at the speed of the fastest or else clip the wings of the fastest by adopting the pace of the average. Groups are often dominated by one, two or a few people, who inhibit the ability of the others to express themselves freely. In any case, the tendency of all groups is towards standardization rather than differentiation, toward the average and the typical rather than the unique and the individual. And what about the individual who prefers to remain silent in the group? How many group members are actually and genuinely hostile to their fellows? The existentialist does not, however, totally reject group in-

[9] Friedrich Wilhelm Nietzsche, *On the Future of Our Educational Institutions.* (New York: The Macmillan Co., 1924), pp. 37–38. See also p. 75.

struction. This method may be used, not in the first instance to raise the standards of the class or group as a whole, but to stimulate the development of each individual within the group. The end of group education is the education of the individual. And *the individual uses the group for his own personal fulfilment.*

Existentialism also deplores the tendency of parents to surrender more and more of their educative responsibilities to the school. In the home the child is cherished as an individual to a degree that is hardly possible in the more impersonal atmosphere of the schoolroom, where he must share his teacher's attention with the rest of the class. Unless the child develops an authentic, independent self within the home, he will tend as a rule to conform to the attitudes and expectations of his schoolmates. Contrary to popular opinion the existentialist extols family life as the most genuine social arrangement and wants the home to be a much greater educative force than it is at present. The freedom to have children entails the responsibility for their fullest genuine development. Parents cannot abrogate the responsibility for the education of their off-spring and rely upon the school to do their job for them.

(3) Probably the most widely held theory of knowledge in educational circles today is that popularized by experimentalism, which states that the best way to acquire knowledge is to propound and test hypotheses to account for particular situations. The ideal to be cultivated is one of detachment—the supposedly impartial calm of the scientist in his search for truth. By contrast the existentialist insists that

if "purely objective" knowledge does not engage the feelings of the knower, it can never be decisive for him. Man is not an intellect alone but a creature of feeling as well, and in order to truly know something, he must be able to relate it to himself personally. Knowledge must be linked to the true end of the individual, which is to become authentically involved with life. For the existentialist there is no such thing as "disinterested knowledge." He asserts that man must not contribute to a cumulative affair so much as to the fact that he must round off his life here and now, and give it meaning while he still has the opportunity. Hence the existentialist lays less emphasis on the gathering of evidence, to which the experimentalist pays so much respect, and more on what the individual does for himself with the evidence. He insists that science is inevitably limited in its scope by the mystery of Being, and that truth in its entirety must always elude us.

Knowledge, properly conceived, brings freedom, since it delivers man from ignorance and prejudice and enables him to see himself as he really is. The school must therefore completely revise its conceptions of knowledge by ceasing to regard subject matter as an end in itself or as an instrument to prepare the student for his future career, and considering it instead as a means for the cultivation of the self. Since authentic existence involves the whole man, we should no longer regard learning primarily as mental discipline. On the contrary, the student should be urged to involve himself intellectually and emotionally in whatever he studies; he must appropriate to himself any exercise or problem or study he tackles. The whole emphasis of the curriculum must shift from the world of objects to the world of the person. Since the meaning of existence lies in man himself, the student should use his knowledge of external realities in order to come to terms more completely with his own nature.

(4) The only values acceptable to the individual are those which he has freely adopted. Indeed, the first principle of all value, and the basis of morality, is the fact of human choice, so that the aim of any moral system should be the expansion of freedom of choice for all. On the other hand, existentialism is no cover for unbridled egoism, for to selfishly seek one's own freedom regardless of its effect on that of other people, is to violate the very meaning of the word.

If the basis of morality is freedom, then we cannot expect the individual to embrace moral standards that have been laid down independently of him and to which he is told to conform irrespective of his personal feelings. Values which are not freely chosen are valueless. The teacher should not impose his own values but should present the principles in which he believes and the reasons for them, and ask the pupil to choose whether he will accept them or not. Existentialism does not require the school to condone moral anarchy in its students. But it does assert that the student can no longer be conditioned by his teacher into accepting supposedly timeless moral principles, which he must uphold inflexibly, whatever their cost in human suffering or their repugnance to himself.

The teacher should bring home vividly to the student that, whatever he does, he cannot escape the consequences of his actions, but must accept them as the issue of his own free choice, however thoughtless that choice may sometimes be. He should insist that each man's life is his own to lead and that no one else can lead it for him. It is pointless for us to blame our failures on external factors such as environment, family, temperament or the influence of others. However important such factors may appear, they do no more than set the scene for the exercise of choice. Although they may explain our mistakes, they do not exonerate them. The child should learn to develop his own principles and a sense of pride in himself, so that he scorns to simply follow the crowd.

Finally the student must recognize that frustration and conflict are not just undesirable states to be avoided at all costs, but that they stem from the inherent "forsakenness" of the human condition, in which man's freedom has set him apart from the rest of the world. Indeed the school should acquaint him with the "darker" side of life, with its pain, its terror and its seemingly inexplicable brutality, as well as with its beauty, ecstasy and joy. The student must become personally concerned with the realization of his own nature and with what Tillich calls the courage to be himself. How different this attitude is from the behavior expected by so many of our youth in the public schools today, who are urged to act and think in teams, to get along with one another at all cost and to adopt as their values only those that can be publicly agreed on! How different, too, from the understanding of so many that individualism is essentially social individualism and that man is inherently a social or political animal!

(5) Existentialists reject traditional conceptions of the relationship between teacher and pupil. The teacher is not at his desk primarily to impart knowledge (realism), or as a consultant in problem-situations (pragmatism) or as a personality to be emulated (idealism). His function is to assist each student personally in his journey towards self-realization. A good teacher acts himself as a free agent; his influence is not temporary but persists into adult life. How often one meets men, perhaps advanced in years, who speak with enthusiasm and respect of a teacher who once inspired them. The teacher of all persons is in the best position to promote the growth of free, creative manhood in those who come before him, inspiring them with a passionate concern for the meaning of life and the quality of their own lives. The good teacher urges his students to challenge and criticize his own views; he advises them not to be daunted by the fear of error, provided the approach they use is genuine. He exhorts them never to take the opinions of others, whether read or heard, for granted, and to scorn mere imitation and the reproduction of ideas second-hand. By virtue of the force of his own commitment to freedom and individuality the teacher can generate a similar enthusiasm for these ideals among his students.

But the teacher's task is not simply to stimulate latent originality. He must also encourage the student to *commit* himself to his work, to reflect on each item of knowledge until it is of importance to him personally. This is not an assertion about the nature of truth but about the nature of learning. The validity and importance of a geometric theorem or an event in history are not affected by the attitude of schools toward them. What are affected are their truth and importance *for him*. Knowledge is not more important than man, but less so, serving his foremost end, which is the search for authenticity.

When dealing with the rebellious adolescent, the teacher should not seek to humiliate him or hold him up to the ridicule of the rest of the class. By all means let him punish the child, pointing out that certain behavior will not be tolerated; but let him not talk down to him or seek to rob him of his self-respect. Again, there is not reason to berate the more backward pupils. The importance of education for them, as indeed for all, lies not in how much they can learn but in how they learn it and what it means to them. If they use the little knowledge they have acquired in order to enhance their own freedom and originality, then they are doing the right thing. Although he should never cease to urge his pupils to greater intellectual efforts, the teacher should not regard proficiency in examinations as an end in itself. The student who can handle what little he learns is far more to be admired than the one who can merely produce a lot of information on demand.

On the more sublime aspects of the relation of the teacher and the student no one has written with greater feeling than Martin Buber, whose remarkable work, *I and Thou,* should be compulsory reading for all who are sincerely dedicated to the task of teaching. The *I* is the teacher; the *Thou* is the student; everything else is the *It:*

> If I face a human being as my *Thou,* and say the primary word *I-Thou* to him, he is not a thing among things, and does not consist of things. This human being is not *He* or *She,* bounded from every other *He* or *She,* a specific point in space and time within the net of the word; nor is he a nature able to be experienced and described, a loose bundle of named qualities. But with no neighbor, and whole in himself, he is *Thou* and fills the heavens. This does not mean that nothing exists except himself. But all else lives in *his* light.[10]

A melody is not composed simply of notes; nor a poem of words; nor a statue of lines. I cannot take from the man to whom I say *Thou* the color of his hair, the sound of his speech, the quality of his goodness, though I must constantly do so, without his ceasing to be *Thou.*

> The life of human beings is not passed in the sphere of transitive verbs alone. It does not exist by virtue of activities alone which have *something* for their object. I perceive somthing . . . I feel something . . . I imagine something . . . I think something. The life of human beings does not consist of all this and the like alone. This and the like together establish the realm of the *It.* But the realm of the *Thou* has a different basis. When *Thou* is spoken, the speaker has nothing for his object. For where there is a thing, there is another thing. Every *It* is bounded by others; *It* exists only through being bounded by others. But when *Thou* is spoken, there is no thing. *Thou* has no bounds. When *Thou* is spoken, the speaker has no thing; he has indeed nothing. But he takes his stand in relation . . . All real living is meeting.[11]

As all real living is meeting, so is all teaching—an intimate relation of two beings who join spontaneity and inventiveness with the discipline of form.

What the pupil desires is his own share in the becoming of things. This is not to be confused with what instrumentalists are apt to call the impulse to activity or the feeling on the part of many that a child needs to be kept busy. Rather the child wants to build or destroy, fondle or hit, accept or reject, never simply to busy himself with no apparent goal. His so-called blind lust for destruction does not arise for the sake of destruction but because the child is curious to discover the things whereof objects are built. Children are by nature pioneers, originators, inventors. And so the teacher must enter into the kind of relationship with his pupil that releases creativity within the framework of these cultural values in which both find themselves immersed. As I shall show in the next section, concrete knowledge and social values are indispensable, and it is the teacher's function skilfully to select those elements of the "feasible world" which are most appropriate to the task of teaching, here considered as a supreme act of meeting. The really talented teacher works on the tissue of human imagination and in the Socratic sense functions as a midwife in helping students give birth to great creations.

(6) What shall we teach and how shall we teach it? The fact that the ex-

[10] Martin Buber, *I and Thou* (Edinburgh: T. and T. Clark), 1950, p. 4.

[11] *Ibid.,* p. 8.

istentialist is less concerned with what is actually taught than the purpose for which it is learned does not imply that he is indifferent to fundamental studies. On the contrary, he insists that there is a considerable body of traditional subject-matter which must be mastered, since it is necessary that the student should realize the "giveness" of the world in which his freedom must be exercised. And although the student may use the world to further his own purposes, it does not follow that he can do what he likes with it. Man and the world do not form a single continuum of experience, as the pragmatist maintains, but are necessarily separate in nature, since man is free whereas things are not. There is no shirking the rigors of study, and the student must discipline himself to learn thoroughly about the reality in which he lives.

Existentialists attach great importance to the humanities, since history, literature, philosophy and art reveal in greater depth and immediacy than other subjects the nature of man and his conflict with the world. The student of the arts becomes acquainted with the reflections of the world's finest spirits on death, guilt, suffering, love, freedom, hate, mortality, joy, mysticism—indeed, on the mind's perennial themes, which are so presented as to engage the student both intellectually and emotionally. Nor should history be taught as a mere catalogue of facts. The so-called "objectivity" of history is a myth, for events must always be interpreted according to the standpoint of the historian. The existentialist sees history in terms of man's struggle to realize his freedom. The student, too, must commit himself to whatever pe-

riod he is studying and immerse himself in its problems and personalities. The history he reads is not there simply to be learned and then played back in an examination. It must fire his thoughts and feelings and become part of him.

Over-specialization is a mistake, because it stunts the growth of the pupil's total inner life. This is particularly the case with science, which has become so ramified and so enormously complicated that as a rule the scientist may concentrate on only one specialty and ignore the rest. As Nietzsche pointed out, "A specialist in science gets to resemble nothing but a factory workman who spends his whole life in turning one particular screw or handle on a certain instrument or machine."[12] It is vital for the student of science to study continuously in the humanities to prevent his mind and sympathies from narrowing. The existentialist also opposes any sort of vocational emphasis on the grounds that, instead of encouraging the pupil to become a free individual, it trains him to be a particular kind of person. The individual may use any career or occupation as a means for the exercise of freedom, but not for immediate and tangible rewards. By all means let us train our students to take up particular careers, but let us educate them more generally at the same time. And let us not commence vocationalism too early!

The Socratic method is the ideal mode of education, since by it the student learns what he personally asserts to be true. The teacher-pupil relationship becomes an intimately personal

[12] Friedrich Wilhelm Nietzsche, *op. cit.,* p. 39.

one. The teacher persuades the latter to think by questioning him about his beliefs, by setting before him other beliefs and thus forcing him to probe the workings of his own mind. In this way the student accepts the truth, but only because it is true for him. The existentialist rejects the problem-centered approach of experimentalism, on the grounds that the problems chosen concern the student chiefly in his role as a social being. He also respects the value of any application of intelligence to a problem which insulates it from the individual's feelings and permits an "impartial" examination. Detached, objective solutions are valueless to the authentic individual.

On the lighter side existentialism emphasizes the importance of "play." Sartre, for example, extols the value of play over seriousness, (*l'esprit de serieus*). For when playing the individual achieves release and gives full rein to uninhibted creativity. Indeed, the more impromptu the game, the freer its players. The player also seeks to impose himself on objects, to make them *his*. The footballer tries to make the ball, the turf, the field, the entire match conform to his will. It is clear, however, that the existentialists see little value in games which subordinate the individual to the team and seek to convert men into a unit for the sole purpose of winning for alma mater. The game is in the playing and in its effect on the individuals who take part, rather than in the result, whether victory or defeat.

Let us conclude, then, with the reflection that existentialism is above all else a philosophy of freedom and individual responsibility. It has not been my purpose in this essay to examine the existentialist analysis of freedom as such, but rather to discuss some aspects of it which concern education; so at this point you should ask yourself, how can you *as a teacher* realize this ideal of freedom? I would personally reply that you should think, act and teach in accordance with your own principles. But do not imagine that this is a light and easy matter, for freedom's path is hardly strewn with roses. Indeed, it can be a hazardous and dispiriting journey, for the true individual meets incomprehension, hostility and, perhaps worst of all, sheer lack of interest. Be prepared to defend your views before school boards, supervisors, administrators, parent-teacher associations, before anyone in authority. Dare to take intelligent risks!

As a teacher you are responsible, not only for your freedom, but also for that of your students. The trend to conformism in our society is only too clear. Where better to fight it than in the school itself, since it is here that it largely begins? As a teacher you should impress each pupil with the need to be himself or herself rather than a stereotype of the group. You should point out that in order to become a man, it is not necessary merely to fill a T-shirt but to have courage and independence. Tell your pupils never to fear unpopularity, for the one who has the courage to be himself risks incurring the hostility of the group, and popularity itself can too often be purchased at the price of integrity. By word and deed demonstrate your own independence. Its effect on your children, if you are a good teacher, will be both immediate and enduring. And this will be your re-

ward, that you will have opened im-
measurably the lives of those who have
at their most formative period both
heard and observed you, and com-

manded in them a respect for you, because you have chosen to be your own
genuine self and nourished in them the
same desire.

∾

Pragmatism and Education

*Frederick C. Neff**

Pragmatism is America's unique
contribution to the history of philosophic thought. In its modern form it is
primarily a theory of meaning, whereby
the truth or falsity of a proposition
emerges from its being experimentally
tested in a concrete situation. In order
to be genuine, propositions must have
"predictive" qualities, i.e., they must be
convertible into demonstrable hypotheses which, when tested, yield in actuality what they claim or predict to be true
as theories. While it would be unwarranted to say that all pragmatists equate
meaning with truth, nevertheless there
is a strong tendency among most pragmatists to hold that the meaning of an
assertion consists in the sum of its verifiable consequences. On the negative
side, pragmatists are prone to regard
assertions that cannot be so treated as
meaningless or "nonsense" statements,
and to view problems that are nonref-
erentially oriented as pseudo-problems.

Attached to the pragmatic theory of
meaning are several auxiliary tenets. In
the first place, it should be noted that
truth "emerges" from the testing of
hypotheses, which is to say that it is not

antecedent to investigation. Instead of
being discovered, truth is formulated,
constructed, or brought into being. The
act of inquiry "yields" truth—it does
not merely "come upon" it as a pre-
formed entity. This is not to hold that
man creates or invents truth, in the
sense of making something out of nothing. Rather, it means that man "forges"
truth out of the responsible process of
careful investigation of evidence. In the
second place, what is labeled true is a
result of the means, methods, and techniques that are used in establishing it,
to say nothing of the particular evidence or data in an examination of
which they are employed. In so far as
improved methods are used and greater
evidence becomes available, truth accordingly is modified, refined, corrected. Truth, in other words, is subject
to change. Thirdly, when emphasis is
placed upon consequences, the role of
the presuppositional or the *a priori* is
correspondingly diminished. Inductive
method is thus more highly regarded
than rationalization, and facts and data
come in for greater consideration than
speculation based upon "authority."
Likewise, processes and relationships
assume greater significance than reified
notions and spiritual "essences."

* An original essay written expressly for
this volume.

As is characteristic of most "new" philosophies, pragmatism has its historical progenitors. In observing that one cannot step twice into the same river, Heraclitus (fifth century, B.C.) perceived the inevitability of change, which suggests a relativism in respect to basic processes. The oft-quoted remark of Protagoras (B.C. 481?–411) that "man is the measure of all things" points to the notion that so-called extramundane truths are reducible to human judgment and human interpretation— hence that truth is neither more nor less than what man assesses it to be. Much of the same attitude characterizes the teachings of Socrates (469–399) and the Sophists. The Biblical directive, "By their fruits shall ye know them," is certainly a bluntly pragmatic maxim. In his advocacy of inductive method Francis Bacon (1561–1626) reviled the older system of logic wherein reasoning consisted in manipulating premises for the purpose of safeguarding predetermined beliefs rather than in seeking after knowledge. Such logic, said Bacon, ". . . rather assists in confirming and rendering inveterate the errors founded on vulgar notions, than in searching after truth; and is therefore more hurtful than useful." August Comte (1798–1857), in holding that laws and relations are more basic than spiritual or physical substance of any kind, urged greater attention to methods and processes than to supposed entities or realms of "being." Hints of pragmatism may likewise be found in the writings of Aristotle, Berkeley, and Hume, while Kant's emphasis upon practical reason may be construed to have further paved the way toward present-day pragmatism.

PEIRCE, JAMES, AND DEWEY

The three greatest contributors to American pragmatism are generally recognized to be Charles Sanders Peirce (1839–1914), William James (1842–1910), and John Dewey (1859–1952). It has been said that Peirce was brilliant, James was witty, and Dewey was profound. Peirce first gained recognition in philosophic circles through his association with the Metaphysical Club, which consisted of a small group of persons interested in philosophy who met in Cambridge for the purpose of presenting papers and arguing philosophic questions. Another member of the Club, William James, was impressed with Peirce's views and encouraged him to give them a wider audience. As a result, Peirce published two essays, "The Fixation of Belief" (November, 1877) and "How to Make Our Ideas Clear" (January, 1878), in the *Popular Science Monthly*. The publication of these essays may be said to mark the "official birth" of pragmatism as a full-fledged philosophy. Peirce had been trained as a mathematician, and his orientation was primarily mathematical and objective, not psychological and subjective. One of Peirce's intentions was to correct what he regarded as a defect in Kant's thinking by establishing a continuity between an inner world of ideas and an outer world of objective realities. To do this he advocated testing the meaning of an idea by putting it to work in the objective world of action; whatever consequences appeared he believed would thus determine what an idea means.

In "How to Make Our Ideas Clear" he wrote:

Consider what effects, that might conceivably have practical bearings, we conceive the object of our conception to have. Then, our conception of these effects is the whole of our conception of the object.

On the same point Peirce further remarks:

In order to ascertain the meaning of an intellectual conception one should consider what practical consequence might conceivably result by necessity from the truth of that conception; and the sum of these consequences will constitute the entire meaning of the conception.

Although it was Peirce who coined the word "pragmatism" and who preferred to regard his philosophy as pragmatic, in certain respects he was, like Whitehead and Russell, very much of a realist and might almost be said to have embraced a metaphysics, as indicated in the following passage.

There are Real things, whose characters are entirely independent of our opinions about them; those Reals affect our senses according to regular laws, and, though our sensations are as different as are our relations to the objects, yet, by taking advantage of the laws of perception, we can ascertain by reasoning how things really and truly are; and any man, if he have sufficient experience and he reason enough about it, will be led to the one True conclusion. The new conception here involved is that of Reality.[1]

Elsewhere, Peirce qualifies and attempts to make clearer what he means by independence.

. . . on the one hand, reality is independent, not necessarily of thought in general, but only of what you or I or any finite number of men may think about it; and . . . on the other hand, though the object of the final opinion depends on what that opinion is, yet what that opinion is does not depend on what you or I or any man thinks.[2]

In commenting upon the realistic overtones in Peirce's writing, John L. Childs interprets Peirce as saying that "the subject matters of existence provide the ultimate ground for all our theories about the nature of reality."[3]

Despite certain shortcomings, Peirce's procedural theory of meaning has been widely adopted as a scrutinizing tool of criticism. This is especially true of the so-called scientific philosophers, e.g., the logical empiricists, positivists, and linguistic analysts. But it serves everywhere to translate into intelligible language the heady verbiage of abstruse philosophy.

We are all liable to confuse highly abstract and erudite conceptions, not only in metaphysics but also in the mathematical and natural sciences; but if one conception does not differ "practically" (in Peirce's sense) from a second, then an employment of it adds nothing to our employment of that second conception. Again, we are sometimes tempted to engage in speculations which have no assignable "practical bearings"; but in that case, according to pragmatism, our thoughts and words have no assignable meaning whatsoever.[4]

In turning to William James, we find a temperament that was almost diametrically opposite to that of Peirce. Born into an affluent New York family

[1] Charles Hartshorne and Paul Weiss (eds.), *The Collected Papers of Charles Sanders Peirce* (Cambridge: Harvard University Press, 1931–1935), Vol. V, p. 384.

[2] *Ibid.,* p. 407.

[3] John L. Childs, *American Pragmatism and Education* (New York: Holt, Rinehart and Winston, Inc., 1956), p. 43.

[4] *Encyclopaedia Britannica* (1960), Vol. XVIII, p. 413.

of considerable social prestige, James might predictably have attached himself to a genteel idealism—a position which he later characterized as "tender-minded," as distinguished from "tough-minded" pragmatism. James was early introduced into a world of books, and extensive travel was almost a routine of his life. Ebullient and charming, James contrasted sharply with the intense and rather frenetic Peirce; yet the two became fast friends and found much in common despite certain differences. From the beginning, James was a more popular philosopher-psychologist than Peirce ever was. It has been said that William James wrote psychology like a novelist and that his brother Henry wrote novels like a psychologist.

Whereas Peirce regarded pragmatism almost mathematically, James viewed it in terms of the moral and the religious. While both James and Peirce conceived meaning and truth to consist in the workability of hypotheses, they apparently differed in the ways in which they construed workability. James, for example, argued that if the God-hypothesis "worked" in experience, it was therefore true. By "worked" James evidently meant that if such belief wrought observable changes for good in people's lives, it was accordingly true. Peirce would probably have retorted that, while such an example might tend to verify the existence of a belief and its ability to affect behavior, it did not testify to its truth. In other words, what was being tested was not whether God exists but whether there was a belief that God exists, which belief might then understandably affect conduct.

It was James, more than Peirce, who succeeded in bringing pragmatism before the public, a feat due in large measure to James's facility with words, to his apt analogies, and to his ability to make pragmatism generally appealing. As James phrases it,

> The pragmatic method . . . is to try to interpret each notion by tracing its respective practical consequences. What difference would it practically make to anyone if this notion rather than that notion were true? If no practical difference whatever can be traced, then the alternatives mean practically the same thing, and all dispute is idle. Whenever a dispute is serious, we ought to be able to show some practical difference that must follow from one side or the other's being right.[5]

John Dewey survived William James by over forty years, and we are likely to forget that the two were at one time contemporaries. Yet each contributed to occasional corrections in the other's thinking, and they were personal friends. Dewey came out of a typical Vermont background, which may be partly responsible for his practicality. His early philosophic training was largely in the tradition of the idealism of Plato, Kant, and Hegel. Gradually his thinking moved from metaphysical idealism to a more functional and empirically oriented idealism, and he later abandoned the notion of a universal mind and a universal selfhood and began to formulate conceptions of social individualism and social intelligence.

Dewey's philosophy is, first, a theory of meaning and of truth; secondly, it consists of a body of fairly flexible philosophic doctrines. Dewey believed that "experimentation enters into the deter-

[5] John Herman Randall and Justus Buchler, *Philosophy: An Introduction* (New York: Barnes & Noble, Inc., 1942), p. 126.

mination of every warranted proposition."[6] To subject ideas to testing is to reveal whatever are pseudo-problems, which then either evaporate or are quickly resolved. In Dewey's words,

> It is no longer enough for a principle to be elevated, noble, universal and hallowed by time. It must present its birth certificate, it must show under just what conditions of human experience it was generated, and it must justify itself by its works, present and potential.[7]

"If certain operations are performed," according to Dewey, "then certain phenomena having determinate properties will be observed."[8] The extent to which a proposition has meaning, then, lies in the effectiveness of its operation; to say that a proposition is true, i.e., has "warranted assertibility," is to say that the results that it predicts actually do occur.

METAPHYSICS—WHAT IS REALITY?

In so far as pragmatism is basically a method or procedure for determining the meaning of an idea, as distinguished from being a body of fixed doctrines or dogmas, most pragmatists are wary of committing themselves to any sort of metaphysics. As Peirce has remarked,

> ✓ Suffice it to say once more that pragmatism is, in itself, no doctrine of metaphysics, no attempt to determine any truth of things. It is merely a method of

ascertaining the meanings of hard words and of abstract concepts.[9]

Traditionally, metaphysical notions have been characterized by other-worldliness and absolutism. To say that an idea is metaphysical is to say that it is beyond the physical, apart from experience, or independent of knowledge. Plato, for example, conceived truth, goodness, and beauty as existing whether man's experience or knowledge enabled him to be aware of them or not. Moreover, he construed them to be eternal and unchanging, hence he had to lodge them in a "metaphysical" realm, that is, outside the world of modifiable human experience. Conversely, the only way by which any notion may be so conceived is to formulate it in nonempirical terms, for the simple reason that ideas generated by experience and formulated on the basis of knowledge are subject to reconstruction as experience is broadened and as greater knowledge is achieved. In short, to root an idea in experience is to recognize the possibility that it may be modified; to lodge an idea in a metaphysical world is to seal it off from inquiry, possible improvement, and reformulation—hence, to make it absolute.

↶Pragmatism holds that no intelligible or verifiable statements can be made about what might lie beyond knowledge, i.e., that we cannot claim to be true what we do not know. For this reason pragmatists tend to view any claims to truth that are not subject to empirical verification as either sheer nonsense or at least as extremely tenuous. Whereas metaphysical philosophies

---

[6] John Dewey, *Logic, The Theory of Inquiry* (New York: Holt, Rinehart and Winston, Inc., 1938), p. 461.

[7] John Dewey, *Reconstruction in Philosophy* (New York: Mentor Books, 1950), p. 59.

[8] Dewey, *Logic, The Theory of Inquiry*, p. 456.

[9] Hartshorne and Weiss, *op. cit.*, p. 464.

have concerned themselves largely with seeking some sort of "ultimate Reality," pragmatism regards such a search as fruitless and focuses its attention instead upon gaining an understanding of phenomena that are knowable. In the words of William James, the pragmatist

turns away from abstraction and insufficiency, from verbal solutions, from bad *a priori* reasons, from fixed principles, closed systems, and pretended absolutes and origins. He turns towards concreteness and adequacy, towards facts, towards action and towards power. [He seeks] the open air and possibilities of nature, as against dogma, artificiality, and the pretence of finality in truth.[10]

In rejecting the notion of "ultimate" reality and "ultimate" truth, John Dewey has pointed out that man's search for absolutes might better have been directed toward an amelioration of the human state, and that instead of looking for one, all-inclusive Purpose, it would be wiser to recognize that there are many, many purposes in life—one, so to speak, for every time, place, and set of conditions. Notions of an ultimate reality, except as they are recognized as poetic adornments, are found to be superfluous. Says Dewey, ". . . the chief characteristic of the pragmatic notion is precisely that no theory of Reality in general . . . is possible or needed."[11] If there is anything resembling a metaphysics in Dewey, it might be likened to what George Santayana has termed "the dominance of the foreground." Yet this

is scarcely a metaphysical conception—certainly not in any traditional sense of the term.

In the language of James, ours is "a universe with the lid off." Like James, Dewey turns away from the older notions of a closed world with fixed limits and restricted possibilities. The world that confronts modern science and modern man is open," . . . a world varying indefinitely without the possibility of assignable limit in its internal make-up, a world stretching beyond any assignable bounds externally."[12] If there is any measure of "reality" or "energy of being" it is no longer fixity but omnipresent change.[13] Dewey feels that a framework of philosophic absolutism serves no long-range useful purpose and attempts to construct a framework of philosophic activity wherein ". . . the interaction of organism and environment, resulting in some adaptation which secures utilization of the latter, is the primary fact, the basic category."[14] Ideas, likewise, are reconceived as "plans of action"; they are given work to do, instead of being viewed as fixed entities lodged in some remote and immutable realm.

So far as ideas are not fancies, framed by emotionalized memory for escape and refuge, they are precisely anticipations of something still to come aroused by looking into the facts of a developing situation.[15]

Whereas truth is assumed as an unexamined starting point in most other philosophies, pragmatism holds

[10] Randall and Buchler, *loc. cit.*

[11] John Dewey, *Creative Intelligence* (New York: Holt, Rinehart and Winston, Inc., 1917), p. 55.

[12] Dewey, *Reconstruction in Philosophy*, p. 63.

[13] *Ibid.*, p. 67.

[14] *Ibid.*, p. 83.

[15] *Ibid.*, p. 120.

that what is true is a matter of scientific formulation, subject to public and critical—as distinguished from private and careless—acceptance. In the words of Dewey,

> Truth means scientific success, or as we ordinarily say, "verification," with all that this term implies. It is what emerges from the critical employment of the best method that we can develop. It *is* a social product, not in the sense that a majority happens to accept a given belief, but in the sense that no belief can be called true unless it is capable of compelling the universal assent of those who understand.[16]

More succinct and dramatic are the words of Peirce:

> The opinion which is fated to be ultimately agreed to by all who investigate, is what we mean by the truth, and the object represented in this opinion is the real. That is the way I would explain reality.[17]

EPISTEMOLOGY—HOW DO WE KNOW WHAT IS TRUE?

It has been the custom of nonempirical philosophers to begin with certain metaphysical assumptions as to what is true and then to utilize selected knowledge and methods of reasoning to support them. The pragmatist, on the other hand, holds that to accept what is true on other grounds than what is knowable is to invite chicanery, since to speak of what is unknowable is at the same time to speak of what is unintelligible. The pragmatist chooses to construct whatever conclusions about truth he may reach upon the solid

foundations of knowledge. Hence to speak of an "unverifiable truth" would be to exhibit an ill-becoming precociousness or to engage in a contradiction of terms, if not to talk nonsense. Being essentially a theory of analysis, pragmatism begins the quest for understanding, not with a prefabricated notion of truth, but with what it regards as responsible methods of knowing. It finds the question, "How do we know what is true?" prior to and more challenging and profitable than the question, "What is truth?" This is another way of saying that pragmatism is epistemologically rather than metaphysically oriented.

It is important to recognize that knowledge needs to be carefully distinguished from belief. The authenticity of what a person may purport to *believe* is scarcely either confirmable or refutable; but what he claims to *know* must, in the pragmatic sense, be capable of demonstration to all who would question, that is, to any impartial, qualified observer. In short, while beliefs may be private, knowledge is to be regarded as public. Although some beliefs may be founded upon knowledge, certainly many of them are not. A statement that purports to be true is one which is convertible into a proposition formulated as a hypothesis, the testing of which will bear out the prediction that the proposition claims to be true. An assertion that is responsible is one which can be phrased in "if . . . then . . ." language. For example, the statement, "Book X has 304 pages," is equivalent to saying that if the assertion were tested, it would be found to be true. It means that whoever claims the statement as true is, in effect, saying, "I

16 *Ibid.*, p. 142.
17 Hartshorne and Weiss, *op. cit.*, p. 408.

know—that is, I am prepared to demonstrate—that Book X has 304 pages." More exactly, what is being claimed is that *if* certain agreed-upon controls were set up—e.g., consensus regarding a way of identifying Book X, of what constitutes a page, of a particular numbering system, etc.—*then* the conclusion that Book X contains 304 pages is inevitable, or, in Peirce's words, "fated to be ultimately agreed to by all who investigate." This is a homely illustration of what the pragmatist requires in order for a thing *to be known*. It follows, then, that one cannot *know* what is not true—although, of course, one may believe it. Similarly, if what is true is restricted to what is knowable, then whatever is at any given time unknowable cannot at the same time be considered true.

Being primarily a method of knowing, pragmatism obviously does not begin with any eternal or universal "truths," which it was the purpose of earlier philosophies to rationalize. Pragmatism is empirical in the sense that it looks to experience as the most responsible arena for resolving conflicts and for validating assertions. Yet it differs from traditional empiricism in rejecting the strictures of proven procedures and outcomes in favor of the untried and the experimental. According to Dewey,

Pragmatism . . . presents itself as an extension of historical empiricism, but with this fundamental difference, that it does not insist upon antecedent phenomena; not upon the precedents but upon the possibilities of action.[18]

[18] John Dewey, *Philosophy and Civilization* (New York: G. P. Putnam's Sons, 1931), p. 24.

Morover, empiricism has traditionally viewed the senses as a means of bridging the gap between the knower and the objects of knowledge, whereas pragmatism views perception, not as a series of discrete acts, but as an interaction that includes both percipient organisms and things said to be perceived. It is understood as a unitary relationship wherein the whole "field" is engaged.

F. C. S. Schiller, the Oxford pragmatist, in his *Studies in Humanism,* goes so far as to say that "in validating our claims to 'truth' . . . we really *transform* them [realities] by our cognitive efforts, thereby proving our desires and ideas to be real forces in the shaping of the world."[19] Such a view, however, comes precariously close to the notion that "wishing will make it so," and it is doubtful that other pragmatists would attach themselves to so extreme a position. Perhaps the possibility of misconstruction led Dewey to prefer the term "transaction," for he was concerned with preserving what might be called the "integrity" of the total human situation by not cutting it off from its environing conditions. The wholeness of things Dewey prized more highly than their separateness, not only in respect to the transactional relationship between knowing and the known, but also in regard to the integration of knowledge through the continuous reconstruction of experience. The holistic emphasis in Dewey's thought is sometimes attributed to the influence of Hegel, study of whom Dewey once said had left a "permanent deposit" in his thinking.

[19] Dagobert D. Runes (ed.), *The Dictionary of Philosophy* (New York: Philosophical Library), p. 246.

Beginning with Peirce, pragmatism has emphasized that knowledge is a prerequisite to the formulation of truth. Before knowledge is attainable, the criteria for validating it must first be set up. Otherwise, although we may raise questions interminably, no solutions would ever be forthcoming. In the words of Randall and Buchler,

The purpose of Peirce's pragmatism was precisely to overcome verbalism in intellectual matters by supplying objective criteria of distinction.

We are now able to say what it is that makes a problem a significant (or soluble) one. A problem is significant or genuine if the possible answers to it are verifiable, that is, if it is capable of scientific investigation.[20]

Ever since he first began to reflect, Peirce was enchanted with methods of inquiry. He studied Kant's *Critique of Pure Reason* for two hours a day for over three years. But the more he studied the more critical he became of systems based upon formal logic and of syllogistic rationalizing, which he regarded as highly authoritarian. He felt that doubt was more to be cherished than imposed or unexamined systems of belief and that it was the former that laid the real basis for inquiry. ". . . the action of thought is excited by the irritation of doubt, and ceases when belief is attained; so that the production of belief is the sole function of thought."[21]

In "The Fixation of Belief" Peirce addressed himself to a consideration of four alternative methods of settling belief, the first three of which he successively rejected in arriving at the fourth.

Briefly, the methods he discusses are as follows:

1. *The method of tenacity,* or the wilful adherence to a belief on the basis of tradition or emotional attachment, such that one makes it a habit "to turn with contempt and hatred from anything that might disturb it."[22] This method, according to Peirce, proposes such extreme individualism that sooner or later it is bound to conflict with social conceptions of law, order, and justice.

2. *The method of authority,* wherein such institutions as church, state, and education are so constituted that their notions of "the correct doctrines" shall prevail and that their will shall override that of the individual acting on his own. Peirce grants that this method has an advantage over the method of tenacity in its concern with the social order. But since institutions have the "power to prevent contrary doctrines from being taught, advocated, or expressed,"[23] such method is actually doctrinaire and authoritarian. In its culmination the method of authority might be likened to the ideological systems of the Nazis and the Communists, or to the political conditions in Franco's Spain and Castro's Cuba.

3. *A priori method,* or resort to "conscience" or intuition, wherein both wilful tenacity to a belief and its arbitrary imposition upon others are superseded by "inclination," "reason," and appeal to transempirical "universals." This method prizes the introspective and the metaphysical, rather than the objective and the demonstrable. While, *prima facie,* it appears to respect indi-

20 Randall and Buchler, *op. cit.,* p. 124.
21 Hartshorne and Weiss, *op. cit.,* p. 394.
22 *Ibid.,* p. 377.
23 *Ibid.,* p. 397.

viduality, in practice it degenerates into a vaunting of "instinctiveness" and sheer taste, whims, and prejudices, which often represent not much more than a following of fashion.

4. *Scientific method,* or the process of inquiry, in which there is a "rejection of the purely private and arbitrary by scientific method—a rejection which necessarily follows from the scientific demand for data, procedures, and findings that are open to the test of criticism of others. . . ."[24] Peirce describes what he means by the scientific attitude as follows:

The scientific spirit requires a man to be at all times ready to dump his whole cartload of beliefs, the moment experience is against them. The desire to learn forbids him to be perfectly cocksure that he knows already. Besides positive science can only rest on experience; and experience can never result in absolute certainty, exactitude, necessity or universality. . . . To set up a philosophy which barricades the road of further advance toward the truth is the one unpardonable offense in reasoning.[25]

The method of science was embraced by Dewey fully as much as it was by Peirce, but Dewey directed its use more deliberately upon social problems than did Peirce. For Dewey science was a quest, not a possession; a means for testing hypotheses, not a collection of immutable truth. In advocating scientific inquiry Dewey, like Peirce, rejected Kant's emphasis upon reason as an arbiter of experience.

Reason, as a Kantian faculty that introduces generality and regularity into ex-

perience, strikes us more and more as superfluous—the unnecessary creation of men addicted to traditional formalism and to elaborate terminology.[26]

Dewey likewise abandoned the notion of a supine intellect capable of not much more than a passive reception of the world's impressions.

. . . historic intellectualism, the spectator view of knowledge, is a purely compensatory doctrine which men of an intellectual turn have built up to console themselves for the actual and social impotency of the calling of thought to which they are devoted.[27]

What Dewey argued for was a conception of ideas that would function significantly in bringing about effective conduct. The core of this principle he called "instrumentalism," by which he meant the conception of ideas as devices for converting the insecurity accompanying an indeterminate situation into a satisfactory resolution or clarification of it.

. . . instrumentalism means a behaviorist theory of thinking and knowing. It means that knowing is literally something which we do; that analysis is ultimately physical and active; that meanings in their logical quality are standpoints, attitudes, and methods of behaving toward facts, and that active experimentation is essential to verification.[28]

Ideas are important in so far as they become instrumental to the reorganization of experience and of the environment, or to the alleviation of a condi-

24 Childs, *op. cit.,* pp. 42–43.

25 Justus Buchler, *The Philosophy of Peirce —Selected Writings* (New York: Harcourt, Brace & World, Inc., 1940), pp. 46–47, 54.

26 Dewey, *Reconstruction in Philosophy,* p. 89.

27 *Ibid.,* p. 103.

28 John Dewey, *Essays in Experimental Logic* (New York: Dover Publications), pp. 331–332.

tion that needs to be remedied. To the extent that an idea succeeds in such an office it is sound, trustworthy, true. In so far as it leads to further confusion, fails to clarify a muddled situation, or promotes an evil, it is to be regarded as false, bad, or unreliable.

That which guides us truly is true— demonstrated capacity for such guidance is precisely what is meant by truth. . . . The hypothesis that works is the *true* one; and *truth* is an abstract noun applied to the collection of cases, actual, foreseen and desired, that receive confirmation in their consequences.[29]

To the pragmatist, man's habitual servitude to prescientific conceptions of mind, life, and reality has resulted in a curious juxtaposition of the scientific and nonscientific, instead of a reconstruction of the nonscientific in terms of the scientific. The present generation is caught between two conflicting epistemologies, viz., between a method of knowing that conceives truth as its product and one which locates truth somewhere else and conceives it as having a prior existence. In the words of Dewey,

If knowing were habitually conceived of as active and operative, after the analogy of experiment guided by hypothesis, or of invention guided by the imagination of some possibility, it is not too much to say that the first effect would be to emancipate philosophy from all the epistemological puzzles which now perplex it. For these all arise from a conception of the relation of mind and world, subject and object, in knowing, which assumes that to know is to seize upon what is already in existence.[30]

[29] Dewey, *Reconstruction in Philosophy*, pp. 128–129.
[30] *Ibid.*, p. 107.

LOGIC—THE NATURE OF THOUGHT

Pragmatists view logic, not as a separate philosophic category, but as part and parcel of all reflective undertakings. But by logic the pragmatist does not mean a formalized system of thought whereby unexamined generalities are arbitrarily applied to concrete problems. Since this is the common acceptance of the term, pragmatists are prone to speak more frequently of problem-solving, mediation, and effective analysis than of "logic," as such. To Dewey, logic is a means of effective inquiry, the techniques and procedures of which grow out of or are adapted to the exact nature of the problem that confronts us. While the general method of science pertains to every empirical situation, nevertheless, the specific directives for procedural analysis are as distinctive as the nature of problems varies. Dewey puts it as follows:

If thinking is the way in which deliberate reorganization of experience is secured, then logic is such a clarified and systematized formulation of the procedures of thinking as will enable the desired reconstruction to go on more economically and efficiently.[31]

The isolation of thinking from confrontation with facts encourages that kind of observation which merely accumulates brute facts, which occupies itself laboriously with mere details, but never inquires into their meaning and consequences—a safe occupation, for it never contemplates any use to be made of the observed facts in determining a plan for changing the situation.[32]

[31] *Ibid.*, pp. 114–115.
[32] *Ibid.*, p. 119.

The role of thought is to enhance freedom in action—it is to emancipate us from blind chance and fatalism. Within the thinking process ends are generated which are undergirded by knowledge, as distinguished from those whose airy origin precludes the possibility of actualization. "The only situation in which knowing is fully stimulated," says Dewey, "is one in which the end is developed in the process of inquiry and testing."[33]

AXIOLOGY—RELIGIOUS AND MORAL ASPECTS OF PRAGMATISM

The writings of Peirce do not deal specifically with "moral" problems as such, although it is of course possible to infer certain axiological conclusions from his naturalistic premises. William James, on the other hand, did address himself to many familiar religious and moral themes, but his treatment of them was more "popular" than philosophic; moreover, James had very definite romantic attachments and inclinations which often obscured what pragmatic commitments he claimed, and his interpretation of moral and religious matters scarcely represents the viewpoint of present-day pragmatism.

While Peirce and James did on occasion voice piecemeal comments on the human condition, there is a sense in which the whole of Dewey's philosophic effort was directed toward an alleviation of man's inhumanity to man. His stringent logic, his epistemology, and his economic, political, and psychological theories all may be viewed as instrumental to making the human condition more rational, more moral, more humane. If Dewey was critical of religion it was because he saw in its "frozen" creeds and dogmas deterrents to the full and free expression of the religious spirit or attitude, without which "one may be very strong in piety but as for the rest very weak and deficient, and a bad man."[34] Dewey found no defensible basis for the idea of a "fixed and immutable" moral law which could be discovered from the essential nature of man. He believed that operating under such a notion obligates us to revert to the past for instruction, thus inviting authoritarianism. It urges us, furthermore, to accept the idea "that one method obtains in natural science and another, radically different, in moral questions." To hold to such a position means ". . . creating disunity in the intellectual life of our time and denying the promise which he [Dewey] believed empirical and scientific methods can hold even in the field of ethics."[35]

Dewey found it inconsistent to hold that inquiry should be limited to physical phenomena and not be permitted to function in the sphere of ethics and values. In commenting upon what he considered to be an illicit dichotomy between the scientific and the moral, he wrote:

I became more and more troubled by the intellectual scandal that seemed to me involved in the current (and traditional) dualism in logical standpoint and method

---

[33] *Ibid.,* p. 122.

[34] John Dewey, *A Common Faith* (New Haven, Conn.: Yale University Press, 1934), p. 9.

[35] *Encyclopaedia Britannica* (1960), Vol. VII, p. 297.

between so-called "science" on the one hand and something called "morals" on the other. I have long felt that the construction of a logic, that is, a method of effective inquiry, which would apply without abrupt breach of continuity to the fields designated by both of these words, is at once our needed theoretical solvent and the supply of our greatest practical want.[36]

To the historical scholar there is a curious conservatism in Dewey that is revealed in his exhortation to purge religion of its nonrational and otherworldly elements and, like the Greeks, cultivate its "daylight" aspects. In effect, he reprimanded society for its indifference to a gradual usurpation of the religious qualities in experience by ecclesiastical bodies and institutions, thus permitting such qualities to lose their one-time civic function and, by implication, their educational and cultural functions as well.

In Dewey's judgment, what we now call supernatural originally meant nothing more definite than events that were extraordinary or unusual—events regarding which insight into their natural causes was lacking. Familiarity with what is ordinary breeds, if not contempt, at least equality, while the unusual and the unfamiliar take on properties of awe and hence are assigned a superior status.[37] As commonplace occurrences came to be viewed with greater indifference, awe and reverence became increasingly attached to the extraordinary, with the result that these two sorts of phenomena were finally separated into two distinct categories, natural and supernatural, to which were assigned an inferior and a superior status, respectively. It has been man's tendency ever since to view as "natural" whatever he could predict and control, e.g., the quenching of fire with water, or the harnessing of energy to produce electricity—so-called "household knowledge"—and to interpret as "supernatural" whatever was understood to be uncontrollable and beyond the scope of mundane affairs, e.g., eclipses of the sun, or the origins of life and the physical universe. Needless to say, this tendency has often persisted even in those instances where science has afforded us natural explanations for events that had hitherto been explained in exclusively supernatural terms.

The choice that religion once had of aligning itself with the world of men or with the supernatural appears to have been made. Whether that decision is final and irrevocable is, of course, open to question. So-called "official" spokesmen for religion, however, for the most part will have it only one way. Accordingly, as Dewey sees it, the association of religion with supernaturalism has bred a dogmatic and divisive spirit that might have been avoided had religion chosen to ally itself with the flexibility and pluralism of the world of experience. Such association has bred "that torpor of imagination which is the uniform effect of dogmatic belief."[38]

What is proposed instead is not simply another religion, but "the eman-

[36] John Dewey, "From Absolutism to Experimentalism," *Contemporary American Philosophy*, ed. G. P. Adams and W. P. Montague (New York: The Macmillan Co., 1930), Vol. I, p. 13–27.

[37] John Dewey, *The Quest for Certainty* (New York: G. P. Putnam's Sons, 1929), p. 13.

[38] John Dewey, "Religion in Our Schools," *The Hibbert Journal* (1908), VI, 808–809.

cipation of elements and outlooks that may be called religious."[39] To Dewey, "religious" is a more functional term than "religion." The former denotes "attitudes that may be taken toward every object and every proposed end or ideal,"[40] attitudes unencumbered with "the apparatus of dogma and doctrine,"[41] while the latter has usually meant acceptance of "something that is isolated and exists by itself."[42]

Let us perfect ourselves within, and in due season changes in society will come of themselves is the teaching. And while saints are engaged in introspection, burly sinners run the world.[43]

Instead of relying upon an "inner perfection," Dewey urges relying upon critical methods of examination and inquiry as represented both by the scientific search for truth and by the democratic way of life. Faith in man's ability to inquire into and verify what is true "is potentially more religious than all it is displacing."[44]

Morality conceived as a philosophic quest for the good life cannot avoid examination. "Moral theory cannot emerge when there is positive belief as to what is right and what is wrong, for then there is no occasion for reflection."[45] In such an attitude there is idealism of the toughest kind, for "an idealism of action that is devoted to

creation of a future, instead of to staking itself upon propositions about the past, is invincible."[46]

Morals is not a catalogue of acts nor a set of rules to be applied like drugstore prescriptions or cook-book recipes. The need in morals is for specific methods of inquiry and of contrivance: Methods of inquiry to locate difficulties and evils; methods of contrivance to form plans to be used as working hypotheses in dealing with them. And the pragmatic import of the logic of individualized situations, each having its own irreplaceable good and principle, is to transfer the attention of theory from preoccupation with general conceptions to the problem of developing effective methods of inquiry.[47]

Dewey's use of the term "God" to denote "the active relation between the ideal and the actual"[48] was perhaps unfortunate, and his appeal to natural forces in attempting to validate the ethics of human experience is likewise open to criticism. The development of aesthetic criteria and descriptive analyses applicable to religious inquiry, while hinted at in Dewey, has not as yet been satisfactorily delineated—certainly it affords one of the most potentially fruitful areas of philosophic inquiry. The active and qualitative aspects of religion Dewey held in higher esteem than its quantified creeds and dogmas. In his words,

Any activity pursued in behalf of an ideal and against obstacles and in spite of threats of personal loss because of conviction of its general and enduring value is religious in quality.[49]

---

[39] Dewey, *A Common Faith*, p. 9.

[40] *Ibid.*, p. 10.

[41] *Ibid.*, p. 44.

[42] *Ibid.*, p. 9.

[43] Dewey, *Reconstruction in Philosophy*, p. 154.

[44] Dewey, "Religion in Our Schools," *loc. cit.*

[45] John Dewey and James H. Tufts, *Ethics* (New York: Holt, Rinehart and Winston, 1932), pp. 173–175.

[46] Dewey, *The Quest for Certainty*, p. 304.

[47] Dewey, *Reconstruction in Philosophy*, pp. 136–137.

[48] Dewey, *A Common Faith*, p. 51.

[49] *Ibid.*, p. 27.

Since qualitative experience rather than verifiable truth-claims is probably what Dewey meant by "religious," perhaps the use of aesthetic terminology would serve to designate "religious" experiences with greater specificity.

Aside from such criticisms, the bulk of Dewey's thought on religion and morals survives as a forceful influence. It remains for education to afford each oncoming generation opportunity to explore with greater accuracy accompanied by warranted fervor the religious and aesthetic dimensions of experience to the end that such endeavor may yield a richness of moral living unparalleled in the human past.

EDUCATION—THE RECONSTRUCTION OF EXPERIENCE

Each of the foregoing categories contains certain educational directives which must be obvious to the alert reader, so that an additional section on education may seem superfluous. Moreover, the impact of pragmatism upon American education has been so great that it is often though of as primarily an educational philosophy. Nevertheless, the very fact of its prevalence has served somehow to obscure its authentic meaning, and it is popularly identified with a movement known as Progressive Education. Accordingly, it seems appropriate to conclude with a few remarks that may correct some of the misinterpretations and distortions that have appeared in attempts to translate the pragmatic philosophy into educational theory and practice.

It was Charles Peirce who did the spade work of pragmatism, it was William James who popularized it, but it was John Dewey who first recognized the social, which is to say, the educational, mission of pragmatism. In fact, Dewey conceived philosophy itself as "the general theory of education." The real test of any philosophy, Dewey believed, is the practical difference it makes in the culture of a people—and education, more than any other institution, is charged with conserving, transmitting, and improving the culture. Hence, the extent to which a philosophy affects education is the measure of its significance, and the extent to which a philosophy refines and corrects educational theories and practices is the measure of its worth.

When most people think of Dewey's educational views they immediately associate them with so-called Progressive Education. While it is true that a few of the original tenets of this movement did stem from Dewey's philosophy, a great deal more sprang from a romantic naturalism largely identifiable with Rousseau and his idealistic views of child nature. Such unqualified cliches as "learning by doing," "child-centered," and "meeting the needs of pupils" scarcely represented an accurate reading of Dewey's educational ideas. Dewey argued that what is done, not the mere doing of it, determines the significance of learning; that subject matter has a rightful place in the educational program, not in a position of isolated autonomy, but in a meaningfully functional capacity; and that the basis on which pupil needs are to be decided is fully as important as meeting them. The most pointed distinction that can be made between Progressive Education and pragmatic education is that the former is substantially founded upon a theory of child nature, while the latter is based upon a distinctive theory of knowledge-getting.

Pragmatic education is unequivocally a philosophy of democratic education, whereas other educational theories might apply with equal effectiveness to aristocratic and totalitarian ways of life. Its social mission is the liberation of human intelligence, which is understood to be realizable in and through the social medium. Whereas closed societies must resort to fixed systems of thought for their perpetuation, the free society requires a public philosophy, that is, one that is open-ended, amendable, open to the criticism of all who would question, and within the power of the people to control. If education is to support the idea of a free, open-ended society, then it cannot at the same time be hemmed in by a closed system of thought. It becomes a unique purpose of education, therefore, to keep all avenues to truth open, free, and ac-

cessible, as well as to point up the irreconcilable conflict between democracy and all forms of absolutism. Education, in Dewey's words, ". . . is that reconstruction or reorganization of experience which adds to the meaning of experience, and which increases ability to direct the course of subsequent experience."[50]

Although pragmatism has had no possessive school of "disciples," it has had many lucid and distinctive interpreters in the field of education. Among them have been William H. Kilpatrick, Boyd H. Bode, John L. Childs, George S. Counts, R. Bruce Raup, George Axtelle, Ernest Bayles, William O. Stanley, Kenneth Benne, Harold Rugg, Theodore Brameld, and Lawrence G. Thomas—to name only a few. It is due largely to the insights and efforts of such men that American education continues to serve as the strongest undergirding of the free way of life.

[50] John Dewey, *Democracy and Education* (New York: The Macmillan Co., 1916), pp. 89–90.

∾

OVERVIEW*

In every culture, at any time, the function of education is to realize the ideals of manhood and of relationships between men that it cherishes. Our own culture, in our time, has come to take the free man, and the process of democratic relationships between free men, as our supreme ideals. These are the fundamental values to which we cling with what might often seem to be masochistic devotion.

* In view of the shortness of Professor Brameld's article the editors have added this Overview, to give the reader a taste of the philosophic flavor of the Reconstructionist basis on which the following article rests.

In every society, also, when there is too great a disparity between the ideal and the factual, between the unrealized potential and the realized situation, then arise conflicts and a subsequent social crisis—whether the frustration of the ideal was promoted by internal causes such as an unequal economic system, or external causes such as a Soviet challenge, or causes such as the frustration of effective world government or effective control of atomic energy, which are both internal and external.

That our culture is in the throes of such a crisis is implicit. Any society is in a state of change and reconstruction, but in such a crisis situation as we know today—and are likely to become increasingly acquainted with for an unpredictable number of years—what is the *distinctive* function of education?

It seems to the Reconstructionist that this distinctive function of education must inevitably involve the giving of direction to this social reconstruction that we so desperately need if we are going to solve our social problems and realize our ideals. And, this giving of direction entails a clear-cut commitment to cooperatively created and tested ends. The distinctive function of philosophy, in a crisis-culture, is to develop an education that can powerfully contribute to the rebuilding of—not merely perpetuating—the dominant structures, habits, and attitudes in the culture. Education must develop individuals who are cooperative in their means, and constantly engaged in achieving agreement about the details and relations of the ends they desire; ends that emanate from their means, and provide purposive actions in behalf of future goals.

If education is to serve this distinctive function, then educational philosophers face the task of determining *what* particular values and *what* particular ends for culture this generation should be asked to adopt and struggle to realize.

ENDS AND MEANS

The problem is partially one of axiology: how do we determine, and what is the relationship between our ends and means, our ideals and values?

If we find the universe closed and possessed already of the good and the true and the ultimately valuable, the task is mechanical: we need only rely on those time-honored values already existent. If we find the universe is not closed, but open and in a condition of constant and relatively unpredictable change, then it would seem values are man-made and relative. Reconstructionism, along with Pragmatism, accepts the latter point of view, and relies upon the capacity of human experience to generate fundamental values, *and to direct a deliberate effort in behalf of their realization.* Since man does not come into this universe with a set of antecedent aims, he must then *develop aims and create means to realize his ends.*

Consistent with his belief that the distinctive function of education in a crisis-culture is the provision of new social ends—*and* the revision of the old —the Reconstructionist is prepared to make a commitment to clear-cut democratic ends that are at the same time commensurate with means.

This commitment to ends is a major theme in the Reconstructionist position, and a theme that a more conservative Experimentalist is perhaps likely to reject, claiming that *any* commitment to ends, however relative, is inconsistent with good methodology. Thus, while both Reconstructionists and Experimentalists insist that ends and means are continuous, the latter would emphasize the means while the former seeks to place a greater emphasis on the ends than has been customary in experimental axiology. It is this end-means relationship that is the bone of contention between Reconstructionists and Experimentalists—and as Professor Sayers so dramatically put it, " . . . our difference is more like the whole skeleton and not just a mere bone." This it may be, but the Reconstructionist finds two objections to a conservative interpretation of this ends-means relationship:

First, the overly-cautious Experimentalist finds his position evasive at the moment of moral choice; by stressing the methodology of such a choice as the be-all and end-all of education, he always has an "out" when the pressure is on. It is this moral flabbiness that has been the favorite target of all critics of Pragmatism. There is something vulnerable in such a position—something which invites opportunism in the name of open-mindedness, liberalism, and methodology.

Secondly, many Experimentalists seem to be unwilling to identify education with the totality of man's cultural efforts to come to grips with himself and his environment. Undoubtedly they will give lip service to this concept, but it is obviously not carried through. For, if it were methodology could not possibly be defended as the distinctive function of education. In real life, life apart from artificial environment, people learn to control their environment *not only* by methods and techniques, *but also by decisions, by commitments, and by choices* that always involve the risk of error and the possibility of failure.

Yet, on the surface, the traditional Experimentalist argument appears to be very telling: Their emphasis on methodology would operate like some fairy godmother, pulling us from the dark forest of recurrent cultural crises. But, we should not deceive ourselves into thinking that this is truly so: there is yet a real need to give direction to social reconstruction, the need to create new aims, new values—and to commit ourselves to those ends developed by the process of social consensus.

SOCIAL CONSENSUS

What concerns us here is the nature of the creation of these ends to which we are going to commit ourselves. Reconstructionists propose to create these ends by the establishment of a social consensus, which is a method of dealing with conflicts which are not only an essential characteristic of democracy, but of the larger conflicts that challenge democracy. That such a method is possible and desirable is supported by the welter of similar methods recently suggested by philosophy and psychology. Max Otto parallels social consensus very closely with his "creative bargaining," inasmuch as both methods imply a getting together for a specific purpose: of coming to grips with a controversial situation in order that it may be made to yield the largest return of good for all who have a stake in the outcome.

If we can successfully utilize social consensus to create social aims to which we are willing to commit ourselves, we must include in our method of value creation an honest attempt to appreciate the aims in conflict, and their relation to the circumstances responsible for those aims. We must search for a new set of aims in which the conflicting ones may be absorbed, and invent a workable program through which the set of aims can come to fruition.

Thus, social consensus is a cooperative search for a new and better state of affairs. That is how it differs from the traditional blind-voting or compromise technique which consists in "splitting the difference" while the original antagonists remain still hostile. This difference is what makes it a novel endeavor. This is why acquaintance with it as a method, and training in its application, are so supremely important to the distinctive function of education.

Beyond all question, social consensus has great elements of strength: it is radically empirical in nature; it is firm in the conviction that within the processes of experience all necessary regulative standards and ideals can be developed with resort or reference of any kind to that which is supposedly "above" or "beyond" experience; it holds that men working together can develop both the ends and means of their community living here and now, and can develop a blueprint for a desirable pattern in the future.

Social consensus assigns a creative role to intelligence in that when it is used collectively it can achieve a reorganization and reinterpretation of existing interests and values. It accepts the fact of difference, but it views these differences among individuals and groups as an invitation to review old premises and project bold new programs which will so change the situation that the forces in conflict may be brought into a functioning unity. Social consensus is democratic in character; it believes that all groups involved in conflict situations should cooperate in the development and evaluation of these new ends.

Throughout Reconstructionism is a sense of urgency, of impending social disaster. Reconstructionists believe that we are today in the throes of a world-wide crisis comparable to none since the breakdown of feudalism, and quite probably more dangerous to survival of the civilization than then. Most Experimentalists do not assess the situation that way, and consequently their program is softer in both ends and means, and they are prone to accuse Reconstructionists of pushing a program that requires hasty commitment to ill-considered and immutable social ends. Reconstructionists do urge commitment to ends, but these ends are democratically created by the use of social consensus, and they are not immutable in that they change with the consensus of social opinion.

We may very well prove to be wrong about some preferred commitments. Indeed, we have learned how easy it is to be wrong. But the first lesson of this learning is not the future avoidance of commitments, it is rather the establishment of every possible safeguard against error or finality while yet aiming to create them. The partialities of Reconstructionists, for example, are confined to those dynamic goals (such as world government and planned democracy) to which they believe the majority of human beings would themselves be committed were they given the opportunity to do so on an international scale. But these goals, too, generate innumerable problems. Far from being self-certainties, they become defensible only in so far as they are scrutinized, compared, and appraised in the full public light of all relevant evidence, appraised in the exercise of communication unhampered by censorship, taboos, or hunters of witches, and defensible in the agreed-upon practice of ceaseless experimentation on the plane of action. Goals are to be created by a democratic social consensus, and defensible only by that sort of democratic education that attains the stature of mature responsibility of the culture which at once shapes its limitations and its reconstructive role.

For the Reconstructionist, then, the distinctive function of education in social reconstruction is not merely a renewed emphasis on the experimental methodology. It includes this, but goes beyond it when it calls for an honest evaluation of the contemporary crisis, and the creation of—and commitment to—those ends toward which we would use the experimental methodology.

Education must give guidance to social reconstruction, and to do so it must know where it is going, why it wants to go there, and how to get there.

Theodore Brameld, the leading proponent of Reconstructionism (see his *Patterns of Educational Philosophy*), exemplifies the spirit of crisis in the following article. Aware, as are all alert educators, that the influence of liberalism in educating is wavering under the recurrent and intensified attacks of the conservatives, he argues that the solution to educational problems in this crisis-culture is not to be found in a retreat to pre-Deweyan conceptions of education but in an advance beyond progressive education.

By way of illustration of the Reconstructionist thesis he applies his educational theories in the construction of a hypothetical junior college, noting how ends and means would be fused to give direction to education now inadequate to meet the challenges of a shrinking world.

Education for the Emerging Age

*Theodore Brameld**

One of the ironies of the Decade Since Hiroshima is that American education—and, I fear, education in much of the world—has not only failed to come to grips with unprecedented problems and tasks but has, if anything, receded from the level it had reached by the early 1940's.

In making this assertion I am aware of the need to qualify. In certain respects there has been progress. One example is the momentous decision of the United States Supreme Court outlawing segregated public schools—a decision that still remains to be implemented in largest part, yet is easily the most important interpretation of educational rights that the Court has made. Another sign of progress is the fact that larger sums are being spent for education today than ever before. Perhaps still more important, in long range, is the operation of the first permanent, internationally sponsored agency concerned with education on a world scale:

the United Nations Educational, Scientific and Cultural Organization (UNESCO). Nor should we overlook the salutary public concern with education as a democratic responsibility, as demonstrated in the White House Conference last year.

Nevertheless, such assets are offset by deficits. The more familiar ones may merely be summarized: the appalling shortage of teachers, equipment and buildings; the fresh inroads of sectarian religious pressure groups upon the public schools; the high rate of functional illiteracy—that is, the inability to use symbols meaningfully; the ignorance and indifference of millions of "educated" citizens concerning political and other crucial issues; the intimidations suffered by uncounted numbers of teachers victimized by Cold War hysteria; and finally, the spread of anti-intellectualism—of contempt for those rational processes typified by scientific method, philosophic analysis, and logical deliberation.

While each of these deficits could be documented at length, I wish to pass on to another that—besides being less

* Reprinted by permission from *The Humanist* (Yellow Springs, Ohio: The American Humanist Association), III (1957), pp. 134–143.

often discussed—supports my opening statement in a still more fundamental sense. Education has retreated from the position it had reached by the early 1940's in that the theory which undergirds its practice has become increasingly sympathetic to what may be called the "new conservatism"—that is, to traditional canons of belief that are, in my judgment, outmoded as guides to the revolutionary age which, for better or worse, we have already entered.

I

The simplest way to support this contention is to look back upon the past decade of public discussion of education, and to recall the voices that have attracted widest attention. For the most part, these voices have attacked the schools for failure to teach "the three R's," for lack of discipline, for disregard of scholarship, and for encouragement of "radical" if not "subversive" attitudes. Often the scapegoat has been something ambiguously called "progressive education"—a witches' brew of iniquitous ideas concocted originally by John Dewey, kept to the boiling point by William H. Kilpatrick, ladled out to innocent teachers by professional hackmen in schools of education, and finally swallowed by generations of children whose brains and spirits are thereby permanently addled.

I have resorted to caricature in order to highlight an opinion widespread among citizens. For example, the books dealing with educational theory and policy that have been most prominently reviewed in general magazines during recent years have seldom been those sympathetic to the experimentalist-progressivist philosophy which is the

key to progressive education. Rather, with few exceptions, they have been books expressing views bitterly hostile both to that philosophy and to the kind of modern schools that result from its consistent application. They have been books that repudiate the scientific and naturalistic thought of such philosophers as Dewey, and that beseech us to accept some classical—if not metaphysical and pre-scientific—doctrine. Therefore their own thought is derived ultimately from ways of life and philosophical systems prevailing in earlier centuries of Western civilization.

While the more competent of these books pay their respects to Dewey and to experimentalism, and all of them of course declare their admiration for science, nevertheless the main impact of their arguments has been to the contrary. Not only do they arouse doubts and confusion about the most original and influential theory in American educational history. They also persuade innumerable citizens—and even many teachers—that such practices in the schools as functional methods of learning to read, first-hand community experience, democratic participation in curriculum planning and school administration, should be thrown on the rubbish-heap and supplanted by their own preferred forms of tradition-grounded theory and practice.

II

These generalizations may be exemplified by the widely disseminated views of the late Gordon Keith Chalmers, president of Kenyon College. One of his last articles, "The Purpose of Learning," is especially revealing as it was the only treatment of educational philosophy included in the issue on "Higher Education Under Stress" of the *Annals* of the American Academy of Political and Social Science. In this article, as in his book, *The Republic and the Person,* Mr. Chalmers seemed so troubled about education that one might suppose, were one unfamiliar with the premises of his discussion, that here indeed was a daring advocate of change in a new direction. "Where," he asked, "shall we find the new philosophy of education so desperately demanded by our country and our times . . .?" He apparently believed that he himself was offering a "radical redirection for American education." When, however, one correctly defines "radical" as connoting a thoroughgoing departure from historically familiar patterns of belief and practice in favor of patterns not hitherto known or experienced, Mr. Chalmers' "radical redirection" proves to be nothing of the sort. In his own words, it "must be based clearly on the classic understanding of the dual nature of man, which characterizes not only Christianity but Greek tragedy, Roman law, and historic Hebrew and ancient Indian thought." Careful inspection of his educational proposals bears out this statement. He would retreat to beliefs and practices that are classical indeed.

Such proposals are unlikely to have anything concrete to say about the burning educational and cultural issues of our day—the attack upon academic freedom, for example, or the implications for learning of such cataclysmic discoveries as atomic energy. Rather, like most neoconservatives, Mr. Chalmers thought that education can solve the great problems of life only by a spiritual and intellectual rejuvenation of the individual "person." And the "person," though described in somewhat different terms by other proponents of his position, turns out to be nothing so much as a twentieth-century prototype of traditional man governed by "right Reason"—the ideal of Renaissance and post-Renaissance aristocratic humanism.

Mr. Chalmers' approach to education was an important and earnest way of reacting, culturally as well as philosophically, to the crisis of our age. But it was a way of reacting that is easily accounted for. As Arnold Toynbee and other philosophers of history have shown, every great crisis in the affairs of men has produced more or less similar types of "solution" by entrenched minorities. In periods of tension and bewilderment, it is perhaps more typical than otherwise for educators, like citizens at large, to react at first shock by listening wistfully to voices that would dissolve their troubles by restoring nostalgic patterns of truth, value, and reality.

III

The recent appeal of traditional patterns is also due in part to the ineffectiveness with which other philosophies and programs have responded to our period of challenge. The experimentalist-progressivist philosophy, particularly, though it has held its own remarkably well since the early 1940's when it was still the dominant educational outlook, has for perhaps twenty years contributed little that can be said to enrich the original formulations of Dewey himself. The fact that the Progressive

Education Association ceased to exist in 1955, after some thirty years of immense influence, is surely due largely to its failure to pioneer any longer. Moreover, there is considerable validity in the common criticism that many schools of education have been guilty of superficial and distorted application of the experimentalist-progressivist philosophy to learning and teaching.

Still more fundamentally, this philosophy, which underlies so much of our modern education, is itself gravely deficient in its capacity to cope with the issues generated by a period of history profoundly altered from that of the first quarter of our century, when it was developed to maturity. Elsewhere I have tried to analyze this deficiency. Here I may only point out that the essential weakness should be diagnosed not only in philosophic but in cultural terms; the experimentalist-progressivist outlook expresses the mood, the values and the practices of a culture *in transition* between two greatly different eras of modern history.

The first era may be bounded roughly by the fifteenth and late nineteenth centuries. It was during these centuries that industrialism, nationalism, capitalist democracy, and individualistic liberalism all achieved maturity. The second era has by no means fully emerged. Indeed, perhaps it may not emerge fully at all before civilization is degraded or even destroyed. Nevertheless, the second era is already more and more recognizable in potential design. And it is likely to be distinguished from all earlier eras by at least these fundamental features: a largely automatic, integrated technology powered increasingly by atomic energy; a world

population sufficiently educated to regulate its own growth according to available resources; a publicly planned and directed system of distribution of these resources so that physical and spiritual deprivation due to inequitable distribution of goods is eliminated; and an *enforceable* international government under democratic and, as far as possible, decentralized control.

To argue the same point differently, the experimentalist-progressivist philosophy is transitional in its basic character in the same way that twentieth-century liberalism (as distinct from the original individualistic liberalism of John Locke) is transitional. Both tend to emphasize the qualities of open-mindedness, of social and political exploration, of regard for "all sides of the question"—above all, of experimental methodology as the key to progress. Both stress the interaction of individual and community, but neither wishes to consider one as, say, the moral criterion of the other. Likewise, both emphasize the reciprocity of means and ends, but both characteristically focus upon means —upon "how we think" (the title of a famous Dewey volume), upon hypothesis rather than solution, upon tolerance rather than conviction, upon process rather than product. Finally, both are critical of the first great era of Western culture: they condemn the evils generated by ruthless industrialism, nationalism, and laissez-faire capitalism. Indeed, their main concern, educationally as well as culturally, has been to alleviate these evils by a more socially responsible and more intelligently directed program.

But neither experimentalism-progressivism nor recent liberalism seems able or willing to go much further than this. Being concerned with the virtues of culture as transition more than with the directions or aims of this transition, each hesitates to commit itself to, or even appraise carefully, the imperatives I have described as potential to the second era. Instead, a characteristic reaction is to label them "utopian" or to condemn them as "dogmatic" without taking the trouble to distinguish between the illegitimacy of dogma and the legitimacy of conviction about these imperatives. In rejecting the desirability of planned designs for the future, experimentalism-progressivism, like typical liberalism, remains in a state of pendulum-like tension between polar values—between individual and community, between means and ends. It prefers to stress the fluid and dynamic experience that has been indigenous to the period of American life which it has so skillfully symbolized.

When neoconservatives attack Dewey's philosophy for glorifying the value of growth for the sake of further growth as the highest measure of good education, they are, then, touching a sensitive nerve. But they cannot, on their own assumptions, account either for the cultural roots of this value or for the emerging values of the second era. They can only suggest that the way to correct an over-emphasis upon process, methodology, and growth is to regress toward traditional standards that are termed "radical" only at the penalty of historic and semantic confusion.

IV

It should now be apparent that the kind of educational philosophy and program required for the second (though still potential) era of modern history cannot be satisfied by the orthodox formulations of the experimentalists-progressivists any more than by the genteel and wishful formulations of the neoconservatives. While the needed philosophy may learn much from both —and especially from the former—it should aim to remove their deficiencies and to reconstruct the principles, methods and contents of education. That the undertaking is tremendous, and that no one person or group can accomplish it alone, is evident. Particularly is it tremendous because the required formulation should be interdisciplinary throughout; not only should it utilize the best available knowledge from philosophy and education, but it should incorporate the most significant new research of the physical, biological and social sciences, and the new creations of every art from literature to architecture. Thus, if it crystallizes at all, it will prove to be vastly more than a formal philosophy of education. It will also be a philosophy of culture, with education conceived as the chief agency through which problems of every kind are attacked, and practices, institutions and values commensurate with the demands of the emerging age are developed and tested.

The primary conviction that should govern every phase of the proposed philosophy is that humanity is now caught in the throes of a planetary transformation. The interweaving characteristics of this transformation are many—scientific, religious, economic, political, esthetic, psychological. Without doubt, the most graphic and monstrous symbol is atomic energy, the consequences of which for good or evil are still far from predictable. No one can guarantee that it will not be utilized to degrade —if not to destroy—human civilization as we have known it. No one can assure us, either, that competing nations will not continue to blunder on for perhaps a very long time—threatening, cajoling, bluffing, fumbling as they now do, yet fearing to release the power stored in their dreadful arsenals because of the reprisals that would surely result. Thus, in epitomizing earlier the salient features of the second modern era toward which experimentalism-progressivism is transitional, I did not say that such an era *will* ever occur. No one knows whether it ever will or not. I described it as a potential design of what the future could be like, and I implied that it is also what it should be like if we reject the alternatives of degradation, destruction, or chronic trepidation.

The point is crucial for educational theory. For, in addition to recognizing the paramount importance of scientific and empirical means, the proposed theory insists upon the equal importance of strong conviction about desirable ends. I wish, therefore, to underscore the argument that the most vulnerable spot in public education, especially as it is influenced by experimentalism-progressivism, is that it has not clearly or unequivocally focused upon either the content or meaning of these ends. Like the American culture of which it is the ideological ally, it has been much more concerned to delineate an effective methodology of intelligent practice than to formulate the goals for which that methodology is indispensable. And while traditional theorists, neoconserva-tive and others, are likewise disturbed by this inadequacy in the philosophy they oppose, they seek to counteract it primarily by restoring a doctrine of ends and purposes adapted to the earlier era of post-medieval culture but entirely unsuitable to the era that should now emerge.

V

How might education, were it reconstructed according to the principles outlined here, actually function?

The question cannot be answered in a single article, but it is possible to illustrate. Let us consider a new type of junior college open to all average young citizens from about seventeen to twenty years old. The four-year curriculum would be organized around one central theme: "What kind of world can we have and do we want?" Each semester would consider different dimensions of this question: political, economic, scientific, moral, esthetic, religious, and many others. Every course of study would utilize the richest possible resources—research, books, community experience, personal contacts with experts of many kinds. In addition, every student would have opportunity to work intensively in fields always related directly and indirectly to the common theme—fields ranging all the way from biology and physics to music and poetry. The entire four years would thus allow ample diversification and concentration, yet would acquire organic unity and purpose.

Methods of learning would depart radically from those typical today. Lectures would be replaced largely by cooperative investigations, by intensive utilization of television and other audio-visual instruments, and by frequent travel and work experience; yet these methods would allow ample room for the gifted student to work independently of groups.

Indoctrination of any proposal or belief would be considered unprofessional. At the same time, teachers would be encouraged to hold and to express their convictions, not for the purpose of compelling acceptance of them but rather for the purpose of inviting critical awareness and opposition to them.

To reduce the likelihood of indoctrination still further, students would be constantly exposed to all kinds of evidence against as well as for every proposal for the new order. Minority dissents to any majority consensus reached by co-operative study would always be respected. Thereby the democratic process, defined as majority agreement tempered by the privilege of minority opposition, would become a basic practice within the school itself—a practice which would provide young citizens with greatly needed sensitivity to the weaknesses and strengths of that process in wider communities.

Such experience with genuinely democratic learning should help students to appreciate that the most important decisions of policy that people reach concerning, say, the public control of atomic energy, are not infallible decisions. Rather, they are subject to error, they require everlasting criticism, and they will probably need continuing correction and improvement. Thus, while emphasis should be placed upon the need for commitment to future-centered goals, every opportunity ought also to be provided to modify or alter any commitment in the light of better evidence, deliberation, and experimental testing. Here, as at other points, the contributions of experimentalism-progressivism to educational theory would not be repudiated but rather supplemented and reinforced.

The curriculum would give continuous attention, furthermore, to the obstacles that stand in the way of cultural reconstruction. These obstacles are mountainous: such blanket terms as lethargy, fear, ignorance, defeatism, hatred, violence, incompetence, superstition, and insecurity scarcely begin to encompass either their scope or complexity. Education, typically, has been derelict in failing to provide understanding of the irrational forces that undermine and destroy the capacity for harmony both within and between individuals and within and between groups. Here the inclusion of much more of the research of such sciences as psychiatry and political psychology is pressing indeed—findings that should not only toughen the student's awareness of himself and his fellows, of power structures and power struggles among classes and nations, but should help to provide therapies essential to their correction and control.

A further concern of the curriculum brings us back to the problem of goals. The problem is not that of determining merely the general purposes of the new era, or even that of specifying its institutional and cultural designs. It is also that of analyzing and selecting the values that these designs should serve and that alone justify them. Axiology, the branch of philosophy concerned with moral, esthetic, and political criteria of value, is indispensable to this task. So, too, are such disciplines as anthropology and history: what can they teach us as to the likelihood of cross-cultural, perhaps even universal, values as these are respected and craved by ordinary people? Both here and elsewhere, the great books of philosophers, artists, and scientists of every era are also indispensable. Unlike educators, however, who would have these classics studied "for their own sake" or for the cultivation of a "faculty" of reason, the proposed theory would have them studied for the insight and guidance they may provide for the means and ends of education conceived in terms of cultural renascence.

This model for a junior college would not, of course, be suitable to the practice of education either below or above that level. While the reconstructed philosophy would affect education throughout the primary and secondary years as well as the years of higher learning, different tasks and obligations apply to each. For example, no one should be qualified as lawyer, doctor, engineer, or teacher unless he has received a general education that acquaints him with the wider problems of a civilization in crisis, and with his own share of responsibility in solving them. There is need, moreover, for new types of training appropriate to new professions that are now emerging: international relations, eugenics and population control, regional social and economic planning, food and soil chemistry, electronic communications, industrial atomic energy—these are but a few of the opportunities in process of creation by the second major revolution of the modern world.

VI

What are the chances that such a philosophy of education as I have outlined for the Hydrogen-Cobalt Age can actually receive sufficient consideration to make it a serious contender for widespread support and experimental action?

To judge by the prevailing American mood, one might answer that there is little chance indeed. Moreover, in Red China and the Soviet orbit, in Fascist Spain and South Africa, there seems at the moment even less. But many variables operate in the present world situation. They will continue to operate in the decades ahead. Even in America, the prevailing fashion of neo-conservatism among many intellectuals —including educational theorists—may be less a long-term trend than a transitory indication of cultural insecurity. Among many young teachers one can already detect both a restlessness and a readiness to respond to better financed, more far-reaching and future-looking educational plans.

In various other countries such restlessness and readiness are even more apparent. Great numbers of people in India, Mexico, Burma and Japan reveal intense dislike both for the American foreign policy of smug paternalism and for Communist authoritarianism. These people are groping, to be sure. But millions of hitherto oppressed and exploited individuals are, for the first time in history, becoming articulate both in their indignation and in their demands. They are opposed to further bloodshed and pillage as much as they are in favor of strong world government. They refuse any longer to accept the fatalistic fallacy that poverty, disease and ignorance are unavoidable. Increasingly they insist upon a life of creative opportunity and fulfillment expressed in their own cultural terms.

It is true, of course, that even minimum education is still lacking in much of the world. Hence one of the first responsibilities of an adequately financed UNESCO should be an international program for the abolition of illiteracy. Yet, essential though this is, it is far from enough. Both the less and the more developed regions of the world are beginning to be aware of, and committed to, the goals of a peaceful, abundant, democratic world, and of the concrete means—of which literacy is but one—by which these goals may be attained.

Here adult education becomes another urgent need. In Puerto Rico, for example, illiteracy is regarded as not merely the inability to read or write but, even more, as the inability to cope with local problems in a co-operative way. Its adult program, reaching deep into the mountains, is affecting the lives of thousands of rural people. So, too, are the programs of Denmark, Israel, and other small countries. Even in the United States enough progress has recently been made in reconstructing the theory of education for adults so that we may anticipate striking improvements in practice as well.

Nor may we overlook the resources of the sciences and the arts in bolstering the required outlook. From the perspective of a layman, I am reasonably certain that consciousness of pervasive crisis and of moral concern to deal with it have never been so acute among natural scientists as they are now. Indeed, quite possibly they are more concerned than are the social scientists: too many of the latter continue belatedly to emulate a now dubious philosophy of "neutrality" and "objectivity" that they acquired from an earlier period of natural science itself. Yet many social scientists also seem deeply conscious of their responsibilities. From them, as well as from artists and philosophers sensitive to the transformations accelerating around us, educators may acquire much that is vitalizing to their own efforts.

For such reasons as these, there is no cause to conclude that the philosophy of education cannot be reconstructed and applied in practice. True, the neoconservative philosophy may continue to appeal to many citizens. True, too, the destructive forces to which I have referred may eventually prevail—in fact, they will almost surely prevail unless we can assess and counteract their strategy and strength. To recognize such possibilities does not, however, preclude recognizing equally powerful potentials in the constructive forces that are now discernible. Opportunity exists for us to throw our loyalties and energies on the side of these constructive forces. Education, reinforced by the assets already at hand and guided by a culture-oriented, goal-centered theory, can also grasp that opportunity while time still remains.

Toward an Analytic Philosophy of Education

*Israel Scheffler**

Various activities may, with historical justification, lay claim to the honored title of "philosophy." These include, among others, e.g., logical analysis, speculative construction, culture criticism, institutional programming, and the expression of personal attitudes toward the world. It is my purpose neither to cast doubt on any of these claims nor to deny the appropriateness of any of these activities. I do, however, wish to stress the ambiguity of the general term "philosophy" and, correlatively, of the narrower term "philosophy of education." It is certainly no striking news that the latter term is currently widely employed to mean practically anything from a well-articulated metaphysics of knowledge to the vaguest expression of attitudes toward, say, the public school system. What *is* worthy of note is that one legitimate meaning is almost consistently ignored: Philosophy of education is rarely, if ever, construed as the rigorous logical analysis of key concepts related to the practice of education. In this paper, arguing for the fruitfulness of such an approach, I shall try, *first,* to explain and illustrate the general notion of philosophy as logical analysis, and *second,* to outline the ways in which logical analysis appears to me relevant to educational problems.

The conception of philosophy as the attempt to clarify key concepts is hardly

a modern invention. For the attempt, by dialectical methods, to clarify the meaning of basic notions is at least as old as Socrates. What distinguishes current analysis is, first, its greater sophistication as regards language, and the interpenetration of language and inquiry, secondly, its attempt to follow the modern example of the sciences in empirical spirit, in rigor, in attention to detail, in respect for alternatives, and in objectivity of method, and thirdly, its use of techniques of symbolic logic brought to full development only in the last fifty years. The result has been revolutionary for philosophic practice. New insights have been achieved in almost every area of traditional philosophy. The individualism so characteristic of its past has, to a marked extent, been tempered by a sense of community of investigation, unified by method rather than doctrine, and by a common search for clarity on fundamental issues. That this development represents no mere doctrinal school is evident from the fact that it comprises sharp differences of opinion within itself, as well as from the fact that a number of its early formulations have undergone orderly revision under the pressure of criticism and new discoveries. Nor can such development be considered entirely negative, for progress has been made in the settling of some older problems and the recasting of new ones, progress which is widely acknowledged by students in this domain. It is, then, this union of

* Reprinted by permission from *The Harvard Educational Review,* XXIV (Fall, 1954), 223–230.

scientific spirit and logical method applied toward the clarification of basic ideas which characterize current analytic philosophy.

Since critical precision rather than doctrine is the essence of such philosophy, its significance is best conveyed by an examination of concrete instances. My first illustration to this purpose is drawn from the theory of meaning, with which current analysts are perhaps predominantly concerned, and in which some of the best work has been done. I must ask you, despite its abstractness and unfamiliarity, to consider it with me in some detail, since for this philosophy detailed precision is all. Yet, I hope such consideration will afford an insight into *general* method and approach, which may emerge even more sharply against an abstract and unfamiliar setting. At a later point, of course, I shall want to suggest educational applications. Meanwhile, it will perhaps be instructive to note how difficult is the attempt to avoid confusion even in a realm removed from the urgencies of practice, and how, even here, increasingly radical departures from common assumptions are necessitated by the quest for clarity.

Consider then, the notions of meaning and existence. Two common assumptions about these notions are: (i) That the meaningfulness of a sentence containing a singular term (i.e. a name, or descriptive phrase purporting to name a single entity) presupposes that this term actually *does* name, that is, that *there really exists* the entity purportedly referred to; failure to name removes the object of discourse and renders both the empty singular term and its context meaningless. (ii) That the

existence-commitments of a theory, i.e. the entities which must exist for it to be true, are revealed by the set of singular terms which it employs. Both assumptions turn out, upon analysis, exceedingly troublesome if we want to construct a consistent and fruitful account of meaning. Let us see why this is so.

Take, for example, a definite singular descriptive phrase of the form "the such-and-such" as it appears in the sentence "The American President in 1953 plays golf." No difficulty here. The descriptive phrase, we would ordinarily say, following (i), *names* some unique entity, Mr. Eisenhower, while the sentence is a *meaningful* statement about this entity, asserting something true of it. The negation of this sentence, though false, we would declare still meaningful, as concerning the same single entity, named by the descriptive phrase in question.

Consider, now, the new sentence, "The American Emperor in 1953 plays chess," and its negation "It is not the case that the American Emperor in 1953 plays chess." Now there is, in point of fact, no entity denoted by the descriptive phrase shared by both these sentences, i.e. "The American Emperor in 1953." It plainly does us no good to declare the first sentence false, since false sentences are meaningful anyway and such a declaration would violate (i). Further, if the first sentence is false, its negation must be true, under the very same condition of failure to name by the identical descriptive phrase. So that a simple resolution to abandon (i) by taking failure to name as always implying falsity turns out impossible.

To hold on to (i) in the face of these two sentences, we must declare them both meaningless. But the consequences of such a course are plainly undesirable on two basic counts: First, it would hinge the very meaning of descriptive phrases inconveniently on fact. In general, we should prefer to keep the meaningfulness of our language independent of specific factual considerations; we want to consider our hypotheses meaningful even prior to any factual confirmation. Following the last proposal, however, we should require factual evidence of the existence and uniqueness of some appropriate named entity before we could even be confident we were *making sense* in using descriptive phrases, let alone asserting a truth by their use. Secondly, and perhaps more paradoxically, to make meaninglessness a consequence of failure to name, as our last proposal does for the two sentences under consideration, means that we cannot, within our language, even *deny* the existence of the American Emperor in 1953. For to do so, we should need to say something like "The American Emperor in 1953 does not exist," and this sentence itself turns out, by our last proposal, to be strictly meaningless.

An analogous problem arises for proper names. Suppose I deny that Zeus exists. A fairly reasonable position. Yet consider: if, in using proper names, I make sense only by talking *about* some actual entity, following (i), what in the world am I talking *about* in saying "Zeus does not exist."? In order for me to make sense, Zeus must exist, but if he does, my denial is false. Must I therefore admit, out of logical necessity, the existence of all members of the Pantheon, all characters in fiction, in short everything bearing an osten-

sible proper name? Furthermore, taking my denial statement as a miniature theory with one proper name ("Zeus"), it is clearly intended that, contrary to (ii), this name should be no clue to its existence-commitments, for it is intended to stand plainly committed to nothing, and certainly not to Zeus.

A well-known, and by now classic solution of the puzzle of descriptive phrases, which, in effect, abandons assumption (i) altogether for such phrases, was proposed many years ago by Bertrand Russell.[1] Briefly, Russell showed how to *eliminate* descriptive phrases in context, in favor of equivalent contexts no longer containing any phrases purporting to name unique entities, but referring quite generally to entities by means of logical variables like "something," "nothing," "everything," etc. Such elimination of contained descriptive phrases together with conversation of asserted content in effect divorces the contextual meaning from the purported naming function of such phrases altogether. For example, Russell's equivalent of our troublesome first sentence above is "something is an American Emperor in 1953 and plays chess and nothing else is an American Emperor in 1953." Though as a whole equivalent to the original, this translation provides no naming unit as a counterpart to the eliminated descriptive phrase. With this, the whole original problem disappears, there now being no difficulty in declaring this equivalent false, together with the original. But the upshot is the denial of (i) for descriptive phrases, since the original

[1] B. Russell, *Introduction to Mathematical Philosophy*, 2d ed. (London: Allen and Unwin, 1920), Chap. XVI.

sentence is now construed as false (and its negation as true), hence perfectly meaningful, though the contained descriptive phrase fails to name. A corollary is denial of (ii) for descriptive phrases, since, if they can be significantly used without naming, they are no clue to the existential presuppositions of the theory.

A solution of the proper name puzzle was recently proposed by Professor W. V. Quine[2, 3] who extends Russell's analysis by showing how all proper names may be construed as descriptive phrases and then eliminated as before. For our above example, we are counseled by Quine to construe "Zeus does not exist" as "The thing that is-Zeus does not exist," Russell's equivalent of which becomes "Either for each entity, it is not the case that it is-Zeus or there is more than one entity which is-Zeus." Again, since no proper name or descriptive phrase purporting to name a unique entity appears at all in this translation, there remains no difficulty in declaring it and its original meaningful, and moreover, true. One upshot is denial of (i) even where a purported *proper name* fails to name. Consequently, a second result is full denial of assumption (ii), since, for this analysis, proper names are clearly no better indicators of the existence-commitments of a theory than are its descriptive phrases, which are, for Russell, no indicators at all, as we have seen. As Quine's extension makes clear, existence-commitents are ultimately re-

vealed solely by the use made of logical variables ("something," "each entity," etc.) when the theory is put into Russellian form. But the details of this judgment are another story.

One further problem, taken from a more familiar area, will illustrate that analysis is capable of touching our most basic notions of practice to the quick. We all talk of confirming general hypotheses by gathering relevant instances. For example, we say that a purported general law is progressively confirmed or disconfirmed by observation of its relevant instances. But consider the puzzle noted by Professor Hempel.[4] What is a confirming instance for the purported law "all ravens are black"? Clearly a raven which is black. A non-raven we would classify as clearly irrelevant altogether. Now, however, consider that our law is logically equivalent to the statement "All non-black things are non-ravens," and for this statement a confirming instance would be a non-black non-raven. But this instance we have decided was irrelevant to the first law. Shall we say that what is to be taken as an instance depends on the accident of linguistic formulation? Let us rather rule that logically equivalent sentences should be confirmed by exactly the same instances. This rule, however, is just as counter-intuitive as ever, since if a non-black non-raven is to confirm our first law, then every time I observe the sky, the sun, my typewriter, or Widener Library, I am progressively confirming the law that all ravens are black. Clearly our ordinary conceptions of what constitutes an instance are

[2] W. V. Quine, "On What There Is," *Review of Metaphysics*, II, 1948.

[3] W. V. Quine, *From a Logical Point of View* (Cambridge, Mass.: Harvard University Press, 1953).

[4] C. G. Hempel, "Studies in the Logic of Confirmation," *Mind*, LIV (1945).

faulty somewhere, and require considerable refinement.

Enough now of general illustrations of analytic problems and methods. I have already intimated that analytic philosophers are by no means exclusively concerned with theory of meaning and philosophy of science. Indeed, much work in ethics, theory of mind, philosophy of law, aesthetics, and theory of social science is presently under way. It is time, I think, to consider how analytic philosophy might be brought to bear on educational problems, as a legitimate and vital pursuit of philosophy of education. In analogy with applications of science to education, I suggest that we conceive of analytic applications in roughly two directions, (a) the utilization of results already achieved in the autonomous development of research, and (b) the use of acknowledged methods directly in the study of educational problems.

(a) To realize fully the extent to which the first mode of application is presently feasible, one would ideally require a detailed survey of current analysis which, as already noted, touches a wide variety of areas. Since one example must suffice, we might consider for a moment the rather fashionable proposal of Dewey,[5] Neurath,[6] and others,[7] to replace the venerable notion of truth by that of probability or verification, or analogous ideas, in view

of the impossibility of complete confirmation of hypotheses. Despite its wide popularity, however, and despite the hasty conclusions drawn for practice, perhaps most analysts are agreed that such replacement would be an error, in view of Professor Tarski's[8] semantic conception of truth. For Tarski, to say that a given sentence, e.g. "the sun is shining," is true, is to say nothing more nor less than "the sun is shining." On the other hand, to say that the latter sentence is confirmed by John Doe to degree d at time t is obviously to make an independent assertion, since it may hold whether or not the sun is shining in point of fact, and vice versa. It follows that truth and confirmation are independent. As Professor Carnap[9] has pointed out, were the impossibility of complete confirmation to rule out the term "is true," it would equally rule out the term "is shining" and, indeed, every scientific term, while if partial confirmation is sufficient for retention of a term, then the term "true" is as acceptable as any. What is ruled out by the pervasiveness of probability is certainty, not truth.

A final illustration from the theory of value. It has been argued, at least since Aristotle, that the pattern of justifying beliefs relative to evidence implies that some beliefs must be certain. For if we justify some belief on evidence and this evidence on further evidence, where do we stop? We cannot

[5] John Dewey, *Logic: the Theory of Inquiry* (New York: Holt, Rinehart and Winston, Inc., 1938).

[6] O. Neurath, *Foundations of the Social Sciences* (Chicago: The University of Chicago Press, 1944).

[7] F. Kaufmann, *Methodology of the Social Sciences* (Toronto: Oxford University Press, 1944).

[8] A. Tarski, "The Semantic Conception of Truth," *Readings in Philosophical Analysis*, ed. H. Feigl and W. Sellars (New York: Appleton-Century-Crofts, Inc., 1949).

[9] R. Carnap, "Truth and Confirmation," *Readings in Philosophical Analysis*, ed. H. Feigl and W. Sellars (New York: Appleton-Century-Crofts, Inc., 1949).

continue to justify every belief relative to evidence without infinite regress. Hence, if any belief is justified, some must be known certain in themselves. Now this persuasive argument for rationalism, as recently shown by Professor Goodman,[10] is somewhat too extravagant. In order to avoid infinite regress, we need only hold some beliefs with some initial credibility. We need attribute certainty to none. While we try to attain and preserve a maximum of initial credibility for the total mass of our beliefs, any single one is subject to withdrawal under pressure of conflict with this total mass. Recently, I have noted[11] the possibility of extending Professor Goodman's argument to ethical justification generally. For it is very widely held that in order to justify any act, goal, or choice, some at least must be held absolutely immune to withdrawal. What we need admit, it seems to me, is only that some choices or goals may have for us some degree of initial committedness, while none is immune to withdrawal. Whereas no act or choice is justifiable in isolation, every act is subject to control by all in our attempt to harmonize them by maximizing initial committedness for the mass of our behavior. If this analysis is not mistaken, then both ethical absolutism and extreme subjectivism are avoided, a corollary with important bearings on value theory and education. The analysis of justification is presently being pursued from a variety of approaches,[12, 13, 14] and may prove fruitful for problems in social theory, theory of democracy, and other areas related to education.

(b) The second mode of application I mentioned above consists of the direct analysis of concepts related to the practice of education. What I have already said perhaps indicates the possibilities in this area better than any catalogue I might offer. Yet it is worth noting at this point that, if obscurity surrounds such basic notions as "existence," "truth," and "confirmation," notions crucially employed and continually refined in the exact sciences, it may surely be expected to hamper the understanding of key notions tied to educational practice, notions like "disposition," "experience," "skill," "achievement," "training," "intelligence," "character," "choice," "growth." How shall we understand, to take but one example, the popular contention that growth is the goal of education? Clearly not every sort of growth is held desirable, witness growth in ignorance or brutality. Even if we eliminate obviously undesirable dispositions, shall we think of growth as simply the increase in dispositions acquired by the learner? This will not do, for a substantial part of growth consists in dropping off dis-

[10] N. Goodman, "Sense and Certainty," *Philosophical Review*, LXI (April, 1952).

[11] I. Scheffler, "On Justification and Commitment," *Journal of Philosophy*, LI (March, 1954).

[12] A. W. Burks, "Justification in Science," *Academic Freedom, Logic, and Religion*, ed. M. G. While (Philadelphia: University of Pennsylvania Press, 1953).

[13] H. Feigl, "De Principiis Non Disputandum?" *Philosophical Analysis*, ed. M. Black (Ithaca, N.Y.: Cornell University Press, 1950).

[14] F. B. Fitch, "Justification in Science," *Academic Freedom, Logic, and Religion*, ed. M. G. White (Philadelphia: University of Pennsylvania Press, 1953).

positions once mastered. We all at one time could shoot marbles pretty well but can do so no longer. Furthermore, in attempting a count of dispositions how shall we classify them? Is playing checkers one and playing chess another? If so, where do we put Chinese checkers? Finally, how shall we weight the progressive intensification of one disposition as against the multiplication of several?

Taking a new direction, we might, along lines reminiscent of Dewey, consider growth as the intensification of some master disposition, e.g. the ability to solve problems intelligently. But how is such intensification itself to be construed concretely? A simple increase in solved problems per unit time may not indicate growth if conjoined with a greater increase per unit time in perceived problems remaining unsolved. Shall we propose, then, as an appropriate indication of our meaning here, the ratio of solved problems to those perceived, per unit time? This would end in absurdity since, other things remaining equal, a decrease in perception would constitute growth, while an increase in sensitivity to problems would constitute regression. We might try a different move (as Dewey appears to in certain of his writings), and construe problems not as relative to the selectivity of a perceiver, but as somehow objectively built into the total situation. But such a move, while it is not obvious that it meets our original difficulties, clearly raises more troubles than we had to begin with: Just what is a total situation, what kind of entities are objective problems, and how do we determine their character?

Now it is important not to confuse the import of my remarks here with the widespread demand for so-called operational definitions. If this were all that is involved, it would be quite easy to define growth operationally as increase in weight as measured in milligrams, or in height as measured in centimeters, or in the average number of hairs per square centimeter of scalp.[15] Such a course would have but one drawback, i.e. it would have nothing whatever to do with our original, predefinitional concept as it figures in the educational statement in question. What is required here, it seems to me, is not the application of operationalist slogans so much as a careful analysis or explication of our original concept, aimed at the distillation of a more precise counterpart, and finally, an examination of what consequences result for educational theory from rewriting it with such newly-achieved precision, or possibly, from failure to attain additional clarity.

Nor do I here intend, by any means, to deny the possibility of a fruitful and significant clarification of the notion of growth as used in educational theory. I am pointing to what seems to me one genuine philosophic problem germane to education, calling for the use of analytic methods. And what I am urging generally is recognition of the need, by a rigorous and thorough application of such methods, to clarify the meaning of our basic educational ideas, as of all ideas we hold important. If philosophy of education accepts this task of clarification, it will be assuming not merely

[15] C. G. Hempel, *Fundamentals of Concept Formation in Empirical Science* (Chicago: The University of Chicago Press, 1952).

a familiar historical role, but one which is proving increasingly fruitful and stimulating in wide reaches of current philosophy, and which cannot fail to deepen our understanding of what we do when we educate.

∽

Philosophical Semantics and Education

Richard W. Dettering*

I. SIGNIFICANCE OF THE PHILOSOPHY OF LANGUAGE

The historical course of western education has reflected most of the important philosophical systems of the past: Greek formalism, Cartesian rationalism, British and French sensationalism, German idealism, and, more recently, American pragmatism. But it has not yet been much affected by the modern philosophies of language which are otherwise beginning to have such vast influence.

Our lifetime has witnessed a phenomenal growth of human self-consciousness, induced in various ways by such pioneers as Darwin, Hegel, Marx, Freud and Einstein. The disposition of man to explore the conditions of his own knowledge and behavior as a prerequisite to understanding the world around him has taken command of wide ranges of contemporary intellectual enterprise. The increasing emphases on epistemology and methodology, on cultural and class determinants, and on psychological insight into one's self and group, now have a powerful new ally in the activity of "philosophical semantics." For to talk about language

is but another way of talking about oneself and one's culture; it is getting "outside" of the subjective situations to look at them "objectively." By using language to study language, what man has thought in the past becomes more subject to immediate and direct analysis. When the study of introspective data was replaced by the study of observable behavior, psychology for the first time established its candidacy as a recognized science. Similarly, when language, rather than private mental states, becomes the object of inquiry, human ideas become objects of continued public inspection. By regarding the media of knowledge as concrete and tangible symbols, their relationship to what is known can be inspected with some hope of scientific consensus. Although symbols are only recognized by what we loosely call their "meaning" instead of by their intrinsic physical properties, there is nothing strange to science about this. Tractors and shovels can only be fully identified by knowing what they *do;* a chess piece can only be defined by giving the rules for moving it and not by what it looks like. The study of language is thus no less empirical than the study of countless other things which are socially and functionally organized into some wider context of our experience.

* Reprinted by permission from *Educational Theory*, VIII (July, 1958), 143–150.

Dissatisfaction with traditional philosophies gave modern philosophical semantics its first great impetus. Metaphysical beliefs had usually been taken at their face value, with interminable argument as to whether they were true or false. Early in this century Bertrand Russell and others began to contend that the *sentences* expressing many of these beliefs were, because of their logical construction or lack of denotative reference, simply not capable of being determined as either true or false, but that—at least until they were further clarified—they must be considered as "meaningless." In this way, many old philosophical problems, including those of educational theory, become interpreted as problems of language. For example, it is regarded as a problem of educational philosophy as to whether or not *reality* is identical with *experience*—the idealists (and many pragmatists) affirming it, and the realists denying it. The "problem" is stated grammatically as though it were like a problem in geometry, e.g., is equilateral triangle identical with equiangular triangle? And the philosopher tries to solve it in the way the geometrician solves his problem. But the results are strikingly different. While geometricians the world over agree quickly and unanimously on the answer to their question, the philosophers violently disagree. Within each philosophical school an answer may be readily forthcoming, but between the schools no common solution is available. Unlike the terms of geometry for which there is an almost universal definition, words like "reality" and "experience" have a bewildering variety of rules for their usage. Thus no neutral logical explication

of these concepts is possible and we cannot venture to explain them *per se.*

The only possible road to agreement in such cases is to restate the problem as one about language. If, instead of asking whether *reality* and *experience* are identical, we ask whether the *words* "reality" and "experience" are synonymous in our standard English, or, if not, what would be the consequences of using them as synonyms, we may get a scientific answer that compels assent. In some sentences (e.g., "He finally met the experience of love") "reality" could easily be regarded as synonymous with "experience" and could be substituted for it without changing the meaning or truth-value of the sentence; in other sentences (e.g., "He had the experience of omnipotence") the two words are clearly not synonymous and substituting "reality" would certainly change the meaning and probably the truth-value of the sentence. While these examples may be enough to show that the two words could not be regarded as *ipso facto* synonymous without seriously disrupting a small but important part of our communicative process, this is not the point at hand; the only concern here is to demonstrate the new kind of inquiry which comes with the linguistic approach to philosophical problems. Whereas the systems of realism and idealism would never by their rules permit their adherents to agree on whether or not *reality* and *experience* are identical, the scientific standards of a lexical study might well *force* agreement on what would happen were "reality" and "experience" to be made interchangeable words. The same kind of linguistic interpretation is possible with such stock metaphysical questions as to whether or not "substance underlies phenomena," or whether or not the universe is mental or a unity, or whether or not "good is convertible with being." In these cases the problem is whether or not the language rules do or should permit such predicates to be used with such subjects. The upshot is to recognize that philosophical problems are often a different kind of problem than they appear to be. They are commonly not so much problems of what is the case as problems of how best to describe what is the case. With this in mind, we shall turn to the history of philosophical semantics.

II. ORIGIN AND DEVELOPMENT OF LINGUISTIC PHILOSOPHY

The direct ancestors of modern linguistic philosophy were the medieval "nominalists" who held that logical classes or universals had no existence in their own right but were simply names for collections of particulars; there was no *dogness* or *doghood* apart from individual dogs. This view led to British empiricism which reduced our concepts of the world to groups of single sense experiences. The only way to cope with general or abstract terms and descriptions is to translate them into equivalent language about individual sense data. Thus the sensationalist philosophies of Locke, Hume and Mill gradually led to the attention to language which arose in the twentieth century. In the meanwhile there appeared on the continent certain movements favoring the scientific unity of all knowledge. Men like Auguste Comte and Ernst Mach not only sought to do

away with metaphysics but to bring all scientific discourse (ranging from mathematics to sociology) into one connected system.

This latter task required a reconciliation of the traditions of rationalism and sensory empiricism. Some way had to be devised to harmonize those statements used in mathematics and logic, based on chains of deductive reasoning, with the statements of descriptive studies based on observation of contingent sensory events—as both kinds of statements are necessary for science. In the twentieth century empiricism was joined for the first time with the logical and mathematical skills which the physical sciences had found so important. This union was the core of what came to be known as "logical positivism," or more appropriately, as "logical empiricism." The fusion still allowed language to contain two kinds of statements: those which are necessary and true independently of experience, like the theorems of mathematics or logic; and those which simply happen to be true on the basis of sense observation. But the two kinds of statements no longer compete with each other. The rational statements simply express the form of the discourse in which we agree to talk, while the factual statements, manifesting this prescribed form, give specific information about the empirical world.

The predisposition of sensory empiricism towards language analysis found its fulfillment in the logical positivist school. Since the time of Bacon, empiricists had tended to discount "reason" because their nominalist and sensory bias had made them unable to explain it. But now reason no longer had to be discounted because it could be explained as the symbolic ordering of knowledge gained and tested through observation. The old "laws of thought," which the rationalists (including Kant) had believed to follow from the nature of the "mind," could now be construed as "the rules of language," of which the principles of logic were simply the most exact and rigorous formulation. This allowed deductive thinking to be granted its essential role, but took all the mystery, all the other-worldliness, out of it. In a way the reconciliation was an assent to Kant's dictum that "concepts without percepts are empty and percepts without concepts are blind." But the *emptiness* of concepts is simply the confinement of formal logic to syntax, to the relations between symbols without regard for their designata, while the *blindness* of percepts is merely the inability of names or descriptions to yield intelligible and socialized assertions unless they are welded into some more or less coherent syntactical system.

With reason thus removed as a *rival* to factual truth, it became the aim of the early logical empiricists like Wittgenstein, Schlick and Carnap to reduce all synthetic knowledge to "atomic facts" based on sense experience. By eliminating from language all the emotive and pictorial terms and by restricting the purely logical terms to roles like those of the sentence connectives (e.g., "and," "or," "if . . . then"), it was hoped to limit the cognitive content of descriptive assertions to their reference to immediate observations. "Protocol statements" (e.g. "Red patch here now," "Pointer reading 5 at time t") were held to be the basis of all "mean-

ingful" discourse, aside from the purely analytic or tautologous truths of logic. While factually true statements were required to abide by the principles of logic (e.g., they could not violate the law of contradiction), they did not become factually true by virtue of their correct logical form. Both their truth and meaning rested on their relationship to the data outside of language.

The subsequent history of logical and linguistic philosophy has shown many divergences and wide departures from these early and somewhat narrow conceptions of the logical positivists. Perhaps the most important of these changes has been the abandonment of the prescription that a synthetic, descriptive statement must be empirically verifiable in order to be significant or meaningful. In 1938, Reichenbach pointed out that unless a highly probable proposition is regarded as true "there are no meaningful sentences at all left in science."[1] And von Mises in 1939 added that verifiability cannot be considered the sole criterion of a sentence's admissibility because "the question of verification depends upon the accepted definitions, and hence upon the linguistic rules."[2] Von Mises formulated his own criterion of the "meaningfulness" of a word or sentence to be its "connectibility" with the rest of the language, indicating the direction in which linguistic philosophy has been moving ever since. Wittgenstein, before he died, revised his notions to introduce the concept of the "language

[1] Hans Reichenbach, *Experience and Prediction* (Chicago: The University of Chicago Press, 1938), p. 189.

[2] Richard von Mises, *Positivism, A Study in Human Understanding* (Cambridge, Mass.: Harvard University Press, 1951), p. 116.

game" as the context in which an expression achieved cognitive significance, and in 1952, J. L. Evans, from the environment of the new British "analytic" school, concluded that to say "that either names or descriptions are meaningful is merely to talk about the rules governing their use."[3] All this trend has made meaning dependent more upon purely syntactical relations and independent of denotative and designatic reference, thus separating the problem of meaning from the problem of empirical truth or falsity. While there are several different branches of linguistic philosophy today, with considerable disagreement on many important questions, there is still a rough consensus that the analysis of language is the appropriate door through which any philosophical type of problem must be approached; and it is with this conclusion that we shall now examine the implications for education.

III. EDUCATIONAL IMPLICATIONS

In the new tradition of linguistic philosophy, the stress has been on critical and logical analysis of the various systems of discourse. Any invitation to build a new philosophic system has been flatly rejected, mainly on the grounds that any such system would either duplicate the descriptions already offered by the empirical sciences, or else go beyond the domain of science into an unproveable and meaningless metaphysics. Thus there stands the question as to how we are to find in such a

[3] J. L. Evans, "On Meaning and Verification," *Mind* (January, 1952), 10.

rebellious ferment any positive insights for a philosophy of education. It is only by examining the negative and critical contributions of such a philosophical trend that we can begin to find some directions for moving forward.

Fundamental to the didactic of linguistic philosophy has been the contention that philosophy and metaphysics cannot provide new knowledge in the sense that scientific findings provide new knowledge. Philosophy, it is asserted, can only linguistically organize and clarify knowledge already afforded by the sciences. Many metaphysical descriptions of the universe have tried to go beyond science—to a higher knowledge—only to yield statements which have played freely upon the metaphorical and connotative aspects of language and which are even theoretically unverifiable. That such descriptions have often altered human behavior, including the practice of the teacher, is not denied; but it is argued that such changes have come from the arousal of emotion and affect rather than from any scientific understanding, prediction or control. While the logical and linguistic philosopher is not blind to such potencies, any more than he is oblivious to the results of advertising, he tends to deplore any changes brought about in this way. Such altered behavior rests on temporary psychological satisfactions which escape the hard tests of experiment and fail to rely on knowledge in any scientific sense.

A second philosophical pretension which linguistic philosophy challenges is the belief in some kind of logical unity between the true and the good, either the conviction that values derive formally from facts or that facts derive formally from values. Each of these will be considered in turn.

It is an old habit of logical empiricism to deny that from true descriptions of the universe, moral imperatives can somehow be deduced. While human values are complex affairs, involving subtle, dynamic relationships between culture, psychology and language, they are still *phenomena* which in the last analysis are to be accepted or rejected by an act of choice. The direction of this choice is not logically implied, although it is usually pragmatically influenced, by either facts or reason. So far as ethics is the study of what *means* best attain certain ends, it belongs in the behavioral sciences, and with educational psychology or sociology. But when it tries to vindicate certain ends through the use of reason, it is simply working within a circular language system which assumes what it means to prove, and whose necessary axioms and rules are accepted dogmatically. The historic Platonic aim to accredit ultimate goals by sheer cognition is thus considered an impossible quest. The most frightening and compelling description of a jealous and exacting deity would, *even if true,* not prove that it was *right* or *good* to obey his will, unless one means by "right" or "good" simply "to obey his will," in which case the argument would be trivial or tautologous and reduce morality to plain respect for naked force. There is no way in which a man can deeply penetrate the meaning of an "is" to arrive at a logical "ought." From this viewpoint, no philosophy or science is allowed to *prescribe* the final objec-

tives of society or the school on the sole basis of its ability to *describe* nature, man or the educational process.

On the other hand, it is equally important to the positivistic position to deny that facts somehow depend on values. Scientific truth is quite independent of other kinds of personal or social goods. Operationally speaking, this does not mean that the moralist or educator should not, in the pursuit of his special ethical ends, *use* true descriptions of certain relevant phenomena. But while such descriptions may be *selected* to serve certain values, they are definitely not to be *created* by such values. It is not the role of either the philosopher or the scientist to report the world in such a way as to make his values seem more palatable or easily attainable. Scientific empiricism and linguistic philosophy take a firm stand here because one of their own primary values requires the avoidance of wishful thinking regardless of how well it might promote other (political, cultural, aesthetic) values a person may also hold. Part of the scientific humanist morality demands that science, whatever the biases and preconceptions on which it may rest itself, remain immune from the influence of non-scientific biases and preconceptions. In this respect, one must also reject the popular belief that "frames of reference," "interpretations," "perspectives," and "points of view" largely determine what is true and false. As Dennes has said, "It is mainly the romantic tradition in philosophy, with its various derivatives, such as mentalism, egoism, pragmatism, Marxism (in part) and the present fashionable so-called sociology of knowledge"[4] which has lent weight to this way of thinking. The question is vital to education. However estimable it is to have empathy, share experiences and see the other fellow's viewpoint, it would be educationally fatal to tolerate the possibility that two ultimately contradicting statements can both be equally "true." In fact, the respect for a rival viewpoint can have democratic significance only in the humble recognition that its difference from one's own outlook still remains to be resolved by an experimental test whose results *both* parties agree in advance to accept. The "social contract" to determine truth in a way which transcends the interests and prejudices of any individual or group is as basic to the democratic process as it is to the community of science.

This logical independence between fact and value judgments, so strongly emphasized in the modern positivist tradition, is also reflected in the ordinary language rules by which we determine what is true and what is good. The ascertainment of fact is normally represented as an externalized problem, decided by an appeal to some "court" independent of the individual, whether it be the authority of the senses, an expert or a scripture. The effort to judge a statement's truth-value requires an initial decision to play and abide by the rules of some publicly accepted epistemological game in which a subsequent coercive experience, like the cards dealt to one's hand, is awaited to give the specific answer. In our west-

[4] William R. Dennes, "Interpretation," *Meaning and Interpretation* (Berkeley and Los Angeles: University of California Press, 1950), p. 10.

ern world, on the other hand, determining what to call "good" has become more and more of an internalized problem, calling for a private intuition, a spiritual resolve, a search within. In times of vast moral integration, such as the medieval period, values were indeed *externalized,* much as scientific truth is today. But the deep effects of Protestant and romantic individualism have gradually freed the super-ego from both the burdens and protections of such moral universalism, at the same time that the industrial revolution was requiring the ego to be bound more and more by a scientific universalism. The change has been to personalize values and socialize truth.

The issue has been confused by philosophy, of course. At one extreme we have been influenced by Platonism which, using a geometrical model, would reduce virtue to knowledge and bind morality in advance to accept the deductions of a rigidly formalized system of inquiry, thus underwriting the belief in moral absolutes. But at the other end, modern pragmatism has tried to reverse this relationship and make truth itself a function of our operating values which are seen to shift so much with the exigencies of living. In many spots our common language resists each of these interpretations. We *"find"* truth," but we *"do"* good"; we *"study"* facts," but we *"act"* in the right"; we *"seek"* information," but we *"show"* honor"; we *"retain"* knowledge," but we *"maintain"* virtue." These idioms reveal an objective pursuit of facts and a subjective pursuit of values. While giving scant support to the notion that descriptive and normative judgments are logically connected, our everyday speech, does, on the other hand, recognize a close psychological and social relationship between the two.

The behavioral relationship between the true and the good involves the pragmatic dimension of language, the way it fits as an *event* into the other events of human experience. The linguistic philosopher, in his concern with the formal (syntactical and designatic) dimensions of language, has usually left the study of the pragmatic dimension to the scientist, or at least to the philosophical pragmatist, whose language he is quite willing to accept in this sphere. There have been recent indications that some of the British analytic philosophers are thinking more and more like pragmatists, however, and in their examination of the actual use of language have seen that not only fact-speech and value-speech functionally interact while maintaining a logical separation, but that what happens in language generally is interdependent with psychological and biological patterns. To use Wittgenstein's favorite analogy, to understand two chess players in action requires a *joint* explanation in terms of two quite different but not incompatible systems. One kind is purely formal, e.g. move p forestalls move q, and permits moves r, s and t to bring checkmate. The other kind is purely behavioral, e.g. player A has agoraphobia which causes him to prefer corner play and will lead him to make move p. To make the best *de facto* prediction of the outcome of the game, one would need *both* kinds of discourse. Such a combination would then consist of alternating sequences of the formal and behavioral languages; each logical statement of the situation on the chess

board would evoke a certain relevant psychological statement, and *vice-versa*. But the logical statements about the game would not change the linguistic rules of the psychological statements (the laws of psychology), and the psychological statements about the players would not change the linguistic rules of the chess-statements (the laws of chess). The determination of human behavior by language rules (or systems of ideas if you will) is equally necessary to grant, provided their application is interwoven with statements of other determinants such as biological, economic and psychological. What happens to a person when he becomes a Communist, for example, can only be predicted by knowing both the Marxian dialectic *and* the drives, conditionings, cues, etc. of the particular individual. With agreement on this point, formal, philosophical semantics can welcome the contributions both of pragmatist philosophy and the behavioral sciences.

While most of the positive applications of the study of symbolism to education have been advanced from the camp of "behavioral semantics," especially the general semantics movement of Korzybski and Hayakawa, there are still certain behavioral and attitudinal components of modern linguistic philosophy which can have significant educational consequences. The teacher influenced by linguistic philosophy will be better equipped to improve the clarity of student vision in respect to discourse. He will be ready to stress the distinction, for example, between a statement and feelings about a statement. A student who learns for the first time that many of America's wars were conditioned and even precipitated by "selfish" economic interests may well have an emotional reaction that will lead him falsely to deny that powerful ethical motives were also often involved. The teacher in such an instance would be prone to encourage that momentary withholding of affect so essential to educational maturity in this age of charged language. His students may become more able to accept and understand ideological, religious and attitudinal differences without making cognitive confusions. By recognizing the inescapable temporal and tentative quality of almost all language, both teacher and student should adjust better to the role of cooperative inquirers rather than of competitors in feeling.

In the last analysis, however, modern philosophical semantics cannot of itself be a great affirmative force in shaping the goals and methods of the school. Because it does not believe that mere philosophy can contribute knowledge, what it can do is to clear the decks for a full, unbiased appreciation of the behavioral sciences. In this way, it is compelled, for example, to give much attention to the theories of John Dewey, whose arm-chair speculations about the learning process—the use of direct experience, motivation, problem-solving situations, transfer, collateral learning, and environmental and social interaction—have received such considerable confirmation from independent psychological researches, even to the point that many of his "methods" have been endorsed by rival educational philosophers. But in its acceptance of experimentalist insights, the linguistic philosopher will not accept the experimentalist's generalized philosophic descriptions of nature, man or experience. For him such descriptions are hortatory, and not based upon the cautious, sober kind of reflection which Dewey used in his evaluation of other points of view. Instead the question will be: what scientific truths will be especially helpful in getting the school to modify student behavior in whatever direction is considered desirable?

∽

Part IV

From Theory to Practice

The Problem of Relating Theory to Practice

Imitating John Dos Pasos, a commentator on the 1950's might begin *U.S.A. Revisited* with the following collection of titles and text:

NEWSREEL I

This is the dead land
This is the cactus land

EDUCATIONAL WASTELANDS: THE RETREAT FROM LEARNING IN OUR PUBLIC SCHOOLS

Americans make a distinction, however, between the school learning which increases a man's earning power and the newfangled, dangerous ideas which unsettle his thinking. "Education spoils a good field hand."
. . . There's a CRISIS BEFORE US, a CRISIS IN EDUCATION. *Much of the elementary and secondary schooling is little more than assemblyline processing with mechanized teaching methods and an intellectual level rarely rising above mediocrity.* It's a CRISIS IN AMERICAN HIGH SCHOOLS, A CRISIS OF PURPOSE.

QUACKERY IN THE PUBLIC SCHOOLS

The New Education, it seems is living, vital, life-related, dynamic, organic, bold, gripping, throbbing, creative, adventurous, rich, significant, forward-looking, thrilling, constructive, child-centered, onward-going, growth oriented, and, of course, democratic, with the variant, democratizing. The Old Education was dead, passive, meager, traditional, abortive, impotent, static, retrogressive, subject-centered, moribund, inorganic, stale, flat, backward-looking, autocratic, Prussian, Alexandrian, bookish, and/on my oath/intellectualized. HARD EDUCATION OR SOFT. WE ARE LESS EDUCATED THAN FIFTY YEARS AGO. EDUCATION FOR ILLITERACY.

351

YOUR CHILD IS THEIR TARGET

LETS' STOP WASTING OUR GREATEST RESOURCE
making a
NATION OF ADVANCED PLUMBERS

European schools are neither social clubs nor finishing schools. Their objectives are limited and clearly defined: They seek to equip the child with all the intellectual tools he can handle: they nourish his mind with as much general culture as he can absorb; and they give his body all the exercise it can take. BACK TO THE THREE R's. This is the WAY OUT OF THE BLACKBOARD JUNGLE.

> And the wind shifts
> and the dust on a doorsill shifts
> and even the writing of the rat footprints
> tells us nothing, nothing at all
> about the greatest city, the greatest nation
> where the strong men listened
> and the women warbled: Nothing like us ever was.

I

The controversy over public school practices and the theories which strive to give them direction achieves high drama. How much sense it makes is another question.

Throughout the development of American education the question of how ideas should be carried into action in the schools has been a heated subject. Like sun spots it recurs systematically and interrupts the normal lines of communication. In the argument about the proper relationship of theory to practice, the constancy of the rhetoric often obscures the fact that the public schools have undergone a profound metamorphosis. If the nature of this change were understood by many critics then less nonsense might be written about what's wrong with the schools today, and how they aren't doing as well now as they did in the critics' earlier generation. Often, when the changes that have taken place in American society concerning the nature and function of public education are ignored, critics conclude that a given conception of education can be examined without considering the problems which provoked it. In such a-historical argument the actual connection between theory and practice is lost, and discussion, no matter how logically precise, remains sterile.

As the phrase "the theory-practice problem" indicates there are two dimensions to the problem: the theoretical and the practical. The former dimension involves the problem of relating educational philosophy to educational practice, or the logical methodology of moving from abstract philosophical statements to concrete educational practices. The latter dimension involves an historical examination of how theories have in fact been connected to practice, or how the changing socio-educational scene has influenced school theories and practices.

The following pages are devoted to a brief review of these two dimensions of the problem and, following this, Part IV concludes with a series of essays in which the authors—using different techniques and subject matters —"use" educational theory to examine educational practices.

"THEORETICAL" DIMENSIONS OF THE THEORY-PRACTICE PROBLEM

There is a widespread assumption that an organic connection exists between formal philosophy, on the one hand, and specific educational practices on the other hand, such that it can be said philosophy provides directives for the conduct of education. Indeed, this is the very assumption that justifies the teaching of courses in philosophy of education.

Implicit in the following remarks is the prior assumption that philosophy of education is neither a discipline *sui generis*[1] nor merely the semi-intellectual hand-maiden of general philosophy,[2] and on that basis the analysis which follows attempts to demonstrate three things:

1. That the connection between formal philosophy and educational practice is not adequately explained or formalized by the logical connective designated by the term "strict implication"
2. That the connection between formal philosophy and educational practice is not adequately explained or formalized by the synthetic connective designated by the term "empirical implication"
3. That if there is an organic connection between formal philosophy and educational practice, it may be most adequately explained and formalized by a psychological connective designated by the term "pragmatic implication"

By way of nomenclature, for purposes of labeling the area of inquiry, let it arbitrarily be defined as "the problem of the educational implication." The

[1] Cf. Foster McMurray, "Preface to an Autonomous Discipline of Education," *Educational Theory* (July, 1955), 129–140.

[2] "The philosophy of education is not a poor relation of general philosophy even though it is often so treated. . . . It is ultimately the most significant phase of philosophy." John Dewey, *Problems of Men* (New York: Philosophical Library, Inc., 1946), p. 165.

problem, of course, is to ascertain the precise nature of the "educational implication," or the rules of connection by which we can justifiably assert that a given philosophic position somehow involves a given educational activity. Put simply, what is the relationship of theory to practice in education, and how can this relationship be formalized?

II

Joe R. Burnett put the question in this way: *"Do* formal philosophies have logical implications for educational theory and practice?"[3] In an unusually competent analysis he identified three possible meanings of the term "logical implication," which he called (1) the "lay implication," (2) the "formal implication," and (3) the "situational implication." The lay conception which ". . . mistakenly assumes that formal philosophies are, *in and of themselves,* rich with implications for specific (educational) practices" is promptly and correctly dismissed as nonsense. Then, having dismissed the lay view as following no reasonable rules of inference, Burnett proceeded to answer his question in the affirmative, saying:

> [Yes,] one can utilize formal philosophy . . . in order to derive logical implications for educational theory and practice; . . . [but only] by conceiving "logical implication" in a . . . "situational" [manner].[4]

It is certainly correct to say that whatever connections are to be made between philosophy and education will be made in that type of experiential matrix which Burnett, following Dewey, has called "situational." But it is tautological that any and all kinds of connections are situational, and it is manifestly evident that there are different kinds of situations and situational connections. By redefining the normal meaning of "logical implication" so that "logical" means "situational," Burnett asserts that it can be said that formal philosophy does hold logical implications for educational practice. Yet, with due respect for his scholarly analysis—and that is not a gratuitous compliment or condemnation by faint praise, for Burnett had the courage

---

[3] Joe R. Burnett, "Some Observations on the Logical Implications of Philosophic Theory for Educational Theory and Practice," *Proceedings of the Fourteenth Annual Meeting of the Philosophy of Education Society* (Lawrence, Kansas: University of Kansas Press, 1958), p. 51. Also see: Hobert W. Burns, "The Logic of the Educational Implication," *Proceedings of the Sixteenth Annual Meeting of the Philosophy of Education Society,* ed. Ernest E. Bayles (Lawrence, Kansas: University of Kansas Press, 1960), pp. 49–55; Joe R. Burnett, "An Analysis of Some Philosophical and Theological Approaches to the Formation of Educational Theory and Practice," *Proceedings of the Seventeenth Annual Meeting of the Philosophy of Education Society,* ed. Robert E. Mason (Syracuse University, The Philosophy of Education Society, 1961), pp. 7–30; and Van Cleve Morris, "The Problem of Application," *Philosophy and the American School* (Boston: Houghton Mifflin Co., 1961), pp. 81–83.

[4] *Ibid.*

and the intellect to tackle a problem philosophers of education have long known about but ignored (for complex philosophical problems evade effective analysis much less often than philosophers evade complex philosophical problems)—it does seem that he has defined the problem away rather than solved it.

The problem of the "educational implication" is not yet solved, for it is not at all clear what *kind* of connection it is that might hold between formal philosophy and educational practice; and certainly it is not clear what is to be meant by the word "implication" when it is asserted that philosophy contains implications for educational behavior.

Some philosophers of education have used the term "logical implication" rather loosely, apparently equating it with the word "assumption." An example of this kind of loose usage is found when the argument is made that metaphysical or epistemological positions contain in themselves certain specific directives for education, and that these differing philosophic positions will produce differing educational consequences. But all too often, as Edward Reisner pointed out years ago,

> The presumption has been too easily accepted that there is a unitary correspondence between a metaphysical principle and a philosophy of education which might be thought of as logically derivable from it . . . (but) such a unitary relationship cannot be substantiated, and . . . from a given metaphysical core a considerable variety of educational philosophies may be and actually has been developed.[5]

(Note that Reisner does not deny the existence of such a correspondence or connection, but only that it is so vague as to permit many and conflicting "implications" from a given set of metaphysical principles. He thus makes the implicit assumption that formal philosophy and educational practice are, in some way, related—the very view which is basic to the intellectual justification of some philosophies of education.)

It is possible, of course, to declare that there is a unitary correspondence between some metaphysical or epistemological principle which is part of a formal philosophy and some philosophy of education, and a corresponding relationship between that metaphysically derived philosophy of education and some specific set of educational practices; in this way it might be said that formal philosophy provides logical implications for the practice of education. The principle of free speech permits such declarations, but the principle of clear speech indicates that to use the term "logical implication" in such a manner is to use the term rather loosely—so loosely, in fact, that the meaning of the term "logical implication" becomes equivalent to the meaning of the

[5] Edward Reisner, "Philosophy and Science in the Western World; A Historical Overview," *Philosophies of Education,* ed. Nelson B. Henry (Chicago: The University of Chicago Press, 1942), p. 32.

word "assumption." Surely an intuitive sense of logic suggests a meaning much stronger than "assumed connection" by "logical implication."

When it is said that "P implies Q," it is meant that one is connected to the other in some *necessary* manner, for it would be a rather useless kind of implication that would permit willful, capricious connections to be made between formal philosophy and educational practice. (For purposes of this essay let "P" stand for some abstract philosophic position, and "Q" for some concrete educational consequent which is said to follow from "P.") By "P implies Q" is meant that one presupposes the other, where the presupposition is characterized by some sense of necessity, some sense of dependency. Thus, "implication," means something like "necessary presupposition" or "dependent condition." But in what sense are implications necessary connections? In what sense are they dependent conditionals? In what sense are they presuppositional?

III

In one sense of "presupposition"—a sense that is characterized by necessity and dependence—it might be said that being human necessarily implies the possession of certain rational faculties and a soul; or that being a fully-licensed physician necessarily implies that the holder of the license is a doctor of medicine; or that being a "tough-minded" pragmatist necessarily implies that one is an empiricist. In these examples the word "implies" means "necessary condition"; it means that the fulfillment of one condition is dependent upon the fulfillment of the other condition.

To say in this sense that "P implies Q" is to say that P necessarily presupposes Q, or that P is dependent upon Q; and therefore, by rule of tautology, if not Q then not P. Thus, if a featherless biped did not possess some set of rational facilities and a soul, he could not possibly be human; if an individual did not possess a doctorate in medicine, he could not possibly be a fully-licensed physician; if an individual were not an empiricist, he could not possibly be a "tough-minded" pragmatist.

Put otherwise, the meaning of the word "implication" in this usage is that the denial of Q is sufficient ground to deny P, but at the same time the affirmation of Q cannot justify the affirmations of P. To return to the examples for clarification, the possession of rational faculties and a soul does not necessarily presuppose or require that their owner be human—he may be an angel (the editors are assuming angels have souls and are rational); nor does the possession of a doctorate in medicine necessarily presuppose that its holder is a fully-licensed physician—he may be an interne; nor does the fact that an individual is an empiricist necessarily presuppose that he is a pragmatist—he may be a positivist.

In this first possible meaning of the word "implication," therefore, it would be erroneous to say that the relationship of a presupposition to those conditions which somehow rest upon it is the relationship of premise to conclusion. Rather it is the consequent which is presupposed by the premise, and the premise cannot be affirmed unless the consequent is valid. In this usage, therefore, the necessity and the dependency in the concept of the term "educational implication" would be one of formal logic, it would be strictly logical.

Yet, it cannot be defensibly maintained that the connection between philosophy and educational practice meets the requirements of formal logic, as this first possible meaning of "educational implication" would suggest, because *there is simply no formal way by which the philosopher of education can logically deduce specific educational practices from metaphysical, epistemological, or axiological premises.*[6]

The import of this strikes deeply into the thought of those who have maintained that a certain set of educational practices are logically derivable from a given philosophy.[7] There may well be some kind of organic connection between philosophy as abstraction and education as practical, but that connection is not logical. At the juncture it might be well to repeat the words of Sidney Hook:

[6] Cf. Burnett, "An Analysis . . . ," p. 11.

[7] This point has practical as well as theoretical import, since critics and defenders of contemporary education have often assumed, conveniently, that educational practices are logically dependent upon some particular philosophy. It is generally assumed, for instance, that specific educational methods and curricula logically depend upon a specific educational philosophy; or more particularly, that those practices called "progressive education" logically presuppose the acceptance or validity of pragmatism.

This type of illogic has been illustrated, in a classic manner, by Albert Lynd, who insists that "progressivist methods [cannot] stand alone . . . without reference to Deweyan pragmatism [since] progressivism is logically consistent with instrumentalism philosophy right down the line" (Albert Lynd, "Who Wants Progressive Education?," *The Atlantic Monthly,* CXCI [April, 1953], 35).

Frederick C. Breed, although considerably more sophisticated in matters philosophic than is Lynd, nevertheless believes that at least some metaphysical principles have applicability to education. He says, ". . . to say that the neo-Thomists are deceiving themselves in linking their pattern for education with the philosophy of Aristotle and St. Thomas Aquinas, or that Dewey's educational progressivism has no necessary connection with his instrumentalism, seems like a sadly erroneous interpretation. [Especially in the case of Dewey] who, as is well known, takes a position directly opposed . . ." (Frederick C. Breed, "A Realistic View of Education," *Twentieth Century Education* ed. P. F. Valentine. [New York: Philosophical Library, Inc., 1946], p. 67).

But Sidney Hook, refuting this type of argument, insists that "Although there is an organic connection in Dewey's own thinking between his philosophical ideas and his educational proposals, they are not related as logical premise to logical conclusion" (Sidney Hook, *Modern Education and Its Critics* [Oneonta, N.Y.: American Association of Colleges for Teacher Education, 1954], p. 7).

There is a great deal of nonsense talked about philosophy of education. This is particularly true of claims that a metaphysical or epistemological position has logical implications for educational theory and practice . . . (thus) To encourage philosophers . . . "to derive (a philosophy of education) from some philosophic position such as Idealism, Realism, Thomism, Pragmatism or Existentialism" is to encourage them to perpetrate garrulous absurdities.[8]

IV

Another kind of connection is suggested when it is said, for example, that mastery of symbolic logic implies mastery of Aristotelian logic; or that the forthcoming trip to the moon implies the techniques of inertial navigation; or that the discovery of physical law presupposes the invention of mathematics. But in the usage indicated by these examples, as contrasted with the earlier usage, the words "implies" and "presupposes" do not seem to involve a necessary connection.

This second type of connection, this second possible meaning of the word "implication," is uniquely different from the strictly logical sense for, in this terminology, it might actually be possible to master symbolic logic without mastery of Aristotelian logic; it might actually be possible to get to the moon without using the techniques of inertial navigation; or it might actually be possible to ascertain lawful relationships among physical phenomena without the use of mathematics. That is, these are empirical possibilities.

To use the word "implication" in this way is to say that when "P implies Q" we do not mean the denial of Q necessarily requires the denial of P. There is no necessarily logical, or logically necessary, connection between P and Q since any possible connection is a question of fact, not logic. All that could be meant by the denial of Q, in this usage, is that if Q is denied that its hypothetical connection with P is more difficult to establish or justify; Q, in this case, is not a necessary condition for P, since P might be valid even though Q is not.

It cannot be said, consequently, that formal philosophy is connected to educational practice in this sense of the term "educational implication"; that is it cannot be said without considerably weakening the criterion of necessity, for one might thus be forced to say that any or all educational practices could be valid while any or all philosophy is unnecessary to guide the conduct of the educational enterprise. This might be the case, of course, but it seems unwise to define the "educational implication" in this way since such a definition would justify the complete divorce of educational theory from practice.

[8] Sidney Hook, "Note on a Philosophy of Education," *Harvard Educational Review*, XXVI (Spring, 1956), 145, 148.

Equally important, if the "educational implication" is not characterized by some quality of necessity, then it could be concluded that philosophy plays no directive role in education; and then educators must find some other source of educational directives, some other justifying source for educational practices.

Yet, to affirm that philosophy plays no such guiding role—to assert, for instance, that the behavioral sciences are the only proper source from which the ends and means of education can come—does not solve the problem of the "educational implication" at all: the term "philosophy" would merely be replaced by the term "behavioral science" as the directive antecedent in the "educational implication," while "educational practice" would remain the consequent. The problem of identifying and formalizing the nature of the connective holding between antecedent and consequent would still constitute the problem of the "educational implication."

The same analysis, therefore, which might reveal that philosophy is not necessarily connected to educational practice would, no doubt, also reveal that the behavioral sciences are not necessarily connected to educational practice.[9] This is only to say that, if it is insisted upon defining the "educational implication" as being a necessary connection, it apparently makes little difference which antecedently directive body of subject matter one tries to connect up to educational practices.

This second possible meaning of "educational implication," then, also falls short of explaining and formalizing the kind of connection that supposedly exists between formal philosophy and educational practice.

What is clear to this point is that the complexities of the concept of the "educational implication" cannot be completely contained or clarified in terms of strict, logical implication or the empirical, synthetic implication, as outlined earlier.

What seems to be required is a definition of the term "implication" such that it will be possible to make inferences not only from proposition to proposition, but from actions and beliefs as well. In short, what seems to be needed to make the concept of the "educational implication" much more intelligible than it is now is some set of rules for non-symbolic implication.

In addition there is the further difficulty that, since education is admittedly a moral affair, many of the assertions, actions, and beliefs about education are normative and have an "ought" or "should" dimension about

[9] The form of the argument is quite justifiable, although the content is of course asinine: quite obviously the behavioral sciences, like philosophy, play an important role in the conduct of education. Yet, as is noted, the form is valid: what are the rules of inference by which we can defensibly assert that philosophy or the behavioral sciences contain or entail directives for educational practice? The answer to that question would constitute a solution to the problem of the "educational implication."

them. That fact alone could unendingly complicate the analysis, for it might well mean that the educational philosopher, in order to solve the problem of the "educational implication," may have to find some rule of inference by which it will be possible to move from the descriptive to the normative and vice versa—he may have to answer the question "how many philosophic is's make an educational ought," and then show how he got his answer. This in itself demonstrates the need for a "new" logic in educational philosophy, or at least a new approach to educational problems with a logical dimension. Since many educational statements are emotive or normative they simply cannot be fed into a two-valued or multivalued logical mill which defines all propositions as being analytic or synthetic or nonsense, or as being true or false—for what does it mean to say that a normative statement is false?

V

A third kind of connection is more psychological than logical, as was the first, or factual, as was the second. To say, for example, that behavior is purposive (rather than random) is to say that a person does certain things because he believes certain things; it is to say that he behaves in a certain way because he has a certain set of beliefs; it is to say that he acts in some manner because he believes his act will have as its consequent some different empirical condition than now exists. In this third possible meaning of the word "implication" the beliefs of an individual are the causal conditions of his actions; in this sense his actions are implied by his beliefs, and his beliefs are to be inferred from his actions.

This is not to suggest that ideas or ideologies, considered apart from the individuals who have them or believe them, or considered apart from the empirical conditions required for their use, operate as causal conditions or agents. That would be to commit the error which Reisner pointed out. However, as Ernest Nagel says

. . . only if one abandons all normal canons of evidence and ignores well-established empirical findings, can one deny that the beliefs men hold, or the reasons men advance for what they do and profess, often are crucial determining factors . . .[10]

By way of illustrating this "psychological" kind of implication, imagine Sherlock Holmes interrogating a witness to a crime. The fact that Holmes questions, examines, cross-questions and cross-examines his witness clearly implies that Holmes believes the witness may be able to produce some clue which would solve the mystery at hand. The implication here is *not* logical in the sense of strict implication nor is it empirical in the synthetic sense; it

[10] Ernest Nagel, *Liberalism and Intelligence* (Bennington, Vt.: Bennington College), p. 1. Fourth John Dewey Memorial Lecture, June 10, 1957.

is *psychological*. This belief of Holmes, this psychological presupposition, not only explains his behavior to some extent but is the causal condition of his behavior; it is a necessary condition, for if he did not believe that his witness could possibly produce some relevant information about the crime, Holmes simply wouldn't bother to interrogate him.

The necessity in this type of "implication" is psychological, not logical (although it is consistent) nor material (although it is factual); the consistency is measured not in terms of formal, sentential rules of inference, but pragmatically—in terms of human behavior, in terms of means-ending.

In this usage, the meaning of "educational implication" is that particular educational practices are presupposed by particular philosophic beliefs about the nature of education or man, else those educational practices would be meaningless and irrational. In this way a necessary connection may be seen to exist between philosophy and educational practice. It is important to note that these educational practices are not logically implied by philosophy, nor are they logically implied by one's belief in a philosophy; rather they are in some manner *psycho*logically implied in a pragmatic means-ending sense. That is what is meant when it is suggested that this kind of "educational implication" is pragmatic.

To say, then, that philosophy implies educational practices is to say that an educator follows some set of educational procedures because he believes certain things about the universe and man; if he believed other things then, to be psychologically consistent, he would follow other practices. Perhaps this type of connection is one defensible explanation of the nature and function of the "educational implication."

Some will object, of course, that there is no room in logical theory for such things as "psychological implication," "non-symbolic implication," or "normative propositions." Yet these critics could not deny Nagel's assertation that ". . . considerable difference exists as to the scope of logical theory and as to which concepts and principles properly belong to logic."[11] To restrict logical theory to metalinguistics or analysis of statements in an object language seems unnecessarily to foreshorten the power of analysis. "Logic," as Dewey reminded us more than a quarter of a century ago, "can hardly admit that it is concerned only with objects having one special mode of production and existence, and yet claim universality."[12] Flowing from this simple contradiction pointed out by Dewey is the fact that the neglect of normative or psychological considerations in contemporary logical theory

---

[11] Ernest Nagel, "Logic Without Ontology," *Readings in Philosophical Analysis,* ed. Herbert Feigl and Wilfrid Sellars (New York: Appleton-Century-Crofts, Inc., 1949), p. 203.

[12] John Dewey, *Philosophy and Civilization* (New York: Minton, Balch and Co., 1931), p. 94.

leaves thought in such areas as education without any logical control or status at all; it is to deny that education has any logical foundation—or, at least, none until it is brought into line with preconceived logical categories, categories which rob education of its distinctive moral meaning.

These are important considerations which fall within the jurisdiction of the problem of the "educational implication," but within the scope of the editors' present essay there is time only to outline a possible manner in which the psychological implication, the "educational implication," might be formalized.

VI

Following the lead of Bar-Hillel,[13] Grant,[14] and Strawson,[15] it is possible to identify at least two types of non-symbolic or psychological implications. (From this point on, the term "pragmatic implication" is used to designate these concepts.) The first involves implications of actions, the second involves implications of belief.

By way of illustrating the first type of pragmatic implication, it is easily seen that the act of selling a new site to a school board implies the proposition that the vender owns the parcel to be transferred; or that a teacher's act in accepting an administrator's offer of a contract implies the proposition that there is an opening in the school district; or that the act of placing a student in a "gifted class" implies the propositions that some instrument exists by which to judge giftedness and that the child has been evaluated and found to meet the requirements of the criterion. In these examples of pragmatic implication language is normally used, since man is a linguistic animal, but it is not strictly necessary and in that sense this kind of pragmatic implication could be called non-symbolic.

A sustained analysis of this first mode of pragmatic implication will reveal some imperfections, but as a general rule the connection that holds between such actions and the propositions they imply can, for now, be expressed thus: *the propositions implied by an action are those which are logically entailed by those other propositions which correctly describe the action.* The meaning of this general rule is simply that if the propositions thus implied by actions are not true, then the actions simply could not be acts of selling, contracting, or evaluating. (Note the influence of *modus tollendo tollens* upon the general rule.) Put otherwise, pragmatic implica-

[13] Yehoshua Bar-Hillel, "Analysis of 'Correct' Language," *Mind,* LV (October, 1946), 328–340.

[14] C. K. Grant, "Pragmatic Implication," *Philosophy,* XXXIII (October, 1958), 303–324.

[15] P. F. Strawson, "On Referring," *Mind,* LIX (July, 1950), 320–344. The analysis in Part VI draws heavily on these and other sources; this reliance is evident and acknowledged.

tions of actions may be defined thus: An act A implies a proposition p if and only if the proposition "person X is performing act A" itself entails p. This type of pragmatic implication is therefore defined in terms of entailment.

By way of illustrating the second type of pragmatic implication, imagine a high-school disciplinarian interrogating an unruly pupil about some missing school property. On the basis of his actions we can infer three sets, or kinds, of propositions: (1) psychological propositions about the beliefs and anticipations of the actor, (2) empirical propositions about the antecedents and consequents of the act, and (3) conditional propositions about the empirical conditions needed if the intended consequences of the act are to be realized.

For instance, we might (1) infer the psychological propositions that "The disciplinarian believes the pupil has information about the crime" and "The disciplinarian anticipates (hopes) his interrogation will cause the pupil to reveal this information"; we might (2) infer the empirical propositions that "A school rule has been violated" and "The disciplinarian is trying to solve the mystery," or "The pupil will reveal his information"; we might (3) infer the conditional propositions "If the pupil was witness or participant, he has information about the crime" and "if the disciplinarian is to solve the puzzle, he must have this information."

As a general rule, therefore, acts of this type always imply psychological propositions about the actor's beliefs, empirical propositions about the "reason for" or "point of" the act, and conditional propositions about the empirical conditions which must obtain if the desired or probable outcome of the act is to be realized. It is true, of course, that this type of pragmatic implication—in contrast to the first type—cannot be defined in terms of logical entailment. That is, the sets of propositions labeled "psychological," "empirical," and "conditional" are not logical consequents of another proposition which might accurately assert that an act A is being performed. Thus, rather than arrive at these three sets of propositions through logical deduction or empirical inference, they are arrived at pragmatically—that is, they are inferences based on (1) what prior experience has shown to be the natural consequences of similar acts and (2) knowledge of the actor's purposes and the situation in which he acts.

This is a clear admission that pragmatic inference makes sense only with reference to intentional actions, to actions that are intended to bring about a certain and specifiable state of affairs; it is a clear admission that pragmatic inferences are means-end inferences because they relate human purposes with ends that are sought or intended by the actor. Pragmatic implication, then, is dependent upon purposive action, and this invariably involves the making of means-ends judgments. Once an action is classified as purposive it is thereby related to its end and cannot be taken out of relation or reference to that end. Thus we see that the meaning of the general rule governing propositions pragmatically implied from an act is that *such propositions come to be the conditions of rational action in that specific situation;* or, put in terms of *tollendo tollens* again, if these propositions are false then the act itself is pointless.

Pragmatic implication, in sum, is based on the assumption of rational action; that is, on the assumption that people usually intend the most probable consequences of their actions. It is obvious, of course, that quite often an actor's intended consequence, or what he took to be the probable consequence, does not follow from his act (who has not made a mistake, for example?); but this fact of error in no way injures the principle of rational action.

Any interested observer of the educational scene is entitled to ask of a teacher "Why did you do that?" when, for instance, she is observed making a homework assignment which involves memorization of Euclidian postulates. This is a request for information in the sense that one wants to know her "reason for" or the "point of" that particular act. If she responds, "I don't know," or if she can't or won't supply an answer to the question concerning the reason for her behavior, one is entitled by definition to declare her action "irrational," "meaningless," or "pointless"—and this would contravene the principle of rational action and therefore make it impossible to find pragmatic implications of her action. But if, as might more reasonably be expected, she responds by saying, "Well, I did that because . . . ," then it is noted at once that she is means-ending or identifying what she takes to be the intended (therefore, desired and probable consequences of her act).

This assumption of rational action is necessary if one expects to understand and explain human behavior; it is an assumption not uniquely different from Locke's statement that "No man ever sets himself about anything but upon some view or other, which serves him for a reason for what he does . . ."[16]

(For analytical philosophers, who may be skeptical about basing a solution to the problem of the "educational implication" upon a more generic pragmatic implication that draws its validity from the assumption of rational action, a reference to game theory might make them more comfortable. That is to say, the assumption of rational action is most useful, as well as necessary, when one tries to analyze situations of incomplete or imperfect

[16] John Locke, "Of the Conduct of the Understanding" *The Works of John Locke,* 9th ed. (London: [printed by and] for T. Longman, B. Law and Son, J. Johnson *et al.,* 1794), Vol. II, p. 323.

information. Thus the game theory concepts of Von Neumann and Morgenstern, being attempts to explain one dimension of human behavior, were based on the assumption of rational action, as their "Minimax Principle" illustrates. The only catch, of course, is whether or not the assumption of rational action is itself a rational action.)

The concept of the pragmatic implication outlined in these pages may be a modest start toward the solution of the problem of the "educational implication."

VII

If the foregoing analysis has shown anything at all, one of those things is that the "educational implication" has not only its obvious logical dimension, but a troublesome axiological and ontological dimension as well.

The axiological dimension, as noted earlier, is that education is inescapably moral, normative, and value laden: hence the solution of the problem of the "educational implication" will have to incorporate a satisfactory formalization of this dimension.

The ontological dimension has to do with prediction: whenever we assert that philosophy guides or directs or influences education, we are saying—if we really think this is so, and if we really ever hope to explain the connection between philosophy and education—that we can predict. It is a truism that prediction is the essence of explanation, and we are thus left with the problem of prediction to solve. But here we meet with a host of new problems and paradoxes—no, they are not new: even the ancient Greeks knew that prediction is either tautological and therefore meaningless, or else arbitrary. For instance, take the proposition—which is so often heard —that "Education is a change in behavior." If "a change in behavior" already qualifies the meaning of "education," then the prediction involved is analytical in some Kantian or Wittgensteinian sense; but if "change in behavior" does not already qualify "education," then what is the justification for adding it on?

Put otherwise, if the assertion "a given formal philosophy implies a certain set of educational practices"—that is, implies a *finite* set of such practices—then the meaning of "educational practices" is already contained in the philosophy; thus the operational definition of the connective "implies" means "equal to." But clearly this is vacuous; and the vacuity is illustrated by the notation that if specific educational practices are contained in philosophy and can be gotten from philosophy by the process of logical deduction, then in the training of teachers we need no courses in method: we need only teach them philosophy and logic, and let prospective teachers deduce the practices that follow logically from philosophy.

But suppose the phrase "formal philosophy implies a certain set of educational practices" refers to an *infinite* set. Then it is necessary for the educational philosophy to show just how to derive or identify each successive practice that is implied, *ad infinitum,* by or from philosophy. Yet this is senseless, for if that could be done then in what way could it be maintained that educational practices are dependent upon philosophy? In what way could practice be thus dependent upon theory?

Thus we come full circle and return to the starting point, although it is hoped that the foregoing analysis may have tightened the ring somewhat.

Educational philosophers assume, evidently with some justification, that there is indeed some kind of organic connection between philosophy and educational practice. This connection is of a kind that lets one in some way draw upon philosophy as a guiding force for our actual educational behavior, but as this analysis has shown there is not yet a clear idea just how this phenomenon operates; it is not known just how we get these clues for behavior from philosophy, and the precise nature of the "educational implication" is not yet explained.

What is known is that the connection between philosophy and educational practice cannot be explained or formalized in terms of strictly logical implication, nor in terms of strictly synthetic implication. Whether or not the pragmatic implication, outlined in parts V and VI of this essay is a promising approach to the solution of the problem of the "educational implication" remains to be seen. Fruitful or not, if the philosophy of education is said to be that kind of intellectual discipline that draws upon philosophy to guide actual educational practices, then its validity is vague and dubious until educational philosophers make explicit the methodology by which philosophy does in fact guide educational practice.

This is perhaps the major theoretical challenge now facing philosophers of education, and it is to be hoped that more of them will turn their attention to this problem.

VIII

"PRACTICAL" DIMENSIONS OF THE THEORY-PRACTICE PROBLEM

Despite the intellectual difficulties involved in translating theory into practice, problems of educational practice had to be resolved (if not solved) if America was going to "keep school." We did keep school, and in the keeping practical as well as theoretical obstacles arose.

Three Historical Stages. In an important sense the problems of educational practice have changed much more profoundly in the past one hundred fifty years than has the language of educational theory. That is, with the language and concepts of educational theory remaining reasonably constant while the problems and practices have changed radically and rapidly, a theory-practice hiatus has arisen in which similar words and phrases possess quite different meanings and implications for educational practice.

Educational practice, in broad overview, has undergone three critical stages of development, each with its unique demands on the society, the economy, teacher training, students, and theory. These stages were the (1) initial development of public instruction, (2) gradual but inexorable expansion to enroll almost all youngsters, and (3) consolidation and correction for quality of accomplishment.

Initial development—1800 to 1880. With all due respect, public schooling can still be characterized as always having been a low-key shoe-string operation. For all the able teachers, there has never been enough teacher talent to go around, nor enough money to build the kind of schools the public has been led to expect. In that sense disappointment and frustration were inevitable. The public was bound to be disappointed with the results, yet it remained reluctant to pay more for a program with which it was not satisfied. And teachers usually undertrained and often ungifted, were bound to be frustrated because they were continually led to expect they would achieve results with youngsters which were expressed in terms of ideals rather than realities. This combination of disappointment and frustration has led to public and professional mutual distrust. Often the public distrusts the teacher's ability, and the teacher distrusts both his professional leaders and the theories he had been trained to believe.

The initial development of public instruction during the first three quarters of the last century set the state for just such disappointment, frustration, and distrust. The first programs, based on the monitorial method and object lesson teaching, could aspire only to minimum accomplishment by students working under minimally trained instructors. Public instruction began in financial famine, and the malnutrition this fostered in teaching has never been fully remedied. Further, it started all over the country, more or less at once, with little plan, less pattern, and no systematic organization. This grass-roots diversity did indeed have the advantage of potential adaptability to local circumstances; but combined with intellectual malnutrition, brought on by economic poverty, it resulted in confusion, duplication, gaps, and all kinds of loopholes through which academic incompetence and pedagogical indolence could slip by often unnoticed, almost always unproven, and sometimes disguised by talk about democracy, adjustment, or permissiveness.

Expansion—1880 to 1940. In just over half a century the American population more than doubled, and the percentage of youngsters attending school increased more than five-fold. Underfinanced and understaffed from the beginning, the school's capacity to fulfill its obligations declined at about the same rate that the task with which it was faced grew. What could not be denied was that more and more youngsters, with more and more diverse backgrounds and abilities, would continue to be forced into the same schoolrooms no matter what this did to the level of instruction or the capacity of the teacher. With every child required to attend classes until age 14 or 16, something had to be made available for him that he could do. If school was truly for everyone, as it surely was becoming, then instruction must have something for everyone.

Eventually all children would go to school because the American public believed that education was a right the society owed to its young. Public money would have to finance this enterprise and this assured a natural conservation. The big hope was that some new pedagogical theories and techniques would be developed to handle this mass of students without a drop in the quality of achievement.

In fifty centuries educators had been able to distill enough wisdom in convenient rules of thumb to be able to cope with the best students, and the hope was that in the next fifty years vastly more progress would be made, enabling teachers to improve their methods of instruction at roughly the same rate that the size of classes and the spread of abilities increased. Educators did not ask "Can this be done?" so much as they conceded, "It must be done!" But regardless of necessity no miraculous new techniques were mothered, no matter how loudly group-process and activity-movements were touted. Yet necessity did father experimentation and even invention. In the context of such diversity of organization, such insufficiency of funds, and such inadequacy in background and training, invention and experimentation were sporadic, spotty, and not at all cumulative in effect. Discouragement and frustration continued to dominate both the public and the practitioner. Talk about new techniques flourished, however, spurred by the realization that something had to be done while nothing seemed to be happening. Theory often became armchair speculation disconnected from widespread, systematic application. And so-called practical experiments become unguided, disparate, trial and error innovation.

Consolidation and Correction—1945 to Present. With time out for the War, by VJ Day public education could mark the close of its expansion period and declare success in enrolling almost everyone and holding most youngsters. What it gave them was another matter entirely. Something for everyone had too often become anything for anyone.

Something for everyone having been achieved, the next step was assurance that the "something" had worth, that it was in fact being learned, and that youngsters were achieving in some measure according to estimates of their capacity. Standardization of content, homogeneous grouping, achievement testing and expert organization of some aspects of the curriculum have been the opening moves toward solving the ultimate problem of how to get the "most" of the "best" to and from the greatest number. This noble end necessitates that someone assert *what* should be taught, *how* it can best be taught, to whom it should be taught, and what level of achievement, constitutes acceptable performance. The problem could be approached more reasonably if there were reliable data to indicate which teaching techniques work best with what kind of students in the mastery of what kind of information, tasks, and skills; but neither in terms of how to teach nor in terms of what to teach do we have anything but the fuzziest notion of consequences. Here again theory becomes synonymous with speculation rather than with generalization drawn from reliable information.

Six Practical Outlooks. Each of these three historical stages presented educational practice with different demands, but the initiation of public education required economy above all else and this was achieved by employing relatively untrained people at low salaries. The expansion of education necessitated broadening course content and the curriculum, as well as lowering the standards of acceptable performance. The improvement of education now (as always) demands, more than anything else, better teachers. Only an increase in teaching talent can bring about better results, if the student body remains the same in size and diversity. The demands of those three historical stages have set the condition under which educational practice has had to develop. Such conditions determined how six major conceptions of instruction would be interpreted: Monitorial Method, Object Teaching, Herbartianism, Child-Study, Experimentalism, and the current Academic Emphasis. (See the diagram on p. 370.)

Monitorial Method (1840). Using the best boy in the class as unsalaried teacher met the demands of economy but necessitated that the schools restrict their objectives to achieving minimum literacy by means of drill and memorization in a climate of strict obedience. Instruction was formal, mechanical, and dealt mainly with abstractions. Control of youngsters was rigid, highly restrictive, constrained.

Object Teaching (1870). The monitorial method succeeded in getting something presented, while object teaching concerned itself with what would be remembered. Instead of bombarding the youngster with words

MAJOR APPROACHES TO THREE ASPECTS OF INSTRUCTION

Aspect of Instruction	Monitorial Method	Object Teaching	Herbartianism	Child Study	Experimentalism	Current Academic Emphasis
Deportment	Strict obedience	Opportunity to examine objects	Attentive compliance	Chance to explore and develop feeling	Opportunity to experiment and choose	Attentive curiosity relative to content
(Attitude)	(Constraint)	(Elbowroom)	(Constraint)	(Elbowroom)	(Elbowroom)	(Constraint)
Organization	Order based on past precedent	Order implicit in classroom activities	Logical or chronological order as established by subject matter	Order natural to creative expression	Order evolved from cooperative planning	Order based on subject matter as determined by experts
(Attitude)	(Established)	(Spontaneous)	(Established)	(Spontaneous)	(Spontaneous)	(Established)
Kind of Learning	Concepts memorized from lessons and books	Sensations & understandings extracted from objects and activities	Cultural concepts from literature and history	Feelings and understandings gained from personal expressions	Changed attitudes & behaviors; social awareness	Skills, ideas, information needed to further academic study
(Attitude)	(Didactic)	(Ostensive)	(Didactic)	(Ostensive)	(Ostensive)	(Didactic)

and ideas drilled mechanically, it sought to offer him sense impressions which he would retain and could build on—a kind of ostensive learning. Concerning control of behavior, this concept advocated the acceptance of a broad range of normal behavior and sympathetic, rather than stern, treatment. Here, was the first step toward making elbow room for a greater range of personalities and abilities, but that room had to be made at the expense of the formally arranged and established curriculum.

Herbartianism (1890). Not being concerned with minimum literacy, since this program for secondary schools assumed everyone in class could read, Herbartianism opposed the seeming softness, poor organization, and merely ostensive learning of object teaching. Herbartians wanted to maximize exposure to well organized academic lessons, taking it for granted that learning would follow as naturally as hearing follows being spoken to —didactic learning. And by way of tightening down on behavior, the Herbartians advocated that the teacher retain pupil respect through social distance and control by force if necessary.

Child-Study (1895). The child-study movement could not accept the idea that mere exposure fostered learning. Expanding the object teaching concept of sense impression learning, this movement sought to maximize individual pupil expression. Since everyone could "express" himself, even those who could not retain much from exposure teaching, there would be something for everyone in such a program. Applying bits of Freudian-type thinking it was reasoned that "good" expression could only take place in a free uninhibited, unfearful environment, designed to capitalize on immediate interests—spontaneous organization. Hence permissiveness gained a hearing both in the name of theory and under the practical pressure that it is easier to get along with students of low ability if they are not pushed too hard.

Experimentalism (1930). Faced with the full impact of having virtually all youngsters in school, the advocates of Experimentalism stretched the curriculum to include what especially in the depression years, seemed most necessary: vocational training. But the 1930's were also a period of intellectual unrest and social revolt. Here was a chance to train a generation of children so that they would not repeat the mistakes of their fathers, but this kind of retraining called for a break from established values and the courage to build new ones. Even if everyone could not do algebra or understand Shakespeare, in one way or another everyone could doubt, everyone could inquire and think. Everyone could think about social problems as well as vocational ones. Hence, it seemed quite natural to foster the "common man" approach to the solution of social problems by giving him practice in this process while he attended school as a youth. Further, such reasoning fit in well with the increased awareness that we, as a democratic nation, had an obligation best discharged by beginning with the enlightenment of our own people. Finally, all the "new break throughs" in psychology, sociology, anthropology, and political science lined up against Spanish, German, Italian, and Japanese fascism to support permissiveness against authoritarian control in the home and the schools. But permissiveness, democratic cooperation in groups, the handling of social problems so as to derive group conclusions, plus vocational training, could only be included at the expense of Latin, some mathematics, etc., in the curriculum.

Current Academic Emphasis (1950). Prosperity made vocational training expendable. The shift of populations away from rural areas, added to the recent growth of corporate farms, made agricultural education almost necessary. The increase in divorce and delinquency rates cast snickers at life adjustment theories, while the high rate of military rejections for physical unfitness put suspicion on physical education. The unruliness of GI's during the war, and the popular accusation of "momism," brought permissiveness into question, while the cold war and Sputnik I brought academic content to the foreground. Today careful organization of academic content is replacing group activities and the development of interest projects, as the suspicion spreads that youngsters can indeed do more than their schooling has challenged them to do. With the great fear of fascism replaced by the greater fear of communism there is a tendency to insist on obedience, and not worry so much about whether it stifled individual expressiveness, so long as it seemed to produce political loyalty and technological skill.

Polar Conceptions of Practice. Throughout these six major practical outlooks, and as a result of the pressures of initiation, expansion, and correction of public school practices, instruction has been organized around certain recurrent Polar Concepts. Three aspects of practice have been involved: (1) the concept of what kind of student behavior to encourage in the classroom, (2) the concept of how to organize content, and (3) the concept of what kinds of learning should be achieved. These three aspects, labeled deportment, organization, instruction, can be associated with the major traditions and with the polar ideologies by the two diagrams on pp. 370, 373.

THE ESSAYS TO FOLLOW

The following seven essays relate educational theory to practice and, in so doing, show how philosophic considerations provide guidance to education.

Van Cleve Morris, in the opening essay, writes directly to the point of connecting theory to practice in terms of schools and students. Following this Fred N. Kerlinger examines the "permissiveness theory" in educational practice and concludes it leads not to freedom but authoritarianism. Virgil S.

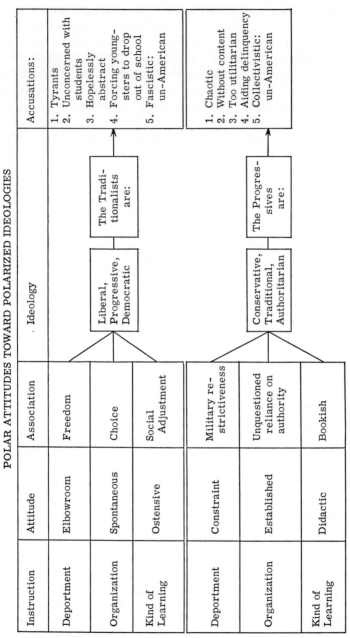

POLAR ATTITUDES TOWARD POLARIZED IDEOLOGIES

Instruction	Attitude	Association	Ideology		Accusations:
Deportment	Elbowroom	Freedom	Liberal, Progressive, Democratic	The Traditionalists are:	1. Tyrants 2. Unconcerned with students 3. Hopelessly abstract 4. Forcing youngsters to drop out of school 5. Fascistic: un-American
Organization	Spontaneous	Choice			
Kind of Learning	Ostensive	Social Adjustment			
Deportment	Constraint	Military re-strictiveness	Conservative, Traditional, Authoritarian	The Progressives are:	1. Chaotic 2. Without content 3. Too utilitarian 4. Aiding delinquency 5. Collectivistic: un-American
Organization	Established	Unquestioned reliance on authority			
Kind of Learning	Didactic	Bookish			

Ward's contribution dwells on the unfortunate separation of theory from practice and, with reference to gifted children, shows the unhappy consequences of divorcing theory and practice. In the fourth essay B. Paul Komisar uses theory to demonstrate that the "child-needs" theory—and educational practices based on "meeting the needs of children"—is surplus intellectual baggage. Then, in the next essay, D. Bob Gowin moves from a consideration of values theories (the philosophic) to the evaluation of educational programs (the practical), and in so doing relates philosophy to education. The sixth essay is an attempt to use theory—more generously, educational philosophy—as a resource for solving the very practical problem of merit salary plans for teachers. Finally, in the last essay, Richard W. Dettering conclusively shows that Rogerian or non-directive psychology (an approach used by many guidance counselors and school psychologists) is the intellectual step-child of an outmoded philosophic Idealism and therefore an inappropriate basis for contemporary educational guidance practices.

Because all seven of these essays are short and non-technical the editors have not provided them with individual overviews.

⌒

Movable Furniture and a Theory of Man

*Van Cleve Morris**

One of the most familiar obscurities of modern life is the connection between theory and practice. Especially is this true in the field of education, where the things that we do in school rooms with boys and girls often seem quite remote from the pronouncements of professors of pedagogy and educational theorists. Fortunately, however, the obscurity is only apparent, for the kinds of things teachers, principals, superintendents, guidance specialists, and all the rest—the kinds of things these people do in their day-to-day practice—can be explained, or as we say in theoretical discourse, "rationalized," by

* Reprinted by permission from *Educational Theory*, VII (July, 1957), 187–193.

referring to basic theories concerning schools and human beings. This paper seeks to examine the linkage between theory and practice with respect to these two subjects—schools and people.

I

First, how about schools? One of the first things to know about the nature of the school in modern American life is that it is a *public* institution. This is well known, of course, but there are some significant specific facts that flow from this fairly obvious general one which are perhaps not so well known. When we say the school is a public institution, we mean that the people who run schools are public employees, and that education is, in the political word we use, a socialized enterprise. And this means of course that teaching in America is a *socialized* profession.

We hear a lot of squabbling nowadays about socialized medicine, as if to socialize any major service function of our society were the so-called kiss of death, politically speaking. But we have had socialized education for over a hundred years now and nobody, to speak of, is clamoring that we are on the road to social ruin. Ironically we have always taken the view that health is a private, individual affair, but that education is a public, social affair. If you get sick and are about to die, that's your own tough luck. I have no special social obligation to see to it that you get proper medical attention. That's up to you. But if you allow your children to grow up uneducated, that becomes of real concern to me and my neighbors, and we can even send the law around to *force* you to get your children into the school.

Now to say that the school in America is public is also to associate it with government, and there are many who believe that too close a kinship with government can be a very distasteful thing. In a recent pamphlet on education published by the National Association of Manufacturers the following appears:

With governmental support and control there is inclined to be:
1. less consideration of minority wishes by the majority,
2. more dependence on the advice of professional experts than on purely local considerations, and
3. more inclination to follow current political and sociological ideologies

which may not be approved by some individualists.[1]

The author of this sentence obviously has never been to his local school. For if he had made the visit he would find quite the opposite. At that school which is governmentally supported and controlled he would find all kinds of minorities, even the minorities of one, being soothed and placated by the agent of the majority, the principal; instead of experts in every corner, he would find just ordinary folks (probably arranged in discussion groups!) trying honestly to solve the troublesome problems of teaching boys and girls; and to crown all, instead of visionary, socialist crackpots lurking in the halls and classrooms, he would discover a group of timid and frightened teachers who would hesitate to admit even a membership in the League of Women Voters —if, of course, they were members, which, of course, they are not.

What the public-izing of education has done to the teaching profession is not all lovely to behold, and many of us can understand the medical profession, though not support it, when it fights the public medicine movement as vigorously as it does. All it has to do is look around the corner to see how the socialized profession of teaching is making out.

To summarize, if the *theory* of public education is more or less as stated here, and if we are committed to it (and we seem to be), perhaps we should more readily recognize and

[1] Educational Advisory Committee and the Educational Advisory Council of the N.A.M., *This We Believe About Education* (New York: The National Association of Manufacturers, 1954), p. 12.

evaluate the kinds of *practical action* which this theory seems to produce in educators. For many thoughtful persons are increasingly of the opinion that the embattled principal and the timid teacher are direct products of the public and socialized character of American education.

II

Much more could be said about the school. But turning now to boys and girls, we might change the procedure a little bit. Instead of developing the theory of boys and girls first and then identifying the practices of teachers consistent with that theory, we might reverse the sequence, i.e., examine some concrete examples of practical action in our schools today and see from what kinds of basic outlooks they seem to originate. Three come immediately to mind.

1. SOCIAL PROMOTION. It could be honestly said that the modern elementary school has veritably fallen in love with social promotion. Boys and girls who are unable to read at the first grade level are moved on to the second grade. Youngsters who have not mastered long division in the fourth grade are moved nonetheless to the fifth. Why?

Contemporary critics of the public schools say that this practice is the outgrowth of a deterioration in standards. Teachers themselves might try to explain it by saying that experimental evidence seems to indicate that repeaters do not often do much better the second time around than they did the first. Still other teachers might openly admit a reluctance to endure a troublesome youngster for another whole year and hence yield to the temptation to move him along.

But these are only the surface reasons. The real reason is this: Boys and girls in our elementary schools learn from many sources other than teachers, books, motion pictures, field trips, and other standard paraphernalia of the typical school. They learn from each other. If you cut off a child from his age group, if you separate him from the social unit in which over nine months he has managed to gain full fledged membership, you are literally cutting him off from one of his "teachers," namely, his psychological and social peers.

To say that children learn a great many things about their environment from each other is to say that we have only within the last half-century awakened to the profound significance of the old cliché that man is a social animal. At one time believing that the sociality of man was primarily manifest in his recreation and play, we now recognize that his very character is formed through intimate association with other human beings. Our colleagues in anthropology and social psychology have demonstrated that in a very real sense our very human nature—our desires and preferences, our outlooks and values, our seemingly natural habits and behavior patterns—are in actuality hammered out in the course of social experience.

This means then that if a young child is cut off from his own kind, he begins to wither a little, and no amount of watering and fertilizing by an adult teacher—a person *not* of his own kind —will make up the deficit entirely. So, it is not through some humanitarian and altruistic softness that we seem to wink at failure in spelling or arithmetic and pass a child to the next level. It is rather through a rational and empirically demonstrable conviction that the kinds of learning available to a youngster by keeping him with his age group are often quantitatively and qualitatively more important than the kinds of learning obtainable by the repetition of a grade in school. It is possible, of course, to question the application of this general theory, or the decision reached on any given child; but if you dispute the theory itself, you are making bold enough to run counter to an ever-increasing body of empirical evidence regarding the social psychology of man.

2. The Grade-less Report Card. Another standard and widespread practice of modern schools is to report the progress of pupils in a variety of ways other than the standard ABC method. Some schools, for instance, attempt to convey a general notion of the quality of pupil work through the symbols of S for Satisfactory and U for Unsatisfactory. Others have adopted the plan calling for short notes to parents regarding the work of their children or brief commentaries on each child recorded and inserted in what we call an anecdotal record file. Still others have tried to do away with grades and report cards altogether, choosing to adopt the dictum of Professor William Heard Kilpatrick who once said that, in education, it ought to be the rule that "No news is good news."

Now again our critics, especially among the lay public, accuse us of lowering academic standards and of becoming indifferent to the values, intellectual and moral, to be found in rigorous study of the standard academic disciplines. And teachers themselves may be a little vague about all of this, saying that you can't really differentiate between the achievement of children, and that letter grades are largely guesswork, or that continual failure for any individual is psychologically unhealthy and, according to the fringe element, that the ABC grading system is to blame for making people fail!

But these are only the superficial and erroneous reasons. The real reasons are to be found elsewhere. In the first place, we have come to realize just within the past couple of generations that the real rewards of learning are intrinsic to the learning itself, that the sense of accomplishment, the awareness of new insights, and the recognition of genuine growth within oneself are payment enough for the effort put forth in learning. I know a first grade teacher who every Monday morning gives a gold star to all of her children who attended Sunday school the day before. Besides being a questionable practice in light of our anxious desire to keep church and state separate, it testifies to the belief on this teacher's part that the rewards of attending Sunday school are not sufficient to attract youngsters and that they need the additional, extraneous bait of a gold star on Monday to overcome their habitual, and in many cases justified, resistance to perform a duty on Sunday. If performing religious rites requires the mild bribery of a secular institution like the school, then perhaps it would be wise to re-examine the religious rites themselves. So likewise, if learning is so purposeless that youngsters require the use of extraneous rewards represented by grades, then perhaps it is time to re-examine the kinds of things we are asking boys and girls to learn.

But on a more basic level of consideration, we are de-emphasizing grades because they measure only one aspect of growth and development, namely, the mastery of encyclopedic content in a prescribed course of study. One of our traditional theories of education is that learning is the mastery of subject matter set out to be learned. In general, this view of education is based on the theory that man is a potential receptacle of knowledge. His peculiar distinction in nature is that he can learn things, store them up in his head, and then withdraw them for use at prescribed times. This goes by the facetious name sometimes of the Two-Gallon Jug theory of education; on other occasions it is referred to as the Cold-Storage theory of education. Man is a psychological warehouse, where treasures from the encyclopedia may be carefully mastered, tucked away in a special place in one's mind, and then withdrawn on request for use. In circumstances like this, grading youngsters with A's and B's and C's is to ascertain *how much* of this material they have mastered and stored away in their heads, and *how much* they can subsequently regurgitate on demand for a paper-and-pencil test.

But man is a lot more than a psychological Sears Roebuck. He is, of course, blessed with the peculiar facility of mastering content, but what makes him such a remarkable creature is his ability to employ this content in reorganizing his life, in constantly modifying the responses he makes to his en-

vironment so that his future conduct can be classified in some way as superior to his past conduct. Mastering content is only a part of the job of learning. The other part is allowing the insights of content mastery to flow into our lives in such a way that our behavior becomes progressively more mature; it is the task of learning things about our environment and seeing to it that these learnings somehow don't get stuck in our brains but flow ultimately into our whole beings, making our lives more meaningful and intelligent and hence more human.

It is this ability of the learner to indicate *by his behavior* that he has learned something that increasingly needs our attention in this business of grading. The ABC's may indicate how much we have put into our heads. But now we need another grading system to show how much we integrate into our daily conduct. In this instance we see that practical action—de-emphasizing grades—is only the protest movement against an obsolete theory of man —a psychological warehouse. The protest must now turn its energies in more affirmative directions so that new practical action, i.e., a new grading system, may fulfill the spirit of a recognized reconstructed theory of man, i.e., a behaving, growing organism.

3. It is perhaps time now to return to the scripture lesson of this little essay —the connection between movable furniture and the nature of man. Just as in the previous instances, there is a demonstrable nexus between those practices we employ in our schools and the theories of man we carry in our heads.

The older school was typified by straight rows of desks, firmly secured to the floor, and all facing the podium as in an auditorium. And of course the classroom was literally an audit-orium, a place where you were supposed to sit quietly and listen. Learning was not only thought of in the receptacle sense discussed above, but was also influenced by the mechanism and inflexibility of an advancing technology. This was the age (the latter 19th and early 20th centuries) of the "mechanical man." It was the age of the discovery and rapid spread of science, of technological applications of science, and ultimately of what we call mass production techniques. If technology and mass production could turn out highly intricate automobiles, refrigerators, and radios, then there was no reason to believe it could not also turn out educated human beings. Under the spell of this mentality, we cooked up a variety of mechanical theories of man all the way from the faculty theory of the mind to Behaviorist psychology.

This was also the age of the interchangeability of parts, probably one of the most important technical discoveries making mass production possible. And so we in education came to see that not only were individuals pretty much alike in their needs and requirements in the school, but the things they studied and learned were more or less interchangeable. It was almost inevitable then that we should eventually stumble upon the Carnegie Unit and the credit-hour. Any course that can get approval of the academic powers and which meets three hours per week may carry three of these credits and is equal to any other course of similar design. If you attend regularly for forty-five class sessions, do what you are told, keep your ears open

and your mouth shut, and in general remain docile and manageable, it is no trouble whatsoever to pick up three of these credits. If you can continue this procedure for four years, you can collect these credits as you would little coupons. And when the final June rolls around, and if you have collected a total of 120 or so of these coupons, you are entitled to gather them up in a bundle, carry them to the box office, and redeem them for one large coupon which hence forward in your life may be modestly produced in polite society to indicate that you are an educated person.

In the light of all this pedagogical technology and psychological mechanism, it is no wonder that we have thought it so important to place children in rows of seats which could not be moved, and to design these seats in such a way that the eyes, ears and mouth should all be pointed forward so as to receive stimuli and emit responses on call in connection with the performance of a teacher on a raised platform up in front.

Now we are hopefully moving out of the age of the mechanical man into what we think is a more humane definition of his psychology. It is true, of course, that many of his needs and requirements are standard and that much of his learning can be mechanically organized and presented, but man is a much more complex creature. Each individual we now recognize has his own peculiar curve of development, each his own special channels of growth, each his particular areas of ability and creative competence. It is this kind of man who now inhabits our school rooms, and if education is to give elbow room to this side of man, if it is to let this creative impulse breathe and live, then its methods must necessarily become less entangled with inflexible seating arrangements, classroom ritual, and administrative bookkeeping, and become increasingly more attuned to the free and open atmosphere characteristic of an unregimented society.

We haven't yet seen any feasible way of doing away with the Carnegie Unit and semester hour bookkeeping systems, and it is probable that in order merely to administer education for the masses we will have to keep them, but there is no particular reason why we cannot change our practices inside the classroom, unscrewing those rigid lines of desks and replacing them with chairs and tables and desk-seats which can be moved about as the requirements of the learning situation demand.

III

Here we have three instances of practical conduct in the performance of educational duties which we have tried to connect to changing theories of man. By indirection this essay has taken a look at a variety of other things we do in the schools and how they relate to outmoded notions of human beings. We might have discussed many, many more. We could have taken a look at the phenomenon of extra-curricular activities, at the project method of teaching, at the idea of free textbooks or free lunches; we might have considered the kindergarten, or the G.I. Bill of Rights. Certainly each of these recent innovations on the educational landscape has its explanation in a changing conception of man and the world he lives in.

But the point of this paper is and ought to be more than simply a rehearsal of some interesting ways in which what we do connects with what we think. We might ask, why have theory at all? If practical action seems to evolve along humane and sensible lines, why must the variety of theories underlying our actions be identified and clarified? In short, what is the special function of theory anyway?

In hasty answer to this question, the least we could say is that all of us should know what we are doing, and knowing what we are doing signifies knowing why as well as how. After all, it is practically impossible to conceive of *doing* anything without having consciously or sub-consciously some motive or object for doing it. In this relatively superficial sense, theory becomes merely the complement of practice, merely the other and necessary side of a coin which in our daily lives is usually turned practice-side up.

But theory has a much more important job to do. It is through theory that we are able to connect one practice with another to see if they are consistent, coherent, and hence intelligent. Is social promotion compatible with the de-emphasis of traditional grading systems and with the introduction of movable furniture? By referring all of these practices to the basic conceptions they stem from, we find they are all of a piece; they come out of an aggregate of modern notions of man that seem to have kinship with one another.

If social promotion is ultimately

based on our new awareness of the sociality of the human species and the discovery that he learns much of his character and personality by mere association with his kind, we may infer that the types of things he learns from his kind are more associated with his social behavior than with the manipulation of intellectual concepts in his mind. Hence a grading system to measure growth in behavior, in addition to the one we already have in measuring growth in intellectual manipulation, is seen to be a necessary hand maiden to the idea of social promotion. And if this social creature called man requires for his developing sociality a geographical proximity to his fellows and a freedom to turn physically toward them and associate himself with them, then there is a clear rationale for the introduction of movable furniture.

Conceived in this sense, theory is the primary unifying agent in our lives. It makes possible a criticism of what we do to see if it is logically coherent with all else that we do. In this special office, theory performs a very *practical* task.

Viewed in this light we can say that a good theory is the most practical thing a man can possess. For as we stumble around from day to day, as we get lost among the trees of practical action, we can often save ourselves by withdrawing and viewing the forest of social reality in which we all move.

It is this connecting of trees with forest, practical action with theory, that is the singular, continuing obligation of modern man.

$\sim$

The Implications of the Permissiveness Doctrine in American Education

*Fred N. Kerlinger**

The doctrine of permissiveness in education and its relation to democratic ideology have been tormenting problems to American educators. Most thinkers apparently agree on a rather large measure of permissiveness in the education of children. The idea seems basically to be that children, if they are to mature into democratic individuals and citizens, must not be too restricted in the pursuit of their own interests and needs, since such restrictiveness

* Reprinted by permission from *Educational Theory*, X (April, 1960), 120–127.

will somehow have the unfortunate consequence of producing undemocratic citizens. If children are not "permitted" a good deal of freedom—more specifically, decision choice—then they will not mature into autonomous, cooperative, and generally democratic individuals. In short, without permissiveness we run the danger of creating authoritarian individuals and an authoritarian society. Certainly, the argument goes, we now have a generally authoritarian school system which is systematically warping millions of children into undesirable types of human beings, human beings who lack autonomy, maturity, and true democratic potentiality.

That there is much truth in the above argument few educators would deny. The underlying undemocratic and even authoritarian quality of many, perhaps most, American schools and classrooms seems evident, if we are to believe responsible critics. Yet it also seems that a good deal of the older restrictiveness and authoritarianism have been mitigated; improvement, while slow, has occurred. The strong reaction against the older restrictiveness in education which started in the early part of the century has had its effect. Old-line authoritarian educational thinking and methods are becoming more and more disapproved as the contemporary permissive influence makes itself felt. The superintendent, principal, or teacher who wants to play the boss role must now do it in a more covert and subtle fashion.

The purpose of this paper is to speculate on the possibility of a new authoritarianism springing from a relatively extreme and basic emphasis on permissiveness. In a previous paper in which the modern origins of permissiveness in American education were traced, it was claimed that the doctrine of permissiveness in education had its origins in the thinking of Freud and Dewey and that the strong impact of these two great thinkers had laid the foundations for modern ideas and practices of permissiveness in education.[1]

It was also suggested that a new authoritarianism might be arising, a phenomenon expressed by two concepts which are becoming influential symbols in American education: permissiveness and group dynamics. It was further suggested that possibly there were manipulatory and authoritarian implications of the doctrines many educators are espousing. Finally, the paper hinted at a covert anti-intellectualism springing from permissivist and group dynamics doctrines. The present essay will be limited to an analysis of the implications of the permissiveness doctrine. Group dynamics doctrine was partially explored in a previous paper.[2] Similarly, the anti-intellectual implications of the permissiveness doctrine will not be directly discussed. It must wait for future treatment.

The argument that follows is based on five main points: (1) that the doctrine of permissiveness is more of a reaction against older restrictive and undemocratic educational ideas than it is a movement for democratic ideas; (2) that the espousal and implementation of relatively extreme permissive ideas imply and lead to manipulation of the pupil by the teacher and of the teacher by the pupil; (3) that while extreme permissive practices are claimed to be democratic they may be in effect autocratic; (4) that when permissive ideas dominate a teacher, when they form the mainspring of her educational being, they lead to a basic violation of the integrity of the individual; and (5) that when permissiveness is a fundamental and overriding concern of

---

[1] Fred N. Kerlinger, "The Origin of the Doctrine of Permissiveness in American Education," *Progressive Education*, XXXIII (1956), 161–165.

[2] Fred N. Kerlinger, "The Authortarianism of Group Dynamics," *Progressive Education*, XXXI (1954), 169–173.

the teacher it leads to a pervasive conformity of the individual to the will of the teacher and/or the class group.

Before beginning the main discussion, an important point should be clarified. This paper is not meant to be a critique of permissiveness in general. It is assumed that a moderate amount of permissiveness is good and that the older educational restrictiveness is bad. The permissiveness to be discussed is the relatively extreme and unilateral doctrine espoused by a number of educational writers, some of whom will be cited. This unilateral doctrine seems to imply a wholesale sort of permissiveness running from the kindergarten through the graduate school, a permissiveness which labels almost any sort of educational direction from a teacher as a sign of autocracy, which says that to lecture is to impose one's will on students and is therefore bad, authoritarian, and to be eschewed by the democratic educator, which says, furthermore, that group processes in the classroom are in and of themselves good, democratic, to be encouraged since they presumably permit the greatest amount of individual expression through democratic interaction with others. In short, it is the unilateral and extreme doctrine of permissiveness which permits nothing but permissiveness and which threatens to become dogma and religion that is the object of scrutiny.

The first point, that a great deal of permissivist doctrine is a reaction against the older authoritarianism and restrictiveness in education rather than a movement for permissiveness and democratic ideas, is apparent from a study of much education literature.

One gets the impression from reading permissivist works that nothing in the older education was much good—except the pupils. This reactivity against traditional education accounts for much of the literature's extreme and rather naive quality, and it leads permissivist authors to be somewhat condescending and patronizing when talking about the older education and about practices with which they disagree. Permissivist literature has mainly negative criticism of traditional education as its ideological foundation. When it comes to the task of constructing a positive philosophy permissivists find themselves in a difficult position since they must "permit" anything but restrictiveness. What permissivists have done, therefore, is to attempt to solve the problem by borrowing quite selectively from Dewey and Freud, mainly, and by manufacturing a new metaphysics on the basis of these borrowings. The character of the movement is heavily moral and, as already indicated, seems to derive most of its force from derogation—derogation of the older education, of subject matter, of teachers. The derogation is often concealed by words and rather vague, even mystical, writing. For example, Rasey says, "And we teachers. We teach nothing. We can no more teach than we can learn a child. We are onlookers while life teaches."[3] As with many such statements there is a kernel of truth here. But there is also obfuscation of the teaching-learning problem. A number of examples of derogation can also be

[3] Marie I. Rasey, *Toward Maturity* (New York: Barnes & Noble, Inc., 1947), p. 231. See, also, the same author's *This Is Teaching* (New York: Harper & Brothers, 1950).

found in Cantor's work. One of the best of these is his castigation of instruction which begins with definitions.[4] He implies that any instructor who uses definitions in approaching a subject is, ipso facto, a bad teacher. In another place, Cantor, like many other educators, derogates those who lecture. He says, "The instructor who lectures deprives the students of their right actively to participate in their class."[5] He then says, very significantly, "The instructor who is aware of his function refrains from using students for displaying his knowledge. He permits himself to be used, in a professional way, by them."[6]

The argument being advanced is that, if permissivism is basically a reactive doctrine it must also necessarily be essentially negative in tone and practice. The teacher must not do anything restrictive; she must not do anything—or think anything—traditional. To be deeply concerned with subject matter, for example, is questionable since it leads to "coercion" of pupils. It seems evident that permissivist educators served a very useful purpose during the early days of reaction against the authoritarian practices of the past. (The battle is of course by no means yet

won.) To continue to espouse a basically negative and reactive ideology, however, can be a defeat of the hard-won victories of a splendid educational movement.

Perhaps the most serious implication and end-result of extreme permissiveness is that it leads to manipulation of pupils. The very permissive teacher sets up few or no limits for her pupils. Few norms of behavior and learning are supposed to be teacher-determined. But a normless social situation is of course impossible; some norms or rules must always govern behavior. If the teacher does not supply the rules or norms, the pupils will. Fine! says the permissivist, and it is fine—to a certain extent. But the teacher is a basic authority ingredient of any learning situation. Many educators may dispute this and say that the learner, or rather, the learner group should be the basic ingredient. But the teacher is a guide to learning; she is the experienced group member who must take a leading role in directing group activities toward educational goals set at least partly by society. She is society's surrogate who must ensure, by norm and rule-setting, that the societal educational goals are reached. Now when she does not take this function, she puts herself into the unfortunate situation of being forced, consciously or unconsciously, to manipulate her charges. She must discharge the societal function; there is, by definition, no alternative. Pupils may take the responsibility adequately; they may decide to teach the societal goals. Then, again, they may not. And this cannot be left to chance, and any teacher knows it. Pupils, even by the age of six, are dimly aware of it, as Piaget's work would seem to indi-

[4] Nathaniel Cantor, *Dynamics of Learning.* Buffalo: Foster and Stewart Co., 1946. Pp. 145, 153.

[5] *Ibid.,* p. 174. See also, Earl C. Kelley and Marie I. Rasey, *Education and the Nature of Man* (New York: Harper & Brothers, 1952), p. 86. This latter work is especially interesting because it is supposed to give the scientific foundations for the authors' educational beliefs. Of the entire list of 131 entries (footnotes), however, only four are reports of actual scientific research, and of these four perhaps one is a significant study.

[6] *Ibid.*

cate. The problem boils down not to whether or not there are norms—there are always norms—but to who sets the norms. Ideally both pupils and teacher should set them. Yet the teacher's role in norm-setting, again by societal definition, must always be dominant. Any other situation is sociologically and psychologically anomalous. To say that this is a violation of democratic freedom is semantic nonsense. Freedom is always relative; it is always bounded by norms and rules for behavior. As Dewey well said, ". . . guidance given by the teacher to the exercise of the pupil's intelligence is an aid to freedom, not a restriction upon it."[7] The argument can be rounded out with another Dewey excerpt.

Sometimes teachers seem to be afraid even to make suggestions to the members of a group as to what they should do. . . . But what is more important is that the suggestion upon which pupils act must in any case come from somewhere. It is impossible to understand why a suggestion from one who has a larger experience and a wider horizon should not be at least as valid as a suggestion arising from some more or less accidental source.

The above argument leads to the third point: that extreme permissivism leads to autocratic rather than, as supposed, to democratic thinking and practice. If the permissive teacher acts upon the precepts of a Kelley or a Cantor, she will find herself in a peculiar predicament. If the group will does not point in the socially desirable direction—and, again, any teacher will know this by the very nature of social norms which

[7] John Dewey, *Experience and Education* (New York: The Macmillan Co., 1938), p. 84.

depend for their efficacy on being interiorized by all or most members of a society—she will be in the unenviable position of manipulating the group so that it will more or less fall into line. The famous expression, "Do we have to do what we want to do today?" while a humorous exaggeration, contains the kernel of this problem. Basically, and somewhat cynically, the teacher who is committed unilaterally to permissiveness must so manipulate the situation, herself, and the pupils that the goals of society which are her goals by definition since she is, at least in good part, a surrogate of society, are achieved. The manipulation comes in when the direction of educational activity strays too far from the societal goals. It should not be thought that this is a defense of education as a preserver of the status quo. No matter what position is taken on education's function, it still remains a fact, by the definition of education as a cultural phenomenon, that schools must teach at least a basic core of values, attitudes, skill, and facts. Variability will be very great in a democracy, naturally, but the common norm must be there.

In other words, the lines must be drawn somewhere, and it is the teacher acting for and as society who draws the lines. And the lines must be clear and unambiguous. To think or act otherwise is to lay the foundation for social and personal chaos. One good definition of a teacher is that he is a person working to put himself out of a job. This means, of course, that a teacher always should try to have his students develop as rapidly as possible into mature people who have learned what he knows, who have his understandings and more. To give a child too much freedom too soon, to force children to make choices they are really incapable of making, is to defeat this definition because, as Fromm has pointed out, we have to grow to independence through dependence, through self-love to love of others. Learning from teachers always has this symbiotic character. It is not undemocratic; it is natural and inevitable.

That an espousal of relatively extreme permissivism can lead to violation of the integrity of the individual follows from the argument on manipulation. Manipulation of pupils, if practiced systematically, is a violation of the integrity of both pupil and teacher for quite obvious reasons. The integrity, the wholeness, of any individual depends upon acting fairly consistently in accordance with both approved social norms and one's approved self-image. The manipulation is of course usually not perceived as manipulation. The teacher has herself been taught that the ideas she is trying to implement are good—and they are good. Democratic cooperation, participation in the learning process, and the like are good values. But the difficulty is how to achieve them. The group way, she has been taught, is the right way. She is also taught not to impose her will on children but to discover their needs and interests and to use these to achieve the learning objectives. All this, too, is good. But somewhere, some time, she must draw lines beyond which children cannot be permitted to go. To do this she sometimes must use methods which, in a permissivist framework, are not good, she believes. Thus there is a conflict. And the conflict be-

tween being democratic and autocratic cannot be resolved, for her at least, by a clearcut choice. She has no choice: she must be democratic. Yet to be democratic, she has learned, is to be permissive. Her only recourse is to use the permissive methods and still achieve societal objectives. And this often means doing things which are "coercive." She often ends up using "nice coercion." Children soon learn the rules of the game, and, as Riesman points out, they become skilled at conforming to these "nice" demands. They also become skilled at manipulating the teacher. But in the process both teacher and pupil lose some of their integrity since life and the classroom are not always so nice, so cooperative, so democratic, and in order to maintain the "nice" fiction, it is often necessary to practice mild but insidious deceptions on others and on oneself.

To complete the argument, we need to examine the relationship between permissiveness and conformity. When permissiveness is the fundamental guide of a teacher's thinking and behavior, pupils must pay the price of conformity. This is perhaps best understood by going through the back door. It can be agreed that in an autocratic setup the social situation is clear to all parties concerned—role relationships are clearly understood as are group norms. The pupils, for example, at least have something concrete to rebel against and, if necessary, to fight. But with the highly permissive teacher, whether manipulatory and autocratic or not, there is nothing to rebel against or to fight. A pupil may have a vague feeling of being used, and he may want to do something about it. But what can he do? Even the other pupils will disapprove of him if he goes against the "nice one." The pressures toward conformity are very strong in such situations. And the conformity goes beyond what was demanded under the outright and open autocratic setup: it is personal and moral as well as behavioral. The pupils should even think like the teacher, or rather, the teacher-pupil group.

Study of a number of contemporary educational writings shows learnings which clearly imply conformity to the group. In fact, permissiveness and group cooperation, as doctrines, usually go hand in hand in much of the writing. They seem to be basic tenets of a new orthodoxy. For example, Kilpatrick, in talking about the effectiveness of group education, says:

> How then is good character best built. . . . In the multitudinous social contacts there will inevitably arise situations of social stress. Under wise guidance the group should be led to see the issues involved and conclude as to just disposition of the dispute. Such a group conclusion no individual will permanently dispute. To defy his group seldom satisfies. In the end he will accept. . . .[8]

Comment here is hardly necessary.

Along with these emphases goes a concomitant rather strong emphasis on emotional learnings. One gathers that the basic function of education is to foster proper emotional attitudes and the ability to get along with people. It is here contended that this "sociometric" approach to education, as Riesman has aptly named it, is actually detrimental

to democratic education, that it leads in effect, to autocratic practices. When the emphasis in a class is emotional, it is difficult for children to learn objective modes of thinking. They learn to focus on the rather slippery ground of affect and only secondarily learn to handle facts and things. It is not contended here that emotional learning is wrong. But it is contended that a basic emphasis on emotional learning is wrong. The emphasis in a classroom should be on work, on things, and on attitudes, but work should be central. Only thus is the child free to develop as a democratic human being. When the central emphasis is on feelings, especially feelings toward other persons, objectivity, independence, and autonomy become difficult or even impossible to learn and to achieve. This is because constant preoccupation with one's own and other people's feelings is an unstable and insecure ground on which to build a basis for learning to make objective and critical judgments of problems and issues since all of one's thinking becomes colored and perhaps distorted by interpersonal affect. This is a major defect of much of the practical application of group dynamics as well as of the classroom dominated by feelings. When one learns always to be concerned with the feelings of others and of oneself as primary in any situation, then one also learns to be careful and circumspect, to be always concerned with not promoting bad feelings. Such affect preoccupation effectively cripples any budding learning of how to approach problems objectively since one's approach to problems becomes strongly conditioned by irrelevant concerns such as what other people may think of your proposed so-

8 William H. Kilpatrick, *Group Education for a Democracy* (New York: Association Press 1940), p. 130.

lution of the problem. Questionable hypotheses, hypotheses that might jar the group and other people's feelings, are entertained timidly if they are entertained at all. Gradually one learns to be sufficiently sensitive to what will or will not disturb other people's feelings. There are always situations, in any problem solution and in any complex learning, in which it may be necessary for someone to say, "You're wrong; this is the right solution." But this is forbidden in the permissive, group-oriented classroom, strange as it may seem. The word "permissive" comes to mean to permit anything but that which will hurt feelings, which will disturb the nice cooperative atmosphere of the class group.

It can readily be seen that permissiveness in education is anything but permissive. Norms, rules of behavior, are set up in any situation. In the traditional classroom they are set up almost entirely by the teacher. In the permissive classroom, they are set up by the group which includes—or may not include—the teacher. In the former situation the norms are usually clearcut and well understood. They may not be liked but they are clear and unambiguous. And traditional classrooms are usually object or subject or problem-oriented. In the latter situation the norms usually lack clarity and definiteness; they are the rather amorphous product of an amorphous social situation where, theoretically, much is permitted but where, in reality, a great deal is restricted. Norms that are amorphous and ambiguous, however, are still rules of behavior, expectations about the right and wrong things to do. The trouble is that

no one is clear as to just what is right, only what is wrong. It is wrong to be uncooperative, not a good group member, not nice. Anything else is right, provided it meets the needs and purposes of the group members. Such an inverted value scale is characteristic of extreme permissive groups, and it is no wonder that manipulation also becomes a characteristic. Manipulation is almost demanded by such a topsy-turvy social situation for, as indicated earlier, the group leader is responsible for achieving the external group goals. But she cannot impose her will; this would not be democratic. Thus she must manipulate the group except in the fortunate case when the group's wishes perhaps fortuitously coincide with the external group goals, i.e., with the goals of society.

The individual psychological consequences of permissiveness have been almost entirely ignored in this essay and can only be touched upon now. It was pointed out in the earlier paper on permissiveness that one of the cogent psychoanalytic reasons for permissiveness was to avoid frustrations to prevent the presumed consequences of frustration, aggression, and possibly mental ill-health. Fenichel has cogently discussed this problem, and I will not repeat his argument.[9] Suffice it to say that in the extreme permissive situation there is probably a good deal of frustration which cannot be dealt with since by definition it is not supposed to exist. Nobody is frustrated if almost anything is permitted everybody (ex-

9 Otto Fenichel, *The Psychoanalytic Theory of Neurosis* (New York: Norton, 1954), pp. 584–589.

cept, perhaps, in the adult group when some members want to get the work done), but as we have seen everything is not permitted. There is a wide band of thinking and activity which is not permitted, even though nothing may be openly said about this verboten area: don't do or say anything which will hurt other people's feelings, which is undemocratic (or that anxiety-provoking word, authoritarian), which is uncooperative, which will prevent the group from reaching its goals and meeting its needs. Above all, don't be an unnice person who is hard to get along with. The autocratic implications of all this should be obvious. Like consensus unanimity thinking, extreme permissiveness carries within itself the seeds of authoritarianism. Conformity, not rational conformity which is necessary for any social life, but irrational and emotional conformity and loss of freedom are the prices paid for this questionable product. Other prices, while not as high, are devastating to the individual, especially to the teacher. Guilt at not being nice, at not being sociometric, at not being a good guy is probably increasing among content-oriented teachers. Anxiety lest one say or do the "wrong" thing, lest one be undemocratic, lest one hurt someone else's feelings, lest one be obstructive (the older word is "argumentative"), lest one not appear right, or—most crushing to the teacher—lest one not be permissive, lest one not let whole children grow as wholes, lest one not be warm and loving, is also increasing. Again, the ultimate price of the permissive-group complex is freedom of the individual. Permissiveness, as preached in some ed-

ucational literature, can be a corrosion of individual freedom, the freedom of the individual intellect to wonder, to speculate, to be daring, to be imaginative, even to be radical. To permit too much is really to permit very little.

Many readers may think that the argument as presented is extreme. And it is. But it is believed that the tendency as outlined exists to an extent little realized by educators themselves. And what is worse, the idea that the philosophy being espoused may be questionable, may be deleterious to children and to teachers, is not even considered. Educators are also often not aware of the metaphysical quality of contemporary permissivist doctrine. Nor are they aware of its dogmatism. As Dewey aptly said, "It is not too much to say that an educational philosophy which proposes to be based on the idea of freedom may become as dogmatic as ever was the traditional education which is reacted against."[10]

A final word is in order. In a healthy democratic classroom the bounds and limits of behavior must be clearly known and understood by teacher and pupils. Pupils must understand authority. Authority of course does not mean authoritarianism. Nor is authority a dirty word. It is an inevitable concomitant of the social process. In the classroom it inheres in the teacher and only seldom in the class group. To be permissive, especially in an extreme fashion, is to blur and confuse the outlines of the class social situation. This does not mean that a teacher should not be permissive. The difficulties men-

[10] Dewey, *op. cit.,* p. 10.

tioned arise when permissiveness is es-poused (explicitly or implicitly) as a basic doctrine of educational practice and is not something a teacher occasion-ally is. When it is espoused as a basic doctrine, it, like all other dogmatisms, leads not to democracy but rather to au-thoritarianism in the classroom.

∽

The Role and Nature of Theory in the Education of the Gifted

Virgil S. Ward*

INTRODUCTION: THE UNFORTUNATE DICHOTOMY BETWEEN THEORY AND PRACTICE

On almost every hand in the pan-orama of American culture a regret-table dichotomy is observed between two broad modes of thought and in-quiry, both of which are essential to the advancement of knowledge and human welfare. We refer to the sys-tems of thought or behavior known as "rational," or speculative, on the one hand, and on the other "empirical," or more narrowly, "experimental." Not since Bacon in the *Novum Organum* explained how either of what he termed the "sophistic or theoretic school" or the "empiric school" of inquiry could, in isolation from the other, "corrupt natural philosophy," have these tech-niques of inquiry been held in proper relationship to each other.

It is known that science, by which term we mean the continuous unfold-ing of reliable information concerning the elements and processes of nature, moves forward through deliberate trans-

* Reprinted by permission from *Educa-tional Theory*, X (July, 1960), 210–216.

actions between reason and delibera-tion on the one hand, and on the other, precise sensory observations, measure-ment, and careful relating of antecedent and consequent conditions in the search for cause and effect. We believe that in American science, research, whether of the "basic" or "applied" nature, has suffered from the neglect of delibera-tive, speculative, and critical play of in-tellect over its diverse enterprises.

Theory goes begging in the aca-demic setting as well. This unfortunate dichotomy between the rational and the empirical is expressed in the pro-duction of dissertations in universities across the nation. Experimental designs, which by their nature are mere instru-ments of inquiry, often receive a de-gree of meticulous attention not simi-larly afforded the idea of the problem into which inquiry is pressed. To render his statistics fool-proof, and to look carefully to the role of what Soro-kin calls "calculating machinery," is ex-pected of the student in far too many institutions, with insufficient regard for the significance of the proposed prob-lem in terms of the existing structure of science. And at the level of the edu-cation of teachers, or lawyers for that matter, what university man has not felt the impact of registration-day inquiries—sometimes timid, sometimes bold—as to whether an anticipated course will for the student be "just more theory" or "something practical and useful."

Now the power of theory to direct the practical activities of scientists, and moralists, and technologists can be experienced merely by invoking such names as Dewey in the progressive education movement, Thorndike in the psychology of learning, Freud in the study of personality, and collectively, Copernicus, Darwin, and Einstein in the pursuit of the natural sciences. Indeed, the writer has never been able to escape the wisdom of Dewey's observation that theory is in the end the most practical of all things because of its widening range of attention beyond nearby purpose and desire (*Sources of a Science of Education*, p. 17).

THE STATUS OF THEORY IN THE EDUCATION OF THE GIFTED

But our concern here is with the status of theory, not in American science or education at large, but in the particular matter of education for the gifted. We have endeavored to analyze this movement with respect to those phases in which some guiding theories appear to have emerged, and those phases which appear still to function largely in accord with arbitrary judgment, local expediences, or simple, unexamined predilections. We submit forthwith that theory exists which is sufficient for the guidance of practical endeavors in two phases of this work:

i.e., in the logical justification of special education for the gifted as grounded in the basic idea of differential education for differential abilities; and in the area of definition and identification. To get the contrasting picture before us immediately, we submit that in two other phases of the enterprise, there is a dearth of theory and a consequent senseless diversity (if not chaos) at the level of practice. These areas are: educational programming and curriculum development.

The very earliest thought in the education of exceptional children spelled out a logic for special education sufficient to embrace all classes of significantly deviant children. The idea that in the differential abilities of children, there exists a demarcation point at which experiences most appropriate for the person of "normal" ability become unsuited for the exceptional child is an adequate notion to support the search for improved experiences both for the mentally handicapped and the mentally gifted.

Now we have suggested further, possibly evoking a marked negative reaction in many thoughtful readers, the adequacy of theory in the problem of definition and identification. But we did not suggest this idly. Throughout the history of this development, and in all the diverse contemporary approaches, essentially two threads of thought prevail. The historically older position, assumed by both Terman and Hollingworth, is that giftedness is a matter of intellectual superiority; the newer position—and one with which the writer takes serious issue—suggests a broader definition, to include specific talents and aptitudes as well as high general intellect. Now all the controversy for and against either of these positions, and all the efforts toward screening and identifying children for differential educational experience, are geared toward one or the other of these theoretical conceptions. This is what we mean by saying that this area of the problem is guided by theory. It does not mean that we think the best of these theories prevails, nor that the best of them is supported by adequate instruments for screening and identifying children. Our point is simply the existence of focal ideas which discipline and lend meaning to practical efforts at the identification of gifted pupils.

In contrast, let us reflect upon the problem of educational programming, the structuring of the daily, weekly, and yearly sequences in subject matter and personal activities so that the child's most excellent total development may occur. The so-called administrative provisions, as the reader may know, usually take such forms as ability grouping, acceleration of the pupil through the grades, or lowering certain subjects within the graded structure. Now we recognize that any of these procedures singly is perhaps intrinsically good, and we are happy, of course, that they are widely practiced. But we submit that the absence of theory is manifest in that schools usually settle upon one or another of these discrete practices and utilize it to the exclusion of the others. For example, the school that practices ability grouping, will most likely not engage in acceleration, but will rather purport that enrichment takes care of subject matter. On the other hand, one hears school after

school suggest to its public that they do have a program for the gifted, they are cooperating in Advanced Placement. Now in spite of all its merits, the Advanced Placement program is merely a form of acceleration, with proper regard to articulation of subject matter. It does not comprise a whole program of special education for the gifted. These various administrative devices are not best utilized in isolation. Various patterns among them should be worked out so that children could, according to their individual needs, benefit from several of these arrangements in combination, as from both moderate acceleration in grade placement and earlier access to individual subjects like Algebra or a foreign language.

We submit as further evidence of the absence of theory in educational programming, the awkward fact that special provisions for the gifted most often have to begin as "extras," external attachments to the required school program, rather than an integral part of it. The gifted student will thus be invited (almost under the discouraging attitude "all right, if you must; but you can't do it on school time") to study the Russian language after school, and on a non-credit basis. In a similar way, "Saturday art classes," and evening seminars on the "Great Books," are sometimes provided. A sound theory of program would arrange for the elevated experiential capacity of the intellectually superior child to exercise itself in a balanced fashion, entirely within the bounds of the normal requirements in time and place, and above all, for full credit.

But possibly the worst consequence of absence of sound perspective is the frequent substitution of what are sheerly administrative re-arrangements of a standard curriculum, for a truly unique program of experience that parallels both the child's superior learning capacity and society's need that he exercise these capacities in appropriate directions and levels. We sincerely hope, for instance, that the emphasis upon "five tough subjects" which the National Education Association and James B. Conant are stressing for the "Academically Talented" pupil will not be translated into an adequate whole program of education for the gifted. A really appropriate paralleling of the child's abilities with the broad range of man's knowledge in a culture in which both science and technology are explosively expanding, and in which problems of the human career are of unsurpassed complexity, simply cannot be arranged out of the traditional content of the American school curriculum. Imaginative and even radical departures will be essential if we attain in this important connection what Lippmann has asked for in general as a "breakthrough" in educational thought. But this criticism of the dearth of theory in curriculum development leads naturally to the inquiry as to the nature of such theory. This is the principal focus of this presentation.

TOWARD A SYSTEMATIC THEORY OF THE CURRICULUM FOR THE SUPERIOR LEARNER

What should be the nature of the educative experience that qualifies as unique, in that it satisfies both the distinguishing capacities and personal needs of the intellectually superior individual, and the social problem of his most proper education for service to mankind? We shall for this occasion refer to three points in the systematic theory embodied in a larger work,[1] in which there have been developed some twelve major "Propositions," and approximately twice as many "Corollaries," which principles we believe to pertain with relative uniqueness to the education of the gifted. We shall think of the three principles just now as involving "reversed ratios," in the sense that each of them suggests a type of reverse emphasis from the usual practice in education. In each case, the extraordinary usage is held to involve the superior abilities of the gifted person, and to provide more appropriately for the range of experiences and responsibilities likely to be assumed or thrust upon him in his life career.

The first of the experiential ratios which we submit must be inverted involves the role of the intellectually superior student in his own education. In the usual instance, educational planning seems to be centered in objective means for engendering within the pupil attitudes and tendencies toward action, and in devices external-to-the-individual for accomplishing the learning act. In planning the curriculum in discussing methods, and in establishing requirements, the governing assumption seems to be that in the individual himself there resides no power which can be utilized, but rather that anything accomplished must take place by means

[1] Virgil S. Ward, "Principles of Education for Intellectually Superior Individuals." Unpublished doctoral dissertation, University of North Carolina, 1952.

of some device struck upon to "cause" the educative experience to be effective.

Typically, the gifted child is interested in school and in learning. Where developmental circumstances or health factors have been conducive to optimum maturity, the intellectual capacity, plus the intrinsic motivation which generally characterizes the gifted individual, provide a combination of psychological qualities that can be utilized in numbers of ways to further his education. Destined to assume social roles in which the continued apprehension of facts, and reflective thinking thereupon, will be urged, the concept of education as "learning how to learn" becomes especially significant for the gifted, and practices which conduce straightforwardly toward increased self-sufficiency in planning and continuing self-education take on added importance.

Teachers serve the individual who can acquire for himself the basic facts and principles of an academic discipline, not by teaching this content per se, but rather by indicating the problems likely to be encountered in learning it. Subsequent to individual learning, the class hour would be given to discussions of the uses and the significance of the ideas involved. In such discussions, if they are handled appropriately, the nature of the problems, insights and concerns to emerge in a special class of gifted children will be radically different from a discussion of subject matter in the usual class. Now this heavier dependence upon the learner for learning without immediate instruction, and the reservation of the class hour for engagement in the complex and elusive subtleties lying in the richest instance just beyond the individual's present unaided grasp, comprise an alteration of usual school practices which we suggest to reverse the ratio of teaching to learning, and of learning to thinking within the class hour.

The second extraordinary process which we extend for consideration involves the treatment of knowledge within the curriculum. Again, in the usual instance the regular school curriculum is shaped through a process that tacitly recognizes a series of maxims such as these: 'Knowledge exists; the direct transmission of knowledge is good; all knowledge cannot possibly be taught; hence a selection must be made of the more reliable and useful details that are to be transmitted.' This transmission is in the order of a one-to-one relationship, i.e., the knowledge that is deemed worthy is passed on in concrete detail to the learner. What is known becomes what is learned.

Now this treatment of knowledge is not the only possible manner of educating youth in necessary skills and understandings. The rapidity of change in culture, as well as the idiosyncrasy of personality suggests the appropriateness of comprehensive exploratory investigations into practically the whole of existing knowledge, sacrificing the particulars of static, accomplished fact (which is available to any upon inquiry) for an introduction to all fields of knowledge in the manner of methodology, problems, applications, limitations, and interrelationships that pertain to each. The school's chief responsibility would thus lie not in transmitting subject matter per se, as at present, but rather in the artful and adequate introduction to fields of knowledge and the laying upon them of a perspective useful throughout the life span.

Through such perspectives—knowledge about knowledge, as it were—the individual's judgment concerning what knowledge were necessary in succeeding problems, and how to acquire such knowledge as were immediately and temporarily essential would be facilitated.

Accordingly, electives from the usual array of courses would be eliminated in general education, in the interest of pursuing in the manner indicated all major fields of knowledge. In practical application, the gifted youth would, instead of selecting Biology, or Chemistry, or Physics, or Geology would be required to understand the nature of all these disciplines at the level, not of existing fact destined so rapidly to become outmoded, but in terms of inherent characteristics of the fields themselves. And his tedious, utterly laborious pursuit of a single foreign language through the artificial instruction of artificially learned teachers would give way to equivalent time in the study of linguistic phenomena, so as to bring within reach of individual mastery the particular forms and uses of any language across the face of the universe, when the exigencies of adult responsibility and opportunity might so indicate.

Now, the full application of this principle, again, bespeaks a very radical departure from pedagogical conceptions as they are, the distinctiveness of the capacity level of the superior learner and his anticipated roles on the frontiers of culture indicating the changed procedure. This form of "preparation for life" is both as possible and as pertinent for the gifted, as it is impracticable and unrealistic in the education of the generality.

The third and final reversal in experiential ratio which we submit as appropriate for the gifted concerns the degree of abstraction involved in the instructional process. The role of direct experience is well recognized in modern educational practices in general. The sand table, the field trip, the school laboratory all testify to an imbedded respect for the inductive mode. "Learning by doing" is truly a foundation stone for modern school instruction.

However, the necessary ratio of concrete experience to the intellective ramification of that experience in the development of generalizations is a variable factor in learning. A rough negative correlation is indicated between the intelligence of the individual and the amount of concrete experience essential to the understanding of a concept. Therefore, it is suggested that at all points in the educative process where the concrete can be abbreviated for gifted youth, in recognition of its diminished necessity, that this be accomplished.

The presentation of curricular material in text and in lecture should be couched at a level of generalization that recognizes the amount of direct experience that the gifted individual will have undergone in formal school and informal environment, and tend to bring to the learning situation. Textbooks written at advanced levels, encyclopedic articles on specific problems (these being noted for compactness and comprehensiveness), and original writings by critics, historians, and scientists on the level of the academic and professional world, as distinct from the standard textual presentation—all these are indicated as more likely to approximate a convenient ratio between the concrete and the abstract than does the text and lesson presentation, at normal grade levels, through which the generality are schooled.

In the education of the gifted, we further note that "ideas" should receive central emphasis. Instruction in ideas as such, and in their relative magnitudes; and curricular traffic in literature conceived at generic levels of ideational structure—these are the zestful educational ingredients for able youngsters. Thus the idea of psychological measurement is likely to be attractive, in addition to the study and application of instruments of measurement; the idea of electricity as a controlled natural energy, in addition to the mechanics of control; the idea of social security, and so on, ad infinitum. Such ideas exist in every subject area. They are found in the history of the subject, from which history "creative moments" may be selected for particular examination. The isolation of "great experiments" in Psychology or in Physics contains the same potentiality. Reflection upon major and minor discoveries in the development of man's complex technology, upon "accidents that have influenced history," are further indications of the educational potential in the selection for study of ideas per se.

It follows finally that the re-presentation of knowledge acquired by the gifted youth should take the more general and the more abstract form. Expectations by the teacher that classroom contributions and individual reports reflect the higher intellectual process are appropriate; merely average quality in thought and performance are not ap-

propriate, and should not be acceptable. In like fashion, teacher-made tests should contain exercises which tap the superiority of the gifted through discussions which demand greater precision in significant fact, more elaborate cognizance of the related variables in a problem, more penetrating inference beyond fact, and more responsible judgment. Without such advanced expectations at all levels in the educative process, the education of the gifted falls short of evoking his finest potential, and school experiences, rather, conduce toward his mediocrity.

CONCLUSION

Now, what have we been saying? A regrettable dichotomy between the empirical and the rational in American culture and science, appears to have manifestations in the field of special education for the gifted. The greatest theoretical vacua appear to be in the areas of programming the special provisions, and in curricular theory. The special curricula being devised so numerously across the nation are far too inadequately buttressed and disciplined by a clear logic, and far too largely the result of spontaneous, unsystematic thought, and immediate exigencies. An intermediate body of principles standing between psychological and sociological fact on the one hand, and school programs on the other—a differential theory of experience to guide the establishment of school practices—may have been the major default of the educator. This presentation comprises certain of the author's attempts at this type of essentially rational endeavor.

Should We Meet the Needs of Students?

B. Paul Komisar*

I. DO WE NEED THE CONCEPT OF NEED?

The weight of evidence, I will try to show, clearly indicates the time has come to dispense with the concept of need in serious discussions of educational policy and theory. Of course the term can continue to claim some utility in the informal day-by-day practice of education. That is, there is no reason for outlawing such "on the job" assertions as "He needs another pencil." But as a central concept in formal talk *about* education, the concept of need is expendable. It confuses rather than clarifies, and it conceals serious issues while flourishing innocuous ones.

This view of the matter seems not to be universal among educationists. There are still many who refer to a "needs-curriculum" and describe the schools' task as "meeting the needs of youth." The *Evaluative Criteria,* one of the most commonly employed set of standards for appraising school performance, is saturated with the language of "need." Thus, there are sufficient grounds for looking again at the concept and surveying some of the grosser consequences of its continued use in educational discussion.[1]

II. THE MEANINGS OF "NEED"[2]

Actually, there is more than one concept of need. As others have noted, the term is equivocal. That there is a motivational concept of need, comes as no surprise to those in education. We say that students have a need for something and mean that the students presently want it or are disposed to want it from time to time when the appropriate provocation arises. Alleged needs for dominance, affection, security or even competence are instances of the motivational concept.

There is also, in education, another meaning of "need." It should be mentioned here although it appears to be a degenerate case of the other meanings. It is the concept of need as a state of lack, as a claim that some specified condition is absent. I do not plan to make further use of this meaning.

There is a third, a prescriptive concept of need which should not be confused with either of these. When we say of an unruly child "He needs discipline," we are not reporting or presupposing that the child now feels a keen desire for discipline. Nor are we

---

* Unpublished manuscript. The analysis is based on the author's "The Pedagogical Concept of Need," *Essays in the Language of Education,* eds. B. O. Smith and R. H. Ennis (Chicago: Rand McNally & Co., 1961).

[1] See almost any standard book on school curriculum and educational psychology; *Evaluative Criteria* (Cooperative Study of

Secondary School Standards, Washington 6, D.C.); *N.E.A. Code of Ethics,* First Principle, Section 2; and *Planning for American Youth* (Washington, D.C.: National Association of Secondary-School Principles, 1951), p. 9.

[2] See the analysis in Paul W. Taylor, "Need Statements," *Analysis,* XIX (April, 1959), 106–111.

reporting or presupposing a propensity on the child's part to seek discipline periodically. Quite the contrary. When we claim (in the prescriptive sense) a need for discipline, we are decrying the absence of such a propensity.

Finally, and this point is often overlooked, a prescription does not assert a lack, though in fact it usually presupposes one. There is an important difference between noting the absence of something and prescribing to remedy it. Statements that report a lack require only criteria of identity, and relevant facts of the case, for their appraisal.[3] For instance, to decide on the correctness of the claim that you lack a car, we require only a way to identify automobiles and information about your possessions. However, the appraisal of the prescription that you *need* a car calls for additional information. We would have to know

1. What goal or objective the car is intended to serve
2. The principles or social expectations which justify this goal
3. Whether the car is in fact necessary to the goal

A students' needs, on this meaning, are not independent things like his blue eyes and brown hair. Rather they are conditional properties, relative to

[3] The same is true of reports of desires and wants, although the criteria of identity may be vastly more difficult to specify. "You can ask a man what he wants, or psychoanalyze him to find out what he *really* wants, but you cannot settle what he needs otherwise than by reaching an agreed decision on the standards to be applied in his case." F. E. Sparshott, *An Enquiry into Goodness* (Toronto: University of Toronto Press, 1958), p. 138.

some posited objective and the principles which justify them. This is revealed, in part, when we are told that a student needs to study *in order to become eligible for football* or that a boy needs discipline *to improve his character*. Without these or other objectives, the needs vanish, and changes in the objectives we uphold for students may result in changes in the students' needs.

Bear in mind, these two concepts of need—the motivational and the prescriptive—as we turn to some of the educational contexts in which they play a role.

III. APPLICATIONS OF CONCEPTS OF NEED

A. "Schools Meet the Needs of Students." Perhaps the minimum objection one can make against this claim is that when it is unaccompanied by a revelation regarding the particular concept involved, some auditors may not know what educational program it suggests. It could either be referring to a school program which caters to motives or one which fulfills prescriptions. Those acquainted with educational literature know the prescriptive meaning is usually adopted, but there must be a way of phrasing this intent which avoids the initial confusion.

But even when the prescriptive meaning is clearly indicated, new difficulties beset us. First, the very nature of the prescriptive concept makes it possible to get "agreement" on the claim among men who agree on little else in education. The claim that schools do or should meet needs of youth becomes nothing but an empty formula.[4] The pseudo-agreement arises from the conditional character of prescriptions. We can all assent to the desirability of "meeting needs" while diverging on the particular goals to be achieved or what manner of content and organization are "really necessary" to achieve them. The emptiness of the formula may not be a disadvantage in some conceivable circumstances, but the statement of a serious educational position is not one of them.

The obverse side of this coin is that having accepted the needs formula as significant, there is a temptation to view the determination of content as just a technical matter, a descriptive task. The specious similarity between the directives "Teach the Students Civics" and "Meet the Students' Needs" renders the view even more plausible. Nonetheless the claim is false. Because of their very nature, the determination of educational needs is a *normative* enterprise. For any prescrip-

tion of need invokes an appeal to social principles or norms for its justification. One may *describe* the balance of powers in government, but the claim that students need to learn this or that, is not a descriptive claim. But, alas, the normative element is implicit, and curriculum-makers, who are understandably not attracted to disputes, may be tempted to keep it that way. This attitude accounts, I suspect, for the presumption that an education based on needs naturally requires a diversified curriculum. To many educationists this is an utterly obvious inference. It seems not to occur to them that with different norms one might just as obviously claim that students need a common, even a common academic, curriculum.

So the use of "need" in the formula we are discussing, engenders two equally abhorrent results: pseudo-agreement to an empty formula and a view that the determination of educational needs is only a descriptive matter. This is what we should expect from a term that is both vacuous and deceptive.

There are other educational contexts in which the term "need" has a role, its disservices to perform. Some of the sharp distinctions which help to isolate variables and distinguish points of contention are obscured when the term is employed to state them. Let me cite a few examples.

B. Remote Versus Immediate Needs. This distinction is popular among educators, though it is not always made in these terms. From what we know of the two concepts of need it is clear that the distinction has several possible interpretations.

(1) This may simply be another, less adequate, way of casting the original distinction between needs as mo-

---

[4] "Woolliness of this sort seems to have a natural habitat in certain fields: in education, in sociology, in metaphysics as well as in aesthetics. Why should these fields be distinguished by so fine an array of empty formulae? One reason, certainly, is that the metaphysician, the sociologist, the educationalist, attempt to reconcile oppositions in a formula so generally applicable, so empty of any intrinsic content, that everyone can interpret it to suit himself. Thus the sociologist engages in dull and pretentious talk about society's being "an organic whole" when he wants to conceal the fact of social conflict, the educationalist talks about "the ultimate welfare of the child and of society" as "the aim of education" when he wants to make it appear that everybody expects the same kind of consequence from educational processes; J. A. Passmore, "The Dreariness of Aesthetics," *Aesthetics and Language,* ed. William Elton (New York: Philosophical Library, Inc., 1954), p. 43.

tives and needs as prescriptions. The prescriptions, presumably, being more "remote" to the student than his own motives.

(2) If we stay within the prescriptive meaning, this distinction could take two forms:

(a) If "remote" is viewed psychologically, a distinction can be maintained between needs prescribed for the student's own goals and those prescribed on the basis of imposed goals. Thus, a high school diploma is an immediate or personal need for the boy who wants to go to college, but it is a remote goal for the boy whose parents uphold this objective against his own wishes.

(b) However, "remote" can have a temporal meaning as well. In this case the difference exists between prescriptions or goals to be achieved soon and those to be realized in the more distant future.

(3) Without developing it in detail, the same two possibilities as in (2) exist when "need" is taken motivationally. There are, psychologically, more and less pressing motives and, temporally, long and short range motives.

Once the opaque reference to needs is pierced a rather startling range of possibilities is revealed. There is no simple dichotomy along a single dimension as the original distinction might lead us to expect. Nor can these differences be rejected as mere pettifogging, if we consider the educational purposes for which this distinction is made. This distinction is important in examining and directing the place of motivation in the classroom. It is a variation on the old question (as phrased by Dewey) of whether objectives of adult life can supply sufficient motive power to sustain contemporary learning in school. What we find, however, is that

the problem is in no way that simple. There are not just two variables which might influence learning but a range of them. Considering that this is an empirical task, it ill behooves us to impede the research by a choice of inappropriate terminology.

C. INDIVIDUAL VERSUS COMMON NEEDS. The question that arises in connection with this particular distinction is not that important differences are embedded in its interstices. It is certainly true that the meaning of it varies with the sense of "need," but the possible interpretations are not particularly obscure.

Prescriptively, given any objective, there may be requirements which apply to all students. Other students, because of unusual deficiencies, may require additional achievements to realize the objective. For example, with some such goal as "essay writing," all students may require assistance in developing style (common need), but one student may require special help with spelling (individual need).

Motivationally, a dichotomy can be set up between those who have the "same" motive and those who have idiosyncratic ones. There is a tendency to overlook some of the difficulties in identifying sameness here. In the physiological domain we can speak of the same motives on the basis of similarity in the physiological processes involved. Regarding the personality or social needs, however, we depend on the kind of behavior which is manifested. The problem connected with this fact, mainly problems of *language,* have not been carefully attended to in education.

But these are not the main objections to be raised against this distinction. Instead, I would ask why the term "need," at least in its prescriptive sense, should be introduced here at all. Since the phenomena involved are already so well known in the verbal garb of "individual differences," why clutter the landscape with new terms?

D. NEEDS OF SOCIETY VERSUS NEEDS OF INDIVIDUALS. Lurking in the recesses of this distinction is the temptation to ignore an issue of contemporary significance, or what is worse, to rationalize the issue away. For some are prone to disregard the distinction for purposes of school policy, claiming that education necessarily involves both individual *and* social considerations. Therefore, the claim that the two are in conflict is erroneous.[5]

There is just enough plausibility in this claim to make it dangerous. For certainly action on any social need requires that we translate the need into individual terms. The need of society for engineers ultimately takes the form of a host of individual prescriptions (John needs to be an engineer, and Harry and . . .). It works in the other direction as well. There is a sense in which all individual needs are based on social considerations. Whenever we require something of an individual, we do so on the basis of certain social expectations or principles. This is part of the very logic of the prescriptive concept of need. Therefore, whenever we deal with needs, both social and individual factors are involved.

But these facts do not preclude the possibility of a conflict between social and individual needs in concrete cases. Suppose we have a student with ability

in two fields, one greatly demanded by industry and government and the other not. Which ability do we exploit in school? I think we all recognize the ethical overtones here.[6] Yet once we phrase the issue in terms of "need," the conflict seems to vanish. We catch ourselves saying, "Yes, but the individual needs X because society needs Y, and both are satisfied together." The temptation is strong, but it arises only because we adopt the rhetoric of need. Strip away the rhetoric and the ethical issue intrudes, not to be solved by sophistry.

E. FUNCTIONAL NEEDS AND FELT NEEDS. Though not intended as a distinction, these are two particularly piquant examples with which to close this discussion. Though the demonstration is probably unnecessary at this point, it could be shown that in the prescriptive sense the notion of a *functional* need is a howling redundancy. The situation is not much better with motivational concept when the description of needs is accompanied, as it so often is, by the codicil that all specific motives serve as ways of satisfying one or a group of "basic" motives (needs). By a *priou* arrangement, then, most needs turn out to be functional.

The expression "felt need" suffers not so much from redundancy as ambiguity. A felt need is usually described as a need which the subject recognizes (or a need of which he is conscious). But this is of no help. A person can "have a requirement" as well as, "have a motive." A person can come to realize

---

[5] For an example, see the section "Individual Needs Versus Social Needs: A False Issue" in Maurice P. Hunt and Lawrence E. Metcalf, *Teaching High School Social Studies* (New York: Harper & Brothers, 1955), pp. 217–222.

[6] Or if we do not, the following, among others, offer reminders: Henry S. Commager, "Education For What?" *Hadassah Newsletter* (March, 1958), p. 4; and Henry M. Wriston, "Education and the National Interest," *Foreign Affairs* (July, 1957), 564–580.

a tendency in his own behavior, thus recognizing a personal motive. But one can also become aware of a requirement. In fact "becoming conscious of a requirement" can have the additional meaning of "accepting the requirement as proper." So a claim to base schooling on felt needs is open to a surprising variety of possible interpretations. It is not at all clear what the injunction means.

IV

The upshot of all this is clear. The continued wanton use of "need" to pose important educational ideas and issues results in vague, indeterminate, often trivial cliches which sacrifice clarity to obfuscation and generally do treason to the cause of understanding. We would do well to objure the term. We would not be losing a word; we would be gaining an audience.

∽

Value Theories and the Evaluation of Education

D. Bob Gowin*

Starting in the fall of 1958, a five-year study will attempt to answer the question: "How good are our schools?"[1] Co-sponsors of the study are the National School Boards' Association and the American Association of School Administrators. The project will attempt to provide techniques that would enable school board members, school administrators and the community "to take an objective and critical look at their schools and determine just how effective they are."[2]

Serious concern with the effectiveness of public education is both a public and professional issue. The public is demanding a better report on the schools: teachers are demanding the opportunity to do a better job of teaching.

Often missed in the many heated discussions, however, is the recognition of the terms "effectiveness" and "better" as value terms. Whether public schools are effective as they ought to be, or whether they could be better, cannot be decided until we can at least recognize the different conceptions of values and then go on, if we need to act, to choose an appropriate conception.

Help with this problem comes from two directions. First, a brief look at where values are located in the different value theories helps to clarify the issue because if we can locate values, then we will know where to turn to evaluate education. Secondly, a more extensive look at some of the confusions as well as positive contributions surrounding the prominent experimentalist theory of value might help to present a program for action.

In classical value theory, values are located in a variety of places. The Aristotelians place value in the being, inherently; and "beings" are usually

* Reprinted by permission from *Teacher Education Quarterly*, XV (Connecticut State Department of Education, Spring, 1958), 78–84.

[1] Leonard Buder, "Five-Year Study Set on School Rating," *The New York Times* (April 17, 1958), p. 33.

[2] *Ibid.*

placed in some hierarchy. From this viewpoint we find that history will always have more value (inherently) than bookkeeping or accounting, as the Carnegie unit indicates. Idealism drives value to an eternal order of the mind. Of highest value is something which is least useful, and a professional group of moralists, aestheticians, and clergymen are necessary to divine the elusive reaches of highest value. Materialism often reduces value to physical conditions. A violin solo is, after all, only the vibration of horsehair over "cat" gut. Each of these classical positions regards value in one fashion or other as absolute. Experimentalism regards value as relative.

What are values relative to? Experimentalism has undergone many criticisms concerning the proposition about the relativity of value. Most of these criticisms spring from misunderstandings. Because an experimentalist expresses relativity of value, he is accused of being a subjectivist—of believing that value is relative to opinion, and that one person's opinion is just as good as another's. Some suggest that relativity means amorality—since there are no absolute standards, then there are no value standards at all, and we can all indulge our suppressed desires and be amoral. Finally, other writers identify the experimentalist notion of value with that of some logical positivists— that values are mere "sensations" or emotions which express preference, preference which ultimately reduces to "Boo" or "Hurrah."

For the experimentalist, however, values are relative to a frame of reference. Values are relative to wants (desires), to possible means (or instru-

ments), and to satisfactions (consequences). Because value propositions are relative (and not merely impulsive, or emotional, or capricious, or spontaneous), they may be intelligently discussed, investigated, and tested. Value is a daily part of the business of scientists, businessmen, economists, educators. The argument that other peoples' tastes suit them just as ours suit us, and that therefore both tastes are equally good, has the underlying assumption that tastes are ultimate bases of value and nothing can be done about it. Merely desired objects may or may not be worth desiring. An obese student who continually eats sugars and starches because he desires them probably needs a doctor to help in valuing the suitable and in learning to like it.

Experimentalist value theory suggests four bases for judging values. These four bases or grounds may be labelled (1) the yardstick (2) the score card (3) the ideal (4) the hypothesis.

THE YARDSTICK

If we could lay down a yardstick alongside one educational system, mark it off at say 29 inches, and then place the same yardstick against another educational system and read a 31, we would know—through the intermediation of the yardstick as an instrument—that one system was "longer" than the other. Notice that the word was not "better." In some evaluating contexts, however, we may have a third piece of information which warrants a high probability that there is a high correlation between "more" of something and "better" of something. This form of evaluating may sound like

Chamber of Commerce bigger-and-betterism, but even so there is a limited truth in the notion that there is some correlation between quantity and quality. The correlation, however, should not be assumed—which is the fallacy of bigger-and-betterism. The correlation must be demonstrated by empirical and experimental work.

For example, there is a correlation between quantitative tests of wheat and the quality of wheat for food uses. Weight, size, color, and hardness may all be measured quantitatively. Also, sample testings of germination of wheat may be recorded in percentages. Experimental testing over the years warrants the proposition that some wheat is better than some other wheat if on each of these yardsticks the amount is higher.

Yardsticks are rare in education. The over-exploitation of the I.Q. and scholastic grade averages indicates the eagerness for some such purely quantitative yardstick. It is not always the case that the higher the I.Q. the better the student; persistence and motivation must be counted, too. Nor does a high grade average mean "better educated"; many students get the grade without getting what the grade is supposed to stand for.

Nevertheless, evaluation should begin with Sir Francis Galton's maxim: whenever you can, count. We can compare system A with system B in purely quantitative terms on (at least) the following three yardsticks: the number of drop-outs, the frequency of the turnover of library books, the salaries paid teachers. A recent empirical study done at Columbia reports that the more money paid to teachers (not just the total amount spent on schools), the better the education.

Newspapers may be compared in terms of the length of space given particular news. When Texas newspapers were measured in this way on the amount of national and international news space given, most were found to be grossly deficient compared to newspapers of many other states. Toynbee compared civilizations in terms of the number of criminals rehabilitated. Political administrations might be compared in terms of the number of unemployed, or the number of civil rights violations.

In using the yardstick, we assume at least two things: (1) that the units of measure are equal units (i.e., that the scale is a cardinal scale) and (2) that the findings of experimental research establish a high correlation between the quantitative and the qualitative.

THE SCORE CARD

This measure may be used in cases where the units are not deemed equal but where a ranking is deemed possible. For example, in judging cattle, expert judges may have a score card with as many as forty items. Each item has a weighting, and the listing of the items on the score card is a useful device for covering all relevant judgments. A perfect specimen is conceivable, but not necessary. All that is needed are examples judged superior. Or to put it differently, the end is assumed, but the need for determining absolute worth is abridged. Complex judgments resulting in a sort of summary statement of rank order—of "A is better than B" and "B is better than C"—instead of a slavish adding up of items, is the purpose of this method of comparison.

Scores from typical psychometric tests, for example, are better thought of as placing individuals in an order rather than as measuring amounts of the characteristic in question. If students X, Y, and Z respectively score 50, 100, and 150 on the Stanford-Binet Intelligence Test, it is generally preferable to think of X as being below Y rather than as having one-half as much intelligence and of Y as above X but below Z, and hence to rank individuals 3, 2, and 1. The same comments may be made about academic grades and the scores obtained from most rating scales. The appropriate statistics for score card ratings are the nonparametric statistics.[3]

The score card in education is a much more generally applicable method of evaluation than the yardstick. The Strong Interest Test, for example, may present to the person tested a summary judgment of the order "You are interested in Social Service area more than Journalism and your interests in Social Service are more like those of teachers of social science and Y.M.C.A. directors than not." In studying father-child relations, rating scales along various continua of conformity, aggression, and positive-negative feeling, make possible summary judgments of more or less.[4] The logical end-points of zero and per-

fect are meaningless in practice and need not be assumed.

THE IDEAL

The ideal is seeing in what is that which would be better. This measure may serve as a standard of comparison for existing factual complexes or for proposed objectives. The end is not assumed, but prior values are assumed. The ideal specifies conditions under which wants or desires will or would be fulfilled, and therefore can serve as a norm for any partial fulfillment, viz., the United Nations.

From the ideal one may be able to deduce the means for bridging the gap between available resources and the ideal solution. Thus the ideal serves as an indirect technique for comparing the value of alternative plans or policies. It is better than not, methodologically, to frame the ideal with reference to the particular problem and with due regard for the realities in the matter of resources. Or as Mitchell wrote, "The ideal is imaginary but it need not be fanciful."[5]

The practical function of the imagination is common to everyday experience. We may be hungry, tired, lonely, thirsty, and crave stimulating surroundings and conversation. We could order these wants in a rank; and, starting with the highest ranked want, satisfy them one after the other. Or we could imagine an ideal dinner which would fulfill all of them satisfactorily. In a similar manner, the ideal of love and home satisfies a variety of wants

[3] Merle W. Tate, and Clelland, Richard C., *Nonparametric and Shortcut Statistics* (Danville, Ill.: Interstate Printers and Publishers, Inc., 1957).

[4] Lois Meek Stolz *et al., Father-Child Relations of War-Born Children* (Stanford, Calif.: Stanford University Press, 1954).

[5] E. T. Mitchell, "Valuing and Evaluation," *Value, A Cooperative Inquiry*, ed. Ray Lepley (New York: Columbia University Press, 1949), p. 190–210.

while transforming and refining them.

The formation of the ideal, viewed as a process of revaluing old wants and satisfactions, transforms old values and creates new ones. The improvement of instruction is a transformation of prior values. The value of an ideal as an organic whole is not fully appreciated until it is experienced. Forming the ideal assumes old values, such as food, drink, and conversation; but it also requires artistry or creative imagination to re-formulate the old values which have been separately experienced into a new end, a new combination of values which are modified, ordered, and related in terms of the proposed end.

In terms of unity and integration, of revaluing factors in a more complex experiential whole, we may get some vision of the continually enriched experience sometimes called qualitative growth, or the artistic intensification of experience. As for artistry in teaching such matters as correlated subjects, the core curriculum, the assaying of community resources, the judging of the available resources of the pupils in each class, teacher-pupil planning, general education, current events frequent testing—all these procedures and methods may be seen as ways to project from where one is, to where one would like to be. Often missed in such proposals to improve instruction, however, is just this principle of evaluation—the principle of imaginative projection into the future of an artistic integration of values experienced earlier. Unless the more complex organic whole is experienced, its value is not fully appreciated. If an ideal stands the test, it is proclaimed to be good; it is useful in the attainment of the good life.

THE HYPOTHESIS

Making and testing hypotheses might seem appropriate only to scientific endeavor. Hence, it is important at the outset to mention the difference between the function of an hypothesis in scientific inquiry which is prompted by an absence of knowledge, such as the search for a medical tool to handle polio, and the function of an hypothesis in educational and social policy where there is absence of agreement on what should be done, how it should be done, and the application of socio-scientific knowledge to get it done. Thus, one does not vote on whether two and two add up to four or apply a microscope to ballots.

In education, absence of agreement is most commonly the problem, although it is obvious that absence of information, or factual knowledge, where factual knowledge may be obtained, can affect agreement. Factual information about the relation between salary and teaching effectiveness, range of intelligence of teachers, number of hours devoted to teaching or to other jobs outside of class, length of time at one grade level or at one school may help us decide about merit pay scales, but hypotheses still need to be made.

The hypothesis functions in general evaluation of policies. We know, or should know, that the changes proposed will have indirect consequences that are difficult to foresee. New satisfactions and dissatisfactions undreamed of will arise. Our only procedure in evaluating policies is discussion, and the only value of discussion is to bring to bear on moot questions as much of human experiences and technical knowledge as possible. Debate boils down to rival hypotheses as to the indirect consequences of the proposed program. The truth as to what the consequences will be is quite hypothetical. The accepted hypothesis is tentative, subject to revision as the actual consequences substantiate or invalidate the predictions. If an hypothesis stands testing, it is proclaimed to be true; it is useful in the progress of knowledge.

In a problem situation, the right choice is the best alternative in view of the anticipated consequences. In choosing, we would want accurate historical evidence about the possible trends of various alternatives; we would want relevant scientific information which seemed to have the greatest predictive validity. But, in so far as the circumstances are unique and particular, our anticipations are highly conjectural.

Nevertheless, we must choose and we must act. The energy found in the compelling human desire for certainty before we act needs to be channelled into discovering historical trends and scientific information. We must choose and act, because as it has frequently been pointed out, to make no choice is to make a choice in favor of the status quo. That is, it is a choice to let someone else do it for us. There are many, many people to do the job; but they are apt to be eager and inept. The yardstick, the score card, the ideal, and the hypothesis are tools the professional educator may use to evaluate education and to improve instruction; and he should have no reluctance to go in and win. In such a situation, the overarching value judgment is that it is better to solve our problems than not to solve them and it is better to solve them better, than worse.

∽

The Merit Plan: Boon or Bane?

*Hobert W. Burns**

If teachers, as an organized group, have driven home any single point to the public that supports the entire educational enterprise, that point is that teachers are underpaid. Indeed, the concept "teacher" almost tautologically implies the concept "underpaid" in the mind of the public.

It is a truism, of course, that teachers *are* underpaid: and for specification instead of generalization the reader is

referred to his journal of opinion, his journal of number, or his newspaper.

Yet, with a philosophic perversity that may be reminiscent of ivory tower days, we should like to dismiss for the time being the question of "how much money" and, by the application of Occam's Razor, consider merely the question of "how."

With philosophic detachment, then, we suggest that the real issue in the determination of teacher salary schedules is not one of how *much* but one of *how* to pay teachers.

* Reprinted by permission from *The Educational Forum*, XXVI (May, 1957), 443–451.

The *much*-ness is basically an empirical question which conjoins with an ethical question, and both are solved only by reference to the body politic: empirically, the question is how much money is available for the entire educational undertaking in any given community; ethically, the question is how much of that total sum the public, as represented by its board of education, is willing to allocate for certificated salaries. These questions, pressing and controversial as they may be, are not here under discussion for our emphasis lies elsewhere.

The *how*-ness, in contrast to the empirical nature of the *much*-ness, is primarily a philosophic question; but its solution depends upon other questions which claim both a logical and psychological priority. The first, and likely the most important and most difficult, of these prior questions turns ultimately upon the definition of teaching as either craft or as profession.

Psychologically we may be inclined to assert that education, on the basis of some *de jure* or *de facto* argument, or on the basis of some self-evident truth, is quite obviously a profession (or a craft, as the case may be). These naive, emotional approaches—too often the trademark of the militant teachers union, and too often the sustaining ethic of the super-professional teachers group—may well serve the purposes of faculty meeting debates, but they are necessarily inconclusive and unconvincing in serious analysis. We need, somehow, to distinguish adequately between the crafts and the professions without reference to dogma in order that we may then, in the light of such criteria, not only assign education its proper role

but apply these criteria to our economic questions of *much*-ness and *how*-ness.

The most significant distinction between the crafts and the professions— assuming that such a distinction does exist, and granting it is not an absolute distinction—lies not in the traditional manual-mental dexterities dichotomy, nor in the possession or absence of skills, nor in the type or amount of energy expended. Rather, on analysis, it seems to lie in that precise area pinpointed by Professors Broudy,[1] Kinney,[2] and Thomas:[3] *in the role that theory plays for both craft and profession, and in the degree to which practice is guided by theory.*

Here, perhaps, we can begin to distinguish measurable differences between occupations: granted that, to some extent, all occupations are possessed of both practice and theory, we notice that some *depend* upon and seek guidance from theory to a considerable extent, while others, if not independent, are less dependent. If, as seems to be the case, some occupations require of their practitioners the mastery of not only the body of empirical knowledge which consists the occupation but also mastery of theoretical knowledge which guides the occupation, then by ascertaining if, in the first place, an occupation does make such a requirement and then, in the second place, the degree to

[1] Harry S. Broudy, "Teaching—Craft or Profession?" *The Educational Forum,* XX (January, 1956).

[2] Lucien B. Kinney and Lawrence G. Thomas, *Toward Professional Maturity in Education* (San Francisco, Calif.: California Teachers Association, 1955).

[3] Lawrence G. Thomas, *The Distinctive Nature of the Philosophy of Education,* unpublished MS, Stanford University, 1955.

which theory actually does give guidance to practice, we have a rather clear-cut method of differentiating between occupations. Further, we may thus find a solution to the *how*-ness, if not the *much*-ness, problem.

With such criteria in mind we can safely assert that those occupations which do have a body of theoretical knowledge as well as practical know-how, which do derive guidance from that body of theory, and which also require mastery of theory on the part of the practitioners are, by definition, professions. Accordingly, those occupations which fail in these respects are not professions in the full sense of the word. This does not imply, of course, that occupations which fail to meet these criteria are thereby crafts.

Undoubtedly there are criteria for craftsmanship which are no less exacting than those we have proposed for the professions. Indeed, it may well be that many crafts *do* have a body of theory to validate their practices. If this is the case, the question then becomes one of guidance and one of theoretical competence on the part of the craftsman. But, consistent with our criteria and the definition that followed from them, the craft that meets all of these requirements is, or becomes, a profession. Thus do our criteria meet the challenge of change, as well as avoid the faulty logic of either-or: there is no immutable characteristic of crafts that prevent them from becoming professions nor, conversely, any convention that guarantees tenured status to a profession.

We have not developed, in any detail, criteria for craftsmanship inasmuch as our primary analysis is to determine whether or not teaching can qualify as a profession, and if so, the subsequently entailed questions of whether or not teachers qualify as professionals, and if so, how professionals ought to be paid. It is entirely possible—more likely, probable—that we shall find no clear-cut answer because education as a whole may be a profession while individual educational practitioners may not be professionals. This unhappy circumstance occurs when the occupation has a theoretical foundation and requires a theoretical competence of its practitioners, but when individual practitioners are either ignorant as to the theoretical base or fail to derive guidance from that base. These variables, it becomes apparent, will have important implications for our concern with the *how*-ness of salary schedules.

From these considerations it follows that teaching is a profession only if it requires, and if required utilizes, theory to give guidance to educational practices. That education has theory is only too evident—witness the theoretical spectrum that runs from scholasticism through essentialism, and from progressivism through reconstructionism. Here, if anything, is an embarrassment of theoretical riches.

The analysis now depends upon the guidance received from such theories, and this being more of an empirical question we temporarily refer it to those operating in the lower levels of our ivory tower.[4] We, preferring to remain aloft for the moment, wish now to note that the issue also reduces to

---

[4] Ultimately, of course, empirical questions are vastly more important than sheer theoretical questions, for theory finds its justification and its value only in practical situations.

the theoretical competence of the educational practitioners. But this too is more of an empirical question, so in keeping with our temporary bias we refer this also to those with their feet planted on firm empirical ground.[4]

I

What we have determined so far, as a result of our analysis, is that education is, or can become, a profession—depending upon the individual practitioners. Or, to put the emphasis in another way, education as an occupation meets the criteria of a profession—but individual practitioners within education may or may not be professional.

This permits us to conclude at this point that educational salaries [remember that our main concern herein is the question of *how*-ness], if they are to be consistent with the occupational and practitioner requirements demanded by our criteria, *ought to be flexible enough and liberal enough to match the degree of professionalism achieved by individual practitioners.* This, of course, presupposes but is not dependent upon individual differences among practitioners.

The question of *how*-ness, thus, turns out on inspection to be prior to and more important than the question of *much*-ness—for if the *how*-ness requires the recognition and reward of individual professional achievement (however we may define achievement), then the degree of *much*-ness needs to be correlated with the degree of professionalism. In this sense quantity depends upon quality, and this indeed implies a differential salary schedule— or, to use the more controversial phrase, it implies merit rating.

As soon as we raise the question of merit, and our prior analysis of professionalism notwithstanding—we come face to face with the Medusa head of the merit-criteria problem. Yet, before we reflect upon this seemingly ugly sight, let us for a moment desert the realm of theory for the realm of fact, and make some observations about the current *how*-ness practices.

Currently teachers are being paid like craftsmen (they may, of course, be craftsmen), and our salary problems reflect our emphasis on *much*-ness. In the overwhelming majority of school districts we find that our teacher salary schedules have a basic, craftsmanlike structure: horizontally across the schedule we find the categories of preparation, and vertically down the schedule we find the categories of experience. The basic dimensions of *how*-ness, then, are training (horizontally, along the x-axis) and seniority (vertically, along the y-axis). The teacher, similarly with the craftsman, is fitted into a general category and rewarded solely upon the basis of his latitude and longitude upon this two-valued schedule which provides for little recognition of individual professional achievement and competence.

The craftsman who has completed his apprenticeship training, and who has been a journeyman for a period of time, achieves the status of master-craftsman when he stands to the far right-hand side of the schedule; further, as he passes through the horizontal categories of apprentice, journeyman, and master, he necessarily moves down on the schedule at the same time until, near the end of his career, he achieves the prestige and economic rewards that two-dimensioned wage scales provide for those who finally settle down in the lower, right-hand corner of the schedule. In the one nomenclature we call such a practitioner a "master-craftsman" and in another nomenclature we call such a practitioner a "master-teacher." It is not difficult to conclude that teachers are rewarded in similar fashion to craftsmen, at least in regard to the *how*-ness (if not the *much*-ness).

There are, as we might expect, many assumptions underlying the theory that pays teachers in accord with such a two-dimensioned scale. Most obviously, it is assumed that the quality of teaching performance increases with the *quantity* of preparation, and with the *quantity* of experience. Yet, we must note that it has been empirically determined that the correlation between quality of teaching and length of service—after the first few years—is not high; indeed, it is not even statistically significant.[5]

Salary increments based on the vertical [length of service] axis are thus not consonant with the underlying assumptions of the two-valued schedule. In point of fact, we need also note that individual teacher differences contradict the assumption that equal training assures equal classroom performance: it is no trade secret that schools of education have long and futilely sought a measure that will successfully predict and correlate classroom competence with academic preparation. Yet an ac-

curate correlation of quantity of preparation with quality of performance is as yet undetermined—if, indeed, it is determinable—and thus salary increments based on the horizontal [amount of pre- or in-service training] axis are not consonant with the assumptions underlying the two-dimensioned scale. Hence, *the two most vital presuppositions justifying the existence of contemporary salary schedules are, to a large and significant degree, faulty.*

We cannot escape the conclusion that our present salary schedules, which exhibit the craft-philosophy of *how*-ness, are not flexible enough to match the varying degree of professionalism that may be achieved by individual practitioners. If we accept our earlier analysis as to the basic distinction between craft and profession, then we must reject the two-valued salary schedule as inadequate, inconsistent, and erroneous.[6]

There are practical, and unfortunate, consequences that follow when we claim professional status and yet cling to a craftsman's schedule: in our salary negotiations we restrict our flexibility by being able to demand only across-the-board increases, or at best, differential increases for all practitioners depending upon their horizontal-vertical position. Such limited mobility not only minimizes the fact of individual differences, it limits each categorical *much*-ness to the lowest common denominator of that category. Further, it makes the salary maximum functionally dependent upon the lowest common denominator within the entire schedule:

[5] If it is even measurable; if it isn't measurable then there is no way in which the presuppositions of the schedule involved can be verified, and we are left with the uncomfortable consequence of merely accepting them on faith. For the devout this may be familiar and reliable, but for the scientist such familiarity breeds only contempt.

[6] Here is an instance of educational philosophy giving guidance to educational policy —in accord with our criteria of professionalism.

thus there is no difference between the salaries of excellent, average, and poor teachers who are, as a consequence of the rigid schedule, in the same training-experience classification. In a real and practical sense, until teachers develop a *how*-ness that is commensurate with their professional ambitions, the public may balk at providing a *much*-ness that is based on an unclear and unsound *how*-ness—and our present salary schedules are not models of clarity. By accepting guidance from the inconsistent theory demonstrated in the two-valued schedule our salary practices have led to unhappy economic consequences for all teachers.

II

Ascending once more into the realm of philosophy, if we are forced to surrender our simple training-experience criteria of *how*-ness as being incompatible with professionalism, what alternatives are left to us?

To answer this question, obviously, we should require an analysis that would pre-empt the pages of *The Educational Forum* for many issues to come. We must, therefore, content ourselves with sketching out the basic issues involved in determining the criteria for a professional salary *how*-ness.

The fundamental requirement is that a professional salary schedule be based upon the traditional values of training and experience, but also contain the vital third dimension designed to reward individual professional merit. Thus it would be presumed that all practitioners must meet fairly stable training requirements, possess fairly variable teaching experiences, and, fi-

nally, it would be presumed that as a consequence of training, experience, and individual ability certain practitioners would be more professionally competent.

This does not preclude, of course, a professional minimum, nor does it imply individual salary negotiations that make room for favoritism, or put each teacher at the mercy of an administrator, or smack of yellow-dog contracts. It requires only that adequate provision be made for the economic recognition of the superior teacher; that the *much*-ness be geared to the *how*-ness, and that the *how*-ness be geared to individual professional competence and achievement. Thus we now re-encounter the Medusa head from which we turned our faces a few moments ago. But, supported now with empirical as well as theoretical weapons, we may confidently focus on the Medusa.

The criteria problem, which seeks to identify "good teaching," is difficult but not insoluble. However, what is required here is not so much an analysis of practice,[7] but an analysis of theory: more specifically, of value theory. But, surely, we cannot solve this. Theoreticians far wiser than we have struggled through the centuries for an infallible definition of goodness, and none has appeared. It is conceivable, then, that no such definition has appeared because there is none to appear; that no definition of good is absolute and infallible. This apparently casts us into the morass of relativism, but on sober reflection it

---

[7] Which is done by all criteria-seekers who utilize the relatively new "critical incident technique" of John C. Flanagan. This technique will accurately describe the *how*-ness being practiced, but it cannot describe or prescribe *how*-ness in theory.

may turn out that our solution does lie in a relative approach.

Presupposing for the moment that the search for an *absolute* criterion of good teaching is foredoomed to failure —for, in this case, the needle is not even in the haystack—we are left, consequently, not with a problem of discovery but with a problem of creation. Immediately the glare of the offending Medusa softens: man may not be able to discover, for what he seeks may not exist—but man *can* create. And our creations need not claim absolute status, they need only to be accepted by other men. With this approach to value theory we can begin to solve our problem: granted that there is no determinable absolute quality of good teaching upon which to base our professional salary schedule, but also grant that each district can create or define qualities which they will accept as constituting good teaching, and then base our salary schedules upon these man-made criteria. Further, let us define these qualities in behavioral terms—and now, it seems, we not only have the criteria of good teaching but the means of measuring and evaluating teaching. Our salary schedules can now be based not upon untested and untestable presuppositions, but upon observable and measurable behavior.[8]

III

Generally, it does not seem that individual practitioners are opposed to

merit plans in principle—they are aware of the basic soundness of a principle that rewards on the basis of individual performance. However, one of our great American "buts . . ." seems to admit the validity of the principle and then deny the practical effectiveness of the theory, and merit salary schedules are no exception—they have almost been "butted" to death.

The "but, it isn't practical" argument has many forms, yet most "buts" usually reduce—after some intellectual exercise—to the basic argument that merit plans necessarily require measurement, that teaching is an elusive, unmeasurable art, and therefore merit plans are impossible in practice. It is then concluded that we had better stick with what we have, because it does work in practice even if it is weak in theory. This is, needless to say, a fairly low-level interpretation of pragmatism.

The argument does, however, appear to have a convincing face validity *if* it is actually the case that teaching is such an elusive process that it defies all measurement. Yet, when we look beneath the surface of the argument we uncover a rather humorous *reductio ad absurdum:* it is the hard and empirical fact that even the two-valued schedule requires that teachers be evaluated and judged in order to determine their positioning upon the two-valued schedule —and all this while protesting that teaching defies measurement! Thus the defense of current schedules which insists that "merit plans require measurement, we can't pay if we can't measure —and we can't measure, therefore we can't pay" is hoist awkwardly by its own petard: if we can't measure then not only do merit plans fail but the

---

[8] Promising as this approach is, it is far from being free of complications. For an insightful analysis of success-criteria problems see Arthur P. Coladarci, "Administrative-Success Criteria," *Phi Delta Kappan,* XXXVII (April, 1956).

two-valued plan fails. And, even more embarrassing, the fact that we do pay does seem to suggest that we can measure.

The alternative, of course, if we affirm that teaching is unmeasurable is to admit not only that we cannot measure teaching, but that we cannot—lacking measurement criteria—even train teachers. Further, if we admit that we do not really know, or cannot determine, what good teaching is and cannot train good teachers, then we must conclude that we cannot evaluate the product of teaching—our pupils. How, then, if we cannot measure teaching can we justify the entire educational enterprise? Without measurement only an act of faith can serve to keep schools in session. This, quite obviously, is an untenable position—but it is precisely the position in which we find ourselves when we deny the possibility of determining criteria of good teaching. Certainly no occupational body which claims professional status would be willing to admit that their professional procedures are so mystical that they defy definition and validation. That is rather the hall-mark of the fortune-teller than of the professional.

Thus, we not only clear away the main objection to merit salary schedules, we demonstrate the internal inconsistencies of the two-dimensional schedule.

There are, however, serious questions of practice to be solved in conjunction with the establishment of merit salary schedules. What should be the relationship of tenure to merit? What are the characteristics on which teaching is to be evaluated? Who shall make these decisions? What kind of evidence is acceptable, and how shall it be gathered? How provide for dissent? There are guiding principles available to aid in the solution of these practical problems [e.g., the bases for collecting evidence of merit should be determined co-operatively by teachers, administrators, and public representatives], but these are mostly of a technical nature and can be solved over a period of time.

Perhaps the one most difficult problem to overcome is the image, the phenomenal picture, or the self-role the teacher assigns to himself. *Until the teacher sees himself as a professional and accepts the consequences of professionalization, he is likely to cling to the security of the two-valued system which permits only of collective bargaining on the best collective terms achievable.* Certainly there is a security, both psychological and economic, in submerging individual merit into collective status, but that is not the type of security compatible with our concept of profession.

There is, aside from this depreciating self-role, no serious theoretical or practical obstacle remaining to militate against the adoption of a merit plan; we need only *do it*.

IV

We should like to note, in conclusion, that while merit schedules are one logical consequence of professional status, that very professional status is dependent upon the role played by theory in the occupation. Yet not just any theory will do, witness the bewildering consequences of the theory that pays teachers on a two-dimensioned craftsman's schedule. We need an educational theory that has firm roots in experience. Our ivory tower must be built upon a solid, empirical foundation.

If our theory is truly meaningful then it has, at the very minimum, the potential of empirical verification—otherwise the guidance we derive from it is useless. By adopting the requirement that theory be empirical in the ultimate test of validity, we can avoid theorizing that is mumbo-jumboish and consists of mystical metalanguages, jabberwocky, and gobbledygook that is mere metaphysical nonsense. Meaningless theory is equivalent to no theory; and to reject theory is to condemn education to the very meanest level of craftsmanship.

But given an empirical philosophy from which we can conscientiously seek guidance, and given practitioners who unite theory and practice, the complete professionalization of education, including both the salary practices of *how*-ness and *much*-ness, becomes only a matter of time.

Satisfactory salary schedules, then, do not ultimately depend upon appeals to the largesse of the public through the media of mass communication, which continually drum home the harsh facts of our current economic shabbiness. The true profession does not depend upon public pity to enhance its financial status.

Rather, the true profession builds upon a sound theory to validate its procedures, requires of its practitioners a theoretical competence, and, having established its status and value in the eyes of the public, rewards its practitioners on the basis of professional merit.

This the public will pay for. It will not pay more for anything less.

$\sim$

Philosophic Idealism in Rogerian Psychology

*Richard W. Dettering**

THE NATURE OF THE ROGERIAN MOVEMENT

The "non-directive," client-centered, student-centered therapy and teaching of Carl Rogers and his followers have begun to assume the proportions of a minor crusade in this country. A unique kind of Rogerian methodology has significantly penetrated the practices of counseling, psychiatry and edu-

* Reprinted by permission from *Educational Theory*, V (October, 1955), 206–214.

cation. The following this approach has already amassed is a tribute to its effect and to the meaning which it has come to have to thousands of able and alert professionals in these respective fields. Nor is it only the extent of influence which excites attention. The professed aim of the movement is revolutionary. "If education is most effectively conducted along lines suggested by client-centered therapy," writes Rogers, "then the achievement of this goal means turning present-day education upside down."[1] This combination of strong support and radical intent entitle some broad questions to be asked in both historical and philosophical, as well as psychological, terms. Where did this movement come from? Why did it arise at this time? Where is it going?

There are a few elementary features of the Rogerian movement which are clear at the outset. Its overt attraction has been to the most extreme anti-authoritarian elements of our culture. It is not only opposed to command and instruction, but also to admonition and advice. The movement is thus directly antagonistic to the classical heritage of moralizing and educating. It rejects any form of "realism" which would have the client or student adjust himself to any body of hard, inflexible facts— whether they be external events, rational norms, or libidinous processes within him. And with even greater force, Rogerian thinking turns down any variety of Aristotelianism, Thomism or Rationalism which would induce the subject to follow, imitate or submit himself to some higher, imposed standard. The stress is all the other way —towards self-direction, self-discovery, self-realization. The reliance is placed entirely on the "fountain within," as Coleridge called it.

Thus it is not surprising to find among Rogers' converts and allies large numbers of psychologists and educators who have been sympathetic with the trends in "group dynamics," "action research," and "field psychology." The new phenomenalists like Snygg and Combs show by ample reference and quotation their abundant goodwill towards Rogers and his works. And receding one more generation, it is not unexpected that a large residue of "progressive educators," enticed by Dewey's repudiation of static absolutes, should find in Rogers a further culmination in their efforts to find truth and value only in the realm of experience. Rogers himself has said that his work "represents a rediscovery of effective principles of Dewey, Kilpatrick and others."[2] Surrounded by such an impressive array of modernists, the Rogerian school may well feel itself to be the latest vanguard of a personal liberation movement in recent Western thought. And this raises a preliminary question of great interest. If Rogerian psychology is the latest leader of a trend, what *is* this trend? How has the trend been exemplified in the past? What are its values and its philosophic rationale?

THE COUNTERPOINT IN PRAGMATISM

We might well suppose, in view of the new alliances, that the experimentalist philosophy of Dewey and his followers would contain significant features consistent with Rogerian principles. And such seems to be the case. Dewey's passion for the continuity and unity of experience and nature, his integration of mind and body, is affirmed by Rogers and the field theorists with their concept of the interrelatedness of the phenomenal field. Both Dewey and Rogers believe in the dynamic character of human experience, in its constant movement and change. Both have seen

[1] Carl Rogers, *Client-Centered Therapy* (Boston: Houghton Mifflin Co., 1951), p. 385.

[2] *Ibid.,* p. 386.

within this matrix of flux, the possibility of freeing the individual and the emergence of a self-directive "purpose." And both have envisioned as the goal of this personal emancipation some kind of social cohesiveness; as Rogers has expressed it, "self-actualization appears to be in the direction of socialization, broadly defined."[3] These four broad similarities cannot be discounted; and they have undoubtedly given the Rogerian school a powerful momentum to ride within the immediate heritage of American philosophic thought.

But there is another side to the picture. Dewey represented a convergence of Hegel and Darwin, of dialectical idealism and empirical science. And it is the Darwinian side that we have been leaving out. Meiklejohn has exposed this conflict in forceful terms:

In two different social moods Dewey gives two different accounts of the activities of problem-solving. One . . . is predominantly individualistic. The other is equally socialistic. . . . If we say that thinking takes place as a result of "strain" in human experience, the most popular and widely accepted pragmatic interpretation of that statement is subjective and individualistic. . . . This view regards a problem as solved, for an individual, when, in the experience of that individual, the feeling of strain out of which the problem came, dies away. The individual in question is no longer disturbed. His problem is solved. . . . But [Dewey] has also another account of problem solving which is far more difficult to construe. . . . The strain of a problem, he often tells us, is not in any individual alone. It is "in the situation." It is objective. It is social. And this means that a problem may remain utterly unsolved even though any

given individual may have been freed from the strain of it.[4]

It is this social, objective, scientific aspect of Dewey's philosophy—his Darwinian side—that we should now seek to compare with Rogers.

THE CONFLICT BETWEEN DEWEY AND ROGERS

Our task, at this point, is to find documentation for Meiklejohn's analysis, such that we can establish points of comparison with the thinking of Rogers. The Darwinian side of Dewey focuses on three major conceptions which we shall now examine in turn.

a. THE CONCEPT OF INTERACTION. Dewey has written that "the word 'interaction' expresses the second chief principle of interpreting an experience in its educational function and force. It assigns equal rights to both factors in experience—objective and internal conditions. Any normal experience is an interplay of these two sets of conditions."[5] Now the problem in interpreting this statement is whether the "interaction" is to be regarded as Darwin undoubtedly would have regarded it— as an objective, scientifically reported phenomenon—or whether it is to be considered as itself a private experience involving only two interacting aspects of the experiential field of any given subject. Dewey may remain ambiguous here, but there is no doubt as to where Rogers stands. For Rogers the individual reacts to the field *as he perceives* it.

[3] *Ibid.*, p. 488.

[4] Alexander Meiklejohn, *Education Between Two Worlds* (New York: Harper & Brothers, 1942), p. 128.

[5] John Dewey, *Experience and Education* (New York: The Macmillan Co., 1938), p. 38.

Snygg and Combs also constantly inveigh against the so-called "normative" or "external" approach of conventional psychology, which, so they contend, views the subject's environment from the position of the *outside* observer and therefore overlooks a considerable amount of stimuli *within* the subject's field and to which he is in fact responding. It is when we consider social interaction, especially in the educational process, that the difference between Dewey and Rogers becomes clear cut. Dewey always emphasized two-way participation between student and teacher. The teacher at least *suggested,*[6] and became an essential correspondent in the relationship. However, even this much intervention would violate Rogers' non-directive ideal. With Rogers the role of teacher or counselor becomes unusually restricted and suspends even the normal non-authoritarian habits of social intercourse; the weight is placed on interaction *within* the subject, not between the subject and agent. The agent serves not as a partner or active cooperator, but as a catalyst. He interacts as does a mirror. In terms of the measured activity of the agent, if nothing more, there is an important difference between the Deweyan and Rogerian learning situations.

b. EXPERIMENT AND CONSEQUENCES. The original pragmatism of Peirce led to Dewey's attention to the consequences of acting from given ideas. The anticipation of consequences stands on conclusions about the regularities of nature. The whole notion of "experiment" falls if there is no constant upon which to experiment. In a completely unpredictable universe an experimental

6 *Ibid.,* p. 84.

act would be nothing more than a random expression. Kilpatrick has construed experimentalism as "the conception that we find out what to expect in life by studying experimentally the uniformities within experience."[7] Thus arises the "operational method" of testing ideas and determining their meaning and truth-value. This is one of the cornerstones of experimentalist philosophy and has given it a unique role among modern systems of thought. But here again Rogers must demur. The introduction of socially acknowledged results as tests of therapy or learning smacks of the "external approach." Rogers does not wish to make such outside criteria matters of anxiety to either patient or therapist, student or teacher. Kerby-Miller has described this aspect of Rogers' thinking as "love *without* consequences." And although Rogers through his clinic has exposed some of the results of his technique, he is basically consistent with his maxim that "the best vantage point for understanding behavior is the internal frame of reference of the individual himself."[8] He stands opposed to *any* external imposition of norms, whether based on authority, custom, logic *or* consequences. It is contrary to Rogers' morality to assess the person from without; intersubjective must yield to intrasubjective verdict. The divergence here from the *social* side of Dewey's thinking is striking.

c. CONFLICT AND PROBLEM-SOLVING. Hegel's dialectical process mingled with

7 William Kilpatrick, "Philosophy of Education from an Experimentalist Outlook," *41st Yearbook, National Society for the Study of Education* (Chicago: The University of Chicago Press, 1942), Part I, p. 44.

8 Carl Rogers, *op. cit.,* p. 494.

the Darwinian struggle for survival to furnish the basis for Dewey's concern with conflict and challenge as a necessary factor in self-development. The belief that not only the specific solution, but the general capacity to solve, comes out of repeated, experimental and self-directed efforts to solve problems, emerged in Dewey's writings as a distinct and arresting program for promoting human education and growth. Whereas Hegel emphasized contradictions appearing in the process of reasoning which required rational reconciliation on a higher level, Dewey dealt with problems as ecological threats or frustrations to be coped with by the maximum expression of both mental and manual skills. The ongoing process is the same in both Hegel and Dewey; a solution merely means passing on to another problem. But unlike Hegel, Dewey did not think the business was structured and predetermined in a diagnosable dialectic. Each problem would be new, fresh, contingent; but it would call for exercise of past training and the full use of knowledge, habits and abilities strengthened by previous problem-solving efforts. Certainly Dewey in his educational theory did not advocate *throwing* problems at students; but he did believe in the value of "upsetting experiences" and he thought that the nature of living and growing up in society was a matter of facing and solving continual problems. Perhaps his most important prescription here was that the problem should be solved by the student and not by his teachers or elders. But then Dewey drew a fundamental distinction between "subject-matter which constitutes the problem and subject-matter that is supposed to resolve the problem. To discriminate and recognize cases of audition, vision . . . merely exposes a problem. No persistence upon the method that yields them can throw any light upon them."[9] In brief, while the problem may be *found* introspectively, in the private world of experience, it cannot be understood or solved except in social and scientific terms.

Rogers' thinking on this question shares the ethics of self-directed solution to problems. But unlike Dewey he would keep the problem within the subject's field, for both its comprehension *and* solution. The only problem to be recognized by the teacher or counselor or society, is that which the subject freely verbalizes; and then society has no right to expect him to solve the problem or to solve it—or even to formulate it—for him. For Rogers the subject's expression of the problem is a complete self-fulfilling act; from the standpoint of the outsider, nothing more needs to be done. If the subject continues to work on the problem, this is his business for which the all-accepting counselor or teacher is ready to help. But the problem never really gets externalized, although its nature may get communicated to society. For this reason Rogerian therapy and teaching discounts the problematic-situation as a socially acknowledged fact and relies instead on the self-determination of both problem and solution by the subject. This is contrary to the position of Dewey quoted above.

It would be possible to go beyond these three points of difference between

[9] John Dewey, *Philosophy and Civilization* (New York: Minton, Balch and Co., 1931), p. 265.

Dewey and Rogers and discuss some of the problems Rogerian psychology would face in adjusting to the naturalistic and scientific basis of experimentalist thinking. But enough has been indicated to show a serious discrepancy in the respective descriptions of the teaching-learning situation. One opposition which seems to run through all these differences we have discussed is between an intersubjective and an introspective concept of knowledge. Here we must especially remember Dewey's criticism of the "introspectionist" view that "consciousness or experience is the organ of its own immediate disclosure of all its own secrets"-—a view, he says, which arose with Descartes and Locke and was "foisted on psychology from without."[10] On this issue above all, Rogers must part with Dewey. Whereas Dewey relied ultimately on the consensus of the scientific community, Rogers rests on the process of self-disclosure.[11]

THE ROGERIAN ADVENTURE INTO IDEALISM

We have seen how the naturalistic and scientific theme in pragmatism is irreconcilable with the personalistic and subjective criteria which Rogers employs for both therapy and learning. On the other hand Rogers' concepts are consistent with the individualistic stress in pragmatism. But Rogers then proceeds to stretch this individualism far beyond the point that any legitimate pragmatist is likely to go. There are at least two important respects in which

Rogerian thinking has treaded into idealistic ground.

a. THE CONCEPT OF SELF-DISCOVERY. Rogers has emphasized that "truth that has been personally appropriated and assimilated in experience cannot be directly communicated to another." He has found with "some relief" that Kierkegaard, the mystic Danish theologian, realized this too—"it made it seem less absurd."[12] Learning, then, cannot be provided from without; it is a process of "self-discovery." Now "self-discovery" is capable of an interesting ambiguity. Dewey too believed in "self-discovery," but he meant discovery *by* the self—discovery of data that were *not* the self. But another interpretation is readily possible. In this view "self-discovery" would mean not only discovery *by* the self but discovery *of* the self—it *is* the self which is discovered. Although Rogers may not have it, the main direction of his therapy indicates that this second interpretation is being used. In the current language of phenomenalist psychology the subject-object distinction is represented as an arbitrary and often transitory differentiation within the phenomenal field. It is only part of the perceptual field itself, as Rogers says, which becomes known as "reality." The distinction is tentative and may be changed with further reflection or development. In some cases, as with the therapist-patient relationship, according to a statement by Rogers,[13] the distinction may be lost altogether and the two individuals in effect merge. It is clear that this "self," originally a *part* of the "phenomenal

10 *Ibid.*, p. 261.
11 Carl Rogers, "Classroom Approaches to Human Behavior." Address at Harvard Conference, April 4, 1952.

12 *Ibid.*
13 Carl Rogers. Address at San Francisco State College, June 12, 1952.

field," has movable walls—it may *become the whole phenomenal field*. And in such a case *any* discovery would automatically be discovery of more of the "self." The mechanics here are akin to the epistemology of traditional mysticism, which involves a successive rejection of subject-object distinctions, ending in speechless identification with the cosmos. And so Rogers says:

This whole train of experiencing . . . seems to have launched me on a process which is both fascinating and at times a little frightening. It seems to mean letting my experience carry me on, in a direction that I can but dimly define . . . The sensation is that of floating with a complex stream of experience with the fascinating possibility of trying to comprehend its ever changing complexity.[14]

The dynamics here are highly subjective—and auto-suggestive—and even that part of the "phenomenal field" called the "external world" is given no credit for pushing Rogers on. While there is a mystic surrender of the self and its controls here, the surrender, as with idealism, is not to an external world, but to a world that was in the self to begin with. The "self" disappears only in the recognition that it is everything; hence there is no "not-self," and "self" becomes meaningless. This is the process by which modern idealism has developed.

b. SELF-DEVELOPMENT AND UNFOLDING. The non-directive method places great weight on trusting the client or student, in encouraging his spontaneity and in maintaining that he already holds the answers within himself. Some of this credo is as old as Socrates, part

of it was used by Dewey, but Rogers carries it about as far as it can possibly go. Now the Western idealist philosophers have differed on the amount and nature of external guidance and direction which should be afforded in the learning process, but there has been general agreement among them that the self contains within it the momentum for its growth and education. Brubacher has pointed this out especially with the Fichtean brand of idealism.

Some idealists are inclined to exalt will rather than intellect or reason to the position of the Absolute. On analysis, they find that primacy must be awarded to a certain activity or striving as the heart of reality. This theory is notably different from the pragmatic in accounting for the activity principle in education. It puts education squarely up to the individual. Neither teacher nor parent, school nor church, can educate him. Only through a voluntary act of his will can he educate himself.[15]

Along the same line, there is an idealist tendency to stress the personality rather than the subject taught. As Horne puts it, "The main thing is to remember that we teach pupils, not subjects."[16] Education here, it is easy to see, moves closer to therapy. But perhaps most significant and reminiscent are the views of the great idealist and theistic educator, Froebel, who stressed the notions of "inner connection" and "self-revelation." Froebel founded the kinder-

---

14 Carl Rogers, "Classroom Approaches to Human Behavior."

15 John S. Brubacher, *Modern Philosophies of Education* (New York: McGraw-Hill Book Co., Inc., 1950), p. 313.

16 Herman H. Horne, "An Idealist Philosophy of Education," *Philosophies of Education* (41st Yearbook, National Society for the Study of Education. Part I). Chicago: The University of Chicago Press, 1942, p. 172.

garten—the child's garden where the children unfolded and blossomed like flowers. In the early nineteenth century Froebel wrote,

> The drawing of direct inferences concerning the inner life of childhood and youth from certain external manifestations of life. is the chief cause of antagonism and contention, of the frequent mistakes in life and education. . . . Therefore, education in instruction and training, originally and in its first principles, should necessarily be *passive, following* (only guarding and protecting), not *prescriptive, categorical, interfering.*[17]

It would be hard to see how the nondirective educator and psychologist could fail to applaud the foregoing statements. The person who cannot be taught but can only learn, the self-enhancing, self-actualizing person of Rogers and the field theorists, seems to have attained an emancipation from the immediate environment and a dependence on "inner connection" that has historically been presented most vigorously in idealism.

CONCLUSIONS

We have tried to show initially that Rogerian psychology has made important departures from the social, scientific, environmentalist strain in pragmatism and experimentalism. Next, we have argued that it has stretched the subjective and individualistic side of pragmatism far over into the idealist camp. Let us return now to our original questions about what all this means.

First, we are presented with an interesting religious phenomenon. The

Rogerian school would seem to be the first major expression in modern psychology of Protestant individualism. The theology which rejected the mediating formalism of the church and stood for direct, personal communion with God, which stressed initiative and self-reliance and abhorred institutional controls, finds its sophisticated counterpart in the little self-enhancing individuals of Rogers' clinic and Rogers' classroom. Far from being a pure weakness, however, this personalism is Rogers' greatest strength. It fits his methods into our religious and economic heritage and undoubtedly accounts for the easy shift so many people have made into his fold. As Kant, who started German idealism, has been called the philosopher of the Reformation, perhaps Rogers, somewhat belatedly, can be called its psychologist. But just as Western individualism has run into constant difficulty in times calling for great social responsibility and organized change, so non-directive therapy and education is apt to fall short of that often needed juncture of the individual with the group. Rogers' thinking is curious here. "Finally, the self-actualization appears to be in the direction of socialization, broadly defined."[18] As Rogers will not permit the counselor, teacher or society to motivate this socialization, he must count on some tendency within the individual to bring it to fruition, as the idealists counted on the individual will to evolve into the social will. Adam Smith, of course, had the same problem; and Rogers' uncaused socializing tendency could be

[17] Friedrich Froebel, *The Education of Man,* trans. W. N. Hailman (New York: D. Appleton, 1887), p. 7.

[18] Carl Rogers, *Client-Centered Therapy,* p. 488.

regarded as the "invisible hand" of a *laissez-faire* psychology. The other problem here is solipsism, long a bane of idealistic philosophies. Rogers' denial of the positive role of the interacting agent makes this problem for him especially acute. If he and the "phenomenalist psychologists" insist on encapsulating the individual in his "phenomenal field," then they must posit some unexplained overlap or "pre-established harmony" between various persons' fields in order to account for socialization. But if they renig at such complete encapsulation they must acknowledge some intersubjective relationship, some norm or agent outside the individual. In either case, the dilemma is not solved.

Secondly, there is a neat factor of historical timing in the emergence and popularity of the Rogerian movement. Personalism in philosophy has always had a paradoxical kinship with certain forms of positivism, as both have stressed the superior validity of immediate, subjective experience. The refusal of Rogers to make interpretations beyond the given experience or to encourage his subjects to do so joins him in this traditional phenomenalistic approach. There are two points to be made about this kind of orientation. It has on the one hand a strong affinity with the mysticism of the East, where enjoyment of the "aesthetic continuum" of pure experience has been given priority over the theoretical interpretations and abstract meanings of experience.[19] And this is perhaps not all regrettable in a period when East-West communi-

cation is of rising moment. But on the other hand, such retreat into the privacy of consciousness or of given sense-data is typical in Western history only when traditional institutions, concepts and values are in a state of collapse; the absolute in such times is found within. As Northrup has expressed it:

> Whereas the Orient is for the most part continuously positivistic, the West tends . . . to be positivistic only during those revolutionary transition periods in its historical development when the traditional scientific and historical doctrine has broken down in the face of new evidence, and before the new, more adequate one has been put forward to take its place.[20]

It is hard to deny that we are going through such a period today, resulting from the collapse of the social values of the New Deal era and the disillusionment with post-war internationalism. One of the clearest symptoms of our contemporary epistemic regression is the sudden new modesty of the psychiatric profession, with its "not sticking your neck out" approach and its trend towards silent, permissive treatment along Rogerian lines. In education, too, scepticism, acceptance and "understanding"—"get the most out of the age of five"—are replacing the theoretic and moralizing strictures of "work for the night cometh." In this one respect, of course, Rogers' methods run counter to traditional Protestantism, with its utilitarian work-ethic; but the emergence of leisure in our society has rendered such frontier values obsolete and is drawing more heavily upon the passive, non-judgmental aspects of Protestant culture, represented best by

19 F. S. C. Northrup, *The Meeting of East and West* (New York: The Macmillan Co., 1947), p. 375.

20 *Ibid.*

the Quakers. When not much work needs to be done, experience gets assessed more for its intrinsic qualities—the depth of its religious content and its immediate and personal meaning. Such is the direction we seem to be taking. Appreciation of the aesthetic component of experience is supplanting our former explanatory and interpretative response.

The main impact of our argument is that the Rogerian movement is a symbol of much more than its adherents realize or are willing to admit. Its psychology is one of *enduring* life rather than *remaking* it—with something akin both to early Christianity and modern French existentialism. One need never deny the personal benefits

and sense of relief that come from this doctrine. The cultivation of empathy, seeing the other person from his own inside, is a long standing humanitarian virtue. But whereas Dewey regarded it as the starting point of social co-operation, Rogers considers it the stopping point as well. Only in some kind of idealistic terms—of an "emergent mind" or a "natural self"—can such a position be justified. Otherwise it would seem to be wanting in the production of effective citizenship or social reconstruction. In view of the present world-crisis, the question is whether we can afford to try such an easy way out. Perhaps the answer is to improve our ability to make judgments rather than to lose it.

∽

Suggestions for Further Reading

PART I: THE NATURE OF EDUCATIONAL PHILOSOPHY

A survey of these suggestions for further reading will provide some indication of the journals which carry articles in the field of educational philosophy. There are two publications, however, which are devoted exclusively to this field. They are: *Educational Theory* (published by the College of Education of the University of Illinois, The John Dewey Society, and The Philosophy of Education Society; Archibald W. Anderson, Editor-in-Chief, College of Education, University of Illinois) and *Studies in Philosophy and Education* (published by Studies in Philosophy and Education, Inc., College of Education, University of Toledo; Francis T. Villemain, Executive Editor).

Basic Texts

BRAMELD, THEODORE. "Philosophy: Its Import and Its Functions," *Philosophies of Education in Cultural Perspective*. New York: Holt, Rinehart & Winston, Inc., 1955. Pp. 19–44.

BROUDY, HARRY S. "Defiintion of Education and Philosophy of Education," *Building a Philosophy of Education*. Englewood Cliffs, N.J.: Prentice-Hall, Inc., 1954. Pp. 3–28.

BRUBACHER, JOHN S. "The Role of Educational Philosophy," *Modern Philosophies of Education* (2d ed.). New York: McGraw-Hill Book Co., Inc., 1950. Pp. 1–21.

BUTLER, J. DONALD. "Philosophy and Education," *Four Philosophies and Their Practice in Education and Religion* (rev. ed.). New York: Harper & Brothers, 1957. Pp. 11–14.

MORRIS, VAN CLEVE. *Philosophy and the American School*. Boston: Houghton Mifflin Co., 1961. Pp. 3–23.

NATIONAL SOCIETY FOR THE STUDY OF EDUCATION. "The Challenge to Philosophize About Education," *Modern Philosophies and Education,* ed. NELSON B. HENRY. (54th Yearbook of the NSSE, Part I.) Chicago: The University of Chicago Press, 1955. Pp. 4–16.

NATIONAL SOCIETY FOR THE STUDY OF EDUCATION. "Scope of Educational Philosophy," *Philosophies of Education,* ed. NELSON B. HENRY. (41st Yearbook of the NSSE, Part I.) Chicago: The University of Chicago Press, 1942. Pp. 292–297.

Books and Articles

BRAUNER, CHARLES J. *Education as a Subject of Study*. (U.S. Office of Education Project 245–7140, School of Education, Stanford University). Washington, D.C.: Department of Health, Education, and Welfare, 1959.

BROUDY, HARRY S. "How Philosophical Can Philosophy of Education Be?" *Journal of Philosophy,* LII (October, 1955), 612–622.

HOOK, SIDNEY. "Modern Education and Its Critics," *AACTE Seventh Yearbook (1954)*. Washington, D.C.: American Association of Colleges for Teacher Education, 1954, 1–22.

LODGE, RUPERT C. "The Essence of Philosophy of Education," *Educational Theory*, III (October, 1953), 352–356.

MARTIN, WILLIAM OLIVER. "The Importance of the Philosophy of Education for Administrators and Teachers," *Educational Theory*, VI (October, 1956), 232–235.

PRICE, KINGSLEY. "Is a Philosophy of Education Necessary?" *Journal of Philosophy*, LII (October, 1955), 622–633.

REDDEN, JOHN D., and FRANCIS A. RYAN. "The Position of Philosophy in Education," *A Catholic Philosophy of Education*. Milwaukee: Bruce Publishing Co., 1942. Pp. 3–32.

REID, L. ARNAUD. "Philosophy and Education," *Education and the Philosophic Mind*, ed. by A. V. JUDGES. London: Harrap and Co., 1957. Pp. 186–205.

SCHILPP, PAUL A. "The Distinctive Function of 'Philosophy of Education' as a Discipline," *Educational Theory*, III (July, 1953), 257–268.

SHIELDS, THOMAS E. "Introduction," *Philosophy of Education*. Washington, D.C.: Catholic Education Press, 1921. Pp. 21–32.

SMITH, B. OTHANEL. "Philosophy of Education," *Encyclopedia of Educational Research*, ed. CHESTER W. HARRIS. New York: The Macmillan Co., 1960. Pp. 957–964.

SMITH, PHILIP G. "Philosophy, Educational Theory, and Pedagogy," *Educational Theory*, VI (July, 1956), 129–134.

VILLEMAIN, FRANCIS T. *Philosophic Research in Education*. New York: School of Education, New York University, 1953. Pp. 1–12.

WENDON, JOHN. "On Philosophy of Education." *Educational Theory*, V (January, 1955), 24–28.

Special Issues

"Philosophy Symposium: What Can Philosophy Contribute to Educational Theory?" *Harvard Educational Review*, XXVIII.

"Symposium: The Aims and Content of Philosophy of Education," *Harvard Educational Review*, XXVI (Spring, 1956), 93–202.

"Various Conceptions of the Role of the Educational Philosopher," *Boston University Journal of Education*, CXLI (October, 1958), 2–31.

PART II: THE DIVISIONS OF PHILOSOPHY

A survey of these suggestions for further reading will provide some indication of the journals which carry articles in the general field of philosophy. There are many such outstanding journals, two of which deserve special mention: *The Journal of Philosophy* (published by the Department of Philosophy, Columbia University; Emerson Buchanan, Managing Editor) and *Mind* (published by Thomas Nelson and Sons, Ltd., Edinburgh; Gilbert Ryle, Editor).

Beginning students, often lacking the general background in philosophy necessary to make the most of a course in philosophy of education, would do well to read an introductory textbook in philosophy. It has been the experience of the editors that any one of the three following books will be of value in this connection:

BECK, LEWIS WHITE. *Philosophic Inquiry*. Englewood Cliffs, N.J.: Prentice-Hall, Inc., 1952.

FULLER, B. A. G. *A History of Philosophy* (rev. ed.). New York: Holt, Rinehart & Winston, Inc., 1945.

RUSSELL, BERTRAND. *A History of Western Philosophy*. New York: Simon and Schuster, Inc., 1945.

Basic Texts

BRAMELD, THEODORE. *Philosophies of Education in Cultural Perspective.* New York: Holt, Rinehart & Winston, 1955. Pp. 101–103, 214–220, 298–302 (metaphysics); 103–112, 220–226, 303–307 (epistemology); 112–121, 227–234, 307–314 (axiology).

BROUDY, HARRY S. *Building a Philosophy of Education.* Englewood Cliffs, N.J.: Prentice-Hall, Inc., 1954. Pp. 128–146 (metaphysics and epistemology), 273–300 (axiology).

BRUBACHER, JOHN S. *Modern Philosophies of Education* (2d ed.) New York: McGraw-Hill Book Co., Inc., 1950. Pp. 22–41 (metaphysics), 71–91 (epistemology), 92–113 (axiology).

BUTLER, J. DONALD. *Four Philosophies* (rev. ed.). New York: Harper & Brothers, 1957. Pp. 82–86, 172–192, 320–331, 451–459 (metaphysics); 86–90, 192–200, 316–320, 445–451 (epistemology); 92–101, 206–220, 334–342, 466–478 (axiology).

MORRIS, VAN CLEVE. *Philosophy and the American School.* Boston: Houghton Mifflin Co., 1961. Chaps. 2–3 (ontology), 5–6 (epistemology), 8–9 (axiology).

NATIONAL SOCIETY FOR THE STUDY OF EDUCATION, *Modern Philosophies and Education,* ed. NELSON B. HENRY. (54th Yearbook of the NSSE, Part I.) Chicago: The University of Chicago Press, 1955. Pp. 17–24 (Realism), 57–67 (Thomism), 91–107 (Idealism), 137–144 (Experimentalism), 215–222 (Existentialism), and 259–271, 304–330 (Empiricism).

NATIONAL SOCIETY FOR THE STUDY OF EDUCATION, *Philosophies of Education,* ed. NELSON B. HENRY. (41st Yearbook of the NSSE, Part I. Chicago: The University of Chicago Press, 1942. Pp. 40–61 (Experimentalism), 87–97 and 104–118 (Realism), 139–151 (Idealism), 251–265 and 276–279 (Thomism), and 297–315 (Comparative treatment).

Books and Articles

BAKAN, MILDRED B. "On the Subject-Object Relationship," *Journal of Philosophy,* LV (January 30, 1958), 89–101.

BAYLES, ERNEST E. "Relativism," *University of Kansas Bulletin of Education,* VII (February, 1953), 39–43, and (May, 1953), 77–82.

CRISSMAN, PAUL. "The Conflict of Values of Ends," *Educational Forum,* XXX (November, 1952), 37–45.

DEWEY, JOHN. "The Construction of the Good," *The Quest for Certainty.* New York: G. P. Putnam's Sons, 1900.

DEWEY, JOHN. "The Significance of the Problem of Knowledge." *The Influence of Darwin on Philosophy.* New York: Holt, 1910. Pp. 271–304.

DRAKE, DURANT (ed.). *Essays in Critical Realism.* New York: The Macmillan Co., 1920.

FREISTADT, HANS. "Dialectical Materialism: A Friendly Interpretation," *Philosophy of Science,* XXIII (April, 1956), 97–110.

HARTMAN, ROBERT S. "Value, Fact and Science," *Philosophy of Science,* XXVI (April, 1958), 97–108.

HOLT, EDWIN B. *et al. The New Realism.* New York: The Macmillan Co., 1912.

HOOK, SIDNEY. "The Quest for 'Being,'" *Journal of Philosophy* (November 19, 1953), 709–731.

KRAEMER, WILLIAM S. "Absolutism and the Rational Good," *Educational Theory,* III (October, 1953), 361–368, 373.

MOWRER, EDGAR ANSEL. "The Open Universe," *Saturday Review* (April 19, 1958), 11–13, 43–45.

MULLER, H. J. "Human Values in Relation to Evolution," *Science,* CXXVII (March 21, 1958), 625–629.

RAPOPORT, ANATOL. "Scientific Approach to Ethics," *Science,* CXXV (April 26, 1957), 796–799.

RUSSELL, BERTRAND. "What is Mind?" *Journal of Philosophy,* IV (January 2, 1958), 5–12.

STEVENSON, CHARLES L. "The Emotive Meaning of Ethical Terms," *Mind,* XLVI (1937).

STRAWSON, P. F. "Ethical Intuitionism," *Philosophy,* XXIV (1949).

TAYLOR, ALFRED. "Mind as the Basic Potential," *Main Currents in Modern Thought,* XIV (March, 1958), 83–86.

Special Issues

"John Dewey in Perspective," *Antioch Review* (Fall, 1959), 293–359.
"Metaphysics: Its Function, Consequences, and Criteria," *Journal of Philosophy*, XLIII (July, 1946), 393–412.

PART III: PHILOSOPHIES OF EDUCATION

For those students who wish to be current with the work being done in educational philosophy, the *Proceedings of The Philosophy of Education Society* are published annually (The Philosophy of Education Society, School of Education, Syracuse University; Hobert W. Burns, Secretary-Treasurer) and are made available to libraries at a special subscription rate.

Basic Texts

BRAMELD, THEODORE. *Philosophies of Education in Cultural Perspective*. New York: Holt, Rinehart & Winston, 1955. Pp. 89–121 (progressivism), 203–234 (Essentialism), 287–314 (Perennialism).

BRUBACHER, JOHN S. *Modern Philosophies of Education* (2d ed.). New York: McGraw-Hill Book Co., Inc., 1950. Pp. 296–340 (Comparative Philosophies of Education).

BUTLER, J. DONALD. *Four Philosophies* (rev. ed.). New York: Harper & Brothers, 1957. Pp. 57–101 (Nationalism), 131–220 (Idealism), 289–342 (Realism), 417–478 (Pragmatism).

MORRIS, VAN CLEVE. *Philosophy and the American School*. Boston: Houghton Mifflin Co., 1961. Pp. 327–330 (Idealism), 330–340 (Realism), 340–351 (Neo-Thomism), 355–372 (Progressivism), 372–389 (Reconstructionism), 383–400 (Existentialism).

NATIONAL SOCIETY FOR THE STUDY OF EDUCATION. *Modern Philosophies and Education*, ed. NELSON B. HENRY. (54th Yearbook of the NSSE, Part I.) Chicago: The University of Chicago Press, 1955. Pp. 24–56 (Realism), 67–90 (Thomism), 107–136 (Idealism), 144–174 (Pragmatism), 222–258 (Existentialism), 271–303, 331–341 (Empiricism).

In addition to the textbooks in philosophy of education which have been cited earlier, there are many books which deal directly with educational philosophy. In the editors' opinions, students would do well to investigate the following texts, reviewing and evaluating each one for scope, sequence, approach, and style in order to find those which would profitably[1] serve his ends.

BAYLES, ERNEST E. *Democratic Educational Theory*. New York: Harper & Brothers, 1960. Pragmatic point of view.

BERKSON, I. B. *The Ideal and the Community*. New York: Harper & Brothers, 1958. Humanistic point of view.

BRACKENBURY, ROBERT L. *Getting Down to Cases in Educational Philosophy*. New York: G. P. Putnam's Sons, 1960. Comparative treatment.

BRAMELD, THEODORE. *Education for the Emerging Age*. New York: Harper & Brothers, 1961. Reconstructionist point of view.

BRAMELD, THEODORE. *Toward a Reconstructed Philosophy of Education*. New York: Holt, Rinehart & Winston, Inc., 1956. Reconstructionist point of view.

BRUBACHER, JOHN S. (ed.). *Eclectic Philosophy of Education*. New York: Prentice-Hall, Inc., 1951. Comparative treatment.

CHILDS, JOHN L. *American Pragmatism and Education*. New York: Holt, Rinehart & Winston, Inc., 1956. Pragmatic point of view.

DEWEY, JOHN. *Democracy and Education.* New York: The Macmillan Co., 1916. Pragmatic point of view.

GRUBER, FREDERICK C. *Foundations for a Philosophy of Education.* New York: Thomas Y. Crowell Co., 1961. Comparative treatment.

HULLFISH, H. GORDON, and PHILIP G. SMITH. *Reflective Thinking: The Method of Education.* New York: Dodd, Mead & Co., Inc., 1961. Pragmatic point of view.

JUDGES, A. V. (ed.). *Education and the Philosophic Mind.* London: George G. Harrap & Co., Ltd., 1957. Comparative treatment.

KILPATRICK, WILLIAM H. *Philosophy of Education.* New York: The Macmillan Co., 1951. Pragmatic point of view.

KNELLER. GEORGE F. *Existentialism and Education.* New York: The Philosophic Library, Inc., 1958. The Existential point of view.

O'CONNOR, D. J. *An Introduction to the Philosophy of Education.* London: Routledge & Kegan Paul, 1957. Analytic point of view.

PARK, JOE (ed.). *The Philosophy of Education.* New York: The Macmillan Co., 1958. Comparative treatment.

REDDEN, JOHN D., and FRANCIS A. RYAN. *A Catholic Philosophy of Education.* Milwaukee: Bruce Publishing Co., 1942. Thomistic point of view.

SAYERS, E. VERN, and WARD MADDEN. *Education and the Democratic Faith.* New York: Appleton-Century-Crofts, Inc., 1959. Pragmatic point of view.

SCHEFFLER, ISRAEL (ed.). *Philosophy and Education.* Boston: Allyn & Bacon, Inc., 1958. Analytic point of view.

SCHEFFLER, ISRAEL. *The Language of Education.* Springfield, Ill.: Charles C. Thomas, 1960. Analytic point of view.

SMITH, B. OTHANEL, and ROBERT H. ENNIS (eds.). *Language and Concepts in Education.* Chicago: Rand McNally & Co., 1961. Analytic point of view.

ULICH, ROBERT. *Philosophy of Education.* New York: American Book Co., 1961. Idealistic point of view.

WEBER, CHRISTIAN O., *Basic Philosophies of Education.* New York: Holt, Rinehart & Winston, Inc., 1960. Comparative treatment.

Articles

BRAMELD, THEODORE. "Imperatives for a Reconstructed Philosophy of Education," *School and Society* LXXXVII (January 17, 1959), 18–20.

BRUBACHER, JOHN S. "Ten Misunderstandings of Dewey's Educational Philosophy," *Bulletin of the School of Education of Indiana University,* XXXVI (January, 1960), 27–42.

BRUMBAUGH, ROBERT S., and NATHANIEL M. LAWRENCE, JR. "Aristotle's Philosophy of Education," *Educational Theory, VIII* (January, 1959), 1–15.

BURNETT, JOE R. "On Professor McMurray's 'Autonomous Discipline of Education,'" *Educational Theory,* VI (January, 1956), 10–19.

HAMPSCH, JOHN H. "Integrative Determinants in the Philosophy of Education of St. Thomas Aquinas," *Educational Theory,* IX (January, 1959), 31–40.

HENLE, ROBERT J. "Philosophy of Knowledge and Theory of Learning," *Educational Theory,* VIII (October, 1958), 193–199. (See also "A Response to 'Philosophy of Knowledge and Theory of Learning,'" by ERNEST E. BAYLES, *ibid.,* 200–202.)

HOOK, SIDNEY. "John Dewey: His Philosophy of Education and Its Critics," *The New Leader* (Section Two, November 2, 1959), 3–23.

KILPATRICK, WILLIAM H. *The Aims of Philosophy of Education in American Democracy.* New Brunswick, N.J.: New Jersey School Development Council, Rutgers University, 1958. Pp. 5–14.

KOROLEV, E. F. "Some Theoretical Problems of Soviet Pedagogy," *Soviet Education,* II (1959), 14–21.

McCall, Raymond J. "The Autonomy of Education: A Thomistic View," *Educational Theory,* I (December, 1951), 248–250.

McGucken, William J. *Catholic Education: Its Philosophy, Its Fundamentals, Its Objectives.* New York: The America Press. Pp. 1–40.

McMurray, Foster. "Preface to an Autonomous Discipline of Education," *Educational Theory,* V (July, 1955), 129–140.

Morris, Van Cleve. "Existentialism and Education," *Educational Theory,* IV (October, 1954), 247–258.

Morris, Van Cleve. "Freedom and Choice in Educative Process," *Educational Theory,* VIII (October 1, 1958), 231–238.

Morris, Van Cleve. "The Other-Directed Man: Outline for a Reconstructionist Philosophy of Man," *Teachers College Record,* LVII (January, 1956), 232–240.

Muuss, Rolf. "Existentialism and Psychology," *Educational Theory,* VI (July, 1956), 135–153.

Olson, Robert G. "The Anguish of Nothingness in Modern Philosophy," *Antioch Review,* XVII (Summer, 1957), 247–254.

Pace, E. A. "St. Thomas' Theory of Education," *Catholic University Bulletin,* VIII (July, 1902), 290–303.

Smith, John Milton. "A Critical Estimate of Plato's and Dewey's Educational Philosophies," *Educational Theory,* IX (April, 1959), 109–115.

Wirth, Arthur G. "Existentialism, the Emperor's New Clothes, and Education," *Educational Theory,* V (July, 1955), 152–157.

Special Issues

"Controversies in Education: The Philosophic Issue," *Phi Delta Kappan,* XL (October, 1958), 6–16.

"Dewey Centennial Issue," *School Review,* LXVII (Summer, 1959), 123–280.

"Educational Theory," *School and Society,* LXXXVII (January 17, 1959), 5–25.

PART IV: FROM THEORY TO PRACTICE

A survey of these suggestions for further reading will provide some indication of the journals which carry philosophic articles of practical interest to educators. For a quick overview of the work being done in this field, however, the reader is referred to the American Educational Research Association monograph, "The Philosophical and Social Framework of Education," *Review of Educational Research,* XXXI (February, 1961), especially Part II ("Philosophy of Education," edited by A. Stafford Clayton) and Part VII ("Educational and Social Policy," edited by William O. Stanley).

Basic Texts

Brameld, Theodore. *Philosophies of Education in Cultural Perspective.* New York: Holt, Rinehart & Winston, Inc., 1955. Pp. 123–158 (Progressivism), 235–259 (Essentialism), 315–346 (Perennialism).

Broudy, Harry S. *Building a Philosophy of Education.* Englewood Cliffs, N.J.: Prentice-Hall, Inc., 1954. Pp. 147–210 (Curriculum), 211–238 (Methodology), 239–270 (Organization).

Brubacher, John S. *Modern Philosophies of Education* (2d ed.). New York: McGraw-Hill Book Co., Inc., 1950. Pp. 114–121 (professional ethics), 218–276 (educative process).

BUTLER, J. DONALD. *Four Philosophies* (rev. ed.). New York: Harper & Brothers, 1957. Chap. IV (Naturalism in education), Chap. IX (Idealism in education), Chap. XV (realism in education), Chap. XX (Pragmatism in education).

MORRIS, VAN CLEVE. *Philosophy and the American School.* Boston: Houghton Mifflin Co., 1961. Chaps. 14–15 (Philosophy in Action).

Books and Articles

ALBERTY, HAROLD. "A Plan for Developing a Philosophy of Education for the High School," *Educational Research Bulletin*, XXII (November, 1943), 199–210.

ARNSTINE, DONALD G. "Aesthetic Experience in Education," *Proceedings of the Philosophy of Education Society.* (14th annual meeting.) Lawrence, Kan.: The University of Kansas Press. Pp. 74–81.

BAYLES, ERNEST E. "Let's Take a Look at Core." *The University of Kansas Bulletin of Education,* IX (November, 1954), 1–5.

BECK, ROBERT H. "The Social and Educational Philosophy of New Humanism and New Conservatism," *Proceedings of the Philosophy of Education Society.* (16th annual meeting.) Lawrence, Kan.: The University of Kansas Press. Pp. 93–103.

BELTH, MARC. "Intelligence and the Teaching of History," *Educational Theory,* III (April, 1953), 126–134.

BROUDY, HARRY S. "Teachers, Strikes, and the Art of Payments," *Proceedings of The Philosophy of Education Society.* (17th annual meeting.) Syracuse, N.Y.: The Philosophy of Education Society, Syracuse University, 1961. Pp. 66–75.

BROUDY, HARRY S. "Teaching—Craft or Profession?" *The Educational Forum,* XX (January, 1956), 175–184.

BURNETT, JOE R. "An Analysis of Some Traditional Philosophical and Theological Approaches to Educational Policy and Practice," *Proceedings of the Philosophy of Education Society.* (17th annual meeting.) Syracuse, N.Y.: The Philosophy of Education Society, Syracuse University, 1961. Pp. 7–30.

BURNETT, JOE R. "Some Observations on the Logical Implications of Philosophic Theory for Educational Theory and Practice," *Proceedings of the Philosophy of Education Society.* (14th annual meeting.) Lawrence, Kan.: The University of Kansas Press, 1958. Pp. 51–57.

BURNETT, JOE R. "Whitehead's Concept of Creativity and Some of Its Educational Implications," *Harvard Educational Review,* XXVII (Summer, 1957), 220–234.

BURNS, HOBERT W. "Philosophical Dimensions of Empirical Research in Education," *California Journal of Educational Research,* X (January, 1959), 10–14.

BURNS, HOBERT W. "Pragmatism and the Science of Behavior," *Philosophy of Science,* XXVII (January, 1960), 58–74.

CHAMPLIN, NATHANIEL L. "Value Inquiry and the Philosophy of Education," *Educational Leadership,* XIII (May, 1956), 467–473.

ECKER, DAVID W. "Toward a Philosophy of Art Education," *Research in Art Education.* (9th Yearbook.) The National Art Education Association, 1959.

ELLIS, FREDERICK E. "The Educational Implications of Philosophy of Transcendence," in *Liberal Traditions in Education: Essays in Honor of Robert Ulich,* ed. George Z. F. Bereday. Cambridge, Mass.: Graduate School of Education, Harvard University, 1958. Pp. 3–26.

GALL, MORRIS. "Some Value Problems of the Classroom Teacher," *Educational Theory,* IV (October, 1954), 297–299.

GRIFFITHS, DANIEL E. *Administrative Theory.* New York: Appleton-Century-Crofts, Inc., 1959.

HALPIN, ANDREW W. (ed.). *Administrative Theory in Education.* Chicago: The Midwest Administration Center, University of Chicago, 1958.

LIEBERMAN, MYRON. "Professionalism and the Voodoo of Education," *Proceedings of the Philosophy of Education Society.* (17th annual meeting.) Syracuse, N.Y.: The Philosophy of Education Society, Syracuse University, 1961. Pp. 53–65.

LEVIT, MARTIN. "Pupil-, Subject-, or Growth-Centered Education," *Progressive Education,* XXXIII, 91–94.

McCLELLAN, JAMES E. "Dewey and the Concept of Method," *The School Review,* LXVII (Summer, 1959), 213–228.

MORRIS, VAN CLEVE. "The Philosophical Premises Underlying Public Education," *Progressive Education* (May, 1957), 69–74.

NEFF, FREDERICK C. "The Retreat from Heresy," *The Scientific Monthly,* LXXVIII (January, 1954), 19–29.

SCHWARZ, BALDWIN V. "The Role of Philosophy in Religious Education," *Religious Education,* LIII (November–December, 1958), 505–511.

SMITH, PHILIP G. *Philosophic Mindedness in Educational Administration.* Columbus, Ohio: The Ohio State University Press, 1956.

THOMAS, LAWRENCE G. "The Meaning of 'Progress' in Progressive Education," *Educational Administration and Supervision,* XXXII (October, 1946), 385–400.

WALTON, JOHN. "The Nature and Function of Theory in Educational Administration," *Educational Theory,* VII (October, 1957), 240–248.

Name Index

Subject Index